A Concise Introduction to

World Religions

SECOND EDITION

Edited by

Willard G. Oxtoby
& Alan F. Segal

OXFORD
UNIVERSITY PRESS

OXFORD
UNIVERSITY PRESS

Oxford University Press is a department of the University of Oxford.

It furthers the University's objective of excellence in research, scholarship, and education by publishing worldwide. Oxford is a registered trade mark of Oxford University Press in the UK and in certain other countries.

Published in Canada by
Oxford University Press
8 Sampson Mews, Suite 204,
Don Mills, Ontario M3C 0H5 Canada

www.oupcanada.com

Library and Archives Canada Cataloguing in Publication

A concise introduction to world religions / edited by Willard G. Oxtoby & Alan F. Segal. — 2nd ed.

Includes bibliographical references and index.

ISBN 978-0-19-543774-4

1. Religions—Textbooks.   I. Oxtoby, Willard G. (Willard Gurdon), 1933-
II. Segal, Alan F., 1945-III. Title: World religions.

BL80.3.C65 2011   200   C2011-905406-X

Cover image: 4 Eyes Photography/Photodisc Gettyimages

Oxford University Press is committed to our environment. This book is printed on paper which contains a minimum of 10% post-consumer waste.

Printed and bound in the United States of America.

5 6 7 — 15 14 13

Contents

1 The Nature of Religion 2
Alan F. Segal and Willard G. Oxtoby

2 Indigenous Traditions 28
Robert M. Baum

3 Jewish Traditions 80
Alan F. Segal

4 Christian Traditions 140
Alan F. Segal and Willard G. Oxtoby

Important Features of this Edition

This second edition of *A Concise Introduction to World Religions* is a significant revision, with four new contributors and five new chapters (on Sikhism, Jainism, Japanese traditions, the religions of China and Korea, and new religious movements). It also includes—in addition to timelines, maps, glossaries, 'Traditions at a Glance', 'Sites' boxes, excerpts from essential texts, and 'Focus' boxes on various subjects—four new pedagogical features:

- bolded key terms (defined in end-of-chapter glossaries);
- study questions;
- lists of recommended websites; and
- comparative tables of sacred and other foundational texts.

A vibrant new full-colour design, with many new photographs, reflects the richness and diversity of the various traditions.

Chapter
6
Hindu Traditions
≈ Vasudha Narayanan ≈

Traditions at a Glance

Numbers
Confucianism: Estimates range from 6 to 8 million, but because most of the East Asian world does not consider Confucianism to be a religion, the true number is impossible to gauge.
Daoism: Estimates range from 2.5 to 3.5 million.
Chinese folk or popular religion includes numerous movements and sects whose devotees may consider their traditions to be more cultural than religious. Estimates range from 385 to 405 million.
Korean shamanism and popular religion: Estimates range from 1 to 7 million.

Distribution
Confucians and Daoists live mainly in East and Southeast Asia, Australia, New Zealand, northwestern Europe, and North America. Adherents of popular religions remain primarily in East Asia, with small pockets in diasporic communities in North America and Europe.

Founders and Teachers
Mythological founders and heroes include Yao, Shun, and Yu in China, and Dangun in Korea. Famous first teachers—some mythical, some historic—include the Yellow Emperor, Confucius, and Laozi in China, and Choe Chung in Korea.

Deities
For Confucians, the place of a deity is filled either by Heaven or by Heaven and Earth together. For some Daoists, the Way functions as a deity; others look to what is in effect a bureaucracy of deities. Popular religions, both Korean and Chinese, include deities from various traditions.

Authoritative Texts
For Confucians, the Classics from the Zhou and Han are the foundational texts. For Daoists, the *Daodejing* (or *Laozi*) is fundamental; other important scriptures vary from sect to sect. Popular and shamanistic religions tend not to be textually oriented.

Noteworthy Teachings
None of the East Asian traditions are exclusive. Daoism and Confucianism share cultural and social space with each other as well as popular religions, even if they differ doctrinally. The two elite religions share a utopian view of a peaceful and harmonious society whose members are devoted to self-cultivation and discipline, live frugally, serve the community, and try to be good.

the inner world of the family. The essential function of rituals, ancestor rituals in particular, was to define, frame, and encourage right relationships, especially between men and women.

Confucian Exemplars and Sages
The prototypes of the Confucian sage are three mythical 'sage kings' named Yao, Shun, and Yu, whose stories are told in the first chapters of the *Classic of Documents*. The virtues they

Traditions at a Glance boxes at the start of most chapters give readers a summary of the basics.

Sites boxes draw attention to locations of special significance to each tradition.

Sites

Bethlehem The traditional birthplace of Jesus.

Nazareth Jesus' home in youth and manhood.

Jerusalem The site of Jesus' crucifixion and centre of the earliest Jewish Christian community; capital of the Latin Christian Kingdom in the Holy Land from 1099 to 1187.

Rome The capital of the Roman Empire, where Peter introduced Christianity and the Roman Catholic Church eventually established its headquarters in Vatican City—the world's smallest independent country.

Anatolia A region (corresponding to modern-day Turkey), evangelized by Paul, that became an important centre of the early Church; the location of the famous councils of Chalcedon. Nicaea, and Constantinople.

Constantinople The capital of the Byzantine Empire and headquarters of the Orthodox Church; conquered by the Ottoman Turks in 1453 and renamed Istanbul.

Wittenberg The German town where Martin Luther posted his 95 theses, beginning the Protestant Reformation.

Worms The German city where an imperial council ('diet') tried Luther for political subversion.

Trent (Trentino in Italian) Site of the Council of Trent (1545–63) and centre of the Catholic Church's response to Protestantism, known as the Counter-Reformation.

Geneva The city in which John Calvin attempted to translate his vision of Christianity into a practising community.

Münster A town in northwestern Germany that became a centre of the Anabaptist movement.

Valladolid City in Spain; the site of a great debate in 1550 in which Bartolomé de las Casas defended the rights of the indigenous peoples of the New World.

Salt Lake City, Utah Founded by the Mormons in 1847; the headquarters of the Church of Jesus Christ of Latter-day Saints.

of the Jaina devotional apparatus. A commanding figure who could just as easily have been a worldly *chakravartin*—the ideal benevolent ruler, endowed with all the powers and possessions the world has to offer—the Jina 'conquers' the world by turning his back on it. Indeed, the Jina is venerated in both his potentialities: as the regal *chakravartin*, magnificently bejewelled and crowned, and as the unadorned **Arhat**, deep in meditation, entirely detached from worldly concerns. World renouncer and world conqueror, though antithetical in their orientations, both trace their beginnings to the auspicious karma accrued from a life of non-violence. Restraint, self-discipline, and commitment not to harm are the starting points for the Jina and the *chakravartin* alike.

To grasp the vigorous, even forceful character of Jainism, we need to keep in mind that the Jaina path of renunciation is one not of retreat from the harshness of the world, but of

Timeline

c. 850 BCE	Parsavanath, the 23rd Tirthankara
599–527 BCE	Traditional dates of Mahavira
4th century BCE	Possible beginning of split within Jaina community with southward migration of one group
2nd century CE	Umasvati, Digambara author of the *Tatthvartha Sutra*
5th century CE	First Jaina temples
9th century CE	Jinasena, Svetambara philosopher
10th century CE	Colossal statue of Bahubali erected in Shravanabelagola, Karnataka
11th century CE	Dilwara temple complex in Rajasthan
12th century CE	Hemachandra, Svetambara philosopher
15th century CE	Lonkashaha initiates reform in the Svetambara tradition
16th century CE	Banarsidass initiates reform in the Digambara tradition
17th century CE	Beginning of Svetambara Sthanakvasi subsect
18th century CE	Beginning of Svetambara Terapanthi subsect
19th century CE	Emergence of modern Jaina reform groups, and the widespread publication of Jaina scriptures
20th century CE	Revitalization of the Bhattaraka tradition within the Digambara sect
1962	Consecration of Jain temple (Svetambara) in Mombasa, Kenya, the first to be built outside India
1966	Jain Centre of New York established
1981	Jain Federation of North America (JAINA) established
1983	Siddhachalam ashram founded in New Jersey by Acharya Sushul Kumarji; the first recognized Jaina pilgrimage site outside India, it is visited by both Svetambaras and Digambaras

Timelines help to place religious developments in historical context.

Informative maps provide useful reference points.

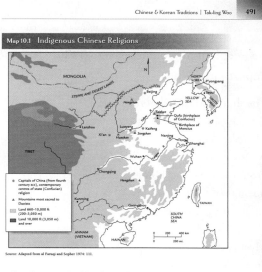

Sacred/Foundational Texts tables give students a convenient summary of the most important texts in each tradition, how and when they were composed or compiled, and how they are used.

Sacred/Foundational Texts boxes present a generous selection of excerpts from scripture and other important writings.

Focus boxes offer additional information on selected subjects.

End-of-chapter study questions enhance understanding of key concepts and glossaries explain key terms (bolded in the text), while further readings and recommended websites provide excellent starting-points for further research and study.

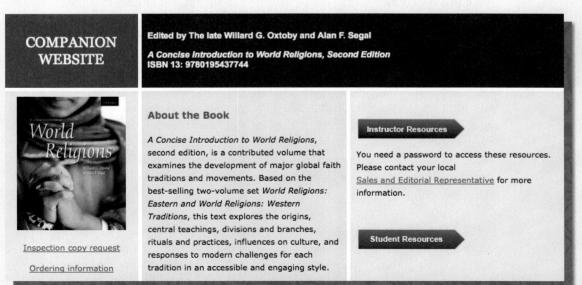

The sample pages (370–371) show the following:

Page 370 — *A Concise Introduction to World Religions*

Study Questions

1. Lay (householder) Jainas are integral to the tradition, which has always recognized the centrality of their role. Explain.
2. What are some of the major differences between Svetambara and Digambara Jainism?
3. What are the main reasons believed to be responsible for the split that gave rise to the Svetambara and Digambara sects?
4. How are women understood within Jainism? What are some of the main differences between Svetambaras and Digambaras in terms of female theology and women's religious roles?
5. Although Jainism envisions final liberation (moksha) as a purely spiritual state, it does not see the spiritual and the material in oppositional terms. Explain.
6. Karma is envisioned as more than a moral law of cause and effect in Jainism. Explain.
7. Non-violence (ahimsa) informs every aspect of Jainism, from cosmology to dietary practices and devotional rituals. Elaborate.
8. Jainas worship beings (Jinas) who they believe to be utterly removed from all worldly matters and unresponsive to their concerns. How do they understand their acts of devotion?
9. What is the significance of 'right faith' (samyak darshan) in Jainism?
10. How do Jainas understand the final state of liberation (moksha)?
11. What are some of the main ways in which diaspora expressions of Jainism differ from Jainism in India today?

Glossary

agama Canonical texts within Svetambara Jainism
ahimsa Literally, non-harm or non-violence. For Jainas it denotes a philosophy of life in which all living beings should be respected and, to the greatest degree possible, protected from harm.
ajiva Non-soul, non-consciousness; ajiva is also referred to as 'matter' or 'karma'.
anavratas Five vows modelled on the great vows of the renouncers but modified to make them applicable to lay life: non-violence, truthfulness, non-stealing, non-attachment, and chastity
caturvidhyasangha Literally, 'four-fold community'; the community consisting of monks, nuns, laymen, and laywomen.
Digambaras Early sectarian node within Jainism with its own sacred scriptures; identified by the male mendicant practice of nudity.
Jina Literally, 'conqueror'; name given to the 24 ascetic-prophets who conquered the world of desire and suffering, and taught the path to eternal happiness; alternatively called Tirthankaras.
jiva Eternal soul/consciousness; all living beings are endowed with jiva.
Mahavira Literally, 'Great Hero'; epithet of the 24th and final Jina of our time cycle, born Vardhamana Jnatrpura in the sixth century BCE.

Mahavira Jayanti A joyous spring festival celebrating the birth of Mahavira.
mahavratas The five 'great vows' adopted by renouncers: absolute non-violence, truthfulness, non-stealing, non-attachment, and celibacy
Namokar Mantra The central prayer in Jainism.
paap Karmic particles of an inauspicious nature ('bad karma').
pratikramana The ritual practice of repentance.
puja Ritual worship, usually of a Jina, for the purpose of self-purification.
punya Karmic particles of an auspicious nature ('good karma').
Rsabha The first Tirthankara of our current time cycle; also called Adinath.
sallekhana A voluntary fast to death, usually undertaken in old age.
samayika A desired state of equanimity achieved through ritual practice of meditation.
samyak darshan Right vision, faith, or intuition into the basic truth of the cosmos; spiritual growth is dependent on the attainment of samyak darshan.
siddha loka Final abode of the liberated jiva.
Svetambara One of two early sectarian nodes within Jainism; mendicants wear simple white robes.

Page 371 — Jaina Traditions | Vallely

Tattvartha Sutra An important philosophical text accepted by all Jaina sects, composed by Umasvati in the second century CE.

Tirthankara Literally, 'ford-maker'; epithet for the 24 Jinas who, through their teachings, created a ford across the ocean of samsara.

Further Reading

Babb, Lawrence A. 1996. *Absent Lord: Ascetics and Kings in a Jain Ritual Culture.* Berkeley: University of California Press.
Banks, Marcus. 1992. *Organizing Jainism in India and England.* Oxford: Clarendon.
Carrithers, Michael, and Caroline Humphrey, eds. 1991. *The Assembly of Listeners: Jains in Society.* Cambridge: Cambridge University Press.
Cort, John E. 2001. *Jains in the World: Religious Values and Ideology in India.* New York and Delhi: Oxford University Press.
Dundas, Paul. 2002. *The Jains.* 2nd ed. London: Routledge. A comprehensive overview of Jainism and an excellent introduction to the subject.

Granoff, Phyllis. 2006. *The Forest of Thieves and the Magic Garden.* Penguin Classics.
Jaini, Padmanabh S. 1979. *The Jaina Path of Purification.* Berkeley: University of California Press. The standard general study of Jainism.
Kelting, Whitney. 2009. *Heroic Wives: Rituals, Stories, and the Virtues of Jain Wifehood.* Oxford: Oxford University Press
Kelting, Whitney. 2001. *Singing to the Jinas: Jain Laywomen, Mandal Singing, and the Negotiations of Jain Devotion.* Oxford: Oxford University Press
Laidlaw, James. 1995. *Riches and Renunciation: Religion, Economy, and Society among the Jains.* Oxford: Oxford University Press.
Long, Jeffrey. 2009. *Jainism, an Introduction.* New York: I.B. Tauris & Co.

Recommended Websites

www.jaindharmonline.com A portal dedicated to Jainism and Jaina dharma, containing information and links to news articles.
www.jainstudies.org The International Summer School for Jain Studies.

www.jainworld.com Jainism Global Resource Center, USA.
http://pluralism.org/wrgb/traditions/jainism Resources from Harvard University's Pluralism Project.

References

Cort, John E. 2001. *Jains in the World: Religious Values and Ideology in India.* New York and Delhi: Oxford University Press.
——— 2005. 'Devotional Culture in Jainism: Manatunga and His Bhaktamara Stotra'. In James Blumenthal, ed. *Incompatible Visions: South Asian Religions in History and Culture.* Madison, WI: Center for South Asia, University of Wisconsin–Madison.
Gelra, M.R. 2007. *Science in Jainism.* Ladnun, Rajasthan: Jain Vishva Bharati Institute.
Jacobi, Hermann, trans. 1884. *Jaina Sutras,* Part 1. In F. Max Müller, ed., *Sacred Books of the East,* 22. Oxford: Clarendon Press.

Jain, S.C. 2008. 'Jain Festivals'. Unpublished manuscript prepared for the International Summer School of Jain Studies.
Jaini, Padmanabh S. 1979. *The Jaina Path of Purification.* Berkeley: University of California Press.
——— 1990. 'Ahimsa'. Inaugural Roop Lal Jain Lecture, Centre for South Asian Studies, University of Toronto.
Laidlaw, James. 2005. 'A Life Worth Leaving: Fasting to Death as Telos of a Jain Religious Life'. *Economy and Society* 34, 2: 178–99.
Lath, M., trans. 1984. *Kalpa Sutra.* V. Sagar, ed. Jaipur: Prakrit Bharati.

Note

1. This text was compiled by Jinendra Varni and published by Sarva Seva Sangh Prakashan, India. It was translated into English in 1993 by T.K. Tukol and K.K. Dixit.

Extensive ancillary package

For Instructors: an Instructor's Manual, a Test Generator, and PowerPoint slides.
For Students: a Students Study Guide.

COMPANION WEBSITE

Edited by The late Willard G. Oxtoby and Alan F. Segal

A Concise Introduction to World Religions, Second Edition
ISBN 13: 9780195437744

Inspection copy request
Ordering information

About the Book

A Concise Introduction to World Religions, second edition, is a contributed volume that examines the development of major global faith traditions and movements. Based on the best-selling two-volume set *World Religions: Eastern* and *World Religions: Western Traditions,* this text explores the origins, central teachings, divisions and branches, rituals and practices, influences on culture, and responses to modern challenges for each tradition in an accessible and engaging style.

Instructor Resources

You need a password to access these resources. Please contact your local Sales and Editorial Representative for more information.

Student Resources

Instructors should contact their Oxford University Press sales representative for details on these supplements and for login and password information.

Contributors

ROY C. AMORE has extensive research experience in Asia. His books include *Two Masters, One Message*, comparing the lives and teachings of Christ and Buddha, and *Lustful Maidens and Ascetic Kings: Buddhist and Hindu Stories of Life*. He is Professor in the Department of Political Science and Associate Dean, Institutional and External Affairs, Faculty of Arts and Social Sciences, at the University of Windsor and is currently writing a book on religion and politics.

ROBERT M. BAUM is Associate Professor of Religious Studies at the University of Missouri and his focus is indigenous religions, especially in West Africa. The author of the award-winning book *Shrines of the Slave Trade: Diola Religion and Society in Precolonial Senegambia*, as well as numerous articles, he is currently working on a history of Diola prophetic movements and a continent-wide history of African religions.

AMIR HUSSAIN is Professor in the Department of Theological Studies at Loyola Marymount University in Los Angeles, where he teaches courses on Islam and world religions. A Canadian of Pakistani origin, he is the author of *Oil and Water: Two Faiths, One God* (an introduction to Islam for North Americans) and current editor of the *Journal of the American Academy of Religion*.

VASUDHA NARAYANAN is Distinguished Professor in the Department of Religion and Director of the Center for the Study of Hindu Traditions at the University of Florida. A past president of the American Academy of Religion, she is the author or editor of seven books and has written more than a hundred articles and chapters in books. Her current research focuses on Hindu traditions in Cambodia.

JOHN K. NELSON is Professor in the Department of Theology and Religious Studies at the University of San Francisco. Trained as a cultural anthropologist, he is the author of two books on Shinto as well a documentary film on

Yasukuni Shrine, and is actively researching contemporary Buddhism in Japan and North America.

The late WILLARD C. OXTOBY, the original editor of the two-volume *World Religions: Eastern Traditions and Western Traditions*, was Professor Emeritus at the University of Toronto, where he launched the graduate program in the study of religion. His books include *Experiencing India: European Descriptions and Impressions* and *The Meaning of Other Faiths*.

The late ALAN F. SEGAL was Professor of Religion and Ingeborg Rennert Professor of Jewish Studies at Barnard College, Columbia University. He wrote extensively in the fields of comparative religion, Judaism, and early Christianity. His books include *Rebecca's Children*, *Paul the Convert*, and *Life After Death: A History of the Afterlife in Western Religions*.

PASHAURA SINGH is Professor and Dr Jasbir Singh Saini Endowed Chair in Sikh and Punjabi Studies at the University of California, Riverside. He has authored three Oxford monographs, co-edited three conference volumes, and contributed articles to academic journals, books and encyclopedias. His recent book, *Life and Work of Guru Arjan: History, Memory and Biography in the Sikh Tradition* (OUP, 2006) was a bestseller in India.

ANNE VALLELY is Associate Professor in the Department of Classics and Religious Studies at the University of Ottawa, where she teaches courses on South Asian traditions (especially Jainism and Hinduism), as well as Nature and Religion. Her book *Guardians of the Transcendent: An Ethnography of a Jain Ascetic Community* (2002) is an anthropological study of Jain female ascetics. Her co-edited volume *Animal Others and the Human Imagination* is forthcoming.

TERRY TAK-LING WOO teaches at York University and Hangzhou Normal University. She is involved with courses that introduce the study of religion, East Asian religions, and human rights.

Foreword

Will Oxtoby seemed to know everything there was to know about the world's religions. Having majored in philosophy, he completed his Ph.D. in Near Eastern Studies at Princeton and, after learning Hebrew and Arabic, began his career as a Bible professor at McGill. Before long, however, he was enticed into the Persian gardens of Zoroastrianism. Exploring the relationships between Zoroastrianism and early Second Temple period Judaism required him to learn Avestan, the classical Persian language, which in turn required a working knowledge of Sanskrit. By the time he began teaching the history of religion at Yale, he already had half the world's traditions within his purview. He had also developed strong views on the teaching of religion.

He put those views into practice as the founding director of the University of Toronto's Centre for the Study of Religions. Will himself had begun his exploration of other faiths from a Presbyterian perspective, and he wanted to emphasize that anyone with strong roots in a particular religious tradition cannot help bringing certain assumptions to the study of other traditions. In this respect, the believer and the non-believer start from a similar place: both may find it difficult to appreciate an unfamiliar tradition from the insider's point of view.

Will also wanted his students to understand that the truths of religion do not reveal themselves to the casual eye. Close observation is required even when the observer is an insider to the faith. And a capacity for critical analysis is no less essential for those exploring their own traditions than a sympathetic openness to difference is for outsiders seeking to understand religious experiences that they do not share.

In a sense, Will's entire career reflected his conviction that religion plays a central role in the lives of most people around the world, and that we cannot understand others without understanding their faiths. He also believed that it is only by making the effort to understand other religions that we can truly begin to understand our own.

Will was among the first to identify Iran's Islamic revolution as an event of worldwide religious significance—an early expression of a much broader revitalization of religion that was likely to bring with it dangers as well as rewards. A decade later, he recognized the collapse of the Soviet Union as another event of enormous religious importance, and not just because it opened the way for a religious revival in Eastern Europe. It was significant, Will suggested, because the demise of an explicitly atheistic, Marxist-inspired state could be attributed—at least in part—to a contradiction within Marxism. Marx himself had justly criticized religion as an instrument of oppression, serving the authoritarian state. Yet some of the fundamental principles on which Marx based his critique would be quite at home in any number of religions, and in many ways Marxism itself could be seen as a religion (especially one of the Western Abrahamic variety). The communist system had gained power by promising to end tyranny and alleviate human misery. Having done the very opposite, it was justly condemned by its own principles.

In the course of his career, Will came to believe ever more deeply in the plurality of truth. With that belief came the conviction that human efforts to understand truth must be plural as well. In Will's view, truth was not the possession of any single religion or school of thought: it was something that emerged in the process of comparison and dialogue. Thus every religion must be recognized as having its own purchase on truth, and every individual—believer, unbeliever, and everyone in between—as having a potentially valid perspective; then all those perspectives have to become part of a wide-open, ongoing dialogue. The spirit behind such dialogue Will called pluralism, and it was in that spirit that this textbook was conceived.

Alan F. Segal
Barnard College
Columbia University
September 2009

A Tribute to Alan F. Segal (1945–2011)

'If I forget thee, O Jerusalem, let my right hand forget' (*Psalm* 137:5)

Those of us who had the privilege to know Alan F. Segal will never forget him. He was our colleague, our editor, our mentor, and above all our friend. He was also left-handed, and so the Psalmist's assumption that the right hand is the one that matters makes us smile and remember how Alan faced challenges, with humour and optimism.

Alan was born in 1945 into a Reform Jewish family in Worcester, Massachusetts. After studies at Amherst College and Brandeis University, in 1975 he completed a PhD dissertation at Yale University, which was published two years later as *Two Powers in Heaven: Early Rabbinic Reports about Christianity and Gnosticism*. The fact that his magisterial first book focused on the relations between Judaism and Christianity prefigured the work that Alan would do for the rest of his career. His next book, *Rebecca's Children: Judaism and Christianity in the Roman Empire* (1986), was revolutionary in that it treated Judaism and Christianity not as parent and child but as siblings who sometimes didn't play well together. As Alan wrote in his introduction:

> Like Jacob and Esau, the twin sons of Isaac and Rebecca, the two religions fought in the womb. Throughout their youth they followed very different paths, quarrelling frequently about their father's blessing. As was the case with Rebecca's children, the conflict between Judaism and Christianity moulded their characters and determined their destinies.

Alan continued to explore the relationship between the two faiths in *Paul the Convert: The Apostolate and Apostasy of Saul the Pharisee* (1990), a study of early Christianity's most important exponent as a Jewish thinker. Finally, he extended his comparative research to the entire Western tradition in *Life After Death: A History of the Afterlife in Western Religion* (2004).

It was as a student at Yale that Alan met Willard Oxtoby. Will was Alan's teacher, and they became colleagues in 1978 when Alan began teaching at the

University of Toronto. Unlike Rebecca's sons, they became close friends and remained so long after Alan accepted a position at Barnard College in 1980.

At Will's invitation, Alan wrote the chapter on 'The Jewish Tradition' for the first edition of *World Religions: Western Traditions* (Oxtoby, ed., 1996) and eventually saw it through two revisions. After Will's death in 2003, he took over the task of editing the first edition of the present work, *A Concise Introduction to World Religions* (2006), for which he also condensed and updated both his own chapter on Judaism and Will's chapter on Christianity.

Alan retired from Barnard College in December 2010 as the Ingeborg Rennert Professor of Jewish Studies. Having lived for years with leukemia, he died less than three months later, shortly before this second edition of the *Concise* went to press. He leaves his wife Meryl, their children Ethan and Jordan, his siblings Eric and Carol, and countless friends and colleagues, including ourselves.

Roy Amore, co-editor, *World Religions: Eastern Traditions*, 3rd edition
Amir Hussain, co-editor, *World Religions: Western Traditions*, 3rd edition

ACKNOWLEDGMENTS

Oxford University Press Canada gratefully acknowledges the assistance of Professor Leslie Hayes of the University of Toronto and Professor Martin Lockshin of York University. We would also like to thank the following reviewers (as well as those reviewers who wished to remain anonymous), whose comments helped to shape this volume:

William Acres, Huron University College
John Cappucci, Algonquin College
Steven Engler, Mount Royal College
Lyle Eslinger, University of Calgary
Tim Labron, Concordia University College of Alberta
Ramdas Lamb, University of Hawai'i
Wayne Litke, University of Alberta
Gillian McCann, Nipissing University
Susan Jean Palmer, Dawson College

On behalf of the late Alan Segal, Roy Amore and Amir Hussain thank Stephen Kotowych for his encouragement, Kathryn West and Patricia Simoes for their developmental guidance, and Sally Livingston for her hands-on editorial work.

The Nature of Religion

≈ Alan F. Segal and Willard G. Oxtoby ≈

Suppose someone asks you: 'Aren't religions all pretty much the same?' The question looks simple enough. Presumably the questioner is suggesting that all religions resemble one another in certain essential respects, and that any differences in the details can be dismissed as secondary.

To answer responsibly, though, we should start by unpacking the question. It could be seeking confirmation that all religions share some essential core in their teachings, or that their practice accomplishes some common result. Or it could be asking about the value of the world's diverse traditions in relation to one another. Questions of value are almost inevitable when we compare faiths, especially when we include our own in the comparison. For the moment, though, let's consider the matter of diversity itself.

The diversity of the world's religions is nowhere more evident than in their representations of supernatural power. Some localize the divine in tangible objects; others claim it to be beyond form altogether. We can marvel not only at the divine itself but at the bewildering array of its manifestations. Still, some groupings do emerge when we begin to sort those manifestations into categories.

THE NATURE OF THE DIVINE

Monotheism and Polytheism

The terms **monotheism** (from the Greek for worship of only one god) and **polytheism** (worship of many gods) first appear in European writing in the seventeenth century: a time of absolute monarchy, when a single God functioned to justify a single monarch on the throne. Sometimes these terms were used in an intra-Christian context; for example, by Protestants who condemned the Roman Catholic veneration of saints as polytheistic. Then as now, however, they referred principally to the contrast between the Hebraic model of exclusive devotion to one god and the Hellenic model of devotion to many. Furthermore, then as now, the concept of monotheism included an implicit judgment not only on polytheism—by far the more common system around the world—but on diversity itself.

Western civilization owes to ancient Israel the idea that there is only one god. Well before the term 'monotheism' was coined, that idea was a distinctive characteristic of the three principal religions in the West: Judaism, Christianity, and Islam. This monotheism is exclusive. It declares that the faithful should worship only the one God, that the worship of any other deity is an abomination to God, and that no other gods even exist. The deity's exclusive status tends to be matched by exclusivity in the communities of followers.

◀ Stonehenge (David MacDonald).

Christians and Muslims, as members of **missionary religions**, tend to draw clear boundaries between themselves and outsiders, and then encourage those on the other side of the line to cross over and join them. Jews, by contrast, think of themselves as a family community. They allow others to join the community if they are truly motivated, but have rarely attempted to attract converts; they also believe that the righteous of all nations will enter paradise in the world to come. When Christians and Muslims have come into contact with Eastern traditions whose communities are less clearly demarcated than their own, they have tended to describe those traditions as if they too followed the boundaried model. But neither Chinese nor Indian religions need to be defined in those terms, and even Judaism does not fit the 'boundaried' definition very well.

Scholars have often tried to identify the forces that produce monotheism in a society. Guy E. Swanson, in his book *The Birth of the Gods: The Origin of Primitive Beliefs*, maintains that monotheism is associated with social complexity, reflecting the establishment of a multi-layered hierarchy. From another perspective, though, multiple gods may simply represent the attribution of human motivations to natural phenomena. In that case the movement towards monotheism could just as easily be seen as marking a society's repudiation of this primitive understanding of causation.

Perhaps scholars should pay more attention to the principles that a society considers important. Polytheistic Greek society eventually adopted the family principle, arranging all the gods into a large extended family. The Greek philosophers also attempted to reduce the complexities of the world to one single, overriding element or principle, whether water, fire, change, time, love, or knowledge. Contemporary cosmological physicists seek a theory of everything—one that will unify gravity, electromagnetism, and the forces that keep atoms together. So far that theory has been elusive.

On the other hand, the search for single causation may be a product of the human mind itself. Some great Eastern religious systems like Hinduism and Buddhism identify a single principle of salvation in which animals, humans, and gods all participate. For them, monotheism and polytheism are not the polar opposites that Jews, Christians, and Muslims tend to consider them.

Dualism: Zoroastrianism, Gnosticism, Manichaeism

Dualism in religion postulates two ultimate principles opposing each other and more or less evenly matched. These principles are usually (though not always) personified as a good god and an evil devil.

Zoroastrianism

Zoroastrianism is a nominally monotheistic religion with dualistic overtones. It developed in Persia (Iran) sometime before the mid-sixth century BCE; it was the state religion of Iran's last great pre-Islamic empire (the Sasanians); and it is still alive today in India and Iran, in small communities that have preserved the tradition over the past 14 centuries.

The supreme creator god of the Zoroastrians is called Ahura Mazda ('Wise Lord'). In ancient times Zoroastrians called themselves Mazda worshippers and their tradition 'the Good Religion'. 'Zoroastrianism' came later, from the Greek name for the tradition's priestly and prophetic teacher, Zarathustra. The time, place, and details of his life are unknown. All we can say with any assurance is that he lived somewhere in Iran before the beginning of the Achaemenian era (559–331 BCE). The scholarly consensus credits him only with 17 psalms, called the *Gathas*, that form part of the sacred book called the Avesta. (The rest of the text consists mainly of ritual hymns and a work on priestly purity regulations.)

The religious thought of Zoroastrianism places it among the great religious traditions of human history. Five features are of particular interest. One is its emphasis on ethics: morality is central, both as an ideal and as an achievement. Another is its **eschatology**, centred on the expectation of a world to come both for the individual and for the world as a whole, when this life will be overhauled and a new utopian age ushered in. A third notable characteristic of Zoroastrian tradition is its vivid personification of evil as a demonic antagonist who, like Satan in the Christian and Muslim traditions, seems beyond the good deity's control. Fourth, it is the Zoroastrian tradition to dispose of the dead by exposing the remains to birds of prey in 'towers of silence'. Fifth and finally, there is the historical influence of Zoroastrianism: although this remains more a question than a fact, it is possible that Zoroastrian ideas about evil and the soul contributed to the development of comparable ideas in Judaism, Christianity, and Islam.

Most Zoroastrians today consider themselves monotheists, perhaps in part because their tradition was maintained under Islamic rule in Iran and under Christian rule in British India. But their monotheism is not exclusive: Zoroastrians revere a host of divine entities (some corresponding to deities in the Hindu Vedas) that they believe to function as agents and deputies of Ahura Mazda. In the early parts of the Zoroastrian scripture, the Avesta, there are statements suggesting that two gods hold sway over the universe. The good god, Ahura Mazda, is the one to whom all praise and thanks are due. His evil counterpart, known first as Angra Mainyu and later as Ahriman, is the one who controls evil and must be exorcised.

The devil is a much more elusive figure in Judaism, Christianity, and Islam, perhaps because theologians wanting to affirm God's purpose and power have been reluctant to make room for a second locus of ultimate power. Nevertheless, he is a visible presence in the art and narratives of the Christian Middle Ages and continues to figure in the folklore and popular piety of all three Abrahamic traditions today.

The devil or Satan is mentioned both in the New Testament and in the Qur'an, where he is known as Shaytan or Iblis. But he does not figure in any Old Testament narrative. The snake of Genesis 2–3 is never described as anything more than a snake. Satan makes no appearance in the Hebrew creation story, and even the book of Job refers only to 'the satan'—a Hebrew word meaning 'adversary' and apparently designating a court official; it is not a personal name. The few other references to 'satan' in the Hebrew Bible are best understood in the same way.

When did 'the adversary' become 'Satan'? Most scholars today would place the transition sometime between the completion of the Old Testament and the beginning of the writing of the New Testament. That is because there is no statement in the Old Testament that can unambiguously be applied to a figure in opposition to God. Yet Satan is a fully developed power, independent of God, in the New Testament, and this same characterization is also present in a series of books composed after the Old Testament and before the

After the Muslim conquest of Persia many Zoroastrians fled to India, where their descendants came to be known as Parsis ('Persians'). Here four priests perform a fire ceremony at a gathering in Bombay. The cloths covering their mouths are intended to prevent any spittle from coming in contact with the fire (Willard G. Oxtoby).

New Testament, which are not included in either the Jewish or the Christian Bible. In fact, the devil appears to emerge in Jewish and Christian tradition just at the moment when Persian influence was at its height. There seems no doubt that the image of Satan as he appears in the Christian and Muslim traditions, and to a lesser extent in Jewish folklore, owes something to Persian depictions of Ahriman.

Gnosticism and Manichaeism

Westerners tend to see monotheism as the culmination of religious development—the final stage in an evolutionary progression away from polytheism. For them, dualism thus represents an intermediary stage. Historically, though, dualism appears to have arisen only after monotheism had established itself. In fact, dualism seems to represent a kind of strategic retreat made necessary by the difficulty of explaining evil in a monotheistic system. The scope of God's power is, in principle, limited by whatever the demonic adversary can control. If God is both physical creator and moral sovereign, then the religious narrative must answer two questions regarding the force of evil. First, why would an all-powerful creator have permitted the introduction of evil? Second, given the present force of evil, how may we be assured that good will triumph in the end?

An influential narrative response to these questions came in the movement we call **Gnosticism**. Spreading mainly among Hellenized Jews and Christians living in an atmosphere of popularized Platonic thought, Gnosticism suggested that humanity could be released from its primal entrapment in the sinful cosmos only through divine redemption. Since pure spirit was seen to have fallen into an evil material existence, it was the task of the faithful to renounce physical satisfaction and seek an ascetic's release from entrapment in matter. Jewish communities were particularly receptive to the Gnostic message because of early Jewish **mysticism**, in which adepts of meditation could ascend to heaven to discover hidden truths. Gnostic mythological systems proliferated in the first few centuries of our era, each with a different story of how the evil world came into being and how the saviour beyond it was to be reached. The Gnostic literary enterprise tended towards stories of origins, but implicitly it was no less concerned with salvation. The awakened person was duty-bound to escape the evil universe, and the only guide was the special redeeming knowledge called *gnosis* in Greek. In many Gnostic systems the spiritually awakened person was called a 'pneumatic', from the Greek *pneuma*, meaning spirit.

In the third century a Syrian Christian named Mani (c. 216–c. 274) organized his own new religion on a largely Christian Gnostic base. Manichaeism attracted many of those who cherished individual Gnostic systems and melded them into a new world religion. It spread westward across the Mediterranean world, and its narratives of conflict between good and evil lingered into the Middle Ages in the Balkans and southern France. It also spread across Central Asia to China, where it survived for centuries before dying out. In the course of its Central Asian dispersion it moved into Buddhist territory, where its emphasis on salvation and its program of asceticism both appear to have landed on fertile soil. But the question to which Manichaeism offered an answer was not one that troubled Buddhism. While the monotheistic religions of the Middle East and Mediterranean might see the problem of suffering and evil as a reason to question divine power, Buddhism does not. The Western traditions ask why a good God allows suffering, but Buddhism (especially the Mahayana school) sees the celestial powers as helping humans along the path to liberation from suffering.

Mani was active in Syria and later Persia, home of Zoroastrianism, and it was just after his time that the latter became the established religion of Persia's Sasanian dynasty (r. 226–51). The Sasanian Zoroastrians' vision of the universe, from the creation to the final judgment and renewal, drew on earlier Persian ideas that may have underlain the biblical and Gnostic–Manichaean narratives as well. Still, Zoroastrian and Manichaean interpretations of the struggle between good and evil differ in one crucial respect. For Gnostics and Manichaeans, spirit is good and material existence is inherently evil. For Zoroastrians, however, the material world is simply the context within which the moral forces of good and evil operate: in itself, that world is morally neutral. Only at certain times in its history, notably during the Sasanian era, has the Zoroastrian tradition seriously explored the philosophical idea that the ultimate power of Ahura Mazda, the Wise Lord, is in any substantial way compromised by the activity of the evil spirit.

Both the ethical struggle of the Zoroastrians and the spirit–matter opposition of the Gnostics and Manichaeans have been termed dualistic. The word 'dualism' was coined in 1700 by the Englishman Thomas Hyde, who was writing about Zoroastrianism and used the term to refer to a system of thought in which an evil being is set over against the being who is the source of good. For Hyde, then, the spirit–matter contrast of the Gnostic traditions was not a defining characteristic of dualism. But within a generation the term came to be used in other contexts, and as a result it acquired additional connotations. The eighteenth-century German philosopher Christian Wolff, for instance, applied it to the contrast between mind and matter in the philosophy of René Descartes.

Since then the term has been applied to such a variety of dualities that it has lost almost all useful meaning. To call Daoism dualistic, for example—as some have done because of its opposition between yin and yang—is not helpful, since Daoists, while privileging yin in conduct, see goodness in the universe as existing in a perfect dynamic balance between the two. Even so, to the extent that 'dualism' refers explicitly to a struggle between good and evil as ultimate powers, it does offer a response to one of the most difficult problems raised by monotheism.

Missionary Religions

We began this chapter by considering the proposition that all religions are pretty much the same. Missionary religions take the opposite view. They believe not only that all religions are different, but that the differences are so consequential that they cannot be dismissed: therefore those who know the truth are obliged to spread it. Missionaries' motives are often profoundly altruistic. They may spend long years far from their homes, living a frugal and sometimes dangerous life, simply in order to help others understand a message that will save their souls. Any hope of gaining otherworldly merit through such service is generally a secondary consideration.

No one can say how many religions there have been in the world, for the boundaries distinguishing them are sometimes fluid or arbitrary, and new religions emerge all the time. Yet a mere three traditions claim the allegiance of half the world's population. Buddhism, Christianity, and Islam have all succeeded as missionary religions, thanks to their worldwide diffusion. Interestingly, all three have presented their messages as 'universal': intended for all humans, not merely for specific groups defined by heredity or descent.

In the early phase of Buddhism's development, Indian society was already stratified into four broad social classes. Buddhism set these caste distinctions aside as irrelevant to the achievement of liberation.

Christianity began as a sect of Judaism, a religion that emphasized the special national destiny and responsibility of the Jewish people but maintained that all righteous persons, regardless of ethnic or religious identity, will achieve God's kingdom. Hence it saw no need for missionary activity. Instead Judaism concentrated on moral teachings that it believed to be intended for everyone, and as a result Jews were able to survive as guests in cultures where other religions predominated.

Christianity was helped towards its missionary course by the apostle Paul, who insisted that converts did not need to become Jews first in order to become Christians. At the same time Christian rhetoric appropriated the divine promises made to Israel and claimed them for the new Israel represented by the ethnically inclusive Christian Church. Early Christian preaching promoted a universal spiritual and moral interpretation of the ideas of community and kingship received from Judaism. Paul's rejection of the distinction between Jew and Greek in Galatians 3 and Romans 10 reverberates through the centuries in the Christian community's consciousness: 'There is no longer Jew or Greek, there is no longer slave or free, there is no longer male and female; for all of you are one in Christ Jesus' (Gal.

3:28). This is a universal declaration of striking generality; yet others have noted that it makes no reference to pluralism. There is only the one faith, to which all must adhere.

The Qur'an maintains that God has used different prophets to deliver his message to different peoples. But Muhammad did not think that monotheism was intended for the Arabs alone, and the message of *islam* ('submission') was inherently universal. In fact, *islam* connotes conversion for Muslims, though it also describes life in community thereafter. Describing its own message—specifically addressed to the people of Arabia—as clear, reasonable, even self-evident, the Qur'an invites comparison with the revelations given earlier to Jews and Christians. But the purpose of the comparison is not so much to prove the previous revelations false as to show them to be incomplete. The words that God has been sending to particular communities are seen as parts of an overall word to humanity at large. What makes humans acceptable in the sight of God is not their ethnic identity but their devotion and obedience.

The community that the Prophet established among his Arabian followers always had the potential to expand beyond Arabia, and Islam did become a world empire within a century of his death. An essential component of the missionary effort was the idea of free choice between one tradition and another; the Qur'an explicitly says: 'Let there be no coercion in religion' (Q. 2:256). In virtually every society, people have the choice to accept or reject the society's prescribed path of conduct. It has been much less common for people to be offered a choice between different paths. In fact, missionary religions are very careful to define the content of their faith and must often combat alternative understandings that develop in the course of their spread. Christianity grew out of Judaism (specifically an early form that attributed a great deal of power to God's chief angel, variously called the 'Angel of the Lord', the 'son of man', or the 'Glory of the Lord'). Islam grew out of the Judeo-Christian tradition, defining itself in contradistinction to Christianity's mediated monotheism. Protestantism too can be understood as a new religion, formed in response to the critiques of the Roman Catholic Church put forward by reformers like Martin Luther, even though it saw itself as a renewal movement within the existing tradition. Many new religions have grown out of reform movements within existing traditions, especially under the influence of a charismatic leader or prophet. A relatively recent example of this phenomenon is the Baha'i Faith (see Chapter 11).

Many liberal Jews, Christians, and Muslims could certainly support the principles encapsulated by the Baha'i Faith. But support and sympathy are not enough for the latter: the Baha'i religion also wants converts. The same is true of most monotheistic religions. They innovate by hiving off into new sects or cults that then seek converts, especially when the prophets of the innovations face significant opposition from authorities within the society. This pattern is true of religion in general, but it is particularly characteristic of monotheistic and missionary traditions.

Missionary Expansion

With the imperial support of Constantine, the missionary religion that was Christianity became a state religion as well. Islam was both a missionary and a state religion from the start. A comparison of their expansion processes may be instructive.

Christianity frequently saw entire populations convert following the conversion of their rulers. If a mission to a particular people could succeed in gaining the ruler's favour,

Hagia Sophia was built as the seat of the Orthodox patriarch of Constantinople and was converted into a mosque after the Ottoman conquest of 1453 (courtesy Evangelos Dimopoulos). Christian iconography was replaced by non-representational Islamic motifs, but over time some of the earlier imagery has become visible. At the top of this photo, for instance, a mosaic depicting the Archangel Gabriel can be seen through the plaster (Photo courtesy of Evangelos Dimopoulos).

an entire nation could be incorporated into the Christian fold. That approach succeeded in the case of the Slavs and some northern European peoples, but failed in the cases of the Chinese and Japanese.

In its earlier centuries, Islam also succeeded in persuading a significant number of nations to convert. (Part of its appeal may have been the juridical status and tax relief it offered to those who accepted Islam.) The Mediterranean from Iraq to Gibraltar became Muslim and adopted the Arabic language. Iran and Central Asia also became Muslim, although they retained Persian as their language. The third great wholesale conversion was that of the Turkish people, who also continued to speak their own language. Nevertheless, both the Persians and the Turks used the Arabic script for writing their languages until the twentieth century, and this became an important mark of their Islamic identity.

Christianity's spread after the 1490s was closely connected with European military and cultural expansion. Priests accompanied soldiers in Mexico and Peru, and the sponsoring Spanish and Portuguese regimes took it as their responsibility to save the indigenous inhabitants' souls even as they were enslaving their bodies. The cultural–religious imperialism of Catholic countries in the sixteenth century was matched in the nineteenth when Protestant Britain extended its influence in Africa.

Muslim rule in northern India began with the establishment of the Delhi sultanate in the thirteenth century. This was the first case in which Islam did not succeed in converting the entire population of the land it had taken over. It was only in the Indus Valley, Bengal, and the mid-southern interior that Muslims become the majority; the rest of the subcontinent remained predominantly Hindu.

In the later centuries of its expansion, Islam grew not so much through military conquest as through trade and the missionary activity of the Sufis in particular. The Sufi devotional life resonated with the Hindu and Buddhist meditational piety already present in Southeast Asia and opened the door for Islam to enter the region, in which it became dominant. Similarly in Africa south of the Sahara, traders and Sufis were the principal vehicles for Islam.

In general, missionaries for the major religions have been more successful in recruiting converts from the traditional religions of small-scale tribal societies than from the other major religions. The reasons may have something to do with the material cultures and technologies of the major civilizations, whose writing systems and scriptural literatures have given the major traditions a special authority among cultures that are primarily oral. As a result, it has been relatively easy for them to use the content of their scriptures to shape the target societies' values.

The credit for the early spread of Buddhism in India and Southeast Asia goes to the missionary effort undertaken by King Ashoka. We do not know enough about the indigenous traditions in the lands converted by his missionaries to understand why their Theravada teachings were so effective. We have a clearer idea in the case of China, where the Daoist interest in magic and healing techniques likely gave Buddhism, especially Mahayana, its initial foothold.

Can we evaluate missionary activity in general? Some missionaries have been ardent advocates for their host peoples, working to defend them against colonial or entrepreneurial exploitation. Missionaries have also produced some of the finest linguistic, ethnographic, and historical studies of indigenous traditions. On the other hand, missionaries have often been intrusive and invasive, blind or insensitive to the inner dynamics of their target cultures. Some have imposed alien customs and cultural values that did not necessarily fit well with the traditions they were preaching. And some have been pawns of their home countries' geopolitical interests. In short, the missionary record has been mixed at best, with some very disturbing undertones.

In the twentieth century some Christian denominations began to curtail their missionary activity. Increasing respect for other communities and traditions was undoubtedly one reason for the retreat. But another reason may have been the recognition that the returns are too small to justify the investment required. In the second half of the twentieth century, when much of Africa gained independence from European colonial rule, European Christian missionaries suffered from identification with colonial interests; this was especially true in West Africa, where Europeans had dominated the slave trade. Increasingly, Christian missionaries in Africa were replaced by indigenous church leaders.

Missionaries were often more welcome for their social contributions than for their theology. Some countries that denied visas to Westerners for evangelistic missionary activity continued to grant them for agricultural development, education, and medical work. The schools and hospitals operated by Christians were influential in many parts of Asia, but their influence declined as government support for educational and medical institutions increased.

PLURALISM

Since the mid-twentieth century, the term 'pluralism' has often been used to mean not just the fact of diversity in itself but the evaluation of that diversity as desirable. This double sense of pluralism reflects a convergence of developments in many areas of life.

The fact of diversity has been reinforced by increasingly close contact between cultures. Today tens of thousands of people cross the Pacific by jet every day, and even without travelling we can be instantly in touch with almost any part of the world. Migration has also increased significantly. Since the end of the Second World War, the demographic profiles of European and North American cities have been transformed by the arrival of immigrants who have brought their Muslim, Hindu, Buddhist, and other traditions with them. Though apprehensive at first, Western societies have made some progress towards recognizing and appreciating these traditions.

Change in the evaluation of diversity is reflected in many details of contemporary life, large and small. In some cases institutions that were originally religious have been given new secular rationales. Sunday, for instance, the Christian day of religious observance, remains the day for reduced business activity in many jurisdictions. But the main arguments for legislation preserving Sunday store closing have shifted from religious observance to reasons involving fairness, family time, and opportunity for recreation.

We should distinguish pluralism from secularism. **Secularism** is the exclusion in principle of all religious groups, institutions, and identities from public support and participation in public decision-making. **Pluralism** is the granting of equal support, acceptance, or influence in decision-making to more than one religious group. Whereas recreational arguments for Sunday closing are secularist, arguments for school holidays at the Jewish New Year and Passover, or at the Ramadan fast, are pluralist. Up to a point, secularism and pluralism go hand in hand in the West because both seek to remove Christianity's privileged influence over social standards and norms. Where they differ is in what they propose to replace it with.

Pluralism places a parallel value on the faith and practice of all religious communities. It often does so on the assumption that the practice of any religion is beneficial to society as long as that practice does nothing to harm others. It can also presume that improving our understanding of our neighbours' religions—whatever they may be—is beneficial to society. Essentially, pluralism downplays the specific commitments of individual religions and concentrates instead on shared values. In its scale of priorities, it subordinates the differences between religions to the value of harmony in the society as a whole.

Responding to Difference

For more than three decades the 1978 Jonestown tragedy has stood as a challenge to any categorical acceptance of religious diversity. An agricultural commune established in Guyana in 1972, Jonestown was populated by Americans, about 70 per cent black and 30 per cent white. The fact that more than 900 of those people committed mass suicide on the orders of their leader, the Reverend Jim Jones, confronts students of religion with a twofold task: to understand how and why the Jonestown community came to take such drastic action, and to determine the grounds on which such action should be accepted or condemned.

Jim Jones was a charismatic leader, a messiah to his followers. He founded the Peoples Temple in Indianapolis, Indiana, in the 1950s and moved with some of his group in the mid-1960s to establish a rural settlement in Redwood Valley, California. In time they also established an urban following in San Francisco. Jones's eschatological goal—an overhaul of the existing world order—was compatible with a reformist and utopian strand in Protestant (and Marxist) thought, but he also sought from his followers an uncritical dedication to his personal leadership that frightened many observers. When the political climate in the United States shifted to the right in the early 1970s, Jones moved his base to rural Guyana. The mass suicide was carried out after a number of investigations convinced Jones and his followers that evil forces were closing in on them and that the only honourable escape was death.

History repeats itself. Suicide has been embraced as martyrdom more than once by members of various religious traditions. In 1993, for example, 75 members of an Adventist sect called the Branch Davidians chose to perish with their leader, David Koresh (Vernon Wayne Howell), rather than escape the flames that engulfed their commune outside Waco, Texas, when it was stormed by US government agents investigating firearms violations.

The Peoples Temple and Branch Davidians—like missionary religions through the ages—set out to recruit converts. Since the late 1960s especially, many other new religious movements have done the same. If modern pluralistic society proclaims the freedom to practise or preach one religion without state intervention, fairness demands that such freedom be extended to all. But that freedom is not total. A group's right to proselytize is limited by the right of others in society to refuse what it offers. Any religious group will forfeit its right to acceptance in a pluralistic society if, in order to maintain itself, it engages in illegal activities (tax fraud, narcotics trafficking, etc.) or if it uses coercion of any kind, physical or psychological.

Critics of new religious movements often refer to them as 'cults'. The word 'cult' originally meant simply 'worship', but in the context of new movements it is used disparagingly, often with the implication that such movements are fraudulent, coercive, or both, and that their leaders demand excessive, unquestioning dedication from their followers. Critics find it particularly alarming when such movements tell their recruits to sever all ties with their families, although there have been parallels to such demands in many other religious traditions, including early Christianity.

The new religious movements spurred an anti-cult reaction. As large numbers of young people left their families and friends for the Unification Church (the 'Moonies') or the International Society for Krishna Consciousness (the Hare Krishna movement), or paid large fees to the Church of Scientology, families intent on 'rescuing' them often resorted to measures that were no less coercive than those of the movements themselves. Young people kidnapped by their parents might be subjected to intense 'deprogramming', which was justified as a matter of fighting fire with fire—in this case, using psychological influence to fight psychological influence. In the same period, sociological and psychological researchers sought to understand why such movements appealed so strongly to the offspring of well-to-do families. One answer was that, for young people whose parents gave them practically everything they wanted, the new religions offered precisely what their parents did not: a strict and demanding discipline, with structured goals to be achieved.

In the last decades of the twentieth century, some new religions achieved a degree of institutional maturity and public acceptance. Most of these organizations were compatible with mainstream religions in that they helped their members cope with their lives and encouraged good citizenship. In effect, like mainstream religions, in one way or another they addressed the human condition.

The last point is important. Religions are not all the same, but many may be humanly acceptable if they benefit human beings. On some occasions, when they have lived up to their ideals, all the major traditions have passed that test; on others, when they have fallen short of their ideals, the same traditions have failed. Humankind is the common denominator of all religions, and human benefit is a fair test of their performance.

Typically, though, every tradition considers its distinguishing features to be eminently valuable in themselves. If all religions were of equal worth, if there were no fundamentally important differences, why would anyone choose one of them over another? Most Christians, for instance, would probably say that there is a fundamental difference between salvation through Jesus Christ and the Buddhist goal of liberation. Most Buddhists would probably agree. Thus pluralism poses a serious theological challenge. Does it require us to modify our own doctrinal claims? We are convinced that it does.

In the past, statements of religious truth tended to be absolute and universal: claiming to explain the entire material universe and report past events exactly as they happened. Today, however, affirmations of religious truth are often perspectival—true 'for me', not necessarily for everyone. Thinkers in several traditions now present their heritages as symbolic accounts of the physical world and metaphorical narratives of past events. What's more, they now contend that this is the way the various traditions should always have been understood, and that literalism has been a mistake through the centuries.

It is not our task here to say how different religions will or should change in the future. That challenge is one for the religious communities themselves to face. What is certain is that, as human society becomes ever more interconnected, the opportunities to see one another in action and to engage in open dialogue will be far greater than they ever were in the past. Observers of religion will want to be alert to the new forms and formulations that emerge.

❧ Defining 'Religion'

One way to approach the question of whether or not all religions are essentially 'the same' is to look at the words we use to talk about the subject. There is, after all, a substantial body of discourse about 'religion'. Bookstores and libraries have sections on religion, schools and universities offer courses and conduct research on it, the Saturday newspaper may devote a page to it, and there are laws that guarantee citizens' freedom to practise and preach it.

Yes, people do seem to have an idea of what they mean by 'religion'. Some find it in historical uses of the term. Others find it in the characteristics shared by the 'short list' of traditions that are generally agreed to constitute mainstream religions. Still others define the concept by contrasting it with what it does not include, refining it through the discussion of borderline cases. We will consider each of these approaches in turn.

'Religion' in the West

In general the Euro-American West has defined the concept of 'religion' mainly by reference to its own principal religion, Christianity. During the European Middle Ages, the

Latin word *religio* and its derivatives had a meaning internal to Christianity: it meant piety, or the faith and action incumbent on a practising member of the Christian community. Even today, 'a religious' is someone who is a member of a Christian religious order.

This is not to say that European Christians were unaware of other traditions. Early Christian writers referred to rival teachings. The medieval Christians knew of the Muslims as a major challenge to the south and east of Europe, the Jews as a distinct minority within medieval Christendom, and 'pagans' as rivals in the classical Mediterranean region and in pre-Christian northern Europe. But they did not refer to those other traditions as 'religions' until after the fifteenth century.

When the Christian West looked at other traditions, it sought to define them in terms parallel to the terms in which it understood Christianity. The Christian historical self-understanding imposed three of its own tendencies on what it described.

First, it insisted on pinning things down as affirmations of belief. One identified oneself as a Christian by stating a creed, by declaring such-and-such a belief about God, Jesus, or the world. Therefore one expected adherents of a different tradition to have a corresponding set of creedal beliefs. Some of Asia's great traditions, such as Buddhism, do present substantial, sophisticated, and challenging doctrines; but in traditions such as Shinto, statements of doctrine are virtually non-existent. Thus to expect every religion to have a systematic doctrine is to exclude a vast and important range of religious activity from consideration. Any definition of 'religion' that depends on 'belief' is not descriptive of a spectrum of phenomena, but prescriptive, restricted to the narrow band within the spectrum that fits the observer's stipulations.

Second, Christianity tended to impose on all religions its own institutional distinction between the sacred and the secular. Having survived for three centuries as a minority faith before receiving state patronage, Christianity was quite accustomed to the idea that some things belong to God and others to Caesar. Even the medieval Latin Church, at the height of its influence, took note of this principle in its power struggles with various European rulers. One of the chief characteristics of modernity in the Euro-American West is a secularity that puts both intellectual and institutional limits on the sphere allocated to religion.

Islam, however, did not share Christianity's formative experience of 300 years as a minority. From the beginning it was a total value system governing every aspect of life, including commerce and even warfare. In the case of Islam, virtually every aspect of culture and civilization is relevant to religion.

The sacred–secular contrast is also unhelpful when we consider Chinese thought of 2,500 years ago, though for different reasons. The principal contribution of Confucius and his early successors was a humane social ethic—what the West might consider moral philosophy. Admittedly, Confucius made rhetorical references to Heaven, but he seems to have been rather agnostic about much of the traditional religion and ritual in his day. Perhaps the closest parallel to Confucius in the West is Socrates, who represents the more secular Hellenic part of the Western cultural heritage, as distinct from the part that is rooted in the religion of the ancient Hebrews.

Still, the tradition stemming from the teachings of Confucius became more religious in later centuries, when the Neo-Confucians cultivated an inner personal spirituality and speculated on the ultimate nature of things. A third Christian expectation concerning 'religion' is the notion of exclusive membership. The idea that God demands loyalty and will tolerate no rivals is part of Judaism and was passed on to Christianity and Islam. Each of these three has been at pains to demarcate the boundaries of its community. In southern and eastern Asia, however, following one tradition has rarely if ever meant that one can't follow another as well.

This point is doubly relevant in the case of the Sikh tradition. The early Sikhs were disciples of a teacher who saw God as transcending all forms, including the boundaries of human communities—boundaries made all the more visible with the arrival of Islam in India. Four centuries after Guru Nanak, however, some Sikh leaders were determined to define their community in contrast to a Hindu community with which they had a great deal in common. And five centuries after his time, Sikhs contend that full recognition of their identity has been denied them.

Do boundaries help us to understand Japan? Studies report that only a small percentage of Japanese see themselves as belonging to any religion. Yet when surveys ask whether they follow Buddhist, Shinto, or other rituals and practices, the positive answers add up to more than the total population of the country.

Pillars at the Ptolemaic temple of Kom Ombo in Egypt show Cleopatra VII with Sobek, the crocodile-headed god of fertility (courtesy Evangelos Dimopoulos). Kom Ombo is unique in that it was devoted to two gods, with one set of halls and quarters dedicated to Sobek and the other to Horus, the falcon-headed god of war (Photo courtesy of Evangelos Dimopoulos).

The Roster of Religions

Perhaps we can arrive at a definition or characterization of religion in general by looking at the most commonly cited examples. For three centuries after the 'discovery' of the Americas, Europe was content to recognize just four religions: Christianity, Judaism, Islam, and paganism. But the 'pagan' category expanded dramatically as new 'discoveries' were made in Asia, Africa, and the Americas. As with stress building up along an earthquake fault, a realignment would have to come sooner or later.

What brought it about was probably the rapid increase in the information available regarding doctrines. One of the first books in English to recognize half a dozen major traditions was written in 1846 by a versatile Anglican theological scholar named Frederick Denison Maurice. The idea of a short list of 'great' or 'living' or 'world' religions was launched. To be included on that list, a religion is required to be both historically influential and still alive today. In addition, it has been expected for the past century and a half that each short-listed tradition will have a well-developed literature or body of doctrine.

As with any canon, there have been a few undisputed nominees and many more marginal cases. In addition to the three great missionary religions (Buddhism, Christianity, and Islam), the list has often included the national religious heritages of Israel (Judaism), Persia before Islam (Zoroastrianism), India (Hinduism), and Japan (Shinto). It can also include two distinct Indian communities (the Sikhs and the Jains) and two distinct Chinese traditions (Confucian and Daoist).

The traditions omitted from that core consensus can be classified in three groups. The first group consists of the religious traditions of indigenous peoples. Despite some overall resemblances, these traditions are diverse and fragmented, and their traditions are oral rather than textual. The second group consists of traditions that, no matter how sophisticated their doctrine or rich their mythology, have essentially died out. Manichaeism is one example; others include the religions of ancient Greece and Rome, Mesopotamia and Egypt, Mexico and Peru. The third group consists of movements too recent for inclusion in the nineteenth-century canon, such as Japan's new religions and the Baha'i Faith.

All these traditions have tended to receive scant coverage in textbooks. But this situation may well change in the future. As some of the new religions gain historical and doctrinal depth, the canon will need reassessment. It is also conceivable that a synthesis of Native American, African, Polynesian, or Melanesian traditions could take shape and gain recognition as a 'new' religion.

If we could identify the characteristics that all the 'world' religions share, it might be possible to define an essence of religion. But when we look at the candidates for inclusion on an 'essential' list, it seems there are always exceptions:

- Belief in a personal god or spirits: Early Buddhist (Theravada) doctrine lacks this feature, and for Hindu Vedanta, ultimate reality is not personal.
- A cohesive worshipping community: Confucianism seems to be deficient in this regard.
- Divinely sanctioned morality: It's hard to see much of this in Shinto.
- A promise of life after death: Classical Hebrew religion offered no such assurance.

In fact, it seems impossible to identify any feature that is absolutely essential in order for a tradition to qualify as a religion. The short list is more about standard examples than about any essence that those examples might share.

If we cannot expect all religions to share any single feature, perhaps a 'syndrome' approach would be more appropriate. As in clinical medicine, perhaps we should identify as a religion any tradition that displays a majority of the characteristics listed above. Such a fuzzy definition is not satisfactory from a logical and philosophical standpoint. All the same, it seems to be what Western civilization has meant by 'religion' for 500 years now.

Defining by Exclusion

Another way of defining religion might be to consider things that look like religion but are commonly agreed to be something different. Examining these other phenomena might allow us to identify some distinguishing feature of religion that they lack.

The modern Protestant theologian Paul Tillich characterized religion as 'ultimate concern': that is, concern for what ultimately matters most in this world, this life, and beyond. His view has sometimes been distorted to suggest that religion is whatever we hold as our highest priority, however mundane; for some people, golf might be a religion. For Tillich, though, such mundane concerns do not qualify. A truly ultimate concern must have something to do with the overall meaning of the universe and of life in it.

For more than seven decades after the Russian revolution of 1917, many thought that the communist system, built on the atheistic socialism of Karl Marx, posed a worldwide threat to religion. As implemented after the mid-twentieth century, from Czechoslovakia to China, it repressed traditional religious institutions while bearing some curious resemblances to religion itself. These resemblances are particularly noticeable vis-à-vis the monotheistic Western religions. Like Judaism, Christianity, and Islam, communism seeks to liberate the poor from exploitation; finds direction, meaning, and significance in history; and idealizes a future moment when evil will be overthrown and justice will prevail. A new order will be ushered in, the classless society corresponding to the kingdom of heaven.

Marx critiqued all religion and politics before his time on the grounds that they had failed to improve the lot of humanity either morally or materially. But communism too can be judged by Marx's standards, and eventually it too was found wanting. Communism, like traditional religions, wants to state an 'is' and derive from it an 'ought'. There is a huge philosophical difference between descriptive laws of nature, which must be modified to conform to the behaviour of phenomena, and prescriptive laws of society, which demand that individuals modify their behaviour to conform and which threaten punishment for failure to do so. Yet both communism and religion seek the benefits of description and prescription simultaneously. Each sees the order of things as a description of the way things necessarily are, and at the same time proposes to derive from that description a prescription for the way individuals should voluntarily behave.

Furthermore, communist ideologues have resembled missionaries in their zeal to spread their teachings. Members of the community of the committed take part in group rituals that reinforce solidarity. Intense pressure is applied to persuade individuals to confess and publicly disavow their faults and shortcomings. In the case of China's Mao Zedong, the cult of the leader even had its own scripture—a pocket-sized anthology of his quotations, bound in red. Yet communism has not thought of itself as a religion, and in practice it has often shown active hostility towards religion.

Another crucial difference emerges if we ask whether a power may exist above or beyond humankind. Religion characteristically says yes: the way or power of the universe governs us. Communism has said no: history is human history, and controllable by humans. The postulation of a transhuman power is sometimes termed faith in transcendence. When communism is disqualified as a religion, it is generally because it lacks that essential ingredient.

It remains to consider one further alternative to 'religion'—namely, philosophy. Are there not philosophies that, like religions, contemplate ultimate reality? When we look at the Chinese moral teachers in their cultural setting, it is not easy to draw a clear line between philosophy and religion. Don't both seek to map out the good that people should seek in their conduct?

If we form a view of the universe or a set of prescriptions for thought and action, we may have stated a personal philosophy, but we have not created a religion in the sense intended in this book. If with a circle of friends and disciples we discuss these views, subjecting them to rational criticism and argument, we may have participated in a philosophical movement, but we have not formed a religion. If our group meets regularly, repeating the same activities each time, we may have ritualized our conduct, but we still may not have become a religion. Where do we cross the line?

Part of the difference is that philosophy is a rational, intellectual pursuit, while religion seeks a commitment of the will and the emotions as well. Philosophical decisions, are by nature, decisions for an individual mind to make, whereas many religious decisions are made by groups. The rituals of philosophers are seldom crucial to the force of their arguments, but the rituals of religion are often seen as essential, creating or confirming centrally important states of affairs.

A Provisional Definition

We can now sum up these efforts at characterizing religion. We have looked at the evolution of our vocabulary, at standard religions as examples, and at communism and philosophy as important counter-instances. In so doing, we have been circling our prey. No single line of definition seems able to trap it, but we can weave a net. Religion is a sense of power beyond the human that is:

- apprehended rationally as well as emotionally,
- appreciated corporately as well as individually,
- celebrated ritually and symbolically as well as discursively, and
- transmitted in conventionalized forms as a tradition that offers people
    - an interpretation of experience,
    - a view of life and death,
    - a guide to conduct, and
    - an orientation to meaning and purpose in the world.

Some Twentieth-Century Analyses

A frequently cited article by the American anthropologist Clifford Geertz expands on each dimension of the previous observations about religion:

A religion is: (1) a system of symbols which acts to (2) establish powerful, pervasive and long-lasting moods and motivations in men by (3) formulating conceptions of a general order of existence and (4) clothing these conceptions with such an aura of factuality that (5) the moods and motivations seem uniquely realistic (Geertz 1966:4).

Some of the wording here seems elastic (what is an 'aura' of factuality? how do symbols, rather than people, 'act'?). Nevertheless, many have found Geertz's article a useful mainstream example of twentieth-century social theory of religion.

In focusing on the social function of religion, social scientists like Geertz stood back from the theories of religious origins contributed by their discipline's nineteenth-century pioneers. Yet most shared with their predecessors the conviction that religion can be treated as a social and psychological phenomenon and analyzed with conceptual tools from outside religion itself.

The Role of the Participant

After the mid-twentieth century, anthropologists increasingly questioned the usefulness, if not the validity, of describing cultural structures in terms alien to the culture in question. Sometimes for intellectual reasons, sometimes for political ones, investigators sought to give voice in cultural description to terms or concepts internal to a tradition or community. They were trying to bridge the classic gulf between participant and observer.

But are the participants in a system always consciously aware of its structure? A common-sense answer must be no. In many aspects of human affairs, investigators have repeatedly identified cases where observers can detect patterns, relationships, and similarities of which participants are unaware. Members of a Siberian indigenous people, for instance, may be very familiar with shamanism as they practise it without being aware of shamanism as a cross-cultural phenomenon.

The Perspective of the Observer

From the 1960s through the 1980s, 'structuralist' approaches were popular in several fields of cultural studies. The specific meaning of 'structuralism' depended on the field, whether anthropology, developmental psychology, linguistics, or literary studies. One common feature of such efforts, however, was to point out that all religions are structured in similar ways and that the structures are accessible to scholarly or scientific observation even if the adherents of those religions do not recognize them. As the French anthropologist Claude Lévi-Strauss explained it:

> Science has only two ways of proceeding: it is either reductionist or structuralist. It is reductionist when it is possible to find out that very complex phenomena can be reduced to simpler phenomena on other levels. For instance, there is a lot in life which can be reduced to physiochemical processes, which explain a part but not all. And when we are confronted with phenomena too complex to be reduced to phenomena of a lower order, then we can only approach them by looking to their relationships, that is, by trying to understand what kind of original system they make up. This is exactly what we have been trying to do in linguistics, in anthropology, and in other fields (Lévi-Strauss 1978:9–10).

The structures so identified had validity if they made sense in the mind of the investigator, regardless of whether they were understood by the populations under study. In short, structuralists assumed that they knew better than their subjects themselves what the latter were doing.

Post-structuralist, deconstructionist, and postmodern writers took that 'We know better' assumption and turned it on the investigators themselves. Scholarship has undergone a kind of politicization, in which the motives of the investigator are considered to be socially and economically determined. Intellectuals are seen as slaves to their political, racial, class, and gender affiliations. Scholars are portrayed as career-driven rather than thirsting for understanding. Where we might have assumed a kind of free will in the history of ideas, we are now confronted with a kind of determinism in the sociology of knowledge. To overstate the development only slightly: scholars do not seek truth, but work in their own self- or group interest.

Recent discussions along these lines may seem new, but the issues are long-standing. In every age, people have striven to comprehend the world. In every age, people have called for fairness in action and fair criteria in judgment. And the determinists are to a considerable extent right: in every age, people have been conditioned to interpret the world in the light of the assumptions current within their own class or community. As debates continue, people will continue to disagree, while seeking (according to different understandings) to do justice to the data. Meanwhile, we must all continue working to recognize and challenge our own parochial assumptions.

Religious Theories of Religion

Adherents of the world's religions have generally believed that their own tradition's message was divinely constituted. The idea that all religions might be equally God-given is a relatively modern phenomenon.

We can see this religion-in-general stance as, in part, a reaction to European social-scientific theories that emerged in the late nineteenth century. Theories such as E.B. Tylor's animism or, later, Émile Durkheim's totemism attributed religion to human causes, describing it as the product of cultural circumstances, or psychological needs, or the human imagination. Religious people were understandably alarmed at such interpretations, for while many might have been willing to dismiss other people's religions as merely human artifacts, they were alarmed at the thought of explaining away their own faiths.

Theologians have a term for this explain-it-away spirit: reductionism. Religion is 'reduced' to the factors claimed to cause it, explained in terms other than its own. Many scholars of religion reject reductionist explanations. Yet before writing them off completely, we should consider what other kinds of explanations, if any, might be more acceptable.

The German philosopher of religion Rudolf Otto was profoundly disturbed by the turn-of-the-century tendency to explain religion as socially conditioned. In 1910 he wrote an article criticizing the cultural-evolutionist perspective of a work on ethnic psychology by the German Wilhelm Wundt—a work that Durkheim admired greatly—and in 1917 he published *The Idea of the Holy*, which became a theological best-seller. Building on Schleiermacher's view of religion as intuitive feeling, Otto described a sense of mystery—at once overpowering and fascinating—that he called the **numinous**:

> We are dealing with something for which there is only one appropriate expression, mysterium tremendum. The feeling of it may at times come sweeping like a gentle tide, pervading the mind with a tranquil mood of deepest worship. . . . It may burst in sudden eruption up from the depths of the soul with spasms and convulsions, or

lead to the strangest excitements, to intoxicated frenzy, to transport, and to ecstasy. . . . It may become the hushed, trembling, and speechless humility of the creature in the presence of—whom or what? In the presence of that which is a Mystery inexpressible and above all creatures (Otto 1923:12–13; italics in original).

Otto believed that the sense of the numinous was a common feature of all religions, although he gave a privileged place to Christian examples of it.

In 1933 a theologian and historian of religions named Gerardus van der Leeuw published a wide-ranging survey whose English title is *Religion in Essence and Manifestation*. Like Otto, van der Leeuw treated religion as a response to a divine stimulus:

Many ancient peoples were familiar with the idea of a World-course, which however is not passively followed but rather itself moves spontaneously, and is no mere abstract conformity to Law such as are our Laws of Nature, but on the contrary a living Power operating within the Universe. Tao in China, Rata in India, Asha in Iran, Ma'at among the ancient Egyptians, Dike in Greece:—these are such ordered systems which theoretically, indeed, constitute the all-inclusive calculus of the Universe, but which nevertheless, as living and impersonal powers, possess mana-like character (Van der Leeuw 1938:30).

Also like Otto, van der Leeuw found his definitive examples in the Christian tradition.

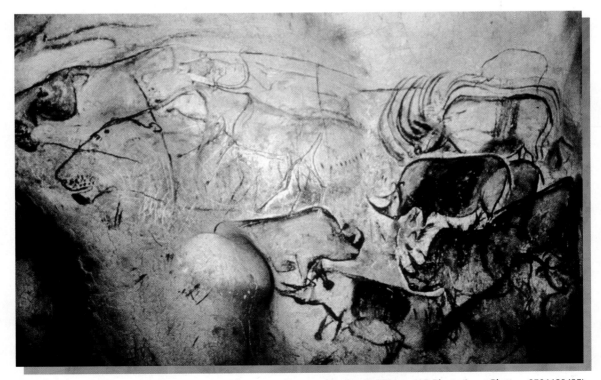

Animal images from the Chauvet cave in southwestern France, dated c. 30,000 BCE (AP Photo/Jean Clottes, 9501180435).

Another important figure in this line of thought was the Romanian Mircea Eliade, whose extensive work in the area of comparative religion drew particularly on Hindu and tribal traditions. Like Otto, who spoke of religion as a response to the holy, Eliade saw religion as a response to a transcendent reality—a reality that he called 'the sacred'. For Durkheim the sacred might have been nothing more than a human social construct, but for Eliade it originated somewhere else entirely:

> Man becomes aware of the sacred because it manifests itself, shows itself, as something wholly different from the profane. To designate the act of manifestation of the sacred, we have proposed the term hierophany. . . . It could be said that the history of religions—from the most primitive to the most highly developed—is constituted by a great number of hierophanies, by manifestations of sacred realities. . . . In each case we are confronted by the same mysterious act—the manifestation of something of a wholly different order, a reality that does not belong to our world, in objects that are an integral part of our natural 'profane' world (Eliade 1959:11).

Do all religions ultimately say the same thing? In the view of these theorists, the answer seems to be yes. The sacred or holy is what all the religions point to, despite their vast diversity.

SIMILARITIES AND DIFFERENCES

Another way of approaching the question of unity is by way of the contexts in which claims have been made for the fundamental similarity of all religions and for crucial differences between them.

We do not have to look far for situations in which religions are treated as different. Every community that undertakes missionary activity is implicitly declaring that its religion stands apart from the rest. Not only must the difference be large enough that prospective converts can be expected to perceive it, but it must be important enough that, ultimately, the missionaries' efforts will be worth the sacrifices they may entail.

Non-proselytizing communities can also assert fundamental differences among religions. Shinto, for instance, is closely linked with Japan's national identity. Given Japan's traditional insistence on the unique character of its heritage, practitioners of Shinto are not likely to see all religions as essentially the same. At the same time, many Japanese practise more than one religion, recognizing distinctive benefits in each one.

Philosophers in particular have been interested in identifying instances of disagreement on specific issues. In cases where two religions have become established in geographic isolation from one another, we might be able to dismiss any philosophical differences between them as circumstantial. Differences between Confucian and Christian notions of duty and morality, for example, might be attributed to the different cultural vocabularies in which they are expressed. It might even be possible to harmonize the Shinto and Hebrew narratives of creation if we were to understand them as metaphorical rather than literal.

Sooner or later, though, we must face up to outright disagreements. For instance, the various Hindu traditions all assert the reality of the self; even in Vedanta, where individual identity is seen as illusory, it merges with reality in a cosmic self. Early Buddhism, by contrast, clearly repudiated the idea of the human self as a persisting reality. Buddhism and Hinduism share many features, among them monastic asceticism and the notion of cyclical rebirth. But the difference between them regarding the self is so radical that it poses a serious problem for anyone who would argue that religions are fundamentally the same.

An equally significant difference exists between Christianity and Islam on the subject of divine incarnation. For Christians, Jesus is the son of God and a manifestation of God's very nature in a human life. For Muslims, the absolute otherness of God forbids the association of any other being with God at God's level. The Qur'an (112:3) explicitly states that God does not beget and is not begotten. There is even a charming passage (5:116) that imagines God asking Jesus at the day of judgment, 'Did you tell them you were to be worshipped as divine?' and Jesus replying, 'No; why would I ever tell them such a thing?'

Yet even in the face of such disparities, people still assert the fundamental unity of religion. There is a Hindu saying: 'Truth is one; the sages call it by different names.' We need to consider how this statement should be understood. Is it rhetoric, meant to persuade, or an apologetic defence against some criticism? Is it a moral necessity? Or a matter of revelation? Is it a conclusion that can be substantiated?

🌿 CONCLUSION

Earlier in this chapter we noted that all the major religious traditions seek in one way or another to benefit human beings. Another fundamental similarity can be seen in the ways their adherents have found to live out their religion.

As late as the 1950s, two things were expected of practising Christians. One was 'faith', generally understood as belief in a particular set of doctrines. The other was 'works' in the sense both of ritual activity and of ethical behaviour. In the 1960s, however, the consciousness revolution gave rise to a new emphasis on what we might call 'experience'. Some sought religious ecstasy in drugs, though most soon found this route a dead end. Others looked to 'exotic' cultural traditions—Zen, Sufism, yoga—for depths of experience that they found lacking in mainstream Western traditions. By the early 1970s charismatic movements were gaining ground in some previously staid denominations, tapping sources of 'feeling' in the Western tradition that, although they were not new, had been largely forgotten by the mainstream. Today experience stands alongside faith and works as an essential dimension of Christianity for many believers.

A similar development took place in the Hindu tradition approximately 2,000 years ago with the composition of the *Bhagavad Gita*. The *Gita* is a remarkable text, not only for its literary beauty and its religious depth, but for its skillful synthesis of three alternative 'ways' in religion. The way of works, *karma marga*, includes both ethical and ritual dimensions, as in the Christian tradition. The way of knowledge, *jnana marga*, parallels the doctrinal or 'faith' component in Christianity. Finally, the way of devotion, *bhakti marga*, is presented in the *Gita* as the climax and fulfillment of the other two ways. This experiential and devotional element has been central to Hinduism ever since.

Islam suggests a similar triad of paths, though it does not identify them as such. They are the *shari'ah*, the law governing ritual and conduct; philosophical theology; and Sufism, the mystical, devotional tradition that gave Islam its entrée to the Hindu and Buddhist cultures of Malaysia and Indonesia and provided a basis for understanding between the Muslim ruling minority and the Hindu majority population of medieval northern India.

It may be tempting to see these broad similarities as reason enough to agree with the proposition that, ultimately, the world's religions are much the same. But the differences are significant too, as we have seen. Perhaps it is less important to answer the question of unity in diversity than to recognize its fundamental moral, political, and intellectual significance for the world we live in.

Study Questions

1. How would you define a missionary religion?
2. Why were religious people in the late nineteenth and early twentieth century alarmed by theories such as E.B. Tylor's animism or Émile Durkheim's totemism?
3. Is there a difference between a personal philosophy and a personal religion?
4. Is there any feature or characteristic that is common to all the forms of expression that we call 'religions'?

Glossary

dualism A conception of the universe that postulates two ultimate principles set in opposition to one another and more or less evenly matched; these principles are usually (though not always) personified as a good god and an evil devil.

eschatology The branch of theology concerned with 'last things' such as death, judgment, heaven and hell, the destiny of human beings, or the end of the world; from the Greek meaning 'study of the end'.

Gnosticism A movement based on the belief (held by a variety of groups but considered a heresy by the early Christian Church) that the material world was evil and that the only way to escape entrapment in it was through esoteric knowledge.

missionary religion A religion that actively seeks converts.

monotheism The doctrine that there is only one God.

mysticism A current in many religious traditions; mystics seek direct experience of communion with ultimate reality or the divine, often through the practice of a specific discipline.

numinous Term coined by Rudolf Otto to describe the overpowering sense of mystery that he believed to be a part of all religions.

pluralism In the context of religion, the principle that all religions are equally valuable, should be treated with equal respect, and should have an equal opportunity to play a role in public decision-making.

polytheism Belief in more than one god.

secularism The principle that no religious group or institution should receive public support or play any role in public decision-making.

Further Reading

Durkheim, Émile. 1915. *The Elementary Forms of the Religious Life*. London: Allen & Unwin.

Hallencreutz, Carl F. 1970. *New Approaches to Men of Other Faiths, 1938–1968: A Theological Discussion*. Geneva: World Council of Churches. Traces the emergence of ecumenical Christian interest in inter-religious dialogue as a wider ecumenism.

Hick, John H. 1995. *The Rainbow of Faiths: Critical Dialogues on Religious Pluralism*. London: SCM Press. (Also published as *A Christian Theology of Religions: The Rainbow of Faiths*. Louisville: Westminster John Knox Press, 1995.) By a leading investigator of the philosophical implications of religious pluralism.

Laymen's Foreign Missions Inquiry, Committee of Appraisal. 1932. *Re-thinking Missions: A Laymen's Inquiry after One Hundred Years*. New York: Harper. A landmark study challenging older missionary assumptions, by a committee chaired by the Harvard philosopher William Ernest Hocking.

Lessa, William A., and Evon Z. Vogt, eds. 1979. *Reader in Comparative Religion: An Anthropological Approach*. 4th edn. New York: Harper & Row. A superb anthology with substantial extracts from nineteenth- and twentieth-century ethnographic and theoretical literature, well introduced. The four editions vary in their content, but some classics survive in all of them.

Oxtoby, Willard G. 1983. *The Meaning of Other Faiths*. Philadelphia: Westminster Press. An appeal to a Christian readership for greater openness toward various religions.

Pals, Daniel L. 1996. *Seven Theories of Religion*. New York: Oxford University Press. Perhaps the best introduction to modern views on religion, especially social-scientific ones.

Segal, Alan F. 2005. *Life After Death: A History of the Afterlife in Western Religions*. New York: Doubleday.

Sharpe, Eric J. 1975. *Comparative Religion: A History*. 2nd edn. La Salle, IL.: Open Court. Very good on nineteenth- and twentieth-century shifts in attitudes regarding the study of religion.

de Vries, Jan. 1967. *The Study of Religion: A Historical Approach*. New York: Harcourt, Brace & World. Reviews theories of religion, with particular attention to European interpretations of myth.

Ziolkowski, Eric J., ed. 1993. *A Museum of Faiths: Histories and Legacies of the 1893 World's Parliament of Religions*. Atlanta: Scholars Press. A useful appreciation of the influence of the parliament.

References

Eliade, Mircea. 1959. *The Sacred and the Profane: The Nature of Religion*. New York: Harcourt, Brace.

Geertz, Clifford. 1966. 'Religion as a Cultural System'. In Michael Banton, ed. *Anthropological Approaches to the Study of Religion*, 1–46. London: Tavistock.

Van der Leeuw, Gerardus. 1938. *Religion in Essence and Manifestation*. London: Allen & Unwin.

Lévi-Strauss, Claude. 1978. *Myth and Meaning*. Toronto: University of Toronto Press.

Otto, Rudolf. 1923. *The Idea of the Holy: An Inquiry into the Non-rational Factor in the Idea of the Divine and Its Relation to the Rational*. London: Oxford University Press.

Swanson, Guy E. 1966. *The Birth of the Gods: The Origin of Primitive Belief*. Ann Arbor: University of Michigan Press.

Indigenous Traditions

❧ Robert M. Baum ❧

Today most scholars define an indigenous religious tradition as one that was created by a particular community or nation, is closely related to that group's sense of identity, and has remained uniquely associated with that group (that is, its adherents have not attempted to spread it to other communities). The fact that indigenous religions reinforce a sense of cultural identity does not preclude borrowing from other traditions, but the borrowed elements—rituals, deities, ideas—are integrated into the indigenous system. Nor does it preclude the spreading of particular religious cults to other groups or the spread of non-ethnically-based devotional practices throughout a cultural region. Adherence to that system is often an essential aspect of membership in the community.

INTRODUCTION

In the past, scholars often described indigenous religions as 'primitive', conjuring images of savagery, superstition, and childish simplicity even though such traditions typically involve extensive instruction and complex rituals. More recently some scholars have preferred terms like 'tribal', 'small-scale', 'oral', or 'traditional'. But these terms too are problematic. Why should the **Yoruba** tradition of West Africa, with some 20 million practitioners on four continents, be labelled 'tribal' or 'small-scale' when the traditions of far smaller communities, such as Jews, Baha'is, and Zoroastrians, are recognized as world religions?

'Primal', for its part, suggests either infancy and raw emotion (as in 'primal scream') or the earliest stage in an evolutionary model of development leading towards some preconceived notion of what a religion ought to be. As for 'oral', it is true that most indigenous religious traditions have been transmitted orally. But to characterize those traditions as '**oral**' or 'preliterate' is to ignore the fact that some indigenous peoples have had written traditions for over a thousand years—and that 'world' religions themselves have important oral dimensions.

Finally, even the term 'traditional' is unsatisfactory, since many other kinds of religion have existed for millennia. Thus 'indigenous religion' has come to be the preferred term for the particular type of tradition created by a particular group of people for whom that tradition is part of what defines them as a distinct community.

Until roughly 3,500 years ago, all the world's religions were 'indigenous' in this sense. The development of religions like Judaism and Hinduism drew adherents away from earlier traditions, some of which disappeared as distinct entities. Still, even those older traditions exerted important influences on the new dominant religions.

Even in the twenty-first century, indigenous religious traditions command significant followings around the world, although reliable statistics in many cases do not exist, and official sources tend to exaggerate the numbers of adherents to 'official' religions. For

◀ A dancer at the Poundmaker Powwow in St Albert, Alberta (Lydia Bociurkiw).

example, indigenous traditions continue to be practised by indigenous peoples throughout the Americas. Some of their practices show clear signs of influence from religions not native to the Americas, notably Christianity; in effect, new traditions have developed that integrate ideas and practices from both indigenous and foreign traditions. This amalgamation process, or **syncretism**, is common wherever different religions have interacted over a long period of time.

Religious syncretism has taken place throughout history and in all parts of the world. The Africans transported to the Americas as slaves brought with them traditions, either African religions and/or Islam, that interacted with indigenous American Indian religions and European-American Christianity to create new religious traditions such as Vaudou (Voodoo), Santeria, Candomblé, and Umbanda. In Africa itself, indigenous religions still flourish despite centuries of proselytizing by Muslims and Christians. Even among those who do not practise indigenous traditions, many have found ways of reconciling the religious duties and understandings of Christianity or Islam with their own religious traditions and knowledge. Indigenous and newer religions have influenced each other and produced distinctively African syncretic traditions.

Indigenous religions remain important in Australasia as well. Southeast Asia, Malaysia, and Indonesia have been influenced by Hindu and Buddhist traditions for nearly two millennia, by Islam for nearly a thousand years, and by Christianity for nearly five hundred. In this region indigenous religions, which tend to be stronger in rural than in urban areas, still exert significant influence on the local practice of world religions. In Australia and the Pacific Islands—Malaysia, Indonesia, New Guinea, Melanesia, Polynesia, and Micronesia—contact with outside communities came later. In Australia British colonization caused radical declines in Aboriginal populations and religions alike. In the Pacific Islands, however, where the European occupation was less harsh, population declines were less dramatic and conversion to other religious traditions less widespread.

Indigenous religious communities in northeast Asia have coexisted with Buddhism for well over a thousand years, with Islam for about 800 years, and with Christianity for about 500 years. In Mongolia, southern Siberia, Tibet, and Japan, the interaction between Buddhism and indigenous religions has been so prolonged that it is difficult to separate the one from the other. Japanese Shinto is closely integrated with Buddhist traditions received from Korea and China.

In fact, it was under the influence of Buddhist teachers that Japanese scholars recorded the oral traditions of early Japan in what became the sacred texts of Shinto religion. For most Japanese the ritual calendar includes both Buddhist and Shinto holidays. Many people in Siberia converted to Russian Orthodox Christianity in the eighteenth and nineteenth centuries, but others continued to practise indigenous religious traditions. For most of the twentieth century, indigenous religions throughout the Soviet Union were somewhat insulated against active missionary work of any kind—Christian, Muslim, or Buddhist—by the Soviet authorities' suspicion of institutionalized religion.

With the exception of some groups in northeast Asia and North America that shared cultural origins and maintained limited contact, indigenous religious clusters generally developed in isolation until the nineteenth century. It was only with the expansion of the Islamic and Christian worlds, when they were forcibly integrated into a Western-dominated world trade system and Western (or Western-inspired) colonial systems, that they were exposed to other religious traditions beyond their cultural regions. Efforts to win indigenous peoples over to Islam, Christianity, and (to a lesser extent) Buddhism have often been aggressive. And even in places where independence movements have succeeded in returning formal sovereignty to the indigenous people, the new political leadership has often been dominated by adherents of world religions who marginalize indigenous traditions. The experience of foreign domination and marginalization within their own countries is one common thread in the religious histories of indigenous peoples. Still, every indigenous religious tradition has its own rich and distinctive history.

INDIGENOUS RELIGIONS AND WESTERN SCHOLARSHIP

Interestingly, the comparative study of religion has focused particular attention on indigenous religions. In the nineteenth century, when religious studies was struggling to break free of theology and establish itself as an independent academic field, Western libraries were beginning to accumulate accounts, by explorers and other travellers, of unusual customs and practices from around the world. These accounts provided a wealth of information for scholars seeking to develop 'scientific' theories of society and religion, who—at a time when most universities were affiliated with state-sponsored churches—did not dare put Western traditions under the microscope for fear of losing their jobs.

As a result, many of the key terms used in the comparative study of religion were derived from indigenous religions, indigenous languages, or both. Scholars would take a word like '**totem**'—a Canadian Ojibwa (Anishinaabe) term for a spiritual kinship between a particular animal or species and a particular individual, family, or clan—and apply it to cultures as different as the Zulu, Hopi, and Maori. In the same way the Melanesian word '**mana**', denoting a free-flowing power in the universe capable of either enhancing or diminishing life, was applied to religious traditions all over the world, and the Polynesian word *tapu*, referring to a sacred prohibition, was borrowed to form '**taboo**'. Perhaps the best-known example is the Siberian Tungus word '**shaman**': the term for the primary ritual specialists in that culture, whose souls could leave their bodies and travel into other realms to encounter spirits. 'Shaman' has become a general term for the visionaries in many cultures who use ecstatic trances and out-of-body experiences to communicate with spiritual beings on behalf of the community.

Terms such as these were rarely applied to the scholars' own religious traditions, however. The dietary laws of Islam and Judaism were not identified as taboos; neither Elijah's ascent to heaven in a whirlwind nor Muhammad's ascent on the angelic steed Buraq is described as a shamanic journey. Yet local customs or ideas were reshaped in the scholar's study to fit a foreign terminology. Accounts of indigenous religions often exaggerated their 'exotic' aspects, minimizing their similarities to the dominant world religions and presenting them as fundamentally different. In the nineteenth and twentieth centuries, scholars tended to perceive indigenous religions as living replicas of the traditions their distant ancestors followed before embracing Judaism or Christianity.

Underlying this view was the assumption that religions developed in stages, beginning at the 'primitive' level and rising until they either reached their 'highest' form (usually monotheism) or withered away into atheism. It is still not uncommon for comparative religion textbooks to discuss 'indigenous religion' as if 'indigenous' were a synonym for **'Paleolithic'** or **'Neolithic'**. This perspective reflects a stereotype of indigenous peoples as 'natural' and unchanging. Yet scholarly research is now finding that every indigenous religion has its own history, and that some of them have experienced more changes over time—in concepts of deities, rituals, ethics, social organization—than some world religions.

It is important to keep in mind that most of the information available about indigenous religions has not come from adherents of those traditions. Most informants have been outsiders, and not many of them have been trained and objective observers. By contrast, most texts describing world religions have been the work of believers. Many of the primary sources on indigenous religions have been explorers, traders, and missionaries—people whose primary attention was focused elsewhere. Accounts written by indigenous people themselves are rare, and those that do exist often reflect the influence of earlier writings grounded in Western theories of religion.

It is also important to remember that most of the descriptions we have were written after the period of initial contact with Europeans, when the political, economic, cultural, religious, and environmental changes initiated by that contact were already well underway. Most accounts of indigenous religions in the Americas, for instance, were recorded well after Aboriginal populations had been devastated by European diseases. Most descriptions of African religions were written by people of European origin sometime after the establishment of the Atlantic slave trade, which generated a unique set of power dynamics between 'Black' and 'White' in the Atlantic world. Furthermore, the traders, missionaries, and scholars who produced those descriptions had the support of Western authorities, and so were operating in a context of profound power inequality in relation to the people they were describing. Typically, the means of communication have been the monopoly of Westerners, while indigenous people themselves have been marginalized.

Many early accounts of indigenous religions were written by explorers and traders who did not stay long enough to learn the local languages and therefore relied on interpreters unschooled in religious concepts and terminology. Making their way to universities in Britain, France, and Germany—far from the actual practitioners who could have corrected any misrepresentations—these reports were then interpreted by 'arm-chair' anthropologists who often imposed on them theoretical frameworks that had little or nothing to do with the traditions in question. The quality of missionaries' reporting was usually much higher because they stayed longer, had some knowledge of local languages, and were specifically concerned with religious issues. Nevertheless, missionaries' desire to convert indigenous peoples tended to limit their empathy and influence their interpretations.

It was not until the late 1800s that professional ethnographers began to undertake extensive field research based on participant observation (in which researchers live among the people they are studying and take part in community activities) and interviews. Interviews allow indigenous people to explain how they understand their religious activities and the roles they play in daily life. They can also provide access to historical source materials in the form of oral traditions—narratives, legends, fables, proverbs, riddles—that are passed down from generation to generation and that, like the scriptures of literate religions, help to make important religious ideas accessible to the general public.

Some cultures emphasize exact memorization of these oral texts; others are more free-flowing. Still, oral traditions depend on individuals' memories, and people living in different circumstances may emphasize different aspects of a shared tradition. In other words, oral traditions are dynamic, subject to change, and this means that other sources may be needed to assist in the interpretation of such data.

Archaeological evidence is also important, especially for the more distant past. Ruins of temples or ritual sites, tombs, images of gods or ancestors, paintings or carvings showing religious activities—all provide valuable insights. Even the debris found at ritual sites, such as bone fragments or seeds, can offer clues to sacrificial practices. Sometimes recognizable features of the local environment, such as waterfalls, grottos, or unusual trees, can assist in the interpretation of traditional narratives.

The study of indigenous religions therefore requires a multi-faceted approach based on written and oral texts, field research, and archaeological evidence. Scholars must be familiar with all the available information, historical, anthropological, and archaeological. Interestingly, scholars of the dominant world religions today are using a similar multiplicity of approaches in their discipline, which in the past focused almost exclusively on sacred texts and commentaries on them.

The rest of this chapter will focus on four major clusters of indigenous religions—African, American Indian, Asian, and Australasian—and how each of them experienced the challenges of European domination.

🦎 AFRICA

If archaeologists are correct in believing that the first human beings came from Africa, then it stands to reason that the first religions also originated there. For decades, a succession of archaeological finds in East Africa, between Ethiopia and Tanzania, has been pushing back the date for the earliest human presence in the region. But evidence regarding religion is scanty at best. Excavations of Paleolithic burial sites, dating back as far as 100,000 years, have revealed that bodies were placed in the ground with their faces turned towards the setting sun, and were often painted with ochre. These practices suggest that early humans valued their dead and may have linked their passage out of life to the setting of the sun, while the personal items (such as hunting weapons, tools, or food) that were often placed in the grave with the body suggest a belief in some form of afterlife.

Graves from the end of the Paleolithic Age, approximately 10,000 years ago, sometimes contain animal bones that appear to have been heated until they cracked—perhaps so that a diviner could study the patterns and use them to foresee the future or understand the causes of current problems. Discoveries such as these suggest that the earliest humans were concerned with making an uncertain world more predictable and controllable. Recent archaeological excavations in the Tsodilo Hills of northwestern Botswana—home to more than 4500 rock paintings—have revealed a cave that may have been used as a ritual site as much as 70,000 years ago; if that estimate is accurate, it would represent the oldest religious sanctuary known to humanity. Inside the cave is a large rock in the shape a python—an animal central to the creation myths of the local Khoi-San peoples—with hundreds of human-carved marks on it, resembling scales, as well as an inner chamber where a shamanic leader could have hidden to perform rituals.

As early as 10,000 years ago, Saharan and southern African rock paintings depicted people hunting various types of animals. Some of these scenes include images of figures with rays coming out of their heads. Commentators have suggested that the latter represent a freely circulating spiritual power that some powerful individuals were able to tap. But we cannot know what these images meant for the people who painted them. Even if the culture in question has an oral tradition explaining the origins of the world, for example, it may provide little information on religious practices or the nature of the deities, spirits, or powers that were active in the formative period. It is also possible that, as early humans slowly migrated to other areas of Africa and other continents of the world, they carried with them religious ideas and practices that originated in quite different places.

Africa is the world's second largest continent, stretching from the Mediterranean Sea in the north to the southern reaches of the Atlantic Ocean. Through most of its history the area north of the Sahara Desert had close connections with the Mediterranean and Middle Eastern cultural regions, and most of its peoples were converted to either Christianity or Islam during the first eight centuries of the Common Era. The Saharan and sub-Saharan regions, however, had relatively little contact with the Mediterranean world. Today the sub-Saharan region is home to the world's largest concentrations of indigenous practitioners—perhaps as many as 200 million.

The first Europeans to visit sub-Saharan Africa were Portuguese navigators who explored the western coastline in their search for a sea route to India and the Spice Islands during the Age of Discovery. Some explorers recorded vivid descriptions of African rituals, though the lack of a shared language and the brevity of their visits made their interpretations questionable. With the beginning of the Atlantic slave trade in the late fifteenth century, European accounts of Africa became increasingly lurid, describing 'brutal' rituals that made the idea of slavery more palatable to Europeans. Some claimed that Africans had no religion at all and maintained that the rituals described by early travellers were only 'superstitions'. The German philosopher Georg Friedrich Hegel (1770–1831) described Africa as a land without history, a place of sorcery and superstition.

By the late 1800s European scholars were developing evolutionary theories that traced the origins of religion to Africa. Such theories typically saw humanity as progressing in stages from a 'primitive' African belief in multiple gods and spirits to the final flowering of Western monotheism. Thus Edward Tylor saw Africans as animists, believing that there were souls in all things. Charles de Brosses and James Frazer thought that Africans worshipped **fetishes** (objects believed to be endowed with special powers), others suggested that Africans were polytheists, worshippers of many gods who were often represented by statues and masks. These images filtered into Western popular culture. The ballet Petrouchka (1911) includes a character called the Blackamoor who worships a coconut, and more recent notions of African religions have been shaped by Hollywood movies, from the Tarzan series to Jim Carrey's "When Nature Calls". The anthropologist E.E. Evans-Prichard described the standard 'recipe':

A reference to cannibalism, a description of Pygmies (by preference with a passing reference to Herodotus), a denunciation of the inequities of the slave trade, the need

Traditions at a Glance

Numbers
There are no reliable statistics on the numbers of people who practise indigenous African religions. Estimates run as high as 200 million, or slightly more than 25 per cent of the continent's total population.

Distribution
Mainly south of the Sahara desert, especially in the forest areas of West and Equatorial Africa and a range of ecological zones in East and southern Africa.

Principal Historical Periods

616 CE	First Muslims arrive in Ethiopia
1444	Portuguese begin exploring sub-Saharan Africa
c. 1480	Beginning of Atlantic slave trade
1885	Africa partitioned by European powers at Congress of Berlin; dramatic increase in Western missionary efforts, primarily in non-Muslim areas.
1956–1974	Various countries enter the post-independence era

Founders and Leaders
Some traditions mention a founder, but most do not. Many notable leaders have emerged in times of crisis. Examples include Kinjikitile and Alinesitoué Diatta.

Deities
Most African religions recognize a supreme being who began the process of creation, is the ultimate source of lesser deities' power, gives or withholds rain, and judges human beings on their behaviour before they enter the afterlife. This deity can be male, female, both male and female (androgynous), or neither. The lesser spirits and ancestors are often the primary focus of ritual activity because they are more approachable than the supreme being. Trickster deities are common.

Authoritative Texts
African religions are fundamentally oral. Most traditions include accounts of the creation of the world and the settlement of particular regions. Recently, indigenous scholars have written down some oral traditions, and these texts are used for religious guidance.

Noteworthy Teachings
The supreme being is the ultimate source of all life and all spiritual power, and determines the fate of people when they die. Reincarnation is an important part of most African traditions. The most favourable afterlife is that of ancestors who can continue to help their descendants before being reborn, often within their original lineage. A communitarian ethic is central to all African religious systems.

for the civilizing influence of commerce, something about rain-makers and other superstitions, some sex (suggestive though discreet), add snakes and elephants to taste; bring slowly to the boil and serve (Evans-Prichard cited in Ray 1976:3)

These were my first images of African religions as well. They reflected the long history of slave trading, colonization, and Western ethnocentrism, which tended to minimize the creative genius of African peoples.

African Religious Thought

So what are African religions really like? First, it is important to recognize that the continent is home to more than a thousand distinct religious traditions. Their diversity reflects the diversity of the communities in which they developed, each of which has its own history, patterns of contact with other cultures, ecological environment, and economic system. One thing they have in common, however, is a focus on life in this world, on human communities and their immediate environments. Reflecting that focus, they are strongly instrumental in emphasis, seeking direct assistance from deities, spirits, or ancestors who might be able to ease the difficulties of daily life.

African religions also share a focus on a supreme being—what English-speakers would call God—who is seen as the source of all life. Individual traditions differ on whether the supreme being actually created the world or delegated that task to subordinates. The Yoruba of Nigeria and Benin maintain that Olodumare, the lord of the heavens, delegated the creation to lesser gods called *orisha*, while the Dogon of Mali believe that their supreme being, Amma, began the task of creating the world but left it to be completed by spirits known as Nummo, also created by Amma. The Nuer and Dinka of the southern Sudan, the BaMbuti of Congo, and the Khoisan of South Africa all emphasize that the supreme being alone was responsible for creation. The fact that almost every African ethnic group already had a term for the supreme being made it relatively easy for nineteenth-century missionaries to translate the Christian idea of 'God'.

Different traditions also differ in their views of the role that the supreme being plays in the daily affairs of their communities. The Yoruba tradition suggests that Olodumare reigns but does not rule—just as the Yoruba kings are sacred symbols of the townships that they oversee but do not rule their city-states. Similarly, the Igbo of southeastern Nigeria have a saying—'God is like a rich man, you approach him through his servants'—that suggests their supreme being is far removed from human beings and has created lesser spirits, divine servants, to handle specific types of problems. In both cases, the implication is that humans should avoid appealing to the supreme being except in matters of great importance or when appeals to lesser spirits have repeatedly failed. To ask the supreme being for help with minor concerns like getting a job or winning a football game would be to show an arrogance bordering on blasphemy.

Most African religious communities do not have specific shrines for the worship of the supreme being, though they have many shrines dedicated to the lesser spirits or deities whose job it is to assist humans in daily life. This pattern has contributed to the false impression in the West that the supreme being is not central to African religious life, but in

Map 2.1   Selected African cultural areas

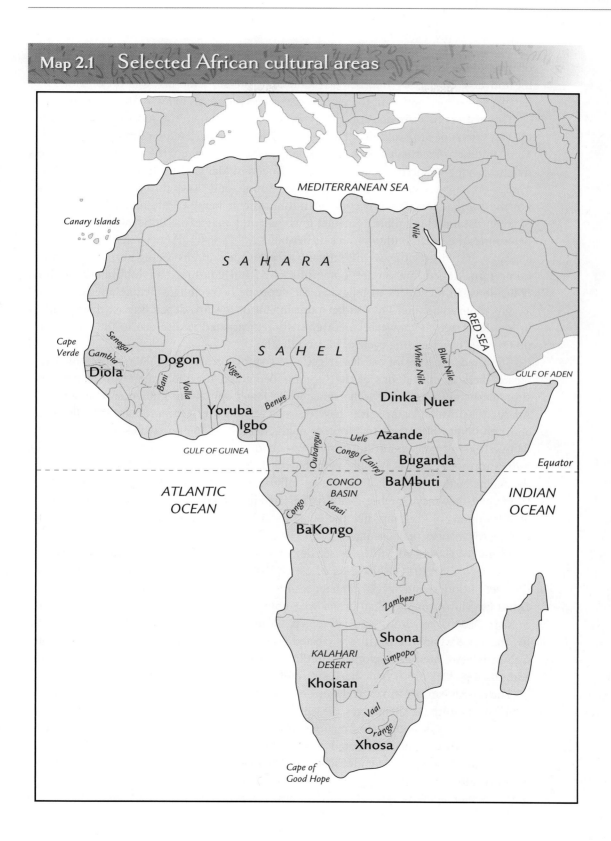

fact it shows the people's reverence for the supreme being, who has no need of sacrificial offerings, and their recognition of how insignificant their concerns are in the context of the universe created by that being. (Sometimes the supreme being is male, sometimes female, sometimes both, but there are no gendered pronouns in West African languages.)

The matters that are controlled by the supreme being are the most critical ones: the life transitions of birth and death, and the precious, life-sustaining resource that is water. Many traditions maintain that the supreme being is the source of the vital force that enters into a woman's womb to create life. For the Dogon of Mali and Burkina Faso, that force—*nyama*—originates with the supreme being, Amma, and flows throughout the universe. For the Yoruba, conception occurs when the supreme being Olodumare allows the spirit of an ancestor seeking rebirth to enter a woman and assigns the unborn infant a fate that determines the broad outlines of his or her life.

Particularly in regions where rainfall is scarce, the supreme being also gives or withholds rain, depending on the community's ethical conduct and fulfillment of ritual obligations. In most African religions, the supreme being judges people after death and assigns them to an afterlife of either punishment or reward, depending on their conduct in life. Most people, however, are eventually reincarnated and return to the living community in a never-ending cycle of life and death.

The precise nature of the lesser gods and spirits varies. The Nuer people of Sudan regard them as emanations of the supreme being and use the same term for both: the supreme being is called Kwoth Nhial, while lesser spirits are known simply as *kwoth*. Among the Yoruba, lesser spirits have distinct personalities, extraordinary independence, and rich bodies of sacred traditions or myths describing their activities. By contrast, the Bantu-speaking peoples of Equatorial, East, and southern Africa tend to emphasize the importance of ancestors: people who, having led basically good lives, have passed into the realm of the dead but continue to influence the lives of their living descendants. Eventually, they may be reborn within their own lineages or extended families. In societies with traditions of kingship, like the Buganda of Uganda and the BaKongo of Angola and Congo, royal ancestors have major shrines dedicated to their memory.

In much of West Africa the lesser deities have their own elaborate mythologies. The Yoruba recognize 401 *orishas*, each of which has a unique personality and history, a distinct set of duties, and special preferences for ritual offerings and behaviour by followers. Oduduwa, for example, is an *orisha* who completed the creation of the world after his brother Obatala got drunk and fell asleep. Oduduwa eventually became the king of Ile-Ife, the place where the world was created (and the oldest of the Yoruba cities). His sister Oshun is associated with women's fertility, sexuality, and beauty, and has acquired the additional powers of her male husbands or lovers.

The *orishas* can possess their devotees, mounting them as if they were horses and using their bodies to make themselves present and communicate necessary information. They also continue to develop new functions in community life. Thus Ogun, the god of iron and war, has come to be associated with the protection of metal workers, car mechanics, and chauffeurs. Shopona, a goddess traditionally associated with smallpox, became linked with HIV–AIDS when smallpox was eradicated and AIDS became a grave threat. At the same time Yoruba religion reserves a vital role for ancestors, people who have crossed over into the realm of the spirit and who continue to assist their living descendants. Throughout most of Yorubaland, the ancestors can become physically present in masked dances.

Trickster deities are particularly important in West Africa. The trickster is not a force for evil, but one who loves chaos and disorder. He encourages impulsive behaviour in humans and often acts impulsively himself, disrupting any kind of social order. For instance, tricksters often serve as messengers for the other gods and purposely make minor changes in their messages so that they can enjoy the resulting confusion. In Dogon religion the Pale Fox or Jackal, a sibling of the Nummo, not only disrupts earthly existence but also possesses the power to see into the future and discern the causes of disorder in the distant past.

The Yoruba trickster, Eshu, is the messenger god who summons the other *orishas* to attend all major rituals in Yoruba religion. Eshu delights in forgetting parts of messages or changing them in small ways, just to see what will happen. He loves to play tricks on human beings, whose greed, laziness, and desire make them easy to fool. He is also described as a kind of perpetual adolescent, over-sexed and promiscuous.

Christian missionaries, who saw good and evil as locked in eternal conflict, often associated tricksters like Eshu with Satan, but for the Yoruba the forces that enhance life and detract from it are commingled. These radically different world views are often described as 'conflict' and 'complementary' dualism. African religions (like most indigenous religions) generally tend towards the 'complementary' model.

Ritual

The purpose of rituals such as prayer, animal sacrifice, offerings of grain and libations of palm wine, water, or milk is to communicate with gods or spirits. Such ceremonies release life forces that nourish the gods and spirits, who then return those life forces to those seeking assistance. In turn, the participants in the ritual commit themselves to the purpose of the ceremony by consuming the food and libations after they have been offered to the gods. In this way the ritual nourishes all the participants, divine and human. Sacrifices may be offered for fertility (of crops, livestock, or humans), for adequate rain, for healing, for protection against dangerous tasks or witchcraft, or to ensure a successful transition from one life stage to another.

The rituals associated with life transitions—puberty, marriage, birth, death—are often referred to as rites of passage. Many of these rituals have a three-stage structure. In the first stage the initiates are separated from their familiar world; thus boys entering puberty may eat a last meal with their mothers before attending a ceremony that will prepare them to separate from the community for a time. The second stage is often described as one of liminality (from the Latin for 'threshold'). It is during this marginal stage, when initiates are between life phases, that much of the work of the transition or passage takes place. Initiates are instructed in their new religious and social responsibilities, and develop a feeling of solidarity with other initiates that the anthropologist Victor Turner has called 'communitas'. Finally they are reintegrated into their communities, with the added powers and responsibilities of their new status.

Most rituals involving life transitions associated with puberty, fertility, birth, and warfare are conducted in single-sex congregations, especially in communities that understand spiritual power to be gendered: restricting participation to a single sex is seen as the most effective way to harness the power of womanhood or manhood. Some spirit cults focused on women's fertility are open only to women who have successfully given birth to a child, since someone whose reproductive powers are still unknown could have a harmful influence on the fertility of others.

Throughout Africa, special containers are used to hold ritual libations, and special spears and knives are used for animal sacrifices and preparation of the ritual meals that follow. Of all the material objects used in rituals, however, the ones that have attracted the most attention are images of gods and ancestors in the form of statues and masks. Non-Africans have dismissed such images as idols—objects of worship in themselves—based on the erroneous assumption that the image contains the god. In some cases statues of gods are ritually prepared with special medicines to summon the presence of the god, but the god can be present in many places at once and is never contained by an object.

Similar confusion has surrounded the masks used in ritual dances. Activation of the dancers' spiritual power may allow them to receive the presence of the gods, spirits, or ancestors represented by the masks they wear, but the dancer's body is just a temporary dwelling place. The masks bring the god, spirit, or ancestor into the community, sometimes symbolically, sometimes by displacing the conscious mind of the dancer so that the spiritual power in question may speak through him or her; but the mask is only the vehicle that allows the spirit to manifest itself.

The design of masks and statues is highly symbolic. Thus spirits associated with women's fertility tend to be depicted with faces that represent idealized forms of beauty, and their bodies have large hips and breasts that evoke the ability to bear and nourish children. Masks of spirits that protect against malevolent forces, such as witches, often emphasize their power to terrorize spirits and humans alike.

Witchcraft

In many African traditions witchcraft serves to explain the presence of evil and suffering in the world. Witches are believed to be people whose souls travel outside their bodies to attack and consume other people's souls, or to take for themselves the spiritual essence of their valuable property. There is no material evidence for witchcraft: it takes place entirely in the realm of the soul. For evidence, witch-finders typically look to dreams, visions, or divination, though sometimes suspects will be forced to drink special witch-finding beverages believed to be capable of making the guilty fall ill or die.

Witchcraft is also used to explain chance misfortune—the sort of thing that Westerners call 'bad luck'. For example, Azande elders told the anthropologist Evans-Pritchard of a man who took a nap under a corn crib and was crushed to death when the crib collapsed. The immediate cause of death did not need explaining, but the fact that the crib collapsed while the victim was sleeping under it was attributed to witchcraft.

In many cases the society of witches is envisioned as the exact opposite of ordinary existence. Diola witches, for instance, organize in hierarchical and authoritarian groups, in stark contrast to ordinary Diola society, which emphasizes egalitarianism and opposes any concentration of authority in a single person or group. Similarly among the Yoruba,

A Diola boy receives gifts from his maternal relatives in preparation for the circumcision ritual he will undergo a few months later. The rice stalks scattered over him symbolize fertility (Photo courtesy of Robert M. Baum).

women are subordinate in ordinary society, but female witches can wield extraordinary power over men. Although most societies recognize witches of both sexes, some believe that witchcraft is restricted to either women or men. These variations may reflect tensions between the sexes, or competition between various social groups.

Five Major Traditions

The rest of this section will take a closer look at the traditions of five peoples in different geographical regions of the continent: the Diola of southern Senegal, the Dogon of Mali, the BaKongo of the central (equatorial) region, the Nuer of southern Sudan, and the Shona of what is now Zimbabwe.

Diola

The Diola people number about 600,000 and form minority communities in Senegal, Gambia, and Guinea-Bissau. Considered to be the best wet-rice farmers in West Africa, they live close to their rice paddies in large townships that were traditionally self-governing through local assemblies and councils of elders. These institutions continue to operate today, although they are not recognized by national governments. The large majority of

Senegambians are Muslim, and the Diola themselves have significant Muslim and Christian communities. But they also have a vital and dynamic indigenous religion.

At the centre of Diola religion is a supreme being called Emitai (literally, 'of the sky'); we know that this name was in use as long as ago as the seventeenth century, since it appears in a slave-trading company's dictionary of the Diola language. In addition to creating life and controlling the rain, Emitai judges individuals' conduct in life and decides what becomes of them in the afterlife. People who have led good lives, who have been generous, honest, and hard-working, become ancestors; their souls live near the Diola communities, so close that you can feel (but not see) their cooking fires. They can advise and guide their living descendants through dreams and visions, and will eventually be reincarnated.

By contrast, people who have led destructive lives—who have harmed others or violated basic community norms—became phantoms, their souls confined to the forest areas or 'bush' beyond the areas of settled habitation. These phantoms cannot speak, but they can trick people wandering alone at dusk, challenging them to wrestling matches that the living will always lose. They too will be eventually reborn, but they will have a dim memory of their misdeeds and will be unable to repeat them in the next life. Finally, some people will die without sufficient grounds for judgment. They will be reborn in a village to the south of where the Diola live now, in an area from which they emigrated centuries ago. It is Emitai who determines the fate of the dead, and Emitai who decides when life will be created.

Emitai may also choose certain individuals to impart some message to the people or to establish a new 'spirit shrine': a term that includes not only the physical shrine dedicated to a particular spirit but that spirit itself and the cult that surrounds it. By the late nineteenth century at least 14 people had been 'sent by Emitai' to assist the Diola. Some founded villages; others introduced lesser spirits, newly created by Emitai, and taught the people how to supplicate them for help in the procurement of rain or in their struggles against European colonization. These people may be considered the equivalent of prophets.

The Diola also have a number of lesser spirits created by Emitai to assist people in specific aspects of life. Thus in many communities there is a spirit shrine dedicated to assisting township elders in their governance role by giving authority to their rulings on matters such as community work, wages, or prices. Similarly, a male initiation shrine helps to ensure proper conduct by men and towards men, while a female fertility spirit is charged with ensuring that women conduct themselves properly and that men respect them. Anyone who does not follow the rules risks punishment in the form of diseases inflicted by the spirits. A man who abuses women, for example, is threatened with developing a disease that gives him a distended belly, resembling pregnancy.

Other spirit shrines are linked to specific economic activities: blacksmithing, hunting, rice farming, fishing, and so on. Some are associated with particular homesteads or extended families. Others protect a certain neighbourhood, village quarter, or township. The large numbers of shrines, whose priesthoods and councils of elders are open to most adult members of the community, ensure that most people will be able to participate in township governance and serve in a position of religious authority at some stage in their lives.

This tendency to provide broad access to leadership roles, together with the idea that the spirits can reveal themselves to people at times of crisis, contributed to an ongoing tradition of innovation that has allowed Diola religion to meet the challenges of missionary

Christianity and Islam. Before colonization, male prophets 'sent by Emitai' established a number of new spirit shrines and rituals designed to address the persistent problem of drought, for example. Existing spirits assumed new roles and new spirits were introduced to regulate the slave trade by establishing rules for raiding, trading, and ransoming slaves, and by inflicting horrible diseases on anyone who violated the rules.

The typical Diola ritual consists of libations of palm wine (believed to contain the life force of the palm tree) accompanied by spoken prayer. Offering wine and prayer together reinforces the power of the life forces contained in each. More important rituals may also include offerings of chickens, goats, pigs, or cattle, whose blood further strengthens the force of the appeal to the spirits whose assistance is sought. By eating the sacrificial meat and drinking the wine, the congregation ingests the words of the prayer and lends its support to the ritual activity. In this way ritual sacrifice can be seen as serving a social purpose as well as a religious one.

Though a few shrines are open to both men and women, most are reserved for one or the other. Male spiritual power is distinct from female power, but both are important. Thus men control the rituals of the hunt, the blacksmithing forge, war, and death, while women control the rituals of female fertility and childbirth. Females are excluded from the cemetery until the day they die, and males are not allowed into the maternity houses from

Diola women celebrate the initiation of a new priestess of a women's fertility shrine. The priestess, dressed in locally made cotton cloth, carries a cow's tail fly whisk, a symbol of ritual authority. She and two of the associates are dancing across someone's cloth in order to bring its owner good luck (Photo courtesy of Robert M. Baum).

the time they leave as infants. The most important rites of passage are the male circumcision ritual, male initiation into the rites for the dead, girls' puberty rituals, and women's initiation into the congregation of mothers.

In most Diola communities, male circumcision ceremonies are held only once every twenty years; thus each group of initiates forms a distinct generation, sharing not only the ordeal of the operation but one or two months of ritual seclusion during which they receive an intensive religious and social education. Girl's initiation, which does not involve any kind of surgery (except in those areas introduced to Islam by the Mandinka people), is held in small groups, whenever several girls are approaching the age of first menstruation. Members of the group attend special festive meals at one another's homes and their mothers and other older women introduce them to some of the religious and social responsibilities they will encounter as adolescents. Full instruction in those responsibilities, however, is not provided until after the delivery of the first child, at which time women are initiated into the fertility cult of Ehugna.

Dogon

The Dogon people of Mali and Burkina Faso number roughly 300,000 and live along the semi-arid ridges south of the Niger River, farming crops such as millet and onions. Like the Diola, the Dogon associate the supreme being with the sky and life-giving rain. However, their lesser spirits have more distinct personalities and a greater degree of independence. In addition—and in sharp contrast to the Diola—the Dogon have a rich tradition of representational art in the form of masks and statues.

The Dogon also possess an extraordinarily complex body of creation myths. According to the oral traditions collected between the 1930s and the 1950s by the French anthropologist Marcel Griaule and his associates, the supreme being, Amma, created the world because he was lonely. Accounts of how he did so differ, but one says he transformed himself into a womb, within which he created four spirit beings called Nummo. Two of the Nummo were predominantly male, but also female; the other two were predominantly female, but also male. They were supposed to stay in the womb for 60 years, but one of the males—the Pale Fox—was impatient to be with his sister/wife. Amma, anticipating this breach of the natural order, had hidden the sister in another part of the womb, and the Pale Fox was unable to find her. In the course of his search he tore away part of the womb, and that part became the earth. To purify the world, Amma sacrificed the sister and then life began.

While their impatient brother continued to wander in search of his mate, the two remaining Nummo clothed their mother Earth with a simple loincloth of living vegetation moistened with the creative power known as the First Word, which emanated from Amma and became the *nyama*: the creative life force that circulates throughout the universe.

But the Pale Fox, anxious for company, stole the loincloth from his mother and, in touching her genitals, committed incest. This pollution led to the first menstruation, from which the Earth had to be purified before she could nurture life. The Pale Fox acquired the simple speech associated with the First Word, an imprecise way of speaking, which became the language of divination. To purify the Earth, the Nummo created a Second Word, a more complex type of clothing.

Then Amma and the Nummo created and placed on the Earth eight beings who were to become the ancestors of humans. Lured into the genitals of Mother Earth, they ascended to the heavens, where they were directed to eight different chambers and given different types of grain, one of which—a small grain that was difficult to prepare, a millet called *fonio*—they all vowed never to eat. But in time they became lonely in their isolated rooms, and when their food ran out they met and cooked the *fonio*. As a result all eight were expelled from the heavens in a Celestial Granary—a model of the universe containing symbols of all the animals, plants, ethnic groups, and seeds of this world, as well as the Third Word, a more elaborate and refined type of cloth and the word that bore the full complexity of speech. When the Granary crashed to the Earth its contents were released, and at that moment human life began.

Dogon communities are organized around four major ritual societies, each of which was organized by one of the four ancestral fathers. The oldest of these, Amma Seru, is associated with the supreme being, and the oldest member of each extended family performs rituals in his honour. Beyond the extended family are lineages or clans, each with its own priest of the Binu cult, which links the clans to particular animal species with whom they share certain powers and spiritual ties. These ritual societies have shrines specially painted to depict important events in the agricultural year. The Binu cult is particularly associated with water.

A third cult is dedicated to a man named Lebe who was sacrificed to preserve the Third Word after the descent of the Celestial Granary and was reborn as a large snake. Lebe is closely associated with Mother Earth; his priest is the oldest man in the community and serves as its political leader as well. Known as a Hogon, this priest judges local disputes and ensures the proper operation of the village market. Because his duties on behalf of his community were seen as exhausting, Dogon tradition held that Lebe, in the form of a snake, would appear to the Hogon on a nightly basis and lick his body, imparting life-enhancing *nyama* and enabling the priest to carry out his duties for another day.

Finally, the fourth cult, linked to a man named Dyongu, controls the transition from life into death. Its members are in charge of funeral rituals, the masks associated with them, and a ritual called Sigi, which commemorates the origins of death itself in the disobedience of Dyongu, a deceased ancestor who used the speech of humans to express anger at the misconduct of some living people.

Nuer

The Nuer people of the southern Sudan number more than 300,000 and inhabit the marshy area known as the Sudd and the surrounding plains. Historically, they earned their livelihood as cattle herders and governed themselves through clan elders and 'leopard skin' priests, who mediated disputes between clans. For most of the past 50 years, however, Nuer life has been severely disrupted by the Sudanese civil war.

The Nuer, as we have seen, call their supreme being Kwoth Nhial. Lesser spirits are seen as emanations of Kwoth Nhial, who is omnipotent and omniscient, but physically distant. According to at least two oral traditions, Kwoth Nhial at one time lived closer to humanity; the divine realm of the sky was connected to earth by a rope. One myth says that the connection was broken after a girl who lived in the sky used the rope to descend to the earth, where she fell in love with a man; when she refused to return to the sky, Kwoth Nhial withdrew the rope and the two realms became separate. Another story blames a prank by a trickster god in the form of a jackal. In any case, following the separation of heaven and earth, Kwoth Nhial either created or extended himself into a host of lesser spirits (*kwoth*), sometimes referred to as Spirits of the Above (celestial spirits) and Spirits of the Below (spirits on Earth).

In the nineteenth century, increasing contact with a closely related group called the Dinka, together with the disruption caused by the northern Sudanese slave trade, led to a dramatic increase in both the numbers of Spirits of the Above and their activity.

Today many such spirits are openly acknowledged to be of Dinka origin. From the 1850s until the 1930s, a number of 'prophets'—people possessed by the spirits—emerged

Ngundeng Bong: A Nuer Prophet

Until the mid-nineteenth century, Nuer and Dinka engaged in intermittent warfare over the pasturelands that both needed for their large herds of cattle. Conflict increased in the 1840s with the arrival of Egyptian slave-traders who, in addition to raiding both groups for slaves themselves, incited the Nuer and Dinka to raid one another for slaves to sell. As this warfare escalated, new religious leaders emerged in both communities, men claiming to have received revelations or experienced possession by Spirits of the Above. These 'prophets' claimed the power to lead their people in battle and to renew the strength of their communities in the face of various threats to their well-being.

The most famous Nuer prophet was Ngundeng Bong, who claimed to have received revelations from a spirit named Deng. One of the many new cults adopted by the Nuer in response to the increasing turmoil in the region, the cult of Deng had originated among the Nuer's Dinka neighbours. In 1878 Ngundeng used the spiritual powers he received from Deng to lead Nuer warriors into battle against a Dinka group that was raiding the Nuer for slaves. As he led his forces into battle, he speared a special ox, which died with its head facing their opponents—a good omen. Then Ngundeng raised a large root in the air. Rain and lightning fell from the skies, and many Dinka were said to fall dead, even before the battle. After the battle he built an earthen pyramid, surrounded by elephant tusks, in which he ritually deposited many of the destructive powers that were held responsible for the threats to the Nuer.

Warfare between Nuer and Dinka eased thereafter, but slave raiding continued unabated until 1902, when the British arrived and established a colonial administration in the area. Ngundeng conceded that he could not defeat them, and in 1906 he died. His son Gwek, who claimed similar powers, assumed the religious leadership of his community. In 1929 he too speared an ox in an effort to inspire a group of warriors confronting British forces, but he failed to kill it. He died in battle and the British destroyed the pyramid that his father had constructed.

Nevertheless, Ngundeng's prophecies of renewed warfare and eventual liberation helped to inspire the southern Sudanese secessionist movement that began in the 1950s. In the 1990s a young male prophet of Kwoth, Wutnyang Gataker, raised an army that fought alongside southern Sudanese forces, and his support of their common cause made him an effective mediator between different ethnic and lineage groups in the region. Finally, in January 2011, a referendum showed overwhelming support for secession. The Republic of South Sudan gained its independence on 14 July 2011.

to play important roles in the Nuer resistance against Sudanese slave raiders as well as British colonizers.

Today Spirits of the Above continue to seize people with illness: sometimes to summon them to the priesthood, sometimes as punishment for moral infractions or neglect of community obligations. In the latter case, a healing ceremony is held that includes public discussion of the social problems that could be responsible for pollution and illness; then the community is cleansed through an animal sacrifice and ritual meal.

Spirits of the Below, for their part, include totemic spirits representing spiritual ties between particular Nuer clans and individuals and particular animal species. Other Spirits of the Below are associated with various natural forces and places that evoke a sense of awe and spiritual power.

In the absence of formal political structures, leopard-skin priests play a crucial role as arbitrators in disputes between clans and lineages. Their charismatic authority and ability to cleanse people of the polluting effects of misconduct allows them to insist that the various parties make a genuine effort to resolve their disagreements.

BaKongo

The BaKongo people number almost five million and live in what are now Congo, the Democratic Republic of Congo, and Angola. Although today they are involved in every aspect of Congolese life, urban as well as rural, historically they were farmers of root crops who also hunted and fished. When the Portuguese arrived in the fifteenth century, Kongo was a highly centralized kingdom with its capital in northern Angola.

The BaKongo king, Alfonso I, invited Portuguese missionaries to his court to teach their religion and share their knowledge of Western technology. To pay for the missionaries' assistance with the establishment of missions and schools, however, the Portuguese crown insisted that the BaKongo provide slaves for sale. The Atlantic slave trade sharply reduced the population, and in the seventeenth century the BaKongo lost control of their kingdom to the Portuguese. The massive disruption brought on by the slave trade, increasing Portuguese intervention in BaKongo affairs, and the presence of an influential Christian elite make it difficult to establish the early outlines of BaKongo religion.

The high incidence of disease and violence in that period led to a proliferation of healing shrines. Of particular importance were the Nkita and Lemba cults. Dedicated to healing disease and protecting people involved in the slave trade, they continue to play an important part in BaKongo religious life today.

The BaKongo emphasize the role of a supreme being, Nzambi Mpungu, who created the world and continues to create life. Lesser gods are not as important in this region as they are in West Africa. Rather, the BaKongo focus on the ancestors who have passed over into the realm of the dead but continue to influence the lives of their descendants through dreams and visions. Matrilineal ancestors are the most important, since ancestry is traced primarily on the mother's side.

The BaKongo conceive of the world as two mountains—the mountain of the living, where one is born in the east and dies in the west, and the mountain of the dead, where one is born in the west and dies in the east—separated by an ocean known as Kalanga. It has been suggested that this worldview may have contributed to the warm welcome the Portuguese received when they arrived in the region: the fact that they came from the Atlantic Ocean

(Kalanga), were deathly pale, and seemed uncomfortable on land may have suggested to the BaKongo that the newcomers were actually ancestors returning from the land of the dead.

In the event of illness or misfortune, a ritual specialist called a *nganga* will identify the spirit or source of power that must be contacted in order to correct the problem. This power is often manifested in consecrated ritual objects known as *minkisi*: carved objects in which the *nganga* conceals powerful medicines. Though normally used to heal the sick or protect people from misfortune, they can be used for malevolent purposes. In that case they are associated with *kindoki* (witchcraft).

Witches are often depicted with a special organ in the digestive tract that both empowers them with witchcraft and creates the appetite to consume the spiritual power of others. In BaKongo thought, kindoki is closely associated with unusual wealth and success, and it is possible that this association dates from the time of the slave trade (1480–1880), when a few people profited at the expense of many others. Even when the immediate cause of a misfortune is clear—when someone is struck by lightning, for example—the fact that it happened to that particular person is often attributed to witchcraft. The destructive power of witchcraft as a force circulating through the world also serves to explain the persistence of evil and suffering.

Because of the region's long involvement in the slave trade, BaKongo made up a large proportion of the slaves taken to the Americas. Their traditions have had a profound influence on the religions that developed in the African diaspora, from the southern United States to the south of Brazil.

Shona

The Shona are the largest ethnic group in the high plateau area of present-day Zimbabwe, numbering more than 8 million. Until the colonial occupation by the British South African Company, at the end of the nineteenth century, most Shona were farmers raising corn and cattle on scattered homesteads under the authority of local chiefs.

The supreme being of Shona religion, Mwari, receives prayer and ritual offerings at various shrines. Like the supreme beings of the Diola and Dogon, Mwari is associated with rainfall—a vital resource in a region where drought is common. At Mlanjeni, a major oracle site, female spirit mediums make the wishes of Mwari known. The medium sits inside a cave and enters a state of possession, during which a voice speaks that is said to be the voice of Mwari. Male priests interpret Mwari's message to pilgrims seeking advice. Messengers and priests of Mwari were seen as playing a vital role in the Shona revolt against British colonization in 1896.

Shona ritual life focuses on the spirits of the dead: not only individual families' ancestors, but **culture heroes**: figures from the distant past who taught the people of a community their basic tasks and obligations. There are also spirits associated with the chieftaincy and with strangers whose souls cannot settle in a particular location. These spirits communicate with the living through dreams, visions, and the persons of the individuals they choose to serve as their mediums. Those so chosen are identified when they are stricken with illness and a diviner determines that the cause is **spirit possession**. Then the chosen person is initiated into the cult, trained to control his or her spirit possession, and instructed in how to perform divination rituals.

These cults are often described as shrines of affliction, because the disease itself becomes a summons to spirit-mediumship. Ancestors continue to offer advice and guidance to their living descendants, just as they did when they were alive. When the living ignore this advice or neglect their obligations to the ancestors, the latter may punish them with illness or problems such as infertility.

The spirits of dead chiefs are known as *mhondoro* ('lion spirits'). They play a particularly influential role in their former domains, and their spirit mediums are among the most powerful people in Shona society. Mhondoro from the people's early days in the region can facilitate the distribution of rain and enhance the fertility of the land, while those from more recent chiefly lineages tend to concern themselves with matters related to the social and political structure of their former territories, including the selection of new chiefs. Two of the most powerful *mhondoro*, Chaminuka and Nehanda, played central roles in uniting Shona communities, first against incursions by the Ndebele people (a Ngoni group based on the coast) and then against British settlers.

Summary

Even the brief overview above reveals important similarities among the religious traditions in different parts of Africa. All the religions surveyed focus on a supreme being who is generally seen both as the source of life (and often rain) and as the judge who determines humans' fate in the afterlife. These beings make their wishes known through prophets and mediums, as well as dreams and visions.

Most ritual sites, however, are dedicated to lesser gods or spirits. These lesser beings are often gendered, male or female, and their powers are described in gender-specific terms. They too communicate with humans through dreams, visions, and prophetic revelation. Among the Yoruba and Dogon they often have distinct personalities and bodies of myth. Some are tricksters who, although they are not evil, enjoy disrupting the orderly and predictable workings of the universe.

Other traditions focus more on the spirits associated with particular aspects of life, such as fertility or hunting, or that serve the needs of particular groups within a community. Thus the Diola have spirits associated specifically with women's fertility, blacksmithing, or male initiation. Finally, ancestors play important roles in many traditions, advising and if necessary punishing their living descendants. In some religions these lesser spirits are sometimes represented by masks or statues that serve as a focus for community ritual or for the transmission of spiritual power. But the supreme being is never represented in physical form.

On the other hand, it is important to recognize how these traditions differ. While many African religions involve ritual worship of the supreme being, some do not. Nor do all have traditions of spiritual possession. Some actively seek to communicate with the supreme being through prophets or mediums, or to receive divine communications through dreams or visions; but others regard the deity as too powerful to concern Itself with the problems faced by humans in their daily lives.

The impact of European conquest on these peoples will be examined in more detail later in the chapter.

🦁 North and Central America

When many people think of Native Americans, they imagine Plains people on horseback wearing feathered headdresses and either hunting buffalo or vigorously resisting European settlement—the image emphasized in movies and on TV. Ironically, this image itself is largely a product of the European presence. The domesticated horse was not introduced to the Americas until the sixteenth century, when Spanish settlers arrived in Mexico. Before the first horses made their way to the Great Plains, buffalo hunters had to stampede the animals over cliffs or drive them into canyons where they could be killed with spears and arrows. The increased mobility offered by the horse allowed a number of mountain and woodland peoples to establish themselves on the Plains and develop a new economy based on the buffalo hunt.

A number of new cultural practices soon developed that reflected the Plains environment. Central to an emerging cluster of Plains religions was the Sun Dance, which focused on the most powerful deity, the god of the Sun. Held near the summer solstice, when the sun appeared to be strongest, it required elaborate preparations. Those who pledged to perform the dance itself offered their bodies to the sun god, either in hope of receiving extraordinary powers or in gratitude for powers already received. Military and religious leaders such as Sitting Bull and Crazy Horse performed the Sun Dance on numerous occasions to empower and guide their leadership.

The details of the Sun Dance vary from people to people; the following description comes from the **Lakota Sioux.** First, to purify the participants, a sweat lodge would be constructed of branches and animal skins with an opening toward the East—the source of all life power. Stones heated over a fire to the east of the lodge were then taken into the lodge to create a dry heat that cleansed the participants' bodies.

To bind themselves to their common purpose, participants also smoked a ceremonial pipe modelled on one given to the Lakota by the goddess Whope (White Buffalo Cow Woman). The pipe was a model of the universe, with a red stone bowl symbolizing the presence of Inyan (the first god, the God of Stone) and Maka, Mother Earth. The wooden stem of the pipe linked these earthly realms to the heavenly realms of Skan, the Sky God, and Wi, the Sun God, while eagle feathers attached to the stem reinforced the association with the celestial powers.

Before the pipe was smoked, the master of ceremonies offered tobacco to the four directions, to the above and below, inviting all the beneficent powers of the universe to be present. Mingling with the smoke of the pipe, the words of prayer were inhaled by the participants and disseminated throughout the universe. The purification ritual of the Sweat Lodge was a common preliminary to most major ceremonies of the Lakota and other Plains Indians.

Following purification, male elders searched out a tall cottonwood tree to serve as the focus of the Sun Dance ritual. The chosen tree was then cut down by young girls who had not yet married or had sexual relations. The girls carried the tree to the ritual site—already purified by the burning of sweet grass—and erected it in the centre of a circle. After four days and four nights of fasting and dancing, those who had pledged to make the sacrifice would have the skin of their chests pierced through with ropes, which were tied to the

North American Traditions at a Glance

Numbers
By the year 2000 the number of Aboriginal people in Canada and the United States had reached nearly five million (a small fraction of the indigenous population when Columbus established a permanent link between Europe and the Americas). There are no reliable statistics for the numbers of people who practise indigenous religions today.

Distribution
Although many Aboriginal people are Christian, indigenous traditions are still practised in some areas. Some more recent traditions that developed in the wake of Euro-American expansion also continue to have significant followings. The Handsome Lake religion has adherents among the **Iroquois** of Quebec and New York, and the Native American Church is influential in many communities in both the United States and Canada.

Principal Historical Periods
c. 1500–1800	First contact with Europeans
c. 1500–1900	European colonization and Christian missionary activity
1799	Handsome Lake's vision
1800s	US Congress bans the Sun Dance
1889	Wovoka revives the Ghost Dance
1890	More than 300 Ghost Dancers killed at Wounded Knee
1930–60	Governments begin to reduce restrictions on Aboriginal life
c. 1960	Aboriginal population numbers begin to recover
1960s–	Revival of indigenous religious traditions

Founders and Leaders
Few of the pre-conquest traditions trace their origins to a particular founder, but the new religious movements that developed in response to colonization are usually closely associated with a particular individual (for example, the Iroquois leader Handsome Lake).

Deities
Most Native American religions do not see any single deity as the source of all life and power. Instead, they attribute creation to a series of gods, and often the most important deity is one of the second or third generation.

Authoritative Texts
The earliest 'texts' are oral traditions, most of which involve the creation of the present world and the beginnings of the community in question. Meso-Americans, however, did have written sacred texts early in the Common Era. More recent religions often have their own sacred texts (for instance, the *Gaiwiio* of Handsome Lake).

Noteworthy Teachings
Native American religions are theistic, but do not necessarily worship the original creator deity. Many emphasize the spiritual powers of the natural world and the ability of religious specialists or visionaries to use these powers on behalf of their communities.

central pole. While dancing until the ropes broke through their skin, they sought visions from the sun god, Wi, which they could use on behalf of their communities.

The Lakota conceived of a universe permeated by a life-enhancing power known as *wakan*. In nineteenth- and twentieth-century cosmologies the supreme being was named Wakan Tanka ('Great Spirit' or 'Great Mystery'), but earlier cosmologies envisioned four primary gods. In the beginning there was Inyan, the Rock. In order to have companions, Inyan sacrificed himself by cutting into his body. The blood that flowed out created Maka, Mother Earth; Skan, the Sky God and god of justice; and Wi, the Sun God. After giving up so much blood to create the other gods, Inyan was left as hard and dry as rock.

The four gods then created partners for themselves: Inyan created Wakinyan, the Thunderbird, who controls rain and storms, while Wi created Hanwi, the Moon. Together each pair created a new generation of deities, including tricksters who worked to disrupt the cosmic order. The sacrifice of Inyan, which led to the creation of the three other gods of the first generation, provided a model for the Sun Dance: the offering of one's own body in order to enhance life.

Another important Lakota ritual is the vision quest. Following purification in the Sweat Lodge, a young man goes into seclusion, often on a hilltop, to fast and await a vision that will shape the rest of his life. For a maximum of four days, he cries out for a vision in which a special relationship will be established with a deity or an animal guardian spirit. In some societies girls are also permitted to undertake a vision quest, but it is more often required of boys as part of their passage to adulthood.

Visions can take many forms. Sometimes they will identify the seeker as having specific gifts to share with the community. Sometimes they will empower him to become a healer, hunter, or warrior. Sometimes a vision will invite the seeker to take up the life of a *winkte*: a biological man who lives as a woman. In the past, such men were not uncommon in Native societies (another common name for them is *berdaches*), which considered them sacred because of their ability to tap into the distinctive spiritual powers of both men and women. Some communities consider biological women who live as men to be sacred as well, though this is less common. The majority of Aboriginal cultures in North America regard the vision quest as a powerful indicator of the roles that young people will assume in their societies.

Among the Lakota, girls begin their formal initiation into womanhood just after menarche. When a girl menstruates for the first time, she goes into seclusion with some of her female elders, who teach her about her responsibilities as a Lakota woman. Her family and tribe celebrate her new powers to create and nurture life within her body and she is given special foods to strengthen her and celebrate this joyous occasion. Her seclusion during the ritual is intended to protect her from malevolent forces which could take advantage of her vulnerable state as she learns to control her new life-giving powers.

First Contacts

Most Native American creation myths describe the world as beginning somewhere in the Americas, if not in the place where the people now live, then in one they migrated from or were removed from by conquest. The majority of scholars, however, believe that the earliest ancestors of 'indigenous' people originated outside the Americas. The dominant theory is that they arrived on the continent from northeastern Asia approximately 30,000 years ago, crossing the Bering Strait in several waves during periods when the sea level was low enough to expose a 'land bridge' between what are now Siberia and Alaska. The first encounters between Europeans and Native Americans took place along the eastern coast of North America, in the Caribbean, and in coastal areas of Latin America.

Early European accounts of North America sparked intense debate about the nature of Native people. Did they have souls? Did they have religions? Should they be treated as human beings, or as brutish savages? Did they have rights that Europeans were obliged to respect? Could they be enslaved? Should they be converted to Christianity? Just two months after arriving in the New World, Columbus wrote that the peoples he encountered had no religion, but were 'very gentle and ignorant of evil' and would readily accept Christianity. Those who shared his view recommended a paternalistic colonial policy in which European governments and missionaries would protect the 'noble savages' from exploitation by less scrupulous newcomers. Others favoured harsher treatment, including enslavement of those who resisted.

The Native societies of North America varied widely in environment, language, economic activity, and social organization, and their religions reflected this diversity. There are some broad similarities, however. Most Native American traditions include a creator god (or series of gods), but they do not generally consider a single deity to be the source of all life and power. Rather, they tend to classify deities in different groups, either by generation (as in the Lakota myth outlined above) or by type. In many instances it is a deity of the second or third generation that is the primary object of veneration. The Swedish historian of religion Ake Hultkranz has argued that Native American deities can be classified according to their primary abode. Thus he describes sky gods (associated with the sun, stars, moon, etc.); atmospheric spirits (the four winds, rain spirits, Thunderbirds); earth spirits (the Buffalo Spirit, the Maize Spirit); and underworld beings (Mother Earth, underwater beings).

Creation Myths

The Tewa of New Mexico belong to the group of peoples that the Spanish called 'Pueblo' because—unlike the hunter-gatherer peoples to the south—they lived in settled villages. According to Alfonso Ortiz, the Tewa believed that the area where their six communities were located was the spiritual centre of the world, surrounded by four mountains, one in each of the four cardinal directions. Closer to the pueblo, on small hills on the outskirts of town, altars were constructed where the people could perform rituals honouring the powers of the north, south, east and west. Their most important rituals, however, were performed in the centre of the pueblo, where the power from all four directions was concentrated.

The Zuni and Hopi similarly believed in what the historian of religion Mircea Eliade called the *axis mundi*: the central point where the spiritual realms of the heavens and the underworld intersected with the earth. In many Pueblo communities, the place of transition between worlds was represented by a ritual centre known as a *kiva*.

In Pueblo creation myths it is the younger gods that are commissioned to create life and left to control it; therefore they are the focus of worship. A Hopi account traces the beginning of life to a third-generation goddess named Kokyangwuti or Spider Woman, who creates two gods from saliva and earth, covers them with a white cape embodying wisdom, and sings the Creation Song. These two gods in turn are entrusted with continuing the process of creation, one of them solidifying the earth and the other filling it with sound. Spider Woman also creates all the plants and animals on the earth; human beings are formed from four different colours of earth, mixed with saliva. For the Hopi, the life essence is embodied in Spider Woman's saliva; songs and wisdom are the forces of creation.

Many creation myths, particularly among the peoples of the Eastern Woodlands, suggest that in the beginning all was water and without form; then an animal or a god dives under the water and returns with earth to begin building dry land. These accounts (which also recall shamanic journeys into other realms) are often referred to as Earth Diver myths. The same motif can be seen in an Iroquois creation account. In this story the first two animals to try bringing earth from under the water are a duck and a fish, both of which fail. Finally a muskrat—well-adapted to life both in water and on land—succeeds and the creation of the land can begin.

Similarly, the Muskogee people of the southeastern United States have a myth in which the gods decide to create dry land so that they can obtain food. First they send Dove out to find land, but all he finds is water. Then they send Crayfish. For three days he too fails, but on the fourth day he returns with a small ball of dirt; from it Eagle fashions a plot of land on which the gods live until the remaining waters recede. Similar motifs are found in early Japanese and other northeast Asian traditions, reinforcing the idea that the human populations of the Americas originated in Asia.

Animals and the Spiritual Order

Indigenous religious traditions across the Americas reflect the people's careful observation of animal behaviours and powers. In many cases, particular gods and humans were said to share in the skills of particular species. Animals were seen as spiritually powerful, both individually and collectively. They played crucial roles in the creation of the lands where humans live. They appeared to individuals on vision quests, offering specific types of powers associated with their particular characteristics. They voluntarily gave up their lives to hunters so that people could live. In turn, humans were expected to offer prayers of thanksgiving for successful hunting or fishing, to treat the deceased animals with respect, and to recognize the relationship between hunter and hunted.

Such rules were enforced by deities known as 'Keepers of the Game'. For example, the Inuit required that a hunter who killed a polar bear place the body facing the direction from which the bear had come, so that its spirit could return. Hunters gave fresh water to the whales and seals they had killed, so that their souls would return to the sea reinvigorated and ready to be reborn. The Algonquian and Iroquoian peoples of the Eastern Woodlands had similar views regarding the animals they killed. When rules were violated, the Keepers of the Game could remove the animals from the area where the offending people lived, depriving the community of an essential food source.

A particular individual, clan, or extended family might also have a spiritual relationship with a particular animal species. Sharing certain characteristics, abilities, or sensibilities with that species, those people would be expected to treat it with special respect: they

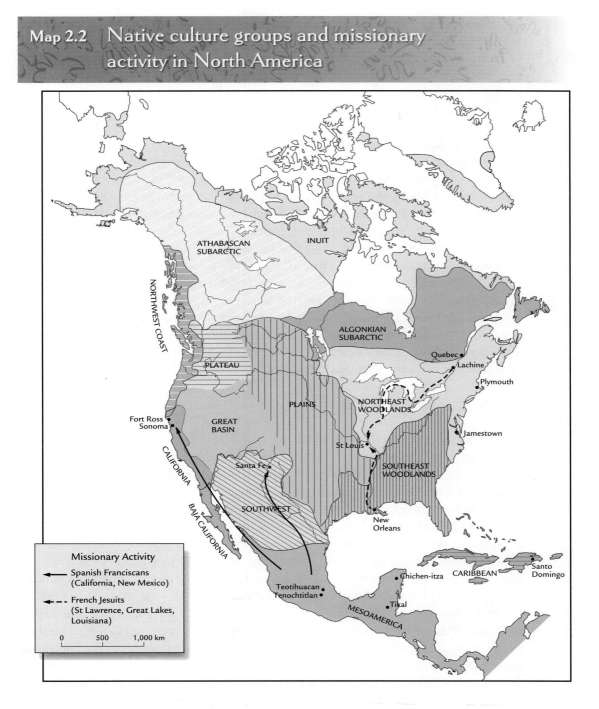

Map 2.2   Native culture groups and missionary activity in North America

would not hunt it, nor would they ordinarily be harmed by it. Such a relationship is described as 'totemic' (from the Ojibwa word for 'family'), and its most familiar expression is probably the Northwest Coast totem pole. It would be a mistake, however, to assume that relationships between humans and the spirit world were always harmonious. There are many accounts of monstrous spirits who devour human beings or drive them to madness, and the world of the animal spirits themselves was sometimes imagined as no less violent than that of humans.

In an Inuit myth recorded by Franz Boas, for instance, the goddess Sedna is initially married to a bird who mistreats her. Her father rescues her and kills her husband, but the husband's kin, a group of sea birds, chase Sedna and her father as they try to escape by boat. The birds stir up a massive storm and Sedna is swept overboard. She clings to the side of the boat, but her father, afraid it will capsize, chops off her fingers. Once the storm subsides, her father lets her back into the boat, but in revenge she sets her dogs on him while he sleeps. When he awakes and sees that they have gnawed off his feet and hands, he curses her. Then the earth opens and swallows them up. Sedna's fingers become the various types of whales and seals and she becomes the keeper of the animals of the sea.

Other sacred traditions emphasize the trickster roles of animal deities like Coyote, Wolf, and Raven, which are seen as wily creatures. Many of the sorrows of this world—death, disease, hunger—are attributed to the chaos-loving nature of trickster deities. Like their African counterparts, these tricksters are forces not of evil but of disorder. Evil and suffering can come from the actions of trickster gods, but so can creative ways of dealing with disorder. For example, the Shoshone and Paiute of the Great Basin (the region between the Rockies and the Sierra Nevada) consider the trickster Coyote to be the creator of the world. Other Great Basin peoples see him as the creator both of death and of mourning rituals (since his own son was the first to die), as well as sexual reproduction, which became necessary after death was introduced.

The Eastern Woodlands

Like the Yoruba, many of the Algonquian and Iroquoian peoples of the Eastern Woodlands saw the universe in complementary dualist terms, with life-enhancing power (*manitou* for the Algonquians, *orenda* for the Iroquoians) circulating through the world in opposition to life-destructive powers (*windigo*, *utgo*). The origins of this dualistic world view can be traced to an Iroquoian creation myth that begins with a group of human-like divinities living in a celestial realm illuminated by a giant tree.

In this divine society, as in the Iroquois society of eighteenth-century Quebec and New York state, dreaming is the way the soul speaks to the conscious mind. Thus when one of the inhabitants of this celestial realm falls in love with a young woman but is unable to communicate his feelings to her, he has a dream in which he is instructed to tell his brothers of his feelings and ask them to tell her how he feels. They do so and she marries him. Shortly thereafter, he has another dream in which he is instructed to tell his brothers to uproot the celestial tree that provides light and warmth. Reluctantly, the brothers do so, leaving a huge hole in sky, but with continued light from the stars. One day, as his wife sits with her feet dangling over the edge of the hole, she is impregnated by the Wind. Angered by this turn of events, the young man pushes his wife through the hole, but her fall is broken by birds and eventually she comes to rest on dry earth that has been gathered on the back of a turtle.

There she establishes a home and gives birth to a daughter who, when she is grown, disobeys her mother's order not to swim in the nearby lake. Impregnated by the waters, she conceives twin boys. The first, Tarachiawagon, embodies the life-enhancing power

Hiawatha

According to Iroquois oral traditions, Hiawatha lived in the fifteenth century. Devastated by the death of his wife and family in one of the many wars dividing the Iroquoian-speaking peoples of the Eastern Woodlands, he retreated to the forest where he lived alone as a thief—some say a cannibal—ambushing isolated travellers and hunters. When he reached his lowest point, he saw a face reflected in a pot of water. Assuming that is was his own, he thought that it did not look like the face of a cannibal. In fact it was not his face but that of the god Dekanawidah.

At that moment Dekanawidah revealed himself and told Hiawatha that he must persuade the Onondaga, Oneida, Cayuga, Mohawk, and Seneca nations to unite and form what came to be known as the Iroquois Confederacy. Hiawatha abandoned his anti-social behaviour, rejoined his community, and set out on this mission. Eventually, he persuaded 49 chiefs to gather at Onondaga and commit their five nations to stand together as one extended family—a Longhouse—within which all blood feuds would be forbidden. (A sixth nation, the Tuscarora, would join them in 1720.) This confederation, initiated by a visionary experience, and consecrated by ritual, united the Iroquois peoples for nearly three and a half centuries. The story of Hiawatha's visionary experience at a time of moral and physical crisis provided a model for later prophetic figures, including Handsome Lake.

of *orenda*; the second, Tawiskaron, embodies the life-destructive powers of *utgo*. (The fact that they could trace their ancestry only on their mother's side formed the basis for Iroquoian societies' emphasis on matrilineal descent and matrilocal marriage.)

Tarachiawagon is born first, in a normal birth, but his brother chooses a short-cut through his mother's armpit, which results in her death. As she is dying, the mother tells Tarachiawagon how to bury her and reveals that corn will grow out of her breasts in the grave. (Corn, grown primarily by women, was the Iroquois' agricultural staple, nourishing the community just as mother's milk nourished an infant.) Using the power of *orenda*, Tarachiawagon creates human beings out of soil and breathes life into them. He creates rivers in which canoeists can travel with the current, along with edible plants and a variety of animals and other things that human beings can use. Tawiskaron, however, uses the power of *utgo* to create rapids in the streams, along with weeds, insect pests, dangerous animals, and diseases.

It is here that the meaning of **complementary dualism** becomes clear, for the *utgo* that Tawiskaron uses to create disease is the same power that is used to cure it. Thus it is Tawiskaron who empowers the most important of the Iroquois healing societies, the False Face Society. In sharp contrast to conflict dualist religions, the Iroquois tradition sees destructive powers as capable of enhancing life. Healing rituals involving the telling of dreams, the confession of misconduct, and ritual offerings are an important part of the Iroquois ceremonial cycle, beginning with the Midwinter festival and continuing through the Green Corn Festival of the summer and the fall harvest ceremony.

Healing and the Afterlife

The **medicine society**—an organization of ritual healers or shamans—was an important part of life in many Native American communities. As in Africa, the summons to take on the responsibilities of a healer was often associated with a particular disease. Initiation took place in stages over the course of an adult life. Each stage was linked to a particular type of animal, beginning with water mammals like beaver and muskrat, continuing with birds, then land animals like snakes or bobcats, and culminating with the animal most closely associated with healing, the bear. The Ojibwa–Anishinaabe Midewiwin society was slightly different in that its members were led to become healers as a result of a dream or vision; this society developed in the early days of the fur trade, before the French and English began taking over Aboriginal lands, and may have represented a way of coping with the devastating epidemics of smallpox, measles, and other diseases that arrived with the Europeans.

Some communities believed that individual healers or shamans could travel into the realms of the gods and bring back healing powers. Shamans could be either men or women. While their bodies remained in a deep trance, their souls were believed to travel under the seas or into the heavens to learn the causes of their patients' illnesses and the appropriate cures (often herbal remedies). Shamans could also use various rituals to divine the causes of illness or to predict the future. Shamanic healing was particularly important among the Inuit, the peoples of the Northwest Coast, and the various communities of the Great Basin.

Disease and calamity could also be interpreted either as punishment for violation of community rules or as the result of witchcraft. Witchcraft also figures in many creation myths. According to Hopi and Navajo traditions, humans began to practise witchcraft in the lower world before they emerged into the present world.

Funeral rituals varied dramatically. Some peoples buried their dead in the ground; some practised cremation; and others constructed scaffolds to offer the bodies of the dead to the celestial powers. In most cases the purpose of funeral rituals was to ensure the safe journey of the soul to the land of the dead while discouraging the spirit from lingering. There were exceptions, however. The Lakota suggested that a portion of the soul could stay with the family while the rest travelled south to the land of the dead. Other peoples, especially on the Northwest Coast, believed that the souls of the dead would be reborn among the living. Some, especially on the Great Plains, believed that the dead could reveal themselves to their living descendants. Others, including the Pueblo and Navajo in the southwest and the Inuit in the far north, feared the souls of the dead.

Meso-America

Urban civilizations dominated large areas of Meso-America, beginning with the Olmecs some 2,000 years ago and continuing with the Mayans, Toltecs, and Aztecs until the Spanish conquest in the early sixteenth century. In sharp contrast to the popular image of indigenous traditions, these were literate cultures with elaborate spiritual practices organized according to a calendar based on complex astronomical calculations. Rituals were conducted at special ritual centres such as the Mayan Chichen Itza and the Aztec Tenochtitlan. Deities associated with corn played a particularly important role in Meso-American religions. In addition, however, the Aztecs offered human sacrifices to their

Detail from 'Pilgrimage to Wirikuta', a 3-metre-long yarn painting by Emeteria Rios Martinez. In this final section the pilgrims gather the peyote cactus they believe the gods have sent to allow the people to communicate with them (Photo courtesy of Eugene Garfield).

war god, Huitzilopochtli, in return for protection, and to the sun god who ensured the continuing vitality of the world.

Just beyond the area of the great urban civilizations lived a number of Chicimec hunter-gatherer groups, among them the Huichol Indians. Although they had originated in the northern desert, they settled in the Sierra Mountains, near Guadalajara, to escape attacks by their more powerful neighbours. Struggling to growing corn, beans, and squash in a physical environment that was not suited to agriculture, they envisioned the corn goddesses as delicate deities who required careful attention and longed to return to Wirikuta, where their gods continued to live. Led by a shamanic priest, small groups of Huichol made annual pilgrimages to their original homeland to gather parts of the peyote cactus, which were used to induce visions and reunite the people with their gods. Beautiful images made of coloured yarn record some of the visions experienced by the Huichol under the influence of peyote.

Summary

Native American religious traditions have many elements in common. Like their African counterparts, they are primarily theistic, centred on divinities rather than abstract forces (as in some schools of Hinduism, Jainism, and Buddhism). Their principal concerns are the concerns of this world: ensuring adequate food, fertility, health, and protection from enemies. Still, as we have seen with the Iroquois and the Hopi, different traditions have different visions of the origins of the world, the nature of the gods, and human relationships both with the environment and with the ancestors who have died before them. Many of the traditions described here are still practised in many areas, but newer traditions developed in response to the massive disruption caused by European settlement. These will be discussed later in this chapter.

🦎 SOUTH AMERICA

South America was inhabited by more than a thousand different ethnic communities at the time of the Spanish and Portuguese conquest. Like their North American counterparts, they are thought to have arrived, mainly from Siberia via the Bering Strait, in a series of waves beginning as early as 30,000 years ago. Each group brought its own language, cultural practices, and religious ideas and rituals, which changed over time as they came into contact with other groups and adapted to new ecological conditions and developed new forms of economic activity.

In broad terms, South America encompasses at least six highly distinct ecological zones to which the human inhabitants had to adapt: the Andean highlands, the tropical rainforests of the Amazon and Orinoco river basins, the coastal mountains and highlands of Brazil, the temperate grasslands of the Argentinian Pampas, and the cold prairies of Patagonia. The human cultures of these widely varied environments combined economic production, social organization, and religious beliefs and practices in different ways. All envision some kind of supreme being who began the process of creation, though the role of this deity is more prominent among some groups (notably those of the tropical rainforests and the Andean highlands) than others. In some cases the supreme being is seen as active and approachable; in others, it creates the world and then withdraws, leaving lesser deities to complete the task of creation and deal with human affairs.

'Masters of animals' are deities that protect particular animal species against violations of the laws surrounding the hunt; they are capable of withdrawing game from communities that break the rules. Jaguar spirits are particularly important in the Amazon region, where their nocturnal habits led them to be associated with various spirits of the underworld, the abode of the dead. Various deities and culture heroes (female as well as male) are credited with the introduction of staple crops such as corn, potatoes, and cassava. One of the most prominent culture heroes was the Quechua Viracocha, who became linked with the Incan sun god during the period of Incan domination of the northern Andes. Other deities are associated with the fertility of plants, domestic animals, humans, and wild game.

In many South American traditions certain musical instruments were considered sacred and were controlled by various ritual groups. The harmonious sounds created by musical instruments were often associated with harmonious relations between the living and their ancestors, or spiritual beings in general.

Indigenous communities in the more remote parts of the continent were largely protected from the unfamiliar diseases that accompanied European settlers. But Indian populations in more accessible regions were decimated. This led to the expansion of healing cults and growing concerns about witchcraft.

The experience of the Mundurucu—a community of farmers and hunters in the southern Amazon region—illustrates many of these points. The Mundurucu focused much of their ritual activity on the spirit mothers who protected different game species from overhunting or disrespect while assisting the animal populations to grow. Hunters who violated the rules could be punished with illness, accidents, snake bites, loss of spiritual energy ('soul loss'), or continuing failure in the hunt. Other spirits associated with forests and waterways were said to attack solitary travellers with illnesses that could be fatal. Shamans performed healing rituals using herbs such as tobacco, knowledge of which was obtained in their journeys into the realm of spirits. Such knowledge could also be used to protect against attacks by witches and sorcerers. Yet the power of shamans was similar enough to the power of witches and sorcerers to cause fear that they might use it to harm others.

Mundurucu men's rituals focused on their ancestors. At the 'men's house'—a place used both for sleeping and for ritual activity—reed trumpets were played to soothe and welcome the ancestral spirits. Women were excluded from public areas and confined to their homes during such ritual performances. Men told visiting anthropologists in the mid-twentieth century that this custom was a reflection of their own dominance in village life. Women, however, said that the trumpets were originally under female control. According to their sacred tradition, a group of women gathering firewood were drawn to a small lake in the middle of the forest, from which a beautiful song was heard. They cast nets into the lake and caught three fish that transformed themselves into reed trumpets.

Thereafter the women would disappear into the forest to play the trumpets, forcing the men to take on the women's traditional tasks of gathering firewood, drawing water, and preparing food in addition to their primary work of hunting. Then one day a man followed the women into the forest and discovered their secret. He demanded that they bring the trumpets into the village, and—because the spirits associated with the trumpets required offerings of wild game—the male hunters were able to wrest control of the instruments from the women and regain their position of dominance. Even though women could no longer take part in trumpet rituals, the memory of a period of female ascendency remained important in Mundurucu life.

🌿 NORTHEAST ASIA AND AUSTRALASIA

Northeast Asian and Australasian religions are extremely diverse, but can be divided into a number of clusters within which interaction and mutual influence were significant: Inner Asia (from Afghanistan and Tibet in the south to Mongolia and Siberia in the north), Southeast Asia (from southern China to Indonesia), Aboriginal Australia, Melanesia, Polynesia, and Micronesia. Indigenous traditions continue to be practised in all these areas, but the great missionary religions of Christianity, Islam, and Buddhism have had a significant impact as well. Similarities in religious practice can probably be attributed to migration from the Asian mainland, but thereafter the various clusters were largely isolated from one another until the period of European expansion that began in the sixteenth century. (Japanese Shinto, Korean shamanism, and Chinese folk religion are discussed in chapters 10 and 11.)

Siberia

Siberia, the vast and sparsely populated eastern region of Russia, extends from northern forests to the Arctic tundra. Until the Russian empire expanded into the region, beginning in the seventeenth century, it was populated mainly by hunter-gatherers and fisherfolk who spoke Paleo-Siberian, Tungus, or Turkic languages. Siberian religious traditions centred on a supreme being, closely associated with the sky, rain, and storms, who created the world in which people live. A second generation of gods, both male and female, were given the tasks of mediating between humans and the sky god and maintaining the world. Although the term 'shaman' (or 'saman') originated with the Tungus people, it could be applied to many of Siberia's most important ritual specialists.

For many Tungus-speaking groups, the universe was divided into three worlds: an upper world inhabited by life-enhancing deities, a lower world inhabited by malevolent and life-destructive spirits, and the middle world (Earth), inhabited by humanity. Tungus-speaking shamans mediated between these worlds, climbing a World Tree or following a sacred river that linked the three realms. Their souls were said to leave their bodies and travel to these other realms where they communicated with the deities and spirits that lived there. In general, the goal of these spiritual journeys was either to enhance the fertility and overall well-being of the community, or to provide spiritual guidance for individuals who sought the shamans' assistance.

Farther south, in Mongolia, indigenous religious traditions developed that have co-existed with Buddhist traditions for over a thousand years. This area, adjacent to the ancient trade routes that linked eastern and western Asia (and Europe), was also influenced by early contact with Zoroastrians, Christians, and Muslims, producing a rich syncretic tradition. Like their Siberian neighbours, Mongolians associated their supreme being (Atagha Trigri) with the sky and placed a strong emphasis on shamanism. Unlike the Siberians, however, they also envisioned ancestors as playing an important role. Ancestors together with many lesser deities communicated their needs and desires through the sha-mans' trance journeys. Some of these deities, such as Bisnu Trigri (the Indian Vishnu) and Qormusta Trigri (the Zoroastrian Ahura Mazda), reflected the influence of other religions.

Australia

Australian Aborigines had little contact with the outside world before the beginning of British colonization in the late eighteenth century. Until then they controlled most of the Australian continent, from the well-watered and temperate southeast to the tropical northern regions and the desert interior. Hunting, fishing, and gathering wild foods were the primary economic activities, and there was little political organization beyond the authority exercised by clan elders.

Together, massive violence against Aborigines, including women and children, and imported European diseases drastically reduced their numbers. Today Aborigines account for less than three per cent of the total population of Australia. Before European settlement, there were nearly five hundred different Aboriginal tribes, each with its own language or dialect and its own particular religious ideas and practices; now there are fewer than one hundred. Written accounts begin with European contact, and most oral traditions were collected after the colonization process had begun.

In sharp contrast to most of the world's peoples, Australian Aborigines had no creation myths: for them the world had always existed. The supreme being was associated with the sky and was the source of all power in the universe, but was not the focus of wor-ship. Instead, ritual practices focused on a number of spirits who were believed to sleep within the earth and periodically emerge to transform it. These earth spirits were said to

The gigantic sandstone formation called Uluru (known in English as Ayers Rock), in the central interior of Australia, is sacred to the local Aboriginal peoples. It is as tall as the Empire State Building and covers an area larger than New York's Central Park (Willard G. Oxtoby).

be capable of assuming either human or animal form and were considered the 'totemic ancestors' of particular Aboriginal clans.

The term 'Dream Time' was coined by nineteenth-century anthropologists to refer to a primordial era that plays a central part in Australian Aboriginal myths. But in fact different groups envisioned that era in different ways. Among the Aranda of central Australia, a more accurate term might be 'uncreated time', referring to the period when the first ancestors shaped the world and established the traditions that their descendants must follow. The actions of those earth spirits or ancestors were thought to be imprinted on the land, whether in distinctive physical landscapes such as Uluru (Ayers Rock), in unusual water holes, or in the particular characteristics of animals and plants. The Dream Time—the physical landscape of the universe and the sacred traditions that describe it—was the foundation of Aboriginal thought and religious practice and its power was believed to be ongoing.

Many ritual practices focused on re-enacting the formative events of that primordial era. Song and dance, as well as body and sand paintings, were used to gain access to the Dream Time and teach the community about it. Many rituals were strictly gender-specific, reflecting the differences in male and female powers, as well as the distinct types of work that men and women do.

The Western Pacific Islands

The islands of the western Pacific Ocean are usually grouped in three clusters: Polynesia, Micronesia, and Melanesia. The easternmost, Polynesia, embraces three widely separated island groups: New Zealand, Tahiti, and Hawaii.

Polynesia

In Polynesian religions the supreme being and creator of the universe, Tangaroa or Kanaloa, was most closely associated with the ocean rather than the sky; in island societies it is not surprising that the sea would be a central force in people's lives. Two other important deities throughout Polynesia were Tane or Kane, the god associated with life-giving fresh water, which he found by plunging a digging stick into the earth, and Lono or Rongo, the deity associated with the fertility of the land, healing, and peaceful relations among people. In addition there was a group of deities, collectively known as Tu or Ku, that assisted humans in daily life and were also invoked in times of crisis, such as famine or epidemic disease.

Among the Maori, the creator god Tane sought female partners to create water, plants, and animals. But he was unable to create human beings until he and his brothers created a female with whom Tane copulated in every orifice. In this way he created saliva, mucus, earwax, and excrement, but also a daughter. Finally, through incestuous relations with that daughter, Tane was able to father human beings.

A cycle of birth, life, and death centred around the idea of reincarnation. The spirits of human beings were said to leave the realm of spirits and enter the womb of a woman to be reborn. Death marked a similar transition to the realm of the spirit.

Polynesian gods entered this world from the spirit realm in order to shape natural forces and make their wishes known. Their priests performed rituals on behalf of the community and served as advisers to kings and local chiefs. Both rituals and priests were subject to rules known as *tapu* (the source of the English 'taboo'), the violation of which would provoke negative spiritual consequences. The term is now applied to many sorts of rules enforced by fear of pollution or spiritual retribution.

The gods made their wishes known through dreams or by temporarily possessing the bodies of human beings and compelling them to speak in their names. Such **spirit possession** may occur spontaneously, but it is often deliberately sought through the performance of specific rituals.

Micronesia

Micronesia is a series of archipelagos in the western Pacific, formed largely from coral reefs. In the early nineteenth century Micronesians relied mainly on fishing and farming (taro, sweet potatoes, coconuts). The arrival of Europeans, especially on whaling ships, brought new diseases which devastated the local populations. But colonization and the establishment of Christian missions created new opportunities for employment in European-dominated sectors of the economy.

Religious life focused on ancestral spirits who made their presence known either through dreams or through spirit possession. Shaking and a trance-like state were interpreted as signs that an ancestral spirit had come to tell the people something about the future or advise them on some current problem. Some of these 'great ghosts' became the subjects of myth and were assumed to have extraordinary powers to influence the world.

Several deities associated with the creation of the world were also important, as were the trickster gods who, despite their penchant for disruption and amoral behaviour, were seen as the providers of necessities such as fire. Other patron deities taught humans essential skills such as sailing. The Micronesian tradition had no counterpart to the wholly evil forces found in many Western religions.

Melanesia

Melanesia consists of the large islands of New Guinea and Fiji together with nearby archipelagos such as the Solomon Islands and New Caledonia. Before the European conquest, most of the peoples of this region supported themselves by hunting, fishing, raising pigs, and farming yams and taro.

It was from Melanesia that scholars borrowed the term 'mana' to refer to a life-enhancing power emanating from deities. Although early anthropologists incorrectly assumed that Melanesian religion was pre-theistic—lower down the evolutionary scale than even polytheistic traditions—in fact its sacred myths describe how various gods created the world and endowed it with mana. It is true, however, that ritual attention tended to focus less on the gods than on the ancestors who sometimes assisted and sometimes punished their living descendants.

Male religious leaders in Melanesia tended to be deeply suspicious of women's power and enforced an elaborate system of menstrual avoidance; sexual intercourse was regarded as causing a dangerous loss of male power, even within marriage. In some areas of central New Guinea, boys were required to ingest the semen of older men so that they would be strong enough to weather the dangers of sexual intercourse with women once they reached adulthood, and married men induced monthly nosebleeds to remove the 'pollution' caused by sexual contact with their wives—the ritual equivalent of menstruation.

INDIGENOUS RESPONSES TO EUROPEAN COLONIALISM

Until the fifteenth century, Europe was a relatively weak and isolated region on the western fringes of the Eurasian land mass. Then the voyages of the great Portuguese and Spanish navigators launched a process of expansion that by the early twentieth century had made Europe the centre of the world economy and the dominant force in global culture, including religion. Most indigenous communities lost their independence, came under the domination of European powers, and were challenged by the new religion of Christianity.

Africa

With a few exceptions—in Algeria, South Africa, Rhodesia, and Kenya—the European powers that colonized Africa were not trying to create settler societies like the ones they established in the Americas and Australia. Thus in most regions of Africa there was no need to remove the indigenous populations from the land to make way for European immigrants. Instead, the colonial powers used African soldiers to establish and maintain their empires.

Disease may help to explain why the imperial enterprise took a different form in Africa. In the Americas and Australia, the job of establishing European control had been greatly facilitated by the vulnerability of indigenous populations to Old World diseases like small-pox, pneumonia, measles, and tuberculosis. In Africa, however, the situation was reversed. Here Europeans were vulnerable to endemic diseases like malaria, yellow fever, and dys-entery, while most indigenous peoples had already developed resistance to the diseases that accompanied European expansion, since they had links to Europe and Asia going back thousands of years.

Europeans first explored the African coast in search of a sea route to South and East Asia, but by the late fifteenth century the Atlantic slave trade had become a central part of their activities. By the time it ended, between 10 and 20 million people had been forcibly taken from Africa and enslaved in the New World. Many more died, either on the way to the coast or in the inter-African wars fuelled by competition in the trade.

The consequences for the societies of West and Central Africa were profound: the bal-ance of power shifted from the interior toward coastal areas and warfare became both more frequent and more violent. As the slave trade was gradually suppressed in the nineteenth century, European traders turned their attention to buying tropical products for export and selling manufactured goods in Africa. Under the influence of economic theories that advocated controlling the sources of raw materials and protecting markets for manufac-tured goods, the European powers moved towards formal colonization. The partition of Africa was largely completed in the later nineteenth century.

The success of the colonization project sparked a crisis of confidence in indigenous religious systems. Several factors contributed to the loss of confidence, including the close association of political and religious authority in African societies, the tradition of relying on religious ritual to secure military success, and the Europeans' disdain for African reli-gious practices. Some people adopted the religion of the European conquerors in the hope of understanding the spiritual basis of their power. Some looked to Christian missionaries for protection against the abuses of colonial rule. Some wanted to succeed in the new colo-nial order and saw a missionary education as the essential first step on the path to success.

Some people, however, experienced a profound conversion, seeing Christianity as a new source of religious authority and a way of understanding the spiritual basis of the Europeans' power. Today approximately one-quarter of Africa's people are Christian. Ironically, Islam also experienced its most rapid growth following the European conquest, perhaps because it represented a new way of explaining the world and offered a connec-tion to a global religious system that did not require converts to embrace European ways.

Many people continued to rely on indigenous religious systems to explain the meaning of the European occupation, contain its influence, and preserve their communities. But those systems themselves were also affected by the experience of colonial rule. Reform movements emerged with charismatic leaders claiming privileged communication with the

Alinesitoué Diatta

In 1941, in a crowded market in Dakar, Senegal, a young Diola woman named Alinesitoué Diatta had the first in a series of visions of the supreme being. Emitai commanded her to return to her village and tell the people that one of the reasons for the prolonged drought they were suffering was that many had abandoned the religious traditions of their ancestors in favour of Islam or Christianity.

But that was not Alinesitoué's only message. Equally important, she said that Emitai was withholding the rain in protest against the changes in Diola agricultural practices that had taken place under French colonial rule: in particular, the replacement of traditional African rice with higher-yield (but less hardy) Asian varieties, and the introduction of ground-nuts (peanuts) as a cash crop, which not only required that forests be cut to create fields but led many men to grow the new crop and leave the job of growing rice for the family to their wives. In effect, Alinesitoué explained that the recent agricultural disasters were directly connected to French intervention in the people's daily lives.

To restore her community's relations with Emitai, Alinesitoué introduced a new cult, cen-tred on the annual sacrifice of a black bull, which was adopted by Diola throughout the region. The priests of this cult, called Kasila, were to be chosen by divination and could rich or poor, male or female, young or old. Challenging the power of a religious elite that had become established during the era of the slave trade, Alinesitoué's new cult made it possible for women, young people, and the poor to become community leaders.

The Kasila ritual lasted six days and six nights, during which the participants slept outside in the public square, ate all their meals together, and sang and danced songs of the ancestors, reaffirming the sense of community that Alinesitoué saw as the basis of Diola society. She also insisted that all members of the Diola community participate, regardless of their individual religious affiliations, and that the former Diola practice of observing a day of rest every six days be restored—contrary to the rules of both Christianity and Islam.

Finally, amid growing unrest, French authorities ordered Alinesitoué's arrest. Convicted in 1943 of obstructing colonial authorities and causing embarrassment to colonial officials, she was exiled to Timbuktu, where she starved to death a year later, at the age of 23. But the move-ment that Alinesitoué started did not end with her arrest.

Within a year, two other Diola women claimed that they too had been sent by Emitai to offer guidance to their communities, and since then more than 20 other people, mostly women, have come forward to teach in the tradition of prophetic authority associated with Alinesitoué. They remain active today, emphasizing the close relationship between the supreme being, agricultural practices, and adequate rainfall. Alinesitoué's legacy is a major factor in the continuing vitality of Diola traditions in a region that is overwhelmingly Muslim.

spirit world. Some of these **revitalization movements** sought to purify African religious practices, seeing the European conquest as punishment for lax observance of indigenous traditions. Finally, some regarded their own time of sorrows as a prelude to a golden age in which the Europeans would leave and the ancestors would return, bringing peace and prosperity for Africans.

South Africa: Nongqawuse and the Xhosa Cattle-Killing

In 1856, in the region that is now South Africa, a young Xhosa woman named Nongqawuse had a vision in which her ancestors told her that the military defeats her people had suffered at the hands of Europeans were their punishment for practising witchcraft. She relayed this message to her uncle and guardian, a chief named Mhlakaza, telling him that it was because many Xhosa had used witchcraft to enrich themselves and harm others that Europeans had been allowed to take over their land and steal their cattle. In order to cleanse themselves of this spiritual pollution, the ancestors demanded that the people destroy their remaining cattle. If they did so, the Europeans would disappear; the Xhosa's ancestors would return from the dead, and their property would be restored to them in greater quantities than they had ever known.

Following Nongqawuse's instructions, many people killed their cattle and burnt their granaries to demonstrate their faith in the ultimate beneficence of their tradition's celestial beings. The result was a devastating famine in which thousands of Xhosa lost their lives. Those who survived lost their independence, the Xhosa resistance to the British collapsed, and many people sought asylum with missionaries, with the result that Christianity made enormous inroads within the Xhosa community. Meanwhile, those who had not agreed to destroy their lands and livelihoods were blamed for the failure of Nongqawuse's prophecy.

How could people put their faith in such a vision? One factor might be desperation after more than century of military defeats. Another might have to do with the tendency of indigenous religious systems to understand catastrophe as punishment: much as the ancient Hebrews considered the Babylonians and Assyrians to be scourges sent by God to punish them for violating his laws, so the Xhosa appear to have seen the Europeans as instruments used by a supreme being to punish and remind them of their religious obligations. As Nongqawuse emphasized, for the Xhosa to regain control over their lives and restore a prosperous and independent community, they had to forsake witchcraft and put their faith entirely in the hands of the ancestors and the supreme being.

When the prophecies failed, Xhosa resistance to the British ended. Many Xhosa sought out Christian missionaries, who offered assistance with the necessities of life and a way of understanding a world in which their own religious resources had failed to provide effective answers. But a significant minority—known as 'Red Xhosa' for the red ochre they used as body paint in certain rituals—remained faithful to their Xhosa religious traditions. Moreover, within a few decades Xhosa Christians began to insist that their churches take ritual action to address the persistent problems of disease and witchcraft afflicting their communities. When the missionaries refused, the Xhosa began breaking away and forming their independent churches, many of which called themselves Zionist because they looked forward to the liberation of their promised land. This blending of indigenous and foreign traditions is an example of syncretism.

Tanganyika: The Maji-Maji Revolt of 1905–7

By the end of the nineteenth century Germany too had established several colonies in Africa, among them Tanganyika (now the largest portion of Tanzania). This region was home to several ethnic groups, and in 1905 a visionary named Kinjikitile set out to regain their independence.

Kinjikitile announced that, some three years earlier, he had experienced a kind of shamanic journey, disappearing into a river for several days and emerging completely dry. In the course of this journey, he said, he was possessed by Hongo (a snake spirit known throughout the region), met the water god Bokero, and learned of a powerful medicine called Maji-Maji (Swahili for 'water-water') that would make those who bathed in it invulnerable to German guns. He called on the people to unite behind his leadership and abandon the practice of witchcraft. He then built a pilgrimage site at Ngarambe, where he said the ancestors would return to life once the Germans had been driven away, and called on the diverse peoples of the region to unite behind his leadership. The call for unity succeeded, probably because of his emphasis on two spirits of region-wide significance. But the consequences were disastrous. Although Kinjikitile himself was captured and executed in the early stages of the rebellion, it dragged on for more than two years. Estimates of the death toll range between 75,000 and 130,000.

The African Diaspora

African religious traditions were carried to the Americas through the Atlantic slave trade. Particularly in the Caribbean and South America, where slaves greatly outnumbered Europeans or free people of mixed ancestry, slave societies developed new syncretic religions that combined African (especially Yoruba) and Native American traditions with elements of Christianity. In these African diaspora religions, saints were identified with specific African deities, initially as a way of concealing African religious practices that slave owners had tried to stamp out. Gradually, though, the characteristics of African gods and European saints merged into one another and new syncretic practices developed that were neither European nor African.

Religions such as Candomblé, Macumba, and Umbanda (Brazil), Vaudou (Voodoo; Haiti), and Santeria or Lucumi (Cuba) all emphasized spirit possession and healing. In Candomblé, Macumba, and Santeria, gods known by the Yoruba term *orisha* were said to ride their followers much as people ride horses. In Vaudou, believers could be possessed both by African deities and by violent local gods known as Petro spirits (often associated with slave masters). Saints and gods acquired new roles and new forms of religious community emerged in response to the trauma of slavery and the continuing struggle to live in societies beset by poverty and political uncertainty. Ritual organizations often reflected a family structure with mothers and fathers of the spirits serving as primary priests and teachers for their 'children'. In nineteenth-century Cuba, religious organizations concealed their activities within dance societies to escape interference by slave owners or the Spanish colonial state. In Haiti, Vaudou leaders played a central role in organizing the Haitian revolution, the most successful slave revolt in the Americas. Part of the reason behind the negative stereotypes attached to Vaudou was the terror that slave owners throughout the Americas felt on learning that Haitian rebels had used ritual means to organize and strengthen their resolve.

Since emancipation, these traditions have also gained some adherents among people of European descent and have been carried by immigrants to Europe as well as Canada and the United States. In recent years, local governments in Florida have sought to curb the practice of Santeria and Vaudou by prohibiting animal sacrifice, but the US Supreme Court ruled that such a ban was an unconstitutional limitation on the freedom of religion.

The Americas

The disruptions that came with European expansion in the Americas were particularly severe. According to some estimates, a total population of perhaps 80 million was reduced by three-quarters within a century of Columbus's arrival, primarily as result of European diseases against which the indigenous peoples had no natural immunity. For central Mexico, some scholars have suggested a 95 per cent loss in the course of the sixteenth century. Entire nations died out, and those that survived in many cases had to join forces with others in order to form sustainable communities. By 1890, when the North American frontier was generally considered to have closed, more than 90 per cent of the land in the United States had been taken from Native Americans and given to newcomers, primarily of European origin. Meanwhile, the animal populations that Native peoples depended on had been devastated by the fur trade, settlement, and (especially in the case of buffalo), 'sport' hunting.

The Eastern Woodlands: Handsome Lake Religion

The Iroquois Confederacy dominated the Eastern Woodlands area from Quebec in the east through New York and southern Ontario to the midwestern US in the seventeenth and eighteenth centuries. Through alliances and military force, the Cayuga, Mohawk, Oneida, Onondaga, Seneca, and, eventually, Tuscarora controlled the fur trade throughout the region, and they were quite effective in playing off the imperial ambitions of the French, Dutch, and British against one another.

But their bargaining power was severely compromised after the fall of New France in 1763, when the British gained exclusive control over most of North America. When the United States won independence from Britain, in 1783, the 'Indian Territory' to the west of the thirteen colonies lost its British protection. By 1800 the fur trade was no longer viable and the once mighty Iroquois were confined to several small reserves in northern New York, southern Quebec, and southern Ontario, where many eventually succumbed to disease, alcoholism, and despair.

Among them was a Seneca named Ganioda'yo or Handsome Lake (c. 1735–1815). As a young man he witnessed the devastating impact of American land annexations, the decline of the fur trade, and the spread of disease, and when his people were confined to small reservations in western New York he sank into despondency. Finally in 1799 he fell into a coma-like state and his family thought he had died. They were beginning to prepare for his funeral when he regained consciousness and described how three angels sent by the Creator, Tarachiawagon, had instructed him to reform his life and begin teaching a new form of Iroquois religion.

As a result of that vision, Handsome Lake taught that the Iroquois should worship only Tarachiawagon—not his destructive twin, Tawiskaron. Two months later, a fourth angel took him on a trip to heaven and hell that became known as the 'Sky Journey'. In hell he saw a jail containing handcuffs, a whip, and a rope knotted into a hangman's noose—symbols of the Euro-American penal system—and a church without exit doors or windows, filled with people wailing. But on the road to heaven he encountered George Washington and Jesus; both of them he saw as good white men.

In further teachings, eventually recorded in a book that became known as the Gaiwiio, 'the good word', Handsome Lake emphasized a new division between good and evil. He urged his people to avoid the 'four evils' (whiskey, witchcraft, love magic, and abortion or anti-fertility medicines), renew themselves, and restore their proper relationship with Tarachiawagon. Although he did not succeed in banning the medicine societies that relied on Tawiskaron's power of *utgo*, he effectively shifted the Iroquois worldview from complementary dualism to **conflict dualism** along the lines of the Christian model. Tawiskaron became identified as the Evil Twin, the Punisher who, like the Christians' Satan, tormented the souls in hell.

Handsome Lake also advocated the public confession of sin, sought to simplify mourning ceremonies, and identified witches as sources of sin and internal enemies of Iroquois communities. As part of his social program he preached accommodation with the economic organization of Euro-Americans, encouraging the practice of agriculture by men as well as women, individual land-holding, and patrilineal, patrilocal social organization (as a result, Iroquoian women lost some of the influence they had enjoyed when the woman's family was the primary kinship unit).

With the assistance of his half-brother, Chief Cornplanter, Handsome Lake's teachings gained a significant following. Many Iroquois abandoned the practices he condemned as evil, such as witchcraft and alcohol consumption. At the same time, his promotion of farming helped to ease the transition to life in the new nation-states of Canada and the United States. Today approximately one-third of the Iroquois people still gather regularly at their meeting houses to study the Gaiwiio and practise what has come to be known as the Handsome Lake or Longhouse religion.

The Ghost Dance

Almost a century after the Iroquois were forced off their land, the Lakota of the northern Plains faced a similar loss. In 1874, just six years after the US Congress had approved a treaty promising the Lakota a vast territory for 'as long as the grass is green and streams flow', it allowed gold prospectors into the sacred territory of the Black Hills. The resistance that followed reached its climax in the Battle of the Little Big Horn (1876), in which General George Armstrong Custer suffered the worst military defeat in the history of the American Indian wars. Pursued relentlessly by Custer's replacement, a group of Sioux led by Chief Sitting Bull took refuge across the border in the territory that would become Saskatchewan.

Four years later, forced by food shortages to accept the confines of reservation life, they returned to the US and surrendered. What they found was not what they had been promised in the 1860s. Parents were pressured to send their children to residential schools where they were forbidden to speak their own language and were forcibly instructed in Euro-American Christianity and concepts of labour. In the 1880s the US Congress passed legislation forbidding traditional healers to practise their craft and banning the Sun Dance along with a custom called Keeping of the Soul, in which a ritual bundle containing a small portion of a deceased relative's scalp was prepared and kept in the house. These laws effectively stripped the Lakota of their primary ways of coping with disease, invoking the sun god, and remaining in contact with their ancestors.

In 1889 a man named Wovoka revived a short-lived movement that a close relative among the Paiute named Wodziwob had started nearly two decades earlier. Like Wodziwob, Wovoka had experienced a vision in which he was told that his people could hasten the restoration of their old way of life if they performed a 'Ghost Dance' for their ancestors. Urging his people to put an end to warfare and embrace a life of hard work, he prophesied that the white people would disappear, the ancestors would return, and the lost buffalo and other game would be restored. As news of these teachings spread, the Lakota were particularly drawn to the Ghost Dance as a replacement for their outlawed rituals.

In 1889 a group of Lakota pilgrims travelled to Nevada to hear Wovoka's teachings. That same year the Lakota performed the Ghost Dance, wearing colourfully painted Ghost Shirts that were supposed to permit them entry to the new world, and carrying bows and arrows in anticipation of the buffalo herds' return. Seeing the weapons, a young Indian agent named D.F. Royer, nicknamed Young-Man-Afraid-of-Indians, panicked and called in the cavalry, which in December 1890 attacked a group of Ghost Dancers at a place called Wounded Knee, killing between 150 and 300 men, women, and children.

In the wake of Wounded Knee the federal government prohibited the Ghost Dance, but the ban was lifted in the 1930s, along with the ban on the Sun Dance. Since then both traditions have been revived.

Australasia and the Western Pacific

In describing religious responses to conquest in East Asia and Australasia, it is important to distinguish between the Asian mainland on the one hand and Australia and the Pacific Islands on the other. After centuries of commercial and religious contact, the former were not unprepared for dealing with foreigners. They had had time to develop some degree of immunity to foreign diseases, and in most cases their territory was not particularly attractive for settlement. Despite the loss of their political independence, therefore, the peoples in those regions were generally able to adapt to the changes that came with colonialism.

In sharp contrast, the peoples of the Pacific Islands had little experience of large imperial states or missionary religions prior to European expansion. They also had far less resistance to foreign diseases. In the case of Polynesia and Australia in particular, the land was considered suitable for European settlement, and the people therefore suffered massive losses of territory. Throughout the region, new religious movements emerged to explain and contain the destabilizing forces associated with European colonization.

Melanesia: Cargo Cults

The peoples of Melanesia first encountered Europeans in the mid-nineteenth century. In coastal regions especially, those first contacts gave rise to a highly distinctive type of religious movement known as a **cargo cult**. The development of the cargo cults reflected the enormous differences in economic organization and manufacturing capability that shaped the Melanesians' early encounters with Europeans. It also reflected a sense that the production of material goods (the 'cargo') was the work of the gods and those to whom the gods had revealed the secret of material success.

Seeing ships arrive carrying manufactured goods for European military, traders, administrators, and missionaries, some Melanesians began to envision a day when similar cargoes of canned goods, iron tools, and firearms would arrive for them, provided by their ancestors rather than the Europeans who were seeking commercial ties and political control. When that day came, they said, Melanesians would no longer have any need for Europeans. During the Second World War, cargo cult prophecies would expand to include deliveries on island airstrips or wharves built by Allied militaries. Although similar cults continued to be reported into the 1980s, this discussion will focus on two earlier examples.

One of the first such movements emerged in Fiji. The Tuka Cult began in 1885, when a man named Ndungumoi claimed that his soul could leave his body and communicate with spirits. He predicted that a revolutionary new world was coming in which Europeans would serve Fijians, ordinary people would rise to positions of authority over their former chiefs, and Fijians would have trade goods—especially cloth and canned food—in abundance. Among the rituals he created was one that involved anointing his followers with sacred water, for which he charged a small fee; then he would use the proceeds to host elaborate feasts. Those who refused to take part in Ndungumoi's rituals were told that they would have to serve his followers or suffer a terrible fate in the afterlife.

When the date of the transformative event drew near, Ndungumoi instructed his followers to place all their faith in his prophecy. The movement came to an end, however, when he began to speak out against European planters and administrators, who arrested him along with his chief aides and exiled them to a nearby island.

Another cargo cult developed in the New Guinean community of Tangu in the late 1930s, when a prophet named Mambu began teaching that white Europeans and black Melanesians were descended from two brothers. The white brother had been given a greater share of material goods in the expectation that he would share them with his brother, but he had failed to do so. Mambu claimed that the gods who had created these commodities had also sent them to the people of New Guinea, but that Europeans had intercepted them. He established a ritual centre near the coast and encouraged his followers to be 'baptized' with sacred water on their genitals and to wear European-style clothes so that they would be prepared for the cargo's arrival. In the meantime, however, they should avoid all contact with European government officials or missionaries. Mambu was arrested by colonial officials before his prophecy could be fulfilled.

New Zealand: The Pai Marire Movement

The Pai Marire ('Good and Peaceful') movement was established during a period of increasing tension between the Maori and British settlers. Its founder, Te Ua Haumene Horopapera Tuwhakararo, had been captured by English travellers as a child in the 1820s and been taken to a Wesleyan Methodist mission station, where he accepted baptism, studied the Bible, and worked for missionaries. When war broke out in 1860 he sided with the Maori king and served him as an adviser during the early campaigns. Two years later, however, he experienced a vision of the angel Gabriel, who commanded him to work for the unification of the Maori and a peaceful separation between them and the British settlers.

Te Ua's teachings reflected Maori understandings of Christian doctrine, focusing on the ancient Hebrews' longing for a messianic leader through whom their land might finally be liberated. His followers rejected what they regarded as missionary paternalism and insisted on their own right to interpret the Bible. Te Ua introduced two new deities alongside the Trinity: Riki and Rura. Rura was associated with the angel Gabriel; Riki was a war god, associated with the angel Michael, who would protect the Maoris against all invaders. Te Ua also emphasized the imminence of Judgment Day; those who followed him would enter heaven and those who refused would be judged harshly. Rituals focused on ceremonial poles, with four carved wooden heads, inserted in the ground, around which dances

A sculpture at the Maori traditional site named Whakarewarewa in Rotorua, New Zealand (Willard G. Oxtoby).

and songs were performed. Although the movement did not survive for long after Te Ua's death in 1866, it inspired a number of later Maori nationalist movements. By relating Christian teachings to the spiritual predicament in which Maori found themselves, it created an opening for Maori interpretations of Christianity and the development of other Maori syncretic movements.

Summary

Indigenous religions were profoundly affected by the experience of conquest and colonization. New religious leaders came forward offering new teachings and practices based on divine revelations. Some urged direct resistance to European expansion. Some focused on reforming their own societies—by eliminating witchcraft, reducing dependence on European trade goods, restoring economic self-sufficiency—and renewing their commitment to their own traditions. Others predicted the coming of a new age when the ancestors would return, depleted animal populations would be restored, and diseases would be eliminated; these movements have often been labelled millennial or millenarian (after the Christian idea that God would establish his kingdom on earth a thousand years after the death of Jesus). All these movements sought to redress the sudden and traumatic loss of autonomy suffered by indigenous peoples under colonial rule. Those that were able to make sense of that loss and restore a sense of order to the world helped to revitalize their communities and continued to attract adherents after their founders had died; the movements founded by Handsome Lake and Alinesitoué Diatta are examples of successful revitalization movements. The resistance movements of Nongqawuse, Kinjikitile, and Wovoka (the Ghost Dance) proved less successful because they directly challenged the European presence—or were perceived as doing so—and therefore were quickly suppressed.

CONTEMPORARY ISSUES

Indigenous religions are the oldest traditions in the worlds, but they continue to play important roles in the contemporary world. Even though Christianity, Islam, Buddhism, and Hinduism have attracted many converts from indigenous religious communities, the ways in which those converts understand and practise their new faiths continue to reflect the influence of their ancient traditions. Throughout the Islamic world, for example, local spirits (*djinn* in Arabic) are still invoked for assistance with matters that Islam does not address: illness, infertility, material success, personal security. Similar examples can be found in the Christian and Buddhist worlds, and Hinduism has a long tradition of incorporating local deities into its devotional traditions. Particularly for women who feel marginalized by the male authorities who still control most Abrahamic and Asian traditions, indigenous women's cults continue, often clandestinely, to play an important role.

Indigenous religions have confronted major challenges, however. Throughout the Americas and Australia, indigenous peoples have become minorities in most of their territories, and as their numbers declined, so did their religions. Meanwhile, the 'world religions' have benefitted from their association with organizations such as political parties and development agencies. Furthermore, nationalist movements and post-colonial political parties have tended to see a Western education and an Abrahamic faith as essential for leadership in a 'modern' state: since independence, every chief executive of an African state has been Muslim, Christian, or secular in their primary religious orientation.

Reinforcing this tendency are the vast resources made available to Christian, Muslim, or Buddhist organizations operating in areas formerly dominated by indigenous peoples. In Senegal, for example, many economic development projects are funded and carried out by religious organizations. Islamic organizations and missionary churches with international resources fund the construction of mosques, churches, and private schools, whereas indigenous religious organizations have to seek funding entirely from their own communities. In Nigeria, many political movements have formed around religious organizations with overseas support, which are able to provide levels of funding that are not available to more secular political movements.

Despite these challenges, however, indigenous religions continue to serve important functions in their societies. Indigenous religious specialists were key to the success of the liberation movements in the regions that became Zimbabwe and Guinea-Bissau, performing rituals to protect the guerrilla soldiers and advising them on how to sustain the correct relations with the spirits associated with the land—for example, by invoking the protective powers of lesser spirits and ancestors, and by avoiding sexual relations.

People in Nigeria, South Africa, and the Democratic Republic of Congo have all established schools for the training of indigenous priests and traditional spiritual healers. Many Africans now take pride in the way the religious traditions developed by their ancestors are transforming themselves to address the religious challenges of the twenty-first century world. In West Africa, for instance, the Yoruba *orisha* Shopona, who used to be feared as the god of smallpox, is now the deity associated with AIDS. And the *orisha* of metal, Ogun, has expanded his area of activity (blacksmithing, war) to include the concerns of factory workers, chauffeurs, and mechanics. Pan-African religious cults like the wealth-oriented maritime deity Mami Wata and the Central and Southern African healing cults (*ngoma*) have become widely followed throughout major colonies of the African continent. Nigerian and Ghanaian religious teachers have used air travel and the internet to create new transnational religious communities, reinforcing connections with African diasporas in the Americas and Europe, while establishing new ties with people around the world who have no personal links to Africa.

Similar forces are shaping the practice of Native American religions today. Rituals such as the Sun Dance and the Ghost Dance are drawing growing numbers of participants. Indigenous healing practices are also attracting clients, especially among those interested in holistic medicines and natural remedies. The intertribal powwow, first popularized by European-American entrepreneurs who saw a lucrative market for exhibitions of Native music and dance, has been taken back by Aboriginal people, who have made it an occasion for celebrating their identity, healing the psychological wounds inflicted by centuries of institutional abuse (e.g., in Canada's residential school system), and expressing their spirituality. Throughout North America, indigenous groups have established legal organizations devoted to protecting the rights guaranteed by various treaties (e.g., special hunting and fishing rights, and rights of access to traditional sacred sites).

In Australia, recognition of the country's Aboriginal heritage has become a standard part of public events such as the opening of Parliament or the ceremonies surrounding international athletic competitions. And the Maoris of New Zealand have specialized in establishing connections with other indigenous communities around the world. They have also led the way in lobbying the United Nations and other international organizations for the protection of their traditions.

CONCLUSION

Despite their diversity, the indigenous religions examined in this chapter share a number of characteristics. First, they have all focused on the worship of personal deities (as opposed to impersonal forces) and have assumed that these deities play an active role in the world. Second, they have been profoundly oriented towards this world (as opposed to the next) and the well-being of the community. Ritual specialists invoke the spiritual powers of the universe to improve the human situation, not just for individuals but for the communities in which they live. Third, they have strong ethical systems: actions are judged to be righteous or destructive on the basis of their impact on the life of the community. Finally, they are capable of dramatic transformation in response to changing political, economic, social, or environmental conditions. This chapter has focused on the changes associated with European colonialism, but equally dramatic changes have taken place in response to situations such as epidemics or prolonged droughts.

For most of human history, all religious traditions conformed to the indigenous model. It was only in the second millennium before the Common Era that a new kind of religion began to emerge in which members of a community defined themselves in terms of shared knowledge and practice rather than shared descent. In the twenty-first century, indigenous traditions persist in some regions, but their practitioners generally make up only a minority of the population. Nowhere do they have the government representation they would need to counteract the assimilationist pressures exerted by institutions such as schools and social service agencies. Furthermore, in sharp contrast to practitioners of world religions like Christianity, Islam, and Buddhism, they are not part of an international community and therefore cannot look to other countries for either moral or financial support. Preserving indigenous religious perspectives will be an even greater challenge in the future, as globalization intensifies the trend towards cultural homogenization.

A Note on Sacred Texts

For most indigenous religions, the only written texts were created as a direct result of contact with Christians, Muslims, or Buddhists. Otherwise, sacred traditions were transmitted orally. Some oral traditions circulated widely through the society and some were closely guarded secrets, shared only with initiates. Some of these traditions were written down by missionaries, colonial administrators, anthropologists, and so on. Others continue to exist only in oral form.

Study Questions

1. Indigenous religions have also been labelled primitive, animist, tribal, fetishist, oral, and traditional. Which term do you think best describes the category of religion discussed in this chapter? Why? Is there a better term? Or is the category itself a problem?

2. In describing African religions, many scholars have focused on lesser spirits and ancestors. What is the role of the supreme being in the traditions outlined here? What is its relationship to lesser spirits and ancestors?

3. Many indigenous religions have understood religious power in gendered terms. How are these gender divisions reflected in the traditions you have read about in this chapter?

4. European colonization of the Americas, Africa, Asia, Australia, and the Pacific Islands profoundly challenged the ability of indigenous religions to explain the world. How did those religions respond? Which responses were the most effective? Why?

5. What kinds of roles have female deities and leaders played in indigenous religions? What does this suggest about the relative status of men and women in indigenous religions?

6. How did Native American religious traditions understand the relationship of humans with other animals and the environment? In what ways would those understandings differ from the views of mainstream North American society today? In what ways would they be similar?

7. How have indigenous religions traditionally explained suffering and evil? Did the arrival of European colonization change the way those questions were posed and answered? How?

8. What do you see as the future prospects for indigenous religions? Can they provide satisfactory insight into the twenty-first century world? If your answer is 'no', do you think they are more likely to yield to other religious traditions or to a secular world view?

Glossary

axis mundi A place believed to be the spiritual centre of the world, where the celestial world and the underworld meet the earth and it is possible to travel between realms; term coined by Mircea Eliade.

cargo cult One of several Melanesian religious movements centred on the belief that one day ships would arrive bringing supplies of food and manufactured goods for the local people rather than Europeans, ushering in a new age of peace and prosperity.

complementary dualism The concept (common to many indigenous religions) that the universe contains life-enhancing and life-diminishing forces that work together and are equally necessary to its survival.

conflict dualism The concept (common to the Abrahamic or Western religious traditions) that the universe contains good and evil forces that are wholly separate and in constant opposition.

culture heroes Individuals from the distant past who taught the people of a community their basic tasks and obligations and who are often seen as both human and divine.

fetish Originally, a valued object in the Portuguese African trade; the term was eventually applied to any object believed to be endowed with spiritual powers. Fetishism is the worship or use of such objects in ritual.

Inuit 'True human beings'; the preferred name for the people that Europeans called 'Eskimo'.

Iroquois A confederacy of five (eventually six) Iroquoian-speaking nations, formed sometime before the arrival of Europeans, that dominated the Eastern Woodlands area of North America from Quebec and New York to the northern Great Lakes.

Lakota The largest of the Siouan-speaking peoples in the Great Plains region of North America.

mana A Melanesian term for a life-enhancing power that can be concentrated in people or objects; widely used by anthropologists in the context of theories about the origins of religions.

medicine society A native American organization of ritual healers or shamans.

Neolithic Age The 'New' Stone Age; the stage in world history when humans first began to develop agriculture and animal husbandry.

oral traditions Narratives, myths, histories, legends, fables, proverbs, and riddles that are transmitted verbally from generation to generation within a community and are seen as authoritative sources of knowledge.

orisha Any one of the 401 lesser gods in the Yoruba traditions of West Africa.

Paleolithic Age The 'Old' Stone Age; the stage of world history that preceded the Neolithic.

revitalization movement A religious movement sparked by a social crisis, which seeks to reform and give new life to a particular tradition.

shaman A ritual specialist trained in the use of visions, ecstatic trances, and out-of-body travel to communicate with the gods on behalf of the community; the term was borrowed from the Tungus people of Siberia.

spirit possession The concept (common to many cultures) that a deity or spirit can enter the body of an individual and use it to communicate to other members of the community. Sometimes such events are spontaneous and sometimes they are deliberately invited by ritual specialists.

Sun Dance One of the most important rituals of the peoples of the Great Plains and northern Rockies.

syncretism The blending of elements from two or more religious traditions; use of the term is often negative, suggesting contamination of a 'pure' religion under the influence of a different tradition.

taboo A Polynesian term for an action or object that is prohibited; any violation of a taboo is believed to have dire spiritual consequences.

totem An Ojibwa term for an animal that is believed to share a spiritual connection with a particular clan or lineage.

Yoruba A West African ethnic group, one of the largest on the continent; because a large proportion of the slaves sent to the Americas were Yoruba, their traditions had the most visible influence on the religions of the African Diaspora.

Further Reading

Baum, Robert M. 1993. 'Homosexuality and the Traditional Religions of the Americas and Africa'. Pp. 1–46 in Arlene Swidler, ed. *Homosexuality in World Religions*. Valley Forge, PA: Trinity Press International.

———. 1999. *Shrines of the Slave Trade: Diola Religion and Society in Precolonial Senegambia*. New York: Oxford University Press.

Bell, Diane. 1993. *Daughters of the Dreaming*. Minneapolis: University of Minnesota Press.

Bockie, Simon. 1993. *Death and the Invisible Powers: The World of Kongo Belief*. Bloomington: Indiana University Press.

Brown, Joseph Eppes. 1971. *The Sacred Pipe*. Harmondsworth, England: Penguin Books

Burridge, Kennelm. 1986. *New Heaven, New Earth: A Study of Millenarian Activities*. Oxford: Basil Blackwell.

Clark, Paul. 1975. *"HauHau': The Pai Marire Search for Maori Identity*. Auckland: Auckland University Press.

Daneel, M.L. 1970. *God of the Matopos Hills*. The Hague: Mouton.

Durkheim, E. 1965 (1915). *The Elementary Forms of the Religious Life*. New York: Free Press.

Evans-Prichard, E.E. 1956. *Nuer Religion*. London: Oxford University Press, 1956.

Griaule, Marcel. 1972. *Conversations with Ogotemmeli: An Introduction to Dogon Religious Ideas*. London: Oxford University Press, 1972.

Harvey, Graham, editor. 2000. *Indigenous Religions: A Companion*. London: Cassell.

Heissig, Walther. 1980. *The Religions of Mongolia*. London: Routledge and Kegan Paul.

Herdt, Gilbert H., ed. 1982. *Rituals of Manhood: Male Initiation in Papua New Guinea*. Berkeley: University of California Press.

Hultkrantz, Ake. 1987. 'North American Religions: An Overview. Pp. 526–35 in Mircea Eliade, ed. *The Encyclopedia of Religion*. Vol. 10. New York: Macmillan.

Hussein, Ebrahim. 1970. *Kinjeketile*. Nairobi: Oxford University Press.

Iliffe, John. 1979. *A Modern History of Tanganyika*. Cambridge: Cambridge University Press.

Janzen, John, and Wyatt MacGaffey. 1974. *An Anthology of Kongo Religion*. University of Kansas Publications in Anthropology, #5. Lawrence: University of Kansas Press.

Lawrence, Peter. 1964. *Road Belong Cargo: A Study of the Cargo Movement in the Southern Madang District of New Guinea*. Atlantic Highlands, NJ: Humanities Press.

Lessa, William. 1966. *Ulithi: A Micronesian Design for Living*. New York: Holt, Rinehart, & Winston.

Martin, Calvin. 1978. *Keepers of the Game: Indian–Animal Relationships and the Fur Trade*. Berkeley: University of California Press, 1978.

Martin, Joel W. 2001. *The Land Looks After Us: A History of Native American Religion*. New York: Oxford University Press.

Mooney, James. 1970 (1896). *The Ghost Dance Religion and the Sioux Outbreak of 1890*. Chicago: University of Chicago Press.

Murphy, Yolanda and Robert F. Murphy 2004 (1974). *Women of the Forest*. New York: Columbia University Press, Third Edition.

Myerhoff, Barbara. 1974. *Peyote Hunt: The Sacred Journey of the Huichol Indians*. Ithaca: Cornell University Press.

Neihardt, John. 1988 (1932). *Black Elk Speaks: Being the Life Story of a Holy Man of the Oglala Sioux*. Lincoln: University of Nebraska Press.

Ortiz, Alfonso. 1969. *The Tewa World: Space, Time, and Becoming in a Pueblo Society*. Chicago: University of Chicago Press.

Peires, J.B. 1989. *The Dead Will Arise: Nongqawuse and the Great Cattle-Killing Movement of 1856—1857*. Johannesburg: Raven Press.

Pelton, Robert. 1989. *The Trickster in West African Religion: A Study of Mythic Irony and Sacred Delight*. Berkeley: University of California Press.

Sullivan, Lawrence E. 1988. *Icanchu's Drum: An Orientation to Meaning in South American Religions*. New York: Macmillan.

Wallace, A.G. 1972. *The Death and Rebirth of the Seneca*. New York: Random House.

Waters, Frank. 1963. *Book of the Hopi*. New York: Ballantine Books.

Williams, Walter. 1986. *The Spirit and the Flesh: Sexual Diversity in American Indian Culture*. Boston: Beacon Press.

Worsley, Peter. 1968. *The Trumpet Shall Sound: A Study of 'Cargo' Cults in Melanesia*. New York: Schocken Books.

Zerries, Otto. 2005. "South American Indian Religions: An Overview," in Lindsay Jones, editor, *The Encyclopedia of Religion*, Second Edition, Detroit: Gage.

References

Ray, Benjamin. 1976. *African Religions: Symbol, Ritual, and Community*. Englewood Cliffs, NJ: Prentice Hall.

Jewish Traditions

❧ Alan F. Segal ❧

J udaism is quintessentially a historical religion. It sees human history as a reflection of the desires and demands of God, and it understands itself to have been founded more than 3,200 years ago at Mount Sinai, when a divine revelation was delivered through Moses to the people Israel. The covenant with God that was sealed at Mount Sinai established a set of moral and ritual obligations that continue to govern Judaism today.

A Ritual Initiation

Those obligations are reaffirmed every Saturday in the rituals that mark the coming of age of thirteen-year-olds. The details of the **Bar Mitzvah** and Bat Mitzvah ceremonies (the Aramaic terms mean 'son of the commandment' and 'daughter of the commandment', respectively) reflect several of the elements that Jews consider most significant in their tradition.

The coming-of-age ritual is a regular part of every congregation's weekly worship. Saturday—the day of rest, called the **Sabbath**—is a day for prayer and public assembly in the **synagogue**, the house of worship and community meeting. The teenager reads two selections from the Hebrew Bible: one from the **Pentateuch** (the five books of Moses, which make up the first section of the Bible) and one from the second section, called the *Prophets*. (The third section, called the *Writings*, is a collection of assorted works.)

The scripture from which the Bat or Bar Mitzvah reads in public for the first time is the **Torah**. In the broadest sense, the Torah (i.e., religious law) includes the entire Hebrew Bible and all the commentaries on it, but here the term refers specifically to the five books of Moses. The Torah used in synagogues is written in ancient Hebrew, transcribed by hand onto a scroll that is treated with the utmost respect. To read from it, the candidate must have learned both the ancient script in which the text is written and the traditional melodies to which the words are chanted. The Torah is considered the ultimate repository of religious truth, and Jews are expected to study as well as obey it throughout their lives.

The candidate also recites a series of blessings that express the values of the community. The congregation responds by reaffirming them. The Bar or Bat Mitzvah then gives thanks for the scripture that has served as a guide for the people Israel. The city of Jerusalem and the dynasty of David are mentioned, and finally the Sabbath itself is extolled for the beauty and quietude it brings. The congregation notes that the only way in which Jews differ from others is that they have been given the special responsibility of studying and keeping the Torah.

In other respects the coming-of-age ceremony may vary significantly. Some congregations conduct their services almost entirely in Hebrew, others in the local language (English, French, etc.). Some insist that candidates prepare by studying Hebrew and learning the traditional chants. Others may substitute essay-writing, social action, and good works for some of the traditional requirements. Although the most traditional synagogues insist that only males can be called to the Torah, they are the minority in North America

◀ A bar mitzvah in a Paris synagogue (Oren Shalev / PhotoStock-Israel.com).

today, and many of them now offer similar (though not exactly equivalent) ceremonies to celebrate girls' coming of age.

After the service the family usually holds a luncheon or dinner to celebrate their child's success and the family's good fortune. This event may be simple, centring on the religious dimensions of the day, but it can be almost as lavish as a wedding reception, with a catered feast and a dance orchestra.

Defining Judaism

In the course of its development Judaism gave rise to two other world religions: both Christianity and Islam, like Judaism, trace their spiritual lineage to the biblical patriarch

Timeline

c. 1280 BCE	Moses leads the Exodus from Egypt
c. 1000 BCE	David takes Jerusalem and makes it his capital
922 BCE	Northern kingdom separates following Solomon's death
c. 800 BCE	Amos initiates literary prophecy
722 BCE	Assyrians conquer northern kingdom and disperse its people
621 BCE	Josiah centralizes worship at the temple in Jerusalem in Deuteronomic reform
586 BCE	Babylonians conquer Jerusalem and exile its leaders to Babylon
538 BCE	Persians conquer Babylon, permitting exiles to return
164 BCE	Rededication of the temple after Maccabean uprising
70 CE	Romans lay siege to Jerusalem and destroy the temple
c. 220	The *Mishnah* of Rabbi Judah ha-Nasi
c. 500	The Babylonian *Talmud*
882	Birth of Saadia, *Gaon* in Babylonia (d. 942)
1040	Birth of Rashi, commentator on Bible and *Talmud* (d. 1105)
1138	Birth of Moses Maimonides, author of *The Guide of the Perplexed* (d. 1204)
1250	Birth of Moses of León, author of the *Zohar* (d. 1305)
1492	Jews expelled from Spain
1666	Sabbatai Zvi is proclaimed the messiah
1698	Birth of Israel ben Eliezer, the Baal Shem Tov, in Poland (d. 1759)
1729	Birth of Moses Mendelssohn, pioneer of Enlightenment in Germany (d. 1786)
1881	Severe pogroms in Russia spur Jewish emigration
1889	Conservative Judaism separates from Reform in the United States
1897	Theodor Herzl and the first Zionist Congress
1938	German synagogues vandalized in prelude to the Holocaust
1948	Establishment of the state of Israel

Traditions at a Glance

Numbers
Approximately 14 million

Distribution
6.5 million in the Americas (mostly in US, Canada, and Buenos Aires, Argentina); 6.5 million in Asia (mostly in Israel); 1 million in Europe (mostly in Russia, Ukraine, France, and England)

Principal Historical Periods

1700 BCE–70 CE	Biblical
c. 70–700	Talmudic
700–1700	Medieval
1700–present	Modern

Principal Founders
The patriarchs and matriarchs: Abraham and his wife Sarah (legendary, c. 1700 BCE); Isaac (their son) and his wife Rebecca; Jacob (their son; also called Israel) and his wives Leah and Rachel (father and mothers, with Bilhah and Zilpah, of the children of Israel). Also Moses (legendary prophet who received the Ten Commandments on Mount Sinai, c. 1200 BCE); Saul, David, and Solomon (semi-legendary kings, c. 1000–900 BCE).

Leaders
Ezra helped build the second temple, 515 BCE. Yochanan ben Zakkai founded the first rabbinic academy, 70 CE. Judah the Prince produced the *Mishnah*, 220 CE. David Ben Gurion was the first prime minister of the state of Israel, 1948.

Deity
One God, called 'Lord' or 'God' in English. His name is never spoken in Hebrew.

Authoritative Texts
The Hebrew Bible, the *Talmud*, and the *Midrash* (commentaries).

Noteworthy Doctrines
All the righteous of the world can be saved; God has commanded the Jews to observe special laws, including dietary laws and dress codes.

Abraham. Judaism is by far the smallest of the three, with a worldwide population just 1 to 2 per cent the size of the others. Yet its historical influence is great, for it was with the Jewish people that monotheism—the belief in one God—originated.

Is the Jewish heritage by definition religious? Yes and no. Yes, because it is possible to join the Jewish community through conversion, and many people have done so. No, because the tradition is far more often inherited than chosen; for that reason Judaism is often considered an 'ethnic' religion.

Some Jews say yes to their ethnic identity while saying no to the religion. A substantial number of North Americans, Europeans, and Israelis identify themselves as Jews—members of a cultural community with distinctive literary and artistic traditions, foods and folkways, and roles in their various social and historical milieux—but do not take part in the religious tradition. Religion for them is a part of their culture, but not necessarily the defining part.

Nor is biological descent defining. The idea that the Jews constitute a genetic race, which was central to the persecution they suffered in the twentieth century, cannot be substantiated. Ever since the time of the ancient Hebrew kings, people of diverse origins have converted or married into the community. Thus any attempt to identify someone as Jewish on the basis of heredity is futile.

In all, Jews today number roughly 14 million, approximately half of whom live in Israel. The next largest population is in the Americas, mostly in the United States and Canada, but with significant numbers in Argentina and Brazil. The rest live mainly in Europe, especially France, England, Ukraine, and Russia (though many Jews from the former USSR and its satellites have immigrated to Israel, Europe, and North America in recent years). The world population of Jews in the early twenty-first century is almost one-third smaller than it was at the start of the Second World War, in 1939. By the end of that war, in 1945, some 6 million European Jews had been put to death by the Nazis—the political party that ruled Germany—in what is known today as the **Holocaust**.

Israel aside, the main centres of Jewish culture today are in Europe and eastern North America. About half of all Jews are unaffiliated with any synagogue. The other half range from liberal and non-observant to intensely traditional and deeply observant. In the United States and Canada there are three major groups: Reform, Conservative, and Orthodox. It's important to note that these divisions primarily reflect differences in ritual practice; differences in belief or doctrine are secondary. The exact divisions depend on the history of Judaism in each specific country. In Christianity, by contrast, differences in belief and doctrine are the main issues separating one denomination from another.

Jews believe that God expects all human beings to follow the same fundamental moral code, which was revealed in a covenant given to Noah after the primeval flood and is accessible to all humanity. Jews, however, are bound by an additional covenant, delivered by the prophet Moses to the Hebrews, in which they were commanded to follow a number of rules that set them apart from all other peoples. It is for this reason that Jews think of themselves as God's special people: not because they are preferred, but because they have been elected to fulfill the special responsibility of serving as God's priests in the world.

ꙮ ORIGINS

The Biblical Period

The history of Israel as it is recorded in the Torah was written from a special perspective, telling the story of a people as they understand and follow a God who chose them to serve as his instrument. Some of that history is well known because the Hebrew Bible is sacred scripture for Christians and Muslims as well. But interpretations of it differ widely, even within Judaism.

Liberal scholars accept modern historical principles and reserve the right to question the historical accuracy of the biblical text, just as their Christian and Muslim counterparts do, distinguishing between myth, legend, and history. But traditionalists believe every word in the text to be true, dictated to the prophets by divine inspiration. Thus there is a range of perspectives on the same events.

The earliest known reference to Israel by a neighbouring people dates to the early thirteenth century BCE and appears on an Egyptian stela (monumental stone) praising the victories of the pharaoh Mer-ne-Ptah: 'Plundered is Canaan . . . Israel is laid waste . . .'. The hieroglyphic expression referring to Israel designates a wandering people rather than one with a fixed territory. Whatever the historical value of the Hebrews' own legends, then, it seems that their neighbours were able to identify them as the people Israel by 1200 BCE.

Creation in Genesis

The first eleven chapters of *Genesis* outline the primeval history of the universe. In Chapter 1 God creates heaven and earth. Interestingly, the text does not actually say that the universe was created from nothing. What it says is that God created different things on each of the first six 'days', in a process that culminated in the creation of humans. Then on the seventh day God rested, setting the pattern of a weekly Sabbath. Because the text says that 'the evening and the morning were the first day,' Jews celebrate the Sabbath starting at sundown on Friday night and ending at sundown on Saturday.

Chapter 2 of *Genesis* tells a slightly different story, however. Here God causes a mist to rise from the ground, out of which vegetation sprouts. Then he creates the primal man, Adam, and plants a garden in Eden, where he places the man before creating the animals and, finally, the woman, Eve.

The Primal Couple

'Adam' is the Hebrew word for 'man' in the sense of humanity, but here it is also used as the proper name of the person created. Thus 'Adam' has connotations similar to those of 'Everyman' in English. 'Eve', according to the biblical text and most interpreters, is derived from the word for 'living'.

In *Genesis* 2 Adam and Eve stand naked without shame, in a state of perfect innocence, peace, and harmony. *Genesis* 3 shows how easily this state can be reversed when a serpent tempts them to defy God's command not to eat the fruit of the Tree of the Knowledge of Good and Evil. The name of the tree is important. Adam and Eve do not lack understanding before they eat the forbidden fruit: what they lack is moral sense, the 'knowledge of good and evil'. The theme of the story is how humans learned to make moral distinctions.

The Eden story explains the human condition through narrative rather than philosophical argument. Thus pain and evil are the consequences of disobedience and lack of moral discernment. Even though Adam and Eve are expelled from the paradise that was the immediate presence of God, he continues to show them his loving care. The narrative purports to explain a wide variety of phenomena: why snakes crawl on the ground, why women have pain in childbirth, why we have to work for a living, why we die. Some of these matters are natural, some are cultural, and others are ultimate issues of human existence.

The dominant Christian interpretation of the Eden story sees the primal couple's disobedience as 'original sin' and identifies a deep and sinister relationship between sexuality, evil, and death. Jewish interpretations are more positive, emphasizing humans' moral capacity to choose good over evil and to obey God's laws.

The Israelite Narratives

The first eleven chapters of *Genesis* present a sequence of narratives that together explain why God had to choose a specific people to convey his ideas to humanity. In these stories, humans left free to follow their own conscience repeatedly fail to govern themselves as God would wish.

The story of the flood was virtually universal in the mythologies of the ancient Near East. In the Mesopotamian accounts, the gods cause the flood because they are disturbed by the din of human life. In the Hebrew version, however, God's motivation is moral: to punish humans for the evil they have done and to clear the way for a fresh start. God floods the earth, allowing only Noah and the creatures in his ark to survive.

But human judgment is no better after the flood. Within a few generations, Noah's descendants arrogantly attempt to approach God's level by building a tower that reaches to heaven. God responds by confounding their language, so that 'they may not understand one another's speech' (*Genesis* 11: 7). Finally, in *Genesis* 12, a sign of hope emerges when God chooses Abraham to serve as an example of a righteous life.

Covenant

The central organizing concept in the Israelites' religion was the covenant: a kind of agreement or contract specifying how God desires humans to behave and giving a divine mandate to their society's laws. The first covenant was given to Noah after the flood. The second is given to Abraham. God promises Abraham that he and his descendants will have the land of Canaan for their own on condition that they live according to the obligations set down in the covenant.

The two other patriarchs—Abraham's son Isaac and Isaac's son Jacob—are similarly portrayed as making covenants with God, as is Moses, centuries later. These accounts of the legendary early leaders foreshadow the ceremonial covenant-making of the part-legendary, part-historical Hebrew kings David, Solomon, and Josiah, and the scribe Ezra. Each of these great figures renews the covenant between himself, his people, and his God.

The nature of the rewards promised in return for adhering to the covenant reflect the values of Hebrew society at the time when the narratives were written. The ultimate rewards are offspring and a homeland, but in addition Abraham himself is assured of a long life and a peaceful death (*Genesis* 15: 15). It is worth noting that no reference is made to any reward after death. The ancient Hebrews understood ultimate rewards in concrete terms: an easy death after a long and comfortable life, with many descendants. The early part of the Hebrew Bible does not suggest any interest in the disposition of souls after death.

Moses and the Exodus

The narratives of the patriarchs are set in a period of migration from one centre of ancient Near Eastern civilization, Mesopotamia, into the land of Canaan. The narratives that follow, presenting the story of Moses as leader and lawgiver, are set during a migration from the other centre of ancient Near Eastern civilization, Egypt. In reality these events may have overlapped, some of the Hebrew ancestors coming from the southwest via the Sinai Peninsula and others from the east and the north. In the Bible, however, the two migrations occur in strict chronological and historical sequence. Thus the descendants of Abraham suffer 400 years of oppression in Egypt before they are led home by Moses. In arranging their material in this way, the compilers of the scripture emphasized a doggedly historical approach, in which God is the author of every event.

The Divine Name

Chapter 3 of *Exodus* relates an encounter that Moses has with God before the escape from Egypt. During a visit to the wilderness, Moses has a vision of God as a flame in a bush that burns without being consumed. God identifies himself as the God of the patriarchal lineage—Abraham, Isaac, and Jacob—and gives his personal name, represented in Hebrew by the letters YHWH.

Scholars conventionally write this Hebrew word as 'Yahweh'. Since biblical Hebrew is written without vowels, it is impossible to know with certainty how the name would have been pronounced. The text of *Exodus* 3: 14, in which YHWH tells Moses 'I am who I am,' suggests a connection with the Hebrew verb *hayah*, 'to be'. Thus YHWH may mean 'the one who causes things to happen'. Over time, partly because of the commandment not to take God's name in vain, it came to be considered blasphemous to pronounce the name at all. Therefore Jews reading aloud from the scripture would substitute the Hebrew word *adonay* (a title similar to 'Lord') for YHWH.

In some branches of Judaism today, not even the four Hebrew consonants are written: instead, the name is represented by a double *y*, or an *h* with an apostrophe. In spoken usage, the Hebrew expression *ha-Shem*, 'the Name', is substituted for YHWH or Adonai. (The name 'Jehovah' is a variation on the same theme, formed by combining the consonants YHWH with the vowels from *adonay*. 'Jehovah' is used only in Christian circles. It gained currency in the sixteenth century, when Protestants with limited knowledge of Hebrew began turning to the ancient biblical texts.)

The Exodus

When the **Exodus** story begins, the Hebrews are working on construction projects in the eastern part of the Nile Delta. God tells Moses to request their release from what amounts to slave labour. When the pharaoh refuses, God sends plagues on the Egyptians but spares the Hebrews, enabling them to escape across Yam Suf (traditionally translated as the 'Red Sea', but literally the Reed Sea) and reach the barren Sinai Peninsula. In time all Jewish people, whatever their individual origins, would come to identify with the Exodus—the focus of the annual **Passover** festival—as a metaphor of the transition from slavery to freedom as a people with a special destiny and purpose.

For the next 40 years the Hebrews live as nomads, and it is in this period that the legal foundations of Israelite society are laid. Moses meets with God at Mount Sinai and receives the Ten Commandments as the terms of a new covenant (*Exodus* 20: 2–17). That covenant is then renewed in *Deuteronomy* 5: 6–21 ('Deuteronomy' means 'second law'), where all the people, not just the leaders, swear a communal oath to obey its terms.

The foundations of Israelite ritual life can also be traced to this period. It is while the children of Israel are wandering in the desert that Moses' brother Aaron becomes

In the shadow of Mount Sinai. There is no archaeological proof that this peak on Egypt's Sinai Peninsula is the one where Moses received the Ten Commandments, but it has been associated with the event since at least the fourth century (Photo courtesy of Andrew Leyerle).

the archetypal priest. In the absence of a permanent temple, worship is instituted in an elaborate tent called the Tabernacle. Kept in the Tabernacle as the central cult object is a chest called the Ark of the Covenant, which serves as the throne for God's invisible presence. No image is placed on this base, for the deity is not to be represented by any image. This prohibition marks a sharp contrast to the image-rich traditions of all the Israelites' neighbours.

The Israelite Kings

The transition from nomadic to settled life in the land of Canaan takes place under Moses' successors, beginning with Joshua. The book of *Joshua* recounts some spectacular victories over the Canaanites. But the following book, *Judges*, suggests a less triumphant view.

The civilization of the Canaanites is so well established that the Israelites are tempted to join them in their worship of a fertility god named Ba'al. But Yahweh abhors the Canaanite religion, which includes ritual prostitution and child sacrifice. He demands that the Israelites repudiate these practices, promising them progeny and long life if they obey.

In this period the Israelites had a loose tribal confederation ruled by informal chieftains or 'judges', among them Deborah, Samson, Shamgar, Jephthah, and Ehud. Their leadership was charismatic, based entirely on divine designation and popular acceptance. According to the book of *Judges*, each of these leaders was chosen by God to save the Israelites from a specific threat of foreign domination.

The shift to a centralized monarchy took place shortly after 1000 BCE. The institution of kingship emerged in response to the threats posed by the Philistines: a people of Aegean origin who had arrived in the land of Israel at the same time as the Israelites and had mastered the art of iron smelting (a significant technological advantage). As the story is narrated in *1* and *2 Samuel*, God chooses first Saul, then David, and finally David's successors to preserve the Israelites from the Philistine menace.

We first meet David as a young boy fit only to care for his father's sheep. But God strengthens him to the point that he is able to defeat the Philistines' champion, Goliath; capture Jerusalem and make it his capital ('the City of David'); and unify the tribes of the north and south as a single Israelite people. He is succeeded by his son Solomon, whose mother Bathsheba was David's favourite wife.

Solomon undertakes ambitious construction projects throughout the kingdom, including a lavish temple dedicated to Yahweh on the hill called **Zion** (a rock-outcrop ridge on the northern side of Jerusalem; the identification of the hill on the southern side as Mount Zion dates from a much later time). But the ten northern tribes are alienated by his emphasis on centralized government and his use of conscript labour, and on his death, about 921 BCE, the kingdom breaks up. The northern tribes, centred on Samaria, take the name 'Israel' for

The Ten Commandments, *Exodus* 20: 2–17

I am the LORD your God who brought you out of Egypt, out of the land of slavery.

You shall have no other god to set against me.

You shall not make a carved image for yourself nor the likeness of anything in the heavens above, or on the earth below, or in the waters under the earth. You shall not bow down to them or worship them; for I, the LORD your God, am a jealous god. I punish the children for the sins of the fathers to the third and fourth generations of those who hate me. But I keep faith with thousands, with those who love me and keep my commandments.

You shall not make wrong use of the name of the LORD your God: The LORD will not leave unpunished the man who misuses his name.

Remember to keep the sabbath day holy. You have six days to labour and do all your work. But the seventh day is a sabbath of the LORD your God; that day you shall not do any work, you, your son or your daughter, your slave or your slave-girl, your cattle or the alien within your gates; for in six days the LORD made heaven and earth, the sea, and all that is in them, and on the seventh day he rested. Therefore the LORD blessed the sabbath day and declared it holy.

Honour your father and mother, that you may live long in the land which the LORD your God is giving you.

You shall not commit murder.

You shall not commit adultery.

You shall not steal.

You shall not give false evidence against your neighbour.

You shall not covet your neighbour's house; you shall not covet your neighbour's wife, his slave, his slave-girl, his ox, his ass, or anything that belongs to him.

themselves; but they are dispersed by Assyrian invaders in 722 BCE and thereafter come to be known as the 'ten lost tribes'. The southern tribes, centred on Jerusalem and using the name Judah, continue until 586 BCE, when the city is invaded by the Babylonians.

The Composition of the Bible

For centuries, the composition of the first five books of the Bible was attributed to Moses, acting under divine inspiration or dictation. Faced with an apparent discrepancy in the text, traditional commentators would assume that it could not be real, and that it was their job to understand what God wanted to say. Therefore they would devote great effort to harmonizing the apparently contradictory passages. Most modern scholars have taken a different approach, asking who would have chosen to make a particular statement, and why. From this perspective, discrepancies are not challenges to faith but clues for investigation. At the root of this approach is a theory, developed in the latter half of the 1800s, called the **documentary hypothesis**, which proposes that the Pentateuch is a composite text consisting of four major blocks.

The documentary hypothesis has been strongly criticized by traditional Jews, Christians, and Muslims alike, who reject its humanizing assumptions. It has also been criticized by many liberal and radical scholars who may share those assumptions but differ on the details of composition and compilation. Still, its broad outlines continue to shape much contemporary scholarship and serve as a basis for further exploration.

The early theory has needed continuous refinement. Nineteenth-century Bible scholars imagined individual persons writing specific documents at specific times. Now we know that the source materials originated with a variety of groups or institutions in the society—including the royal bureaucracy and the priesthood—and that in each case the process of composition continued in oral and written form over several generations.

For example, the material that uses the name 'Yahweh' is thought to be the product of an author (or school) called the Yahwist. This material is referred to as J, because in German—the language of the scholars who first suggested the hypothesis—'Yahweh' is spelled with a 'J'. The Yahwist, who emphasized southern localities and the role of Abraham, presumably wrote in the southern kingdom of Judea, probably beginning before the division of the kingdoms late in the tenth century BCE.

The second source, E, is the work of an author or school termed the Elohist for its use of the word 'Elohim' to refer to God. We assume that E wrote in the northern kingdom after its separation, probably starting during the ninth century BCE, and emphasized northern local traditions. E calls the sacred mountain Horeb, not Sinai; and refers to the people displaced by the Hebrews as Amorites rather than Canaanites. God is a more remote and transcendent figure for E than for J, and the covenant relationship is less nationalistic.

Nevertheless, the J and E strands were woven together in many places. The result is a great Hebrew epic in a voice—JE—that can be recognized by its use of the term 'the LORD God' to speak of the divinity. The Garden of Eden story beginning in *Genesis* 2 is a good example of JE, whereas *Genesis* 1 represents a 'priestly' prologue to the whole story.

During the reign of Josiah, in 621 BCE, a copy of the law was reportedly found in the course of repairs to the temple in Jerusalem (*2 Kings* 22: 8). On the authority of that document, Israelite altars elsewhere were suppressed and for the first time worship was centralized at Solomon's temple in Jerusalem. Since *Deuteronomy* 12: 13 restricts worship to a single location, it is assumed that the document found in Jerusalem was *Deuteronomy* and that it, the D source, was a new production.

Ostensibly *Deuteronomy* is a sermon by Moses, which would place it 600 years earlier. But its vocabulary and concerns are those of Josiah's day, when the prophet Jeremiah was active. In fact, Moses speaks of himself as a prophet in *Deuteronomy* 18: 15 and describes his role in terms typical of the prophetic movement as it existed in the eighth and seventh centuries BCE, but hardly earlier. Central to the D source is a rewards-and-punishments theology of national morality, not unlike that of the prophetic books.

In some ways the most striking aspect of the documentary hypothesis is its suggestion that P, the priestly source, was a late contribution to the Pentateuchal corpus. Scholars originally thought that it originated in 586–539 BCE—the period following the Babylonian invasion, when the temple was destroyed and the Judean leadership sent into exile. It includes detailed descriptions and measurements of the temple and its furnishings. As long as the temple stood, these details would not have been necessary; but after its destruction P offered a literary blueprint for its restoration. It's now clear that many of the P legal traditions predate *Deuteronomy*. We have to distinguish between the time when the P document was edited and the times when the traditions within it originated. Though priestly materials may be very old, they are the most recent additions to the document.

The Prophets

Alongside the echoes of priestly and legal voices in the Hebrew Bible there is another and perhaps equally important voice: that of the prophets. Since both Christianity and Islam also claim to be founded in prophetic insight, the prophetic movement may have influenced more people than any other religious movement in human history.

The great prophetic books that constitute the section of the Bible called the *Prophets—Isaiah*, *Jeremiah*, and *Ezekiel*, as well as *Amos*, *Hosea*, and *Micah*—date from about 750 BCE onwards. But the prophetic tradition began much earlier, in the period of Hebrew settlement of the land and the early monarchy, with figures such as Micaiah ben Imlah, as well as Elijah and Elisha perhaps. Later ecstatic visions and utterances from God are recorded in the books of *Zachariah*, *Zephanaiah*, *Joel*, *Habbakuk*, *Haggai*, *Obadiah*, *Malachi*, and *Nahum*.

The Babylonian Exile

In 586 BCE the Judean kingdom fell, the temple was razed, and the society's leaders were deported to Babylonia. As much as any single event, the **Exile** marks the transition of the Hebrew tradition from the national cult of an ancient kingdom to the religious heritage of a widely dispersed people. From that time on, we speak of Jews (i.e., 'Judeans') and Judaism rather than Hebrews or Israelites and Hebrew or Israelite religion.

The transition did not happen overnight. But the Babylonian invasion disrupted many ancient Israelite institutions, while the Exile gave focus and impetus to significant social and religious changes. The heritage was now more that of a subject or minority population than of a national state. Especially among Jews dispersed abroad, life became more urban than agricultural, so that many of the old agriculturally based laws and rituals had to be rethought. At some time during the Exile, the institution known as the synagogue was born, and even after the ruined temple was rebuilt, three generations later, congregational life retained the importance it had developed. Aramaic gradually replaced Hebrew as the vernacular language, moving Hebrew into a ritual role.

The people's longing for the restoration of Yahweh's sovereignty manifested itself in a variety of forms, including visions of a deliverer king (messianism) or an overhaul of the cosmos in battle and judgment at the end of the age (apocalyptic literature). The destruction of the temple caused a crisis of confidence. The problem was not that Yahweh's dominion was limited to the region of Judah, for he was lord of all creation. But he had been worshipped in a single place for centuries. Did the destruction of that building mean that Yahweh had finally abandoned his people? The author of *Lamentations* 5: 20–2 expressed the general fear:

> Why dost thou forget us for ever, why dost thou so long forsake us?
> Restore us to thyself, O LORD, that we may be restored! Renew our days as of old!
> Or hast thou utterly rejected us? Art thou exceedingly angry with us?

The Second Commonwealth

In 538 BCE Cyrus the Persian conquered Babylon and allowed the Jews who had been captive there to return home, to the land of Israel. The Israelites saw his victory over their oppressors as part of God's plan to bring a new order to the world (see *Ezra* 1: 1; *Isaiah* 41: 2, 44: 28, 45: 1). With prophetic rhetoric, a postexilic author of later chapters in *Isaiah* announced the theme of homecoming, declaring that a new heaven and a new earth would be created, and this new commonwealth would mark a fresh beginning: 'Arise, shine; for your light has come, and the glory of the Lord has risen upon you' (*Isaiah* 60: 1).

Not all the exiles chose to go home; many prospering artisans and aristocrats stayed behind in Babylon, where they laid the foundations of a community that would eventually play a major role in the composition of the *Talmud*. Archaeological evidence suggests that, for those who did return, life was far from easy. The beginnings of the postexilic community, or 'second commonwealth', were so meagre that very little is known of events in that period.

Among the unknowns is the fate of the Davidic royal line. A Davidic king who adopted the Babylonian name Sin-Ab-Usuru (Sheshbazzar in Hebrew) arrived in Jerusalem shortly after the return began. But thereafter the descendants of David were called *nasi* ('prince') rather than *melekh* ('king'), perhaps in deference to the country's Persian rulers. Zerubbabel, another descendant of David, apparently arrived in Judea to succeed Sheshbazzar. The second temple was then completed in 515 BCE. After that, neither Zerubbabel nor the kingship is mentioned again.

Ezra and Nehemiah, who established a stable government in Judea, went there as court officials of the Persian Empire. The dates of their administrations are not certain, but the government they set up was explicitly based on the covenantal formula used in the first temple period. In the absence of a king, most affairs of state were handled by the priests. This system is often described as a 'theocracy', but in fact God did not rule directly. Rather, the ruling priests claimed to be carrying out God's purposes, though some of them operated mainly as

> ### From Isaiah
>
> In the days to come the mountain of the LORD's house shall be set over all other mountains, lifted high above the hills. All the nations shall come streaming to it, and many peoples shall come and say, 'Come, let us climb up on to the mountain of the LORD, to the house of the God of Jacob, that he may teach us his ways, and we may walk in his paths.' For Torah issues from Zion, and out of Jerusalem comes the word of the LORD; he will be judge between nations, arbiter among many peoples. They shall beat their swords into mattocks and their spears into pruning-knives; nation shall not lift sword against nation nor ever again be trained for war (*Isaiah* 2: 2–4).

political bureaucrats. The Torah served as the foundation document of the nation in somewhat the same way that the collected body of British law serves as Britain's constitution.

An inhabitant of this region, the former tribal territory of Judah, was known as a *yehudi*, a Judean. This is the source for the English word 'Jew'. Although the term did not gain its modern religious sense until the New Testament was written, ethnicity already had religious overtones in the Persian period.

Hellenistic Judaism (331 BCE–65 BCE)

The conquest of the Persian Empire by Alexander the Great in 331 BCE marked the end of the Hellenic age—the time of the city states in classical Greece—and the beginning of the Hellenistic (from *hellenizo*, 'I speak Greek' or 'I learn to speak Greek'). Thereafter many peoples of the eastern Mediterranean adopted the Greek language, and it remained the primary language of trade even after the Romans arrived.

Yet the common culture of the period had little to do with the values of ancient Athens. Trade and cultural contact fostered a cosmopolitan outlook that gradually eroded the Jews' connections to their traditions. This was especially true for those—now the majority—who lived outside the ancient land of Israel, throughout the Mediterranean and Mesopotamia. The reality of the **Diaspora** (from the Greek for 'sowing of seed', hence 'dispersal') meant that Judaism had to evolve new ways of understanding and explaining itself.

The Jewish community of Alexandria in Egypt adopted Greek names as well as Greek styles of architecture and dress, and by the early third century BCE knowledge of Hebrew had declined to the point that the Bible had to be translated into Greek. The **Septuagint** translation brought the Bible to a community with a new set of cultural expectations. Jews in Alexandria regarded their Greek Bible more as an object of meditation or literary study than as the covenant charter of the Hebrew state.

In the fourth century BCE the Greek philosopher Theophrastus described the Jews as 'a race of philosophers' because they 'discourse[d] on the divine . . . observe[d] the stars at night . . . and call[ed] to them in their prayers'. Not all pagan responses to Judaism were so positive, though. Most anti-Jewish comments by Greek and Roman writers in the Hellenistic period merely expressed a general dislike of foreigners. But in one case, xenophobia crossed the line into anti-Semitism. According to the first-century Jewish historian Flavius Josephus, Apion—a Hellenistic educator who wanted to keep Jews out of the great schools of Alexandria—had 'the effrontery' to claim that the Jews at the temple in Jerusalem worshipped the head of a golden ass.

The Maccabean Revolt

For over a century Judea was under the control of the Ptolemies—the Greek dynasty that had ruled Egypt since 305 BCE. Then in 198 BCE the territory passed into the hands of a rival Greek dynasty called the Seleucids, the rulers of Syria. Identifying the Hebrews' Yahweh with the supreme god of the Hellenized world, the Seleucids transformed Jerusalem's temple into a cult place of Zeus in 168 BCE. The Seleucid king, Antiochus IV, raided it for its riches, then moved troops into the temple area and suspended the local Torah constitution. He may not have intended specifically to crush the Judeans' religion; his motives may have been primarily economic and political. But from the Judeans' perspective, his actions amounted to an attack on their religion. In 166 BCE a general revolt broke out, led by a group of fighters called the Maccabees (from 'hammer', the Hebrew nickname of their leader, Judah). Though its immediate objective was to expel the Seleucids, this action also reflected a dispute within the Jewish community, between traditionalists and those who favoured assimilation to the dominant Hellenistic culture. In *1 Maccabees* the traditionalists accuse the Hellenizers of 'abandon[ing] themselves to evil ways': repudiating the covenant, intermarrying with gentiles, and even 'remov[ing] their marks of circumcision' (*1 Maccabees* 1: 11–15). Those who favoured assimilation probably hoped it would advance the political and economic interests of Jerusalem, but in the less Hellenized rural areas they were seen as undermining the religious basis of Judean life and violating the Torah constitution. Worse, some of the main proponents of Hellenization were priests.

The Maccabees prevailed, recapturing Jerusalem from the Seleucids and expanding the Jewish state to its pre-exilic boundaries. The rededication of the temple in 164 BCE brought the divided community together and is commemorated in the minor holiday called Hanukkah. Thereafter, however, the rebel leaders set themselves up as client kings of the Seleucids and Romans, readily adopting Hellenistic culture. Their descendants, known as the Hasmonean dynasty, ruled in shaky independence for more than a century, until the Roman general Pompey captured Jerusalem and brought Judea under Roman occupation in 64 BCE.

Dynamics of Hellenism

The Maccabean revolt was a watershed. Once the Hellenization process came into conflict with the traditional constitution—the Torah—it could no longer be tolerated. But the converse was also true: Greek ideas, no matter how foreign, could be incorporated into Judaism as long as conflict with Torah could be avoided. Life under a foreign empire was possible as long as the political situation allowed for the Israelite constitution to operate as well. Thus a second, subtler phase of Hellenization began, in which Judaism began to adapt Hellenistic ideas and use them for uniquely Judean purposes.

First-Century Sects

Hellenistic society was not merely cosmopolitan but individualistic, and Hellenistic culture encouraged opposing concepts of truth. These qualities were reflected in Hellenistic

Judaism, which comprised a variety of sects. Any attempt to impose a single orthodoxy would have led to wholesale defections, but accommodating diversity promoted stability. As in North American party politics today, power was balanced between two major groups—the Sadducees and Pharisees—who together ran the Sanhedrin, a communal council with juridical functions. Representing the upper and middle classes respectively, both these groups faced challenges from two smaller, more radical sects: the Essenes and the Zealots.

Sadducees

The Sadducees represented the aristocracy that embraced Hellenization. The upper class both politically and occupationally, they were also the party of the priestly establishment and the custodians of the temple, in charge of its operations. They insisted on a narrow, literal interpretation of the law.

Pharisees

The Pharisees represented the middle classes. Some were landowners, some were skilled workers, and many were professional scribes serving the aristocratic Sadducees. From time to time the Pharisees also held power in the temple, but they were more at home in the synagogues of Judea.

The Pharisees tended to interpret the scripture more broadly than the Sadducees did, though they tried to establish principles and procedures for scriptural interpretation. They were also punctilious about rules of purity and tithing, which distinguished members in good standing from the general populace. Special groups called *havurot* ('brotherhoods') were even more strict about these matters. Disdaining the Sadducean priests as cultic functionaries, the *havurot* considered themselves to be the proper custodians of the law.

The Christian writers of the New Testament, not surprisingly, depicted the Pharisees as hypocrites, more interested in the outward forms of ritual than in the inner substance of righteousness. From the Pharisees' own perspective, however, careful observance of external forms made the sacred law part of everyday life.

Essenes

The Essenes are widely believed to have been the authors of the Dead Sea Scrolls—a collection of manuscripts from the Maccabean and early Roman period discovered in 1947 near the Dead Sea at Qumran. They were a group of rigorously observant priests under the leadership of a man they called the Teacher of Righteousness, or Righteous Teacher. When a candidate they disapproved of was appointed high priest, they left Jerusalem and moved to the desert. There they established a centre of priestly purity in expectation of the coming apocalypse: the final battle between the forces of darkness and light at the end of time.

Zealots

At the far end of the political spectrum were several groups that rejected Roman authority under any circumstances. Most of what we know about these groups comes from Josephus, who describes them as bandits. But in fact their motives appear to have been purely political.

The most famous of these revolutionaries were the Zealots (also characterized by Josephus as the 'Fourth Philosophy'), who came together expressly to liberate Judea from Roman control. Beginning in the northern region called Galilee in 66 CE, their revolt was effectively crushed with the destruction of Jerusalem in 70, but a group of perhaps a thousand rebels defended the fortress of **Masada** for another four years.

Masada was a natural high mesa near the Dead Sea, fitted out by Herod the Great as a self-sufficient fortified palace, which the Zealots captured from the Romans shortly after the revolt began. It remained the Zealot headquarters until the rest of Judea had fallen. But after a four-year siege, it too was finally conquered in 73. When the Romans entered the fortress they found all the remaining defenders—men, women, and children—dead by their own hands. According to Josephus, the mass suicide followed a stirring speech by their leader Eleazar ben Yair:

> But since we had a generous hope that deluded us, as if we might perhaps have been able to avenge ourselves on our enemies . . . let us make haste to die bravely. Let us pity ourselves, our children, and our wives, while it is in our own power to show pity to them; for we were born to die, as well as those were whom we have begotten. . . . But certainly our hands are still at liberty, and have a sword in them. Let them then be subservient to us in our glorious design; let us die before we become slaves of our enemies, and let us go out of the world, together with our children, and our wives, in a state of freedom (Whiston 1802, 3: 471–2).

The emergence of the Zealots upset the balance between the Sadducees and the Pharisees. The revolt against Rome left Jerusalem and the temple in ruins and also destroyed Qumran. It was from the ashes of these disasters that the **rabbinic movement** would emerge to carry on the traditions of Pharisaism.

Samaritans

The Samaritans were descendants of the northern Israelites, but their ancestors began marrying outside the Hebrew faith around the end of the eighth century BCE. By the Hellenistic period they were becoming a separate group on the fringes of Judaism. Rejecting the *Prophets* and *Writings* of the Hebrew Bible, they accepted only the first five books of Moses as canonical, and their version of those books differed significantly from the Hebrew Pentateuch in that it contained several references to a messianic figure who was expected to be 'a prophet like Moses'.

Christians

Christianity also began as a sect within Judaism, and it is the only Jewish sect of its day whose origins are well known. If we understand Christianity better by considering it as a first-century Jewish sect, therefore, we may also understand the first-century Jewish sects better by considering Christianity as one of them.

The Christian message that, with repentance, all are equal before God was typical of all apocalyptic thought in first-century Judea. The Christian practices of public repentance, purification through baptism, and chaste communal living were also typical of contemporary apocalyptic groups. Yet these similarities only emphasize the striking difference between Christianity and Essenism, for example. Essenism was limited to an elite whose members were preoccupied with the cultic purity rules that allowed them to approach God's holy places, whereas Christianity was interested in reaching out to the distressed or sinful.

Jewish Thought in the Hellenistic Period

The Concept of God

Contact with Greek culture challenged Judaism's concept of God. Most philosophical Greeks had already abandoned the traditional pantheistic theory of the universe. Now they saw the universe as depending on a single principle (love, beauty, the good) and regarded the traditional gods as allegorical figures representing the virtues. For the Greeks, change of any kind implied imperfection, and since creation implied change, the ultimate good could not be a creator. Rather, creation had to take place at some level below that of the divine, through the action of a semi-divine intermediary or 'demiurge'.

It was in this cultural context that some Jews in the Hellenistic period tended to understand Judaism. Under the influence of Greek thought, Jewish philosophers like Philo—a first-century Alexandrian whose views reflected those current among Hellenized Jews in Judea as well as the Diaspora—reasoned that there must be intermediaries of some kind to carry out Yahweh's actions on earth. For Philo, the principal mediator was the **logos**: a kind of instrumental divine intelligence. The notion of an intermediary was taken up by Christianity, which understood Jesus to have a double nature, divine and human at the same time. The idea that God's essence included a son as well as a father represented a fundamental alteration of the unitary divinity envisioned by Judaism.

At the same time Christians presented the Israelites with a competing claim for the role of God's chosen people—with a significant difference. Whereas Judaism emphasized the responsibility entailed by the covenant, Christianity emphasized the fulfillment of the promises made at Mount Sinai, without the obligation to obey the specific ordinances of Jewish law.

Resurrection

The Jewish Bible is full of predictions regarding the fate of the world at the end of this age. Yet it says almost nothing about the fate of the individual at the end of this life. A genre of Jewish literature that emerged in the later prophetic books and flourished in the Hellenistic era is termed 'apocalyptic', from the Greek for 'unveiling' (the Latin equivalent is 'revelation'). Most apocalyptic literature is eschatological in nature and visionary in presentation. Whereas the prophets had claimed to report Yahweh's words, the apocalyptists generally claimed to report their own visions: 'I saw, and behold . . .'.

Regarding the individual, the ancient Hebrews were not preoccupied with the idea of a continuing existence after death—perhaps in part because they made no strict distinction between body and soul. The original answer to the question of where personality goes after death was Sheol, an underground place (similar to the Greek Hades) where the individual resides in greatly attenuated form. Sheol is not equivalent to either heaven or hell: it is a pit, a place of weakness and estrangement from God, to which all the dead go and from which their spirits issue on the rare occasions when they can be seen on the earth. Occasionally, the psalmists and prophets seem to suggest that the righteous live in God's presence (*Psalm* 139: 7–8, 11–12; *Psalm* 90: 9–10, 12).

What mattered was not to continue as a spirit but to live on in one's descendants. Nothing in Hebrew thought anticipates the post-biblical idea of paradise or resurrection as a reward for a righteous human life. The book of *Ecclesiastes* is clear about the finality of death:

> For the fate of the sons of men and the fate of beasts is the same; as one dies, so dies the other. They all have the same breath, and man has no advantage over the beasts; for all is vanity.
> (*Ecclesiastes* 3: 19)

Even so, it seems that Judaism did develop a doctrine of resurrection specifically for martyrs. The concept of the martyr—one who chooses to die rather than renounce his or her faith—appears to date from the Maccabean revolt (166 BCE). And the first indisputable reference to resurrection in biblical literature comes from the book of *Daniel*, which is set during the Babylonian captivity but is now generally believed to have been written during the years of oppression leading to the Maccabean revolt. *Daniel* 12: 2 prophesies that

> many of those who sleep in the dust of the earth shall awake, some to everlasting life, and some to shame and everlasting contempt. And those who are wise shall shine like the brightness of the firmament; and those who turn many to righteousness, like the stars for ever and ever.

In *Daniel's* vision, the righteous martyrs will be restored to everlasting life, while their persecutors will endure everlasting punishment. Until the late first century, the idea of resurrection was still a matter of debate. The Sadducees rejected it, while the Pharisees accepted it, as did the Christians. (The idea of Jesus' resurrection was consistent with the idea of resurrection for martyrs.)

The Messiah

The term 'messiah' comes from the Hebrew *mashiah*, 'anointed one'; anointing (pouring oil over the head) was a standard ritual signifying divine sanction, usually of a new king. Like the doctrine of resurrection, the idea of a messiah developed in the context of Israel's historical experience. Before the collapse of the Judean monarchy, the term 'messiah' almost always referred to the current king. But the idea of a future king began to take on a new significance after the last heir to the Davidic throne had disappeared. In Hellenistic times the term 'messiah' came to refer to an ideal future leader—king, priest, or prophet—who would finally bring God's justice to the world.

By the late first century CE, however, the disastrous wars against Rome and the spread of Christianity had made the rabbis wary of messianic movements. Their view was summed up in the advice of Rabbi Yochanan ben Zakkai: if a farmer in the midst of planting a tree should hear that the messiah had come, he should finish his planting and only then go to see whether the reports were true (Avot of Rabbi Nathan 31b). The message was clear: while Jews should not give up hoping for the messiah, they should not be too quick to put their faith in claimants who might be fomenting rebellion or heresy.

🦎 CRYSTALLIZATION

The Rabbinic Movement

The fall of Jerusalem to the Romans in 70 CE marked a turning-point comparable to the Exile. Once again the temple was destroyed, and this time it was not rebuilt. Institutions and practices associated with temple worship, such as animal sacrifice, vanished from Jewish life. The Sadducees, having lost both their power base and their *raison d'être*, disappeared, as did the Essenes, whose base at Qumran had been razed to the ground by the Romans. The Zealots had been wiped out. And although a second independence movement did emerge in 132–5, it too ultimately failed. (Its leader, Simon bar Cochba, was seen by some as a messianic figure, and his death gave rise to a tradition—clearly reminiscent of the early Christians' response to Jesus' death —that the messiah must suffer and die.) In this way it fell to the Pharisees to preserve Judaism. Although they too eventually disappeared, their traditions became the base on which the institutions of rabbinic Judaism were built. Thereafter, the chief custodians of the Jewish heritage would not be the priests but the teachers and legal specialists—the rabbis.

Politically, the Pharisaic–rabbinic movement worked out a *modus vivendi* with the Romans. The rabbis conceded that the Jews in any location would be subject to the law of the host community. Palestinian Jewish community government was re-established, and although it had no significant political power, limited local authority was eventually granted to the Patriarch (the highest position in Palestine). Gradually, what had been one of two Jewish sects vying for power transformed itself into a legal and religious establishment that consciously sought to avoid sectarian divisions.

As the tradition from which Christianity emerged, Judaism might have been expected to stay closer to the original culture. But in fact rabbinic Judaism, like Christianity, can be seen as both a continuation and a transformation of the biblical tradition. The rabbinate was not a hereditary priesthood. All that was required for ordination was the appropriate education, available to any male at the local school (the institution of the **yeshivah** evolved over the centuries). Students were ordained as soon as they had completed their studies to the satisfaction of their teachers, though many continued to study the Torah for the rest of their lives.

The rabbis directed a new attention to religious observance in daily life, and in so doing provided the new structure that Jewish society needed to survive the loss of the temple. By emphasizing formal laws, rituals, and rules of conduct, they gave Jews a new way of living their part of the covenant. In the past, the sense of the sacred had been concentrated in the temple, where sacrifice effected atonement (reconciliation with God). Now that sense was relocated at the table of every Jew who observed the rules of the Torah, and the faithful found another path to atonement in performing good deeds. At the same time, the rabbis' emphasis on close textual analysis ensured that the community's traditions were recorded and preserved. The Judaism that we know today is founded on the Judaism of the rabbis in late antiquity.

The Synagogue

The locus of public worship in rabbinic times was no longer the temple but the synagogue. Jews continued to pray three times a day and to attend special services in commemoration of the special services in the temple. But Jewish prayer never again revolved around a central temple, or even the local synagogue.

Synagogues may have come into being as far back as the destruction of the first temple in 586 BCE, but they became especially important as places of assembly, study, and prayer in the Diaspora. After 70 CE, many of the activities that used to take place at the temple were transferred to the synagogue, along with much of the temple liturgy (augmented over the years by prayers and poems written by rabbinic Jews).

By the third century synagogues were beginning to develop the specific architecture that now characterizes them. The congregation prayed facing Jerusalem, the site of the temple. Cut or painted in the wall in front of the worshippers was a niche in which the Torah was placed during the service. Thus most synagogues in Western countries today face east, and for prayer at home, many Jews mark the direction with a plaque reading 'Mizrah' ('east' in Hebrew). Eventually the Torah niche became an elaborate piece of furniture at the front of the synagogue: the holy ark permanently houses the Torah scrolls. In later tradition a lamp above the ark is tended continuously, as were the lamps in the temple. The rostrum from which the Torah is read may be placed either in the centre of the congregation or at the front near the ark containing the Torah.

The use of the seven-branched **menorah** ('candlestick' or 'lamp stand') dates back to the days of the temple. The menorah became a symbol of Jewish culture and sovereignty; today it is the official symbol of the state of Israel.

Scripture and Commentary

The period after 70 marks the beginning of 'classical Judaism'. As in the sixth century BCE, the loss of the temple raised the scriptural texts to a new level of authority. The five scrolls of the *Law* (ascribed to Moses but perhaps not completed until about 400 BCE) were central, as were the writings collected in *Prophets* (probably stabilized around 200 BCE). In addition there were the works that had been chosen for translation in the *Septuagint*: the book of *Psalms*, the temple hymn collection, 'wisdom' writings such as *Job* and *Proverbs*, and various apocalyptic and historical texts. With the diversity of sectarian emphases, the number of writings that might be candidates for scriptural status was growing.

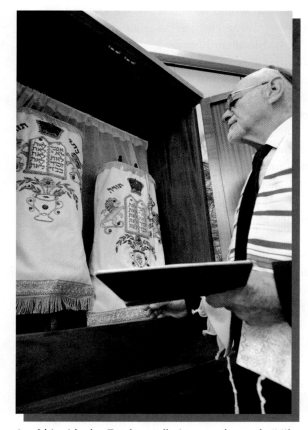

A rabbi with the Torah scrolls in a modern ark (Mike Cherim/istockphoto).

The contents of the third portion of the Hebrew canon, the sacred *Writings*, had presumably been determined by the second or third century BCE, but they were not finalized by the rabbis until about the year 90 CE. Then the Bible came to consist of three sections: the *Teaching* or *Law* (Torah), the *Prophets* (Hebrew *Nevi'im*), and the sacred *Writings* (Hebrew *Ketuvim*). Jews often refer to the complete corpus as the **Tanakh**—an acronym based on their titles (T–N–KH).

After the biblical corpus had been fixed, the rabbis proceeded to collect and add to the body of Bible interpretation, known as **midrash** ('interpretation' or 'commentary'). Most midrashic commentaries are line-by-line interpretations following the sequence of the biblical text. The early *midrashim* include three books of legal discussions from the first and second centuries, when the Pharisees were working to derive rulings about contemporary customs from the written text of the Bible. Although this effort sometimes required imaginative application of exegetic principles, they claimed that their interpretations were based on an oral tradition that had existed alongside the written Torah from the very beginning. But the process of commenting continued for centuries. The rabbinic writers of *midrash* took it as their task to understand the full significance of the biblical text—a task that in their view included resolving the frequent contradictions between one passage and another.

Books of the Hebrew Bible (Tanakh)

Torah ('Teaching', 'Law')	Nevi'im ('Prophets')	Ketuvim ('Writings')
Genesis	Joshua	Psalms
Exodus	Judges	Proverbs
Leviticus	Samuel (I & II)	Job
Numbers	Kings (I & II)	Song of Songs
Deuteronomy	Isaiah	Ruth
	Jeremiah	Lamentations
	Ezekiel	Ecclesiastes
	The Twelve Prophets	Esther
	– Hosea	Daniel
	– Joel	Ezra-Nehemiah
	– Amos	Chronicles (I & II)
	– Obadiah	
	– Jonah	
	– Micah	
	– Nahum	
	– Habakkuk	
	– Zephaniah	
	– Haggai	
	– Zechariah	
	– Malachi	

The *Mishnah*

A major achievement in the rabbis' restructuring of the tradition was their elaboration of the Jewish legal heritage. Forms that had been passed down orally in the Pharisaic tradition were now organized and codified in writing. This basic legal system consists of two parts: the **Mishnah** and the *Talmud*.

Unlike the midrashic commentaries, which follow the sequence and structure of the books that made up the Hebrew canon at the end of the first century, the *Mishnah* had its own topical arrangement in six 'orders' or divisions: Seeds (agriculture), Festivals, Women, Damages, Holy Things (sacrifices), and Purifications. Summarizing the Pharisaic–rabbinic movement interpretation of the traditional law, the *Mishnah* is the oldest datable rabbinic document, produced shortly before 220 by Rabbi Judah, known as 'ha-Nasi' ('the prince'). But it is not the only repository of the legal rulings of the early rabbis (often called the **Tannaim**, or 'repeaters' or 'teachers'). Alternative Tannaitic traditions are also found in a book called the **Tosefta** (Aramaic for 'addition'), and they provide precedents of equal value in rabbinic discussions.

Claims for the authoritative nature of the *Mishnah* were based on the notion of the 'oral law'—the idea that, alongside the five books traditionally ascribed to Moses, there was another body of precedent and interpretation that had been passed down from Moses in a direct line of oral transmission. This doctrine allowed the rabbis to claim that their own interpretations were just as authoritative as the doctrines written explicitly in the Torah.

The development of Pharisaic traditions is reflected in two first-century schools of interpretation, one led by Hillel and the other by his contemporary Shammai. The earliest stages may well have involved the codification of laws on the issues of greatest interest to the Pharisees—Sabbath law, purity, and tithing. However, the early rabbis also paid close attention to marriage and divorce, for rules of personal status contributed to the definition of membership in the Jewish community.

The *Talmud*

By about 220 the formerly open and growing body of interpretation had, like the Bible, become a fixed, written text. And, like the Bible, the *Mishnah* of Rabbi Judah itself now became the subject of passage-by-passage commentary. With its six 'orders' subdivided into a total of 63 tractates (treatises), the *Mishnah* became the skeleton of the collection known as the *Talmud*.

The *Mishnah* itself is no longer than a desk dictionary, but there are two different *Talmuds*, each roughly the size of a multi-volume encyclopedia. Each *Talmud* consists of the Hebrew *Mishnah* of Rabbi Judah together with one of the two bodies of commentary, known as a **Gemarah** (from an Aramaic word meaning 'study).

One *Gemarah* comes from the Jewish community in Palestine, the other from the Jewish community in Babylonia. The *Mishnah* and the Palestinian *Gemarah* form the *Palestinian Talmud*; this material is also known as the *Jerusalem Talmud*, though it was likely produced in the Galilee region north of Jerusalem. The same *Mishnah* and the other *Gemarah*, produced in Babylonia, form the *Babylonian Talmud*.

The *Mishnah* is in Hebrew, the language of the past, of liturgy and scholarly study (the Christian equivalent would be Church Latin); both *gemarahs*, however, are in Aramaic, a vernacular language of the time, related to Hebrew. Typically, a selection from the *Talmud* starts with a short passage from the *Mishnah* followed by the text of the related *Gemarah*, which is often much longer. In printed editions the *Mishnah* and *Gemarah* appear in a small column in the centre of the page, surrounded by later additions and commentaries, together with various study aids such as cross-references.

The *Jerusalem Talmud* is an interesting source of history, lore, and tradition in Judaism, but it was produced under difficult circumstances. Not only was the economy in decline, but with the Christianization of the Roman Empire, Jews were increasingly subject to discriminatory laws, including a law, enacted about 425, that abolished the office of the Patriarch (the head of the leading Palestinian academy).

In Babylonia, by contrast, the ruling Sasanian Persians were relatively tolerant of the Jewish community. Perhaps as a consequence, the legal discussions undertaken there were more acute and substantial than their Palestinian counterparts, and the *Babylonian Talmud* became the more authoritative version for the Jewish community as a whole. At first Palestine was in charge of the ritual calendar: thus the arrival of each new month was determined in Palestine (by direct observation of the moon) and the news was then communicated to other lands. When the calendar eventually came to be calculated mathematically, the Babylonian community embarked on an independent ritual life. This change formalized the primacy of the Babylonian Talmudic academies, which had been gaining in talent and prestige for generations.

The Babylonian *Gemarah* records the discussions of more than 2,000 sages arguing over specific ways to resolve issues by reference to the text of the *Mishnah*. In contrast to the ordered discussions of the *Mishnah*, the *Gemarah* discussions tend to be quite complex and far-ranging, even free-associational. Nevertheless, brief technical terms identify the formal characteristics of the specific arguments that are about to be mounted.

Since the text of the *Mishnah* is a law code, much of the *Gemarah* commentary on it is strictly legal in nature. Some legal discussions (though not all) prescribe specific legal procedures; together, these prescriptions make up the body of religious law known as **halakhah** ('the way' or 'procedure', or more specifically, the proper legal procedure for living life). Another, more anecdotal type of expansion is called **aggadah** ('narrative'). While *halakhah* directives are explicit statements arrived at through legal analysis, *aggadah* teaches a moral lesson, often by telling a story or interpreting the meaning of a word.

Jews conventionally regard the topically arranged legal material of the *Talmud* as *halakhah* and the expansion on biblical narratives in the *midrash* as *aggadah* because they emphasize law and story, respectively. But examples of both genres can be found in each collection, though in vastly different proportions. As a result, the terms *halakhah* and *aggadah* are often used very loosely.

The Status of Torah

Definitions of the term 'torah' are similarly elastic. In the period of the first temple, 'torah' apparently referred only to the laws that governed priestly behaviour. Starting with the book of *Deuteronomy*, however, the term was used to refer first to a written book of law and then to the Pentateuch.

In biblical times books were written on scrolls, and this form has been retained for the copy of the sacred text used in synagogues. Called a **Sefer Torah** ('book of the Torah'), it is written by hand on parchment and mounted on wooden rollers. For other uses (such as personal study) the Pentateuch is bound as a book (the form that replaced scrolls in late antiquity).

In a broader sense, the 'Torah' is the entire Hebrew Bible (the Tanakh), and in some cases the term may even be extended to include the books of the oral law—the *Midrash*, *Mishnah*, and *Talmud*. That is because every discussion of holy law and procedure is considered part of the same divine revelation, continuing over the millennia. Thus 'Torah' can refer to any revelatory or canonical literature. The *Talmud* and the commentaries on it are all part of Torah.

The study of Torah continued unabated while the *Talmud* was being completed. Together, the two principal rabbinic academies in Babylonia were the intellectual centre of the Jewish world from the fourth to the ninth century and even after. There, the leader of the *yeshivah*, known by the honorific term **gaon** ('excellency'), often enjoyed greater power and respect than the ostensible head of the Jewish community, the exilarch. This was because the *gaon* supervised the rabbinic enterprise of legal interpretation.

Further Development of Jewish Law

Tradition says that the compilation of the *Talmud* was completed by the end of the sixth century. Thereafter the development of Jewish law took three main forms.

The first consisted of passage-by passage commentary on the Talmudic text. Perhaps the most famous contributor to this literature was Rabbi Shlomo ben Yitzhak (1040–1105) of Troyes, north of Paris, widely known by the acronym Rashi (R–Sh–Y). His commentaries are invaluable for understanding the simple sense of difficult passages. In addition, great medieval rabbis commented on individual problems in the *Talmud*. A selection of these later annotations appears on a printed *Talmud* page. They are known as **Tosafot** ('additions' or 'footnotes') and are not to be confused with the *Tosefta* of the first rabbis, which accompanies the *Mishnah*.

The second development of the legal tradition was a collection of rulings made by expert rabbis in response to questions posed by individual communities. This *Teshuvah* ('answer') or (in Latin) *responsum* ('response'; plural *responsa*) literature always took the form of public letters. It is possible that the New Testament letters of Paul are early examples of this genre, since they contain Paul's answers to questions asked by the early church communities. Although Paul is now part of Christian rather than Jewish tradition, the questions he addresses are of the same type as the ones that Jews have asked over the centuries. Orthodox rabbis today still issue *responsa*, extending Talmudic reasoning to questions on issues such as the use of birth control or new medical procedures.

Finally, the law codes developed in the medieval period served to clarify complicated legal material and explain what had been done in similar situations. Two influential medieval codes were the **Mishneh Torah** ('The Repetition of the Torah'; c. 1180) of Moses Maimonides and the *Arba'a Turim* ('Four Columns) of Jacob ben Asher (c. 1270–1340). Following the outline of that work, Joseph Karo, a sixteenth-century Spanish Jew who moved to Palestine, brought diverse legal opinions together in a massive compilation entitled *Bet Yosef* ('House of Joseph') and later produced a condensation of that work under the title *Shulhan Arukh* ('Set Table', an allusion to *Psalm* 23). The latter work is still consulted today as a practical guide to Torah observance.

Applying Legal Principles

Originally the civil law of the Israelites, the Torah thus became the religious law of rabbinic Judaism and the guide to moral conduct for Jews far removed in time and space from the ancient state. For such an ancient law to adapt and stay relevant to later ages, a healthy tradition of study and commentary was essential.

Rabbinic Judaism gave enormous emphasis to proper ethical conduct. The tradition called for numerous specific actions of both a ritual and a moral nature, but it recognized that no two circumstances are ever fully identical. Therefore every situation must be analyzed individually. The study of the *Talmud* provided training in the principles of ethical analysis from every conceivable perspective.

'An eye for an eye, a tooth for a tooth,' says the book of *Exodus*. As harsh as this principle may sound today, it may well have been unusually humane in the second millennium BCE, when some societies would put a serf to death for injuring his master. The Bible limited the penalty to the extent of the injury. By the rabbinic period, however, even this relatively lenient principle was considered too severe. After very little debate, the rabbis concluded that compensation for the loss of a body part (for instance) should take the form of a financial payment.

To a modern interpreter, this shift away from physical punishment clearly reflects a moral evolution that led the Israelites to see the original injunction as unjust. Yet most Orthodox Jews hold the scripture to be incapable of error and therefore maintain that the *Exodus* verse called for financial compensation all along: the only evolution required was in the human ability to interpret the text correctly, in which the rabbis were guided by divine inspiration.

For centuries the principles of Torah have been applied to the problems of everyday life. In the Hellenistic period, for instance, many people were reluctant to lend money when a sabbatical year (the year when fields lie fallow and debts are forgiven) was approaching, for fear that they would not be repaid. Even though the Torah does not provide a remedy for this problem, the rabbis were confident that a solution could be found. In this case the solution—derived from a *takkanah* ('remediation') attributed to Hillel—was that the court itself take over debts for the sabbatical year.

Rabbinic law was hardly unanimous or monolithic. For example, classical rabbinic law says nothing directly about abortion, and later rabbinic law offers no single answer. The biblical precedent is found in a text about a miscarriage that is caused accidentally: 'When men fight, and one of them pushes a pregnant woman and a miscarriage results, but no other damage ensues, the one responsible shall be fined according as the woman's husband may exact from him, the payment to be based on reckoning' (*Exodus* 21: 22). Rabbinic interpretation takes this to mean that the destruction of a fetus is a tort but not a capital crime. Thus a pregnancy that endangers the life of the mother may be terminated.

Even so, whether abortion is acceptable in any particular case depends on subtle distinctions. Some Jews would perform an abortion only if the life of the mother was truly endangered. Others, interpreting more broadly, might require only that the mother feel she is psychologically unfit for motherhood. Reform Jews would say that past rulings should be consulted, but that they are not automatically binding on contemporary life. They might extend one principle or another discussed by the rabbis and follow it to a conclusion never reached in the past, then justify their decision on the basis of what a rabbi operating under similar principles might do today.

Purity and Community

Some of the most arcane Torah laws involve ritual purity. When the rabbis turned their attention to these laws, they were codifying a complex symbolic system. Today purity laws are generally thought to have served a hygienic function for primitive societies by prohibiting contact with harmful substances, such as corpses or human excreta, and controlling behaviour around them. Yet various cultures have made some harmful substances central to ritual events, while treating some completely harmless ones as taboo. The same is true of the Hebrew rules, some of which have no obvious medical value.

Hebrew society, like many non-Western societies, had a series of food taboos. Probably the best known is the commandment not to eat the meat from pigs (pork, ham, bacon, etc.). Other forbidden foods include shellfish, blood, and any carnivorous bird or mammal. Another rule forbids eating meat and milk together, but this one is not biblical. Although *Exodus* 23: 19 forbids Jews to eat a young goat boiled in its mother's milk, the Bible says nothing about keeping meat and milk separate. That rule was introduced by the rabbis, perhaps as a safeguard against violating the biblical rules. (The creation of rules to prevent inadvertent violations is known as 'making a fence around the Torah'.)

Other rules rooted in the Bible forbade willful contact with 'polluting' substances such as menstrual blood or semen. Touching them was not a sin in itself—such contact was inevitable—but the resulting pollution had to be removed by visiting a *mikveh* (ritual bathhouse) for purification. Other purity laws required ritual immersion for both spouses after sexual intercourse, and prohibited intercourse entirely for the first week of every menstrual cycle. Christian baptism is widely thought to have grown out of the Jewish immersion ritual. As symbolic boundary markers, separating the ritually pure from the less pious, purity laws also separated Jews from the host society and imposed a high degree of group coherence. Although Jews were permitted to eat with gentiles, dietary and purity laws helped to limit contact.

In biblical society priests were a separate hereditary class that maintained a high degree of ritual purity. With the temple gone, there was no longer any need for such a priesthood. In a sense, though, maintaining ritual purity became a personal obligation for every member of the Jewish community in its priestly role among the nations of the world.

Repentance

The rabbis also put great emphasis on repentance. They did not design a 'scoreboard' religion in which good deeds could be totalled against bad. Rather, they taught that human life is constantly balanced between good and evil deeds, and that for this reason the need for repentance is constant.

There are several stages to repentance. The rabbis recognized that those who do wrong seek to do right, but the human ability to rationalize misbehaviour prevents them from seeing where they go wrong. Thus the first step is to acknowledge openly the wrong one has done. The next stage should be true sorrow for one's misdeeds. People may admit their sins without actually feeling sorry for committing them. Or they may rationalize them as necessary under the pressure of circumstances. True repentance means acknowledging that all these thought patterns are traps.

If God forgives the sincere penitent, humans should do the same. The person wronged may seek repentance and restitution, but if the wrongdoer is sincere, forgiveness must not be unfairly withheld. Only when restitution and forgiveness have been accomplished may the sinner expect that God will accept the repentance offered on Yom Kippur, the annual Day of Atonement.

Some damage cannot be repaired. In the case of murder, for example, nothing can bring back the life of the victim. Therefore compensation may require the death of the perpetrator. A murderer who truly repents and is willing to accept death may enter God's presence as a forgiven sinner. Although the rabbis had no authority to impose the death penalty, the Bible clearly prescribed it for murder, and therefore they had to admit capital punishment as a possibility. But they imposed so many legal strictures on it that there was virtually never a situation sufficiently clear-cut to justify the death penalty.

The rabbis developed a very sophisticated notion of intention. Just as English common law recognizes several degrees of intention in murder cases, so the rabbis recognized the role that subtle differences in intention play in determining the significance of any action. To find someone guilty of murder, they usually required a degree of intentionality that would be very difficult to ascertain in court. This was possible because they believed God to be a witness to every human action.

Thus even in cases where lack of evidence makes it impossible for a human court to determine the truth, it is assumed that, if a wrong has been done, God will see that the wrongdoer is punished. This brings us to a subtle but important distinction: rabbinic law, unlike secular law, assumes God to be a constant participant in the legal process. Sometimes people find rabbinic writing legalistic. But this is a category mistake. The fact is that a great deal of rabbinic writing *is* law, albeit highly theological law.

Commandments for Jews and Gentiles

If, as the rabbis believed, the Torah was God's gift to the Jews, what did God intend for the gentile nations (*goyim* in Hebrew)? Did they too have a part in the divine plan, with their own privileges and responsibilities? By what standards should their conduct be judged?

In the biblical account, the covenants that Yahweh makes with Abraham and Moses establish specific privileges and responsibilities for the people of Israel. The Ten Commandments are at the heart of the law, but the classic interpretation of Torah holds that the people Israel must also obey more than 600 additional commandments (*mitzvot*). (The number is conventional; the rabbis of the Middle Ages enumerated exactly 613 of them.)

It was the covenant with Abraham that marked the formation of a distinct Israelite people. But there was an earlier covenant—the one that God made with Noah and sealed with the rainbow. The rabbis linked the salvation of the gentiles explicitly to this covenant in which God promises mercy and deliverance to all humanity. They also believed that in it God gave to everyone a set of laws known as the Noahide (or Noahic) commandments that included prohibitions on blasphemy, idolatry, bloodshed, incest, and theft.

Medieval rabbinic commentators seeking to understand God's plan for Christianity and Islam—religions founded on Jewish principles but far greater in numbers and power—looked to the Noahide commandments for guidance. Since Islam was strictly monotheistic and rejected the making of images, the rabbis came to see it as consistent with the Noahide commandments. Some of them saw Christianity in the same light. But others balked at Christianity's trinitarian doctrine and its rich traditions of devotion to *eikons* or 'images'.

Jews willingly accept converts to Judaism. However, since salvation is available to all righteous people, they believe that conversion is appropriate only for those who sincerely wish to join their fate with that of the people Israel.

DIFFERENTIATION

The Medieval Period

The Jews of the premodern world were divided geographically: **Sephardim** in the region of the Mediterranean and **Ashkenazim** in central and eastern Europe. By the medieval period Sepharad was identified primarily with Spain, which with Portugal came to dominate Sephardic intellectual history. European Jewish settlement in the New World began with Sephardim from Spain and Portugal—the pioneering lands of exploration and colonial empire-building. There have also been important Sephardic centres in Italy and the Turkish Empire, and Jews across North Africa and the Middle East can all be counted among the Sephardim.

Ashkenaz was identified primarily with Germany and soon thereafter with France and England, but in time came to include Poland, Hungary, Romania, and Russia. Living as a minority under Christian domination, all Ashkenazim were subject to treatment that varied from ignorance and insensitivity at best to repression and persecution.

Medieval Jewish Philosophy

Medieval Jewish philosophy flourished primarily in Muslim lands, where intellectual life had been deeply influenced by Greek philosophy.

Saadia

The earliest notable Jewish philosopher of the medieval period was Saadia (882–942), the *gaon* of an important rabbinic academy in Babylonia. He translated the Hebrew Bible into Arabic and defended rabbinic Judaism against the teachings of the Karaites—a popular movement that held only the Bible to be authoritative and rejected the *Talmud*.

A major theme in all Jewish philosophical writings was the tension between reason and revelation. But Saadia believed there was no such conflict: whenever biblical events or texts appeared to contradict rational principles, they should be understood allegorically rather than literally. In his best-known work, *The Book of Beliefs and Opinions*, he argues that Judaism alone is the divinely revealed truth. Human reason would eventually arrive at the same truth, but revelation is a gift from God that makes it available instantaneously.

Yehuda Ha-Levi

Yehuda Ha-Levi (1075–1141) was born in the Spanish city of Toledo shortly after it fell under Christian control. He is known for his poetry as well as his philosophy. His prose work *The Kuzari* was based on a famous legend concerning the Khazars, a Tatar people who converted to Judaism in the eighth century. In Ha-Levi's version, the decision is made following presentations by spokesmen for all three Abrahamic faiths. He suggests that Islam and Christianity are appropriate religions for naïve nations, but that when those nations mature in their faith, they will be ready for Judaism.

Maimonides

Moses Maimonides, or Moses ben Maimon (1138–1204), is undoubtedly the most famous of all Jewish philosophers. In religious texts he is usually known as 'Rambam': R–M–B–M, the acronym of 'Rabbi Moses ben Maimon'.

Born in Spain, he became a refugee at the age of 13 when the Almohads, a Muslim fundamentalist group from North Africa, took control there. He fled first to Morocco, then to Palestine, which was under the control of the European Crusaders, and finally to Egypt. There he found employment—and the freedom to practise his religion—as physician in the court of the Muslim sultan of Egypt, the famous Salah al-Din (Saladin).

Maimonides' accomplishments were prodigious. He wrote the famous code of Jewish law, *Mishneh Torah*, in Hebrew; several treatises on medicine; a treatise on logic; and a number of **responsa** advising Jewish communities around the world on matters such as false conversion, the concept of resurrection, and the arrival of the messiah.

His most important philosophical treatise, *The Guide of the Perplexed*, was ostensibly a letter of advice to a single student, but in fact was aimed at the many cosmopolitan, acculturated Jews who had begun to question the truth of their own religion.

Maimonides' deep knowledge of Aristotle put him at the forefront of the intellectual life of his day. But the Aristotelian emphasis on analytic observation of physical phenomena and human behaviour was suspect because it suggested a somewhat mechanistic explanation of the universe. Provisionally accepting Aristotle's principles for the purpose of proving the existence of God, Maimonides set out to demonstrate that the world was God's free creation out of nothing, using Greek philosophy to show that biblical religion is true.

Rambam's greatest contribution was his effort to resolve the tension between knowledge and faith, reason and revelation. Like most Jewish philosophers before him, he suggested that the Bible speaks a special metaphoric language; thus passages that attribute human forms and feelings to the divine should be systematically reinterpreted as allegory. He also tried to demonstrate that the commandments were all rational in principle, even if humans could not always understand the reasoning behind them.

The last part of *The Guide of the Perplexed* tackles difficult questions regarding God's providence. How can God's sovereignty be perfect if individual humans have free choice? Maimonides asked the question in a traditional scholastic way: 'How far does God's knowledge extend into our imperfect world?' For the Arabic Aristotelian philosophers, God's knowledge extended only to the level of the species. In the case of sparrows, for instance, God knows the species—he brought it into existence—but his knowledge does not extend to the fate of any individual bird. Whether a particular sparrow lives or dies is not part of God's general providence. Maimonides accepted that description up to point, but suggested that humans represent the unique exception to the rule.

In his view, the capacity for thought means that individual humans also have the benefits of God's special providence. To the extent that they use their rational facilities,

God is able to perceive them as individuals and guide their actions. Prophets are the models for human behaviour because they have perfected their rational and imaginative facilities. And since true morality is truly rational, the more we develop our rational faculties, the more moral we become and the more able we are to be guided by God's special providence. For Maimonides, then, the truly rational person is the truly moral and good person. Reason and revelation are identical processes, and they are both identical with the power by which God creates and preserves the universe.

The idea of Judaism as rational had existed even among the ancient rabbis, but the intellectual structure that Maimonides forged has characterized Jewish self-understanding to this time. Yet it cannot be said that his system was universally accepted by the Jews of his day. Maimonides wrote for an elite steeped in the Aristotelian thought of the medieval Islamic world. The situation was very different in Christian lands such as France, where

Map 3.1   Expulsion and migration of Jews from Europe, c. 1000–1500 CE

• Town from which Jews were expelled

■ Town, at the time under Christian ruler, providing Jews with refuge

◉ Town, at the time under Muslim ruler, providing Jews with refuge

→ Direction and date of major migration of Jews following expulsion

Dates accompanying name of town or region refer to expulsion of Jews

Source: I.R. al Fārūqī and D.E. Sopher, *Historical Atlas of the Religions of the World* (New York: Macmillan, 1974): 148–9.

his writing set off a century of fierce dispute within Judaism—punctuated by book burnings and edicts of ostracism—which historians term the Maimonidean controversy.

On the whole, Maimonides' emphasis on reason has served the Jewish community well in times of peace and prosperity, when intellectual life has been able to flourish. In times of trial and tribulation, however, Jews have been more likely to turn to mysticism for consolation.

The Early Modern Period

It was the toleration of Jews in Islamic Spain that allowed Maimonides' thought to flourish. But that 'Golden Age' came to an end in 1492, when the Christian monarchs Ferdinand and Isabella took control of Granada, the last remaining Muslim stronghold. The Jewish presence might have been helpful to the Christians in a culture shared with Muslims, but once the Reconquista—the campaign to reconquer Spain and take it back into Christendom—was largely complete, the regime wasted no time in expelling the Jews. When Columbus set out for the New World in August 1492, he had to sail from a small port in southern Spain because all the major ports were clogged by Jews leaving their centuries-old home.

Ferdinand and Isabella were not the first western European monarchs to expel Jews. But the effect was particularly devastating for the Iberian Peninsula, where a highly sophisticated Jewish culture was well established. To avoid expulsion, some Jews converted to Christianity while continuing to practise their ancestral faith in secret. Yet even the *conversos* ('New Christians') who abandoned Judaism faced persecution by the Spanish Inquisition. An arm of the Church established in 1478 to root out heresy, it specialized in uncovering Jewish beliefs and observances among the *conversos* or Marranos ('pigs'), as they were sometimes derisively called.

Most of the Jews who left Spain found their way to the Ottoman Turkish Empire. When its ruler heard of the Jewish expulsion, he mocked the Spanish monarchs and suggested that Turkey would take advantage of the 'wealth' they had squandered. Then he encouraged the dispossessed Jews to take shelter in his empire.

Jewish Mysticism

The spiritual crisis caused by the expulsion sparked a new interest in Jewish mysticism. For mystics the most interesting biblical passages are the ones where God manifests himself to his people in a human form or presence known as the *kavod* ('glory of God'). The earliest phase of Jewish mysticism, stretching from the sixth-century BCE prophecies of *Ezekiel* through the twelfth century, is known as Merkabah ('chariot') mysticism. Its central characteristics were (1) an anthropomorphic concept of God and a keen interest in questions such as his size, (2) heavenly ascents, (3) theurgic (magical) spells and motifs, and (4) apocalyptic and revelatory writings.

The central experience in the Merkabah tradition was the ecstatic journey to the heavenly throne room. Although the figure seated on the throne was usually referred to by some angelic name (such as Metatron or Zoharariel), it was understood to represent 'the king in his glory'. The texts, called the *Hekhaloth* ('Palaces') texts, were edited and re-edited throughout the first millennium of Jewish mysticism. In the form in which we have them, they reflect many of the characteristic concerns of the Hasidei Ashkenaz, a pietist group that flourished in fourteenth-century Germany.

The gradual diminution of Merkabah mysticism can probably be traced to the rise of the teaching called **Kabbalah** ('received tradition') in the twelfth century. In Kabbalah the heavenly journey of the Merkabah mystics became a journey into the self. In place of the heavenly palaces, Kabbalah developed a notion of ten *spherot* ('countings' or 'spheres'), which are emanations of God and objects of meditation. By correctly aligning these *spherot* through rituals, pious deeds, and mystical meditation, the Kabbalist can affect the future course of events and so participate in the divine plan for the universe.

The *Zohar*

The principal text of Kabbalah is the *Zohar*. Although it purports to be the work of Rabbi Shimon bar Yohai, a famous second-century rabbi, its real author was probably the thirteenth-century Spanish Kabbalist Moses ben Shemtov of León. The *Zohar* has a special mystical agenda. It describes God as an unlimited divine principle, *En Sof* ('without end'), who produces the universe indirectly through the series of emanations called the *spherot*.

Sometimes the *spherot* recall the heavenly spheres of philosophical discourse; but sometimes they suggest more imaginative configurations of the different powers of God. They can be envisioned as forming a tree of life or even a kind of primeval, cosmic man that may be related to the earlier notion of a gigantic angelic mediator who somehow embodies the name of God. The correct alignments or 'unifications' of the *spherot* will bring about the most harmonious balance of divine forces.

The *Zohar* suggests that this insight is implied in the biblical text. In form, then, the *Zohar* resembles a midrashic exposition of scripture; but instead of explaining the sense of a verse, it explains the secret knowledge that could be derived from it:

> He who desires to understand the wisdom of holy unity, let him contemplate the flame which rises from coal or from a candle, for the flame rises only when it is attached to a material thing. Come and see: in the rising flame there are two lights, one a white shining light, and the other a dark bluish light that holds on directly to the candle. . . . Come and see: there is no stimulus for the kindling of the blue light that it might provide the basis for the white light save through the people of Israel who . . . unite with it from below and continue in their endurance (*Zohar* III, 290a; Caplan and Ribalow 1952: 161–2).

In this passage the blue light symbolizes the aspect of divinity, the *spherah* known as **Malkhut** ('kingship') or **Shekhinah** ('God's indwelling'), which in turn is identified with the spiritual presence of the people Israel. This particular *spherah* has an explicitly feminine identity and is imagined in sexual union with the masculine aspect of God.

The white light conventionally symbolizes the higher *spherah* of *hesed*, God's aspect of 'loving-kindness'. Thus even a simple flame reveals something about the relationship between God and Israel: specifically, that the existence and behaviour of Israel are integrally related to God's loving-kindness in the world. The purpose of such manifestations of God in the world is to ensure the correct flow of divine effulgence (*shefa*), which is generally thought to be balanced when the upper *spherah* (usually Tiferet, 'beauty') is properly related to the *spherah* Malkhut or Shekhinah, the feminine aspect of God that signifies Israel.

The mystic tradition maintains that this balance is affected by human behaviour, ritual and otherwise. Thus sexual intercourse between Kabbalistically sophisticated spouses, when performed with the proper meditations, could help to align the heavenly dimensions of God. But any properly completed ritual action—-like the blessing over wine before a meal—could have a beneficial effect on the universe.

Many of the deepest Jewish minds have seen Kabbalah as irrational and condemned it as undermining the fundamental principle of monotheism. Yet it has appealed to great numbers of people troubled by the suffering that Jews have experienced and the enormous part that evil plays in the world. Kabbalah explains evil as the result of a misalignment of divine effulgence and offers humans the hope that their action will help the divinity progress towards the goal of cosmic perfection:

> The story of Jonah [the name literally means 'aggrieved'] may be construed as an allegory of the course of a man's life in this world. Jonah descends into the ship: this is parallel to man's soul descending to enter into his body in this world. Why is the soul called Jonah? For the reason that she becomes subject to all manner of vexation when once she enters into partnership with the body. Thus, a man in this world is as in a ship crossing the vast ocean and like to be broken, as it is written 'so that the ship was like to be broken' (*Zohar* on *Jonah* 1: 4; Scholem 1949: 103).

In this view, the 'vexation' of the body has a purpose: to motivate the soul to strive towards perfection.

Isaac Luria and Sabbatai Zvi

Until Isaac Luria (1534–72), Kabbalah was largely a private, individual, contemplative discipline. Luria, who lived in the century after the expulsion from Spain, had settled in the Galilee region. It is in Luria's mysticism that the consequences of the expulsion are most clear.

Luria explains the tragedy of Jewish life in terms of a split in the Godhead that occurred in the process of creation, when God had to retreat from the area that was to become the universe, to make room for it. Then, when creation began, sparks of the divine light became contaminated with the gross and evil material of creation. According to Luria, mystics can help God return the divine sparks to their correct place—and thereby assist in the rectification (*tikkun*) of the universe—through meditation and acts of piety, including rituals. The community that Luria founded practised asceticism and observed the rules of Judaism with special intensity, to help God in the enterprise of redemption and hasten the coming of the messiah.

Messianic expectations came to a head in 1666, when Sabbatai Zvi, an adept of Lurianic Kabbalah in Istanbul, was proclaimed the messiah. Influenced by the quickening of millennial expectations among Christians—who associated the year 1666 with '666', the supposed 'number of the beast'—Zvi's followers marched on the sultan in Istanbul. At first, the sultan ignored the rag-tag army; then he had Zvi imprisoned. Finally he offered

Zvi the choice between conversion to Islam and death. Zvi chose the former, and most of his followers gave up in despair.

Those who did not repudiate him understood Zvi's choice as a way of fulfilling the commandments by taking on evil directly and conquering it. This idea, which they called 'the commandment that comes by infraction', gave further impetus to the aspect of mysticism called 'antinomian' ('counter to rule or law'). Some of Zvi's most devoted supporters followed his lead, converting to Islam but continuing to practise their Sephardic traditions in secret, mystical ways. (There are still some members of this sect in modern Turkey, known as the Dönmeh, 'returners'.)

From the Orthodox point of view the Sabbatians resembled Christians: a mystical and antinomian messianic group who took their original teachings from Judaism but who abandoned it over issues involving Jewish law. Roughly a century later, another group of this type, in Podolia (western Ukraine), became outwardly Christian under the influence of a later Sabbatian named Jacob Frank.

Hasidism

The founder of **Hasidism** was Israel ben Eliezer (1698–1759), known as the Baal Shem Tov ('master of the Good Name') or Besht (an acronym). As a youth in eastern Europe he was known for the delight he took in telling stories to children. As an adult he worked at various jobs, wandering from one community to another, meeting ordinary people and making disciples. Everyone who met him was impressed by his humility. The title 'Baal Shem' is thought to refer to his success as a healer who brought about cures through the use of God's name.

The common folk who were his main audience were largely uneducated, and Talmudic scholars had little to offer them. By contrast, the Baal Shem Tov proclaimed the simple and accessible message that the best way of communing with God was through humility, good deeds, prayer (ecstatic and otherwise), and joy. He preached the importance of virtues such as forbearance and mutual help, sought the presence of God in everyday life, and became the model for a Hasidic leader, a *zaddik* ('righteous person').

Like *aggadah*, Hasidic stories teach moral lessons, typically through the most mundane aspects of ordinary life; in one famous Hasidic tale, a student learns about the divine from watching his master tie his shoes. The stories of Hasidic masters often recall the paradoxical wisdom of the Zen *koan*.

The Besht's pietistic Judaism became very popular. The name given to its adherents, Hasidim ('pious ones'), recalls the virtue of *hesed*, the steadfast loyalty that each party to the biblical covenant owes to the other. After the death of the Besht, the leadership passed to his disciple Rabbi Ber of Mezeritz, also known as the Maggid ('preacher'). His successors, who took the title 'Zaddik' or 'Rebbe', were empowered to pass their authority on to their children, and came to be seen as a kind of intermediary between the people and God.

Hasidism changed character when it reached Latvia and Lithuania, where Talmudic training was quite common. For Hasidism to attract adherents there, it needed Talmudic credentials. When a respected Talmudist named Shneur, author of a tract known as *Tanya* ('It Is Taught'), joined the movement, he began synthesizing the scholarly tradition with Hasidic pietism. Zalman's Habad movement was centred in the Belorussian town of Lubavitch, and his followers came to be commonly known as Lubavitcher Hasidim (see p. 125).

❧ PRACTICE

Prayer

Among the commandments given in *Deuteronomy* 6: 4–9 is one that calls on Israel to speak of the Lord's laws morning and evening. The rabbis interpreted this to mean that Jews should offer private prayers when they rise and before they retire. Public prayer follows the order of the temple service, which was performed in the morning, afternoon, and evening. Although these prayers may be private, they are often performed in a synagogue. For convenience a number of the daily prayers can be performed together. Additional prayers are acceptable anytime and in any setting that does not detract from the dignity of the prayer or make it impossible to achieve the proper spiritual state of mind (*kavvanah*).

The Content of Prayer

It is permissible to pray for God's special favour, but only if the advantage sought would not adversely affect anyone else. Thus someone who sees a plume of smoke in the distance is not allowed to pray that the fire not be in his house, because to do so would amount to praying for it to be in someone else's. Prayer for the benefit of others is strongly encouraged.

By tradition, the language of prayer is Hebrew, and many prayers end with the word *amen*: 'so be it'.

Items Worn in Prayer

To help foster the appropriate *kavvanah* for prayer and other ceremonial functions, many Jewish men wear special garments and other articles of dress. The **tallit** or prayer shawl is a rectangular piece of cloth, usually striped in blue and white, that comes in two sizes. A short *tallit* is simply draped around the shoulders like a scarf, while a large one can be drawn over the head when the wearer is concentrating in prayer. Very Orthodox Jews virtually always wear a short 'half *tallit*'—a kind of undershirt with the fringes of the longer garment—under their street clothes. At the other extreme, most Reform Jews have given up the prayer shawl altogether.

The Shema

In Jewish liturgy, the following passage (from Deuteronomy 6: 4–9) *is called the Shema, after its first word in the Hebrew. It is the watchword of Israel's faith, repeated 'morning and night'.*

Hear O Israel, the LORD our God, the LORD is One. You shall love the LORD your God with all your heart and with all your soul and with all your strength. These words which I command you this day are to be kept in your heart. You shall repeat them to your children, speaking of them indoors and outdoors, morning and night. You shall bind them as a sign upon your hand and wear them as signs upon your forehead; you shall write them on the doorposts of your houses and on your gates.

A young man at prayer wearing *tefillin* (AFP/Getty Images).

Many Jewish males also wear a skullcap (*kippah* in Hebrew, **yarmulke** in Yiddish) in observance of the injunction to cover the head when praying. Devout Orthodox Jews wear a *kippah* at all times, even under ordinary hats or baseball caps. Reform Jews may never wear it, even to pray. But today it is not uncommon to wear a skullcap as a public statement of Jewish identity. In the spirit of equality, some Jewish women have begun to wear the *tallit* and *kippah* as well.

Finally, **tefillin** (or **phylacteries**) are two small black boxes that hold passages from scripture. Long leather straps attached to the boxes are used to tie one box to the forehead and the other to the upper arm, facing the heart. Pious Jewish men put on *tefillin* for morning prayers every day except Saturday, the Jewish Sabbath, and other Jewish holy days. Orthodox Jews use them regularly, to concentrate the mind and fulfill the commandment in *Deuteronomy* 6 to bind the words of Torah 'upon the hand and as frontlets between the eyes'. Reform Jews have abandoned them almost entirely, however.

Blessings

Jews take care to bless all the gifts that God provides. Most blessings follow a formula that begins 'Blessed art Thou, O Lord our God, King of the Universe' and continues with words of thanks appropriate to the occasion. Short blessings are said over any item of food before it is consumed, and after a meal a fairly long doxology (series of blessings and praises to God) is recited or—if there are enough people—sung communally.

Jewish prayer is both a comfort and an expression of joy in God's creation. Some Jews feel that God responds to prayer; others do not, but still feel that the regular sequence of prayers throughout the day helps to concentrate attention on the ethical goals of life.

Sabbath Observance

The Sabbath runs from sunset on Friday to sunset on Saturday. On Friday night many Jews attend synagogue services: Orthodox services tend to be short and close to sunset, but most Conservative and Reform congregations now favour a longer service in the evening, after the Sabbath dinner.

Even though it occurs every week, the Sabbath is the most sacred day in the Jewish calendar, consecrated by special prayers. Observant Jews cease all work by sundown on Friday so that they can experience to the fullest the special quiet of a day devoted entirely to song, prayer, and contemplation.

A Devotional Prayer for Women

Women developed special prayers to recite as they prepared for the Sabbath and holidays. Here is one that has traditionally been said on placing a loaf of challah for the Sabbath in the oven on Friday.

Lord of all the world, in your hand is all blessing. I come now to revere your holiness, and I pray you to bestow your blessing on the baked goods. Send an angel to guard the baking, so that all will be well baked, will rise nicely, and will not burn, to honour the holy Sabbath (which you have chosen so that Israel your children may rest thereon) and over which one recites the holy blessing—as you blessed the dough of Sarah and Rebecca our mothers. My Lord God, listen to my voice; you are the God who hears the voices of those who call to you with the whole heart. May you be praised to eternity (Umansky and Ashton 1992: 55).

Jews return home early on Friday afternoon so that they can complete all the preparations for the Sabbath meal—cooking, cleaning, lighting candles—before sundown. Typically, the meal is served on the best dishes and accompanied by special prayers celebrating God's work of creation, psalms, hymns, and Sabbath songs, as well as all the customary blessings of bread and wine. On Saturday, synagogue services continue through the morning, and the afternoon is devoted to learning or quiet contemplation. Later, many Jews return to synagogue for the Havdalah service, which marks the distinction between the Sabbath and the rest of the week. Using wine, a braided candle, and a spice box (symbolizing the sweetness of the Sabbath), the service also highlights the promise of the new week and mentions the prophet Elijah, presumably in the hope that he will appear in the course of the week to mark the arrival of the messianic age.

Dietary Laws

Jewish dietary laws address three subjects: (1) permitted and prohibited foods, (2) food preparation, and (3) the foods that may be combined in the same meal. Meat that is not **kosher** (ritually acceptable) may not be eaten under any circumstances. In addition to pork, all animals that prey on others are excluded, and land animals must have a split hoof and chew the cud; thus beef is a typical Jewish meat dish. In North America chicken has become the classic Sabbath evening meal. Fish are kosher if they have both scales and fins: shark and shellfish are prohibited.

Kosher meat is thoroughly drained, washed, and salted to remove any trace of blood. Animals must be slaughtered in such a way that they die immediately without feeling pain. In practice, this means one quick stroke from a very sharp knife with no nicks in it, and the animal may not be stunned beforehand. The carcass is then inspected for various impairments that would disqualify it.

At Passover, a time of 'spring cleaning' and fresh beginnings, all the equipment used to prepare and serve food must be either new or thoroughly cleaned. In addition, all food eaten during the festival must be free of yeast or leaven.

Many Jews take great care not to combine milk with meat. Observant Jews will never eat a cheeseburger, and if they have eaten meat they will wait a specified period of hours before consuming a dairy product. Many keep two complete sets of dishes, silverware, pots and pans, and cooking utensils for use with milk and with meat. Some also insist on two different dishwashers, sinks, and ovens as well.

Today many younger Jews are simplifying their lives by choosing vegetarianism. Reform Jews vary widely: most do not observe dietary laws at all, some observe them symbolically by abstaining from shellfish and pork only, and a few observe them in full. Conservative Jews usually try to observe the rabbinic ordinances and will eat in a restaurant only if there is fish on the menu. Orthodox Jews avoid any restaurant that does not have a certificate of *kashrut* ('fitness'). The care that individuals devote to observing the dietary laws is taken as an indicator of their piety, and the distinctions between degrees of care can be quite subtle.

Synagogue Service

The chanting in the synagogue reaches a crescendo with the reading of the Torah scrolls, which is traditionally done on Monday, Thursday, the Sabbath (Saturday), and any special holiday. The service is conducted largely by laypersons, although in North America, Reform and Conservative rabbis have taken on the role of a minister, leading parts of the service and usually giving the weekly sermon.

The basic order of service follows the order established at the ancient temple, which consisted of song, musical accompaniment, and animal sacrifice. With the destruction of the temple, the practice of sacrifice came to an end, but other elements of the temple service were transferred to the synagogue and incorporated into individual piety.

In time, services came to include professional singers called 'cantors' who lead the congregation by singing lines from the prayer books—in effect, marking the progress of the service—while members of the congregation pray quietly (but audibly) at their own rate. The Reform movement adopted a more formal European model in which prayers were recited in unison, but some congregations are now returning to the more traditional Jewish style.

In North America most synagogues include a large social hall, a library, and classrooms that reflect their traditional role as houses of study. Many also offer temporary shelter for the homeless, especially in winter.

The Annual Festival Cycle

The Jewish calendar is lunar, not solar. Each month starts with the new moon, which is a time for special prayers, and the fifteenth of the month coincides with the full moon. Since twelve lunar months add up to only 354 days, a leap month is added in the early spring every few years.

Most of the holidays observed today have their roots in the agricultural and pastoral festivals of the ancient Hebrews, but even in biblical times they were associated with specific events in the historical narrative of the people Israel. Eventually rabbinical interpretation gave them new dimensions of symbolic meaning. The fall holidays were associated with contrition in the Bible and this association has been strengthened since they have been celebrated according to the rabbinic liturgy. Rosh Hashanah and Yom Kippur especially have become spiritual holidays of repentance and contemplation.

Rosh Hashanah and Yom Kippur

Rosh Hashanah (New Year) and Yom Kippur (the Day of Atonement) are celebrated at the time of the autumn harvest and were traditionally marked by the blowing of the ram's horn (*shofar*) to metaphorically wake people from moral slumber and remind them to consider carefully the deeds of the past year. The Day of Atonement is the most solemn day of the year and a strict fast day. The liturgy on these days uses the imagery of the shepherd counting his sheep or the commander counting his troops to evoke God's yearly judgment of his people.

Sukkoth

At Sukkoth (the festival of booths or 'tabernacles'), which concludes the autumn harvest, many Jews still build a *sukkah*, a small temporary shelter, outside the house and sleep (or at least eat) in it for some or all of the eight-day festival. This tradition likely originated in the ancient farmers' practice of camping out in the fields to protect the ripening crops. In the biblical interpretation, however, it recalls the Israelites' reliance on temporary shelters during their migration from Egypt under the leadership of Moses.

Hanukkah

Unlike the other festivals, Hanukkah did not originate with the ancient biblical Hebrews. It dates from the mid-second century BCE, when the Maccabean Jews drove their Seleucid oppressors out of Jerusalem. It celebrates the purification and rededication (*hanukkah*) of the temple after its profanation by the Seleucids.

Apparently the rabbis did not consider Hannukah a major part of the Hebrew tradition, but they gave it a spiritual dimension by turning it into a celebration of deliverance through divine intervention: the miraculous eight-day duration of one day's quantity of oil is symbolized by the special nine-branched Hanukkah menorah.

Purim

Purim, another minor festival, usually falls in March. Its narrative comes from the book of *Esther* and recalls the deliverance of the Jews in Persia from destruction by an evil Persian official named Haman. Purim celebrations are reminiscent of the North American Hallowe'en, with costume parties, merrymaking, and gifts of food.

Passover (Pesach)

The major festival of Passover comes in the spring, the season of agricultural rebirth and renewal. It ritually enacts 'spring cleaning' in the home. But its real significance is spiritual, for it commemorates the Exodus—the critical moment when Moses led the Israelites out of slavery in Egypt and towards freedom in the promised land. Like the Sabbath, Passover is closely associated with the home, and is celebrated with a family meal called a **seder**. The Passover liturgy, the **Haggadah** ('narrative'), recounts the story, explains the significance of the symbols associated with it—most notably the unleavened bread eaten in memory of the Israelites' hasty departure, when they had to leave before the bread they were making could be baked—and emphasizes the participation of all Jews, past and present, in that experience of divine deliverance.

A brother and sister read from the Haggadah at the Passover seder (Ira Block/National Geographic/Getty Images).

Shavuot

Shavuot ('weeks'), in late spring, can be traced to the barley harvest, but its observance came to be associated with the eating of dairy foods, perhaps because spring is also calving time. In rabbinic Judaism it celebrates the giving of the Torah on Mount Sinai. Coming 50 days after the first day of Passover, it is also known as Pentecost (from the Greek for 'fiftieth').

The Ninth of Ab

The ninth day of the month of Ab is a fast day observed in late summer in memory of the destruction of the first and second temples. The fast extends from sunset to sunset, and includes the avoidance of all luxurious display. Because leather was a luxury item in rabbinic times, Orthodox Jews today will not wear leather shoes on either the Ninth of Ab or Yom Kippur.

From the Passover Haggadah Liturgy

This is the bread of affliction, the poor bread which our fathers ate in the land of Egypt. Let all who are hungry come and eat; let all who are in need come to our Passover seder. Now we are here; next year may we be in Jerusalem. Now we are slaves; next year may we be free!

Life-Cycle Rituals

Birth

The most characteristic ritual concerned with birth is circumcision: the removal of the male foreskin, usually on the eighth day of life. The procedure is carried out by a ritual circumciser called a *mohel*, hired for the occasion. Today the *mohel* may also be a physician, but there are still many 'paramedical' people who have been thoroughly trained in the rabbinic procedure.

Circumcision usually takes place in the home, in the presence of family members. The liturgy emphasizes the parents' commitment to giving the child a proper Jewish education, to prepare him for learning, doing good deeds, marriage, and a life within the community.

Marriage

Marriage is universally praised in Judaism. Though some great scholars may be forgiven for remaining single, everyone is encouraged to marry and raise children. Sexual relations within the sanctified bounds of marriage are encouraged both for procreation and for the pleasure they bring to the couple; sexual fulfillment is generally included among the responsibilities that a man owes his wife. Thus Jewish marriages are occasions for great happiness in a context of religious seriousness and sanctity. A marriage can be celebrated almost anywhere: in a home, a synagogue, a hotel, a catering establishment. A rabbi is present in a legal capacity, to make sure that the marriage contract is properly prepared and the proper procedures are followed. Orthodox couples will observe Orthodox marriage customs as well as the legal formalities required by the state.

Divorce

Divorce is mentioned several times in the Bible (most explicitly in *Deuteronomy* 24: 1–4) and Judaism accepts it as a legal institution. As in Islam, the grounds for divorce are theoretically quite wide, but in practice divorce was frowned on and hence until recent times was relatively rare.

Even today, Jewish divorce rates in the Americas are lower than those of the non-Jewish majorities. A divorce must be instigated by the husband, though in some cases a court will ask a husband to divorce his wife on her request. On the other hand, no woman can be divorced against her will; mutual consent is required. The divorce decree, called a *get* in Hebrew, is presented to the wife by the husband.

Death

Jews believe that death should be faced resolutely and without illusion. The customs that surround it are intended to help the bereaved come to terms with their loss. The funeral liturgy states that God will resurrect the righteous, that they will shine as the brightness of the firmament, and that they will be bound up in the bonds of life. Even here, however, Judaism is not specific about how those promises will be fulfilled.

The remains are placed in a plain coffin, without embalming, and interred as soon as possible, though no funerals are held on the Sabbath. In some communities, especially in Israel, the remains are simply wrapped in a sheet and are not placed in a coffin.

Community members band together to free the bereaved family from mundane responsibilities so that they can spend the week after the funeral 'sitting Shiva' (from the Hebrew for 'seven'): receiving visitors who wish to pay their respects. Mirrors are covered, while family members dress in sombre colours and either rip their clothing or wear a short black ribbon with a cut in it to symbolize ripping. The children (traditionally the sons) honour the memory of the deceased parent by reciting a special prayer called the Kaddish every day for eleven months.

Religious Education

Traditionally, religious education was restricted to males and began at about the age of five. Young boys began by learning the Hebrew alphabet, and the first subject of study during the school years was the Bible, followed by the medieval Bible commentator Rashi. Advanced education took place in a *yeshivah*, where young men worked with Talmudic masters to understand the difficult text and study various commentaries.

Today, of course, education is no longer restricted to boys. Growing numbers of Jewish parents in North America are now sending their children to private Jewish day schools, which typically devote half the day to Jewish subjects and half to the standard curriculum. In other cases girls and boys attend special classes three or four days a week, after regular school hours, to study Jewish literature, history, customs, and ceremonies, and often Hebrew. In addition, more traditional families ensure that children are taught at least the rudiments of Jewish law. The end of this 'elementary' phase of religious education is marked by the Bar Mitzvah or Bat Mitzvah, which serves as a kind of graduation ceremony.

Pupils at a Hebrew school in Newton, Massachusetts (Michele McDonald/Boston Globe/Landov).

But the Bar Mitzvah need not mark the end of the young person's religious education. Many young people continue their Jewish studies, and Reform Judaism has instituted an additional graduation ceremony known as confirmation, held several years after Bar Mitzvah.

🌿 INTERACTION AND ADAPTATION

Judaism and Modernity

Both the Sabbatian movement and Hasidism may be seen as reform movements. Another early move towards reform may be seen in the work of the seventeenth-century philosopher Baruch Spinoza. Living in the tolerant Netherlands, Spinoza challenged many of the traditional tenets of both Judaism and Christianity.

A more far-reaching desire for reform emerged as Jews came into closer contact with European life. Before the French Revolution, they had lived in various degrees of isolation from their host societies, concentrated in enclaves that in some cases were legally separate entities known as 'ghettos'. After the Revolution, they were swept into the political and cultural unrest sparked by the ideals of *liberté*, *égalité*, and *fraternité*, especially in western Europe.

The Reform Movement

The movement for reform reflected the progressive ideas of the Enlightenment. Until that time many Ashkenazim who left the ghetto converted to Christianity and simply disappeared into the mainstream society. Others, however, wanted to reform Judaism in such a way that Jews could take an active part in modern European life. This movement took its most significant form in Germany around the turn of the nineteenth century.

The first and most influential reformer, Moses Mendelssohn (1729–86), may be seen as the father of modern Orthodoxy as well as Reform Judaism, because his formula for the relationship between Jewish identity and European nationality became the model almost everywhere. Mendelssohn was born in a ghetto in Dessau, Germany, and educated in traditional Judaism. But he also studied German language and philosophy, and he brought those skills to the translation of the Pentateuch and *Psalms*.

In his treatise *Jerusalem*, published in 1783, Mendelssohn argued that the Jews of Germany, instead of resisting German culture, should absorb as much of it as they could. Enjoying the same intellectual freedom as other Germans, he argued, would in no way affect the essence of Judaism, which he described as a religion of reason combined with a revealed law. Mendelssohn separated Jewishness from personhood, suggesting that Jews could be Germans in the same way that Protestants and Catholics were Germans.

Yet a great many rabbis rightly suspected that full participation in German society would pose its own threat to Jewish survival. In 1807 Napoleon called for an assembly of Jewish rabbis and laymen, modelled on the ancient Sanhedrin, to determine whether the Jews of France were truly committed to French citizenship. The delegates' answers suggested that they wanted the privileges of French nationality. But it was not long before the fears of more traditional thinkers were confirmed: as Jews' freedom to participate in secular society increased, so did the number of converts to Christianity. One response to this trend was religious reform.

The Reform movement, which was centred in Germany, sought to minimize the temptations of conversion by creating a new kind of Jewish religious life, more in tune with the times, that came to be known as Reform or (in Britain) Liberal Judaism. They reformed synagogue services to resemble church services, introducing Western musical instruments as well as vernacular prayers and sermons, and cut out numerous repetitions. They even experimented with changing the day of worship from Saturday to Sunday, though most Reform congregations eventually returned to the traditional Sabbath observance. Reformers adopted Western dress, and treated dietary and purity observances as personal or congregational decisions rather than immutable laws.

Taken to North America in the mid-nineteenth century, Reform Judaism continued to modernize, taking on the intellectual assumptions of the time. Inherent in Reform Judaism, especially in North America, is a philosophical preference for ethics over ritual. Emphasizing the moral value of the commandments, it tends to regard traditional practices as non-essential artifacts of a particular historic context, not necessarily valid for all time. Reform groups in the United States today continue to adapt: for instance, they have begun referring to the matriarchs as well as the patriarchs in prayer, and addressing God in feminine as well as masculine terms.

The Reformers' emphasis on the present rather than the past was clear in the principles set out at a meeting of American Reform rabbis in Pittsburgh in 1885:

- The Bible reflects primitive ideas of its own age, clothing conceptions of divine Providence in miraculous narratives.
- The laws regulating diet, priestly purity, and dress do not conduce to holiness and obstruct modern spiritual elevation.
- We are no longer a nation but a spiritual community and therefore expect no return to Palestine.

Conservative Judaism

A more conservative reform movement called *Jüdische Wissenschaft* ('science of Judaism') was founded in Germany in 1819 by Leopold Zunz and enlisted scholars such as Zecharias Frankel. Instead of actively promoting change, these men examined traditional practices to see if their retention could be justified. Frankel, for instance, argued that there were legal and aesthetic grounds for retaining some of the ancient rituals. These scholars were in the forefront of the movement that came to be known in North America as Conservative Judaism.

Conservative Judaism takes an intermediate position between Reform and Orthodoxy. If a particular custom can be shown to be relatively recent, there is no reason it can't be changed or even eliminated. Thus the black caftans worn by Hasidic Jews are not obligatory because they did not become customary until the fifteenth century or later. But the order of prayers goes back at least as far as the first-century temple service and therefore is firmly established by Jewish law. Some aspects of the tradition have been modified in response to changing social realities. Thus most Conservative congregations in North America now seat men and women together, allow women to participate in the services as freely as men, and train women to lead worship as cantors and rabbis (as Reform congregations have been doing for decades).

Orthodox Judaism

Orthodox Judaism emphasizes the preservation of Jewish tradition. Although many Orthodox Jews in North America have adopted modern dress, they still conduct services in Hebrew, observe the Sabbath obligations based on the ancient rules, insist on kosher meals, and reserve the leadership roles in worship and ritual exclusively for males.

At the same time the Orthodox have to live in the modern world, and they have tried to find a modern idiom for their traditions. Among the most effective spokespersons for this perspective in the nineteenth century was Rabbi Samson Raphael Hirsch. Instead of merely condemning the reformers, he outlined a positive program for modern Orthodoxy. Essentially he gave credence to the modern world as well as the traditional sources of Jewish identity, calling for both Torah (in the sense of 'Jewish religious truth') and *Derekh Eretz* (literally 'the way of the land'; in this context, European life).

The Hasidim have evolved to become some of the strictest Orthodox Jews. The Lubavitcher Hasidim have moved towards messianism since their last leader, Rabbi Menachem Schneerson, died in 1994 without an heir. Many Lubavitchers have declared Rabbi Schneerson to be the messiah and are expecting his return. These and other Hasidic sects have often been in sharp competition both with one another and with the Orthodox mainstream, which remains hostile to much of the Hasidic program.

Twentieth-Century Theology

Historically, periods of acculturation and assimilation have tended to stimulate Jewish theological and philosophical inquiry. In the twentieth century, as in the heyday of Arab–Jewish cooperation in Muslim Spain, Judaism entered a period of rich theological expression.

The life of Franz Rosenzweig (1886–1929) is a good example. His family—cultured, affluent, and assimilated, without any deep religious commitments—wanted him to become a physician. Instead he chose philosophy, and eventually decided that he could be the kind of liberal Christian described by the philosopher G.W.F. Hegel. But his path took a new direction following a conversation with a relative who had already converted. He decided that if he were going to convert, he should do so 'not as a pagan but a Jew'. Thus he set out to deepen his understanding of Judaism. After attending an Orthodox Yom Kippur service in Berlin, he chose Judaism over Christianity because Jews were already with 'the Father' and therefore had no need to apply to 'the Son' for mediation.

Drafted into the German army in the First World War, he began writing his first book, *The Star of Redemption*, on postcards to his mother. Arguing that both Judaism and Christianity are true in the subjective sense, he maintains that each has a particular role to play in the world: by constantly projecting the purposes of God into the world, the politically powerful Christian countries are helping to convert and transform it, while Jews are politically powerless but in eternal communication with God through the eternally repeated rituals of Judaism and the Jewish law. Like many Europeans of his time, Rosenzweig left Islam out of the equation; nor did he ever systematically address the great

Asian faiths. For Rosenzweig, the rules governing Jewish life helped to insulate Judaism and prevent the dilution of its spiritual power. Christianity benefits from its engagement with world, but also risks diminution and dilution.

Tragically, Rosenzweig developed amyotrophic lateral sclerosis (Lou Gehrig's disease) in the early 1920s and for several years before his death was able to communicate only through his wife. His personal courage and his understanding of the value of traditional Judaism from the perspective of modern liberal, secular thought attracted a following across the spectrum of modern Judaism. However, his concept of Judaism as standing outside of history can no longer be sustained in a literal sense: since the Holocaust and the formation of the modern state of Israel, Jews have fully re-entered history.

Another thinker whose theological work has been significant to Judaism and to religious people everywhere is Martin Buber (1878–1965). A friend of Rosenzweig, Buber was a student of two important German intellectuals—Wilhelm Dilthey and Georg Simmel—but he also felt the influence of Hasidism through his family (his grandfather, Solomon Buber, was a famous scholar of *midrash*). Buber published his most famous work, *I and Thou*, in 1923. As much a poem as a treatise, this work suggests that all human beings have two ways of relating to the world. Most of our interactions are functional, aimed at manipulation and control; these Buber describes as 'I–It experiences'. But there are also moments of epiphany, or 'I–Thou experiences', in which the divine presence can be felt and true dialogue with God is possible.

In the 1930s, a former Conservative rabbi named Mordecai Kaplan founded a movement known as Reconstructionism. Kaplan attempted to define Judaism as a religious civilization or (in today's terms) a religious culture. He felt that belief in God was important to the people's self-understanding but was not essential to the definition of the group, and translated the terms 'God' and 'Lord' with phrases such as 'The Eternal'.

For many years Reconstructionism was a kind of ideological position that attracted followers across the spectrum of North American Judaism. It became a separate entity only in the 1960s, with the founding of a Reconstructionist rabbinical seminary in Philadelphia. Today there are several Reconstructionist synagogues in North America, but the movement still represents only a very small segment of the community. Ideologically, many Jews who think of themselves as an ethnic group espouse Reconstructionist ideals but remain within a Reform or Conservative synagogue.

Zionism

It was in the mid-1800s, when nationalism was becoming a powerful force in Europe, that Jews first began to explore the possibility of returning to their ancient homeland in the Near East. The idea of return was hardly new: medieval Jewish literature frequently evoked the sense of absence from the land of Israel; Yehuda Ha-Levi wrote poetically of his sadness to be in the West (Spain) when his heart was in the East; and the words of the Passover seder, 'next year in Jerusalem', attest to an ongoing spiritual longing for return. But the nineteenth century introduced several other currents that flowed together to give modern Zionism its impetus.

Among those currents was the desire to revive the Hebrew language. In the age of emerging nation-states, the importance of a common language was widely recognized.

Praying at the Western Wall in Jerusalem. The lower part of the wall dates to Roman times, when it stood as the enclosure of the temple precincts (Andrea Pistoleis/Ponkawonka.com).

Hebrew, which was still widely used in prayer but otherwise rarely spoken, was the only language that all Jews had in common.

Another current was the desire for a haven from persecution. The principal founder of the Zionist movement was Theodor Herzl (1860–1904), a Viennese journalist who became committed to the goal of Jewish statehood in response to the Dreyfus Affair: the French political scandal in which a Jewish army officer convicted of treason in 1894 was later found to have been framed. Although Herzl himself had grown up in an assimilated home, he came to believe that anti-Semitism was so entrenched in European society that the only way for Jews to lead a normal existence would be to live as a people in their own political state (or something approximating it). His Zionist ambitions were entirely secular and nationalistic; for a time he even considered locating a Jewish national homeland somewhere other than in the land of biblical Israel.

Although the Zionist movement coalesced around Herzl's leadership, some intellectuals suggested that a Jewish homeland could represent more than a haven from persecution. The Russian Asher Ginsberg (1856–1927), who wrote under the name Ahad Ha-'Am ('one of the people'), thought that a national homeland should be a spiritual centre for the development of the world and the Jewish people. For him, Jewish nationalism meant pride in the moral virtues that Jews had always valued.

Some Orthodox Jews believed that in the absence of the messiah, the Jews' return to Zion could not be legitimate. They would not work for the creation of a modern state, and after Israel came into being in 1948, they refused to recognize it. Many settled in Israel anyway, and accept the subsidies it provides, but continue to live as if the state did not exist.

Of course there are also Orthodox Jewish Zionists who fully support the Jewish state. This movement has accounted for most of the immigration to Israel from North America in recent decades, and religiously motivated Zionists are represented by several political parties in contemporary Israel. But religion is by no means essential to the notion of Jewish peoplehood. Many Jews without any religious commitments still feel ethnically or nationally attached to Israel and consider its existence important to their Jewish identity.

Furthermore, although Reform Jews initially felt estranged from or inimical to Zionism because they were completely at home in Europe or North America, contemporary Reform Judaism came to accept many Zionist premises. Many North American Jews developed strong feelings for Israel at the time of the Six-Day War in 1967, perceiving it to be surrounded by hostile nations, and those feelings were strengthened in 1973, when the country was attacked on Yom Kippur, the holiest day of the Jewish calendar. Pro-Israel sentiment was somewhat weakened, however, following Israel's invasion of Lebanon in 1982, and opinion regarding its current policies in the West Bank and Gaza is sharply divided. Nevertheless, North American Jewish support for the state of Israel remains very strong.

Judaism in the Americas

Jews from different European countries have different understandings of their Jewish identities. The first wave of Jewish immigration to the Americas—mainly to South America, the Caribbean, and the United States—came from Spain and Portugal in the eighteenth century. German Jewish immigration began in the 1840s after the failure of liberal political reforms in Germany. It brought a number of Reform-influenced Jews who considered themselves Germans but happened to be Jewish in religion. They settled mostly in the United States, often in the same areas as other German immigrants, especially in the midwest. However, the Jewish immigrants tended to be peddlers and shopkeepers rather than farmers.

It was this wave of immigrants that produced the great German Jewish mercantile families of the late nineteenth century—families such as the Bambergers (who owned the Macy's department store, among others, and helped to found the Institute for Advanced Study at Princeton) and the Guggenheims (American mining entrepreneurs who founded the Guggenheim Museum and the Guggenheim Fellowship). They brought with them many German customs, including what we know as the Christmas tree (*Tannenbaum*, 'fir tree'—a term with no religious connotation in German). Such customs were associated with nationality rather than religion in Germany because they were based on ancient pre-Christian traditions.

The next and largest wave of Jewish immigration to America arrived from eastern Europe, some from the *shtetlach* (or *shtetls*—Yiddish for 'little towns') and some from the Jewish quarters of the major cities. The 3 million Jews living in areas controlled by Russia had not benefited from the social changes that allowed for Jewish liberation in western Europe and the Americas. Jews did make some political and economic gains under the relatively benign rule of Czar Alexander II, but his successor, Alexander III, openly encouraged pogroms (massacres) and deportations of Jews.

His policies were directly responsible for the enormous wave of Jewish immigrants who landed mostly on the eastern coasts of Canada and the United States. At first most of the new arrivals went to New York. The German Jews donated massively to help the indigent *Ostjuden* ('eastern Jews'), but were not particularly friendly towards them. Not literate in either German or English, the eastern European immigrants found jobs in the sweatshops of Manhattan's Lower East Side.

In Russia each ethnic group was treated as a separate nationality, and until very recently the passports of Russian Jews continued to identify their nationality as 'Jewish'. Thus Jews arriving from eastern Europe have tended to think of themselves as Jewish by nationality as well as religion. Ironically, some thought they were sacrificing their religion in crossing the Atlantic, because Orthodox rabbis in Europe described North America as a land of non-kosher iniquity.

In 1922, new immigration quotas stopped the flow of Jewish immigration to the United States, but Jews continued to arrive in Canada, Cuba, Mexico, and South America. In Canada, they settled mainly in urban Quebec and Ontario. French-speaking Jews from North Africa and the French possessions understandably favoured the Montreal area. Some English-speakers also settled there, but others headed for Ontario and the West (especially Winnipeg).

The doors of the United States remained largely shut to Jews fleeing from Nazi oppression in the 1930s, and Canada too refused most Jewish refugees during the Second World War. Most of the Jews who arrived in North America after 1945 were concentration-camp survivors.

The Holocaust

No event since the destruction of the second temple and the expulsion from Spain has so affected the Jewish people as the Holocaust. By the time Adolf Hitler's National Socialist ('Nazi') party came to power in 1933, most German Jews were fully assimilated members of German society. Yet Hitler was able to convince many Germans that their country's economic woes should be blamed not on the worldwide depression, or on government policy, or on the punishing reparations that it was required to pay after the First World War, but on their Jewish neighbours.

The Nazis, fearing that the Jewish presence among them would sully their 'racial' superiority, stripped Jews of German nationality. They looted Jewish stores and prevented Jews from practising their livelihoods. They sent Jews to concentration camps to work as slaves. Finally, they erected gas chambers and crematoria to kill the Jews, a program the Nazis called the 'Final Solution' to the 'Jewish problem'. A major factor in the success of Hitler's campaign, of course, was European Christianity's long tradition of vilifying the Jews as 'Christ killers'. Those wishing to foment hatred against the Jews for their own purposes could find ample ammunition in the New Testament, whose editors painted Jews in an extremely bad light for their own theological reasons.

It can be argued that Hitler's war against the Jews was the most successful of all his campaigns. For whatever reasons, the Allies did not strike back strongly enough even when they clearly understood what he was doing. There were no Allied raids on the railway tracks that took tens of thousands of Jews to their deaths every day. Worse still, in eastern Europe, especially in Poland, Hitler found some willing accomplices.

Yet many individual Christians risked their own lives to hide Jews or help them escape, and those who were found out often suffered the same fate as the Jews they had tried to help. The 6 million Jews who died in the Second World War accounted for as much as one-third of the total death toll in Europe. The Holocaust killed roughly a third of all the world's Jews in the space of a few years.

Jews shuddered when the enormity of the crime became known. They had always assumed that, even though they might sin, the eternity of the people Israel was a sign of God's continuing favour. That God could have allowed the wholesale killing of so many innocent, non-combatant men, women, and children raised questions that may never be satisfactorily answered. For most Jews the only possible response is to continue interpreting historical events as the unfolding of God's design, in which their people have a special role.

Among those who have tried to formulate answers is the world-famous author Elie Wiesel. Wiesel was a traditional *yeshivah* student in Romania when the Nazis arrived. His first novel, *Night*, chronicles the murder of his family and his own survival of the extermination camps. Since then he has written movingly of the predicament of modern Jews. The faith he has articulated is ambivalent and often tentative, but in combining doubt with a solid affirmation of Jewish and human values, he seems to speak to the complex feelings that Jews and gentiles alike experience when they contemplate the horrors of the modern world.

'Jews must continue to live so as not to grant to Hitler a posthumous victory,' wrote Emil Fackenheim, a rabbi and professor who escaped Germany in 1939 and worked in Canada for more than 40 years before moving to Israel in 1984. In this regard Fackenheim spoke for many Jews who believe that Hitler's attempt to exterminate an entire people must be remembered and must never be repeated, anywhere in the world. The Holocaust has made it unacceptable for Jews to accept martyrdom (considered honourable since the Hellenistic era), no matter how good the cause. To the traditional 613 commandments spoken by God to the Jewish people, Fackenheim proposed that the Holocaust had added a 614th: to deny Hitler a posthumous victory and ensure the survival of the people Israel, Jews are commanded to live as Jews in the modern world.

The State of Israel

For most Jews, the founding of the state of Israel is closely associated with the Holocaust. In no sense did Israel compensate for the lives that were lost, but it did represent a place in the world where Jews might at last be safe. After 1945, the Zionist campaign for a haven from persecution attracted support not just from Jews but from non-Jewish leaders around the world. The United Nations voted to partition Palestine and create two states, one Jewish and one Arab. The creation of Israel did a great deal to resolve the problem of Jewish refugees in Europe. But the proposed Arab state does not yet exist, and peace has not come to the area.

For many years the neighbouring Arab states of Egypt, Jordan, Syria, and Lebanon vied with each other as well as with Israel for control of the region. Unable to defeat Israel militarily, they eventually ceded to Palestinians—though not to Israelis—the right to control their own territory. But the Palestinians have not been able to agree on a policy to deal with Israel's existence or with its occupation of lands gained in either the 1948 or the 1967 war. Many seem willing to negotiate a state of Palestine that would live in peace with the neighbouring state of Israel. Others refuse to negotiate and have taken up arms against

Israeli civilians. Israel has imposed strenuous controls on the civilian population, to try to prevent attacks on its citizens. Nearly six decades after its creation, Israel still has not managed to resolve some problems fundamental to accommodating an emerging Palestinian nationality. The question of control over the old city of Jerusalem, for example, has been a constant and so far insoluble difficulty.

One can hope that peace negotiations will eventually resume, after all hostilities have proved pointless. But it does not lie in the hands of Israel alone to bring this about.

North America

American culture has long assumed that assimilation should be the goal of every immigrant, and that all ethnic groups should blend together in one great 'melting pot'. But the range of ethnicities that the American pot has succeeded in blending is actually quite small, consisting mainly of a few northern European groups (English, Irish, Scottish, Scandinavian). Other European groups have remained largely separate, as have 'visible minorities' such as Blacks and Asians.

One could argue that Jews have much to gain by staying out of the melting pot. Jewish leaders have traditionally railed against intermarriage. And for two generations, most American Jews did marry within their own community. Yet since 1985 roughly 55 per cent of all American Jews have married non-Jewish partners. If enough non-Jewish spouses were to convert, that might help to stabilize the Jewish population. Still, some predict that within a few generations the Jewish community will consist only of those most resistant to intermarriage: the Orthodox.

The situation in Canada is different. Like the US, Canada is a country built on immigration, but Canadians tend to describe their society as a mosaic rather than a melting pot. From its beginnings Canada has contained at least two distinct cultural communities, French and English, and the nation was founded on the idea that the different communities have the right to live their own lives. Even before 'multiculturalism'—a type of cultural pluralism—became official policy in the 1970s, new Canadians of other ethnic backgrounds may have experienced somewhat less pressure to assimilate than their counterparts in the US. The percentage of Jews who intermarry in Canada is less than half the percentage in the United States.

CONTEMPORARY ISSUES

Perhaps the most crucial distinction between the different Jewish religious groups today is the extent to which each relies on classical Jewish values to find solutions to modern problems. If the Torah really is eternally relevant and divinely inspired, it makes sense that Jews would turn to it for guidance on matters such as the relations between Israel and the Palestinians. This helps to explain why the people, both in Israel and in North America, who are most committed to a life of strict Jewish religious observance also oppose any compromise with the Palestinians: the biblical model of Jewish sovereignty in the promised land is the ideal they aspire to. More liberal Jews who take a positive view of the modern world (and in some cases believe ancient religious texts to be unreliable as guides to modern problems) are more likely to favour compromise with the Palestinians. Of course, there are notable exceptions to this pattern on both sides of the spectrum.

On rare occasions the more fundamentalist Jewish world-view has inspired violence. An example was the 1994 massacre of 29 Muslims worshipping in the Cave of the Patriarchs in Hebron (a site holy to both Jews and Muslims) perpetrated by Baruch Goldstein, an American-born Orthodox Jewish physician who had immigrated to Israel. In general, though, religious violence has been much less common in Judaism than in many other religions. Today the traditional Jewish values of peace and respect for human life (based on the principle that all human beings are created in the image of God) continue to make religiously inspired violence unacceptable even in the most strictly observant communities. Rabbis of all denominations condemned Goldstein and speak out loudly against terrorism of any kind.

Israel and North America Today

The modern world, like the Hellenistic one, offers many ways of living a Jewish life. Different denominations provide a range of options broad enough to accommodate most lifestyles within Judaism.

Jews in North America, as in Israel, are becoming more and more involved in political life. Even though Orthodox Jews usually tend to lean to the right, surveys have found that Jews in general are more likely than the population at large to vote for parties on the left or centre-left.

At the same time, Judaism itself means different things in North America and Israel. North American Jews in general agree that Jews should not only participate fully in the life of their society, but should also support its cultural pluralism. Of course there are exceptions to this rule, notably in the Orthodox and Hasidic communities. There is also a small but growing minority who call themselves *haredim* ('tremblers', after a verse in *Isaiah* describing the true worshippers of God); they scorn the modern world and are selective in their contact with it. On the whole, though, North American Jews accept the risks that come with assimilation because of the undeniable benefits of Western democratic life. North American Jews' identity is thus a blend of ethnicity and religion.

A different concept of Judaism has emerged in Israel. For most Israeli Jews (again excepting the *haredim*, who make up a larger proportion of the population there and have been gaining political power), Judaism is a nationality. The majority observe the Sabbath because it is the national day of rest; the Jewish holidays, because they are national holidays. But most do not observe Sabbath regulations in the traditional sense. On a sunny Saturday, the beaches of Tel Aviv are just as busy as the beaches of Long Island in New York. And although most Israelis are willing to give the Orthodox parties some say in the governance of the state, they refuse to live their lives by Orthodox standards.

So there is another kind of acculturation underway in Israel. Even though the state is predominantly Jewish, most Israelis are in the process of formulating an entirely new way to live Jewishly. This transformation is no less sweeping than the one that is taking place in North America. How well these different Jewish communities understand each other is not clear. Israelis see American Jewry as threatened by street violence and anti-Semitism, whereas North American Jews see threats in Israel's ethnic polarization and confrontation with the Palestinians.

Despite moves towards peace with neighbouring Arab states, conflict between Jews and Arabs living under Israeli jurisdiction continues. The peace process with the Palestine Liberation Organization has made remarkable progress towards recognizing the rights of both communities, but the other major Palestinian organization, Hamas (the Islamic Resistance Movement), remains committed to the destruction of the state of Israel. In the end, even if a formal peace agreement could be reached, actual peace would require mutual trust between two peoples who have been bitter adversaries for a century. Thus the prognosis for the future is clouded.

Hope for the Future: A Jewish Wedding

An optimistic vision of the future can be seen at any wedding where both the bride and the groom are Jewish, whether by birth or by conversion. Whatever the setting—home or synagogue, hotel or catering hall—what weddings have in common is the *huppah*: a tent-like canopy under which the marriage ceremony is conducted. Often the bride and groom are escorted to the *huppah* by their parents, but the bride may also enter in a procession reminiscent of a standard church wedding. In the Orthodox ritual she will circle the groom seven times before the ceremony begins with the bride and groom drinking from a consecrated cup of wine.

The wedding represents a legal agreement in which the husband and wife pledge mutual support and aid. The groom declares, 'Be consecrated unto me as my wife according to the laws and traditions of Moses and Israel.' These simple words complete his legal obligation. Today the bride often makes a similar declaration: 'In accepting the wedding ring, I pledge you all my love and devotion, and I take upon myself the fulfillment of all the duties incumbent upon a Jewish wife.' Then the groom presents the bride with a gift (in

A bride and groom stand under the *huppah* (David Furst/AFP/Getty Images).

the West, usually a ring) to formalize the legal transaction; in liberal ceremonies, the two will exchange rings.

After the legal formalities are concluded, seven blessings are recited over a second cup of wine. The blessings recall the creation and the joy that ancient Judah took in the celebration of a marriage. In fulfillment of the last blessing, which prays for the sound of joy in Judah and Israel, the wedding usually concludes with an enormous feast.

In many ways the Jewish wedding ceremony encapsulates the community's hopes for survival. In consecrating the union of two young Jewish lives, the community thanks God for creation and sustenance, remembers its past, pledges its responsibilities publicly, and prays for its continuation. These themes are particularly poignant today, in the face of an uncertain future.

In ancient times the prophet Hosea likened the covenant between Israel and its God to a wedding. Just as the wedding, in uniting two people, commits them to play their part in the life of their community, so the covenant between God and Israel continues to commit all Jews to play their part in the fulfillment of the Jewish people's special purpose in the world.

Sacred Texts Table

Religion	Text	Composition/ Compilation	Compilation/ Revision	Use
Judaism	Hebrew Bible (or *Tanakh*): 24 books organized in three sections: Teaching or Law (Torah), the Prophets (Hebrew *Nevi'im*), and the sacred Writings (Hebrew *Ketuvim*).	Written in the first millennium BCE.	Canon fixed sometime between 200 BCE and 100 CE.	Doctrinal, inspirational, educational, liturgical.
	Mishnah	Teachings of rabbis in the land of Israel between 100 BCE and 220 CE.	Compiled by Rabbi Judah the Prince c. 220 CE.	One of the foundations of Jewish law; the object of ongoing study.
	Babylonian Talmud	Teachings of rabbis in the land of Israel and in Babylonia between 100 BCE and 500 CE.	Compiled in Babylonia in 6th century CE.	Another foundation of the law; also the object of ongoing study.
	Mishneh Torah	Codification of legal decisions based on legal texts from the previous 1000 years.	Compiled by Maimonides c. 1180 CE.	Legal interpretation, study.
	Zohar	Mystical teachings of various rabbis.	Composed/edited in the 13th century.	Study, inspiration, contemplation.

Sites

Mount Sinai The place where *Exodus* 20–31 says the children of Israel received the Ten Commandments and the subsequent Book of the Covenant. The mountain called Mount Sinai today may or may not be the same one.

Jerusalem A fortress of the Jebusites that was conquered by David around the year 1000 BCE (2 *Samuel* 5: 5–10); also known as 'The City of David'.

Samaria The capital city of the Northern Kingdom.

Alexandria A city in Egypt, founded by Alexander the Great, that became the home of an important Greek-speaking Jewish community.

Masada The mountain fortress where Jewish Zealots made their last stand against the Romans in 73 CE, three years after the destruction of the temple in Jerusalem.

Okop, Podolia A small village in the Polish Russian pale of settlement where the founder of the Hasidic movement, Israel ben Eliezer, the Baal Shem Tov, was born in 1698.

Cincinnati, Ohio The capital of the Reform movement in the United States and the location of the principal Reform seminary.

New York City The home of the largest Jewish population in the Americas and headquarters of the (Conservative) Jewish Theological Seminary.

Study Questions

1. Historians now think that many elements of the literature and law attributed to Moses in fact date from later times. What are some examples?
2. The geographic centre of Jewish intellectual life has been forced to shift more than once over the millennia. Where did that centre move to after the Babylonian conquest? The expulsion of Jews from Spain? The annihilation of Germany's Jews by the Nazis?
3. Which Jewish religious holidays originated in ancient agricultural festivals? What historical and symbolic associations came to be attached to each of them?
4. How did Jewish immigrants to the US after 1900 differ from those who arrived before 1870?
5. Several of the elements that gave impetus to the Zionist movement were already in place before the time of Theodor Herzl. What were they?

6. What is Judaism's perspective on the status of non-Jews? What are its teachings regarding their ethical and religious obligations?
7. Is it still legitimate to categorize all branches and movements of modern Judaism as 'religion'? What elements besides religion make up modern Jewish identity?
8. What are the most important contributions that Judaism has made to Western civilization?

Glossary

aggadah Anecdotal or narrative material in the *Talmud*; see also **halakhah**.

apocalypse From the Greek for 'unveiling' (the Latin equivalent is 'revelation'); the final battle between the forces of darkness and light expected at the end of time. Apocalyptic literature flourished in the Hellenistic era.

Ashkenazim Jews of northern and eastern Europe; see also **Sephardim**.

Bar Mitzvah 'Son of the commandments'; the title given to a thirteen-year-old boy when he is initiated into adult ritual responsibilities; some branches of Judaism also celebrate a Bat Mitzvah for girls.

cantor The liturgical specialist who leads the musical chants in synagogue services.

Diaspora 'Dispersal', the Jewish world outside the land of ancient Israel; it began with the Babylonian Exile, from which not all Jews returned.

Documentary Hypothesis The theory (1894) that the Pentateuch was not written by Moses but was compiled from multiple sources over a long period of time.

Exile The deportation of Jewish leaders from Jerusalem to Mesopotamia by the conquering Babylonians in 586 BCE; disrupting local Israelite political, ritual, and agricultural institutions, it marked the transition from Israelite religion to Judaism.

Exodus The migration of Hebrews from Egypt under the leadership of Moses, later understood to mark the birth of the Israelite nation.

gaon Title of a senior rabbinical authority in Mesopotamia under Persian and Muslim rule.

Gemarah The body of Aramaic commentary attached to the Hebrew text of the *Mishnah*; together the *Mishnah* and *Gemarah* make up the *Talmud* (both the *Jerusalem Talmud* and the *Babylonian Talmud*).

Haggadah The liturgy for the ritual Passover supper.

halakhah Legal material in the *Talmud*; see also **aggadah**.

Hasidim 'Pious ones'; the mystically inclined followers of the Baal Shem Tov in eighteenth-century Poland and their descendants.

Holocaust 'Burnt offering' or 'burnt sacrifice'; one of the ancient sacrifices mandated in the Hebrew Bible; term now applied to the persecution and murder of 6 million European Jews by the Nazis before and during the Second World War (1939–45).

Kabbalah The medieval Jewish mystical tradition; its central text is a commentary on scripture called the *Zohar*.

kippah 'Dome' or 'cap'; the Hebrew word for skullcap or *yarmulke*.

kosher Term for food that is ritually acceptable, indicating that all rabbinic regulations regarding animal slaughter, etc., have been observed in its preparation.

logos 'Word'; a kind of divine intelligence thought to mediate between God and humanity and carry out God's intentions on earth.

Masada The fortress whose Jewish defenders are said to have committed suicide rather than surrender to Rome.

menorah The seven-branched candlestick, a Jewish symbol since ancient times; a nine-branched menorah is used at Hanukkah.

midrash Commentary on scripture.

minyan The quorum of ten required for a prayer service in the synagogue.

Mishnah The Hebrew summary of the oral law—inherited from the Pharisees and ascribed to Moses—arranged by topic; edited by Rabbi Judah ha-Nasi before 220 CE, it has an authority paralleling that of the written Torah.

Mishneh Torah A topically arranged code of Jewish law written in the twelfth century by Moses Maimonides.

mitzvah A commandment; in the Roman era, the rabbis identified exactly 613 specific commandments (*mitzvoth*) in the Torah.

Passover The major spring festival of agricultural rebirth and renewal, given a historical dimension by association with the hasty departure of the Israelites from Egypt under Moses' leadership.

patriarchs and matriarchs Ancestors of the Israelite nation in the Hebrew Bible's narratives of origins; 'patriarch' was also a title given to the head of the Jewish community in early rabbinic times.

Pentateuch The first five books of the Hebrew Bible, traditionally ascribed to Moses but now regarded as the product of several centuries of later literary activity.

rabbi A teacher, in Roman times an expert on the interpretation of Torah; since priestly sacrifices ceased with the destruction of the temple, the rabbi has been the scholarly and spiritual leader of a Jewish congregation.

rabbinic movement The legal teachers and leaders, initially Pharisees, who became the dominant voices in Judaism after the destruction of the temple and eventually became the rabbis as we know them.

responsa **literature** From the Latin for 'answers'; accumulated correspondence by medieval and recent rabbinical authorities, consisting of rulings on issues of legal interpretation; also known as *Teshuvot*.

Rosh Hashanah The new year festival, usually celebrated in September.

Sabbath The seventh day of the week, observed since ancient times as a day of rest from ordinary activity.

seder 'Order'; the term used for the ritual Passover supper.

Sefer Torah 'Book of the law'; a special copy of the first five books of Moses, hand-lettered on parchment scrolls for use in the synagogue.

Sephardim The Jews of the premodern Mediterranean and Middle East; see also **Ashkenazim**.

Septuagint The Greek translation of the Hebrew scriptures, produced in Alexandria in Hellenistic times.

Shekhinah The divine presence or 'in-dwelling', often described in visionary terms.

Sukkoth The festival of 'Tabernacles', named for the temporary shelters used by farmers in autumn to protect their ripening crops and given a historical interpretation recalling the Exodus migration.

synagogue From the Greek meaning 'assembly' or 'gathering': the local place of congregational worship, which became central to Judaism after the destruction of the Jerusalem temple.

tallit A shawl worn for prayer, usually white with black or blue stripes and with fringes at the corners.

Tanakh An acronym referring to the entire Hebrew Bible: Torah (or law), Nevi'im (or prophets), and Ketuvim (or sacred writings).

Tannaim The rabbinic authorities whose opinions are recorded in the *Mishnah*.

tefillin Small black leather boxes, also termed phylacteries, containing words of scripture, tied to the forehead and forearm by leather thongs.

Torah A word meaning 'teaching' or 'instruction'; applied most specifically to the Law of Moses (the Pentateuch) but may also refer to the entire scripture, including commentaries.

yarmulke The Yiddish word for the **kippah** or skullcap.

yeshivah A traditional school for the study of the scriptures and Jewish law.

Yiddish The language spoken by many central and eastern European Jews in recent centuries; though it is written in Hebrew characters and contains some words derived from Hebrew, its structure and vocabulary are essentially German.

Yom Kippur The day of atonement, ten days after Rosh Hashanah; the day for the most solemn reflection and self-examination.

zaddik 'Righteous person', a title conveying the Hasidic ideal for a teacher or spiritual leader.

Zion In biblical times, the hill in Jerusalem where the temple stood as God's dwelling place; by extension, the land of the Israelites as the place of God's favour; in modern times, the goal of Jewish migration and nation-state settlement.

Further Reading

Abrahams, Israel, ed. 1927. *The Legacy of Israel*. Oxford: Clarendon Press. Chapters on Jewish contributions in various fields of Western culture.

Agus, Jacob B. 1959. *The Evolution of Jewish Thought: From the Time of the Patriarchs to the Opening of the Modern Era*. London: Abelard-Schuman. Good source, especially on the Middle Ages.

Ausubel, Nathan. 1974. *The Book of Jewish Knowledge: An Encyclopedia*. New York: Crown. Handy, simple explanations, understandable to non-Jewish readers.

Barnavi, Elie, ed. 1992. *A Historical Atlas of the Jewish People: From the Time of the Patriarchs to the Present*. New York: Knopf. Excellent on the Diaspora in medieval and modern times.

Ben-Sasson, Haim H., ed. 1975. *A History of the Jewish People*. London: Weidenfeld and Nicolson. A social and cultural history.

De Breffny, Brian. 1978. *The Synagogue*. London: Weidenfeld & Nicolson; New York: Macmillan. A survey of synagogue architecture.

Casper, Bernard M. 1960. *An Introduction to Jewish Bible Commentary*. London: Thomas Yoseloff. The genre and spirit of *midrash*, especially as pursued in the Middle Ages.

Cohen, Arthur A. 1962. *The Natural and the Supernatural Jew: A Historical and Theological Introduction*. New York: Pantheon. Treats the meaning of modernity for Judaism.

Encyclopedia Judaica, 16 vols. 1971. *Jerusalem: Encyclopedia Judaica*. New York: Macmillan. Some of the articles, such as the one on Jerusalem, are almost books in themselves.

Gaster, Theodor H. 1952. *The Festivals of the Jewish Year*. New York: William Sloane Associates. Shows how agricultural festivals received historical interpretations.

Glazer, Nathan. 1972. *American Judaism*. 2nd ed. Chicago: University of Chicago Press. A sociological interpretation.

Grollenberg, Luc H., ed. 1956. *Atlas of the Bible*. London: Nelson. Good for the archaeological and historical context of ancient Israel.

Hertzberg, Arthur. 1972. *The Zionist Idea: A Historical Analysis and Reader*. New York: Atheneum. A standard, well-documented source on the Zionist movement.

Idelsohn A.Z. 1932. *Jewish Liturgy and Its Development*. New York: Holt. Written by an expert on Jewish music and chanting.

Kaniel, Michael. 1979. *Judaism*. Poole, Dorset: Blandford. A volume on Jewish art, from a series on world art.

Kanof, Abraham. 1969. *Jewish Ceremonial Art and Religious Observances*. New York: Abrams. Contains pictorial illustrations of items used in worship.

Montefiore, Claude G., and Herbert Loewe, eds. 1938. *A Rabbinic Anthology*. London: Macmillan. A good collection of basic rabbinic texts.

Newman, Louis I., ed. 1934. *The Hasidic Anthology: Tales and Teachings of the Hasidim*. New York: Scribner. Contains many of the most frequently cited Hasidic texts.

Rabinowicz, Harry. 1960. *A Guide to Hasidism*. London: Thomas Yoseloff. A concise survey of Hasidic spirituality.

Scholem, Gershom G. 1974. *Kabbalah*. Jerusalem: Keter. The medieval mystical tradition surveyed by one of its most distinguished modern interpreters.

Schwarz, Leo W., ed. 1956. *Great Ages and Ideas of the Jewish People*. New York: Random House. A survey of religious and social history.

Segal, Alan F. 1986. *Rebecca's Children: Judaism and Christianity in the Roman World*. Cambridge, Mass.: Harvard University Press. Treats the Christian and early rabbinic movements as parallel developments.

Simon, Maurice. 1950. *Jewish Religious Conflicts*. London: Hutchinson. A masterful and readable survey of the development of religious authority across the centuries.

Steinsaltz, Adin. 1989. *The Talmud, the Steinsaltz Edition: A Reference Guide*. New York: Random House. Valuable explanations of technical rabbinic terminology and usage.

Trattner, Ernest R. 1955. *Understanding the Talmud*. New York: Nelson. A lucid introduction.

Wilson, Robert R. 1980. *Prophecy and Society in Ancient Israel*. Philadelphia: Fortress Press. Contextualizes the prophets, making excellent use of sociological and anthropological approaches.

Yerushalmi, Yosef. 1982. *Zakhor: Jewish History and Jewish Memory*. Seattle: University of Washington Press. Themes from the medieval Jewish experience.

Recommended Websites

The following selection is based on the helpful list put together by Behrman House Publishing (www.behrman house.com/popular_jewish_websites.htm).

Israel

www.inisrael.com/3disrael/index.html   Israel in 3D
www.goisrael.com   Israel Ministry of Tourism
www.centuryone.com/hstjrslm.html   Jerusalem history
www.knesset.gov.il/vtour/eng/index.htm   Knesset Virtual Tour

Education

www.jewishvirtuallibrary.org/index.html   Jewish Virtual Library

www.jbooks.com   The Online Jewish Book Community

Jewish History

www.nmajh.org/exhibitions/index.htm   National Museum of American Jewish History
www.ushmm.com   United States Holocaust Memorial Museum
www.fordham.edu/halsall/jewish/jewishsbook.html   Internet Jewish History Sourcebook
www.cjh.org/   Center for Jewish History
www.americanjewisharchives.org/syna/websites.php   American Jewish Archives; a list of website resources for the study of Jewish history and American Jewish history

References

Alexander, Philip, ed. 1984. *Textual Sources for the History of Judaism*. Manchester: Manchester University Press.

Caplan, Samuel, and Harold U. Ribalow, eds. 1952. *The Great Jewish Books and Their Influence on History*. New York: Horizon.

Grunfeld, Isidor, trans. 1956. *Judaism Eternal: Selected Essays from the Writings of Rabbi Samson Raphael Hirsch*. 2 vols. London: Soncino Press.

Lowenthal, Marvin, trans. 1977. *The Memoirs of Glückel of Hameln*. New York: Schocken.

Scholem, Gershom G. 1949. *Zohar: The Book of Splendor*. New York: Schocken Books.

Umansky, Ellen, and Dianne Ashton, eds. 1992. *Four Centuries of Jewish Women's Spirituality: A Sourcebook*. Boston: Beacon.

Whiston, William, trans. 1802. *The Genuine Works of Flavius Josephus*. Edinburgh: Thomas and John Turnbull.

Chapter
4
Christian Traditions
❧ Alan F. Segal and Willard G. Oxtoby ❧

Throughout the Christian world, the year reaches a climax in late December, when the Christmas season marks the birth of Jesus in Palestine approximately 2,000 years ago. Christians see Jesus as the manifestation of divine nature and purpose in a human life and believe that in him God reached out to conquer humanity's weaknesses.

To identify oneself as a Christian is to declare Jesus lord and saviour of the world. The heavy emphasis that Christians place on this declaration is crucial for understanding Christianity's function as a religious tradition. To be a Christian requires a commitment of faith that is expressed not only in the way one lives one's life but also in the affirmation of doctrine. Christians 'confess' or 'believe' Jesus to be the incarnate son of God and saviour of the world.

Timeline

c. 3 BCE	Birth of Jesus
c. 30 CE	Death of Jesus
c. 65	Death of Paul
312	Constantine's vision of the cross
325	First Council of Nicaea
337	Constantine is baptized on his deathbed
c. 384	Augustine's conversion experience
451	Council of Chalcedon
529	Benedict establishes monastery
842	Iconoclastic controversy ends
862	Cyril and Methodius in Moravia
c. 1033	Birth of Anselm (d. 1109)
1054	Break between Rome and Constantinople
1095	Urban II calls for the first crusade
1187	End of the Latin Kingdom of Jerusalem
c. 1225	Birth of Thomas Aquinas (*Summa Theologiae*) (d. 1274)

◀ Built on foundations that were laid around 220 CE, the basilica of Santa Maria in Trastevere may be the oldest church in Rome (Photo courtesy of Zeke Livingston). These mosaics date to the thirteenth century.

1517	Luther posts his 95 theses
1534	Henry VIII becomes head of the Church of England
1536	Calvin's *Institutes*
1563	Council of Trent concludes
1738	John Wesley's conversion experience
1781	Immanuel Kant's *Critique of Pure Reason*
1830	*Book of Mormon*
1859	Charles Darwin's *On the Origin of Species*
1870	First Vatican Council concludes
1910	Publication of *The Fundamentals*
1948	First assembly of the World Council of Churches
1965	Second Vatican Council concludes

❧ CELEBRATING A BIRTH

The word 'Christmas' means 'the mass of Christ'. The mass or Eucharist is Christianity's central rite: a symbolic meal, offered at worship services throughout the year, that recalls or re-enacts the self-sacrificing death of Jesus. Its solemnity figures as a theme even amid the optimism of Christmas, pointing towards the death and resurrection that will be commemorated at Easter, the central Christian festival. For Christians, the reports of Jesus' followers that they saw him risen from the dead confirm his divine lordship.

Christians recognize that many of the cultural trappings around Christmas are secular rather than religious. In theory, they distinguish between the sacred and the secular—a distinction that reflects the early Christians' experience as a minority movement before Christianity became the established religion of any state. In practice, however, the distinction has not always been easy to apply; separating the spheres of church and state was a problem in the European Middle Ages and remains a problem today.

Christians are found in every part of the world. Persons who identify themselves as Christian, whether or not they are observant, constitute the world's largest religious community. Estimates place their number at roughly one-third of the global population.

❧ ORIGINS

The Gospels

The gospels are four biographies of Jesus believed to have been written by his disciples Mark, Luke, Matthew, and John. The word 'gospel' (*evangelion* in Greek, the language the New Testament was written in) means 'good news'—the news of redemption that the Hebrew prophets had promised.

Traditions at a Glance

Numbers
2 billion around the world.

Distribution
Christians constitute the majority of the population in Europe and the Americas, Australia, New Zealand, sub-Saharan Africa, and the Philippines; over a third of the population of Lebanon; and almost a third of the population of South Korea.

Principal Historical Periods

c. 3 BCE–c. 30 CE	Lifetime of Jesus
c. 30–c. 120	The New Testament or Apostolic age
c. 120–451	The early Church
1517–c. 1600	The Protestant Reformation
17th century–present	The modern period

Founders
Founded by the followers of Jesus of Nazareth, called the Christ, on the basis of his teachings and resurrection. Among the early founders, the apostles Peter and Paul were especially important.

Deity
One God, called 'God' or 'Lord', who exists in three persons: as Father, Son, and Holy Spirit.

Authoritative Texts
The Christian Bible consists of the Old Testament (the Hebrew Bible) and the New Testament. The Roman Catholic and Orthodox churches include as part of the Old Testament a number of books from the *Septuagint* that Protestants set apart as Apocrypha. In addition, Roman Catholics hold the teaching office (*magisterium*) of the Church to be authoritative.

Noteworthy Doctrines
Jesus is the second person of the Trinity, truly God as well as truly human, and his resurrection is the sign that those who believe in him will have eternal life. The authority of the Church has been passed down from the **apostles** (the followers who were commissioned to preach the gospel of Jesus after the resurrection).

In Mark's gospel, a Roman soldier who sees Jesus gasp his last breath on the cross is moved to comment: 'Truly this was a son of God.' It is fitting that Mark attributes this observation to a Roman soldier rather than one of Jesus' followers, for the Christian movement soon spread beyond its initial base as a Jewish sect. Within a generation of his death, the Christians decided that their message was not for the Jews alone—that anyone could be a Christian. In that decision lay the seeds of Christianity's development as a missionary religion.

More than three centuries later, when Christianity became the established religion of the Roman Empire, Church leaders made a list of the writings they acknowledged to be scripture. That standard list, or canon, of books and letters is what Christians call the New Testament. It includes the four gospels that had achieved acceptance throughout Christendom. But in the late first and early second centuries, when these and a number of other gospels were first written and circulated, the situation was much more fluid.

Mark

Although Mark's gospel comes second in the New Testament, it is thought to be the earliest of the four gospels that were eventually accepted as canonical. Certainly it is the simplest and most straightforward. Mark says nothing about Jesus' life before the beginning of his ministry. Instead, he begins with John the Baptist, who is preaching 'the baptism of repentance for the remission of sins'. John performs the ritual of baptism on Jesus. Then a vision of the Holy Spirit sends Jesus into the desert for 40 days, during which he wrestles with God's arch-enemy Satan. On his return Jesus launches his ministry in the region of Galilee, proclaiming that the kingdom of God is at hand. His local reputation spreads as he performs healing miracles. When he is challenged for violating the Sabbath by picking grain and healing the sick, he takes the notion of Jewish legal authority into his own hands and declares that the Sabbath is made for people rather than people for the Sabbath. It is in response to this apparent arrogance, Mark suggests, that the Jewish priests conspire to do away with him.

Sayings of Jesus

The following passages come from the body of teachings in Matthew *conventionally known as the 'Sermon on the Mount'* (Luke *presents similar material). The translation is from the* New English Bible.

If, when you are bringing your gift to the altar, you suddenly remember that your brother has a grievance against you, leave your gift where it is before the altar. First go and make your peace with your brother, and only then come back and offer your gift (5: 23–4).

You have learned that they were told, 'Eye for eye, tooth for tooth.' But what I tell you is this: Do not set yourself against the man who wrongs you. If someone slaps you on the right cheek, turn and offer him your left. If a man wants to sue you for your shirt, let him have your coat as well. If a man in authority makes you go one mile, go with him two. Give when you are asked to give; and do not turn your back on a man who wants to borrow (5: 38–42).

Pass no judgment, and you will not be judged. For as you judge others, so you will yourselves be judged, and whatever measure you deal out to others will be dealt back to you. Why do you look at the speck of sawdust in your brother's eye, with never a thought for the great plank in your own? Or how can you say to your brother, 'Let me take the speck out of your eye,' when all the time there is that plank in your own? First take the plank out of your own eye, and then you will see clearly to take the speck out of your brother's (7: 1-5).

Jesus selects twelve of his followers to form an inner circle of disciples. Accompanied by them, he continues to heal, teach, and challenge the priorities of religious authority. Eventually he goes to Jerusalem, arriving with a crowd that shouts 'Hosanna' (a cry for divine deliverance in Hebrew prayer) and proclaims the coming of the messiah: a king in the line of the dynastic founder, David, who brings deliverance. Over the course of a week in Jerusalem, he disputes with the religious authorities, celebrates the Passover with his disciples, is betrayed by one of them (Judas), is arrested, and is brought to trial before the Roman governor, Pontius Pilate. When he does not deny that he is the king of the Jews, he is sentenced to crucifixion.

At the height of his suffering on the cross, Jesus cries out, 'My God, my God, why have you forsaken me?' He expires and, before the beginning of the Sabbath, his body is placed in a tomb that is sealed with a large stone. The day after the Sabbath, when three of his female followers go to the tomb, they find the stone rolled away and the body missing.

Children in Asuncion, Paraguay, take part in the annual celebration of Palm Sunday, commemorating Jesus' entry into Jerusalem (AFP/Getty Images).

Luke

Luke's gospel includes two chapters of material not found in Mark. In addition to recounting events in Jesus' life before his baptism, this material includes visions and portents anticipating his birth and that of John the Baptist. Luke tells how Jesus was born in Bethlehem, how angels (divine messengers) announced the birth to shepherds in the fields, and how the shepherds went to pay their respects to the newborn messiah. Although Luke does not mention any wise men from the East (the magi, Persian for 'priests', appear only in Matthew), he does say that, at a newborn-purification ceremony in the Temple, a devout man proclaimed the infant to be the messiah.

Luke also provides more detail than Mark regarding the trial and crucifixion of Jesus. In his version, the charge is that, by claiming kingship, Jesus has incited rebellion. Here Pilate himself declares Jesus innocent of any crime, but nevertheless yields to mob pressure to have him executed. Luke's Roman centurion does not say that Jesus is a son of God, but does declare him to be innocent. Finally, according to Luke, after the tomb is found empty, Jesus appears among his followers and speaks to them.

Matthew

Matthew's account includes much of the same material as Luke's, but his focus is noticeably different. As a writer, Matthew has clearly designed his narrative to persuade a Jewish

Sources of the Gospel Narratives

Much of the Gospel material consists of Jesus' teachings. Some of these take the form of **parables**: narrative stories designed to teach a moral lesson. Others are short sayings that could stand alone, apart from any narrative, as universally applicable proverbs or maxims. In chapters 5 through 7 of his gospel, Matthew describes Jesus as delivering several of these on a mountain in northern Palestine; the material is thus known as the Sermon on the Mount. Luke presents the same material, though in his gospel it is delivered on a plain.

In general, the accounts of Luke and Matthew overlap, and it has been assumed that both of them used Mark's narrative as a source for their accounts. Yet some of the material they both include is not found in Mark.

These discrepancies led German scholars in the nineteenth century to postulate that the material not in Mark must have come from a different source, one that both Luke and Matthew used and that has since been lost. This hypothetical document has come to be known as 'Q', from the initial letter of Quelle, the German word for 'source'.

audience of the truth of Jesus' claim to be the messiah. For example, it has been suggested that his account of the infant's escape from the slaughter ordered by King Herod was specifically intended to echo the Exodus account of the Israelites' escape from the wrath of the Egyptian pharaoh. Though Herod was a tyrant, no other source records this barbarity.

Matthew opens his gospel by giving a genealogy of Jesus as the descendant of King David, in a lineage that runs through Joseph, the husband of Mary. But he then bypasses this genealogy, saying that Mary conceived the child—by the Holy Spirit—before her marriage to Joseph. Apparently it was part of Matthew's purpose to show that the birth of Jesus exactly fulfilled a prophecy in the seventh chapter of *Isaiah*: 'Behold, a virgin shall conceive and bear a son, and his name shall be called Emmanuel (which means, "God with us").'

The Hebrew text of *Isaiah* mentions only a 'young woman', but the Greek version is ambiguous and can be read as 'virgin'. The stage is thus set for one of Christianity's more problematic teachings: Luke and Matthew are the only New Testament sources for the doctrine of the virgin birth.

John

Despite their differences, Mark, Luke, and Matthew have much more in common with one another than any of them does with the fourth gospel. For this reason scholars often refer to the first three as the 'synoptic gospels', underlining the similarity of their perspectives in comparison with the very different perspective of John.

John's purpose is not simply to recount Jesus' life or (as in the case of Matthew) to show how it fulfilled the Hebrew scriptures. Rather, he is expressly concerned to assert the cosmic significance of that life and to declare Jesus' identity as messiah and saviour. John is candid at the end of his twentieth chapter:

Now Jesus did many other signs in the presence of the disciples, which are not written in this book. But these are written that you may come to believe that Jesus is the

Messiah, the Son of God, and that through believing you may have life in his name' (*John* 20: 30–1).

John shows his theological interest in his opening passage or prologue. 'In the beginning,' he writes (echoing the opening words of *Genesis* in the Hebrew scriptures), 'was the *logos*, and the *logos* was with God, and the *logos* was God; all things were made through him.' As we saw in Chapter 3, *logos* is a Greek term with an important range of meaning in the philosophy and religion of the Hellenistic world at the time of Jesus. Although translated simply as 'word', it signifies something far more—a divine blueprint or pattern or divine intelligence.

A few verses later John declares Jesus to be the incarnation of that divine Word. 'The *logos* became flesh and dwelt among us, full of grace and truth; we have beheld his glory, glory as of the only Son from the Father.' For John, the eternal divine purpose has now become a personal presence in human form, and this incarnation took place only a short while ago, in the community's recent experience.

Here John is in step with Paul, an early convert who probably contributed as much as anyone to the shaping of the early Christian message. Like Paul, John is now using the title 'Christ' (the Greek translation of the Hebrew word for messiah, 'anointed') almost as if it were a second personal name for Jesus. John's view of the significance of Jesus is encapsulated in a frequently quoted passage: 'For God so loved the world that he gave his only Son, that whoever believes in him should not perish but have eternal life' (John 3:16).

From Sect to Church

The handful of Jesus' disciples who were left at the time of his execution were peasants from rural Galilee whose teacher had stirred in them the hope that low-status and marginalized people—the poor, sinners, Samaritans, women—had a place in God's plan. As a group, they amounted to a minor Jewish sect that expected the end of the age and the glorious return of their teacher at any moment.

Various explanations have been offered for how such a small group was able to transform itself first into an independent missionary religion and then, within four centuries, into the state church of the Roman Empire. The New Testament book *Acts of the Apostles*, which is Luke's sequel to his gospel, describes a miraculous event. In *Acts* 2 the disciples are gathered on Shavuoth, the festival held seven weeks after the Passover during which Jesus was executed (Luke uses the Greek word Pentecost for this holiday). Experiencing the Holy Spirit as a rush of wind and fire, they begin to speak—and be understood—in diverse languages, thus capable of preaching to all people.

Paul

The principal influence on the direction of the early Church was not one of Jesus' band of twelve, but an educated, cosmopolitan convert with the privileged status of a Roman citizen. According to Luke, the man who took the name Paul was a Pharisee from the diaspora Jewish community in Tarsus, a large ancient city located on the southern coast of contemporary Turkey, who had gone to Jerusalem for religio-legal study.

Paul had not known Jesus himself. Rather (according to Luke), he was on the way to Damascus to persecute Christians when he experienced a personal encounter with the post-resurrection Jesus that changed the direction of his life. Today this experience would be called a conversion. For the next quarter-century he travelled tirelessly around the eastern Mediterranean, initially directing his message to the diaspora Jewish communities, but eventually preaching that Jews and gentiles (non-Jews) alike were heirs in Christ to the promises of God.

Paul carried on a correspondence with the scattered communities of Christian converts in places like Corinth and Rome in letters whose content ranged from personal greetings and liturgical blessings to essays on questions of theology. Paul's letters, which come from a time before the gospels were written, are the earliest Christian literature, and their formative effect on Christian theology cannot be overestimated.

In his letters Paul refers to himself as 'the apostle to the gentiles'. He opposes the view that in order to follow Jesus one must first become a Jew, be circumcised (if male), and follow the dietary regulations and other commandments of Pharisaism. For Paul, it is not through observance of ritual laws or even correct moral conduct that salvation is attained, but through faith in Jesus and the divine grace that comes through him.

In addition, Paul introduces what will become a pervasive theme in subsequent Christian theology, contrasting life 'in the spirit'—life centred on lasting religious values such as faith, hope, and love—with life 'in the flesh', the pursuit of what passes away, including worldly ambition or pleasure.

Thanks to Paul's travels, Christian communities were established in many of the port cities of the Roman Empire by the time he died, about the year 65. At the beginning of his involvement with Christianity, Paul had held the coats of the people who stoned the apostle Stephen to death. At the end he became a martyr himself, executed in Rome in the course of the emperor Nero's persecution of Christians.

Marcion

If Paul was the principal architect of the early Church, then we might describe Marcion (d. c. 160) as a draughtsman whose blueprint was rejected. Marcion lived a century after Paul. The son of a bishop, he was a wealthy ship-owner from Sinope, on the south shore of the Black Sea. He made his way to Rome, the capital, where his views led to his excommunication (formal expulsion) from the Church in 144, but this did not deter him from communicating his views.

Marcion's theology takes Paul's ideas to astonishing lengths. Paul's contrast between law and gospel becomes for Marcion a contrast not only between the Old and New Testaments but between two distinct deities. The creator God of the Hebrew scriptures, the one who gave the law to Moses, becomes what Marcion calls the 'Demiurge': a stern and fearsome deity, capricious, despotic, and cruel. The coming of Jesus reveals an utterly different God of love and mercy, who will overcome and replace the Demiurge of the Hebrew scriptures. Therefore, Marcion reasoned, the Christian scriptures should not include any part of the Old Testament. In fact, he rejected almost all Christian writings as well, except for an abridged version of the Gospel of Luke and 10 of Paul's letters.

Not surprisingly, given that the Old Testament prophecies justified its own claims to historicity, the Church rejected Marcion's canon and affirmed that the Christian message was rooted in the faith of ancient Israel. But it took the notion of a scriptural canon from him and set out to define its own.

The Gnostics

Another spiritual and doctrinal challenge for the early Christian Church was Gnosticism: a school of interpretation that claimed to have privileged, secret knowledge (*gnosis* means 'knowledge'). To its Christian adherents Gnosticism offered an inner meaning of Christianity (and to Jewish Gnostics, of Judaism). It developed within the network of the Christian churches, and at first the Gnostics did not form a separate community.

The Gnostic philosophical narrative is dualistic: the divine powers of good are opposed by demonic forces of evil, and spirit is engaged in a cosmic struggle with matter. In the beginning, the material world was created through the entrapment or fall and fragmentation of spirit into matter. Although accounts differ on the details—in some, spirit falls victim to temptation; in others, to treachery or attack—all agree that there will be a long struggle before spirit is restored to its proper place.

The Christian Gnostics saw Jesus as an emissary from the realm of the spirit who appeared in human form but did not take on full material existence. Critics within the Church objected that this view was inconsistent with the doctrine of divine incarnation in human form.

In 1945 a major collection of Gnostic manuscripts was discovered at Nag Hammadi in Egypt. Since then a more sympathetic picture of Gnostic ideas has become available to historians. Among the Nag Hammadi texts is the Gospel of Thomas, one of many writings, Gnostic and otherwise, that were not ratified as scripture by the Church at large. Although it was probably written after Jesus' death, it presents his sayings as though he were still alive and does not describe his death.

❧ CRYSTALLIZATION

The Early Church

In its earliest years the Christian movement had no formal organization. With the Easter story as their model, Christians simply gathered in one another's homes on Sundays to pray and affirm their faith. Various individuals emerged as teachers, and some became evangelists, spreading the word and forming new groups. Eventually a process of ordination was established whereby certain individuals were qualified to perform ritual and administrative functions. The most basic grade was deacon, and women as well as men were so designated in the early Church. The ranking priest in a political jurisdiction was the bishop (from the Greek *episkopos*, 'supervisor'). By the third century four episcopal jurisdictions or 'sees' had gained prominence because of the importance of their cities: Jerusalem, Rome, Alexandria in Egypt, and Antioch in Syria. The bishops of these cities came to be known as patriarchs. A fifth patriarch was added in the fourth century, when Constantinople replaced Rome as the imperial capital.

The Ascetic Tradition

Jesus was not the first religious figure to remove himself from his society and retreat into the desert for a period of intense contemplation. John the Baptist and his followers were closely associated with the desert, and the Essenes had a well-established community near the Dead Sea until it was destroyed by the Romans in the first century. During the anti-Christian campaigns of the second and third centuries, life in the desert must have offered some security from persecution. But exchanging the comforts of normal life in society for the harsh discipline of the desert also became a way of repudiating the laxity and complacency of the broader Christian community, especially after Christianity won the official sanction of Rome.

The earliest Christian ascetics or 'desert fathers' were hermits such as Antony (c. 251–356), whose solitary life in Egypt became the model for the monastic tradition, and Simeon Stylites (c. 390–459). After 10 years as a hermit in the Syrian desert, Simeon wanted to practise an even more extreme form of asceticism. Therefore he built a small platform on top of a pillar, installed himself on it, and remained there for the rest of his life, using a basket to haul up the necessities of life provided by his admirers. Simeon's dedication attracted converts and pilgrims, and set an example that other 'stylites' (pole-sitters) copied.

Although the term 'monasticism' (from a Greek root meaning 'one' or 'alone') suggests a solitary life, in time various hermits took up locations near one another for safety and mutual support. Such groupings were at first informal, but by the mid-fourth century nine monasteries for men and two for women had been established in Egypt alone. Basil, bishop of Caesarea in east-central Turkey, drew up regulations for such communities that included poverty and chastity, specified hours of prayer, and assigned manual tasks. Monasticism was becoming formalized as a corporate discipline.

Roman Persecution

Roman society had civic gods and rituals that the population at large was supposed to support. But the Christians refused to participate in the public religion, which from their point of view violated both the Hebraic tradition of monotheism and the biblical prohibition on idol worship. From the Roman point of view, their loyalty to their faith made them guilty of insubordination.

In the mid-third century the emperor Decius commanded public sacrifices to the Roman civic gods and threatened those who would not comply with penalties that ranged from imprisonment to death. Throughout the empire, Christians were systematically persecuted as a matter of policy. The last and fiercest campaign against the Christians began in 303 under the emperor Diocletian. For the next nine years, Christians were killed, Church properties destroyed, and Christian sacred writings burned. But the 'Great Persecution' was no more successful than its predecessors. The Christians who were put to death for their faith modelled their conduct on that of their self-sacrificing lord, accepting martyrdom in the expectation that their reward would be an afterlife in eternal fellowship with him.

'The blood of the martyrs is the seed of the church,' wrote Tertullian (c. 160–c. 220), who came from Carthage in North Africa and was the first theologian to write in Latin.

The Roman policy of persecution had the unintended effect of helping Christians to establish a reputation for courage and fidelity that attracted many new converts.

Constantine

A shift of policy under Diocletian's successor forever changed Christianity's place in the world. Constantine (r. 306–37) gradually abandoned the persecution policy and in 313 granted Christians the liberty to practise their religion.

According to Eusebius, bishop of Caesarea in Palestine, who lived through the transition, the emperor's conversion was sparked by a vision he experienced—on the eve of a decisive battle in 312—of a cross in the heavens and the words 'conquer in this sign'. The following day his troops won the battle and gave him control of the western half of the empire.

Modern historians have speculated about Constantine's motives and sincerity. The allegedly sudden vision does not square with the gradual pace of policy change. Christian symbols appeared on Constantine's coinage alongside pagan symbols for several years; Sunday did not become a public holiday until 321 and even then it coincided with popular worship of the sun. Finally, although his mother was a Christian, Constantine was not baptized until he was on his deathbed. One explanation for this delay might be that baptism in his day represented a once-in-a-lifetime opportunity for total cleansing from sin: therefore Christians hoping to maximize their chances of salvation would postpone the ritual as long as possible.

Whatever his religious motives might have been, as a politician Constantine was probably shrewd enough to recognize that the Church could help to stabilize his regime. The Church was dispersed throughout the entire empire. It had a system of regional government supervised by bishops. It seemed to be arriving at a coherent sense of its teaching, in response to doctrinal challenges. And it had remarkable discipline, at both the institutional and the personal level.

Even so, Christianity did not replace paganism overnight. The etymology of the word 'pagan' hints at the process: like 'peasant', it comes from the Latin word meaning 'rural' (similarly, the pre-Christian traditions that lingered on the remote heaths of northern Europe were called 'heathen'). Christianity spread in the towns and along the trade routes, but in more remote areas the old ways were slow to change. The emperor Julian (r. 361–3) attempted unsuccessfully to bring back the old religion, and although he stopped short of persecuting Christians, it was only with Theodosius I (r. 379–95) that Christianity became the official religion of the Roman Empire.

Doctrinal Issues

By the fourth century the Church had formulated at least two formal statements of belief called **creeds** (from the Latin for 'believe'). The importance attributed to such statements has had a lasting influence on Christians' understanding both of themselves and of others. Because Christians define themselves by their beliefs about Jesus and God and the world, they have often mistakenly expected other traditions to define themselves in terms of belief as well.

Perhaps as early as 150 but certainly by the early third century, a formulation known as the Apostles' Creed was coming into use, especially in the Latin-speaking western part of the Mediterranean. Named for the first group to carry the message of Jesus to the world, the Apostles' Creed is still widely used. A somewhat more detailed formulation is the Nicene Creed, named for the Council of Nicaea in 325 and ratified in its present form in 381. It is still recited in Eucharistic services in the Catholic tradition.

The Trinity

The Nicene creed reflects the emergence of the explicit doctrine of the Trinity: that God has three manifestations or 'persons': father, son, and Holy Spirit. Christians today often assume that this doctrine has been part of the tradition from the beginning, but it has not: although the New Testament speaks of God as father and of Jesus as son, and of God's spirit, it almost never puts the three together.

In fact, the Trinity was the subject of intense controversy at the time of Constantine. In Alexandria, a presbyter ('elder') named Arius (c. 250–c. 336) proposed that the son of God was not eternal, but was created within time by the father as part of the creation of the world; in other words, 'there was an existence when the Son was not'. This meant that the son was not eternal by nature but was subject to change. This view was opposed by another Alexandrian, Athanasius (c. 296–373), who asserted the coeternity and coequality of father and son. One argument for this interpretation was that it emphasized the power of the son to be a saviour. The conflict has been termed a battle over a Greek diphthong, the Athanasians calling the son *homoousion* (of the same substance) in contrast to the Arian *homoiousion* (of similar substance).

Hoping that a unified Church would promote stability in his empire, Constantine called the bishops to meet at the Council of Nicaea, not far from Constantinople, in 325. The dispute between Arius and Athanasius was part of the agenda, and the decision went against Arius. But Arian views still attracted support, and for half a century they continued

---

The Nicene Creed

We believe in one God, the Father almighty, maker of heaven and earth, and of all things visible and invisible; and in one Lord Jesus Christ, the only-begotten Son of God, begotten of the Father before all worlds, God of God, light of light, very God of very God, begotten not made, being of one substance with the Father, by whom all things were made, who for us men and for our salvation came down from heaven, and was incarnate by the Holy Spirit of the Virgin Mary, and was made man, and was crucified for us under Pontius Pilate. He suffered and was buried, and the third day he rose again according to the scriptures, and ascended into heaven, and sits on the right hand of the Father, and he shall come again with glory to judge both the living and the dead; whose kingdom shall have no end. And we believe in the Holy Spirit, the Lord and giver of life, who proceeds from the Father (and the Son), who with the Father and Son together is worshipped and glorified, who spoke by the prophets. And we believe in one holy catholic and apostolic church. We acknowledge one baptism for the remission of sins. And we look for the resurrection of the dead, and the life of the world to come.

to surface in various efforts to develop a compromise formula, before they were defini-
tively rejected at the Council of Constantinople in 381.

Yet no sooner had the Athanasian position become orthodoxy than a corollary to it
cried out for attention. If the eternal son was coequal with the father, then how did the
eternal divinity of Jesus relate to his historical humanity? There were three principal
options, around which regional divisions emerged. The incarnate Christ could be:

- Two separate persons, one divine and one human (the position of the Nestorian
  churches, stretching eastward across Asia);
- One person, with a single, exclusively divine nature (the position of the Monophy-
  sites, from Ethiopia and Egypt to Syria and Armenia); or
- One person, but with both a divine nature and a human one (the position of the
  Greek- and Latin-speaking churches).

Each of these fifth-century options still has adherents today. In a sense, the theological
debate gave intellectual justification to the desire of local, regional, and national churches
for greater independence from Rome. Yet the position of the Roman Church—that God
is one single divine essence, which has eternally had three distinct persons, one of whom
is the Christ, who was both truly God and truly human—is itself a synthesis. Although it
glosses over many intellectually interesting solutions to this intractable problem, it reflects
the Church's desire to appeal to the widest possible clientele.

Two Christian Worlds: Byzantium and Rome

The Council of Chalcedon in 451 was composed almost exclusively of eastern bishops,
but it steered a middle course between the Nestorians, who compromised the eternal deity
of Jesus, and the Monophysites, who compromised his humanity. In this way it arrived at
a Christological formulation that accommodated Rome as well as Constantinople. That
middle position—that the incarnate Christ was one person but with both a divine and a
human nature—was still ambiguous, however. And so the debate continued.

The early seventh century, for instance, saw what amounted to a rerun of the
Monophysite controversy. In an attempt to win back the Monophysite Christians, the
Eastern (Byzantine) emperor Heraclius advocated a compromise suggesting that Christ
had two natures, divine and human, but only one will (*thelema* in Greek; hence the term
Monothelite). But this effort was soon repudiated, and by now much of the region that
had been home to the Monophysites was converting to Islam in any case.

Greek and Latin Christianity grew further and further apart. The underlying reasons
were differences in language and culture, but once again a theological formulation provided the rallying point for rival factions whose differences were primarily political. At
issue was a single word, *filioque* (Latin, 'and from the son'). Did the Holy Spirit 'proceed'
from God the father, as the Greek Church had maintained in the Nicene Creed, or from
the father and the son, as the Latin Church came to hold? In 867 Photius, the patriarch of
Constantinople, denounced both the intrusion of Latin missionaries into Bulgaria, which
he considered Greek territory, and the insertion of *filioque* into the creed. For the next

Christianity in Egypt, Ethiopia, and Armenia

The indigenous Christians of Egypt, the Copts, believe that their faith was taken to Egypt by the gospel writer Mark, and that their ancestors were pioneers, with Anthony, in the development of monasticism. After the Islamic conquest in the seventh century, Egyptians who remained Christian were a minority, but a significant one. The Copts have retained a sense of cultural pride as 'original' Egyptians.

By the fourth century Coptic Christian influence had extended to Ethiopia. A few centuries later, Ethiopia gave asylum to Muslim emigrants, but it was not subjugated by Islam. It remained Christian, recognizing the authority of the Coptic patriarch in Cairo and maintaining a window on the world through its own priests and monks in Jerusalem. The Ethiopian church has remained essentially Coptic, although it has been formally independent of Cairo since the mid-twentieth century.

In Armenia as in Egypt, legend traces the introduction of Christianity to the missionary activity of the apostles, in this case Thaddeus and Bartholomew. Armenian Christians maintain that their king Tiridates III, who was baptized by Gregory the Illuminator around 301, was the first ruler anywhere to establish Christianity as a state religion.

two decades, one party in Constantinople repudiated the term and condemned the pope, while another supported the term and condemned Photius.

Behind the theological niceties lay the basic issue of authority, for Rome had added *filioque* to the creed without the consent of a universal Church council. In so doing it had staked its claim to be the single centre of authority against the Greek view of Rome as just one of five equally important patriarchates, and its own notion that authority was vested in the bishop of Rome (the pope) against the Greek notion that it was vested in a council of bishops. The final result was a break between Rome and Constantinople that is conventionally dated to 1054, although it was in the making well before then and efforts to heal it continued for some time.

The Eastern Orthodox Tradition

'Eastern Orthodox' is a kind of umbrella term for the various churches centred on the patriarchates that refused to accept Rome's claim to supremacy. Among the features that distinguish the Eastern tradition from the Western is the veneration of icons.

The Iconoclastic Controversy

The Byzantine Church developed a distinctive form of portraiture for depicting religious figures. An icon (from the Greek word for 'image') might be an entirely two-dimensional painting, often on a piece of wood, or it might be overlaid in low relief, in wood or precious metal, and ornamented with jewels. While the robes clothing the figure were executed in relief, the hands and face typically remained two-dimensional, so that the parts of image representing flesh appeared as openings in the relief. In the seventh and eighth centuries these images became the subject of a heated dispute known as the iconoclastic controversy.

A mosaic map on the floor of a Byzantine church in Madaba, Jordan, depicts Jerusalem before the arrival of Islam (Tomi Junger / PhotoStock-Israel.com).

Pitting a faction called the iconoclasts ('icon breakers') against one called the iconodules ('icon worshippers'), the debate was in part a vehicle for political and other disagreements. But points of principle were nonetheless at stake, and Byzantine intellectuals engaged in serious theological discussions concerning the role of images in worship. In the end the Second Council of Nicaea in 787 decided that icons were permissible and could be venerated, as long as the faithful did not actually worship them.

Today in Orthodox sanctuaries a massive screen in front of the altar shields it from the main portion of the sanctuary. The screen is called an iconostasis ('place for icons') and is designed to hold a number of icons, each one the size of a newspaper page. Smaller icons are hung in private homes, and travellers will sometimes carry icons the size of a pocket diary, equipped with folding covers.

Christianizing the Slavs

The Greek Orthodox form of Christianity was carried from Byzantium to a number of peoples in eastern Europe. Orthodox missions to the Slavs made significant headway in the ninth century, and language played a role in their success. Though the language of the Byzantine empire was Greek, missionaries working beyond the imperial frontier used local vernaculars, encouraging the development of independent local churches with a strong sense of national identity based on language.

The missionary effort was sparked by two brothers, Cyril (826–69) and Methodius (c. 815–85). In 862 they travelled to Moravia (the region of the modern Czech Republic), where they preached in the vernacular and produced Slavonic translations of the Bible and liturgy. After Cyril's time a new alphabet, a modification of the Greek, was devised for Slavic languages such as Bulgarian, Serbian, Ukrainian, and Russian, and named 'Cyrillic' in his honour. Romania, much of which had been colonized by Rome in the second century, was Christian from about the fourth century. Although it eventually came into the eastern Orthodox orbit, its language continued to use the Latin alphabet.

The early centre of Russian Orthodoxy was the Ukrainian city of Kiev, where the fearsome pagan ruler Vladimir had become a vigorous advocate of Christianity after marrying the sister of the Byzantine emperor around the year 987. Although some accounts say that his new faith made him a more gentle ruler, others suggest that he continued to rely on coercive methods even in his promotion of Christianity. It was only after Kiev fell to Mongol invaders in 1237 that Moscow replaced it as the centre of Russian religion and politics.

Slavic peoples in regions such as Croatia, Slovakia, Poland, and Lithuania were converted by Roman Catholic missionaries and adopted the Latin alphabet. Roman Catholicism also became the dominant form of Christianity among Hungarians. Rome's recruitment efforts in the Eastern Orthodox world eventually led to the formation of several new churches. Even though they were aligned with Rome rather than Constantinople, these Eastern-rite Catholic churches retained important elements of the Orthodox tradition, including immersion baptism, married priests, and the use of local languages rather than Latin. Since most of them originated in Orthodox churches, most continue to have Orthodox counterparts today. The exception is the Maronite Church of Lebanon; founded in the fifth century by a Syrian monk named Maron, it has always been in communion with Rome.

The Latin Tradition

The Papacy

The Church centred in Rome thought of itself as 'catholic': that is, universal. Its interaction with political regimes in the Latin world (the western Mediterranean and northern Europe) produced the synthesis of religion, culture, and governmental and social structure often referred to as Christendom (the 'domain' of Christianity).

The bishop of Rome had unchallenged ecclesiastical authority in the Latin-speaking western part of the empire, parallel to that of the bishops of Greek-speaking centres such as Alexandria and Antioch. The special status attributed to his office was in part a consequence of Rome's own status as the capital of the empire, but it also reflected the fact that the first bishop of Rome was believed to have been the apostle Peter: the 'rock' on whom Jesus was supposed to have said he would build his church (Matthew 16: 18). Christians of other traditions did not accept the Roman claim that Peter's successors as bishops of Rome inherited any special status from him. Nevertheless, by the third century the popes (from *papa*, 'father') were claiming theological primacy as successors of Peter, and their practical influence increased dramatically after the Germanic invasions of the fifth century, which caused government in the western part of the empire to collapse.

Augustine's Conversion

The quotation at the end of this extract comes from Paul's letter to the Romans:

I was greatly disturbed in spirit, angry at myself with a turbulent indignation because I had not entered thy will and covenant, O my God, while all my bones cried out to me to enter. . . . It was I who willed and I who was also unwilling. In either case, it was I. . . . Suddenly I heard the voice of a boy or a girl—I know not which—coming from the neighbouring house, chanting over and over again, 'Pick it up, read it.' . . . In silence I read the paragraph on which my eyes first fell: 'Not in revelling and drunkenness, not in lust and wantonness, not in quarrels and rivalries. Rather, arm yourselves with the Lord, Jesus Christ; spend no more thought on nature and nature's appetites' (Outler 1955: 170–6).

Augustine

By the early fifth century the differences between the eastern and western branches of Christianity were becoming clear. The dominant issue in the East was the nature of divinity in God and Christ, while in the West it was human sinfulness and the possibility of divine redemption.

A landmark figure in the evolution of Christianity in this period was Aurelius Augustine. The son of a devout Christian mother and a pagan father, he was born in 354 in what is now Algeria, raised as a Christian, and as a youth studied classical philosophy and Neoplatonism. He also sowed his wild oats, living with a woman who bore him a son. In his twenties he explored the intense dualism of Manichaean thought, and it was not until 386 that, following a dramatic conversion experience, he turned to Christianity, albeit a far more sophisticated form of Christianity than his mother's. He became a priest, a prolific theological writer, and, as bishop of Hippo in North Africa, an active campaigner against heretics such as Pelagius, who believed that it was possible for humans to achieve perfection through their own moral efforts.

The ideas that had preoccupied Augustine in his Manichaean days—the struggle between good and evil, spirit and matter, the transcendent and the carnal—remained prominent in his Christian writing. His conviction that humans can achieve nothing without divine grace shaped the medieval Christian view of the human self and personality, and his guilt regarding the body's appetites was reflected in the medieval Church's central concern with liberation from sin.

Augustine's best-known book is probably his *Confessions*—an account of his own spiritual struggles and how he came to the Christian faith—but his most influential work was likely *The City of God*: a monumental theology of history in which he contrasts the earthly, human city with the city of God symbolized by the Church.

Medieval Christianity

The Middle Ages are generally considered to stretch from the collapse of the western Roman Empire, around 500, to the beginning of the Renaissance, around 1500. It was during this period that many Christian doctrines and practices became established.

The Monastic Tradition

Monastic communities, male and female, played an important role in both Greek and Latin Christianity. Technically, monks were not priests but laymen, who followed a demanding schedule of prayer and worship. A distinction was drawn between 'religious' or 'regular' clergy, who followed a monastic rule, and 'secular' clergy, who worked in the world. The Greek Church permitted its secular clergy to marry, but the Latin Church did not.

For Latin Christianity monastic life came to be defined by St Benedict, who founded a small community of monks south of Rome in about 529 and established a set of guidelines for monastic life that were eventually adopted by many other communities. In addition to prayer services at regular hours throughout the day and night, the 'rule' of St Benedict included manual labour: medieval communities had to be economically self-sufficient, not only growing their own food but often selling the products of their field and vineyards. It also included serious scriptural study. In this way the medieval monasteries became the custodians of culture, and their libraries preserved many ancient texts that might otherwise have been lost.

Cluniac Fathers

Founded in 910 by William the Pious, Duke of Aquitaine, the monastery at Cluny, north of Lyon in France, became the centre of a movement to reform monasticism by bringing its institutions under the control of religious rather than secular authorities. Over the next two and a half centuries, the Cluniac order established a network of more than 300 satellite houses across Europe. Like the Church itself in Constantine's day, the order served as a stabilizing influence at a time of political fragmentation and turbulence. Within a century of its founding, however, it was growing rich on endowments and beginning to emphasize prayer services over study and manual labour.

Cistercians

In reaction against the changes in Benedictine practice introduced at Cluny, Robert of Molesmes founded the Cistercian order in 1098. The Cistercians wore simple undyed wool habits, ate no meat, worshipped in sparely decorated churches, and put renewed emphasis on manual labour.

One group of Cistercians in particular became known for the austerity of their rule, which included strict regulation of the circumstances under which speech was allowed. The Cistercians of the Strict Observance, or Trappists, were founded in the 1600s by Armand de Rancé, abbot of the monastery of La Trappe in Normandy. Probably the best known Trappist in modern times was Thomas Merton (1915–68), a mystic, poet, and social activist with a deep interest in Eastern spiritual traditions, especially Zen.

Carthusians

The Carthusian order, founded in 1084 and named after its base at La Grande Chartreuse, near Grenoble in France, also emphasized silence and austerity. Like the abbey of Fécamp, which began distilling a kind of herbal liqueur (eventually marketed as 'Benedictine') in the fifteenth century, the Carthusians' abbey at Chartreuse supported itself in part by producing a famous alcoholic concoction based on plant extracts (the brilliant green colour of Chartreuse is attributed to chlorophyll).

The Prayer of St Francis

Although this prayer is not found in the writings of St Francis of Assisi, it has been attributed to him by Franciscan oral tradition.

Lord, make me an instrument of your peace. Where there is hatred let me sow love; where there is injury, pardon; where there is doubt, faith; where there is despair, hope; where there is darkness, light; and where there is sadness, joy.

O divine master, grant that I may not so much seek to be consoled as to console; to be understood as to understand; to be loved as to love. For it is in giving that we receive; it is in pardoning that we are pardoned; and it is in dying that we are born to eternal life.

Mendicant Orders

Monastic orders had from the beginning turned their backs on the secular world. In the 1200s, however, poverty was becoming a serious problem in the growing towns and cities of Europe. In response, a new type of religious order emerged that was dedicated to pastoral work, serving the people. Members of these new **mendicant** orders either worked or begged for their living and were not bound to any one convent.

Franciscans

Francis (1182–1226) of Assisi grew up as the privileged son of a wealthy cloth merchant in central Italy, but a serious illness in his twenties led him to rethink his life. On a pilgrimage to Rome, he was so moved by the presence of beggars outside St Peter's Basilica that he exchanged clothes with one of them and spent the day begging for alms.

When he returned to Assisi he dedicated himself to serving the poor and gradually attracting a small group of like-minded companions for whom he established a rule of life that emphasized poverty. The simple sandals and rope belt they wore became distinctive features of the Franciscan habit. The order received papal approval in 1209 and within a few years Clara of Assisi formed a parallel order for women, known as the Poor Clares. An offshoot of the Franciscans called the Capuchins drew up their own rule in 1529

St Francis preaching to the birds; a detail from an altarpiece (c. 1295) by the early Renaissance master Giotto di Bondone (Photo Credit: Réunion des Musées Nationaux/ Art Resource, NY).

and are still known today for their soup kitchens, which offer free meals in impoverished neighbourhoods.

In 1224 Francis experienced a vision of an angel from whom he received the 'stigmata': wounds in his own body replicating those suffered by Christ on the cross. Proclaimed a saint in 1228—just two years after his death—he quickly became a beloved figure and the subject of many legends, among them several that emphasized his love of the natural world. In one of the most famous tales, he preaches to a flock of birds, telling them how fortunate they are to be provided for by God.

Dominicans and Carmelites

In 1216–17 a priest from northern Spain named Dominic Guzmán received a papal mandate to establish a preaching order dedicated to combatting the so-called Albigensian heresy (named for the city of Albi in southwestern France). Albigensianism was a dualistic doctrine, not unlike Manichaeism, centred on a view of existence as a struggle between light and darkness, and was highly critical of Roman Catholicism. Dominicans like Thomas Aquinas (1225–74) rapidly established their influence as itinerant preachers of doctrine in university towns such as Paris. In England they became known as 'Black Friars' for the black mantle worn over their white habits.

The Carmelites (hermits of Mount Carmel) were organized in Palestine in 1154, during the Crusades, and given a rule by the patriarch of Jerusalem. As the numbers of crusaders in the Holy Land declined, the Carmelites established themselves in Europe and in England, where they were termed 'White Friars'.

The Crusades

In the course of Islam's expansion across the Middle East, the Arab Muslims had captured Jerusalem in 637. The minority of local populations that remained Christian were formally tolerated, and European Christians were still free to make pilgrimages to Jerusalem. In 1071, however, the city was taken by the Seljuq Turks, who—as recent converts to Islam—were less accommodating than the Arabs. The Byzantine emperors felt threatened and appealed for Western help.

In 1095, when Pope Urban II called on Western Christians to liberate the holy places of Palestine, thousands of French, Norman, and Flemish knights committed themselves to the cause. The crusaders won some bloody victories, capturing Antioch and Jerusalem in 1099. They held Jerusalem for almost a century, until their power was broken by Salah al-Din (Saladin) in 1187.

Several more expeditions eventually set out to bolster the crusader enterprise, but too often were distracted by objectives that had little to do with their professed goal. In 1148, the second crusade was diverted to the unsuccessful siege of Damascus, which had been at peace with the kingdom of Jerusalem. In the third crusade, Richard I ('the Lionhearted') of England took Cyprus from the Byzantines in 1192. And in 1204 the troops of the fourth crusade set out for Egypt but went to Constantinople instead, plundering the city and placing a ruler from Flanders on its throne. Although the Byzantines recaptured the city in 1261, relations between Western and Eastern Christians did not recover. Furthermore, although trade relations between Europe and the Middle East eventually resumed, in modern times Muslims have come to regard the crusaders as precursors of Western infiltration and intrusion into their territory.

Beliefs and Doctrine

Sainthood

Over the centuries the Church developed criteria for sainthood (including the performance of attested miracles) and a rigorous procedure for screening new nominees for the title. The first person to become a saint under these regulations was a German bishop, in 993.

The saints collectively came to be thought of as a kind of heavenly senate or honour society whose members could intercede with God on behalf of the faithful. By praying to the saints, or making pilgrimages to their shrines, believers might win release both from punishment in the next existence and from guilt in this one. Particular saints are honoured on particular days, and many European explorers named places in the New World for the saints on whose days they were 'discovered'. Thus St John's, Newfoundland, was so named by John Cabot because he first entered its harbour on the feast of St John the Baptist (24 June).

The Figure of Mary

Early Christianity, both Greek and Latin, accorded a pre-eminent place among the saints to Mary, the mother of Jesus. From scanty biblical details, Christian regard for Mary developed along two parallel lines. She became the focus of popular devotion both as the principal feminine point of access to the Trinity and as a model of sorrow-enduring love in her own right. The holidays marking events in her biography developed first in the Greek east; among them are the Annunciation (when the angel Gabriel announced to her that she had been chosen to bear the Son of God), the Purification (the ritual following childbirth), and the Dormition (the 'falling asleep, or death').

At the same time Mary was the subject of theological speculation. According to the doctrine of the virgin birth, she remained a virgin before, during, and after the birth of Jesus, while the doctrine of the assumption maintained that her body was taken up into heaven, where she now reigns with her son and mediates between him and the faithful. The notion of the immaculate conception, according to which she herself was born without the 'stain' of original sin, was the subject of a centuries-long debate, but was finally proclaimed official doctrine in 1854. As the 'Mother of God' in the Roman tradition and *theotokos* ('bearer of God') in the Eastern, Mary also came to be regarded as the mother of the Church itself.

Pilgrimages and Relics

In the early Church, the bodies of saints and martyrs were interred in churches. This practice marked a break from Jewish tradition, which considered the dead unclean and required prompt burial in cemeteries. By the fourth century it had become customary for the altar cloths used in Eucharistic services to have fragments of saints' bones sewn into their hems. And the Second Council of Nicaea declared it mandatory for every church sanctuary to contain a relic—part of the body or personal paraphernalia of a venerated individual. The function of relics in medieval popular piety can hardly be overestimated. As tangible things, they were easy for people with little or no schooling to understand, and in the Middle Ages people began to make pilgrimages to see them. The only opportunity that most people ever had to travel beyond the fields and towns where they worked, a pilgrimage was an experience to look forward to. The fourteenth-century English pilgrims travelling to the shrine at Canterbury in Geoffrey Chaucer's *Canterbury Tales* represent a variety of social types (including one who is ready to make a quick profit by producing fraudulent relics).

The most treasured relics were naturally those associated with Jesus himself. Chips or slivers of wood and assorted nails purported to be from the 'True Cross' were highly prized, as were spines from the Crown of Thorns worn by Jesus on the cross. A piece of cloth known as Veronica's veil was believed to carry an impression of Jesus' face en route to the crucifixion, and a linen shroud that turned up in France in the fourteenth century was said to bear an impression of his entombed body; now kept in Turin, Italy, it is known as the Shroud of Turin.

The Problem of Evil

Does the devil exist? Today many Christians who are quite ready to talk about God in personal terms are very reluctant to suppose that a comparable being exists as his adversary. In 1999 Pope John Paul II advised the faithful to think of hell not as a place but as a condition of spiritual estrangement. Things were different in the Middle Ages. Not only did God have an angelic host, but the devil—Satan, or the Antichrist—commanded a corresponding host of demons. Satan is still a reality to a huge number of Protestant Christians who are committed to literal interpretation of the Bible.

The Hebrew Bible contains little evidence for an independent evil creature. The word 'satan'—Hebrew for 'adversary'—is found in the Hebrew Bible, but does not refer to a fallen angel. At most this figure is one of God's courtiers (as in the book of *Job*), dependent on God's command. The term 'antichrist' originally referred to a false teacher in the New Testament letters of John. But notions of a supernatural opponent to God emerged in Apocalyptic Judaism around the time that Christianity did.

A view common since the early Christian writers is that the devil started as an angel, but through pride tried to take over God's role and so fell from grace. This is the implication of the name Lucifer ('bearer of light'): a star that has fallen from heaven. Christian theology identified the snake in the garden of Eden with Satan, and this story is central to its notion of the 'original sin' innate in humanity.

In Christian tradition, Lucifer falls to the realm of hell, which is the destiny of the wicked. The medieval imagination depicted in gory detail the torments that the wicked suffered there, far from the divine light; images of hell often showed the damned prodded by pitchforks, speared, and boiled in cauldrons.

Sin, Heresy, and Witchcraft

To the modern mind, the Latin Christianity of the Middle Ages seems obsessed with sin. Referring to the first New Testament letter of John (*1 John* 5: 16), medieval theologians identified two kinds of sin. A 'mortal' sin deprived the soul of God's grace: to qualify as a mortal sin, an act had to concern a 'grave matter' and be committed both knowingly and willfully. The Church required that such an act be reported in private confession to a priest, who had to prescribe penance and absolve the offender before he or she could receive the Eucharist. Lesser sins were termed 'venial' and did not require confession.

For moral edification, the Church also warned the faithful against the Seven Deadly Sins: pride, covetousness or avarice, lust or lechery, envy, gluttony, anger or wrath, and sloth. A list of seven was established as early as the beginning of the seventh century by Pope Gregory I, although his seventh sin was despair rather than sloth.

During the eleventh century it became increasingly common for secular authorities to execute those convicted of heresy by burning them alive at the stake. Groups considered heretical, such as the Albigensians or the Waldensians (a similar group in northwestern Italy) tended to seek refuge in regions where the risks of apprehension were relatively low. Church councils in the twelfth century prescribed a range of penalties for heresy that included expulsion from the Church, imprisonment, and confiscation of property but stopped short of death.

By the beginning of the thirteenth century, however, the Church was prepared to take more severe action against heretics. Bishops were instructed to carry out 'episcopal inquisitions' in their dioceses and turn offenders over to secular authorities for punishment. And in the 1230s a special institution was established to identify and prosecute heretics. Staffed mainly by Dominicans, the papal Inquisition was particularly active in southwestern France, where the trial procedures it established set a pattern that would be followed for centuries. In 1252 Pope Innocent IV stipulated that torture could be used and that heretics handed over to secular authorities should be executed within five days.

The Inquisition was at its most brutal in Spain, where Ferdinand and Isabella used it specifically to target those Jews and Muslims who converted to Christianity in order to avoid expulsion. The Grand Inquisitor Tomás de Torquemada (c. 1420–98) ordered more than two thousand executions. The standard handbook for Christian witch-hunting was the *Malleus Maleficarum* ('Hammer of Witches'), published in 1486 by two Dominicans authorized by Pope Innocent IV to eradicate witchcraft from Germany.

The efforts of religious authorities to root out heresy combined with peasant superstition to encourage the medieval belief in witches as agents of the devil, practitioners of malevolent magic who were said to have intimate sexual relations with him. In reality, records of sixteenth- and seventeenth-century witchcraft trials in England suggest that accusations of witchcraft were often inspired either by personal grudges or by fear of non-conforming behaviour. Widows and women with knowledge of herbal cures were particularly likely to attract accusations of witchcraft. It is also possible that the symptoms of 'demonic possession' suffered by some accusers may have been physiological; records of the witchcraft trials of 1692 in Salem, Massachusetts, have suggested to some modern researchers that the accusers were accidentally poisoned by ergot—a grain fungus that produces a hallucinogen quite similar to LSD. Many people who ingest ergot-infected grain die, but those who survive often report strange experiences and wild visions.

Scholastic Philosophy

As the first European universities developed in cities like Paris, Bologna, and Oxford, theology became a central subject in the curriculum. Scholasticism was the school of thought devoted to understanding scripture through reason.

John Scotus Erigena was a ninth-century scholastic philosopher who was born in Ireland and taught in Paris. He believed that scripture was authoritative, but that it was the duty of reason to examine and expound it. Early scholastic teaching was based on the reading of scripture. At this early stage the scholastics were seeking to distill and summarize scripture and arrive at a rational grasp of its meaning, but in time their teaching developed a dialectical structure in which a proposition of doctrine was stated and then objections to it were systematically dealt with.

Anselm

Anselm (c. 1033–1109), a native of the Italian Alps who became archbishop of Canterbury in England, moved away from the principle of scriptural authority, asserting that faith itself has a kind of rationality. One of his best-known formulations is the statement 'I believe so that I may understand.'

The most tantalizing of the medieval proofs for the existence of God is Anselm's ontological argument ('ontology' is the study of being or existence). Unlike later thinkers who inferred God's existence from inspection of the universe (the 'cosmos'), Anselm found it implied in the idea of God itself. Characterizing God as 'a being greater than which nothing can be conceived', Anselm argues (in a treatise called the *Proslogion*) that such a being must exist not only in the mind but in reality, since if it did not exist, some other being that did exist would be greater. Anselm then pursues the argument in a second and more substantial form: a being that cannot be conceived not to exist is greater than one that can. In philosophical terms, all other being is contingent, whereas God's being is necessary.

Thomas Aquinas

The greatest of the Aristotelian scholastics was the Dominican Thomas Aquinas, who taught in Paris. In his *Summa Theologiae* ('Summation of Theology') and other writings Thomas sharpened the distinction between reason and faith. He argued that a number of Christian faith assertions, such as the doctrines of the Trinity and the incarnation of God in Christ, lie beyond reason (although that does not mean they are contrary to reason). Other Christian affirmations, however, such as the existence of God, he did believe to be provable by reason.

Thomas Aquinas identified five 'ways' of proving God's existence. The first three are variations on what philosophers call the 'cosmological argument' for God's existence; that is, they are based on observation of the universe. First, change or motion in the universe is evidence that there must be a Prime Mover to sustain the process. Second, the pattern of cause and effect points to God as the First Cause. Third, things have the possibility of existing or not existing, being generated or corrupted, but in order for there not to have once been nothing at all, there must have been some being that existed out of necessity, and that being is God.

The fourth argument is that there are gradations of goodness, truth, and nobility in what we experience, and that therefore there must be a being that is supremely good, supremely true, and supremely noble; in a sense, this is also a type of cosmological argument. Finally, the fifth 'way' consists in the idea that the plan observable in the universe is evidence of a divine planner; this is an example of the 'teleological argument' (from Greek *telos*, 'end' or 'purpose').

Three years after Thomas Aquinas died, the archbishop of Paris formally condemned a list of propositions similar to his. But later generations appreciated the comprehensive nature of Thomas's system. In 1567, at the time of the Catholic Reformation, Pope Pius V declared him 'Doctor of the Church'. In 1879 Pope Leo XIII opened a modern era for Thomism when, in an effort to counteract modern thinking, he made Thomas required reading for theology students.

Mysticism

Today the word 'mysticism' often suggests something unclear, uncertain, or mysterious. In the context of Christianity, however, mysticism is defined as the knowledge of God from (personal) experience. The certainty of God that a mystic has is based not on logical proof but on a moment of vivid, intense awareness. At such a moment one may experience ecstasy (from Greek, 'standing outside oneself') or displacement from one's ordinary mode of awareness. Characteristic of that experience is a sense of union with, or a vision of, the divine—a temporary dissolving or bridging of the gulf that separates the human person from God. Human beings are created in the image of God, but our divine nature is obscured because our life is finite and creaturely. However, the mind of the spiritual person permits an actualization of the divine nature that the human soul contains. The individual mystic becomes aware of the divinity of his or her being. Eckhart's mysticism is unitive, seeking to dissolve distinctions between self and God.

The most formidable systematizer of mystical thought in medieval Europe was the German Dominican Johannes ('Meister') Eckhart (c. 1260–1327). For Eckhart human beings are created in the image of God, but our divine nature is obscured because our life is finite and creaturely. The mind of the spiritual person permits an actualization of the divine nature that the human soul contains. The individual mystic becomes aware of the divinity of his or her being. Eckhart's mysticism is described as 'unitive' because it tends towards dissolving distinctions between self and God.

Bonaventure (1221–74), an Italian Franciscan who taught at Paris in the thirteenth century, wrote a text entitled *Journey of the Mind to God*. In it meditation on the humanity of Christ becomes the point of experiential contact with the divine. Later, in the writings of St John of the Cross, a sixteenth-century Spanish Carmelite, the soul seeks to purify itself. John speaks of the 'dark night of the soul' when it is purged of its attachments and rises to God in a union described in the language of a pure flame.

A striking feature of late medieval mysticism is the scope it afforded for women. Though women were prevented from participating fully in clerical activities and were limited to supporting roles in their religious orders, there was no limit to the experiential depth they could attain in their devotion. Hildegard of Bingen (1098–1179) was a Benedictine abbess who had a rich creative life in writing and music. She was also involved in politics, and became known as the 'Sybil of the Rhine' among the clergy and nobles who sought her advice. When she became abbess in 1141, she had a vision of tongues of flame from the heavens settling on her, and over the next ten years she wrote a book of visions called *Scivias* ('Know the ways [of God]').

Mysticism

Hildegard of Bingen

From Scivias (*Know the ways [of God]*), *written between 1141 and 1151, Book II, section 2.6:*

On the Trinity: Just as the flame contains three essences in the one fire, so too, there is one God in three persons. How is this so? The flame consists of shining brightness, purple vigour and fiery glow. It has shining brightness so that it may give light; purple vigour so that it may flourish; and a fiery glow so that it may burn.

In the shining brightness, observe the Father who, in his fatherly devotion, reveals his brightness to the faithful. In the purple vigour contained within it (whereby this same flame manifests its power), understand the Son who, from the Virgin, assumed a body in which Godhead demonstrated its miracles. And in the fiery glow, perceive the Holy Spirit which pours glowingly into the minds of believers.

But where there is neither shining brightness, nor purple vigour, nor fiery glow, there no flame is seen. So too, where neither the Father nor the Son nor the Holy Spirit is honoured, there God is not worthily revered.

And so, just as these three essences are discerned in the one flame, so too, three Persons are to be understood in the unity of Godhead (Bowie and Davies 1990: 53, 75).

Teresa of Ávila

From Chapter 18 of her autobiography:

Previously, . . . the senses were permitted to give some indication of the great joy they feel. But now the soul enjoys incomparably more, and yet has still less power to show it. For there is no power left in the body—and the soul possesses none—by which this joy can be communicated. At such a time anything of the sort would be a great embarrassment, a torment and a disturbance of its repose. If there is really a union of all the faculties, I say, then the soul cannot make it known, even if it wants to—while actually in union I mean. If it can, it is not in union.

How what is called union takes place and what it is, I cannot tell. It is explained in mystical theology, but I cannot use the proper terms; I cannot understand what mind is, or how it differs from soul or spirit. They all seem one to me, though the soul sometimes leaps out of itself like a burning fire that has become one whole flame and increases with great force. The flame leaps very high above the fire. Nevertheless it is not a different thing, but the same flame which is in the fire (Happold 1963:321).

Catherine of Siena (1347–80 or 1333–80) was a member of the Dominican lay order in Italy. She was actively involved in the religious politics of the day, but her *Dialogue* records her mystical visions.

Julian of Norwich (c. 1342–c. 1413) was an English mystic who experienced visions one day during a five-hour state of ecstasy, and another vision the next day. At 50, after two decades of reflection, she wrote a description and analysis of her visions in her *Sixteen Revelations of Divine Love*. To her, evil is a distortion introduced by the human will, serving to reveal by contrast all the more clearly the divine love of God.

Teresa of Avila (1515–82), a Spanish Carmelite living in the same spiritual milieu as John of the Cross, decided at the age of 40 to seek spiritual perfection. Sometime later she experienced her first mystical ecstasy, and over the next 15 years, while actively working to establish religious houses, she deepened her spiritual life until in 1572 it reached the state of 'spiritual marriage'.

A woman who was not a contemplative mystic but nonetheless experienced intense spiritual visions was Joan of Arc (1412–31), who in 1429 led a military expedition to relieve the French forces under siege by the English at Orléans, south of Paris. Captured the following year, she was convicted of witchcraft and heresy, and burnt at the stake in 1431. On a review of her trial in 1456 she was posthumously found innocent, and in 1920 she was declared a saint.

DIFFERENTIATION

The Protestant Reformation

By the early sixteenth century, pressure for change in the Latin Church had been build-ing for decades. Princes north of the Alps were challenging the power of the papacy in Rome. The period of cultural rebirth known as the Renaissance was well underway, as was the revival of classical learning central to humanism, exemplified in the Dutch scholar Desiderius Erasmus (1466–1536). Condemning complicated scholastic theology, Erasmus urged a return to the simple morality of Jesus through the critical study of scripture in local languages; he also wrote a scathing satire of Catholic doctrine and Church corruption called *The Praise of Folly* (1509). A few years later, Ulrich von Hutten and Crotus Rubianus published *Letters of Obscure Men* (1513–15), mocking the futility of Church regulations.

Literacy was spreading and local vernacular dialects were developing into regional languages. But suggestions that the Bible might be translated into the languages of the people were firmly rejected by the Church, which was well aware that direct access to scripture would pose a serious threat to its authority. When John Wyclif (1329–84) in England and John Hus (c. 1369–1415) among the Czechs proposed to replace Latin with the vernacular in worship and to translate the Bible into the languages of the people, the church condemned them as heretics.

Martin Luther

Although the danger signals had been in evidence for decades, it was the stubborn and uninhibited personality of one man that ultimately enabled the Protestant Reformation in Germany to erupt as it did. Martin Luther (1483–1546) was a monk (a member of the mendicant Augustinian order) and theological scholar at the university in Wittenberg who objected to the Church's practice of selling indulgences: releases from time in purgatory (the supposed holding area for the soul in its passage from death to the next existence). At that time the standard way of raising a topic for debate was to post a notice about it on the church door. Thus in 1517 Luther posted a list of 95 propositions or 'theses' criticizing various aspects of Church practice.

In 1521 Luther had to defend himself against charges of political subversion at an imperial council called the Diet of Worms, held at the German city of Worms. When he refused to retract his views, he was first censured and eventually excommunicated. But support for his ideas spread and took on a concrete political form.

Luther was hardly the first to object to the Church's extravagance and corruption. The core of his challenge, however, was theological. Luther wanted to reform the very understanding of the nature of sin and redemption. He rejected the idea of redemption as a transaction in which the individual confesses particular sins and expiates them through particular acts of penance. Instead, he maintained that through Jesus divine grace reaches out to save and redeem human beings regardless of their merit or deeds. Taking up a key theme in Paul's letter to the Romans, Luther insisted that humans are 'justified'—freed from the penalty of sin—not by works but by faith alone. Like Paul, he based his stand on experiential certainty, which he described as the inner guidance or testimony of the Holy Spirit. For Paul, the works in question were Jewish ritual observances; for Luther, they were the rituals of confession and penance in Latin Christianity.

From 1517 until 1521 Luther had the opportunity to withdraw his challenges to the Church. Had a settlement been negotiated, the pressure for reform might have dropped off; but Luther stood his ground. Historians doubt that he actually spoke the words attributed to him: 'Here I stand; I can do no other.' But the sentiment is in keeping with what he likely did say at the Diet: 'Unless I am convicted by Scripture and plain reason—I do not accept the authority of popes and councils, for they have contradicted each other—my conscience is captive to the Word of God, I cannot and I will not recant anything' (Bainton 1974, 15:551).

The emperor, Charles V, called Luther a threat to order and banished him. During the few days he was given to leave under safe conduct, Luther was intercepted by some armed men along the highway and disappeared for more than a year. Many thought him dead, but he was actually in hiding under the protection of his patron, Prince Frederick. Luther used this period of seclusion to produce a string of theological writings and to translate the New Testament from the original Greek into a direct, lively German that eventually gave the Luther Bible a profoundly influential place in German literature.

In the form it took, the Protestant Reformation could not have come about much earlier than it did. The technology of printing from movable type had been introduced in Europe only half a century earlier—a Latin Bible came off Johann Gutenberg's press in 1456. Though prohibitively expensive at first, printed materials soon became less costly to produce. Luther's challenges to the Church were rapidly disseminated in pamphlets that reached a wide popular audience. As many as a million pamphlets were reportedly produced between 1521 and 1524. Of Luther's own short tracts or pamphlets there were at least 1,300 different printings by 1523. His very readable translation of the Bible had an impact, too (the New Testament appeared in 1522 and the Old Testament in 1534).

By the mid-1520s Luther's teachings had inspired a dozen nuns to leave the convent in Wittenberg. Three of them went back to their families, but the other nine were now homeless. Luther found husbands for eight of them and then married the last, Katherina von Bora, himself. In the course of time they had six children and also adopted four orphans. In his writing *Concerning Married Life*, Luther suggests that even such ordinary activities as diaper-washing can be ennobled by faith.

In effect, Luther removed the priesthood from the pedestal it had occupied since the time of Constantine. Replacing institutional tradition with the authority of the Bible and the inner guidance of the Holy Spirit meant that there was no longer any need for an intermediary between Christians and God to transmit human petitions or dispense divine grace. Protestants use the phrase 'the priesthood of all believers' to refer to the egalitarianism of spiritual access that Luther introduced.

In 1524–5, when an uprising broke out among German peasants, Luther refused to endorse all their demands. As a consequence, the more radical among them left Luther to follow a more strident leader, Thomas Müntzer. Eventually they founded the Anabaptist movement, so-called because it held that baptism should be reserved for adults capable of making a mature decision for faith, and therefore rebaptized people who had already been baptized as infants.

Luther also broke with the Swiss reformer Huldrych (Ulrich) Zwingli over the interpretation of the Eucharist. Both men rejected the Roman Catholic view of the Eucharist as a literal re-enactment of Christ's self-sacrifice. But whereas Luther continued to believe that Jesus was physically present, if unseen, during the rite, Zwingli insisted that the words 'this is my body' meant only 'this represents': in other words, that the rite was purely symbolic.

Branches of Protestantism: Sixteenth Century

From the beginning, the Reformation was marked by division and diversity. Protestants had rejected the central institutional control of Rome, but many early reformers were no less authoritarian than the church they had rejected. Those who disagreed with a particular leader would often break away and establish their own denominations. This tendency towards denominational fragmentation has continued to the present day. Three main 'establishments' emerged from the Reformation in the course of the sixteenth century: Lutheran, Anglican, and Calvinist. (Other branches, such as the Anabaptists, are considered non-establishment.)

Lutheranism

Luther's followers became the majority in Germany and Scandinavia. Like him, they stressed the authority of scripture and the guidance of the Holy Spirit. There was ample scope for rational and intellectual argument in the exposition of scripture, but Lutheranism also encouraged a deep sense of personal piety. In Lutheran hymns God is a friend and companion as well as a warrior and judge.

In worship and ecclesiastical organization Lutherans departed in only some respects from the precedents set by the Roman Church. They retained a Eucharistic service; but they celebrated it in the vernacular rather than Latin and rejected the doctrine of transubstantiation, according to which, at a certain moment during the service of the mass, the wafer and the wine are actually transformed into the body and the blood of Christ. They held that although Christ's body became present during the ceremony, it was not produced out of the bread and wine. In addition, the Lutheran Church retained a priesthood governed by bishops, but permitted its clergy to marry. (Ordination of women as priests is a recent phenomenon among Lutherans.)

Map 4.1 Christianity: Major spheres of influence

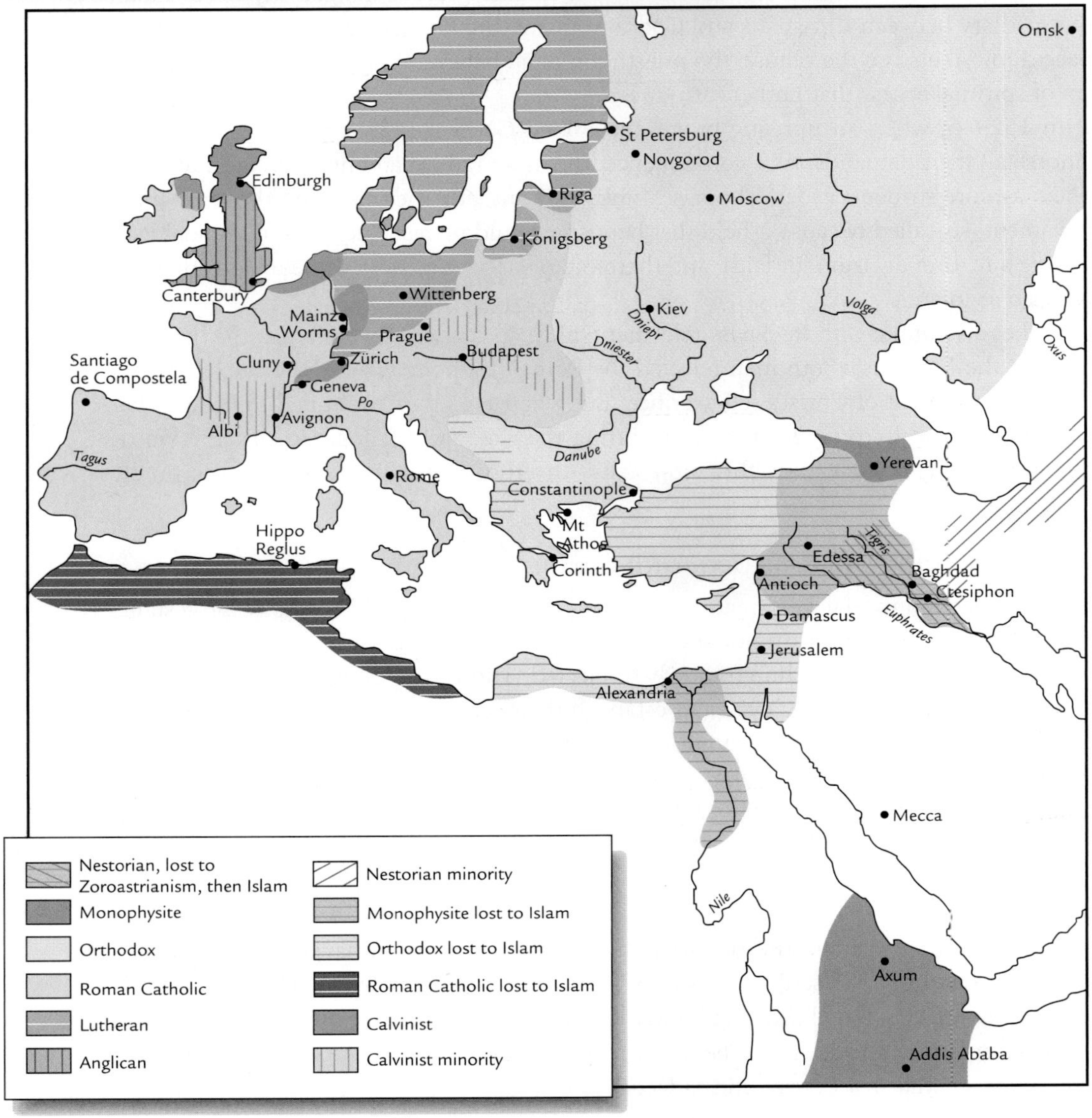
Omsk
St Petersburg
Novgorod
Moscow
Edinburgh
Riga
Königsberg
Canterbury
Wittenberg
Mainz
Worms
Prague
Kiev
Dniepr
Volga
Oxus
Santiago de Compostela
Cluny
Zürich
Budapest
Dniester
Geneva
Po
Albi
Avignon
Tagus
Danube
Yerevan
Rome
Constantinople
Hippo Reglus
Mt Athos
Edessa
Tigris
Corinth
Baghdad
Antioch
Ctesiphon
Damascus
Euphrates
Jerusalem
Alexandria
Mecca
Nile
Axum
Addis Ababa
Nestorian, lost to Zoroastrianism, then Islam
Monophysite
Orthodox
Roman Catholic
Lutheran
Anglican
Nestorian minority
Monophysite lost to Islam
Orthodox lost to Islam
Roman Catholic lost to Islam
Calvinist
Calvinist minority

Outside Germany and Scandinavia, Lutheranism has spread through both missionary activity and migration. In the nineteenth century, German immigrants took Lutheranism to regions such as Pennsylvania, Ohio, Missouri, Ontario, and the shores of Lake Michigan, while Scandinavian immigrants took it mainly to Minnesota and Wisconsin. Since then the ethnic character of North American Lutheran churches has generally become diluted over time, except in areas where German and Scandinavian immigration has continued.

Anglicanism

Whereas in Germany the Reformation had been a popular movement, in England it was royal policy. Henry VIII wanted a male heir, but his queen, Catherine of Aragon, had borne only a daughter. Hoping that Anne Boleyn would produce a son, in 1527 Henry requested an annulment of his first marriage on the grounds that it was invalid because Catherine had previously been married to his deceased brother. Although Pope Clement VII refused the request, Henry found some support in European universities. In 1533, therefore, he secretly married Anne and then had the Archbishop of Canterbury, Thomas Cranmer, annul the first marriage and pronounce the second valid.

At Henry's instigation, the English parliament in 1534 passed an Act of Supremacy, which 'for corroboration and confirmation' proclaimed the king and his successors the only Supreme Head in earth of the Church of England'. Although the wording implied that the monarch had always held that distinction, in reality he had not; the act itself was the first statement in which the king replaced the pope as head of the English Church.

But divorce and a male successor were not the only things on Henry's mind. While the break with Rome could be interpreted as stemming from a high-minded principle of secularity, it is more likely that Henry was motivated by the desire to expropriate the Church's vast landholdings.

The key Protestant reformer under Henry's successor Edward VI (r. 1547–53; the son of Henry's third wife) was Cranmer, who made an enduring contribution in the 1549 *Book of Common Prayer*. Though it has undergone a number of revisions, it is still a model for Anglican worship.

In the end, even though the English Reformation was often directed from the top down, the church it produced had much in common with the one produced by the grass-roots Lutheran Reformation: an established state church without links to Rome; a traditional mass, but conducted in the vernacular; a hierarchy with bishops, but with clergy who could now marry. The Church of England has remained a state church, with the monarch as its titular head. (When the monarch is in Scotland, she or he is head of the Church of Scotland, which is Presbyterian—governed by elders or 'presbyters' rather than bishops.) The ranking bishop of the Church continues to be the archbishop of Canterbury. In most European countries, and in Canada, the established or state churches receive significant financial support from the government.

The tradition of the Church of England is generally called Anglican, although it is known in the United States as Episcopalian, after its form of government by bishops. It has taken root wherever British influence has been strong: not only in North America, Australia, New Zealand, and South Africa, but also in the former British colonies and protectorates in East Africa, West Africa, the Caribbean, India, and the Polynesian islands.

The diversity of the human community is reflected among the participating bishops at international meetings of the Anglican communion. In recent years, the relative liberality of the American and English churches in approving homosexual priests and bishops has led to a serious disagreement with the more conservative bishops of the former colonies and protectorates, one that may yet end in schism (a split).

A tension of much longer standing is the one between what came to be called 'high-church' and 'low-church' Anglicanism. The high-church side can approach Roman

Catholicism in its emphasis on ritual, whereas the low-church side is more spontaneous and committed to spreading the gospel. Although this tension had existed for centuries, it came to a head in the nineteenth century, when the 'Oxford movement' within the Church of England feared that the church might lose its established status. The response of the Oxford movement was to emphasize that the Anglican Church was not dependent on the state, but instead derived its authority from 'catholic' tradition—by which they meant not the Roman Catholic Church but the tradition that began with the apostles.

From 1833 to 1841 John Keble, John Henry Newman, and others published 90 *Tracts for the Times*, arguing for the continuity of that apostolic tradition. The Tractarians, as they came to be called, also promoted a revival of Anglican interest in the aesthetics of the liturgy and the dignity of priesthood.

Calvinism

From the 1520s to 1560s, the Reformation movement in and around Switzerland departed from Luther's position on several points. While Zwingli in Zürich disputed Luther's Eucharistic theology, Martin Bucer in Strasbourg promoted a more active role for lay people as ministers, elders, deacons, and teachers.

The intellectual leader of the Reformation, however, was John Calvin (1509–64), a lawyer and classical scholar (even a Renaissance humanist) who imposed rigorous norms of doctrine and conduct on the city of Geneva. Calvin's Geneva has been termed a theocracy comparable to Iran under the rule of religio-legal scholars after 1979. Yet to his followers Calvin's trust in God's power and caring providence brought at least as much joy as it did fear.

Calvin's principal theological treatise, published in 1536 (just before he became actively involved in Geneva's civic life) and expanded in later editions, bears a title that is commonly translated as 'Institutes of the Christian Religion'. In form it is a manual of spiritual discipline that might be more aptly titled 'instruction in Christian piety'. Echoing Augustine in his *Confessions*, Calvin maintains that humans are created for communion with God and cannot rest until they arrive at it. The human approach to God is both intellectual and spiritual; Calvin uses the term 'knowledge' almost as a synonym for 'faith'. Unlike the writings of Luther, which were usually responses to specific situations, Calvin's Institutes has a systematic overall structure.

For Calvin, God is absolutely sovereign, initiating all actions, both creating and redeeming the world. Two implications of this teaching were given a central place by Calvin's interpreters, and the Reformed tradition has struggled to defend them ever since: first, humans are dependent on divine grace and are utterly sinful and powerless to achieve salvation; second, the sovereign God, who is both omniscient and omnipotent, predestines every person to either salvation or damnation. Strictly speaking, in Calvin's thought, no one could know who was saved or damned. From sixteenth-century Geneva, the ideas of the Swiss Reformation spread to other lands, notably France (where the adherents of the Reformation came to be known as Huguenots), the Netherlands, Hungary, England, and Scotland.

In the Netherlands Calvin's doctrine of predestination was challenged by Jacobus Arminius, who believed that God's sovereignty was compatible with human free will.

Arminian views were condemned by an assembly in Dordrecht (Dort) in 1518, which sentenced their sympathizer, the scholar and jurist Hugo Grotius, to life imprisonment. Grotius escaped in a box of books being shipped to his wife and settled for a time in Paris, but strict predestinarian doctrine carried the day in Holland.

Calvinist churches in the Netherlands and Hungary are termed Reformed. In England the same tradition is called Presbyterian, as is the established state Church of Scotland. Reformed churches do not have bishops; instead, the regional representative assembly, the presbytery, corporately performs the traditional tasks of a bishop, including the supervision, examination, and ordination of candidates for ministry. Presbyterians call a multi-presbytery gathering a synod—the old term for a meeting of bishops.

Presbyterianism has taken root on other continents through migration. Presbyterians from England and Scotland settled in eastern Canada and the middle Atlantic American states, as well as in New Zealand and Australia. Dutch Reformed settlers carried their tradition to South Africa and to New Amsterdam (New York) and Michigan. In the nineteenth and twentieth centuries, Presbyterian missions from Britain and North America reached many parts of Asia and Africa. In most lands the 'younger churches' founded by missionaries remained small, and in the Islamic world they found most of their recruits not among Muslims but among Eastern Orthodox populations. Presbyterians did become a sizable minority in Korea, however.

Anabaptists

All three branches of the Reformation named so far were willing, even eager, to take over the governance of their respective societies and replace established institutions by becoming establishments themselves. The situation was different with the somewhat more diverse and less cohesive group called Anabaptists. Essentially antiestablishment in its orientation, the Anabaptist movement emerged in response to dissatisfaction with the pace of change in the first decade of the Reformation. One of the first breaks with the 'establishment' Reformation came in 1525, when some of the more radical followers of Zwingli began administering adult baptism in defiance of Zwingli himself.

The Anabaptists' emphasis on adult rather than infant baptism reflected their belief that baptism should not be imposed but actively sought on the basis of mature personal commitment. The Church should seek to restore the close-knit sense of community of the apostolic era, and should remain apart from political institutions and structures. Anabaptists rely on lay preachers rather than trained clergy and in times of war they have tended to pacifism. In 1533–5, Anabaptist efforts to establish the kingdom of God by force in the northwestern German town of Münster prompted a severe crackdown by Catholic and Protestant authorities. Thereafter a former Dutch priest named Menno Simons led the movement in a largely otherworldly and non-violent direction. Since there was virtually no chance of removing the authorities, he urged his followers to remove themselves from society. In the course of their withdrawal his followers—the Mennonites—spread eastward through Germany and Austria to the Ukraine.

Some Mennonites escaped hardship or persecution in Europe by migrating to the Americas. In Pennsylvania, where some arrived as early as 1663, they came to be known as Pennsylvania Dutch (from *Deutsch*, meaning 'German'). While most Mennonites today use modern technology, some branches, such as the Old Order Amish farmers in Pennsylvania and Ontario, prefer traditional modes of dress and conduct. They continue to farm with the draft animals and simple tools of a century ago, resisting more advanced technology as part of the moral temptation and corruption of the modern world.

Unitarianism

Unitarianism rejects the doctrine of the Trinity. So what does it have to do with a tradition that may be strictly defined as faith in Jesus as the son of God? Its relevance lies in the fact that it reflects the experience of those who have struggled with the doctrine of the Trinity and concluded that they could not affirm the divinity of Jesus. Historically, it is only in the context of traditional Christianity that Unitarianism makes sense.

In Strasbourg, Martin Cellarius rejected the doctrine of the Trinity as early as 1527, choosing to speak of God as a single person. Unitarian communities later emerged in several lands. In Poland an Italian named Giorgio Biandrata launched Unitarian ideas in 1558 and was followed by Fausto Sozzini in 1579; Socinianism, as the teaching was called, was banished from Poland in 1658. In 1553 Biandrata planted Unitarian ideas in Hungary, where he won the support of the king, John II Sigismund Zápolya, but after the end of his reign the movement was persecuted.

In England the figure considered the father of Unitarianism was John Biddle, who began to publish tracts in 1652, but a Unitarian denomination was not organized until 1773–4, when Theophilus Lindsey resigned from the Church of England and opened a Unitarian chapel in London.

In the United States a sermon delivered by the left-wing Congregationalist William Ellery Channing in 1819 is generally taken as a kind of denominational manifesto. But Channing himself did not regard Unitarians as a separate group, and claimed to belong 'not to a sect, but to the community of free minds'.

In the nineteenth and twentieth centuries North American Unitarianism continued to appeal to a humanist and rationalist clientele, often in university circles. In 1961 the Unitarians merged with a kindred group called the Universalists.

Puritanism

Puritanism was not a denomination but a movement in English and colonial American Protestant churches that flourished from the mid-sixteenth to the mid-seventeenth century. It began as an effort to 'purify' the Church of England of the remnants of Catholicism in church vestments, furnishings, and ecclesiastical organization that it retained after the accession of Elizabeth I in 1558, when Protestants who had been exiled during the reign of the Catholic Mary I returned to England from Calvinist Geneva.

Among the influences the exiles introduced from Geneva was the idea of predestination. Individuals who believed themselves to have been chosen by God for salvation tended to display a strict, sometimes smug, sense of moral vocation that was reflected in the Puritan movement. Puritans were morally activist and stressed moderation in behaviour. Well-known literary expressions of Puritan ideals include the poems of John Milton and John Bunyan's allegorical narrative *Pilgrim's Progress.*

In the 1650s Oliver Cromwell sought to unite Congregationalists, Presbyterians, and Baptists in a Puritan state church. But with the restoration of the monarchy in 1660, Puritanism ceased to have a coherent existence as a movement in England. It had a ripple effect, however, in non-conformist (i.e., non-Anglican Protestant) denominations such as the Congregationalists. By the time Puritanism waned in England, it had already spread to the New World, carried by Puritan immigrants to New England.

Protestant Denominations: Seventeenth Century

More reformist denominations emerged and were carried from England to America in the seventeenth century. Though they differed in the details of their beliefs, each in its own way reflected the Reformation's rejection of external human authority. The Congregationalists insisted on autonomy for every local group of believers; the Baptists refused state interference; and the Quakers looked inward for insight.

Congregationalism

The Congregational movement traces its roots to 'separatist' clergy in the time of Elizabeth I, but it did not become a significant force until the era of Cromwell. As far as doctrine is concerned, there is little to distinguish Congregationalists from Presbyterians. Where they differ is in their form of governance. Carrying the notion of the priesthood of all believers to its logical conclusion, Congregationalists reject the idea of elders and accord each individual congregation the ultimate authority to manage its theological and institutional affairs: for them, the only higher power is God.

In England Congregational churches formed a Congregational Union in 1832 and were active in political and missionary causes throughout the nineteenth century. But the tradition's stronghold was Massachusetts, where Congregationalists founded Harvard University in 1637 in order not 'to leave an illiterate ministry to the churches, when our present ministers shall lie in the dust'. Yale University (1701) and other educational institutions in the American northeast were also founded by Congregationalists.

Baptists

Like the Anabaptists on the European continent, the English Baptists practised the baptism of mature believers rather than infants. Yet they had more in common with the English Puritan movement than with the continental Anabaptists. They believed that people should choose their religion and that this choice ought to be private and beyond any interference by the state. England's non-Calvinist Baptists, called General Baptists because they proclaimed a general redemption for humanity, were augmented in the 1630s by Calvinist or Particular Baptists, so called because they limited redemption to a particular sector of humanity. By that time the Particular Baptists were already practising the ritual of baptism by total immersion.

The real growth of the Baptists in the United States began after the revivalist movement known as the Great Awakening (1740–3). Though the Baptists were not among its principal protagonists, they made massive numerical gains in its wake. They positioned themselves to become the largest American Protestant denomination in part by appealing

Major Branches of Christianity

Nestorians (about 200,000)
  'Assyrians' of Iraq, Iran, and Turkey
  Nestorian Malabar Christians in India
Monophysites (about 30 million)
  Copts in Egypt
  Ethiopians
  Jacobites or Syrian Orthodox
  Jacobite Malabar Christians in India
  Armenians
Orthodox (about 300 million)
  Greek
  Bulgarian, Serbian, and Romanian
  Russian and Ukrainian
Catholics (about 1 billion)
  Roman Catholics
  Eastern 'Uniate' churches
  (some Anglicans)

Protestants (about 600 million)
  Sixteenth-century divisions
    Lutherans
    Anglicans
    Reformed (Presbyterian) churches
    Anabaptists
    Unitarians
  Seventeenth- and eighteenth-century divisions
    Congregationalists
    Baptists
    Quakers
    Methodists
  Nineteenth-century divisions
    Disciples
    Seventh-Day Adventists
    Jehovah's Witnesses
    Christian Scientists
    Mormons

to the Black population; by the middle of the twentieth century, two out of every three African-American Christians were Baptists.

Quakers

George Fox (1624–91) was an English dissenter or non-conformist who in 1646, after three years of seeking, achieved spiritual enlightenment and began to preach that moral and spiritual peace was to be found not in institutional religion but in the experience of the 'inner light' of the living Christ. He called his followers Friends of the Truth, but in 1650, when Fox was charged with blasphemy, a judge referred to him as a 'Quaker' because Fox had advised him to tremble at the word of the Lord. The movement now calls itself the Religious Society of Friends.

William Penn founded the colony of Pennsylvania in 1682 as a place where Quakers might find religious toleration and free expression. There Fox's initially impulsive group became staid, solid citizens. Quakers at worship combine intellectual and spiritual reflection without any fixed ritual, sitting in silence until they are moved by the Holy Spirit to speak. Though they number only about 100,000 worldwide, their humanitarian involvement in peace and refugee-relief causes has been significant and has earned the movement great respect.

Protestant Denominations: Eighteenth Century

Pietism

The term **Pietism** designates not a formal denomination but a movement that rippled through several Protestant denominations, including the Lutherans in Germany and the Reformed (Calvinist) churches in the Netherlands, beginning in the late 1600s. Dissatisfied with what they perceived as doctrinal and institutional rigidity in the Protestant churches that emerged from the Reformation, Pietists emphasized individual piety and renewal of faith accompanied by certainty of divine forgiveness and acceptance. For many, the feeling of that certainty was all the evidence they needed—a position that in Germany pitted Pietism against the emerging rationalism of the eighteenth-century Enlightenment, but that found intellectual expansion in the emphasis that Schleiermacher gave to feeling (see p. 188).

Pietism spread in Lutheran circles both in Europe and in the Americas. In the form articulated by the Moravian Brethren—who traced their origins to the early Czech reformer John Hus—it also influenced John Wesley and contributed to the development of Methodism.

Methodism

In the late 1720s a number of Anglican students at Oxford formed a group to study the Bible and attend church together. This methodical approach inspired others to call them 'Methodists'. Among them were John Wesley (1703–91), his brother Charles, and George Whitefield, all three of whom embarked on careers as itinerant preachers. In 1735 John and Charles set out on a mission to evangelize Native Americans in Georgia, but their condemnation of slavery made them unwelcome in the American South and they returned to England in 1738. A few months later, after a visit to a Moravian Pietist community, Charles experienced conversion, and three days later John felt his heart 'strangely warmed' in Pietist fashion.

John Wesley began to preach to public gatherings, often of miners and workers, outside the established churches. In the 53 remaining years of his life he preached more than 40,000 sermons, averaging 15 a week, and travelled 320,000 km (200,000 mi.), mainly on horseback. Though he had at first hoped his movement would revitalize the Church of England from within, Wesley eventually oversaw the organization of his following as an independent denomination and personally ordained leaders for it.

Revivalism

By the mid-1700s the Pietist model of spiritual rebirth or conversion had spread to a number of denominations. Efforts to promote a reawakening of spiritual enthusiasm resulted in a wave of revivals, especially in the American colonies. The Great Awakening was a revival that swept New England in 1740–3, sparked by the preaching of the gifted and versatile Calvinist theologian Jonathan Edwards.

The influence of the Great Awakening extended well beyond New England, and it altered the shape of American Protestantism as the nation expanded westward after the Revolutionary War. Camp meetings held by itinerant preachers from various denominations would often inspire mass conversions. Although Edwards had preached mainly to Congregationalists and Presbyterians, Methodists and Baptists were more success-ful in making new recruits. In time the Methodists emerged as the largest Protestant denomination in the American Midwest, and were second only to the Baptists in the American South.

Roman Catholicism after 1500

The Roman Church recognized the need to correct the abuses that Luther had condemned. Beginning with the Council of Trent (1545–63), it undertook a process of renewal that has often been called the Counter-Reformation.

The Catholic (Counter-) Reformation

The Council of Trent

After several delays, the Council of Trent opened in 1545 at the northern Italian city of Trent and continued on and off until 1563, when it finished with a burst of decisive energy. Although participation was restricted to Catholic bishops, some sessions were attended by Protestants as well.

The decrees formulated at Trent—the adjective for them is 'Tridentine'—would stand as the Roman Catholic Church's self-definition for four centuries. They covered the whole range of issues, both practical and theoretical, that had come to a boil in the Reformation. The council acted to enforce discipline and end the abuses and excesses that had so weakened the Church's credibility as an institution. But it stood its ground against some of the Protestants' theoretical positions. It reiterated the traditional understanding of the mass as a sacrifice, reaffirmed the authority of institutional tradition alongside scripture, and upheld the idea of a distinct status and function for priests as intermediaries. It also reaffirmed the tradition of celibacy for priests and instituted seminaries for training.

The Society of Jesus (Jesuits)

Established shortly before the Council of Trent, in 1540, the Jesuit order or Society of Jesus exemplified three crucial areas of Counter-Reformation renewal: spiritual discipline, education, and missionary expansion. Its founder, Iñigo Lopez (c. 1495–1556) came to be known by the name Ignatius of Loyola. As a young man he was a soldier who served with bravado in the retinues of various nobles until he was wounded in the leg by a cannonball. The fact that books available during his convalescence included the lives of saints may have contributed to the decision he made, around the age of 30, to take religious vows of poverty, chastity, and obedience.

While following a regimen of prayer and bodily self-denial, he wrote a short text called *Spiritual Exercises* in 1522–3. A manual for Christian meditation, a theological reflection on Christ's incarnation as a divine intervention in human history, and a call to arms to join a spiritual crusade, it is a classic of Catholic piety; in 1922 Pope Pius XI named Ignatius, who had been canonized exactly 300 years earlier, the patron saint of spiritual exercises.

In the course of time the Jesuits became a highly influential teaching order, renowned for the rigorous intellectual training they provided.

The Ursulines

The most prominent Catholic teaching order of women dates from the same period. The Ursulines were founded in 1535 in Italy by Angela Merici and received papal approval in 1544. They became particularly influential in France and Canada. One of the most famous Ursulines was the French mystic Marie Guyard (1599–1672), better known as Marie de l'Incarnation. Left a widow before she was 20, at the age of 27 she entrusted her young son to her sister and entered the Ursuline convent at Tours, where she was inspired by the Jesuits' accounts of their mission in New France. In 1639 she sailed for the small French settlement at Quebec, where she established a convent, a school, and a 'seminary' for young Aboriginal women. Her numerous letters are an invaluable source of information on early New France. She also wrote of her personal development as a mystic.

Catholic Missions

India

Roughly four decades after Vasco da Gama had opened a trade route to India, the king of Portugal sent the Spanish Jesuit Francis Xavier to minister there. He arrived in 1542, made Goa his base, and began to establish communities of converts elsewhere along the Indian and Sri Lankan coasts as well as on the Malay peninsula. Seven years later, despite chronic seasickness, he sailed on to Japan and introduced Christianity there. He set out for China in 1552 but fell ill and died en route from Goa. The Jesuits have attributed 700,000 conversions to Francis.

Japan

The first Christian missionaries in Japan found remarkable success. The Portuguese priests admired the military discipline of the Samurai class, and the Japanese apparently found the Jesuits to resemble their own Zen monks in their discipline and learning. As many as 500,000 Japanese may have become Christians by 1615.

But later Japanese rulers saw the Christian and foreign influence as a threat. In 1587 the shogun Hideyoshi Toyotomi banished the missionaries, though he did not enforce the ban until 1597, when he executed nine missionaries and 17 Japanese Christians. The Tokugawa shogun Hidetada intensified the persecution, and by the early 1620s those who refused to step on an image of Christ or Mary faced torture. The Roman Catholic Church counts 3,125 as martyrs

A descendant of Japan's 'Kakure Kirishitan', or 'Hidden Christians', conducts a ritual in front of holy relics on Ikitsuki Island (Kiyoshi Ota/Reuters/Landov).

in this period in Japan. Around Nagasaki, where Christianity had been strongest, resentment of the central Tokugawa government prompted an uprising in 1637–8, but the crushing of this resistance marked the end of Japan's 'Christian century'.

China

Three decades after the death of Francis Xavier, a party of missionaries led by the Italian Jesuit Matteo Ricci landed at the southern Chinese port of Macau. The emperor in Beijing was so pleased with their gifts—including mechanical clocks, European maps, and lenses and prisms—that they were invited to stay, and even received a monthly stipend. Ricci spent the remaining nine years of his life in Beijing. This was a time of active cultural exchange, in which Chinese philosophical and religious texts were translated into Latin, and European scientific and mathematical texts were translated into Chinese.

In the latter part of the 1600s, however, Dominicans and Franciscans began to complain to the pope about the Jesuits' willingness to accommodate indigenous cultural traditions. Three issues in particular raised questions about the compatibility of Chinese customs and Christianity. First, the Jesuits allowed Chinese converts to take part in rituals honouring Confucius, presumably endorsing his moral system as compatible with Christianity. Second, they permitted converts to continue practising ancestor rituals, honouring deceased family members with prostrations, incense, and food offerings. Third was the question of 'terms': whether Chinese terms such as 'Tian' ('heaven') and 'Shangdi' ('the Lord above') meant the same thing as the Christian term 'God'. By the 1740s the Jesuits' ability to present Christianity in indigenous terms had been severely restricted, and with it their ability to attract new converts.

Central and South America

From the very beginning of Spanish and Portuguese influence in the New World, relations between church and state were intimate. Barely a year after Columbus landed at Santo Domingo, a papal bull effectively divided the non-European world between the two powers: Portugal was awarded all the territory east of a certain point west of the Azores, and Spain everything to the west. Thus Portugal received Africa, Asia, and Brazil, while the rest of Latin America went to Spain.

When Hernán Cortés reached Mexico in 1519 and Francisco Pizarro reached Peru in 1532–3, they encountered highly sophisticated social and religious institutions. Yet the great civilizations of the Aztecs and Mayans in Mexico and the Incas in Peru seemed to fall like dominoes before the relatively small Spanish forces. In the past, some historians attributed the collapse of those civilizations to Spain's advantage in weapons, or its use of horses, which the indigenous peoples of the Americas did not have. More recent theories have emphasized the devastating effect of European diseases on populations that had no natural immunity to them. With the allocation of territory went the responsibility to evangelize its population. Hence the expeditions that followed always included missionaries. Some made no effort to learn the local language, relying instead on pictures, symbols, and gestures. Others made it their business not only to learn the people's language but to document their myths, symbols, and rituals. Among the latter was the Spaniard Bernardino de Sahagún, whose *Historia de las cosas de Nueva España* ('History of matters in New Spain') is a valuable ethnographic record of Mexico at the time of its conquest by Cortés. Other priests devoted themselves to defending the rights of Native people against European exploitation.

The greatest of these was Bartolomé de Las Casas (1474–1566), a Spanish priest who had served as a chaplain during the conquest of Cuba in 1513. As a veteran of that campaign he was allotted a parcel of land and a number of local people to work it, effectively as slave labour. But Las Casas soon renounced his allotment of serfs and set out to win a hearing for the rights of the Indians. He eventually joined the Dominican order and wrote a monumental *Historia de las Indias* ('History of the Indies'), which detailed Spanish abuses in Mexico and was published only after his death. Named bishop of Chiapas in Guatemala in 1544, he denied absolution to any slave-holders in his diocese, and in 1550 he defended the Indians' case in a great debate—held at the request of the king of Spain—on the moral justification for European Christian conquest of the peoples of the New World. The issues that Las Casas raised concerning cultural imperialism and the use of force are still relevant today.

In terms of numbers, the missionary effort appears to have been a tremendous success. One Franciscan friar estimated that he had baptized 200,000 Mexicans within ten years of Cortés's arrival—as many as 14,000 in a single day. Today half the world's Roman Catholics live in Latin America, and from southern California to Tierra del Fuego Catholic Christianity appears to have no serious rivals.

Yet on closer inspection it becomes clear that conquered populations did not necessarily abandon their traditions when they accepted Christianity. Behind the Christian altars in Mexico were pagan images. Inside early Mexican crucifixes are Aztec cult objects. And in coastal Brazil, where West African Blacks were taken as slaves, African tribal deities persist in the guise of Catholic saints in the cult or folk religion known as Candomblé.

Across the hemisphere, syncretism—the combination of elements from more than one religious tradition—has given local people religious figures that they can identify as their own. The most important of these figures in Mexico is the Virgin of Guadalupe, whose cult goes back to a hill near Mexico City that was sacred to the Aztec goddess Tonantzin, herself a virgin mother of gods. In 1531 a Christian convert named Juan Diego reported an apparition of a beautiful lady who said she was 'one of his own people' and instructed him to gather roses from the hilltop and present them to the bishop. He wrapped them in a piece of cloth, and when he opened the package before the bishop, an image of the Virgin appeared to be visible on the cloth. Preserved in a basilica at the foot of the hill, the cloth is still venerated today. The cult that surrounds it is reminiscent of popular piety in medieval Europe.

North America

Roman Catholic influences in North America reflect migration as well as missionary activity. Florida was an area of early settlement direct from Spain. Texas and New Mexico were part of Mexico until the mid-nineteenth century. In California the Franciscans established a chain of missions, the last and northernmost of them at Sonoma, north of San Francisco, in 1823. A short distance to the north, Russian settlers had already established Fort Ross, the site of the first Orthodox chapel south of Alaska. Arguably, the encounter between the Spanish and the Russians in California marked the moment when Christianity's overland spread finally encircled the globe.

But the Spanish and Portuguese were not the only missionaries to the New World. Farther north were the French. In 1535–6 the explorer Jacques Cartier had sailed up the St Lawrence River as far as the first rapids. Because he was looking for a route to China, he called the spot—near the site of the future Montreal—Lachine. But a permanent French settlement on the St Lawrence had to await the arrival of Samuel de Champlain, who established a fur-trading post at Quebec in 1608 and travelled upstream to the Great Lakes.

Missionaries followed: four Récollet friars in 1615 and five Jesuits in 1625. The Jesuit Jacques Marquette arrived in Quebec in 1666 and two years later founded a mission at Sault Ste Marie, at the northern end of Lake Michigan. With the layman Louis Jolliet, a native of New France, he explored southward along the Mississippi River. French missionary activity among the Iroquois and other Aboriginal peoples was handled largely by the Jesuits, whose respect for indigenous ways attracted many converts.

The other major inroads of European Catholicism in North America were the result of migration. French settlements developed not only along the St Lawrence but in Acadia (Nova Scotia) and along the lower Mississippi (Louisiana), while the colony of Maryland was established in 1632 by George Calvert, Lord Baltimore, as a refuge for English Catholics fleeing persecution in Britain. Other regions, including Atlantic Canada and the future Ontario, also attracted Catholic settlers from the British Isles. From the mid-nineteenth century on, the growth of industrial cities along the east coast of North America attracted large numbers of immigrants from Ireland and, later, Italy. To some extent the ecclesiastical hierarchy of the Catholic Church in North America today mirrors the more recent history of immigration.

❧ PRACTICE

Worship

Prayer

Prayer is reverent and contemplative conversation with the divine. Christians can pray individually as well as in groups; in fact, Jesus tells his disciples not to make a public show, but to pray in private (*Matthew* 6). The prayer he teaches them is known both as the Lord's Prayer and as the Our Father or (in Latin) *Pater noster* (from its opening words). It was already in fairly wide use around the end of the first century, when the gospels were produced, and is common to all branches of Christians. From the beginning, music was also part of Christian worship, for the Church inherited from Judaism the biblical psalms that had been sung in the temple.

The Rosary

A rosary is a string of beads used in prayer, especially by Roman Catholics. It consists of 58 beads arranged in five groups of 10 (separated by single beads of a different colour or size) and a small crucifix—a cross bearing an image of the suffering Christ. Following the sequence of the beads, the person using the rosary will say one Our Father (the Lord's

Prayer) and then 10 Hail Marys ('Hail, Mary, full of grace, the Lord is with you; blessed are you among women, and blessed is the fruit of your womb, Jesus. Holy Mary, mother of God, pray for us sinners now and at the hour of our death').

The Eucharist

The central Christian ritual, the Eucharist (from the Greek word for thanksgiving), re-enacts the story of the 'last supper': the Passover supper that Jesus shared with his disciples on the Thursday night of his final week in Jerusalem. In the story, Jesus breaks some bread and passes around a cup of wine, declaring these to be his body and his blood, given for the disciples, and asking them to do the same in remembrance of him.

This sacrament is common to all branches of Christianity, though it goes by a variety of names and is understood in different ways by different denominations. Roman Catholics commonly refer to the Eucharist as the mass, from the final words of the Latin ritual: *Ite, missa est* ('Go; it has been delivered'), while Eastern Orthodox Christians often call it the Liturgy, from a Greek word meaning 'service'. Many Protestants use the terms Holy Communion or Lord's Supper.

Some Protestant denominations also departed from Rome in their interpretations of the sacrament. Some Anglicans and Lutherans have retained the traditional understanding of the ritual as a sacrifice, believing that the body and blood of Christ are present in or together with the bread and wine of the ceremonial meal. In Switzerland, however, the sacramental theology of reformers such as Zwingli and Calvin led most Protestants to understand the Eucharist less as a sacrifice than as a memorial in which the bread and wine symbolize Christ's body and blood.

Baptism

Baptism is the ritual in which a person is admitted into the Christian community. It recalls the ritual bathing practised by a number of movements at the time of Jesus (including the one with which Jesus' forerunner, John the Baptist, was associated): a symbolic washing away of prior uncleanness in preparation for beginning a new life. As long as Christianity remained a minority religion, joined at considerable personal risk, baptism was not undertaken lightly. People were initiated into the faith only after a course of instruction called catechism.

The Christian Year

The liturgical year for Christians is calculated largely from the two main festivals of Christmas and Easter. It begins with Advent, the series of four Sundays that precede Christmas.

Christmas

Although no one knows the time of the year when Jesus was actually born, by the fourth century his birth had come to be celebrated around the winter solstice—a season that coincided with a number of Roman festivals, including the celebration of the unconquered sun on 25 December. Apparently the Christian idea of a birth bringing new blessing was readily associated with the annual renewal of the sun's radiance.

Easter

Christmas has a fixed date because it is related to the solar year, but Easter is related to the phases of the moon and therefore has a variable date. The first Easter occurred just after the Jewish spring festival of Passover, but in the course of time Christianity abandoned the lunar calculations of Judaism. The Latin Church eventually fixed Easter as the first Sunday after the first full moon after the spring equinox. Thus it can fall anywhere in a period of five weeks from late March to late April. The date of Easter in the Greek Church is calculated in a slightly different way, with the result that it coincides with the Latin Easter only about one year in every four.

As the feast of Jesus' resurrection, Easter comes as the climax of a period of six and a half weeks known as Lent, which concludes with Holy Week. For most Christians Lent is the time of the year for the greatest solemnity, the most serious reflection, and the most stringent discipline, often including abstinence from pleasures and luxuries such as meat. Accordingly, the last day before the beginning of Lent has traditionally been a time of wild partying. Shrove Tuesday, as it is called in English, is Mardi Gras ('fat Tuesday') in French, notably in New Orleans, and Carnival ('goodbye, meat') in the Hispanic culture of the Caribbean.

Lent consists of 40 days before Easter, not counting Sundays. The English name refers to the season, when the days are 'lengthening'. Lent begins on Ash Wednesday, so named because in some Christian churches the foreheads of worshippers are daubed with ashes. The ashes come from the dried palm leaves used as church decorations the preceding year on Palm Sunday—the day that begins Holy Week, when churches are often decorated with palm leaves recalling the branches that welcomed Jesus as he entered Jerusalem.

The day of Jesus' last Passover supper with his disciples is called Maundy Thursday in English, for the commandment (*mandatum* in Latin) to love one another that, according to *John* 13, Jesus gave on that occasion. Friday of Holy Week is known as Good Friday. Some think the name refers to the idea that Jesus' self-sacrificing death on the cross was 'good' for humanity, but a more convincing explanation suggests that the original term was 'God's Friday'. This most solemn day of the Christian year is marked by services recalling the 'Passion' (Jesus' suffering on the cross).

Easter day commemorates the disciples' discovery, on the morning after the Sabbath, that Jesus has risen from the dead. Among the layers of meaning that Christians may find in the story of the resurrection is a sense of cosmic triumph over sin and death.

Like Passover, Easter is a spring festival associated with the renewal of life. Some of the most common Easter symbols in popular Christian culture probably antedate Christianity and connote fertility: the egg, for instance, and the rabbit. The English name 'Easter' itself comes from Eostre, a pagan goddess. In most other European languages the term for Easter is derived from Pesach, the Hebrew name of Passover; in French, for instance, Easter is Pâques.

The fiftieth day counting from Easter is Pentecost, from the Greek for 'fifty'. In England Pentecost is often called Whitsunday, on account of the white garments formerly worn by

Greek Orthodox worshippers at the Church of the Nativity in Bethlehem light their candles from the 'Holy Fire' (AFP/Getty Images).

persons baptized on that day. In Latin countries the day is generally referred to as the feast of the Holy Spirit.

CULTURAL EXPRESSIONS

Medieval Church Architecture

In the western Mediterranean, as in Byzantium, the round arch developed by the Romans was the characteristic shape used in the churches. In northern Europe, however, a new pointed arch came into fashion sometime after the eleventh century. This 'Gothic' arch made it possible to achieve greater height, and in the course of the Middle Ages church architects learned to build cathedrals with naves as much as five times as high as they were wide. It has often been suggested that these structures were designed to direct the thoughts of worshippers heavenward.

As architects pushed the capacity of their material—stone—to its limits, many Gothic churches had to be supported on the outside to keep the weight of the roof from forcing the upper parts of the walls outward. When these supports stood free of the wall and were bridged to it with half-arches, they were called 'flying buttresses'.

Gothic churches were usually much more elaborately decorated than their Byzantine or Romanesque counterparts, both inside and out. Carvings in stone and wood, usually brightly painted, depicted events in the lives of Christ and the saints. Also developed in the Middle

Flying buttresses support the walls of the Cathedral of Notre Dame in Paris (Photo courtesy of Andrew Leyerle).

Ages was the stained-glass window made up of thousands of pieces of coloured glass—especially in deep, clear blues and reds—joined by strips of lead. Whether in sculpture, painting, tapestry, or stained glass, scenes from the Bible were often arranged in sequence like the panels of a comic strip, to serve as teaching aids in an era when literacy was limited.

Unique to Roman Catholic churches is a feature known as the stations of the cross: a sequence of 14 locations, usually along the side of the nave of the church, recalling the events from Jesus' trial to the placing of his body in the tomb. The stations may be paintings, or plaques, or sculptures, or even, in austerely decorated churches, simply Roman numerals or crosses. During Lent worshippers move from one station to the next, meditating on Jesus' final suffering.

Protestant Art and Music

Protestant architecture in northern Europe was not very different from earlier Catholic forms, since in many cases Protestants took over existing churches. In the sanctuary, however, Reformed churches rearranged the furniture to suit their sacramental theology. In place of the traditional altar that the priest faced with his back to the worshippers, Protestants adopted a communion table behind which the minister would stand and face the congregation.

The sixteenth-century reformers, who strongly disapproved of what they considered image worship, preferred an empty cross to a crucifix with the suffering Jesus on it.

Statues and paintings were destroyed with fanatical zeal, though many stained-glass windows were spared. Some denominations have kept their church interiors bare and austere. Others have at least an aesthetic affection for Renaissance paintings of the Madonna (Mary) with the infant Jesus. Mary does appear in Protestantism at the Christmas season, but is clearly subordinated to Jesus himself and is associated mostly with his infancy.

In music Protestantism made a major cultural contribution, often taking over the tunes of folk songs and using them in worship. Martin Luther himself wrote one of the most widely cherished Protestant hymns; since the 1960s it has been adopted by Catholics as well:

A mighty fortress is our God, a bulwark never failing;
Our helper he amid the flood of mortal ills prevailing.
For still our ancient foe doth seek to work us woe;
His craft and power are great; and armed with cruel hate, on earth is not his equal.

Musically, most Protestant hymns are simple, but their texts express a wide range of religious concerns—from praise to God as creator to calls for social justice and world peace. In the sixteenth century, the Calvinists in Switzerland and Scotland produced a collection of musical settings of the biblical psalms known as the 'psalter'. The psalms were also the principal focus of congregational song in the Church of England following the Reformation.

From the middle of the eighteenth century to the end of the nineteenth, a frequent theme for hymns was the experience of receiving divine favour. An example is 'Amazing Grace', which is often sung to a familiar early American tune; the words date from 1779:

Amazing grace—how sweet the sound—
that saved a wretch like me!
I once was lost, but now am found,
was blind, but now I see.

INTERACTION AND ADAPTATION

The Modern Era

Together, the eighteenth-century Enlightenment and the American and French revolutions loosened the official ties between church and state. But the shift towards secularism did not mean that Christian symbols and values ceased to play an important role in Western culture and political life. Nor did the increasing emphasis on reason and scientific investigation—even of scripture—necessarily diminish Christians' faith.

Philosophy and Christianity

The eighteenth century was a period of philosophical skepticism about claims for the transcendent. Enlightenment thinkers argued that the objects of religion cannot be substantiated through the operation of reason. Particularly decisive were the critiques of such philosophers as the Scotsman David Hume (1711–76) and the German Immanuel Kant (1724–1804). Aquinas's argument for 'God as First Cause' cannot be proved; as Kant argued, causality is not part of the physical world but part of the framework of thought within which human minds interpret it.

Yet what Kant showed to be in principle unprovable is by the same token undisprovable. Instead of making cognitive assertions about the divine or transcendent, modern philosophers of religion since Kant have generally preferred to speak of experience and feeling—the dynamics of the human response to the transcendent. The German philosopher Friedrich Schleiermacher (1768–1834), for instance, characterized religion as an 'intuitive sense of absolute dependence': if we cannot prove the existence of what we intuitively feel that we depend on, at least we can describe that intuition. In the same post-Kantian vein, the German philosopher of religion Rudolf Otto (1869–1937) adopted the word 'numinous' to refer to what people perceive as an overpowering mystery.

Schleiermacher also contributed to a 'subjective' understanding of Christ's atonement. In the traditional Christian understanding, it is through Christ's sacrifice that humanity is saved and restored to its proper relationship with God. For Schleiermacher, though, Jesus functions above all as a moral example, an embodiment of human awareness of God: salvation comes first as a change in spiritual awareness, and atonement follows in the form of reconciliation between the divine and the human.

Meanwhile, the nineteenth-century Danish philosopher Søren Kierkegaard pioneered the line of inquiry called existentialism, in which the focus shifted from knowledge (already limited by Kant) to commitment. It is no accident that many modern intellectual defences of religion treat it as analogous to love, which likewise depends on commitment rather than argument.

Commitment-based theologies have been influential, but they do not rule out one powerful classic argument against religious faith: the problem of evil and suffering. We find it already in ancient literature (including the biblical book of *Job*): how can one regard as both powerful and good, and hence worthy of worship, a deity that would allow either the evil that results from some human actions or the suffering that results from accidents or chaos in nature? Even in a mechanistic theory, where after creation the deity does not intervene in the world, the creator does not escape responsibility. The modern world has in no way eliminated evil and suffering as objections to theistic faith, nor has it come up with any striking new ways of answering them.

Protestantism after 1800

Protestant Missions and Colonialism

The colonial policies of the northern European nations and the missionary efforts of Protestants peaked in the second half of the nineteenth century. In Africa—one of their main targets—the aims of church and state went hand in hand. The British established themselves on large stretches of the African coastline and then moved into the interior of the continent by river, road, and eventually rail. Although formerly active in the slave trade between West Africa and the New World, Britain had outlawed slavery in 1834, and by mid-century its opposition to the ongoing slave trade in East Africa had become one of the arguments it used to justify its colonization efforts. Even the Scottish missionary David Livingstone made an explicit connection between evangelism and empire. On a visit to Britain from Africa in 1857, he told a Cambridge audience:

> [Africa] is now open; do not let it be shut again! I go back to Africa to try to make an open path for commerce and Christianity. Do you carry on the work I have begun (Livingstone 1858: 24).

Comparable opportunities were identified elsewhere in the world as well. A missionary to the southwestern Pacific reported in 1837 that 'at the lowest computation 150,000 persons, who a few years ago were unclothed savages, are now wearing articles of British manufacture.'

New American Denominations

A defining feature of Protestantism is the freedom it allows for individual expressions of faith. The result has been a bewildering diversity, which is illustrated by the new denominations that emerged on the American scene in the nineteenth and twentieth centuries.

Disciples of Christ

Following Presbyterian opposition to a revival in Kentucky in 1804, Barton Stone left the Presbyterians to become a 'Christian only' and attracted a number of followers. Meanwhile, when Thomas Campbell, a Presbyterian from Northern Ireland, became disaffected with the sectarian character of his church, he and his son Alexander joined Baptist associations, calling themselves Reformers. In 1832 the Stone and Campbell movements merged to form the Disciples of Christ (also called the Christian Church or Churches of Christ).

Seventh-Day Adventists

In 1831 a Baptist lay minister in upstate New York began to preach that the second coming of Christ—the 'Advent'—was imminent. Interpreting the reference to 2,300 days in *Daniel* 8: 14 as 2,300 years, William Miller predicted that the apocalypse would arrive in or around the year 1843. When that did not happen (a 'great disappointment'), the Millerites revised their millenarian calculations several times before giving up on specific predictions.

Originally guided by the 'gift of prophecy' of Ellen Gould White (1826–1915), who experienced trances and visions, the Adventists began sending medical missionaries around the world in the 1880s, and in the twentieth century their ranks grew dramatically in the Third World. At the same time, Adventist intellectuals and scholars in the US were becoming more willing to ask critical questions about biblical interpretation and the claims of Ellen White. By the late twentieth century, the Adventists had completed the transition from millenarian sect to established denomination. (Their name reflects their emphasis on the Advent and their belief that the true Sabbath is the 'seventh day'—that is, Saturday rather than Sunday).

Jehovah's Witnesses

The Witnesses are another millenarian group centred on the belief that the Advent is imminent. Their founder was Charles Taze Russell. Born in 1852 and raised near Pittsburgh, where he was exposed from an early age to forecasts of the apocalyse, he became intensely interested in Bible study, but was largely self-taught. He formed a study group and in 1879 began publishing *Zion's Watch Tower and Herald of Christ's Presence*. Initially Russell and his followers expected the world to end in 1914; when that prediction proved false, they came to believe that 1914 was the year when Jehovah's Kingdom was inaugurated in anticipation of the end.

Russell himself died in 1916. It was under his successor, J.F. Russell, that the movement adopted the name Jehovah's Witnesses, using the version of the name 'YHWH' introduced by the translators of the King James Bible. Their principal activity is door-to-door missionary work distributing their publications *Awake!* and *The Watchtower*. They reject the doctrine of the Trinity and regard Jesus Christ as a created being (as Arius did), although they believe that in dying he gave humanity a second chance to choose righteousness and escape the punishment expected at the end. They also refuse to salute flags or serve in armies, not because they are pacifists but because they see themselves as citizens of another kingdom and therefore reject the authority of secular states.

Christian Scientists

The Church of Christ, Scientist, was founded in Boston in 1879 by Mary Baker Eddy (1821–1910), a New England woman who had become interested in spiritual healing after receiving help for a spinal condition from a healer named Phineas Quimby, who worked without medicines. She began to write about spiritual healing, and her book *Science and Health* (1875), came to be regarded by her followers as an inspired text second in authority only to the Bible.

Although she insisted on the primacy of Christian scripture, Mrs Eddy departed from standard Christian views in several respects, believing that the material world and its evils—sickness, suffering, even death—could be transcended, and that spiritual existence was possible in the here and now. The quest to live those beliefs has occupied most of Christian Scientists' energy. Although the *Christian Science Monitor*, founded in 1908, is known for the integrity of its journalism, the Church's main focus is on spiritual healing rather than social action.

Mormons (Church of Jesus Christ of Latter-day Saints)

The Church of Jesus Christ of Latter-day Saints was founded in 1830 by Joseph Smith, Jr. who claimed that in 1820, as a boy in upstate New York, he had had a vision of God and Jesus in which he was told not to join any of the existing denominations. Subsequent visions persuaded him that he had been divinely chosen to restore the true Church of Christ. The textual basis for Smith's new faith was an account of God's activity in the Western hemisphere, paralleling the biblical account of events in the East, entitled *The Book of Mormon*, which Smith said he had translated from gold plates, inscribed in 'reformed Egyptian', that had been divinely entrusted to him. Under the leadership of one of his disciples, Brigham Young, the main branch of the Mormons settled in Utah, but smaller groups are found in Illinois and elsewhere.

Whether Mormonism is a new form of Christianity or a new religion that has emerged out of Christianity depends on one's perspective. For a more detailed discussion, see Chapter 12.

Holiness Churches

In time, the main Methodist bodies in America became more organized and conventional, more sedate and mainline. But new independent churches and movements continued to spring from Methodism's revivalist roots. Because these congregations emphasized the experience of receiving the gift of holiness, they are often referred to as 'Holiness' churches. Among them are the Church of God (founded in 1881) and the Church of the Nazarene (1908).

The intensity of feeling associated with that experience can spark ecstatic behaviour—rolling in the aisles of the meeting, for example, or 'speaking in tongues' (technically, 'glossolalia')—that is believed to be inspired by the Holy Spirit. The term 'charismatic', from the Greek for 'spiritual gifts', is sometimes used to describe such groups. Though initially a Protestant phenomenon, since the 1970s charismatic activity has been emerging among Catholic Christians as well.

Pentecostal Churches

Protestant congregations that actively cultivate 'speaking in tongues' are called Pentecostal. Although the name recalls the Pentecost experience recounted in *Acts* 2, the 'tongues' that modern Pentecostals speak are understood to represent the mystical language of heaven.

Many locate the birth of the modern Pentecostal movement in a revival held at a church in Los Angeles in 1906. Its leader was William J. Seymour, whose parents had been slaves. Newspaper coverage described the sounds of Seymour's meetings as a 'weird babble'. At the outset Blacks and Whites worshipped together, but as Pentecostalism diversified, it developed segregated congregations.

With its emphasis on immediate personal experience rather than any textual or doctrinal tradition, Pentecostalism can take a variety of forms and appeal effectively to people with little formal education. It also has a cross-cultural appeal, and Pentecostal missionaries enjoy remarkable success in Latin America and Africa. Some consider Pentecostalism the fastest-growing segment of Christianity today.

Evangelicals and Fundamentalists

Seen in its broadest compass, twentieth-century Protestant evangelicalism is a movement that cuts across the major denominations. It is not a denomination as such, although some denominations are solidly evangelical. Like the Pietist and revivalist movements of earlier centuries, it emphasizes the personal experience of conversion as a spiritual rebirth that brings the assurance of God's grace and acceptance. As the term 'evangelical'—which comes from the Greek for gospel or 'good news'—suggests, many evangelicals make it their business to spread their message.

Gospel music evokes the personal experience of conversion (Getty Images North America).

Because Protestantism had put so many of its eggs in the basket of scriptural authority as opposed to the institutional church, critical study of the Bible was bound to provoke a particularly sharp reaction among Protestants. Committed to the literal authority of the scriptures, evangelicals fought a rearguard battle against both the findings of modern historical and literary study of the Bible in the late nineteenth and early twentieth centuries and the Darwinian theory of human evolution.

In 1910 a series of booklets entitled *The Fundamentals* affirmed the inerrancy—that is, the infallibility—of the Bible and traditional doctrines. Three million copies were distributed free to Protestant clergy, missionaries, and students in the US through the anonymous sponsorship of 'two Christian laymen' (William Lyman Stewart and his brother Milton). By 1920 advocates of inerrancy were being called 'fundamentalists'.

The test case for fundamentalism was the 1925 trial of a high-school teacher named John T. Scopes for violating a new Tennessee law that banned the teaching of evolution. Thus began the famous 'Scopes Trial', used by fundamentalists as a demonstration of the truth of their religion. The court ruled in favour of the prosecution (conducted by William Jennings Bryan) and fined Scopes $100. So extensive was the news coverage, however, that in effect fundamentalism itself was put on trial in the court of public opinion. Darwin, Scopes, and the defence attorney, Clarence Darrow, emerged the clear victors among the population at large, although supporters of fundamentalism believed they had been vindicated. Scopes's conviction was overturned in 1927 on appeal, on the technicality that the fine was too high, and the Tennessee law was eventually repealed in 1967.

Fundamentalists (and some evangelicals) often perceive a struggle between good and evil forces in the world. Many believe that evil, personified in Satan, is tangibly manifested in social groups with which they disagree, such as proponents of evolution, defenders of free choice in abortion, or advocates of gay rights. They also tend towards the apocalyptic conviction that a final battle between the forces of good and evil is imminent. Though their views on complex social and ethical issues are often criticized as simplistic, evangelicals give generously to charitable causes such as famine relief.

In the twentieth century, a number of Protestant evangelical preachers—heirs to the revivalist tradition—became famous for their 'crusades', attracting huge audiences and calling on them to make 'decisions for Christ': to convert from a lapsed or inactive form of the faith to a revitalized one. Pioneered by the Southern Baptist Billy Graham (b. 1918), the use of television to take the evangelical message into people's homes gave rise to a succession of 'televangelists' who solicited contributions from viewers. Several highly entrepreneurial preachers who operated outside established denominations built what amounted to personal empires. Financial and marital scandals brought a few of the most visible televangelists into disrepute in the late 1980s. But audience ratings remain high, particularly for the success-oriented 'Hour of Power' broadcast from the Crystal Cathedral of Robert Schuller in southern California.

The Second Vatican Council

In 1958 the Italian cardinal Angelo Giuseppe Roncalli was elected Pope John XXIII. Few at that time had any inkling of the changes that lay in store for the Roman Catholic Church. Though already in his late seventies, this man of great human warmth proved to have both a vision for his church and a fearless openness to change. Calling for *aggiornamento* ('updating'), John XXIII convoked the Second Vatican Council (1962–65; the First Vatican Council, held in 1869–70, had established the doctrine of papal infallibility).

Shortly after Vatican II, however, a major breach developed between the Catholic Church and the laity, when John XXIII's successor, Pope Paul VI, issued an encyclical (letter) entitled *Humanae Vitae* ('On Human Life'; 1968) that prohibited the use of artificial birth control by Catholics. Since then the gap between the Church's official stand on sexuality and the actual practice of many Catholics has continued to widen. Some of the faithful have ceased to take their church's teachings seriously in large areas of their lives.

At the same time *Humanae Vitae* intensified the theological tension between reform and traditionalist wings in the Church's hierarchy. Progressive Catholics saw the document, which was issued by the pope without the consensus of bishops in council, as an attempt to undermine the accomplishments of Vatican II, turn back the clock, and reaffirm the papal authority established by Vatican I.

Ecumenism

One of the principal concerns of Vatican II was to promote reconciliation with other branches of Christianity. For Rome the ultimate goal was what the Council, in its 1964 decree on ecumenism, called 'the restoration of unity among all Christians' within 'one Church and one Church only'.

In fact, ecumenism was by that time a reality within Protestantism, although on a more modest scale. The mainline denominations had begun overcoming centuries of separation in the early 1900s, partly as a consequence of their collaboration in mission fields where distinctions between Anglicans and Presbyterians, Baptists and Congregationalists, meant little or nothing. Even if they disagreed on matters such as Eucharistic theology, the different denominations had no trouble supporting one another on issues such as social justice.

In Canada, Methodists, Congregationalists, and a majority of the country's Presbyterians merged to form the United Church of Canada in 1925. In the United States, a Congregational–Christian merger with the Evangelical and United Brethren produced the United Church of Christ. In England the Presbyterians and Congregationalists formed the United Reformed Church in 1972. And in Australia a similar group of churches joined to form the Uniting Church in 1977. Meanwhile, most of the major Protestant and Orthodox churches had come together to establish the World Council of Churches in 1948.

The spirit of reunion was in the air. By the end of the 1960s Protestant and Catholic institutions for the study of theology and the training of clergy were making collaborative arrangements, their students attending the same lectures and reading the same books. A gulf that had divided Western Christendom for four centuries was being bridged.

Reforming Society

The denominations influenced by Puritanism expected personal morality to bear fruit in society. To Quakers, English Congregationalists, and some Methodist-derived movements such as the Salvation Army (organized by William Booth in London after 1865), one test of any renewal was whether it improved the conditions of life for the population at large.

In the mid-nineteenth century, when the US was torn apart by the issue of slavery, some Christian denominations, including the Presbyterians, separated into northern and southern churches that took a century to reunite. By and large, the Christian conscience was anti-slavery, but there were more interests to be offended in southern White constituencies than in their northern counterparts.

Political issues around race erupted again in the mid-twentieth century. When the civil-rights movement was developing during the early 1960s, the Black community had few institutional structures other than churches, with the result that almost all the early Black leaders emerged from the ranks of the ministry. Martin Luther King, Jr, and his colleagues in the Southern Christian Leadership Conference were the pivotal figures, but the support of White religious leaders was also important.

Religion has been invoked on both sides of the race issue. Some conservative Protestants have argued that God created different races and clearly intended them to remain separate. The Mormons for many years resisted Black membership, let alone leadership. And in South Africa, the Afrikaner population, who came from a Dutch Calvinist background, put forward theological as well as practical justifications for their government's policy of apartheid (segregation), although other South African Christians, many of them Anglican, vehemently opposed it. Yet by 1994, when Blacks for the first time voted in South African elections, even Reformed Church leaders had begun to repudiate apartheid.

Similarly, Christians have not been of one mind on economic policy. During the Industrial Revolution the ownership and managerial classes in many parts of the English-speaking world were largely Protestant, while the industrial workers were largely Roman

From Martin Luther King, Jr, 'Letter from Birmingham Jail'

In the spring of 1963 the Baptist minister and civil-rights leader Martin Luther King, Jr, was arrested and imprisoned for leading a protest against racial segregation in Birmingham, Alabama. When eight fellow clergymen criticized him for taking part in the protest, King responded with an open letter that came to be known as the 'Letter from Birmingham Jail'.

You express a great deal of anxiety over our willingness to break laws. . . . One may well ask: 'How can you advocate breaking some laws and obeying others?' The answer lies in the fact that there are two types of laws: just and unjust. . . . One has not only a legal but a moral responsibility to obey just laws. Conversely, one has a moral responsibility to disobey unjust laws. I would agree with St Augustine that 'an unjust law is no law at all'. . . .

I have beheld the impressive outlines of [the South's] massive religious-education buildings. Over and over I have found myself asking: 'What kind of people worship here? Who is their God? . . . Where were they when Governor Wallace gave a clarion call for defiance and hatred? Where were their voices of support when bruised and weary Negro men and women decided to rise from the dark dungeons of complacency to the bright hills of creative protest?'. . .

There was a time when the church was very powerful—in the time when the early Christians rejoiced at being deemed worthy to suffer for what they believed. In those days the church was not merely a thermometer that recorded the ideas and principles of popular opinion; it was a thermostat that transformed the mores of society. Whenever the early Christians entered a town, the people in power became disturbed and immediately sought to convict the Christians for being 'disturbers of the peace' and 'outside agitators'. . . .

But the judgment of God is upon the church as never before. If today's church does not recapture the sacrificial spirit of the early church, it will lose its authenticity, forfeit the loyalty of millions, and be dismissed as an irrelevant social club with no meaning for the twentieth century. Every day I meet young people whose disappointment with the church has turned into outright disgust. . . .

I hope the church as a whole will meet the challenge of this decisive hour. . . .

Let us all hope that the dark clouds of racial prejudice will soon pass away and the deep fog of misunderstanding will be lifted from our fear-drenched communities, and in some not too distant tomorrow the radiant stars of love and brotherhood will shine over our great nation with all their scintillating beauty (King 1964: 76–95).

Catholic. From the 1860s onward, socialism in Europe addressed the growing gulf between owners and workers. On the continent, socialism was largely anti-Church, but in Britain there was a significant Christian socialist movement.

A principal moral concern of late nineteenth-century Protestants had been alcoholism; thus much of their energy was devoted to the temperance movement. But as the twentieth century opened, broader issues of social and economic justice moved to the fore: in Canada the Methodist Board of Temperance, Prohibition and Moral Reform was renamed Evangelism and Social Service, and in the US Christian critics of the civic and corporate order called for the Christianization of the economy. The leading theologian of the 'social gospel' movement was Walter Rauschenbusch, a former Baptist pastor who campaigned to make the gas company, the transit system, and the public schools more responsive to people's needs. Another leader was Washington Gladden, a Congregational minister who served on the city council in Columbus, Ohio, coordinated social service agencies, mediated in labour disputes, and lobbied the US Congress to create a commission on industrial relations.

In Canada, the Nova Scotia Presbyterian George M. Grant, who became head of Queen's University in 1877, was a spokesman for interdenominational and national unity as well as a social conscience in public affairs. A more dramatic voice was that of James S. Woodsworth, who left the Methodist ministry to become a Vancouver longshoreman and eventually one of the founders of the Co-operative Commonwealth Federation (CCF), the forerunner of the New Democratic Party. Thus the roots of Canada's political left can be located not only in secular socialism but in Christian calls for economic justice, especially during the Depression of the 1930s.

Some three decades later, in 1968, the Latin American Council of [Catholic] Bishops, meeting in Colombia, called on their Church to identify with the poor rather than the ruling élite. The 'liberation theology' propounded by South American churchmen such as the Peruvian Gustavo Gutiérrez and the Uruguayan Juan Luis Segundo makes use of Christian biblical and theological resources that have parallels in Marxist thought. Like Marxism, liberation theology argues on behalf of the rural peasantry and the urban working class for a share in the material benefits of their economy and society. It offers a rationale for social action that addresses an enduring problem, and has attracted the attention of concerned Christians, Catholic and otherwise, outside Latin America as well.

Twentieth-Century Theology

In the last century a number of Roman Catholic theologians and philosophers have explored the Aristotelian principles and methods of Thomas Aquinas for modern purposes. One of the most innovative and wide-ranging was the German Jesuit Karl Rahner (1904–84). Another influential Jesuit concerned with the theory of knowledge was the Canadian Bernard Lonergan (also 1904–84), who taught in Rome for half his career. Jacques Maritain (1882–1973) was a French neo-Thomist with conservative views on many issues who converted to Catholicism while a student. Widowed at the age of 78, he joined the Dominicans in a French monastery for his last years.

Tradition-based theologies have also continued to attract adherents among Protestants. A commentary on Paul's letter to the Romans propelled the Swiss theologian Karl Barth (1886–1968) into prominence at the end of the First World War—a time of disillusionment with the idea that human progress was inevitable. Barth's theology is termed 'dialectical' because it draws a sharp distinction between what humans can do or know by themselves and the saving grace given to them by God; the Barthian position has been popular in conservative Protestant circles.

For existentialist thought, the unprovability of religion is irrelevant: what matters is individual commitment and experience. Existentialism has been particularly important among theologians trained in Europe. The German Paul Tillich (1886–1965), who settled in the United States in the 1930s, characterizes the movement of religious awareness not from God downward, as Barth does, but from the human experience upward: religion is, in Tillich's words, 'ultimate concern'. Tillich's formulations were widely influential during the second half of the twentieth century.

A distinctly American movement is process theology. Drawing on the process thought of Alfred North Whitehead (1861–1947), it has appealed especially to people who associate modernity with change. For its principal thinkers, such as the American Charles Hartshorne (1897–2000), creation is unfinished and God is a dynamic power open to virtually unlimited possibility.

Recent liberal theology has concentrated on social liberation, feminist empowerment, the global environment, and equality for homosexual, transsexual, and transgendered Christians. In particular, liberal theology has seemed reactive in its relationship to modern life, shifting and rethinking its priorities in response to the demands of the culture.

By contrast, fundamentalism in both its Protestant and Catholic forms is a defensive reaction against modernity that promises a return to the basics of Christian faith. Where the two varieties of fundamentalism differ is in what they look to as the ultimate authority: scripture in one case and the tradition of the Church itself in the other.

Women and Gender

The twentieth century, particularly its second half, brought dramatic changes in the status of women in Western society. Traditional notions of females as inferior to, or the property of, males were discredited and the range of roles open to women expanded significantly.

Liberal Protestant denominations in North America were ordaining women as clergy by the middle of the twentieth century, and the Anglican communion did so after the mid-twentieth-century. Barbara Harris (b. 1930) became an Episcopalian bishop in Massachusetts in 1989, and Lois Wilson (b. 1927), a minister and also moderator of the United Church of Canada, served as one of the presidents of the World Council of Churches from 1983 to 1991.

The Roman Catholic and Eastern Orthodox churches, however, do not yet ordain women as priests, let alone admit women to their senior hierarchies. (The Old Catholics, who broke away from the Roman Catholic Church after Vatican I, began ordaining women in 1996.) Both the Greek and Latin churches put special emphasis on historical precedent, and the tradition of women's subordination is so entrenched that it has proven particularly difficult to overturn. Formerly women were not allowed by Rome to take degrees in theology, but in recent decades Catholic women, both lay and religious, have made substantial contributions as scholars in the subject.

Efforts to redress two millennia of patriarchal bias have taken a variety of forms. Some scholars have directed their attention to female figures and symbols in the history and psychology of religion. Comparative studies have suggested parallels between the mother goddesses of various other religious traditions and the function of Mary as the archetypal mother in Roman Catholic piety.

Some theologians suggest that the real problem is the traditional conception of the Christian God as male. They see the deity as equally masculine and feminine, and they address their prayers to 'Our Father and Mother'. Others argue that a gender-balanced God is still anthropomorphic—a deity in human form. For them, the God who transcends the world must necessarily transcend gender.

Contemporary Issues[1]

Approximately one-third of the people in the world today identify themselves as Christians. Yet fewer than 40 per cent live in Europe and North America. The decline in the numbers of Christians in developed regions and their increase in developing regions is a growing trend in the twenty-first century. Christianity has become an indigenous religious tradition in the developing world, independent of Western ecclesiastical structures or missions.

Questions about the relationship between the Church and society, between the individual Christian and her cultural world, have existed since the beginning of Christianity. Christ said that Christians should 'render unto' Caesar what belongs to Caesar and to God what belongs to God (e.g., *Matthew* 22: 21). His Apostles said that Christians should live in the world but not be of the world. The twenty-first century confronts Christians with a number of issues that call for renewed reflection on these scriptural principles.

Globalization, identity, and tradition

Globalization entails both increasing interdependence of national economies and increasing social and political connections across the world. It has made Christians in the West more aware of the consequences—political, economic, cultural, environmental—that follow the introduction of Western-based economic activity to developing regions. It also confronts traditional societies with Western social influences such as materialism and consumerism. The Roman Catholic Church, the Orthodox Church, and the World Council of Churches have all expressed formal concern that globalized capitalist economic development may aggravate inequalities in the distribution of power and wealth.

Globalization can promote closer contact among Christians, especially through the Internet, creating new opportunities for international ecumenical communion and evangelical outreach. But it can also have the effect of highlighting differences among Christians. Some liberal Protestants accept non-traditional gender identities, both for church members and for ordained clergy, while more conservative Christians resist them. The question of the ordination of women, for example, challenges unity within single denominations and among different denominations across the world. More conservative Christians oppose such developments, in part, as secular (or Western) encroachment on sacred traditions, and the increasingly rapid pace of change is likely to increase its unsettling impact. Conservative evangelicalism, the tendency toward fundamentalist retrenchment, and apocalyptic expectation are also stimulated by globalization.

Violence

The Christian Bible and tradition provide Christians with a fundamental orientation against violence as a form of sin. Yet history shows that social structures and cultural influences involve some Christians in domestic, political, and religious violence. In the twenty-first century, church leaders increasingly call the universal Church to repentance and reconciliation. Numerous Western churches have made formal apologies for the role that Christian institutions played both in the transatlantic slave trade and in the violence inflicted on indigenous peoples around the world through the centuries of Western colonialism. Christian churches denounce anti-Semitism, and in recent years they have striven to protect Muslims from violence inspired by fear and suspicion. At the same time, Christians themselves are targets of religious violence in regions where they constitute a minority.

Geopolitical instability, terrorism, and abuses of human rights have led many Christians to work for peace and justice. National and international Christian organizations of many denominations have been motivated by Christ's 'Golden Rule' ('whatever you wish that others would do to you, do also to them'; *Matthew* 7: 12) to provide spiritual and material aid to Christians and non-Christians alike in conflict zones around the world. The global shifts that have developed since the end of the Cold War make the twenty-first century another critical testing ground for Christian precepts and ideals of peace, justice, and non-violence.

Science, technology, and the environment

The acceleration of scientific research and advances in technology confront Christians with serious questions about the balance between human responsibility and divine prerogative. The uneasiness surrounding abortion and euthanasia is rooted in the fact that they entail the destruction of human life. And the tensions multiply where stem-cell research and in vitro fertilization (IVF) are concerned, since they involve both the creation of human life and its destruction when unneeded cells are discarded; for some Christians, the possibility of creating life outside marriage is an additional concern. Contraceptive technologies for women and methods of prevention of HIV-AIDS likewise provoke tension among Christians. Decisions regarding issues such as these call for theological and moral reflection on the divine prerogative over creation and destruction of life, the divine mandate for compassion, the belief that physical health is continuous with spiritual health, and the belief that suffering has redemptive value.

Environmental concerns such as climate change, species extinction, habitat loss, and the use of nuclear technology are also prominent. Opinions differ but tend to follow familiar theological patterns. Foremost among these patterns are two beliefs: that the created world is sacred, and that God gave human beings dominion over it (*Genesis* 1: 26). But what 'dominion' means is a subject of debate. For some Christians it entails the use of creation for human prosperity and ease. For others it entails a responsibility of stewardship, which has led many Christians to become active in 'green' movements of various kinds. The statements on environmental ethics issued by the Roman Catholic and Orthodox churches, as well as many Protestant denominations represented by the World Council of Churches, all attempt to balance the needs of humanity with those of the creation as a mark of Christian faith.

Connecting past, present, and future

Change and diversity are characteristic of Christian tradition. Yet continuity—of creeds, symbols, sacraments—is central to Christian community: 'There is one body and one Spirit, just as you were called to the one hope of your calling, one Lord, one faith, one baptism, one God and Father of all, who is above all and through all and in all' (Ephesians

4:4–6). Together, the apostolic injunction to be in the world but not of it and Jesus' commandment to love God with all your heart and to love your neighbour as yourself (e.g., *Mark* 12:28–34) provide the common orientation for Christian identity and the common starting-point for ethical reflection. Thus the overriding question remains how to live in the ever-changing world as a faithful Christian. Denominations with highly centralized leadership structures, such as the Orthodox and Roman Catholic churches, are consistent, if not uniform, in their responses to that question. Denominations with the decentralized leadership patterns characteristic of many Protestant churches vary widely.

Acknowledging difference while recognizing continuity, achieving renewal and reconciliation, defining the relationship between the material and the spiritual: these are some of the challenges, both internal and external, that Christians around the world face in the twenty-first century.

Christianity and Pluralism

By the beginning of the third millennium, diversity had become part of the national fabric not only of societies built on immigration—like Canada, the US, and Australia—but also of European societies whose citizens were much more likely to share in a common cultural background, including the Christian faith. At the same time those societies have become more and more secular.

Many factors have contributed to the process of secularization. The most obvious is science, but there is good reason to think that Christianity itself has played a part. Certainly the first modern attempts to create secular states took place in Christian societies: England, France, the United States. The distinction between sacred and secular, which was fundamental to Christianity from the beginning, was undoubtedly a factor in the diversification of Protestant Christianity, and it has been reflected in a general recognition of the right to freedom of religion.

Thus Christianity has largely ceased to play a significant official role in the public life of these secular societies. Although many Christians remain convinced that the truth of their gospel leaves no room for other beliefs, today they have no choice but to live as one faith group among many. And even if that were not the case, Jesus' commandment to love our neighbours as ourselves would demand full openness to the identities of our fellow human beings. The plural nature of religious life today is a fact that must be accepted. To see that fact as desirable is to embrace what has come to be known as pluralism.

Pluralism presumes a human community whose common values may yet override the particularism of traditional Christian theology. An early proponent of pluralism was the Canadian scholar of comparative religion Wilfred Cantwell Smith (1916–2000). Smith suggested that to be modern is to be self-conscious about change and to take an active hand in shaping it. This chapter's overview of the Christian tradition makes it clear that change has been a feature of Christian history in every age. One would be ill advised to rule out the possibility of further creative change in the future.

Sacred Texts Table

Religion	Text(s)	Composition/ Compilation	Compilation/Revision	Use
Christianity	The Bible (components are listed below)	The Bible has two parts. The 'Old Testament' (OT) is the ancient Greek edition of the Hebrew Bible called the *Septuagint*. The New Testament (NT) comprises Christian sacred writings produced in Greek between 49 CE and 130 CE which were incorporated with the Septuagint.	Christians accepted the *Septuagint* as scripture from the beginning. The term 'Old Testament' came into use beginning in the 2nd century CE.	
	Old Testament, consisting of the same materials as the Jewish Tanakh, but in a new arrangement that produced 39 books (as opposed to the 24 of the Tanakh).	Translated 3rd century BCE–1st century CE	Early Christian editors organized the *Septuagint* materials in four groups (as opposed to the three of the Tanakh): Pentateuch (the five books of Moses that make up the Torah), Historical Books, Wisdom and Poetry, and Prophets. The placement of the Prophets section at the end of the OT (in contrast to the Jewish tradition) reflected the Christian belief that the life and teachings of Jesus Christ are anticipated in the Prophets. Thus the Christian arrangement makes the first four books of the NT (the Gospels) continuous with the OT Prophets, in accordance with the Christian understanding of salvation.	Liturgy, catechism, worship, devotion, contemplation, doctrine, canon law, theology, ethics, edification.
	Deuterocanonical Books/Apocrypha: 10–15 additions to the OT's Historical Books, Wisdom and Poetry, and Prophets sections.	Composed 3rd century BCE–1st century CE.	The *Deuterocanonical Books* were included in both Latin and Greek Christian Bibles in the 4th century. Their canonicity was re-confirmed by the Roman Catholic Church in the 16th century (in response to the Protestant Reformation) and by the Greek Orthodox Church in the 17th. ……… In the 16th century, most Protestant churches designated the Deuterocanonical Books apocryphal and excluded them from the OT (hence the alternative name 'Apocrypha').	Liturgy, catechism, worship, devotion, contemplation, doctrine, theology, ethics, edification. ……… No divine authority for Protestants, but acceptable for edification.

(continued)

Sacred Texts Table (continued)

Religion	Text(s)	Composition/ Compilation	Compilation/Revision	Use
	The New Testament contains 27 books classified in four groups: • Biography (four 'gospel' accounts of the life, ministry, passion, and resurrection of Jesus Christ):	Approximate dates of composition	The formation of the NT canon began c. 150 CE, after Marcion decided that some writings by Paul and Luke were sacred scripture but the OT was not. Church leaders rejected Marcion's 'canon' as heretical and set out to determine which among the growing body of Christian writings were religiously authoritative. Selection was guided by three criteria—traditional use, theology, and historicity. Slight variations among the lists produced by Church leaders show that consensus was not reached until the late 4th century. The Festal Letter of Bishop Athanasius (367 CE) lists all of the books that make up the NT as we know it today.	Liturgy, catechism, worship, devotion, contemplation, doctrine, canon law, theology, ethics, edification.
	Mark	c. 70 CE		
	Matthew	c. 80–90 CE		
	Luke	c. 80–90 CE		
	John	c. 90–100 CE		
	• History (one account of the Apostolic origins of the Church):			
	The Acts of the Apostles	c. 80–120 CE		
	• Epistles (21 letters containing instruction for theology, doctrine, and practice; classified in 4 groups): 'Pauline':	c. 49–58 CE		
	1 Thessalonians			
	1-2 Corinthians			
	Galatians			
	Philippians			
	Philemon			
	Romans			
	'DeuteroPauline':			
	Ephesians	c. 90–100 CE		
	Colossians	c. 60–90 CE		
	2 Thessalonians	c. 80–100 CE		
	'The Pastorals':	c. 100–130		
	1 Timothy			
	2 Timothy			
	Titus			
	'General' (letters, tracts, sermons):			
	Hebrews	c. 65–100 CE		
	James	c. 80–100 CE		
	1 Peter	c. 112 CE		
	Jude	c. 125 CE		
	2 Peter	c. 140–150 CE		
	1 John	c. 100–110 CE		
	2 John	c. 100–110 CE		
	3 John	c. 100–110 CE		
	• 'Apocalypse' (one account of the apocalyptic culmination of the divine plan of salvation):			
	Revelation	c. 95–96 CE		

Sites

Bethlehem The traditional birthplace of Jesus.

Nazareth Jesus' home in youth and manhood.

Jerusalem The site of Jesus' crucifixion and centre of the earliest Jewish Christian community; capital of the Latin Christian Kingdom in the Holy Land from 1099 to 1187.

Rome The capital of the Roman Empire, where Peter introduced Christianity and the Roman Catholic Church eventually established its headquarters in Vatican City—the world's smallest independent country.

Anatolia A region (corresponding to modern-day Turkey), evangelized by Paul, that became an important centre of the early Church; the location of the famous councils of Chalcedon, Nicaea, and Constantinople.

Constantinople The capital of the Byzantine Empire and headquarters of the Orthodox Church; conquered by the Ottoman Turks in 1453 and renamed Istanbul.

Wittenberg The German town where Martin Luther posted his 95 theses, beginning the Protestant Reformation.

Worms The German city where an imperial council ('diet') tried Luther for political subversion.

Trent (Trentino in Italian) Site of the Council of Trent (1545–63) and centre of the Catholic Church's response to Protestantism, known as the Counter-Reformation.

Geneva The city in which John Calvin attempted to translate his vision of Christianity into a practising community.

Münster A town in northwestern Germany that became a centre of the Anabaptist movement.

Valladolid City in Spain; the site of a great debate in 1550 in which Bartolomé de las Casas defended the rights of the indigenous peoples of the New World.

Salt Lake City, Utah Founded by the Mormons in 1847; the headquarters of the Church of Jesus Christ of Latter-day Saints.

Study Questions

1. Do you think it's likely that Constantine's conversion was sincere? What are the arguments on either side?

2. Over what issue (or issues) did Latin and Greek Christianity separate? How do the two branches differ—in worship, organization, and theology—today?

3. How do Catholics and Protestants differ in their views of Mary, the mother of Jesus?

4. Why did the development of modern biblical criticism represent more of a threat to Protestants than to Roman Catholics?

5. What are the main obstacles that stand in the way of efforts to overcome the historic bias against women in Christianity?

Glossary

Advent The beginning of the Christian liturgical year, a period including the four Sundays immediately preceding Christmas.

apostles The early followers who were commissioned to preach the gospel of Jesus after the resurrection.

atonement Christ's restoration of humanity to a right relationship with God, variously interpreted as divine victory over demonic power, satisfaction of divine justice, or demonstration of a moral example.

baptism Sprinkling with or immersion in water, the ritual by which a person is initiated into membership in the Christian community. Baptism is considered a cleansing from sin.

bishop The supervising priest of an ecclesiastical district called a diocese.

canon A standard; a scriptural canon is the list of books acknowledged as scripture; the list of acknowledged saints is also a canon. Canon law is the accumulated body of Church regulations and discipline.

charismatic Characterized by spiritual gifts such as glossolalia.

Christ The Greek translation of the Hebrew word for messiah, 'anointed'.

conversion Spiritual rebirth, accompanied by certainty of divine forgiveness and acceptance.

cosmological argument An argument that infers the existence of God from the fact of creation, based on the assumption that every effect must have a cause and that there cannot be an infinite regress of causes.

creeds Brief formal statements of doctrinal belief, often recited in unison by congregations. The Apostles' Creed has been widely used in worship services since the third century. The Nicene Creed, named for the Council of Nicaea (325

CE), is longer and more explicit and is recited in Catholic Eucharistic services.

crucifix A cross with an image of the suffering Jesus mounted on it.

ecumenism The movement for reunion or collaboration between previously separate branches of Christianity.

Eucharist The ritual re-enactment of Jesus' sacrifice of himself, patterned after his sharing of bread and wine as his body and blood at the final Passover meal with his disciples. Orthodox Christians term it the liturgy, Catholics the mass, and Protestants the Lord's Supper or Holy Communion.

Evangelical In Germany, a name for the Lutheran Church; in the English-speaking world, a description of conservative Protestants with a confident sense of the assurance of divine grace and the obligation to preach it.

excommunication Formal expulsion from the Church, particularly the Roman Catholic Church, for doctrinal error or moral misconduct.

friar A member of a Latin mendicant order such as the Dominicans, Franciscans, or Carmelites.

fundamentalism A twentieth-century reaction to modernity, originally among Protestants who maintained the infallibility of scripture and doctrine. Implying insistence on strict conformity in conduct and militancy in defending tradition against modernity, the term has been used more broadly in recent years; thus traditionalist Roman Catholics, for example, have also been described as 'fundamentalist'.

glossolalia Speaking in 'tongues'; a distinguishing feature of charismatic movements.

Gnosticism An ancient movement that believed the material world to be the evil result of a fall from pure spiritual existence. Christian Gnostics viewed Jesus as the bearer of a secret, saving knowledge through which the faithful would be redeemed from this material realm.

Good Friday The solemn holy day, two days before Easter, that commemorates the Passion or suffering and death of Jesus on the cross.

gospel 'Good news' (*evangelion* in Greek); the news of redemption that the Hebrew prophets had promised. The gospels are the accounts of Jesus' life attributed to his disciples Mark, Matthew, Luke, and John.

Holiness Churches Protestant churches that believe their members have already received 'holiness' (spiritual perfection) as a gift from God.

icon From the Greek for 'image'; a distinctive Byzantine form of portraiture used to depict Jesus, Mary, and the saints. The 'iconoclastic controversy' of the seventh and eighth centuries centred on an ultimately unsuccessful attempt to ban the use of icons.

Immaculate Conception The doctrine that the virgin Mary was without sin from the moment she herself was conceived; defined as Roman Catholic dogma in 1854.

incarnation The embodiment of the divine in human form.

indulgence A release from time in purgatory; the selling of indulgences was one of the abuses that led to the Protestant Reformation.

justification by faith alone The Lutheran belief that humans are saved only by faith, not by 'works'—specifically, the Catholic rituals of confession and penance.

Lent The period of forty days, not counting Sundays, leading up to Easter; the season for the most serious Christian spiritual reflection.

logos 'Word' in the sense of eternal divine intelligence and purpose, an idea prominent in Greek thought at the time of Jesus.

Manichaeism An intensely dualistic religion, founded by Mani in the third century, that grew out of Syrian Christianity under the influence of Gnosticism.

mass The Roman Catholic Eucharistic ceremony, in which bread and wine are eaten as the body and blood of Christ; celebrated in Latin until 1965 and in local languages since then.

mendicant orders Medieval religious orders operating in the cities and towns rather than in monasteries set apart from them. Members worked or begged for a living, originally as a protest against the monasteries' wealth.

Monophysites Fifth-century advocates of the view that Christ's nature was fully divine.

mysticism A tradition cultivating and reflecting on the content of moments of intensely felt spiritual union with the divine.

Nestorians Fifth-century advocates of the view that the incarnate Christ was two separate persons, one divine and one human.

ontological argument The eleventh-century theologian Anselm's argument based on logic holding that God must necessarily exist.

original sin The sinfulness, or tendency towards sin, supposedly innate in human beings as a consequence of Adam's Fall.

parables Narrative stories designed to teach a moral lesson.

Passion The suffering and death of Jesus on the cross.

patriarchs The five bishops who together represent supreme authority in the Eastern Orthodox tradition.

Pentecost The fiftieth day after Easter, commemorated as the dramatic occasion when Jesus' followers experienced the presence of the Holy Spirit and the ability to preach and be understood in different languages.

Pentecostal Churches Modern Protestant groups that emphasize speaking in 'tongues' as a mark of the Holy Spirit's presence and of the individual's holiness or spiritual perfection.

Pietism A movement that originated in late seventeenth-century Lutheran Germany, expressing a spontaneity of devotion and a confident certainty of forgiveness, over against institutional rigidity. It contributed to the emergence of Methodism in eighteenth-century England.

pope From *papa*, 'father'; the bishop of Rome, who represents supreme authority in the Roman Catholic tradition.

predestination The notion, based on faith in God as all-powerful and all-knowing, that God anticipates or controls human actions and foreordains every individual to either salvation or damnation.

purgatory In Catholic doctrine, the realm to which the soul proceeds after death for some unspecified period in preparation for entering heaven; the concept of purgatory developed in the medieval period.

Puritanism A Calvinist-inspired movement (1558–1660) that sought to 'purify' the Church of England of Catholic influences; before running its course in England, it became a major influence in Congregational churches in New England.

Reformed Churches Churches that are Calvinist in doctrine and often Presbyterian in governance; strong in the Netherlands and Scotland and also found in France, Switzerland, Hungary, and other places populated by settlers from those lands.

rosary A string consisting of 58 beads and a small crucifix, used in Catholic devotion to keep count when repeating Our Father and Hail Mary prayers.

sacrament A ritual action seen as signifying divine grace. The most widely accepted sacraments are baptism and the

Eucharist, although the Catholic Church also recognizes five others.

Stations of the Cross Fourteen locations marked in the nave of a Catholic church, recalling events along the route in Jerusalem from Jesus' trial to his crucifixion.

syncretism The combination of elements from more than one religious tradition.

teleological argument From Greek *telos*, 'end' or 'purpose'; an argument inferring the existence of God from the perception of purpose or design in the universe; as much a strategy for discussing God as a formal proof of his existence.

transubstantiation The Catholic doctrine that, at the moment of consecration in the Eucharistic service, the bread and wine are miraculously transformed into the body and blood of Christ.

Trinity The concept of God as having three 'persons' or manifestations: as father, as son, and as Holy Spirit; the doctrine of the Trinity emerged in the late third century and was adopted after vigorous debate in the fourth.

Uniate Churches Churches in the Eastern Orthodox world and farther east with which the Roman Catholic Church established relations, recognizing their distinctive rites, conducted in languages other than Latin, and their married clergy.

Further Reading

Allen, E[dgar] L. 1960. *Christianity among the Religions*. London: Allen and Unwin. Still one of the most perceptive discussions of historical and contemporary issues of religious pluralism.

Aulén, Gustav. 1930. *Christus Victor*. London: SPCK; New York: Macmillan. A classic discussion of Christian theories of the atonement.

Barraclough, Geoffrey, ed. 1981. *The Christian World: A Social and Cultural History*. London: Thames and Hudson; New York: Abrams. Combines authoritative text with ample pictorial material.

Barrett, C.K. 1989. *The New Testament Background: Selected Documents*. Rev. ed. San Francisco: Harper & Row. Provides a context for understanding Christian origins.

Barrett, David B., ed. 1982. *World Christian Encyclopedia*. Nairobi: Oxford University Press. Current facts and figures, country by country.

Barbour, Ian G. 1966. *Issues in Science and Religion*. Englewood Cliffs: Prentice-Hall. A perceptive historical account by a scholar with scientific training.

Bettenson, Henry S., ed. 1999. *Documents of the Christian Church*. 3rd edn. London: Oxford University Press. Strong on the early Church and Anglicanism.

Buttrick, George A., ed. 1962. *The Interpreter's Dictionary of the Bible*. 4 vols. New York: Abingdon Press. Authoritative articles on Old and New Testament topics.

Forristal, Desmond. 1976. *The Christian Heritage*. Dublin: Veritas. A uniquely readable survey of Christian literature, art, architecture, and music across the ages.

Gilson, Étienne. 1955. *History of Christian Philosophy in the Middle Ages*. New York: Random House. Magisterial synthesis by one of the leading medievalists of his generation.

Isichei, Elizabeth. 1995. *A History of Christianity in Africa: From Antiquity to the Present*. London: SPCK. Traces the emergence of Christian identities in Africa south of the Sahara.

Küng, Hans. 1976. *On Being a Christian*. London: Collins; New York: Doubleday. A comprehensive review of Christian theology by a leading progressive Roman Catholic thinker.

McManners, John, ed. 1990. *The Oxford Illustrated History of Christianity*. Oxford: Oxford University Press. Comprehensive; well-written chapters by reliable authors.

van der Meer, F., and Christine Mohrmann. 1958. *Atlas of the Early Christian World*. London: Nelson. Illustrated guide to the geographical spread and the monuments of Christianity's first seven centuries.

The New Catholic Encyclopedia. 15 vols. 1967. New York: McGraw-Hill. A good place to start for many medieval and Roman Catholic topics.

Pelikan, Jaroslav. 1985. *Jesus through the Centuries: His Place in the History of Culture*. New Haven: Yale University Press. An erudite, wide-ranging review.

Placher, William C. 1983. *A History of Christian Theology: An Introduction*. Philadelphia: Westminster Press. A lively review of major thinkers, particularly useful for Protestantism since the Reformation. For primary texts, Placher's sourcebook in two volumes (early and modern), Readings in the History of Christian Theology (Philadelphia: Westminster Press, 1988) offers what may be the best selection currently available.

Roeder, Helen. 1951. *Saints and Their Attributes*. London: Longmans, Green. A useful guide to Christian iconography.

Ruether, Rosemary R., and Eleanor McLaughlin, eds. 1979. *Women of Spirit: Female Leadership in the Jewish and Christian Traditions*. New York: Simon and Schuster. One of the best feminist collections.

Zernov, Nicholas. 1961. *Eastern Christendom: A Study of the Origin and Development of the Eastern Orthodox Church*. London: Weidenfeld and Nicolson; New York: Putnam. A comprehensive survey.

Recommended Websites

www.christianity.com

www.ncccusa.org   Site of the National Council of Churches USA.

www.oikoumene.org/   Site of the World Council of Churches.

www.religionfacts.com/christianity/index.htm   A wide-ranging source of information on Christianity as well as other religions.

www.vatican.va/phome_en.htm   English-language version of the official Vatican site.

http://virtualreligion.net/forum/index.html   Site of the Jesus Seminar.

www.wicc.org   Site of the Women's Inter-Church Council of Canada.

www.worldevangelicals.org   A global association of evangelical Christians.

References

Bainton, Roland H. 1974. 'Reformation'. In *Encyclopaedia Britannica*, vol.15, 547–57. Chicago: Encyclopaedia Britannica Inc.

Bowie, Fiona, and Oliver Davies, eds. 1990. *Hildegard of Bingen: Mystical Writings*. New York: Crossroad.

Durkheim, Émile. 1915. *The Elementary Forms of the Religious Life*. London: Allen & Unwin.

King, Martin Luther, Jr. 1964. *Why We Can't Wait*. New York: New American Library.

Livingstone, David. 1858. *Cambridge Lectures*. Cambridge: Deighton.

McManners, John, ed. 1990. *The Oxford Illustrated History of Christianity*. Oxford: Oxford University Press.

New English Bible. 1970. New York: Oxford University Press; Cambridge: Cambridge University Press.

Outler, Albert C., trans. 1955. *Augustine: Confessions and Enchiridion*. Philadelphia: Westminster Press; London: SCM Press.

Smith, Wilfred Cantwell. 1963. *The Faith of Other Men*. New York: New American Library.

Whitehead, Albert North. 1929. *Process and Reality*. Cambridge: Cambridge University Press; New York: Macmillan.

Note

1. This section was kindly contributed by Leslie Hayes of the University of Toronto.

Chapter
5
Muslim Traditions

❧ Amir Hussain ❧

Islam is the third of the three monotheistic faiths that arose in the Middle East. Its name means 'submission' in Arabic and signifies the commitment of its adherents to live in total submission to God. A person who professes Islam is called a Muslim: 'one who submits to God'. Another translation of Islam is 'engaged surrender', signifying both the surrender to God and the activities associated with this surrender.

Who is a Muslim? The Qur'an, the Islamic scripture, presents Islam as the universal and primordial faith of all the prophets from Adam to Muhammad, and of all those who have faith in the one sovereign God, the creator and sustainer of all things. According to the Qur'an, Islam is God's eternal way for the universe.

Inanimate things, plants and animals, even the angels, are all by nature *muslims* to God. Only human *islam* is an *islam* of choice. Humans may voluntarily accept or wilfully reject faith, but they will face the consequences of their choice on the Day of Judgment, when they will either be rewarded for their faith or punished for their rejection of it.

Most Muslims are born into Muslim families. But it is also possible to become a Muslim simply by repeating with sincerity before two Muslim witnesses the profession of faith called the *shahadah*: 'I bear witness that there is no god except God, and I bear witness that Muhammad is the messenger of God.' Anyone who does this becomes legally a Muslim, with all the rights and responsibilities that this new identity entails.

❧ ORIGINS

Jewish and Christian communities existed in Arabia long before Islam emerged in the seventh century. The city of Mecca, where Muhammad was born, was dominated by people of the Quraysh tribe, but it was open to a broad range of cultural and religious influences, including Jewish and Christian moral and devotional ideas. There were desert hermits who practised holiness and healing, and a group of Meccan Arabs known as *hanifs* ('pious ones') who concurred with Jews and Christians in their ethical monotheism. The majority of the society, however, was polytheistic, and many of the images of the gods and goddesses they worshipped were housed in an ancient structure called the Ka'ba, believed to have been built by Abraham and his son Ishmael.

◀ The Dome of the Rock in Jerusalem, built between 687 and 691 by Caliph 'Abd al-Malik b. Marwan, is not a mosque but a shrine. It stands on the site of the Hebrew temple destroyed by the Romans in 70 CE (Zafer Kizilkaya/Ponkawonka.com).

Hadith: A saying of the Prophet

The Messenger of God (may God bless him and give him peace) said: 'Whoever has faith in God and the Last Day should not hurt their neighbour, and whoever has faith in God and the Last Day should serve their guest generously, and whoever has faith in God and the Last Day should speak what is good or keep quiet' (*Sahih al-Bukhari*, vol. 8, book 73).

Timeline

c. 570	Birth of Muhammad
622	Muhammad's *hijrah* from Mecca to Medina
632	Muhammad dies and leadership passes to the caliph
642	Birth of al-Hasan al-Basri, early Sufi ascetic (d. 728)
661	Damascus established as capital of Umayyad caliphate
680	Death of Husayn at Karbala, considered martyrdom by Shi'is
711	Arab armies reach Spain
762	Baghdad established as 'Abbasid capital
922	al-Hallaj (born c. 858) executed for claiming to be one with the Truth
1058	Birth of al-Ghazali, theological synthesizer of faith and reason (d. 1111)
1071	Seljuq Turks defeat Byzantines in eastern Anatolia
1165	Birth of Ibn 'Arabi, philosopher of the mystical unity of being (d. 1240)
1207	Birth of Jalal al-Din Rumi, Persian mystical poet (d. 1273)
1258	Baghdad falls to Mongol invaders
1492	Christian forces take Granada, the last Muslim stronghold in Spain
1529	Ottoman Turks reach Vienna (again in 1683)
1602	Muslims officially expelled from Spain
1703	Birth of Ibn 'Abd al-Wahhab, leader of traditionalist revival in Arabia (d. 1792)
1924	Atatürk, Turkish modernizer and secularizer, abolishes the caliphate
1930	Muhammad Iqbal proposes a Muslim state in India
1947	Pakistan established as an Islamic state
1979	Ayatollah Khomeini establishes a revolutionary Islamic regime in Iran
2001	Osama bin Laden (d. 2011) launches terrorist attacks on America
2005	London transit bombings
2006	Orhan Pamuk becomes the second Muslim (after Naguib Mahfouz) to win the Nobel Prize for Literature
2010	Islamic scholars at the Mardin Conference in Turkey issue a ruling against terrorism
2011	The self-immolation of Mohammed Bouazizi in December 2010, in protest against police and government corruption in Tunisia, sets off a series of protests that spread to several other countries, including Egypt, Libya, Yemen, Syria, and Bahrain

The Life of Muhammad (570–632 CE)

Muhammad was born into the Quraysh tribe around the year 570. His father died before his birth and his mother died a few years later. The orphaned child was cared for first by his paternal grandfather, 'Abd al-Muttalib, and then, after his grandfather's death, by his uncle Abu Talib.

Traditions at a Glance

Numbers

There are more than 1 billion Muslims around the world; approximately 800,000 in Canada; and 7 million in the United States.

Distribution

Although Islam originated in Arabia, the largest Muslim populations today are in Indonesia, Pakistan, India, and Bangladesh. Muslims are the second largest religious community (behind Christians) in many Western countries, including Canada, Great Britain, France, and Germany.

Principal Historical Periods

570–632	Lifetime of the Prophet Muhammad
632–661	The time of the four caliphs
661–750	Umayyad caliphate
750–1258	'Abbasid caliphate
1517–1924	Ottoman caliphate

Founder and Principal Leaders

All Muslims place authority in Muhammad as the last prophet. Shi'a Muslims give special authority after Muhammad to his son-in-law 'Ali and 'Ali's descendants.

Deity

Allah is Arabic for 'the God' and is cognate with the Hebrew '*Eloh* (plural '*Elohim*), 'deity'. Muslims believe Allah to be the same God worshipped by Christians, Jews, and other monotheists.

Authoritative Texts

The essential text is the Qur'an (literally, 'The Recitation'), believed to have been revealed by God to Muhammad between the years 610 and 632 CE. Second in importance are the sayings of Muhammad, known as the *hadith* (literally, 'narrative').

Noteworthy Doctrines

Islam, like Judaism and Christianity, is a faith based on ethical monotheism. Its prophetic tradition begins with the first created human being (Adam) and ends with the Prophet Muhammad. Muslims believe that the first place of worship dedicated to the one true God is the Ka'ba in Mecca, built by Abraham and his son Ishmael.

Little is known about Muhammad's youth. He worked as a merchant for a rich widow, named Khadijah, whom he married in his mid-twenties. Muhammad is described in the early biographical sources as a contemplative, honest, and mild-mannered young man. He was called al-Amin ('the faithful' or 'trustworthy') because of the confidence he inspired in people.

Once a year, during the month of **Ramadan**, Muhammad spent days in seclusion in a cave on Mount Hira, a short distance from Mecca. Tradition reports that it was during one of those retreats he received the call to prophethood and the first revelation of the Qur'an.

As Muhammad was sitting one night in the solitude of his retreat, an angel—later identified as Gabriel (Jibril in Arabic)—appeared. Taking hold of him and pressing him hard, the angel commanded, 'Recite [or read]!' Muhammad answered, 'I cannot read.' After repeating the command for the third time, the angel continued, 'Recite in the name of your Lord who created, created man from a blood clot. Recite, for your Lord is most magnanimous—who taught by the pen, taught the human being that which s/he did not know' (Q. 96: 1–5). Shivering with fear and apprehension, Muhammad ran home and asked the people of his household to cover him.

Yet the angel returned to him often, saying, 'O Muhammad, I am Gabriel, and you are the Messenger of God.' Khadijah consoled and encouraged him, and eventually took him to her cousin, a learned Christian named Waraqah bin Nawfal. Waraqah confirmed Muhammad to be a prophet with a sacred mission to deliver a new message from God.

The idea of a prophet like Moses—nabi in both Arabic and Hebrew—was not new to Muhammad's people. But for twelve years Muhammad the Prophet preached the new faith in the One God to them with little success. The Meccans did not wish to abandon the ways of their ancestors, and they feared the implications of the new faith, both for their social customs and for the religious and economic status of the Ka'ba.

Major Branches of Islam

Islam has two major branches, Sunni and Shi'a. The majority of the world's Muslims (about 850 million) are Sunni. They take their name from the sunnah or tradition of the Prophet Muhammad.

About 15 per cent of the world's Muslims (some 150 million people) are Shi'a. Their name comes from the Arabic for 'partisans' and refers to the group of Muslims who, after Muhammad's death, gave their allegiance to 'Ali (his son-in-law) and 'Ali's descendants, collectively known as the Imams. The Shi'a are divided into two groups: Imami or Twelver (about 135 million), who follow a lineage of twelve Imams, and Ismaili or Sevener (about 15 million), who have a living Imam in the person of the Aga Khan.

'Sufism' is not a separate branch of the faith. The term simply refers to Islam's mystical dimension. Sufis may be either Sunni or Shi'a.

Muhammad's message was moral and social as well as religious. He instructed the Meccans to give alms, care for the orphans, feed the hungry, assist the oppressed and destitute, and offer hospitality to the wayfarer. He also warned of impending doom on the day of the last judgment. The first to accept the new faith were his wife Khadijah, his cousin and son-in-law 'Ali bin Abu Talib, his slave Zayd bin Harithah—whom he later freed and adopted—and his faithful companion Abu Bakr.

Like the first disciples of Jesus, Muhammad and his followers were often vilified. Around 615, one group of Muslims without tribal protection faced such severe persecution from the polytheistic people of Mecca—especially the Quraysh—that the Prophet advised them to migrate across the Red Sea to the Christian country of Abyssinia (Ethiopia), where they were well received. And in 619 the Prophet himself was left without support or protection when Khadijah and his uncle Abu Talib both died within the space of barely two months.

It was soon after these losses that the Prophet experienced what came to be known as the *mi'raj* or 'night journey', travelling from Mecca to Jerusalem in the course of one night and then ascending to heaven. There he met some of the earlier prophets and was granted an audience with God. For Muslims, these miraculous events confirmed that Muhammad still had the support of God. Even so, it would be another three years before he found a place for the Muslims to establish their own community, free of the persecution they suffered in Mecca.

The First Muslim Community

Finally, in 622, an invitation was offered by the city of Yathrib, about 400 kilometres (250 miles) north of Mecca. The migration (*hijrah*) to Yathrib, which thereafter came to be known as 'the city of the Prophet' or Medina ('the city'), marked the beginning of community life under Islam, and thus of Islamic history. In Medina Muhammad established the first Islamic commonwealth: a truly theocratic state headed by a prophet who was believed to be guided by the dictates of a divine scripture.

The Qur'an calls the people of Medina Ansar ('helpers') because they were the first supporters and protectors of Islam and the Prophet. An oasis city with an agricultural economy, Medina had a heterogeneous social structure that included a substantial Jewish community as well as two feuding Arab tribes whose old rivalries had kept the city in a continuous state of civil strife. Muhammad was remarkably successful in welding these disparate elements into a cohesive social unit. In a brief constitutional document known

Islamic Dates

The migration from Mecca to Medina provided the starting-point for the dating system used throughout the Muslim world. Years are counted backwards or forwards from the *hijrah* and accompanied by the abbreviation AH, from the Latin for 'year of the *hijrah*'. Because Muslims use the lunar year—which is 11 days shorter than the solar year—*hijri* dates gain one year approximately every 33 solar years. Thus the year 1400 AH was reached in 1979 CE, and the new year of 1433 AH was celebrated in 2011 CE.

as the covenant of Medina, he established the city as a Muslim commonwealth within which both Jews and non-Muslim Arabs would be guaranteed full religious freedom and equality, on condition that they support the state and refrain from any alliance with enemies of Islam such as the Quraysh.

The Qur'an's narratives and worldview are closely akin to the prophetic view of history laid out in the Hebrew Bible. The Prophet expected the Jews of Medina, recognizing this kinship, to be natural allies, and he adopted a number of Jewish practices, including the fast of the Day of Atonement (Yom Kippur).

But the Medinan Jews rejected both Muhammad's claim to be a prophet and the Qur'an's claim to be a sacred book. The resulting tension is reflected in the Qur'an's treatment of the Jews. Some references are clearly positive: 'Among the People of the Book are an upright community who recite God's revelations in the night, prostrate themselves in adoration, believing in God and the Last Day . . . these are of the righteous, whatever good they do, they shall not be denied it' (3: 113–15). Others are just as clearly negative: 'Take not the Jews and Christians for friends' (5: 51). Increasingly, Islam began to distinguish itself from Judaism, so that within two years of the Prophet's arrival in Medina, the fast of Ramadan took precedence over the fast of Yom Kippur and the **qiblah** (direction of prayer) was changed from Jerusalem to the Ka'ba in Mecca.

The Conversion of Mecca

The Muhajirun ('immigrants') who had fled Mecca for Medina had left all their goods and property behind. Without the means to support themselves in their new home, they began raiding Meccan—mainly Quraysh—caravans returning from Syria. In 624, when the Meccans sent an army of roughly a thousand men to Medina, they were met at the well of Badr by a 300-man detachment of Muslims.

Though poorly equipped and far outnumbered, the Muslims inflicted a crushing defeat on the Meccans. Thus the Battle of Badr remains one of the most memorable events in Muslim history. It is celebrated in the Qur'an as a miraculous proof of the truth of Islam: 'You [Muhammad] did not shoot the first arrow when you shot it; rather God shot it' (Q. 8: 17); 'God supported you [Muslims] at Badr when you were in an abased state' (Q. 3: 123).

To avenge their defeat, however, the Meccans met the Muslims the following year by Mount Uhud, not far from Medina, and this time they prevailed. Following the Battle of Uhud, the Jews of Medina were expelled from the city on the grounds that they had formed alliances with the Meccans against the Muslims. The real reason for the decision, however, may have been to free the Muslim state of external influences at a critical stage in its development.

The Muslims were growing in strength. Meanwhile, they continued to raid the caravans of the Quraysh, and before long they received word that the latter were planning to attack Medina itself. On the advice of Salman the Persian, a former slave, the Prophet had a trench dug around the exposed parts of the city to prevent the enemy cavalry from entering. Thus when the Quraysh, along with a large coalition of other tribes, tried to invade Medina in 627, the city was able to withstand the attack. The 'Battle of the Trench' marked a tipping point in relations between the Muslims and the Meccans, and in 628 the latter were impelled to seek a truce.

Two years later, when the Quraysh breached the truce, the Prophet set out for Mecca at the head of a large army. But there was no need to fight. When the Muslims arrived, the Meccans surrendered to them and accepted Islam en masse.

Whenever an individual or tribe accepted Islam, all hostilities were to cease and enemies were to become brothers in faith. Therefore the Prophet granted amnesty to all in the city. Asked by the Meccans what he intended to do with them, the Prophet answered, 'I will do with you what Joseph did with his brothers. Go; you are free.' Then he quoted Joseph's words to his brothers: 'There is no blame in you today; God forgive you' (Q. 12: 92).

Muhammad took no credit for the conquest of Mecca, attributing the victory solely to God, as prescribed in the Qur'an: 'When support from God comes, and victory, and you see people enter into the religion of God in throngs, proclaim the praise of your Lord' (Q. 110). He returned to Medina and died there two years later, in 632, after making a farewell pilgrimage to Mecca and its sacred shrine, the Ka'ba.

Muhammad was always known as *rasul Allah* ('the Messenger of God') rather than as a ruler or military leader. But he was all of these. He waged war and made peace. He laid the foundations of a community (**ummah**) that was based on Islamic principles. He firmly established Islam in Arabia and sent expeditions to Syria. Within 80 years, the Muslims would administer the largest empire the world had ever known, stretching from the southern borders of France through North Africa and the Middle East into India and Central Asia.

At the time of his death, however, no one could have foreseen that future. The majority of Muslims—the **Sunni**, meaning those who follow the *sunnah* ('traditions') of the Prophet—believed that he had not even designated a successor or specified how one should be chosen. But a minority community known as the Shi'a ('partisans'), believed that Muhammad had in fact appointed his son-in-law 'Ali to succeed him. Muhammad's death precipitated a crisis, which grew into a permanent ideological rift.

A *khalifah* is someone who represents or acts on behalf of another. Thus after Muhammad's death, his close companion Abu Bakr became the *khalifat rasul Allah*—the 'successor' or 'representative' of the Messenger of God—and Abu Bakr's successor, 'Umar ibn al-Khattab, was at first referred to as the 'successor of the successor of the Messenger of God'.

From the beginning, the institution of the caliphate had a worldly as well as a

In the courtyard of the Rustem Pasha mosque in Istanbul, Turkey (Photo courtesy of Andrew Leyerle).

religious dimension. As a successor of the Prophet, the **caliph** was a religious leader. At the same time, as the chief or administrative head of the community, he was the *amir* or commander of the Muslims in times of peace as well as war. Perhaps conscious of this temporal dimension of his office, 'Umar is said to have adopted the title 'commander of the faithful' in place of his cumbersome original title. Nevertheless, the caliph continued to function as the chief religious leader ('imam') of the community. In all, there were four caliphs who ruled after Muhammad, from 632 to 661. Thereafter the Muslim world was ruled by a succession of hereditary dynasties, of which the most important were the Umayyads (661–750) the 'Abbasids (750– 1258), and the Ottomans (1517–1924)

❧ CRYSTALLIZATION

Prophets and Messengers

According to the Qur'an, God operates through prophets and messengers who convey God's will in revealed scriptures and seek to establish God's sacred law in the lives of their communities. From the Islamic point of view, therefore, human history is prophetic history.

Islamic tradition maintains that, from the time of Adam to the time of Muhammad, God sent 124,000 prophets into the world to remind people of every community of their obligation to the one and only sovereign Lord and warn them against disobedience: 'There is not a nation but that a warner was sent to it' (Q. 26: 207). The Qur'an mentions by name 26 prophets and messengers. Most are well-known biblical figures, among them Abraham, Moses, David, Solomon, Elijah, Jonah, John the Baptist, and Jesus. It also mentions three Arabian prophets: Shu'ayb, Hud, and Salih.

Islamic tradition distinguishes between prophets and messengers. A prophet (*nabi*) is one who conveys a message from God to a specific people at a specific time. A messenger (*rasul*) is also a prophet sent by God to a specific community; but the message he delivers is a universally binding sacred law (**shari'ah**). The Torah given to Moses on Mount Sinai

Abraham

In the Qur'an, it is the innate reasoning capacity of the Hebrew patriarch Abraham—Ibrahim in Arabic—that leads him away from his people's tradition of idol worship and towards the knowledge of God. Even as a youth he recognizes that idols made of wood or stone cannot hear the supplications of their worshippers, and therefore can do them neither good nor harm.

One night, gazing at the full moon in its glory, Abraham thinks that it must be God. But when he sees it set, he changes his mind. He then gazes at the bright sun and thinks that, since it is so much larger, it must be the real God. But that night the sun too sets, leading Abraham to declare: 'I turn my face to the One who originated the heavens and the earth, a man of pure faith, and I am not one of the Associators [those who associate other things or beings with God]' (Q. 6: 77–9).

was an example of the latter: though delivered to the ancient Hebrews, it remained binding on all those who knew it, Hebrews and others, until the arrival of the next revelation—the gospel of Jesus. In other words, every messenger is a prophet; but not every prophet is a messenger. Among the messenger-prophets, five—Noah, Abraham, Moses, Jesus, and Muhammad—are called *ulu al-'azm* ('prophets of power or firm resolve', Q. 46: 35). Their special significance lies in their having received universally binding revelations from God.

In the context of Muslim piety, respect for Muhammad is shown by speaking (or writing) the phrase 'peace [and blessings of God] be upon him' every time his name or title is mentioned. In writing, the formula is often abbreviated as PBUH. When the prophets as a group, culminating in Muhammad, are mentioned, the formula changes to 'peace be on them all'.

From the Qur'an: Abraham Destroys the Idols

When [Abraham] said to his father and his people, 'What are these idols that you so fervently worship?' they said, 'We found our fathers worshipping them.'

He said, 'Both you and your fathers are in manifest error'. They said, 'Have you come to us with the truth, or are you one of those who jest?'

He said, 'Your Lord is indeed the Lord of the heavens and the earth, for your Lord originated them; and to this I am one of those who bear witness. By God, I shall confound your idols as soon as you turn your backs.'

He thus destroyed them utterly except for the chief one, so that the people might turn to it [for petition].

They said, 'Who did this to our gods? He is surely a wrongdoer.'

Some said, 'We heard a youth called Abraham speaking of them.'

Others said, 'Bring him here in the sight of the people, so that they may all witness.'

They said, 'Did you do this to our gods, O Abraham?'

He said, 'No, it was their chief who did it. Question them—if they could speak.'

The people then turned on one another, saying, 'Indeed you are the wrongdoers!' Then they bowed their heads in humiliation, saying, 'You know well, [O Abraham], that these do not speak.'

He [Abraham] said, 'Would you then worship instead of God a thing that can do you neither good nor harm? Shame on you and on what you worship instead of God; do you not reason?'

They said, 'Burn him and stand up for your gods, if you would do anything.'

We [God] said, 'O fire, be coolness and peace for Abraham.'

They wished evil for him, but We turned them into utter losers. And We delivered him and Lot to a land that We blessed for all beings. We also granted him Isaac and Jacob as added favour, and We made them both righteous. We made them all leaders guiding others by our command. We inspired them to do good deeds, perform regular worship, and give the obligatory alms; and they were true worshippers of Us alone (Q. 21: 51–73).

The Qur'an

The Qur'an was revealed (literally, 'sent down') to the prophet Muhammad over a period of 23 years. According to both the Qur'an and Muslim tradition, the angel Gabriel appeared to him, often in human guise, transmitting the *ayahs* (verses) and **surahs** (chapters) that came to constitute the Qur'an.

The Prophet's role as transmitter of revelation is reflected in the Qur'an's characteristic phrasing: God ('We') instructs the Prophet ('you') to 'say' something to the people (that is, to deliver a particular message to them). Yet the first instruction was the command that Muhammad himself 'recite' or 'read' *(iqra')*. The term Qur'an is derived from the same root: q–r–', meaning 'to read' or 'recite'.

In size the Qur'an is nearly as long as the New Testament. The individual portions revealed to Muhammad vary in length and content from short verses on a single theme or idea to fairly lengthy chapters. The early Meccan *surahs* are generally brief admonitions couched in terse and powerful verses, while the later ones are didactic narratives or illustrative tales of earlier prophets and their communities. Through commands and warnings, stories and parables, the Qur'an seeks to create an *ummah*: a community united by faith.

The *surahs* revealed in Medina are fewer in number but longer, presenting didactic arguments, discourses, and legal pronouncements, often in response to questions or situations arising in the life of that community.

The Status of the Qur'an

Muslims believe that the Qur'an is an immutable heavenly book containing the eternal Word of God. In fact, there is an interesting theological parallel with Christian understandings of Jesus, who in the prologue to John's gospel is proclaimed to be the eternal Word of God made incarnate at a certain moment in history. For Christians Christ is the Word of God made flesh, while for Muslims the Qur'an is the Word of God made into a book.

Muslims understand the Qur'an to have been revealed specifically in the Arabic language—not surprising, given that Arabic was the language of its first audience. Hence any translation is considered to constitute an interpretation, not the Qur'an itself. Even in places where few if any Muslims speak the language, the Qur'an is always recited in Arabic. Of course, each passage is usually followed by a translation in the appropriate language.

The words of the Qur'an are recited in a newborn child's ear as a blessing. They are also recited to bless and seal a marriage contract or a business deal, to celebrate a successful

---

From the Qur'an: On the Day of Judgment

This short surah *(chapter) is known by the title 'The Earthquake'.*

When the earth shall be shaken with a great quake, and the earth yields up her burdens, and the human being exclaims, 'What has happened to her!' On that day the earth shall recount her tidings—as her Lord had inspired her. Whoever does an atom's weight of good shall then see it, and whoever does an atom's weight of evil shall then see it (Q. 99).

venture, or to express sorrow and give solace in times of misfortune. Throughout the Muslim world, the Qur'an is recited on most special public occasions and daily on radio and television. Qur'anic recitation is an art of great virtuosity and hypnotic power. For private devotional recitation over the course of a month, the Qur'an has been divided into 30 parts of equal length. The words of the Qur'an, in the form of calligraphy, have also been a central motif in Islamic art, and are used to decorate Muslim homes, mosques, and public buildings.

Compiling the Qur'an

By the time of the Prophet's death in 632, many people had committed the Qur'an to memory. The only physical records, however, were fragments written on stones, bones, palm leaves, and animal parchment, which were held in a variety of private collections. In some cases the same material existed in several versions, and since the vowel marks were not added until later, different readings of certain words or phrases were possible. These variants became identified with specific readers through the generations of Muslim scholars.

The process of producing an official text of the Qur'an was completed under the third caliph, 'Uthman ibn 'Affan, within twenty years of the Prophet's death. One of the first copies of the complete text was given to Hafsah, a widow of the Prophet.

As an earthly book, the Qur'an has been shaped by Muslim history. Tradition maintains that the verses of each individual *surah* were arranged by the Prophet at Gabriel's instruction, but that the order of the *surahs* in relation to one another—roughly in decreasing order of length—was fixed by a committee that 'Uthman appointed to compile an official version. Of the 114 *surahs*, 113 are preceded by the invocation *bism-illahi ar-rahman ar-rahim* ('in the name of God, the All-merciful, the Compassionate'); the exception is the ninth *surah*, which most commentators believe to be a continuation of the eighth.

Qur'anic Commentary (Tafsir)

The term for commentary on the Qur'an, *tafsir*, means 'unveiling' or elucidating the meaning of a text. Any such interpretation is based on one of three authoritative sources: the Qur'an itself, Prophetic **hadith** (tradition), and the opinions of the Prophet's Companions and their successors. Like the Qur'an and the *hadith*, the earliest commentaries were transmitted orally, but by the tenth century Qur'anic interpretation had developed into a science with several ancillary fields of study.

In fact, every legal or theological school, religious trend, or political movement in Muslim history has looked to the Qur'an for its primary support and justification. The result has been a wide range of interpretations reflecting the diversity of the sects, legal schools, and mystical and philosophical movements that emerged as the Islamic tradition developed.

The Qur'an's Concept of God

The Qur'an presents its view of the divinity in direct and unambiguous declarations of faith in the one and only God, creator, sustainer, judge, and sovereign Lord over all creation. For Muslims, it is a sin to associate any other being with God or to ascribe divinity to any but God alone.

'Allah' is not the name of a particular deity but the Arabic word for God, 'the Lord of all beings' (Q. 1: 2), who demands faith and worship of all rational creatures. It was used in the same sense by the pagan Arabs before Islam, and is still used in that sense by Arab Jews and Christians today.

Islamic theology holds that God's essence is unknowable, inconceivable, above all categories of time, space, form, and number. Materiality and temporality cannot be attributed to God. Nor, properly speaking, can masculinity or femininity, although references to God in the Qur'an and throughout Islamic literature use masculine forms ('he', 'his', and so on).

God's attributes are referred to in the Qur'an as the 'most beautiful names' (sometimes translated as 'wonderful names'). These divine attributes are manifested in creation, in life and knowledge, power and mercy, might and wisdom. The Qur'an (59: 22–3) declares:

> God is God other than whom there is no
> god, knower of the unknown and the visible.
> God is the All-merciful, the Compassionate.
> God is God other than whom there
> is no god, the King, the Holy One, Peace,
> the Faithful, the Guardian, the Majestic, the
> Compeller, the Lofty One.

Faith and Action

Righteousness as it is expressed in the Qur'an has several components. In addition to faith in God, God's angels, books, and prophets, and the judgment of the last day, it includes good works: Muslims should give of their wealth, however cherished it may be, to orphans and the needy or for the ransoming of slaves and war captives. It also includes patience and steadfastness in times of misfortune or hardship and war, and integrity in dealing with others.

Because all men and women belong ultimately to one humanity, they are all equal before God, regardless of race, colour, or social status. They may surpass one another only in righteousness: 'Humankind, We have created you all of one male and one female and made you different peoples and tribes in order that you may know one another. Surely, the noblest of you in God's sight is the one who is most aware of God' (Q. 49: 13).

The Arabic word *iman* means faith, trust, and a personal sense of safety and well-being in God's providential care, mercy, and justice. In the context of inner personal commitment, *iman* is synonymous with *islam*: total surrender of the human will and destiny to the will of God. The opposite of *iman* is **kufr**, rejection of faith. To have faith is to know the truth and assent to it in the heart, profess it with the tongue, and manifest it in concrete acts of charity. *Kufr*, by contrast, means knowing the truth but willfully denying or obscuring it by acts of rebellion against the law of God. The word *kufr* literally means 'to cover up, deny, or obscure'.

The Qur'an also makes an important distinction between Islam and faith. Outwardly, Islam is a religious, social, and legal institution, whose members constitute the worldwide Muslim *ummah*, or community. *Iman*—faith—is an inner conviction whose sincerity God alone can judge, a commitment to live in the worship of God and in moral relations with other persons. This is described beautifully in the Qur'an (49: 14), where the Bedouin come to Muhammad and say, 'we have faith.' Muhammad is commanded to respond: 'Do not say that you have faith, rather, say that you have submitted [you have *islam*], for faith has not yet entered your hearts.' Faith, as a comprehensive framework of worship and moral conduct, is explicitly depicted in the answer that the Prophet is said to have given to the question 'What is faith?': 'Faith is seventy-odd branches, the highest of which is to say "There is no god except God" and the lowest is to remove a harmful object from the road.'

Above Islam and *iman* stands *ihsan* (doing good or creating beauty). On the level of human interrelations, *ihsan* is a concrete manifestation of both Islam and *iman*. On the level of the personal relationship of the man or woman of faith with God, *ihsan* constitutes the highest form of worship, expressed in this hadith: '*Ihsan* is to worship God as though you see God, for even if you do not see God, God sees you.'

Religious Sciences

In Arabic a learned person is termed an *'alim*. The plural, *'ulama'*, refers to the religio-legal scholars, or religious intellectuals, of the Islamic world as a group. What Muslims call the 'religious sciences' were part of a comprehensive cultural package—including theology, philosophy, literature, and science—that developed as Islam expanded geographically far beyond the religio-political framework of its Arabian homeland. Cosmopolitan, pluralistic Islamic cultural centres like Baghdad, Córdoba, and Cairo offered ideal settings for intellectual growth. Beginning in the eighth century, the development of philosophy, theology, literature, and science continued in different parts of the Muslim world well into the seventeenth.

Islam is a religion more of action than of abstract speculation about right belief. Hence the first and most important of the religious sciences, Islamic law, stresses that the essence of faith is right living. The Prophet characterizes a Muslim thus: 'Anyone who performs our prayers [i.e., observes the rituals of worship] and eats our ritually slaughtered animals [i.e., observes the proper dietary laws] is one of us.' For Muslims, inner submission to the will of God is God's way for all of humankind. At both the personal and the societal level, Islam is a way of life that is to be realized by living within the framework of divine law, the *shari'ah*: that is, a way of life based on moral imperatives.

The Sources of Islamic Law

The Qur'an
The Qur'an and hence the *shari'ah* are centrally concerned with relationships among individuals in society and between individuals and God. The most particular and intimate human relationship is the one between husband and wife; the second is the relationship between parent and child. The circle then broadens to include the extended family, the tribe, and finally the *ummah* and the world.

Islam has no priesthood. Every person is responsible both for his or her own morality and for the morality of the entire Muslim *ummah*: 'Let there be of you a community that calls to the good, enjoins honourable conduct, and dissuades from evil conduct. These are indeed prosperous people' (Q. 3: 104).

The Qur'an places kindness and respect to parents next in importance to the worship of God. These are followed by giving alms to support the needy. Usury—the charging of interest on a loan—is prohibited as a means of increasing wealth. But renunciation of material possessions is no more desirable than total attachment to them. Rather, the Qur'an enjoins the faithful to 'Seek amidst that which God has given you, the last abode, but do not forget your portion of the present world' (Q. 28: 77).

In short, the Qur'an is primarily concerned with moral issues in actual situations. It is not a legal manual. Of its 6,236 verses, no more than 200 are explicitly legislative.

The *Sunnah*

The life-example of the Prophet includes not only his acts and sayings but also his tacit consent. His acts are reported in anecdotes about situations or events in which he participated or to which he responded. In situations where he expressed neither approval nor objection, his silence is taken to signify consent. Thus the *sunnah* of consent became a normative source in the development of Islamic law.

Accounts that report the Prophet's *hadiths* (sayings) must go back to an eyewitness of the event. The *hadith* literature is often called 'tradition' in English, in a quite specific sense. Islamic 'tradition' (or 'Prophetic tradition') is the body of sayings traced to the Prophet Muhammad through chains of oral transmission (**isnad**). *Hadith* is the most important component of *sunnah* because it is the most direct expression of the Prophet's opinions or judgments regarding the community's conduct.

To qualify as a *hadith*, a text must be accompanied by its chain of transmission, beginning with the compiler or last transmitter and going back to the Prophet. The aim of the study of *hadith* is to ascertain the authenticity of a particular text by establishing the completeness of the *isnad* (chain of transmission) and the veracity of its transmitters.

There are six canonical collections of *hadiths*. The earliest and most important collectors were Muhammad bin Isma'il al-Bukhari (810–70) and Muslim bin al-Hajjaj al-Nisaburi (c. 817–75). As their names suggest, the former came from the city of Bukhara in Central Asia and the latter from Nishapur in northeastern Iran. The two men did not know each other, but they were contemporaries and both spent many years travelling across the Muslim world in search of *hadith* traditions. The fact that their independent quests produced very similar results suggests that a unified *hadith* tradition was already well established.

Both men are said to have collected hundreds of thousands of *hadiths*, out of which each selected about 3,000, discounting repetitions. Their approach became the model for all subsequent *hadith* compilers. Their two collections, entitled simply *Sahih* (literally, 'sound') *al-Bukhari* and *Sahih Muslim*, soon achieved canonical status, second in authority only to the Qur'an. Within less than half a century, four other collections—by Abu Dawud al-Sijistani, Ibn Majah, al-Tirmidhi, and al-Nasa'i—were produced. It is worth noting that, like al-Bukhari and Muslim, these four also came from Central Asia and Iran. Each of these collections is entitled simply *Sunan* (the plural of *sunnah*).

As legal manuals, all six collections are organized topically, beginning with the laws governing the rituals of worship and continuing with the laws regulating the social, political, and economic life of the community.

The Scope of Islamic Law

For Muslims God is the ultimate lawgiver. The *shari'ah* is sacred law, 'the law of God'. It consists of the maxims, admonitions, and legal sanctions and prohibitions enshrined in the Qur'an and explained, elaborated, and realized in the Prophetic tradition.

The term *shari'ah* originally meant 'the way to a source of water'. Metaphorically it came to mean the way to the good in this world and the next. It is 'the straight way' that leads the faithful to paradise in the hereafter. Muslims believe the *shari'ah* to be God's plan for the ordering of human society.

In the framework of the divine law, human actions range between those that are absolutely obligatory and will bring rewards on the Day of Judgment, and those that are absolutely forbidden and will bring harsh punishment. Actions are classified in five categories:

- lawful (**halal**), and therefore obligatory;
- commendable, and therefore recommended (*mustahabb*);
- neutral, and therefore permitted (*mubah*);
- reprehensible, and therefore disliked (*makruh*); and
- unlawful (**haram**), and therefore forbidden.

These categories govern all human actions. The correctness of an action and the intention that lies behind it together determine which category it falls into, and hence its consequences for the person who performs it.

Jurisprudence (Fiqh)

Jurisprudence, or **fiqh**, is the theoretical and systematic aspect of Islamic law, consisting of the interpretation and codification of the *shari'ah*, or sacred law. A scholar who specializes in this exacting science is called a *faqih* ('jurist').

Islamic jurisprudence as it was developed in the various legal schools is based on four sources. Two of these sources, the Qur'an and *sunnah*, are primary and two are secondary: the personal reasoning (*ijtihad*) of the scholars and the general consensus (*ijma'*) of the community. All schools of Islamic law recognized these four sources: where they differed was in the relative importance they attributed to each one.

Personal reasoning is the process through which legal scholars deduce from the Qur'an and *sunnah* the laws that are the foundations of their various schools of thought. It requires reasoning from analogous situations in the past: modern software piracy, for instance, would be considered analogous to theft. The term *ijtihad*—from the same root as *jihad*, 'struggle'—draws attention to the effort that such an endeavour demands. *Ijma'* was meant to ensure the continuing truth of the three other sources. In the broadest sense, *ijma'* refers to the community's acceptance and support of applied *shari'ah*. More narrowly, it encouraged an active exchange of ideas among the scholars of the various schools, at least during the formative period of Islamic law. The Prophet's declaration that 'my community will not agree on an error' is understood to indicate that consensus remains the final arbiter of truth and error.

Yet even this important principle has been the subject of debate and dispute. Is the consensus of earlier generations binding on the present one? Can the necessary consensus be reached by the scholars alone, without the participation of the community at large? These are among the many questions that divide scholars of the various schools.

Islamic Philosophy and Theology

An important subset of the religious sciences (also known as the transmitted sciences) contained the 'rational' sciences of philosophy and theology. Theology is discourse about God, God's attributes, and God's creation and nurture of all things. It is also concerned with human free will and predestination, moral and religious obligations, and the return to God on the Day of Resurrection for the final judgment. Insofar as theology addresses human faith and conduct, it is part of the science of *fiqh*, or jurisprudence.

In time, however, Islamic theology also came to concern itself with more philosophical questions about the existence of God, creation, and the problem of evil and suffering. In these areas Islamic theology reflects the influence of Hellenistic philosophy, whose principles and rationalistic methodology it adopted.

The rapid spread of Islam out of Arabia into Syria and Mesopotamia brought Muslims into increasing contact with people of other faiths and ethnic backgrounds, including Hellenized Jews and Christians. With the rise of the 'Abbasid dynasty in the mid-eighth century, interest in Greek philosophy, science, and medicine increased, and Arabic translations of Greek works began to appear.

The quest for knowledge reached its peak in the ninth century under the caliph al-Ma'mun, whose Bayt al-Hikmah ('House of Wisdom') in Baghdad was the first institution of higher learning not just in the Islamic world but anywhere in the West. Christian scholars had already translated many Greek medical, philosophical, and theological treatises

Muhammad ibn Idris al-Shafi'i

A decisive stage in Muslim jurisprudence came in the ninth century with Muhammad ibn Idris al-Shafi'i (767–820). Having travelled widely and studied in various centres of learning across the Muslim world, he spent his last years in Egypt, where he wrote the first systematic treatise on the subject. This work radically changed the scope and nature of Islamic jurisprudence. Rejecting personal opinion in favour of absolute dependence on the two primary sources, the Qur'an and *sunnah*, Shafi'i based his system on a vast collection of *hadith* and legal traditions entitled *Kitab al-Umm*, which he compiled in order to write his work. In opposition to the majority of jurists of his time, he argued that they should not base their judgments on the opinions of people, but should rely exclusively on the Book of God and the *sunnah* of God's Prophet.

Although Shafi'i's legal system was later adopted as the basis of a school of thought bearing his name, he himself expressly opposed the idea. He saw himself not as the founder of a new legal school, but as the reformer of Islamic law. The Shafi'i school took root early in Egypt, where its founder lived and died. It then spread to southern Arabia and later followed the maritime trade routes first to East Africa and then to Southeast Asia, where it remains the dominant legal school.

into Syriac and commented on them, but the House of Wisdom, which housed an impressive library of Greek manuscripts, provided additional support for their work. Families of translators worked in teams, rendering into Arabic the ancient treasures of Hellenistic science and philosophy. Smaller centres of philosophical and medical studies in Syria and Iran also made notable contributions.

The Early Period

Early Islamic philosophy had a distinctive character: Aristotelian in its logic, physics, and metaphysics; Platonic in its political and social aspects; and Neoplatonic in its mysticism and theology. Two figures stand out in this early period. The first was the Iraqi theologian-philosopher Abu Yusuf Ya'qub al-Kindi (d. 870), who used philosophical principles and methods of reasoning to defend fundamental Islamic teachings such as the oneness of God, the creation of the universe by God's command out of nothing, the inimitability of the Qur'an, and the necessity of prophets. In his argument for the latter, Al-Kindi underlined the distinction between the philosopher who acquires his knowledge through rational investigation and contemplation and the prophet who receives his knowledge instantaneously, through divine revelation.

In sharp contrast to al-Kindi, Abu Bakr Zakariyah al-Razi ('the one from Rayy, Iran'; c. 865–926) was a thoroughgoing Platonist who rejected the doctrine of creation out of nothing. Drawing on the theory that Plato elaborated in his *Timaeus*, al-Razi argued that the universe evolved from primal matter, floating gas atoms in an absolute void. The universe or cosmos came into being when God imposed order on the primeval chaos, but it will return to chaos at some distant point in the future, because matter will revert to its primeval state.

The Flowering of Islamic Philosophy

Abu Nasr al-Farabi (c. 878–950), who moved to Baghdad from Turkestan, in Central Asia, was not only a great philosopher but an important musical theorist and an accomplished instrumentalist. His Platonic philosophical system was comprehensive and universal. According to al-Farabi, God is pure intellect and the highest good. From God's self-knowledge or contemplation emanates the first intellect, which generates the heavenly spheres and a second intellect, who then repeats the process. Each subsequent intellect generates another sphere and another intellect.

Al-Farabi agreed with al-Kindi that a prophet is gifted with a sharp intellect capable of receiving philosophical verities naturally and without any mental exertion. He then communicates these truths to the masses, who are incapable of comprehending them on the philosophical level.

Although al-Farabi was called 'the second teacher', after Aristotle, even he was excelled by 'the great master' Ibn Sina (known in Latin as Avicenna, 980–1037). Ibn Sina, who was born in Bukhara, Iran, was a self-taught genius who mastered the religious sciences at the age of ten and by the age of eighteen had become a leading physician, philosopher, and astronomer. His encyclopedic manual of medicine, *al-Qanun fi al-Tibb* ('The canon of medicine'), and his philosophical encyclopedia, *al-Shifa'* ('The book of healing'), were studied in European universities throughout the Middle Ages.

Ibn Sina built on al-Farabi's Neoplatonic ideas to construct a comprehensive system of mystical philosophy and theology. He accepted and developed al-Farabi's emanationism, placing it in a more precise logical and philosophical framework. Although he affirmed the prophethood of Muhammad, the revelation of the Qur'an, and the immortality of the soul, he rejected the Qur'anic traditions of the resurrection of the body, the reward of paradise, and the punishment of hell.

According to a widely accepted Prophetic tradition, at the beginning of every century God raises a scholar to renew and strengthen the faith of the Muslim community. Such a person is known as a *mujaddid* ('renovator') of the faith. Abu Hamid Muhammad al-Ghazali (1058–1111) of Tus, in Iran, has been regarded as the *mujaddid* of the sixth Islamic century. His work went far beyond theology and philosophy, encompassing mysticism and all the religious sciences.

In 1091 al-Ghazali was appointed a professor of theology and law at the prestigious Nizamiyah college in Baghdad, where he tirelessly defended mainstream Sunni Islam against the innovations of the theologians and the heresies of the philosophers. Four years later, however, he suffered a deep psychological crisis and gave up teaching. After a long quest, he determined that true knowledge could not be attained through either the senses or the rational sciences, but only through a divine light that God casts into the heart of the person of faith.

His reason thus enlightened, al-Ghazali produced one of the most ambitious works in the history of Islamic thought: *The Revivification of the Religious Sciences* examined all religious learning from a deeply mystical point of view. In another important work, *The Incoherence* [or 'Collapse'] *of the Philosophers*, al-Ghazali rejected the philosophical principle of causality (which said, for instance, that created things could be the efficient causes of events) and argued that the only cause of anything in the universe is God.

Al-Ghazali's critique in turn became the subject of a critique by the Andalusian philosopher Ibn Rushd (1126–98). The greatest Muslim commentator on Aristotle, he came from a long line of jurists and was himself a noted scholar of Islamic law. His legal training decisively influenced his philosophy. In his response, entitled *The Incoherence of the Incoherence*, Ibn Rushd methodically criticized al-Ghazali for misunderstanding philosophy and Ibn Sina for misunderstanding Aristotle. The first to construct a true Aristotelian philosophical system, Ibn Rushd essentially shared his Eastern predecessors' belief in the primacy of philosophy over religion. But in his famous double-truth theory he argued that both were valid ways of arriving at truth: the difference was that philosophy was the way of the intellectual elite, while religion was the way of the masses.

The great thirteenth-century philosopher-mystic Ibn 'Arabi will be discussed later, in the context of Sufism. A more empirical philosopher than any of those mentioned so far was the Tunisian-born 'Abd al-Rahman Ibn Khaldun (1332–1406). Through his extensive travels and the positions he held as a jurist and political theorist, Ibn Khaldun gained insight into the workings both of nations and of political and religious institutions. This insight led him to write a universal history. The most important part of this work is its introduction (*Muqaddimah*), in which Ibn Khaldun presents the first social philosophy of history in the Western world.

Islamic philosophy had a profound influence on medieval and Renaissance thought in Europe, particularly through its interpretation of Aristotelianism. Europeans came to know many Muslim philosophers by Latinized forms of their names: Rhazes for al-Razi,

Alpharabius or Avennasar for al-Farabi, Avicenna for Ibn Sina, Algazel for al-Ghazali, Averroës for Ibn Rushd.

🌿 Differentiation

Shi'ism

As we have seen, the Muslim community was permanently divided soon after the death of the Prophet, when a political party (*shi'ah*) formed around his son-in-law 'Ali in support of his right to succeed Muhammad as Imam (leader). 'Shi'ism' is a broad term covering a variety of religio-political movements, sects, and ideologies, but they all share a general allegiance to 'Ali, his descendants, and their right to spiritual and temporal authority in the Muslim community after Muhammad.

For Sunni Muslims, the term 'imam' refers to anyone who serves as the leader of prayer at the mosque—a role that the caliph sometimes performed. For Shi'is, however, the title of 'Imam' is reserved for the one individual they believe to be the rightful, divinely mandated leader of the Muslim community.

In general, Shi'is believe that the Qur'an attributes a special status to Muhammad's family ('the people of the house'): 'Surely, God wishes to take away all abomination from you, O people of the House, and purify you with a great purification' (Q. 33: 33). Furthermore, God instructs Muhammad to declare that the only reward he wishes for his work in conveying God's revelation 'is 'love for [my] next of kin' (Q. 42: 23). The expressions 'people of the house' (*ahl al-bayt*) and 'next of kin' (*al-qurba*) are usually interpreted as referring to the Prophet's daughter Fatimah, her husband 'Ali, and their two sons, Hasan and Husayn.

The foundation of the Shi'i claim is a *hadith* according to which the Prophet, on his way back from Mecca to Medina, stopped at a place called Ghadir Khumm, took 'Ali by the hand, and made the following declaration:

> O people, hear my words, and let him who is
> present inform him who is absent: Anyone of
> whom I am the master, 'Ali, too, is his master.
> O God, be a friend to those who befriend
> him and an enemy to those who show hostility
> to him, support those who support him
> and abandon those who desert him.

On the basis of this *hadith* and others in which they believe the Prophet directly or indirectly designated 'Ali as his successor, Shi'i specialists constructed an elaborate legal and theological system centred on the doctrine of *imamah*, according to which the source of all legitimate authority is the office of the Imam.

Ashura

In the year 680 the Prophet's grandson Husayn (the son of 'Ali) was leading an uprising against the Umayyad Caliph Yazid when he was killed in battle at Karbala in Iraq.

The anniversary of his death, on the tenth day of the month of Muharram, has become a focal point for the Shi'i community's hopes and frustrations, as well as its messianic expectations.

'Ashura' ('ten'), as the anniversary came to be known, is still commemorated by the Shi'i community throughout the Muslim world. Blending sorrow, blessing, and mystery, it has inspired a rich devotional literature, as well as numerous popular passion plays re-enacting the events leading up to the death of Husayn. Above all, it is observed by the Shi'i community as a day of suffering and martyrdom. Its symbolism is expressed in a variety of devotional acts, including solemn processions, public readings, and a pilgrimage to the sacred ground of Karbala. Sunni Muslims commemorate 'Ashura' with a day of fasting.

Imami ('Twelver') Shi'ism

According to the Shi'i doctrine of *imamah*, the Prophet appointed 'Ali as his viceregent. 'Ali in turn appointed his son Hasan to succeed him as Imam, and Hasan appointed his brother Husayn. Thereafter, each Imam designated his successor, usually his eldest son.

'Twelver' Shi'is believe that the line of Imams descended from Husayn continued until 874, when the twelfth Imam, a four-year-old child named Muhammad ibn Hasan al-'Askari, disappeared into hiding ('occultation'). Thereafter he communicated with his Shi'a through four successive deputies until 941, when he entered a new phase known as the 'greater occultation', which will continue until the end of the world. Then, before the Day of Resurrection, he will return as the **Mahdi**, 'the rightly guided one', and with Jesus will establish universal justice and true Islam on earth. In the absence of the Hidden Imam, the community looks to jurists for guidance.

Shi'is agree with Sunni Muslims on the centrality of the Qur'an and *sunnah* as the primary sources of Islamic law. However, they understand the *sunnah* to include not only the life-example of the Prophet Muhammad and his generation, but the life-examples of the Imams—the men they believe to be his rightful successors. Hence the period of the *sunnah* for Twelver Shi'i Muslims extends over three centuries, until the end of the lesser occultation of the twelfth Imam in 941.

'Sevener' or Isma'ili Shi'ism

The majority of Shi'is accepted the line of Husaynid Imams down to Ja'far al-Sadiq (d. 765), the sixth in the succession. But a major schism occurred when Ja'far's oldest son and successor, Isma'il, died about ten years before his father. Ja'far then appointed a younger son, Musa al-Kazim, as his successor.

Many of Ja'far's supporters considered this appointment irregular and insisted that the seventh Imam should be Isma'il's son Ahmad. For this reason they came to be known as Isma'ilis or 'Seveners'. The largest faction, called Nizaris, carried on the line of Imams through Ahmad and his descendants down to the present. Over the centuries Isma'ili philosophers and theologians developed the doctrine of the divine mandate of the Imam and his absolute temporal and religious authority into an impressive esoteric system of prophetology.

For centuries the Isma'ilis lived as an obscure sect in Iran, Syria, East Africa, and the Indo-Pakistani subcontinent. Nevertheless, they have played an important intellectual and political role in Muslim history. Since 1818 their Imam has been known as the Agha Khan, an Indo-Iranian title signifying nobility. The third Agha Khan (1877–1957) initiated a movement for reconciliation with the larger Muslim community, and efforts to resolve differences have continued under his Harvard-educated successor, Karim Agha Khan (b. 1936). In modern times Isma'ilis have migrated in large numbers to the West. Prosperous and well-organized, they now number roughly 15 million and are the best-integrated Muslim community in the West.

Sufism: The Mystical Tradition

The early Muslim mystics were said to wear a garment of coarse wool over their bare skin in emulation of Jesus, who is represented in Islamic hagiography as a model of ascetic piety. For this reason they became known as Sufis (from the Arabic word meaning 'wool'). Asceticism was only one element in the development of Sufism, however.

At least as important was the Islamic tradition of devotional piety. Since the ultimate purpose of all creation is to worship God and sing God's praises (see Q. 17: 44 and 51: 56), the pious are urged to 'remember God much' (33: 41), 'in the morning and evening' (76: 25), for 'in the remembrance of God hearts find peace and contentment' (13: 28). The Prophet's night vigils and other devotions, alluded to in the Qur'an (73: 1–8) and greatly embellished by hagiographical tradition, have served as a living example for pious Muslims across the centuries. *Hadith* traditions, particularly the 'divine sayings' (*hadith qudsi*) in which the speaker is God, have also provided a rich source of mystical piety. Above all, the *mi'raj*—the Prophet's miraculous journey to heaven—has been a guide for numerous mystics on their own spiritual ascent to God.

The early Muslim ascetics were known as *zuhhad*, meaning 'those who shun [the world and its pleasures]'. One of the earliest champions of this movement was a theologian named al-Hasan al-Basri, who was born in Medina in 642 and lived through both the crises and the rise to glory of the Muslim *ummah*. In a letter addressed to the pious caliph 'Umar ibn 'Abd al-'Aziz, Hasan likened the world to a snake: soft to the touch, but full of venom.

The early ascetics were also called weepers, because of the tears they shed in fear of God's punishment and in yearning for God's reward. Significantly, this early ascetic movement emerged in areas of mixed population where other forms of asceticism had existed for centuries: places such as Kufa and Basra in Iraq (long the home of Eastern Christian asceticism); northeastern Iran, particularly the region of Balkh (an ancient centre of Buddhist ascetic piety, now part of Afghanistan); and Egypt (the home of Christian monasticism as well as Gnostic asceticism).

Asceticism for its own sake, however, was frowned on by many advocates of mystical piety. Among the critics was the sixth Imam, Ja'far al-Sadiq, who argued that when God bestows a favour on a servant, God wishes to see that favour manifested in the servant's clothing and way of life. Ja'far's grandfather 'Ali Zayn al-'Abidin is said to have argued that God should be worshipped not out of fear of hell or desire for paradise, but in humble gratitude for the gift of the capacity to worship God.

What transformed ascetic piety into mysticism was the all-consuming love of the divine exemplified by an early woman mystic named Rabi'a al-'Adawiyah of Basra (c. 713–801).

Rabi'a al-'Adawiyah

When Rabi'a's fellow Sufis urged her to marry, she agreed in principle, but only on the condition that the prospective husband—a devout man named Hasan—answer four questions. In the end she remained unmarried, free to devote all her thoughts to God.

'What will the Judge of the world say when I die? That I have come forth from the world a Muslim, or an unbeliever?'

Hasan answered, 'This is among the hidden things known only to God. . . .'

Then she said, 'When I am put in the grave and Munkar and Nakir [the angels who question the dead] question me, shall I be able to answer them [satisfactorily] or not?' He replied, 'This is also hidden.'

'When people are assembled at the Resurrection and the books are distributed, shall I be given mine in my right hand or my left?' . . . 'This also is among the hidden things.'

Finally she asked, 'When mankind is summoned (at the Judgment), some to Paradise and some to Hell, in which group shall I be?' He answered, 'This too is hidden, and none knows what is hidden save God—His is the glory and the majesty.'

Then she said to him, 'Since this is so, and I have these four questions with which to concern myself, how should I need a husband, with whom to be occupied?' (Smith 1928: 11).

Born into a poor family, Rabi'a was orphaned and sold into slavery as a child, but her master was so impressed with her piety that he set her free. She lived the rest of her life in mystical contemplation, loving God with no motive other than love itself:

> My Lord, if I worship you in fear of the fire,
> burn me in hell. If I worship you in desire
> for paradise, deprive me of it. But if I
> worship you in love of you, then deprive me not
> of your eternal beauty. (Smith 1928)

Mystics of all religious traditions have used the language of erotic love to express their love for God. Rabi'a was perhaps the first to introduce this language into Islamic mysticism. She loved God with two loves, the love of passion and a spiritual love worthy of God alone.

The love that Rabi'a spoke of was the devotional love of the worshipful servant for his or her Lord. A more controversial tradition within Sufism pursued absolute union with God. Among the proponents of this ecstatic or 'intoxicated' Sufism was Husayn bin Mansur al-Hallaj (c. 858–922), whose identification with the divine was so intense as to suggest that he made no distinction between God and himself. For this apparent blasphemy he was brutally executed by the 'Abbasid authorities.

Al-Hallaj had been initiated into Sufism early in life and travelled widely, studying with the best-known Sufi masters of his time. But he eventually broke away from his teachers and embarked on a long and dangerous quest for self-realization. It began when he went

Farid al-Din 'Attar

Farid al-Din 'Attar lived in Iran at the turn of the thirteenth century. In this extract, the words 'Ask not' echo a phrase used by theologians to express paradox—bila kayf, 'without asking how'—but here they evoke the mystic's sense of ineffability.

His beauty if it thrill my heart
If thou a man of passion art
Of time and of eternity,
Of being and non-entity,
   Ask not.

When thou hast passed the bases four,
Behold the sanctuary door;
And having satisfied thine eyes,
What in the sanctuary lies
   Ask not. . . .

When unto the sublime degree
Thou hast attained, desist to be;
But lost to self in nothingness
And, being not, of more and less
   Ask not.
   (Arberry 1948: 32–3)

one day to see his teacher Abu Qasim al-Junayd. When the latter asked who was at the door, Al-Hallaj answered, 'I, the absolute divine truth' (*ana al-Haqq*)—calling himself by one of the 99 'wonderful names' of God mentioned in the Qur'an. Al-Junayd reprimanded his wayward disciple and predicted an evil end for him.

At its core, al-Hallaj's message was moral and intensely spiritual, but it was interpreted as suggesting that God takes the form of a human person (as Christians believe of Jesus)—an idea that most Muslims of his time found deeply shocking. Whereas a less extreme predecessor, Bayazid Bistami, had preached annihilation of the mystic in God, al-Hallaj preached total identification of the lover with the beloved:

I am He whom I love, and He whom I love is I.
We are two spirits dwelling in one body.
If thou seest me, you see Him; and if thou seest Him, you see us both
   (Nicholson 1931: 210–38).

After eight years in prison, al-Hallaj danced to the gallows, where he begged his executioners to 'Kill me, O my trusted friends, for in my death is my life, and in my life is my death.' For many Muslims, al-Hallaj lives on as the martyr of love who was killed for the sin of intoxication with God by the sword of God's own *shari'ah*.

The Crystallization of Sufism

The mystical life is a spiritual journey to God. The novice who wishes to embark on such an arduous journey must be guided by a master who becomes in effect his or her spiritual parent. As Sufism grew, however, many well-recognized masters attracted too many disciples to allow for a one-to-one relationship. By the eleventh century, therefore, teaching manuals were being produced to impart the ideas of great masters to eager disciples. A high point in this process of crystallization was al-Ghazali's *Revivification of the Religious Sciences.*

Roughly half a century after al-Ghazali, Shihab al-Din Suhrawardi (c. 1155–91) became known as the great master of illumination. He grew up in Iran and eventually settled in northern Syria. Drawing on a verse in the Qur'an (24: 35) that speaks of God as the light of the heavens and the earth, Suhrawardi described a cosmos of light and darkness populated by countless luminous angelic spirits.

The most important Sufi master of the thirteenth century was Muhyi al-Din Ibn 'Arabi (1165–1240), who was born and educated in Muslim Spain and travelled widely in the Middle East before finally settling in Damascus. The central theme of Ibn 'Arabi's numerous books and treatises is the 'unity of being'. According to this doctrine, God in God's essence remains in 'blind obscurity', but is manifested in the creation through an eternal process of self-disclosure. Thus even as human beings need God for their very existence, God also needs them in order to be known.

Ibn 'Arabi's doctrine had many implications, among them the idea that, if God alone really is, then all ways ultimately lead to God. This means that all the world's religions are in reality one. Ibn 'Arabi says:

> My heart has become capable of every form: it is a pasture for gazelles and a convent for Christian monks,
> And a temple for idols, and the pilgrim's Ka'ba, and the tables of the Torah and the book of the Koran.
> I follow the religion of Love, whichever way his camels take. My religion and my faith is the true religion
> (Nicholson 2002 [1914]: 75).

Ibn 'Arabi remains one of the greatest mystic geniuses of all time.

Rumi

The most creative poet of the Persian language was Jalal al-Din Rumi (1207–73). Like Ibn 'Arabi, he was the product of a multicultural, multi-religious environment. Rumi was born in Balkh, Afghanistan, but as a child fled with his parents from the advancing Mongols. At last they settled in the city of Konya in central Anatolia (Turkey), a region that had been part of the Roman Empire.

In 1244 Rumi met a wandering Sufi named Shams of Tabriz. The two men developed a relationship so intimate that Rumi neglected his teaching duties because he could not bear to be separated from his friend. In the end, however, Shams disappeared, leaving Rumi to pour out his soul in heart-rending verses expressing his love for the 'Sun' (the name Shams means 'sun' in Arabic) of Tabriz.

Jalal al-Din Rumi

Here Rumi expresses the mystic's experience of union with God in terms of the dissolution of individual identity.

I died as mineral and became a plant
I died as plant and rose to animal,
I died as animal and I was Man.
Why should I fear? When was I less by dying?
Yet once more I shall die as Man, to soar
With angels blest; but even from angelhood
I must pass on: all except God doth perish (Q. 28: 88).
When I have sacrificed my angel-soul,
I shall become what no mind e'er conceived.
Oh, let me not exist! for Non-existence
Proclaims in organ tones, 'To him we shall return' (Q. 2: 151)
　　(Nicholson 1950: 103).

Rumi's greatest masterpiece is his *Mathnawi* ('Couplets'), a collection of nearly 30,000 verses. The spirit of this vast panorama of poetry is clearly expressed in its opening verses, in which the haunting melodies of the reed flute tell the sad tale of its separation from the reed bed. In stories, couplets of lyrical beauty, and at times even coarse tales of sexual impropriety, the *Mathnawi* evokes the human soul's longing for God.

Sufi Orders and Saints

The religious fraternity is an ancient and widespread phenomenon. The earliest Sufi fraternities were established in the late eighth century, and by the thirteenth century a number of these groups were becoming institutionalized. Usually founded either by a famous *shaykh* (master) or by a disciple in the *shaykh's* name, Sufi orders began as teaching and devotional institutions located in urban centres, where they would often attach themselves to craft or trade guilds in the main bazaar.

It became a common custom for lay Muslims to join a Sufi order. Lay associates provided a good source of income for the order, participated in devotional observances, and in return for their contributions received the blessing *(barakah)* of the *shaykh*.

The truth and authenticity of a *shaykh's* claim to spiritual leadership depended on his or her spiritual genealogy. By the thirteenth century, Sufi chains of initiation (similar to *isnad* in *hadith* transmission) were established. Such chains began with the *shaykh's* immediate master and went back in an unbroken chain to the Prophet, 'Ali or one of his descendants, or in some cases to other Companions of the Prophet or their successors.

Through this spiritual lineage, a *shaykh* inherited the *barakah* of her masters, who inherited it from the Prophet. In turn, the *shaykh* bestowed his *barakah*, or healing power, on his devotees, both during his life and, with even greater efficacy, after his death.

Dervishes at the Galata Mevlevihanesi (Mevlevi Whirling Dervish hall) in Istanbul (Images & Stories/Alamy).

The *shaykhs* of Sufi orders are similar to the saints of the Catholic Church in that the faithful ascribe miracles or divine favours to them. Unlike Christian saints, however, they are recognized through popular acclaim rather than official canonization.

Devotional Practices

The most characteristic Sufi practice is a ritual called the *dhikr* ('remembrance') of God, which may be performed in public or in private. The congregational *dhikr* ritual is usually held before either the dawn or the evening prayers. It consists of the repetition of the name of God, Allah, or the *shahadah*, 'There is no god except God' (*la ilaha illa Allah*). The *dhikr* is often accompanied by special bodily movements and, in some Sufi orders, by elaborate breathing techniques.

Often it is their performance of the *dhikr* that distinguishes the various Sufi orders from one another. In some popular orders it is a highly emotional ritual (similar to charismatic practices in some Pentecostal churches) intended to stir devotees into a state of frenzy. By contrast, in the sober Naqshbandi order (founded by Baha' al-Din al-Naqshbandi in the fourteenth century), the *dhikr* is silent, an inward prayer of the heart.

Another distinctly Sufi practice is the *sama'* ('hearing' or 'audition'), in which devotees simply listen to the hypnotic chanting of mystical poetry, accompanied by various musical instruments. As instrumental music is not allowed in the mosque, *sama'* sessions are usually held in a hall adjacent to the mosque, or at the shrine of a famous *shaykh*.

Music and dance are vital elements of devotional life for members of the Mevlevi (Mawlawi) order, named after Mawlana ('our master') Rumi and founded shortly after his death by his son. As practised by the Mevlevis—also known as the 'Whirling Dervishes'—dance is a highly sophisticated art symbolizing the perfect motion of the stars; the haunting melodies of the reed flute and the large orchestra that accompanies the chanting of verses by Rumi and other poets echo the primordial melodies of the heavenly spheres.

Sufism has always shown an amazing capacity for self-reform and regeneration. It was the Sufis who preserved Islamic learning and spirituality after 1258, when Baghdad fell to Mongol invaders, and Sufis who carried Islam to Africa and Asia. Today in the West it is primarily Sufi piety that is attracting non-Muslims to Islam.

Women and Sufism

Women have played an important role in the Sufi tradition, often serving as role models for men as well as women. This may help to explain part of the historical tension between orthodox Islam and Sufism. One of the most beloved stories about Rabi'a, the early female Sufi, has her roaming the streets of Basra carrying a bucket of water and a flaming torch, ready to put out the fires of Hell and set fire to the gardens of Paradise so that people will worship God for the sake of Love alone.

The Sufi tradition provided one of the few outlets for women to be recognized as leaders. Since the Sufis believed the Divine to be without gender, the gender of the worshipper did not matter. After Rabi'a, women could be Sufi leaders even though they were forbidden to train as imams. The shrines of Sufi saints, whether male or female, are often cared for by women. As places where women have some measure of control, such shrines tend to attract more women than men, inverting the usual gender breakdown of attendance at mosques. It isn't hard to imagine how some men, accustomed to thinking of public space as male space, might feel threatened by a public space where women are the dominant presence.

🌱 THE SPREAD OF ISLAM

Islam, like Christianity, is a missionary religion. Muslims believe that the message of their faith is intended for all humankind, to be practised in a community that transcends geographical, cultural, and linguistic borders.

Islam is ideologically and historically a post-Jewish, post-Christian religion. Ideologically, it sees itself as the last of three religions 'of the Book', hence the one that confirms the books that preceded it: the Torah and the Gospel. Historically, Muslims from the beginning responded to and interacted with the communities of other faiths, particularly Christians and Jews. It was therefore necessary for Islam as a religio-political institution to regulate its relations with non-Muslim citizens.

Because the Qur'an considers Jews and Christians to be, like Muslims, People of the Book, they were promised full freedom to practise their faith in all Muslim lands in return for paying a poll tax that also guaranteed them physical and economic protection and exemption from military service. Legally such communities came to be known as *dhimmis* ('protected people'). In the course of time, this designation was expanded to encompass other communities with sacred scriptures, including Zoroastrians in Iran and Hindus in India.

In its first century Islam spread through conquest and military occupation. Much of the Byzantine and Roman world and all of the Sasanian Persian domains yielded to the Arab armies and came under Umayyad rule. In later centuries, politico-military regimes continued to contribute to Islam's dominance, especially in regions under Arab, Persian, or Turkish rule.

Over time, however, the influence of mystics, teachers, and traders has reached farther and endured longer than the power of caliphs and conquerors. It was principally through the preaching and the living examples of individual Muslims that Islam spread to China, Southeast Asia, and East and West Africa. In modern times, migration and missionary activity have carried Islam to the Western hemisphere as well.

North Africa

After conquering what came to be the historical heartland of Islam—Syria, Egypt, and Persia—the Muslims moved into North Africa in the second half of the seventh century. Before that time North Africa had been first an important Roman province and then an equally important home of Latin Christianity. With its indigenous Berber, Phoenician, Roman, and Byzantine populations, North Africa was rich in cultural and religious diversity, and it has always maintained a distinct religious and cultural identity that reflects its ancient heritage.

The Umayyads had established their capital in Damascus in 661. With the shift of the capital from Damascus to Baghdad under the 'Abbasids in 762, the main orientation of the eastern Islamic domains became more Persian than Arab, more Asian than Mediterranean. Meanwhile, the centre of Arab Islamic culture shifted from Syria to the western Mediterranean: to Qayrawan, the capital of North Africa, in what is today Tunisia; and to Córdoba in Spain, Islam's western capital, which rivalled Baghdad and Cairo in its cultural splendour. North African mystics, scholars, and philosophers were all instrumental in this remarkable achievement. In the nineteenth and twentieth centuries, North African religious scholars and particularly Sufi masters played a crucial role in the region's struggle for independence from European colonial powers. They helped to preserve the religious and cultural identity of their people and mobilized them to resist Italian and French colonization in Libya and Algeria. In spite of the deep influence of the French language and secular culture, North African popular piety still reflects the classical Islamic heritage.

Spain

When Arab forces arrived on the Iberian Peninsula in 711, Jews who had lived in Spain for centuries were facing harsh restrictions imposed by rulers recently converted to Catholic Christianity. They welcomed the Arabs as liberators.

With astonishing rapidity, Umayyad forces conquered the land of Andalusia, or al-Andalus, as the Arabs called southern Spain, and laid the foundations for an extraordinary culture. Arab men married local women, and a mixed but harmonious society developed that was Arab in language and expression and Arabo-Hispanic in spirit. Muslims,

Map 5.1   Language and culture in the spread of Islam

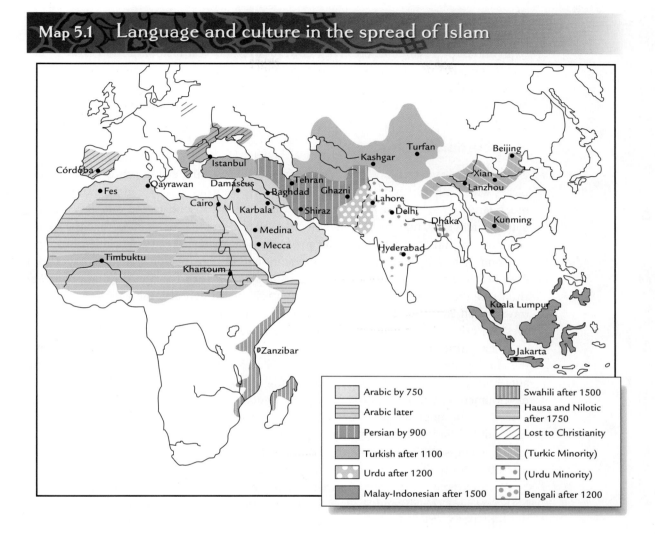

Arabic by 750

Arabic later

Persian by 900

Turkish after 1100

Urdu after 1200

Malay-Indonesian after 1500

Swahili after 1500

Hausa and Nilotic after 1750

Lost to Christianity

(Turkic Minority)

(Urdu Minority)

Bengali after 1200

Christians, and Jews lived together in mutual tolerance for centuries before fanatical forces on all sides stifled one of history's most creative experiments in interfaith living.

Arab Spain produced some of the world's greatest minds, including not only Ibn 'Arabi, Ibn Tufayl, and Ibn Rushd but the jurist and writer Ibn Hazm (994–1064), and the mystic-philosopher Ibn Masarrah (d. 931). Islamic Spain was the cultural centre of Europe. Students came from as far away as Scotland to study Islamic theology, philosophy, and science in centres of higher learning such as Córdoba and Toledo. It was in these centres that the European Renaissance was conceived, and the great universities in which it was nurtured were inspired by their Arabo-Hispanic counterparts.

In Muslim Spain the Jews enjoyed a golden age of philosophy and science, mysticism, and general prosperity. Jewish scholars, court physicians, and administrators occupied high state offices and served as political and cultural liaisons between Islamic Spain and the rest of Europe. Arab learning penetrated deep into western Europe and contributed directly to the West's rise to world prominence.

In addition to symbiotic creativity, however, the 900-year history of Arab Spain (711–1609) included the tensions and conflicts typical of any multi-religious, multicultural society ruled by a minority regime. In the end, Islamic faith and civilization were driven out of Spain and failed to establish themselves anywhere else in Europe.

Sub-Saharan Africa

Islam may have arrived in sub-Saharan Africa as early as the eighth century. As in other places where it became the dominant religion, it was spread first by traders and then on a much larger scale by preachers. Finally jurists came to consolidate and establish the new faith as a religious and legal system. Sufi orders played an important part both in the spread of Islam and in its use as a motivation and framework for social and political reform.

Islam always had to compete with traditional African religion. Muslim prayers, for example, had to show themselves to be no less potent than the rain-making prayers or rituals of the indigenous traditions. In the fourteenth century, the Moroccan Muslim traveller Ibn Battutah wrote a vivid account of the efforts of Muslims in the Mali Empire of West Africa to adapt the new faith to local traditions.

In East Africa Islam spread along the coast, carried mainly by mariners from Arabia and the Gulf trading in commodities and also in slaves. From the sixteenth century onward, after Portuguese navigators rounded the southern cape of Africa, the cultural and political development of East African Islam was directly affected by European colonialism as well.

Unlike the populations of Syria, Iraq, Egypt, and North Africa, the peoples of East Africa did not adopt the Arabic language. But so much Arabic vocabulary penetrated the local languages that at least one-third of the Swahili vocabulary today is Arabic, and until recently, most of the major African languages were written in the Arabic script.

An important element of East African society has been the Khoja community. Including both Sevener (Isma'ili) and Twelver Shi'is, the Khojas immigrated from India to Africa in the mid-1800s. They have on the whole been successful business people with Western education and close relationships with Europe and North America. These relationships have been strengthened by the migration of many Khojas to Britain, the United States, and Canada.

Iran and Central Asia

Central Asia had a cosmopolitan culture before Islam. Buddhism, Gnosticism, Zoroastrianism, Judaism, and Christianity existed side by side in mutual tolerance. The Arab conquest of the region took more than a century: beginning in 649, less than two decades after the Prophet's death, it was not completed until 752.

Under the Samanid dynasty, which ruled large areas of Persia and Central Asia in the ninth and tenth centuries, Persian culture flourished, as did classical *hadith* traditionists, historians, philosophers, and religious scholars working in the Arabic language. Particularly important centres of learning developed in the cities of Bukhara and Samarkand, located in what is now Uzbekistan, which owed much of their prosperity to trade with India, China, and the rest of the Muslim domains. With the first notable Persian poet, Rudaki (c. 859–940), Bukhara became the birthplace of Persian literature.

While their contemporaries the Buyids promoted Shi'i learning and public devotions in the region that is now Iraq, the Samanids firmly established Sunni orthodoxy in Central Asia. Many Sunni theologians and religious scholars lived and worked in Bukhara and Samarkand under Samanid patronage. Among the great minds of the tenth and eleventh centuries were the theologian al-Maturidi, the philosopher Ibn Sina, the great scholar and historian of religion Abu Rayhan al-Biruni, and the famous Persian poet Ferdowsi. In this intellectual environment, Islam was spread by persuasion and enticement rather than propaganda and war.

Early in the eleventh century, the Samanids were succeeded by the Seljuq Turks in the Middle East and the Karakhanid Mongols in Persia and Central Asia. The Mongols profoundly altered the situation in that region, as they would in the Middle East a century later. The devastating consequences of the Mongol conquest of Persia and Central Asia were compounded by the loss of trade revenues when the traditional caravan routes were abandoned in favour of sea travel to India and China. Central Asia never recovered from the resulting decline in culture and prosperity.

The Turks

As Turkic tribal populations from Central Asia moved into parts of the Middle Eastern Muslim heartland, they were converted to Islam mainly by Sufi missionaries. They became influential from the tenth century onward in Central Asia, Armenia, Anatolia, and Syria. Mahmud of Ghazna in Afghanistan (r. 998–1030), of Turkish descent, broke away from the Persian Samanid dynasty; his successors, the Ghaznavids, extended Muslim power in northern India. Mahmud was the first person to be called 'sultan', a term that until his time had referred to the authority of the state.

The Seljuqs, another Turkic family, prevailed in Iran and farther west a generation after Mahmud. The second Seljuq sultan, Alp Arslan, inflicted a crushing defeat on the Byzantines at Manzikert, in eastern Anatolia, in 1071. Bit by bit, eastern Anatolia (today's Turkey) fell to the Seljuqs, who ruled until they were conquered by the Mongols in 1243.

Osman I took over the caliphate from the 'Abbasids in 1299, establishing a dynasty— the 'Ottomans'—that was to endure until 1924. In the fourteenth century they absorbed former Seljuq territory in eastern Anatolia and took western Anatolia from the Byzantines, and they reached the height of their power in the sixteenth century, occupying the Balkans as far north as Vienna, the Levant (i.e., the Syro-Palestinian region), and all of northern Africa except Morocco. So widespread was their empire that Christian Europe until the nineteenth century thought of Islamic culture as primarily Turkish.

As their imperial symbol the Ottomans adopted the crescent, an ancient symbol that the Byzantines had also used. Conspicuous on the Turkish flag, the crescent was considered by Europeans and eventually by Muslims themselves to be the symbol of Islam. Turkic languages continue to prevail across a large part of the region of Central Asia ruled by the Soviet Union for much of the twentieth century. From Azerbaijan to Uzbekistan and Turkmenistan, a dominant element in the population is Turkic. The same is true of Chinese Central Asia, in the vast region of Xinjiang.

China

Islam may have made contact with China as early as the eighth century, although the first written sources referring to Islam in China do not appear till the seventeenth century. For earlier information we have to rely on Chinese sources, which unfortunately focus on commercial activities and have little to say about the social and intellectual life of Chinese Muslims.

The extent of the Muslim presence in any area may often be gauged by the number of mosques. There seem to have been no mosques in the main inland cities of China before the thirteenth century. Along the coast, however, the minaret of the mosque in Guangzhou (Canton) and various inscriptions in the province of Fujian suggest that maritime trade was under way considerably earlier, in 'Abbasid times.

From the beginning, Persian and Arab merchants were allowed to trade freely so long as they complied with Chinese rules. But it was not until the thirteenth century that Muslim traders began settling in China in numbers large enough to support the establishment of mosques. The presence of Islam in China before that time was probably limited.

Muslim communities in China prospered under the Mongol (1206–1368) and Ming (1368–1644) emperors. After the Mongol period Chinese Muslims were assimilated culturally but kept their distinct religious identity. Since it was through trade that they kept in touch with the rest of the Muslim *ummah*, however, the decline of the overland trade with Central Asia in the 1600s had the effect of isolating the Chinese Muslim community. It became virtually cut off from the rest of the world, so that our information about Muslims in China after the seventeenth century is largely a matter of conjecture.

Unlike Buddhism, centuries earlier, Islam never came to be seen as culturally Chinese. The Uighurs—the Muslim population of Xinjiang (Chinese Turkestan), in the far northwest of the country—are an identifiable minority in Chinese society, distinguished by their language as well as their religion. Yet even the Chinese-speaking Muslims in the principal eastern cities of 'Han' China are set apart by their avoidance of pork—a staple of the Chinese diet. The presence of *halal* (ritually acceptable) restaurants and butcher shops is a sure sign of a Muslim neighbourhood.

Chinese Muslims experienced their share of repression under the Communist regime, particularly during the Cultural Revolution of 1966–76. While the overall situation for Muslims has improved since then, Uighur demands for independence have been met with a severe crackdown, and Chinese authorities often describe Uighur nationalists as 'terrorists'. Today there are approximately 50 million Muslims in China. Like other religious communities in contemporary China, they face an uncertain future, but the ethnic base of the minorities in China's Central Asian interior is not likely to disappear soon.

South Asia

Islam arrived early in India, carried there by traders and Arab settlers. Umayyad armies began moving east into India in the early eighth century, and since that time Islam has become an integral part of Indian life and culture.

The Muslim conquest of India was a long process. In the second half of the tenth century the city of Ghazni, in what is today Afghanistan, became the base from which the armies of the sultan Mahmud the Ghaznavid and his successors advanced over the famous Khyber Pass onto the North Indian Plain. By the fourteenth century most of India had come under Muslim rule, with the exceptions of Tamil Nadu and Kerala in the far south.

The Muslim rulers of India came from Iran and Central Asia. Thus maintaining and expanding Muslim power over a large Hindu population meant continuous warfare. For Hindus, the Muslim regime was undoubtedly repressive; yet Indian Islam developed a rich and unique religious and intellectual culture.

India was something new in the history of Islam's territorial expansion. For the first time, the majority of the conquered population did not convert to the new faith. Islam had been able to suppress and supplant polytheism in ancient Arabia, but in India it had to learn to coexist with a culture that remained largely polytheistic.

At the same time Islam was something new to India. In a land where people often had multiple religious allegiances, and community boundaries were fluid, Islam's exclusive devotion to the one God and its clear delineation of community membership represented a dramatically different way of life.

Together, the three countries of the Indian subcontinent—India, Bangladesh, and Pakistan—have the largest Muslim population in the world. The Muslims of India alone make up the world's third-largest Muslim population (after Indonesia and Pakistan), numbering some 140 million. Even so, they are a minority whose future appears bleak in the face of rising Hindu nationalism.

Southeast Asia

The earliest evidence of Islam's presence in Southeast Asia dates from the tenth century, when Arab Muslim traders were active in the Kingdom of Champa (present-day Southern Vietnam). But Yemeni traders are reported to have sailed into the Malay archipelago before the time of the Prophet, and this suggests that the Malay people could have come into contact with Islam some time before that. Whatever the date may have been, the region was already home to a wide variety of languages and cultures, and its religious life had been strongly influenced by the Hindu and Buddhist traditions. Scattered evidence from Chinese and Portuguese travellers, as well as passing references by Ibn Battutah, indicate that by the fifteenth century Islam had spread widely, and when British and Dutch trading companies arrived two centuries later Islam was the dominant religion and culture of the Malay archipelago.

By the thirteenth century Muslim communities existed in a handful of small states ruled by sultans. The earliest of these was Pasai, on the east coast of northern Sumatra. As more such states emerged in the fifteenth century, their growing prosperity attracted Muslim religious scholars from India. In the early 1600s, in an effort to expand and strengthen his realm, the sultan Iskandar Muda of Acheh became the first Muslim ruler in Southeast Asia to establish alliances with European powers. Acheh also produced some noteworthy Islamic scholarship, which is still used in the Malay world today.

In Southeast Asia even more than elsewhere, Sufi orders played a crucial part both in the process of Islamization and, later, in various struggles for political and social reform. Modernist reform movements in the Middle East inspired similar movements in Indonesia and elsewhere in the late nineteenth and early twentieth centuries. At present Islam is the majority religion in Malaysia, Brunei, and Indonesia (now the largest Muslim country in the world, with over 200 million Muslims). When the Muslim minorities in all the other countries of Southeast Asia are added to the total, Southeast Asia can claim to be home to at least one-third of the world's Muslims.

🦟 PRACTICE

The Five Pillars of Islam

- the shahadah (the profession of faith through which one becomes a Muslim);
- regular worship, including participation in all five of the obligatory daily prayers;
- almsgiving;
- the Ramadan fast; and
- participation in the annual pilgrimage to Mecca.

The Five Pillars are the foundations on which Islam rests as a system of faith and social responsibility, worship, and piety. Each pillar has both an inner or private voluntary dimension and an outer or public obligatory dimension. Fulfilling the public obligations of Islam can be difficult in societies where Muslims are a minority within the population.

Bearing Witness

The *shahadah* consists of two statements: 'I bear witness that there is no god except God, and I bear witness that Muhammad is the messenger of God.' The first statement, affirming the oneness of God, expresses the universal and primordial state of faith in which every child is born. The Prophet is said to have declared, 'Every child is born in this original state of faith; then his parents turn him into a Jew, Christian, or Zoroastrian, and if they are Muslims, into a Muslim.'

The second statement, affirming Muhammad's role as messenger, signifies acceptance of the truth of Muhammad's claim to prophethood, and hence the truth of his message.

Prayer

The second pillar consists of the **salat**: prayers that are obligatory for all Muslims. These are distinguished from voluntary devotional acts, such as meditations and personal supplicatory prayers (which may be offered at any time), in that they must be performed five times in a day and night: at dawn, noon, mid-afternoon, sunset, and after dark. The *salat* prayers were the first Islamic rituals to be instituted.

The *salat* prayers must always be preceded by ritual washing. *Wudu'* ('making pure or radiant') or partial washing involves washing the face, rinsing the mouth and nostrils, washing the hands and forearms to the elbows, passing one's wet hands over the head and feet, or washing the feet to the two heels.

Five times a day—on radio and television, through loudspeakers, and from high minarets— the melodious voice of a **mu'adhdhin** invites the faithful to pray together, either in a mosque or at home. Whether a Muslim prays alone or behind an imam in congregation, he or she is always conscious of countless other men and women engaged in the same act of worship. Each phrase of the call to prayer is repeated at least twice for emphasis:

> God is greater. I bear witness that there is no god except God, and I bear witness that Muhammad is the Messenger of God. Hasten to the prayers! Hasten to success (or prosperity)! [Shi'i Muslims add: Hasten to the best action!] God is greater. There is no god except God.

The prayers consist of cycles or units called *rak'ahs*, each of which includes a pre-scribed sequence of movements (bowing, kneeling, prostration). The dawn prayers consist of two cycles, the noon and mid-afternoon prayers of four each, the sunset prayer of three, and the night prayers of four cycles.

Apart from some moments of contemplation and personal supplication at the end of the *salat*, these prayers are fixed formulas consisting largely of passages from the Qur'an, especially the opening *surah* (the *Fatihah*):

> In the name of God, the All-merciful, the Compassionate:
> Praise be to God, the All-merciful, the Compassionate, King of the Day of Judgment.
> You alone do we worship, and to you alone do we turn for help.
> Guide us to the straight way, the way of those upon whom you have bestowed your grace, not those who have incurred your wrath, nor those who have gone astray (Q. 1: 1–7).

The *Fatihah* is repeated in every *rak'ah*—at least 17 times in every 24-hour period. It is as fundamental for Muslims as the Lord's Prayer is for Christians.

Islam (unlike Judaism and Christianity) does not set aside one day of the week for rest. Instead, it designates Friday as the day for *jum'ah* ('assembly') and congregational prayers. In the Friday service the first two *rak'ahs* of the noon prayers are replaced by two short sermons, usually on religious, moral, and political issues. The place of worship is called the *masjid* ('place of prostration in prayer') or *jami'* (literally, 'gatherer'). The English word 'mosque' is derived from *masjid*.

Other congregational prayers are performed on the first days of the two major festivals, 'Id al-Fitr (at the end of the Ramadan fast) and 'Id al-Adha, (at the end of the *hajj* pilgrimage).

Faithful Muslims see all things, good or evil, as contingent on God's will. Hence many take care to preface any statement regarding hopes for the future with the phrase *in-sha' Allah,* 'if God wills'.

Almsgiving

The third pillar of Islam reflects the close relationship between worship of God and service to the poor and needy. Traditionally, all adult Muslims with any wealth were expected to 'give alms' through payment of an obligatory tax called the **zakat** (from a root meaning 'to

The hours of prayer are posted on the door of a small mosque in Paris (Photo courtesy of Andrew Leyerle).

A Muslim Ritual: The Call to Prayer

It is Friday afternoon, a few minutes before the start of the weekly congregational prayer. In this mosque in Southern California, perhaps 200 men and 30 women are gathered; the difference in numbers reflects the fact that this prayer is obligatory for men but optional for women. A young man walks to the front of the large men's section (the women are seated in a second-floor gallery), raises his hands to his ears, and begins the call to prayer: 'Allahu akbar, God is greater . . .'. When he has finished, the people behind him line up in rows and wait for the imam—the person who will lead the prayer—to begin.

Were this service in a different location, the call to prayer might already have been sounded in the traditional way, broadcast from minarets (towers) beside the mosque. But there are no minarets here, as the mostly non-Muslim residents of this neighbourhood wanted a building that would 'fit in' with its surroundings. Nor does this mosque have the characteristic dome. Instead it is a two-storey building designed to look more like a school than a mosque. In this non-traditional context, the function of the call to prayer has changed. Instead of being broadcast outside, to let the community know that it is time to pray, the call is broadcast inside to those already assembled for the prayer. This is one of the ways in which the Muslims who come to this mosque have adapted to their surroundings.

purify or increase'). Offering alms in this way served to purify the donor, purging greed and attachment to material possessions.

The *zakat* obligation was 2.5 per cent of the value of all accumulated wealth (savings, financial gains of any kind, livestock, agricultural produce, real estate, etc.). During the early centuries of Islam, when the community was controlled by a central authority, the *zakat* revenues were kept in a central treasury and disbursed for public educational and civic projects, care of orphans and the needy, and the ransoming of Muslim war captives. Now that the Muslim world is divided into many independent nation-states, most of which collect some form of income tax, payment of the *zakat* has become largely voluntary. Many ignore it; others pay through donations to private religious and philanthropic organizations.

In addition to the obligatory *zakat* alms, Muslims are expected to practice voluntary almsgiving (*sadaqah*). The Qur'an calls *sadaqah* a loan given to God, which will be repaid in manifold measure on the Day of Resurrection (Q. 57: 11). *Sadaqah* giving is not bound by any consideration of race, colour, or creed: the recipient may be anyone in need.

The Ramadan Fast

The fourth pillar of Islam is the month-long fast of Ramadan. Fasting is recognized in the Qur'an as a universal form of worship, enjoined by scriptures of all faiths. In addition to the Ramadan fast, the Prophet observed a variety of voluntary fasts, which are still honoured by many pious Muslims.

The Ramadan fast is mandated in just one passage of the Qur'an:

> O you who have faith, fasting is ordained for you as it was ordained for those before you, that you may become aware of God. [. . .] Ramadan is the month in which the Qur'an was sent down as a guidance to humankind, manifestations of guidance and the Criterion. Therefore whosoever among you witnesses the moon, let them fast [the month], but whosoever is sick or on a journey, an equal number of other days (Q. 2: 183, 185).

Marking the month in which the Qur'an was revealed to the Prophet, the Ramadan fast extends from daybreak till sundown every day for a month. It requires complete abstention from food and drink of any kind, as well as smoking and sexual relations. The fast is broken at sunset, and another light meal is eaten at the end of the night, just before the next day's fast begins at dawn.

With respect to the rules governing the fast, the Qur'an notes that 'God desires ease for you, not hardship' (2: 185). Therefore children, those who are sick or travelling, and women who are pregnant, nursing, or menstruating are exempted from the fast, either altogether or until they are able to make up the missed days.

Before the introduction of Islam, the Arabs had followed a lunar calendar in which the year contained only 354 days. To keep festivals and sacred months in their proper seasons, they (like the Jews) added an extra month every three years. But the Qur'an abolished this custom, allowing Islamic festivals to rotate throughout the year. When Ramadan comes in the summer, particularly in the equatorial countries of Asia and Africa, going without

Beginning the Fast

Ms Becker teaches grade four in a public elementary school. Eleven of the school's pupils are Muslim, and one of them is in Ms Becker's class. This year seven of the Muslim students have decided that they will fast during the month of Ramadan. Some of them have fasted before, but for the nine-year-old in Ms Becker's class this will be the first time.

There is no set age at which Muslim children are expected to begin observing the fast. It may be as early as 8 or 9, or as late as adolescence. In certain Muslim cultures, girls begin at an earlier age than boys, who are usually exempted on the grounds that they 'aren't strong enough'. While their non-Muslim classmates have lunch, those who are fasting gather in Ms Becker's classroom to work quietly on school projects. They are also excused from their physical education classes, and instead do a writing assignment about physical fitness. In this way, a public school accommodates the needs of its Muslim students.

water can be a real hardship. But when it comes in winter, as it did in the 1990s in the northern hemisphere, it can be relatively tolerable.

Ramadan ends with a festival called 'Id al-Fitr, a three-day celebration during which people exchange presents and well-wishing visits. Children receive gifts and wear brightly coloured new clothes, special sweet dishes are distributed to the poor, and people visit the graves of loved ones. Before the first breakfast after the long fast, the head of every family must give special alms for breaking the fast, called *zakat al-fitr*, on behalf of every member of his household. Those who are exempted from fasting for reasons of chronic illness or old age must feed a poor person for every day they miss.

The fast of Ramadan becomes a true act of worship when a person shares God's bounty with those who have no food with which to break their fast. True fasting means more than giving up the pleasures of food and drink: it also means abstaining from gossip and anger, and turning one's heart and mind to God in devotional prayers and meditations.

The Pilgrimage to Mecca

The fifth pillar of Islam is the *hajj* pilgrimage, instituted by Abraham at God's command after he and his son Ishmael were ordered to build the Ka'ba. Thus most of its ritual elements are understood as re-enacting the experiences of Abraham, whom the Qur'an declares to be the father of prophets and the first true Muslim.

Before the pilgrims reach the sacred precincts of Mecca, they exchange their regular clothes for two pieces of white linen, symbolic of the shrouds in which Muslims are wrapped for burial. With this act they enter the state of consecration. They approach Mecca with the solemn proclamation: 'Here we come in answer to your call, O God, here we come! Here we come, for you have no partner, here we come! Indeed, all praise, dominion, and grace belong to you alone, here we come!'

Once in Mecca, the pilgrims begin with the lesser *hajj* ('umrah). This ritual is performed in the precincts of the Great Mosque and includes the *tawaf* (walking counter-clockwise around the Ka'ba) and running between the two hills of al-Safa and al-Marwa. In the traditional narrative, Hagar, Abraham's wife and the mother of his son Ishmael, ran between these two hills in search of water for her dying child. After the seventh run, water gushed out by the child's feet, and Hagar contained it with sand. The place, according to Islamic tradition, is the ancient well of Zamzam ('the contained water'). The water of Zamzam is considered holy, and pilgrims often take home containers of it as blessed gifts for family and friends.

The *hajj* pilgrimage proper begins on the eighth of Dhu al-Hijjah, the twelfth month of the Islamic calendar, when throngs of pilgrims set out for Arafat, a large plain, about 20 kilometres (13 miles) east of Mecca, on which stands the goal of every pilgrim: the Mount of Mercy (Jabal al-Rahmah). In accordance with the Prophet's *sunnah* (practice), many pilgrims spend the night at Mina, but others press on to Arafat. As the sun passes the noon meridian, all the pilgrims gather for the central rite of the *hajj* pilgrimage: the standing (*wuquf*) on the Mount of Mercy in Arafat.

In this rite, the pilgrims stand in solemn prayer and supplication till sunset, as though standing before God for judgment on the last day. The *wuquf* recalls three sacred occasions: when Adam and Eve stood on that plain after their expulsion from paradise, when Abraham and his son Ishmael performed the rite during the first *hajj* pilgrimage, and when Muhammad gave his farewell oration, affirming the family of all Muslims.

The sombre scene changes abruptly at sundown, when the pilgrims leave Arafat for Muzdalifah, a sacred spot a short distance along the road back to Mecca. There they

The Sultan Ahmet or Blue Mosque in Istanbul, built in 1609–16 (Photo courtesy of Andrew Leyerle).

perform the combined sunset and evening prayers and gather pebbles for the ritual lapidation (throwing of stones) at Mina the next day. The tenth of Dhu al-Hijjah is the final day of the *hajj* season, and the first of the four-day festival of sacrifice ('Id al-Adha). The day is spent at Mina, where the remaining pilgrimage rites are completed.

Tradition says that on his way from Arafat to Mina, Abraham was commanded by God to sacrifice that which was dearest to him—his son Ishmael. Satan whispered to him three times, tempting him to disobey God's command. Abraham's response was to hurl stones at Satan, to drive him away. Thus at the spot called al-'Aqabah, meaning the hard or steep road, a brick pillar has been erected to represent Satan. Pilgrims gather early in the morning to throw seven stones at the pillar, in emulation of Abraham. Three other pillars in Mina, representing the three temptations, are also stoned.

Following the ritual of stoning, the pilgrims offer an animal sacrifice—a lamb, goat, cow, or camel—to symbolize the animal sent from heaven with which God ransomed Abraham's son (Q. 27: 107). Then, to mark the end of their state of consecration, pilgrims ritually clip a minimum of three hairs from their heads (some shave their heads completely). The *hajj* ends with a final circumambulation of the Ka'ba and completion of the rites of the lesser *hajj* ('*umrah*) for those who have not done so.

Tradition asserts that a person returns from a sincerely performed *hajj* cleansed of all sins, as pure as on the day when he or she was born. Thus the *hajj* is regarded as a form of resurrection or rebirth, and its completion marks a new stage in the life of a Muslim. Every pilgrim is henceforth distinguished by the title *hajji* or *hajjah* before his or her name.

❧ CULTURAL EXPRESSIONS

Islamic Architecture

The functions of the mosque include not only prayer, implied in the Arabic *masjid* ('place of prostration'), but other community activities, implied in Arabic *jami'* ('gatherer'). Early mosques functioned as treasuries, where financial records were kept; as law courts, where judges heard cases; and as educational centres, where classes and study circles were held. In time these other activities moved into their own buildings, but the functions of public assembly and prayer continued to dictate the architectural form of mosques. Two other types of building with religious functions—the *madrasah* or religious school, and the tomb or mausoleum—drew on much the same repertory of styles that mosques did.

Every mosque includes four essential features: a fountain for washing hands, face, and feet upon entering; a large area for kneeling and prostration in prayer; a pulpit (*minbar*) from which the leader of Friday noon worship delivers the sermon; and an imageless niche in the middle of the wall closest to Mecca, indicating the *qiblah* (direction of prayer). Not part of the earliest mosques in Arabia but characteristic of Islam in many places is the minaret, the tower from which the *mu'adhdhin* delivers the call to prayer. The Turks in the sixteenth century made much use of the dome, an important feature of church architecture among the Byzantines who had preceded them. A high central dome, resting on four semi-dome apses, enclosed the prayer space. Some major Turkish mosques had

Inside the bin Yousuf madrasa (religious school) in Marrakech, Morocco (Jonathan Brown). The building was constructed in the sixteenth century and restored in 1982. There are no animal or human figures in the decoration: only inscriptions and either geometric or floral patterns.

four or more minarets, marking the corners of the mosque. Central dome architecture, though often simpler and without minarets, is also characteristic of mosques in Malaysia and Indonesia, where the rainy climate dictates that the prayer space must be roofed over.

Ultimately, Islamic architecture tends to reflect the distinctive idioms of different geographic regions. The keyhole arch, for instance, is characteristic mainly of North Africa and Islamic Spain. A shallow pointed arch emerged in Iraq, became the predominant form in Iran, and spread to Central Asia and India. The bud or onion domes of Indo-Muslim architecture have been picked up in Southeast Asia. In China many mosques are built like Chinese temples, with tiled roofs resting on wooden columns and bracket structures. A number of Chinese minarets are built in the form of the East Asian Buddhist pagoda.

Islamic Art

Islamic art is rich, elaborate, and exuberant. Three elements are particularly distinctive: calligraphy (the decorative use of script and units of text); geometrical decoration (particularly the interlaced motifs called arabesques in the West); and floral designs (especially common in Iran). All three are more abstract than pictorial and therefore point beyond themselves in a way that pictorial images may not. Design using these elements captures the viewer's attention and directs it to the larger structure on which the decoration appears, whether a page of the Qur'an, a prayer rug, or the tiled entrance of a mosque.

Mohamed Zakariya

Mohamed Zakariya (b. 1942) is the most celebrated Islamic calligrapher in the United States. Born in Ventura, California, he moved to Los Angeles with his family and saw Islamic calligraphy for the first time in the window of an Armenian carpet store. Travelling to Morocco in his late teens, he became fascinated with Islam and Islamic calligraphy. On his return to the United States he converted to Islam.

He made other journeys to North Africa and the Middle East, and spent some time studying manuscripts in the British Museum in London. After studying with the Egyptian calligrapher Abdussalam Ali-Nour, Zakariya in 1984 became a student of the Turkish master calligrapher Hasan Celebi. In 1988 he received his diploma from Celebi at the Research Center for Islamic History, Art and Culture in Istanbul, the first American to achieve this honour. He received his second diploma, in the *ta'lik* script, from the master calligrapher Ali Alparslan in 1997.

Zakariya lives with his family in Arlington, Virginia. His work has been displayed in various museums and galleries, and is in a number of private collections. He was the artist commissioned by the United States Postal Service to design its Eid stamp, which made its debut on 1 September 2001.

In addition to teaching calligraphy according to the Ottoman method, producing new work, and exhibiting it around the world, Zakariya writes contemporary instructional material and translates classic texts. In 2009, he was commissioned by US President Barack Obama to create a piece of calligraphy that was presented to King Abdulaziz of Saudi Arabia. Mohamed Zakariya's work shows that American Islam has become an integral part of the Muslim world. Now students from that world travel to the United States to study with an American master of an ancient Islamic art.

Religious content is most obvious in the decorative use of calligraphy in mosques, where the texts used are often passages from the Qur'an. But even the craft items sold in bazaars are often adorned with some of the 99 'wonderful names' of God.

Three-dimensional sculpture is prohibited in Islam, but the two-dimensional representation of living creatures is highly developed. Some Persian carpets include animals in their garden scenes. Persian and Indian manuscripts are illustrated with miniature paintings of legendary heroes and current rulers. Among Iranian Shi'a, portraits of 'Ali are a focus of popular piety. While representations of the Prophet himself are avoided, Buraq—the steed that carried him on his heavenly journey—is portrayed in popular art as a winged horse with a human head; this is a common motif on trucks and buses in Afghanistan and Pakistan. In addition, Arabic calligraphy has been used ingeniously to create the outlines of birds and animals, as well as crescents, mosques, minarets, and other forms to the present day.

🌿 INTERACTION AND ADAPTATION

Islam and Modernity

Throughout the history of Islam, many Muslims have taken it on themselves to reform the rest of the community. An external impetus for reform has been Muslim interaction with

Western Christendom. The first major challenges to Muslim power were the crusades. Fired by a spirit of Christian holy war to liberate Jerusalem from Muslim domination, the armies of the first crusade captured the Holy City in 1099 after massacring its Jewish and Muslim inhabitants. For nearly two centuries, Frankish Christian kingdoms existed side by side with Muslim states along the eastern Mediterranean shores, sometimes peacefully, but most of the time at war.

In the end most of the crusaders returned home and those who remained were assimilated. But the spirit of the crusades lived on, as did the distorted images of Islam and its followers that the crusaders took back with them. The equally distorted images of Christianity and Western Christendom that the crusades left in Muslim lands also lived on, and have been reinforced and embellished in recent years.

Premodern Reform Movements

We shall examine Islam in the modern era from two perspectives: internal reform and the challenge of the West.

Common to all reform movements has been the call to return to pristine *islam*, the *islam* of the Prophet's society and the normative period of his 'rightly guided' successors. Among those who championed this cause was the religious scholar Ibn Taymiyyah (1263–1328), a jurist of the conservative Hanbali school who fought relentlessly against Shi'i beliefs and practices, Sufi excesses (e.g., claims that the law was no longer binding on them since they had reached God), and the blind imitation of established legal traditions, while fighting to revive the practice of *ijtihad*. Perhaps his most famous *fatwa* (religious legal opinion) was one that allowed Muslims in the city of Mardin (in what is now Turkey) to wage war against the occupying Mongols, even though the latter had converted to Islam after their conquest of Baghdad. In so doing, Ibn Taymiyyah contradicted the standard teaching that Muslims should not wage war against Muslim rulers. The 'Mardin fatwa' was to exert a powerful and long-lasting influence on subsequent reform movements.

Some four centuries later, Ibn Taymiyyah's ideas became the basis of the reform program advocated by the Wahhabi movement, named for its founder Muhammad Ibn 'Abd al-Wahhab (1703–92). Significantly, this uncompromising and influential revivalist movement began in the highlands of Arabia, the birthplace of Islam itself. Ibn 'Abd al-Wahhab's long life allowed him to establish his movement on a firm foundation. He allied himself with Muhammad al-Sa'ud, a local tribal prince, on the understanding that the prince would exercise political power and protect the nascent movement, which would hold religious authority. This agreement remains operative today: the kingdom of Saudi Arabia is a Wahhabi state, ruled by the descendants of Al-Sa'ud.

The Wahhabis preached a strictly egalitarian Islam based solely on a direct relationship between the worshipper and God. They repudiated the widely cherished hope that the Prophet and other divinely favoured individuals would intercede with God to grant the pious blessing and succour in this life and salvation in the next. The Wahhabis regarded the veneration of saints, including the Prophet, as a form of idolatry. They even called for the destruction of the sacred black stone of the Ka'ba, on the grounds that it stood as an idol between faithful Muslims and their Lord.

The Wahhabis held all those who did not share their convictions to be in error. They waged a violent campaign aimed at purging Muslim society of what they considered to be its un-Islamic beliefs and practices. They destroyed the Prophet's tomb in Medina and levelled the graves of his Companions. They attacked the Shi'i sacred cities of Najaf and Karbala, massacred their inhabitants, and demolished the shrines of 'Ali and his son Husayn. They also went on a rampage in Arab cities, desecrating the tombs of Sufi saints and destroying their shrines.

The basic ideals of Wahhabism have appealed to many revivalists and played an especially significant role in eighteenth- and nineteenth-century Sufi reforms. In the present day, however, a number of extremist groups influenced by Wahhabi ideology, including Al-Qaeda and the Taliban, have transformed the internal struggle to 'purify' Islam into an external war against all perceived enemies, Muslim and non-Muslim alike.

Nineteenth-Century Revivalism

Jihad—Arabic for 'struggle'—has two components. Inner *jihad* is the struggle to make oneself more Islamic; outer *jihad* is the struggle to make one's society more Islamic.

A number of Sufi *jihad* movements arose in the nineteenth century, partly in response to Wahhabism and partly in reaction against European colonial encroachment on Muslim domains. Several of these movements were able to establish short-lived states, among them those led by Usman ('Uthman) dan Fodio (the Sokoto caliphate, 1809–1903) in Nigeria, Muhammad al-Sanusi (the Sanusi movement, 1837–1969) in Libya, and Muhammad Ahmad al-Mahdi (the Mahdi rebellion, 1881–9) in Sudan. Common to all these movements was an activist ideology of militant struggle against external colonialism and internal decadence. They also strove for reform and the revival of *ijtihad*.

Because of their broad appeal, these Sufi reform movements exerted a lasting influence on most subsequent reform programs and ideologies. In North Africa in particular, Sufi *shaykhs* and religious scholars not only helped to preserve their countries' religious, linguistic, and cultural identity but in some cases spearheaded the long and bloody struggles for independence from French and Italian colonial rule. In the nineteenth century, for example, the Sufi *shaykh* Abdelkader ('Abd al-Qadir) played an important political role in the long campaign for Algeria's independence. King Muhammad V of Morocco, who negotiated his country's independence from France in 1956, was himself a Sufi *shaykh* and a 'venerable descendant' (*sayyid*) of the Prophet. And the grandson of al-Sanusi, Idris I, ruled Libya as king from independence in 1951 until he was overthrown in a revolution in 1969.

The movement begun by al-Sanusi in Libya promoted reform and Muslim unity across North and West Africa. By contrast, the goal of al-Mahdi's movement in Sudan was more eschatological: its founder saw himself as God's representative on earth and set out to establish a social and political order modelled on that of the Prophet. He believed the Ottoman–Egyptian occupation of Sudan to be un-Islamic and waged a war of *jihad* against it. In 1885 he triumphed over Egyptian forces and established an Islamic state based on strict application of the *shari'ah* law. Although al-Mahdi himself died within a few months, the regime lasted until 1889, when it was overthrown by British and Egyptian forces.

Ahmadiyah

The career of Mirza Ghulam Ahmad (1835–1908) reflects the social and the religious diversity of the Punjab in the 1880s, a time of various movements for renewal of Hindu and Muslim identity, as well as a growing emphasis on self-definition among the Sikhs. To this mix Ghulam Ahmad contributed several volumes of commentary on the Qur'an and claims of his own leadership status.

In 1889 he accepted from his followers the homage reserved for a prophet like Muhammad. Ahmadis, as they are known, have also revered him as the *mujaddid* (renewer) ushering in the fourteenth century of Islam, as the Mahdi expected by the Shi'i, as the tenth incarnation of the Hindu deity Vishnu, and as the returning Messiah of Christianity (Ahmadis also maintain that Jesus did not die in Palestine but went to Afghanistan, in search of the ten lost tribes of Israel, and was buried in Srinagar, Kashmir).

Active proselytizers, Ghulam Ahmad and his followers preached in the streets, engaged in debates, and published translations of the Qur'an. The movement has spread widely. Including 4 million in Pakistan, Ahmadis now total at least 10 million, or 1 per cent of the world's Muslims. Leaders since the founder's death in 1908 have been termed 'successors of the Messiah'. Although those successors are chosen by election, since 1914 the title has stayed in Ghulam Ahmad's family, held first by a son and then by two grandsons. Because they identified themselves as Muslims, on the partition of India in 1947 the Ahmadis were displaced from their base near Amritsar and relocated across the border in Pakistan, west of Lahore.

Many Muslims, however, have not accepted the Ahmadis as fellow Muslims. As early as 1891, Ghulam Ahmad's claim to prophethood was rejected by orthodox Muslim authorities. In Pakistan Ahmadis have been the target of riots and demonstrations; in 1984 they were declared to be a non-Muslim minority (hence ineligible for opportunities available to Muslims); and they have been prohibited from calling themselves Muslims or using Islamic vocabulary in their worship and preaching.

Ahmadiyah's future, therefore, may lie in its diaspora. Missions have been notably successful in lands that were not historically Islamic, such as West Africa, the Caribbean, and the overseas English-speaking world. The largest mosque in North America, opened in 1992, is the Ahmadi Baitul Islam mosque in the Toronto-area suburb of Maple.

Modernist Reformers

As the nineteenth century opened, European influence in the Muslim world was growing. Napoleon, who landed in Egypt in 1798, brought with him not only soldiers but also scholars and the printing press; in this way the Middle East discovered Europe. The great Ottoman Empire, which in the early decades of the sixteenth century had threatened Vienna, had by the nineteenth become 'the sick man of Europe'. Meanwhile, the British Empire was extending its rule in India and its control over much of the Muslim world.

Muslim thinkers everywhere were awed by the West and resentful of the political inertia into which the Muslim *ummah* had apparently fallen. Even so, many areas of the Islamic east did experience an intellectual and cultural revival in the nineteenth century. Egypt, for instance, was the home of an Arab intellectual renaissance. Unsettled social and political conditions in Syria and Lebanon drove a number of Western-educated Christians to

The Badshahi or great Mosque in Lahore, Pakistan, was built by the Emperor Aurangzeb in 1673–4 (Christine Osborne/ Alamy).

Egypt, where they established newspapers and cultural journals and participated actively in the recovery of the Arabo-Islamic heritage.

The Arab renaissance of the nineteenth century was largely stimulated by the cultural and intellectual flowering that was taking place in the West. Undermined first by the Protestant Reformation and then by the Enlightenment, Christian faith and institutions were now giving way to secularism and romantic nationalism. Those ideas had a similar appeal for Muslims in the region of the eastern Mediterranean, encouraging the development of nationalistic identities that came to compete with, and in some cases even supersede, Islamic identities.

These and other Western influences were reinforced by the proliferation of Western Christian missionary schools and institutions of higher learning throughout the Muslim world. In short, Islamic reform movements of the nineteenth and twentieth centuries in Asia, Africa, and the Middle East arose in a context of widespread cultural and intellectual ferment.

The Indian Subcontinent

The Mughal dynasty, founded by Babur in 1526, reached its peak under his grandson Akbar (r. 1556–1605). With the decline of the Mughals in the seventeenth century, calls for a revival of traditional Islamic principles intensified. One of the strongest voices for

Islamic reform was that of Ahmad Sirhindi (1564–1624), who called for a return to the *shari'ah*, regarded Sufis as deviants, and condemned Ibn 'Arabi in particular as an infidel.

The most important movement of Islamic reform on the Indian subcontinent in modern times was begun by Shah Wali Allah of Delhi (1702–62). Although a disciple of Ibn 'Abd al-Wahhab, he was a Sufi himself, and instead of rejecting Sufism he sought to reform it. He also attempted to reconcile Shi'i–Sunni differences, which had been (and sometimes are still) a source of great friction on the Indian subcontinent in particular.

Shah Wali Allah's grandson Ahmad Barelwi transformed his program into a *jihad* movement against British rule and the Sikhs. In 1826 he established an Islamic state based on the *shari'ah* and adopted the old caliphal title 'commander of the faithful'. Although he was killed in battle in 1831, his *jihad* movement lived on. For Barelwi, India had ceased to be an Islamic domain after the end of Mughal rule, and therefore Muslims should wage a *jihad* to liberate it. If independence from infidel sovereignty was not possible, Muslims should undertake a religious migration (*hijrah*) to an area where Muslims did rule.

The shock that Indian Muslims suffered with the consolidation of imperial rule was intensified by the fact that the colonial government tampered with the legal system. The result was a hybrid of Islamic law and the humanistic British tradition known as Anglo-Muhammadan law.

At the opposite end of the spectrum of reaction to British rule from *jihad* movements like Barelwi's was the approach of Sayyid Ahmad Khan (1817–98). Like all reformers, Khan called for modern *ijtihad* or rethinking of the Islamic heritage, but unlike most of them he rejected the *hadith* tradition as a legitimate basis for modern Islamic life. He founded the Aligarh Muhammadan College (later Aligarh Muslim University), where he attempted to apply his ideas in a modern Western-style program of education.

Muhammad Iqbal

The ideas of Sayyid Ahmad Khan and his colleagues culminated in the philosophy of Muhammad Iqbal (1876–1938), the greatest Muslim thinker of modern India. Central to Iqbal's work is the idea of an inner spirit that moves human civilization.

Iqbal argued that Western science and philosophy were rightfully part of the Islamic heritage and should be integrated into a fresh *Reconstruction of Religious Thought in Islam* (the title of his only major work in English, published in the 1930s). A poet as well as a philosopher, Iqbal frequently repeated this call for a dynamic rethinking of Islamic faith and civilization in his verse.

Twentieth-Century Secularism

Many of the early Muslim reformers were at once liberal modernists and traditional thinkers. For this reason they are known as *salafis*: reformers who sought to emulate the example of 'the pious forebears' (*al-salaf al-salih*). This important ideal of equilibrium between tradition and modernity disappeared by the 1920s. Thereafter, Islamic reform meant either revivalism, apologetics, or secularism.

Following the Ottoman defeat in the First World War, a young army officer named Mustafa Kemal Atatürk (1881–1938) launched a movement for national liberation. On taking power in 1923, he abolished the caliphate and transformed the Turkish state from a traditional Islamic domain into a modern secular republic. Although for centuries the caliphate had been a shadowy office without any power, it had nevertheless embodied the only hope for a viable pan-Islamic state. Its disappearance therefore had far-reaching consequences for Islamic political thought.

Atatürk banned Sufi orders, dissolved Islamic religious institutions, replaced the Arabic alphabet (in which Turkish had traditionally been written) with the Latin, and mounted a nationwide campaign for literacy in the new script. His express aim was to westernize the Turkish republic and cut it off from its Islamic past. He encouraged the adoption of Western-style clothing and even went so far as to ban the fez—the brimless conical red hat that, like all traditional Muslim headgear, allowed the faithful to touch their foreheads to the ground during prayer.

Though Atatürk's secular ideology has remained the official state policy in Turkey, the people's Islamic roots were not easily destroyed. Islamic faith and practice remain strong among the Turkish people, and the country has its own powerful revivalist movements.

Twentieth-Century Islamic Revivalism

The previous century had shared a dynamic and courageous spirit of progress. The premature stifling of that spirit may have reflected the lack of a coherent program of reform that post-colonialist Muslim thinkers could implement or build on. In any event, the liberal reform movements of the nineteenth century were transformed in the twentieth into traditional revivalist movements.

On the eve of Atatürk's abolition of the caliphate in 1924, Muhammad Rashid Rida (1865–1935) published an important treatise on the Imamate, or Supreme Caliphate, in which he argued for the establishment of an Islamic state that would be ruled by a council of jurists or religious scholars. Such a state would recognize nationalistic sentiments and aspirations, but would subordinate them to the religio-political interests of the larger community. With Arab nationalism, Rida's Islamic revivalism came to represent a major trend in twentieth-century Muslim thinking, and his plan for a council of jurists would be implemented in Iran following the revolution of 1978–9.

Contemporary Revivalist Movements

It remains the ideal of Islamic reform to establish a transnational Islamic caliphate. The reality, however, has been a proliferation of local movements reflecting local needs and ideas.

Common to most revivalist movements in the second half of the twentieth century was the ideal of an all-inclusive and self-sufficient Islamic order. This ideal had its roots in the Society of Muslim Brothers (Jam'iyat al-Ikhwan al-Muslimin), founded in 1928 by an Egyptian schoolteacher named Hasan al-Banna. The aim of this society was to establish a network of Islamic social, economic, and political institutions through which the total Islamization of society might in time be achieved. Working through social and educational institutions such as schools, banks, cooperatives, and clinics, the Muslim Brothers penetrated all levels of Egyptian society.

The political and militaristic aspects of revivalism also had their beginnings in the Muslim Brothers, particularly after the assassination of the populist and generally peaceful al-Banna in 1949. He was succeeded by hard-line leaders who advocated active *jihad* against the Egyptian state system, which they regarded as un-Islamic. Among the products of the Muslim Brothers' ideology were the young officers, led by Gamal Abdel Nasser, behind the 1952 socialist revolution that abolished monarchical rule in Egypt.

A charismatic proponent of Arab nationalism in the 1950s and 1960s, Nasser nevertheless clashed with the Muslim Brothers, and in the mid-1960s he imprisoned, exiled, or executed most of their leaders. One of those leaders was Sayyid Qutb, who is important as a link to modern Islamist groups. As a theoretician he influenced Islamist ideology; and as an activist—whose defiance of the state led to his execution—he provided younger militants with a model of martyrdom to emulate. Following the Arab defeat in the six-day Arab–Israeli war of June 1967 the Muslim Brothers were driven underground and superseded by more powerful revivalist movements, some of which advocated the use of violence to achieve their goals.

Banned in Egypt under Anwar Sadat and Hosni Mubarak, the Brotherhood has spread in other Arab countries; but in exile, without its social infrastructure, it has been more influential on the level of ideology than of political action. A similar organization, the Jama'at-i Islami (Islamic Society), was established in 1941 by Mawlana Sayyid Abu al-A'la Mawdudi. Like Hasan al-Banna, Mawdudi was committed to pan-Islamic unity. But also like al-Banna, he concentrated his efforts on his own community—in this case the Muslims of India and (after 1947) Pakistan. The influence of both organizations spread far beyond their original homes.

Most contemporary revivalist movements, including the two organizations noted above, have been open to modern science and technology. But they have rejected many Western values and practices—including capitalist democracy, women's liberation, and the free mixing of the sexes—as decadent. Therefore, unlike the nineteenth-century reformers who looked to the West for ideas and models, contemporary revivalist reformers have insisted on finding Islamic alternatives. Mawdudi, for instance, wishing to distinguish his Islamic state model from Western democracies, described it as a 'theodemocracy' based on the broad Qur'anic principle of consultation (*shura*) and the *shari'ah* law.

State Islam and the Islamic Revolution

Following a coup in 1969, Gaafar Mohamed el-Nimeiri made *shari'ah* the law in Sudan. The result was a bloody conflict between the Muslim north and the generally Christian south that continued for decades, reducing a formerly rich agricultural country to famine. Likewise in Pakistan, which for three decades had been a constitutionally Islamic but modern state. The introduction of *shari'ah* by General Mohammad Zia-ul-Haq following a coup in 1977 led to violent social and political conflict.

In Egypt and Algeria, revivalist movements continued to resort to violent means in their quest to establish Islamic states. Again, the results were social strife and instability.

In almost every Muslim country there is at least one revivalist movement advocating some form of Islamic state. In countries like Malaysia and Indonesia, the governments themselves espouse Islamic national policies in order to silence extremist demands for radical reform. Nevertheless, in most Muslim countries feelings continue to run high between Islamic movements made up of educated middle-class men and women and despotic regimes determined to hold on to power at any cost.

On 19 December 2010, a Tunisian named Mohamed Bouazizi set himself on fire to protest police and government corruption that made it impossible for him to sell fruits and vegetables from a cart without paying bribes to officials. His immolation sparked widespread protests that led to the overthrow of the Tunisian president. These dramatic events in turn sparked protests in Algeria and Egypt. The largest coordinated protests began in Cairo in late January 2011 and on 11 February Egyptian President Hosni Mubarak stepped down from power. Among the other Arab countries swept up in the 'Arab Spring' were Syria, Yemen, Bahrain, and Libya. On 18 March the UN Security Council authorized a resolution to protect civilians under attack in Libya, and the following day the first Western air strike was launched against the military of Muammar Gaddafi.

In such highly charged social and political conditions, religion serves as a powerful moral, social, and spiritual expression of discontent—not only for Islamic activists, but for a broad spectrum of the community as well. It was on precisely such mass discontent that Imam Ruhollah Khomeini (1901–89) and his fellow Shi'i *mullahs* (religio-legal functionaries) built the Islamic Republic of Iran, in which social, political, economic, and religious life are all under the control of a religious hierarchy headed by a supreme Ayatollah (*ayat Allah*, 'sign of God').

Throughout the centuries of Shi'i secular rule in Iran (1501–1979), the authority of the religious '*ulama*' operated in more or less continuous tension with the secular authorities. This tension was greatly increased during the reign of Shah Mohammad Reza Pahlavi, who sought to westernize the country and obscure its Islamic identity by emphasizing Iran's pre-Islamic cultural past. In 1963, during the Muharram observances of Husayn's martyrdom, matters came to a head when the Shah's dreaded secret police ruthlessly put down mass demonstrations led by the '*ulama*'. Khomeini, already a prominent religious leader, was sent into exile, where he elaborated his theory that religio-legal scholars should have all-embracing authority in the community. In 1979 Khomeini returned to Iran at the head of the Islamic revolution. The Islamic republic he founded has had a turbulent history, including an eight-year war with Iraq (1980–8), out of which it emerged greatly weakened but still intact. Pro-democracy protests and challenges to the authority of the '*ulama*' came to international attention with the controversy that surrounded the 2009 election and the protests that erupted in March 2011.

Islam in Western Europe

The Islamic presence in western Europe began with the establishment of Umayyad rule in southern Spain in 711. Commercial, political, and cultural relations were initiated with both Latin and Byzantine states, but medieval Europe would not tolerate a permanent Muslim community on its soil. The campaign to drive the Muslims out of Spain succeeded in 1492 with the conquest of Granada. As a result, the Muslim communities in western Europe today are a relatively recent phenomenon.

In the twentieth century some Muslims migrated to Europe from various colonies as students, visitors, and merchants. Many also went as menial labourers and factory workers, especially after the Second World War. The majority of these post-war immigrants were men ranging in age from their teens to their forties.

The ethnic makeup of the Muslim communities in Europe was largely determined by colonial ties. Muslims from the French colonies in North Africa, for example, went to France. Indian and, later, Pakistani and Bangladeshi Muslims tended to go to Britain. Those from Turkey and the former Soviet Turkic republics went to Germany and the Netherlands, while Bosnians went to Austria. These patterns were established in the early decades of the twentieth century and continued in spite of many restrictions imposed by the host countries.

Muslim communities in Europe tend to reflect ethnic and linguistic rather than sectarian affiliations. In recent years hundreds of mosques and cultural centres have been established in European cities, and Muslim communities have become a dynamic religious and intellectual force in European society. France and Britain no longer confine Muslims to the status of 'guest workers', as most other European countries do. Yet even there, the long histories of European racism, ethnocentrism, and colonialism have ensured that many Muslims continue to be treated as second-class citizens. This has created serious problems.

After the Islamic revolution of 1978–9, many Iranians immigrated to Europe, adding yet another layer of ethnic and religious diversity to European Muslim society. The 15-year Lebanese civil war of 1975–90, as well as the disturbances in other Arab countries, including the Gulf War of 1991, also sent many political and economic refugees to the West. Meanwhile, intermarriage and conversion have infused new blood into the Muslim community in the Western world.

Many Muslims born in Europe to foreign-born parents are assimilating into European society and culture. On the other hand, most European countries have taken legal measures to limit immigration, and since the mid-1980s a number of them have repatriated some of their Muslim immigrants. Such actions may have been prompted in part by economic considerations, but also perhaps by nationalistic fears that Muslim immigrants might alter the social and ethnic character of these countries. At the end of 2009, for instance, Swiss citizens voted into their constitution a ban on minarets for new mosques—even though only four of the roughly 150 mosques and Islamic centres in Switzerland have minarets. At the same time, European discrimination against ethnic minorities and the Islamic awakening precipitated by the Iranian revolution have made Muslims more aware of their own religious and cultural identity.

Islam in North America

When the first Muslims arrived on American shores is a matter of conjecture. Suggestions that Muslims from Spain and West Africa may have sailed to America long before Columbus are far from conclusive. But it is very likely that the fall of Granada in 1492 and the harsh treatment imposed on Muslims and Jews by the Inquisition led many to flee to America soon after his historic voyage. Scattered records suggest that Muslims were present in Spanish America before 1550.

In the sixteenth and seventeenth centuries, hundreds of thousands of Africans were taken as slaves to the Spanish, Portuguese, and British colonies in the Americas. Although the majority were from West Africa, Muslims made up at least 20 per cent of the total. And among the slaves taken from Senegal, Nigeria, and the western Sudan, the majority were Muslims, many of whom were well educated in Arabic and the religious sciences. Some were able to preserve their faith and heritage, and some tried to maintain contact with Muslims in their home areas, but many others were quickly absorbed into American society, adopting their masters' religious affiliations along with their family names.

Islamic customs and ideas can still be traced in the African-American community, and today efforts are underway to reconstruct the story behind them from slave narratives, oral history, and other archival materials, including observations of Islamic activities by white travellers in the mid-1800s.

African-Americans began trying to recover their Islamic heritage in the late nineteenth century. In the early 1930s, Elijah Muhammad (born Elijah Poole, 1897–1975) founded the Nation of Islam in America. He saw Islam as a religion of Black people only, misrepresenting the universalistic and non-racial nature of Islam. But his sons and successors, after travelling in the Muslim world and observing the international and multiracial character of the *hajj* pilgrimage, have drawn closer to classical Islam. African-American Muslims often refer to themselves as Bilalians, after Bilal, an African Companion of the Prophet's time and community. Islam continues to be the fastest-growing religion in the United States, particularly among African-Americans.

Before the African-American revival of Islam, small numbers of Muslims travelled to Canada and the United States, mainly from Syria and Lebanon. Those early immigrants were uneducated men who intended only to work in North America for a few years and then return home. Instead, many married North American women and were soon completely assimilated.

The first Muslim missionary in America was Muhammad Alexander Webb, a jeweller, newspaper editor, and diplomat who converted to Islam in 1888, while travelling in India. On his return, Webb created an Islamic propaganda movement, wrote three books on Islam, and founded a periodical entitled *The Muslim World* (not to be confused with the academic journal of the same name). He travelled widely to spread the new faith and established Islamic study circles or Muslim brotherhoods in many American cities. With his death in 1916, however, his movement died as well.

The numbers of Muslim immigrants coming to North America increased markedly during the twentieth century. Most were of South Asian origin. Many were students who eventually chose to stay, or well-educated professionals who came in search of better opportunities. But others came to escape religious or political persecution in their homelands. Interestingly, many recent newcomers who arrived as staunch anti-Western revivalists have soon forgotten their hostility and settled in as peaceful, responsible, and law-abiding citizens.

Although these and other religiously committed Muslim immigrants may have moderated their political convictions, they retained a high degree of religious zeal, which they put to good use in the service both of their own community and of the society at large. They have played a crucial role in preserving the Islamic identity of fellow immigrants and promoting a better understanding of Islam through media activities and academic meetings.

The first mosque in the US was established in 1915 by Albanian Muslims in Maine; another followed in Connecticut in 1919. Other mosques were built established in South Dakota and Iowa in the 1920s and 1930s. In 1928, Polish Tatars built a mosque in Brooklyn, New York, which is still in use. The first Canadian mosque was built in Edmonton in 1938, and a number of smaller towns in Alberta also have Muslim communities. In Toronto, the first Muslim organization was the Albanian Muslim Society of Toronto, founded in 1956. In 1968, this organization purchased an unused Presbyterian Church and converted it into a mosque. Toronto currently has the largest population of Canada's Muslims.

The exact numbers of Muslims in Canada and the US are a matter of debate. The 2001 Canadian census counted almost 600,000 Muslims, making Islam the second-largest religion in the country. As of 2011, that number is estimated to have grown to over 800,000 Canadian Muslims. The United States has not had a religious census since 1936, but the current Muslim population there is estimated to be about 7 million. Whatever the numbers may be, Islam in North America is no longer an exotic rarity: it is the faith of many people's co-workers and neighbours.

Women and the Family

Islam strictly forbade the practice of female infanticide, and it required that those who had killed their daughters in pre-Islamic times (often by burying them alive) make expiation for their crime. The Qur'an states that on the Day of Resurrection, it will be asked of the child who was buried alive, 'For what sin was she slain?' (Q. 81: 8–9). Victims are to be vindicated and recompensed on the Day of Judgment for the wrong done them in this life.

Marriage under Islam is essentially a contractual relationship negotiated between the prospective husband and the woman's father or guardian. But the Qur'an emphasizes that the true contract is between the husband and the wife, based on mutual consent: the woman's father or guardian, 'he in whose hand is the tie of marriage' (Q. 2: 237), is expected to act on her behalf and, ideally, in her interest. Divorce is allowed, but only as a last resort, to be used only after every effort has been made to save the marriage.

The Qur'an allows polygyny (simultaneous marriage to more than one wife). But it places two significant restrictions on such marriages. First, it limits to four the number of wives that a man can have at one time, whereas before Islam the number was unlimited. Second, it demands strict justice and equality in a man's material and emotional support for all his wives. If this is not possible, the Qur'an stipulates that he can have 'only one'. It also insists that 'You cannot act equitably among your wives however much you try' (Q. 4: 3 and 129). As a result, the vast majority of Muslim marriages are monogamous.

Even more significantly, the Qur'an treats polygyny not as an entitlement but as a social responsibility. The verses dealing with this subject open with this proviso: 'If you [men] are afraid that you would not act justly towards the orphans [in your care], then marry what seems good to you of women: two, three, or four' (Q. 4: 3). This statement may be interpreted in two ways. It may mean that a man could marry the widowed mother of orphans in order to provide a family for them. It may also mean that a man could marry two, three, or four orphan girls after they have attained marriageable age, again to provide a home and family for them. In either case, marriage to more than one wife was explicitly allowed as a way of providing for female orphans and widows in a traditional society beset with continuous warfare, where a woman could find the love and security she needed only in her own home.

In addition the Qur'an allows women to own property and dispose of it as they please. Women may acquire property through bequest, inheritance, and bride dowry. These rights may seem inadequate today. Yet the Qur'an clearly recognizes in women a human dignity that in many societies denied until recently.

Islamic law and social custom have been not been so generous and forward-looking, however. In general, they have tended either to restrict the rights laid out in the Qur'an or to render them virtually inoperative. Of all the social and political issues that are currently being debated within the Muslim community, one of the most important is the age-old question of women's rights, with all its ramifications.

The Qur'an does not refer at all to the **hijab** or veiling of women as we know it today. It only demands that women dress modestly; and in the very next verse it demands modesty of males as well. The *hadith* tradition indicates that the practice of veiling was adopted during the time of the caliphate, probably under the influence of Eastern Christian and ancient Greek customs. An extreme extension of the practice, which may also be attributable to non-Arab influences, is the seclusion of women. Under the South Asian system of *purdah*, for instance, women are not only veiled but isolated from men. And seclusion became a hallmark of Turkish life under the *harim* system of the Ottoman aristocracy. In Afghanistan, the *burqa* covers the entire body; even the woman's eyes (and her vision) are obscured by a screen.

In the twenty-first century, the *hijab* has become a powerful—and powerfully ambiguous—symbol, widely condemned (especially by non-Muslims) as a limitation on women's rights, but often defended by Muslim women themselves as a freely chosen affirmation of their Islamic identity. The question at issue is to what extent women can be excluded from public life. A closely related issue, of course, is access to education for both women and men. Increasingly, social and economic conditions throughout the world call for equal participation and equal rights for women and men alike.

In March 2005 Professor Amina Wadud led a mixed-gender Muslim prayer service in New York City. The event caused a great deal of controversy because it broke a number of Islamic conventions. It involved a woman leading a mixed gender group, even though convention says that women can lead prayer only among other women or within their own family. Some of the women attending the service had their hair uncovered. And men and women were not separated. The only time such interspersing of genders is accepted by all Muslims is during the pilgrimage to Mecca, where men and women encircle the Ka'ba and pray beside one another. The New York prayer service has started a new trend; similar events have been held in a number of North American cities, including Toronto. Mixed-gender and female-led prayers are likely to become an increasingly important issue for North American Muslims.

Muslim women activists have also acquired a more prominent voice within at least some mainstream organizations, challenging Muslim leaders to adopt more inclusive language and develop policies to encourage women's participation. They are also becoming more vocal in their engagement with Western feminism over issues such as head covering.

Although their positions on questions of gender equality sometimes diverge from those of Western feminists, controversies over issues such as veiling have created significant openings for Muslim women to engage in political debate within their own religious communities.

Sexual Diversity

Issues of gender equality and sexual diversity are rarely discussed in North America's largest Muslim political and religious organizations (e.g., the Islamic Society of North America), partly because such groups tend to be quite traditional in outlook and partly because they have been preoccupied with matters such as community-building, immigration policy, discrimination, and (to some extent) foreign policy. But as the size of their constituencies has grown, and the range of perspectives within them has increased, there has been growing pressure to address matters involving gender and sexuality.

Ms Dia', a Pakistani-American college student and DJ in Chicago, IL. The mural was an interfaith community project involving Christian, Jewish and Muslim youth (© 2007 Kauthar Umar, isl • am • erica).

Diasporic communities in large urban centres tend to become more open to questions about traditional religious and cultural ideas as they become more deeply rooted (or 'assimilated') in their new societies. As contact with the 'host' community increases, those who question traditional ideas are likely to have much easier access to information and networks of like-minded people than their counterparts in their countries of origin. Some will 'exit' their communities of origin and seek full assimilation to the dominant society; but in large communities particularly, some who remain connected will begin challenging traditionalism from within.

In general, Muslims born and raised in North America are more open to diversity than those born abroad. This is especially true in communities that are not sufficiently homogeneous to support separate schools. The likelihood of dissent is further amplified in North America by relatively high levels of education. Higher levels of education tend to increase openness both to diversity and to equity claims on the part of women and sexual minorities. The fact that Muslim minorities in North America are less economically marginalized than those in Europe also helps to reduce the likelihood of strict adherence to religious tradition.

On the other hand, the great majority of Muslims in Canada and the United States are still relatively recent immigrants from places where social norms regarding gender and sexuality are starkly conservative, and the mosques to which new immigrants become attached are almost invariably conservative on moral questions. Groups seeking to challenge conservative ideas are developing—among them is Al-Fatiha ('the opening'), a group for LGBTQ (lesbian, gay, bisexual, transgender, and queer) Muslims based in Los Angeles—but homosexual Muslims in particular continue to face discrimination from mainstream Muslim society.

An increasingly important source of support for gay Muslims is the Internet, which protects their anonymity while providing access to groups such as the South Asian Gay and Lesbian Association of New York (its site includes a description of the first LGBTQ Muslim conference, held in Boston in 1998) and Queer Jihad. Based in West Hollywood, Queer Jihad defines itself as 'the queer Muslim struggle for acceptance: first, the struggle to accept ourselves as being exactly the way Allah has created us to be; and secondly, the struggle for acceptance and tolerance among Muslims in general'.

Muslims for Progressive Values (MPV) is the leading progressive Muslim group in North America. Its principles regarding gender and sexual equality are stated on its website:

> **Women's Rights:** We support women's agency and self-determination in every aspect of their lives. We believe in women's full participation in society at every level. We affirm our commitment to reproductive justice and empowering women to make healthy decisions regarding their bodies, sexuality and reproduction.
>
> **LGBTQ Rights:** We endorse the human and civil rights of lesbian, gay, bisexual, transgender, intersex, and queer (LGBTQ) individuals. We support full equality and inclusion of all individuals, regardless of sexual orientation or gender identity, in society and in the Muslim community. We affirm our commitment to ending discrimination based on sexual orientation and gender identity.

One sign of progress came in 2008, when the first Muslim ever elected to the US Congress, Keith Ellison, agreed to join the Bipartisan Congressional LGBT Equality Caucus as vice-chair, and was quoted as saying: 'I believe when my gay, lesbian, bisexual or transgender neighbour suffers from discrimination, then I suffer, and so does our whole community'. Ellison is not only the first elected Muslim member of Congress (2006; André Carson became the second in 2008) but the first African American to be elected from Minnesota to the federal House of Representatives. He is respected by virtually all major Muslim organizations in the United States. Even so, queer Muslims in the United States continue to face widespread condemnation or at best silence within their families, among religious leaders, and in mainstream Muslim groups.

Bioethics

Another important challenge facing all religious communities in the twenty-first century is the unprecedented power over human life and death made available by developments in biological research and medical technology. This power is especially troubling for Western religions, which have traditionally considered humans to be sacred, set apart from all other beings. For Muslims, the human being is created expressly to serve as God's repre-sentative on earth:

> Behold, your Lord said to the angels: 'I will create a vicegerent on earth.' They said: 'Will You place therein one who will make mischief there and shed blood, while we celebrate Your praises and glorify Your holy name?' God said: 'I know what you do not' (Q. 2:30).

Central to the notion of the human being as sacred is the notion of the soul. The Christian understanding of the soul was economically expressed by the Anglican writer C.S. Lewis: 'You don't have a soul, you are a soul. You have a body.' According to one *hadith*, the soul enters the body after 120 days in the womb. Another *hadith* puts the time earlier, at 40 days. While the Qur'an makes no explicit reference to this question, there is a verse that talks about stages of creation in the womb:

> And truly We created the human being out of wet clay, then we made it a drop in a firm resting place, then We made the seed a clot, then We made the clot a lump of flesh, then We made (in) the lump of flesh bones, then We clothed the bones with flesh, then We caused it to grow into another creation, so blessed be God, the best of the creators (Q. 23: 12-14).

The majority of scholars identify the 120th day as the moment when the embryo is ensouled and therefore would permit abortion before 120 days' gestation but not after. However, Shi'a scholars as well as some of their Sunni colleagues have cautioned against this distinction because they believe that the pre-ensouled embryo is alive, and that to destroy it is a sin.

Modern Muslims take great pride in Islam's historic contributions to science and medi-cine. Following an injunction of the Prophet 'to seek knowledge even unto China' (that is, to the end of the then-known world), Muslims never really experienced the kind of tension between religion and science that Western Christianity did. To discover scientific truths about the world was to learn more about God who created it. Thus universities were established in the Islamic world as early as the ninth century; one of the earliest accounts of the duties of the doctor was written by a ninth-century physician named Ishaq ibn Ali Rahawi; and in the tenth century another Muslim physician named al-Razi (known in the West as Rhazes) wrote numerous treatises on medicine, pharmacy, and medical ethics.

The Islamic system of moral deliberation is even older. Jonathan Brockopp, in his edited volume *Islamic Ethics of Life: Abortion, War and Euthanasia* (2003), identifies the sources of Islamic ethics as the Qur'an and *hadith*, together with the commentaries on them written over the centuries. Traditionally, the scholars and jurists who interpret those texts in order to rule on the ethical questions brought before them have tended to prefer cases and examples over abstract principles.

Perhaps this traditional preference for the specific over the general helps to account for Muslims' general reluctance to approach medical issues from the perspective of 'bio-ethics' (as is usually done in the West). The tradition has been to let God and the family decide. Although advances in medicine are welcomed and medical expertise is honoured, the wishes of the individual or the family have taken priority over the opinions of either doctors or religious scholars. And because it is impossible to know God's will, Muslims have preferred what Brockopp calls a 'stance of humility' when it comes to decisions on questions of life and death. In the West the notion of human dignity has often been used to justify a patient's right to die, but for Muslims human dignity has traditionally been a function of the patient's relationship to God. In other words, human life is not inherently valuable: it is valuable only because it is a gift from God. So, while active euthanasia (mercy killing) would be forbidden for the same reasons that suicide would, someone who was brain-dead could be removed from life support if the family so wished.

Nevertheless, 'Let God and the family decide' is not always adequate to the conditions under which most North Americans, including Muslims, now live and die. Amyn Sajoo, in his book *Muslim Ethics: Emerging Vistas* (2004), writes not only as an academic but as an insider to the Muslim tradition, and he shows that tradition responding to medicalized death in a more activist mode. Sajoo reprints extracts from the Islamic Code of Medical Ethics adopted by the Islamic Organization for Medical Sciences in 1981. The organization upheld the traditional position on euthanasia: 'A doctor shall not take away life even when motivated by mercy.' With respect to the artificial prolongation of life, however, it advised the doctor

> to realize his limit and not transgress it. If it is scientifically certain that life cannot be restored, then it is futile to diligently keep on the vegetative state of the patient by heroic means of animation or preserve him by deep-freezing or other artificial methods.

Thus in cases where family members wish to continue life support even when there is no hope of recovery, they may not necessarily be the primary decision-makers: the doctor may take over that role.

Another organization that is working to bring traditional religious standards and ideals into modern medical situations is the Islamic Medical Association of North America (IMANA). IMANA has developed a number of principles and policy statements (available on its website) to guide Muslim medical practice and attempt to answer questions about controversial current issues. This organization may not represent a universal Muslim consensus about such issues, but it is a vivid example of accommodation and creative adaptation to new circumstances.

Environmental Issues

The Qur'an tells us that God offered a 'Trust to the heavens and the earth and the mountains; but they refused to undertake it, being afraid thereof: but the human being undertook it; he was indeed unjust and foolish' (Q. 33:72). This passage seems to suggest an understanding that human beings will act foolishly and without justice to the earth. Humanity's stewardship of the earth entails a profound responsibility, requiring both wisdom and justice. All of creation is considered Muslim in the literal sense of the word: submitting to God. The creation itself, in all its diversity and complexity, may be thought of as a vast universe of 'signs' of God's power, wisdom, beneficence, and majesty:

With God are the keys of the unseen that no one knows but God. God knows whatever there is on the earth and in the sea. Not a leaf falls but with God's knowledge: there is not a grain in the earth's shadows, not a thing, freshly green or withered, but it is (inscribed) in a clear record' (Q.6:59).

As North American Muslims become more aware of environmental issues, they are taking seriously the challenge of environmental stewardship. Many are now beginning to talk about 'greening their deen' (*deen* being the Arabic word for 'religion'), following the title of the 2010 book *Green Deen: What Islam Teaches About Protecting the Planet* by Ibrahim Abdul-Matin.

Islam and the Future

A major development in the history of Islam is now underway in the West. Muslims who, through migration, have moved from majority to minority status are being spurred to define the priorities of their faith. Their decisions about what to pass on to their Western-born children will shape the contours of Islam in the twenty-first century and beyond. At the same time, the Western emphasis on open discussion calls on Muslims from different cultural and regional backgrounds to think clearly about what they do and do not share. Muslims living in the West will use Western technology and democratic institutions to help their brothers and sisters revitalize the Muslim communities in their countries of origin, as well as the rest of the Muslim *ummah*. The potential of modern communications to contribute to this process became clear during the 'Arab Spring' of 2011.

Many hoped that the end of the cold war in 1989 and the moves made in the 1990s towards ending the long and bitter conflict between Israelis and Palestinians might allow for better relations between the Western and Muslim worlds in general. But the Israeli–Palestinian conflict has only deepened, and new conflicts have emerged in recent years.

One major political development was the Iranian revolution of 1979. Three decades later, the prospect of an Iran with nuclear weapons has only increased the tensions between the Islamic regime and the West. A second development can also be traced to 1979, when the Soviet Union invaded Afghanistan. Muslims from around the world volunteered to fight with the Afghans for their liberation, and the United States contributed heavily to their training. They were called *mujahidin* (the word is derived from *jihad*), and at the time—before the end of the cold war—they were seen as 'freedom fighters' by much of the world, including the American president, Ronald Reagan.

Among the other contributors to Afghanistan's 'holy war' was Osama bin Laden, the son of a wealthy Saudi Arabian family, who created Al-Qaeda ('the base') to help fund and train *mujahidin*. The Soviet troops were withdrawn in 1988. But Al-Qaeda was not disbanded. In 1996 bin Laden issued a *fatwa* calling for the overthrow of the Saudi government and the removal of US forces in Arabia, and in 1998 he declared war against Americans generally. A series of terrorist actions followed, culminating in the attacks on the United States of 11 September 2001. In response, the US and its allies went to war, first in Afghanistan and then in Iraq.

Muslims around the world have repeatedly condemned terrorist activity. Muslim leaders have pointed out that the use of suicide bombers violates mainstream Islamic teachings that prohibit both suicide and the killing of civilians during war, and in March 2005, on the first anniversary of the 2004 Al-Qaeda train bombing in Madrid, Spanish clerics issued a *fatwa* against bin Laden himself. Even so, it would be another seven years before bin Laden was tracked down and killed by US forces. An important reference point in discussions of martyrdom is the Mardin Conference, held in March 2010 in the city that was at issue in the famous fourteenth-century *fatwa* legitimizing the use of violence against unjust Muslim rulers. Because many modern terrorists have used this *fatwa* to justify their actions (among them bin Laden), the Mardin conference brought together 15 senior Islamic scholars from across the Muslim world to discuss the context in which it was issued some 700 years earlier.

In condoning violence against authoritarian rulers in order to re-establish true Islamic rule, Ibn Taymiyyah broke with the teachings of his own conservative Hanbali school. As the scholars who met at Mardin pointed out, however, the fatwa was issued in a very particular historical context, in the aftermath of the Mongol conquest and devastation of Baghdad (the seat of Islamic authority at the time). They concluded that 'anyone who seeks support from this fatwa for killing Muslims or non-Muslims has erred in his interpretation.' They also asserted that 'It is not for a Muslim individual or a group to announce and declare war or engage in combative jihad . . . on their own.' Unfortunately, extremists seem impervious to mainstream Muslim opinion.

Muslims can accomplish much in the West if they work with their non-Muslim neighbours to promote justice and moral consciousness. But many non-Muslims see 'Islam' and 'the West' as mutually exclusive realities, and do not recognize their shared heritage. If future generations of Muslims are to remain active as Muslims in pluralistic Western societies, it is more important than ever to change old images and ideas.

Sacred Texts Table

Religion	Text	Composition/ Compilation	Compilation/ Revision	Use
Islam (Sunni and Shi'a)	Qur'an	Revelations received by Muhammad between 610 and 632 CE	Authoritative Codex produced between 644 and 656 CE	Doctrinal, ritual, inspirational, educational
Islam (Sunni and Shi'a)	Hadith	Sayings of Muhammad and his early companions collected during their lifetimes	Earliest authoritative collection produced by al-Bukhari (d. 870 CE)	Doctrinal, ritual, inspirational, educational
Islam (Shi'a only)	Nahj al-Balagha ('the peak of eloquence'; the sayings of 'Ali)	Sayings and sermons of 'Ali, the first Shi'i Imam	Collected by Al-Radi (d. 1015)	Doctrinal, ritual, inspirational, educational
Islam (Ismaili Shi'a only)	Ginans (hymns of praise and worship of God)	Collection begun by Pir Nur in the 12th century	Composition and collection continued until the beginning of the 20th century	Doctrinal, ritual, inspirational, educational

Sites

Mecca Home to the Ka'ba, the first place of monotheistic worship. Also the place where Muhammad was born and received his first revelations.

Medina The home of the first Muslim community and the place where Muhammad was buried.

Jerusalem The area of the ancient city called Haram al-Sharif (the 'Noble Sanctuary'; known to Jews and Christians as the Temple Mount) contains two sacred buildings: the Masjid al-Aqsa—the 'farthest mosque', from a passage in the Qur'an (17: 1) referring to Muhammad's miraculous journey—and the Dome of the Rock, a sanctuary built on the spot from which tradition says Muhammad made his ascent to heaven.

Karbala The city in Iraq where Husayn (the third Imam and the grandson of Muhammad) was martyred; of special importance to Shi'i Muslims.

Cairo Home of Al-Azhar University, one of the oldest universities in the Western world and an important centre of Sunni learning.

Istanbul Captured by the Turkish ruler Muhammad II in 1453, Istanbul had been called Constantinople under the Byzantines. It became the capital of the Ottoman Turkish Empire and the centre of the sultan's power. It contains many imperial buildings, including the famous Topkapi Palace and the Western-influenced Dolmabahce Palace.

Study Questions

1. What is the significance of the *hijra* in Muslim history? Why is this event so important to Muslims?

2. Muslims consider the life of Muhammad to be of fundamental importance to their faith. Write a brief biography of the Prophet highlighting two events in his life that are particularly significant to Muslims. In your answer, explain why the events you have chosen are so central.

3. What is the Qur'an? How is it understood in the Muslim tradition?

4. Discuss the differences between Sunni and Shi'i Islam. What are the two primary groups within Shi'i Islam?

5. Outline the development of Sufism, the mystical dimension of Islam.

6. What are the Five Pillars of Islam?

7. How does Islam respond to contemporary questions of bioethics or environmental responsibility?

8. What are some of the issues that come up in feminist interpretations of the Qur'an and the Muslim tradition?

Glossary

caliph From the Arabic *khalifah* ('one who represents or acts on behalf of another'). The caliph was the Prophet's successor as the head of the Muslim community; the position became institutionalized in the form of the caliphate, which lasted from 632 to 1924.

dhikr 'Remembering' God's name; chanted in Sufi devotional exercises, sometimes while devotees dance in a circle.

dhimmis 'Protected people': non-Muslim religious minorities (specifically Jews and Christians, as 'People of the Book') accorded tolerated status in Islamic society.

faqir A Sufi ascetic, from the Arabic word for 'poor'; the corresponding Persian word is *darvish*.

Fatihah The short opening *surah* of the Qur'an, recited at least 17 times every day.

fatwa A ruling issued by a traditional religio-legal authority.

fiqh Jurisprudence, or the theoretical principles underpinning the specific regulations contained in the *shari'ah*.

hadith The body of texts reporting Muhammad's words and example, taken by Muslims as a foundation for conduct and doctrine; a *hadith* is an individual unit of the literature.

hajj The annual pilgrimage to Mecca.

halal Ritually acceptable; most often used in the context of the slaughter of animals for meat; also refers generally to Muslim dietary regulations.

hanifs 'Pious ones'; a group of pre-Islamic Arabs who shared the ethical monotheism of Jews and Christians.

haram 'Forbidden', used especially in reference to actions; similar in its connotations to 'taboo'.

hijab A woman's veil or head covering.

hijrah The Prophet's migration from Mecca to establish a community in Medina in 622 CE. In dates, the abbreviation AH stands for 'year of the *hijrah*' (the starting-point of the Islamic dating system)

'Id al-Fitr The holiday celebrating the end of the Ramadan fast; the festival traditionally begins following the sighting of the new moon.

ijma' The consensus of religio-legal scholars; one of the two secondary principles used in jurisprudence; some legal schools give it more weight than others.

ijtihad Personal reasoning applied to the development of legal opinions.

Imamis ('Twelvers') Shi'is who recognize twelve imams as legitimate heirs to the Prophet's authority; the last, in occultation since 874, is expected to return some day as the **Mahdi**.

Isma'ilis ('Seveners') Shi'is who recognize only seven imams; named after the last of them, Isma'il, whose lineage continues to the present in the Agha Khan.

isnad The pedigree or chain of transmission of a *hadith*, with which the individual unit begins.

jihad Struggle in defence of the faith; some *jihads* are military, waged in response to threats to the community's security or welfare; others are spiritual, waged to improve moral conduct in society.

jinn Spirits or demons (the singular is *jinni*).

kufr Rejecting belief; implies lack of gratitude for God's grace.

Mahdi The Shi'i twelfth Imam, understood in his role as the 'rightly guided one' who will emerge from hiding at some unspecified future date to restore righteousness and order to the world.

mi'raj The Prophet's miraculous journey to heaven.

mu'adhdhin The person who calls people to prayer.

qiblah The direction of prayer, marked in mosques by a niche inside the wall nearest Mecca.

Ramadan The month throughout which Muslims fast during daylight hours.

sadaqah Alms given voluntarily, in addition to the required *zakat*.

salat The prescribed daily prayers, said five times during the day.

shahadah The Muslim profession of faith in God as the only god, and in Muhammad as God's prophet.

shari'ah The specific regulations of Islamic law (jurisprudence, or theoretical discussion of the law, is *fiqh*).

shaykh The Arabic term for a senior master, especially in the context of Sufism.

Shi'is Muslims who trace succession to the Prophet's authority through imams in the lineage of 'Ali; the smaller of the two main divisions of Islam, accounting for about one-sixth of all Muslims today.

sunnah The 'life-example' of Muhammad's words and deeds, based mainly on the Hadith literature; the primary source of guidance for Muslims.

Sunnis Muslims who trace succession to the Prophet's authority through the caliphate, which lasted until the twentieth century; the larger of the two main divisions of Islam, accounting for about five-sixths of all Muslims today.

surah A chapter of the Qur'an; there are 114 in all, arranged mainly in decreasing order of length except for the first (the *Fatihah*).

tafsir Commentary on the Qur'an.

taqlid Following the *ijtihad* or legal opinion of a particular jurist.

ummah The Muslim community.

zakat The prescribed welfare tax; 2.5 per cent of each Muslim's accumulated wealth, collected by central treasuries in earlier times but now donated to charities independently of state governments; see also *sadaqah*.

Further Reading

Alvi, Sajida Sultana, et al., eds. 2003. *The Muslim Veil in North America: Issues and Debates*. Toronto: Women's Press. A good collection of essays about the issues surrounding *hijab*.

Coulson, N.G. 1964. *A History of Islamic Law*. Edinburgh: Edinburgh University Press. Traces the development of Islamic jurisprudence from its inception in the ninth century through to the influence of modern Western legal systems.

The Encyclopedia of Islam, rev. ed. 1963–. Leiden: E.J. Brill. (First published in 4 vols, 1913–38.) Vast and technical, but authoritative. Entries appear under Arabic head-words, sometimes in unfamiliar transliterations, and so pose a challenge for the beginner.

Esposito, John, ed. 2009. *The Oxford Encyclopedia of the Islamic World*. New York: Oxford University Press. An indispensable reference.

Grabar, Oleg. 1973. *The Formation of Islamic Art*. New Haven: Yale University Press. Concentrates on Islamic art in the Middle East in the early Islamic centuries.

Haddad, Yvonne Y., and Jane I. Smith, eds. 1994. *Muslim Communities in North America*. Albany: State University of New York Press. An examination of Islamic tradition and identity in the modern Western diaspora.

Mottahedeh, Roy. 2002. *The Mantle of the Prophet: Religion and Politics in Iran*. Oxford: Oneworld Publications. One of the best single-volume studies of the events leading up to the Iranian revolution.

Peters, Francis E. 1994. *A Reader on Islam*. Princeton: Princeton University Press. An anthology of historical source readings.

Qureshi, Emran, and Michael A. Sells, eds. 2003. *The New Crusades: Constructing the Muslim Enemy*. New York: Columbia. An excellent collection of essays on Western representations of Islam and Muslim lives.

Safi, Omid, ed. 2003. *Progressive Muslims: On Justice, Gender and Pluralism*. Oxford: Oneworld. A collection of essays by Muslim scholars of Islam on these contemporary topics.

Schimmel, Annemarie. 1975. *Mystical Dimensions of Islam*. Chapel Hill: University of North Carolina Press. A survey of Sufism by one of its most respected Western interpreters.

Taylor, Jennifer Maytorena. 2009. *New Muslim Cool*. Documentary film. Educational DVD available from Seventh Art Releasing at <http://www.7thart.com>. The story of Hamza Perez, a Puerto Rican American hip hop artist who converted to Islam.

Wadud, Amina. 2006. *Inside the Gender Jihad: Women's Reform in Islam*. Oxford: Oneworld. An autobiographical account by one of the leading feminist Muslim voices.

Watt, W. Montgomery. 1962. *Islamic Philosophy and Theology*. Edinburgh: Edinburgh University Press. A masterly survey of Muslim religious intellectuals, especially in the first six centuries of Islam.

Recommended Websites

www.uga.edu/islam/ The best academic site for the study of Islam, presented by Professor Alan Godlas of the University of Georgia.

www.cie.org/index.aspx The Council on Islamic Education offers useful resources for teachers.

http://acommonword.com/ An interfaith initiative supported by a wide range of Muslim scholars and leaders.

www.imana.org/ The Islamic Medical Association of North America is a great resource for Islamic medical ethics.

www.msawest.net/islam/ An excellent selection of resources on Islam, including searchable translations of both the Qur'an and the Hadith literature, presented by the Muslim Students Association.

http://theamericanmuslim.org/tam.php/features/ articles/muslim_voices_against_extremism_and_ terrorism_2/ A comprehensive list of Muslim statements against terrorism, extremism, and violence.

References

Arberry, Arthur J. trans. 1955. *The Koran Interpreted*. London: Allen and Unwin.

Brockopp, Jonathan E., ed. 2003. *Islamic Ethics of Life*. Columbia: University of South Carolina Press.

Nicholson, Reynold A. 1931. 'Mysticism'. In *The Legacy of Islam*, ed. T. Arnold and Alfred Guillaume, 210–38. London: Oxford University Press.

———, trans. 1950. *Rumi: Poet and Mystic*. London: G. Allen and Unwin.

———. 2002 [1914]. *The Mystics of Islam*. Bloomington: World Wisdom.

Sajoo, Amyn. 2004. *Muslim Ethics: Emerging Vistas*. New York: I.B. Tauris.

Smith, Margaret. 1928. *Rabi'a the Mystic*. Cambridge: Cambridge University Press.

Chapter
6
Hindu Traditions
❧ Vasudha Narayanan ❧

The earliest compositions in the Hindu tradition are said to have been 'revealed' to *rishis* (visionaries or seers) through both sight and sound; thus the sacred words are called *shruti* ('that which is heard').

When Hindus go on a pilgrimage or visit a temple, they seek an experience known as a *darshana*: to see and be seen by a particular deity or **guru** (holy teacher). But Hindus also believe in the importance of uttering prayers aloud. Reciting Sanskrit texts in the temple or retelling in everyday language the stories of the gods, chanting a prayer or singing a devotional song or meditating on a holy **mantra**—these are just some of the ways in which Hindus actively live their tradition through its sacred words. In short, Hindus experience the divine through both sight and sound.

'Hinduism'

The word 'Hinduism', like the word 'India' itself, is derived from 'Sind': the name of the region (now in Pakistan) of the river Sindhu (Indus). The term was given currency by the British colonizers of India in the eighteenth and nineteenth centuries. To them, 'Hinduism' essentially meant the religion of those Indians—the majority of the population—who were not Muslims, although a few smaller groups, including Jainas, Parsis, Christians, Jews, and sometimes Sikhs, were also recognized. As a term for religious identity, 'Hinduism' did not catch on until the nineteenth century. Thus anyone who tries to look for the term in books printed earlier is unlikely to find it.

There are approximately a billion Hindus in the world today. When they are asked about their religious identity, however, they generally refer not to Hinduism but rather to their particular caste, community, or linguistic group. An alternative term designating a comprehensive tradition is *sanatana dharma* ('eternal faith'), but it is common in only a few regions and in certain classes of Indian society. It is seldom used to refer to local manifestations of the faith.

Under Indian law the term 'Hindu' applies not only to members of a Hindu 'denomination' such as Vira Shaiva or Brahmo Samaj, but also to 'any other person domiciled in the territories to which [the Hindu Family Act] extends who is *not a Muslim, Christian, Parsi, or Jew* by religion' (italics added). In effect, India's legal system uses 'Hindu' as a kind of catch-all category that includes anyone who does not profess one of the specified religions, all of which originated outside India. Jainas, Buddhists, and Sikhs are all officially covered by the 'Hindu' umbrella.

In the same way, what we call 'Hinduism' encompasses an amazing plurality of traditions, and no single holy book, dogma, or religious leader is authoritative for all of them.

◀ The Gangaur festival, honouring the goddess Parvati, is celebrated throughout Rajasthan every spring (© Craig Lovell/Corbis).

We can trace lines of historical continuity and make some generalizations, but only as long as we keep in mind the limits of their validity.

The very concept of religion in the Western, post-Enlightenment sense is only loosely applicable to the Hindu tradition. Some Hindus consider the Sanskrit word **dharma** to come close to 'religion', but they recognize that this is true in a limited way. 'Dharma' for Hindus means righteousness, justice, faith, duty, a religious and social obligation, but it

Timeline

c. 2700 BCE	Evidence of Indus Valley civilization
c. 1750?–1500	Earliest Vedic compositions
c. 600	Production of Upanishads
c. 500	Production of Hindu epics begins
326	Greek armies in India under Alexander the Great
c. 200	First contacts with Southeast Asia
c. 200 BCE–200 CE	Composition of the Bhagavad Gita
c. 200 CE	Compilation of *Laws of Manu* and *Natya Sastra* completed
c. 500	Beginnings of tantric tradition
c. 700–900	Alvars and Nayanmars, Tamil *bhakti* poets
c. 700–800	Shankara's Advaita Vedanta
1017	Traditional birth date of Ramanuja, Vaishnava philosopher (d. 1137)
1100–1150	Angkor Wat built in Cambodia
1398	Traditional birth date of Kabir, North Indian *bhakti* poet (d. 1518)
c. 1400	Major endowments at Tirumala–Tirupati temple
1486	Birth of Chaitanya, Bengali Vaishnava *bhakti* leader (d. 1583)
c. 1543	Birth of Tulsidas, North Indian *bhakti* poet (d. 1623)
1757	British rule established in Calcutta
1828	Ram Mohan Roy founds Brahmo Samaj
1836	Birth of Ramakrishna Paramahamsa (d. 1886)
1875	Dayananda Sarasvati founds Arya Samaj
1893	Vivekananda attends World's Parliament of Religions in Chicago
1905–6	Vedanta Temple built in San Francisco
1959	Maharishi Mahesh Yogi brings transcendental meditation to America and Europe
1965	A.C. Bhaktivedenta Swami Prabhupada, founder of ISKCON, sails to America
1977	Hindu temples consecrated in New York and Pittsburgh
2011	Sathya Sai Baba passes away

does not cover all that is sacred for the Hindu. Hindus may consider many things—from astronomy and astrology to music and dance, from phonetics to plants—essential in the practice of their religion. It would be impossible to do justice to all the subjects that fall under the rubric of the sacred for Hindus. Therefore the following discussion will include a number of features not usually covered by the term 'religion' in the Western world.

🦎 ORIGINS

The origins of Hinduism have been much debated. The standard view in the early twentieth century was that it had grown from a fusion of the indigenous religions of the Indus Valley with the faith of the Aryans, an Indo-European people usually thought to have migrated there sometime between 1750 and 1500 BCE. More recently, however, several different theories have been proposed. Some scholars maintain that the Indo-Europeans migrated into India from other parts of Asia; others insist there is demonstrable evidence that the Indian subcontinent itself was their original homeland.

The Harappa Culture

In 1926 excavations revealed the remains of several large towns on the banks of the Indus River in what is now Pakistan. Two of these towns, known today as Mohenjo Daro ('Mound of the Dead') and Harappa, were more than 480 kilometres (300 miles) apart. Yet archaeological evidence suggested certain cultural similarities across the entire northwestern part of the subcontinent. Similar objects found in towns hundreds of kilometres apart suggest continuous travel and communication between them, and although the culture is still widely identified with the Indus Valley, some scholars prefer to call it the Harappa culture because it extends well beyond the Indus basin itself. Others call it the Sarasvati civilization, after the mighty river that is said to have run through the region in ancient times.

Most historians believe that the towns were in existence by about 2750 BCE (some put the date several centuries earlier). Inscriptions on carved seals show that this culture had a written language, though no one has yet been able to decipher the script with any assurance. What we do know is that the people of the Harappa civilization were impressive builders who lived in what appear to have been planned cities. In the citadel mound at Mohenjo Daro there is a huge swimming-pool-like structure (archaeologists call it 'the Great Bath'), surrounded by porticos and flights of stairs. The care with which the complex was built has led scholars to believe that it was designed for religious rituals of some sort. Some of the houses also appear to have included a room with a fire altar, suggesting a domestic fire ritual. Stone sculptures and terracotta statuettes of what looks like a mother goddess may have been used as icons in worship.

From the buildings tentatively identified as worship halls archaeologists have unearthed some stone sculptures and large numbers of terracotta figurines. Scholars surmise that some were used as icons in worship. These include statuettes of what seems to be a mother goddess—a female figure wearing a short skirt, abundant jewellery, and a fan-shaped head-dress with two little cups on either side. Smoke stains in these cups suggest that they were used for offerings of fire or incense. Because these images were common in this civilization and are similar to figures found in other excavations, it is thought that they

Traditions at a Glance

Numbers

Approximately one billion around the world.

Distribution

Primarily India; large numbers in the United States, Canada, and Western Europe, as well as many parts of South and Southeast Asia, East and South Africa

Principal Historical Periods

c. 2500–600 BCE	Indus Valley civilization; composition of the Vedas
c. 500 BCE–1000 CE	Composition of epics and Puranas
600–1600	Devotional poetry in local languages
13th–18th centuries	Northern India under Muslim rule
mid-1700s–1947	British colonial period
19th century	Indentured workers take Hindu traditions to many parts of the world
late 20th century	Religious teachers (gurus) travelling abroad

Founders and Leaders

Important early figures include Shankara, Ramanuja, Madhva, Vallabha, Ramananda, Chaitanya, Swami Narayanan, Ramakrishna, and Vivekananda. Among the hundreds of teachers who have attracted followings in the last century alone are Aurobindo, Ramana Maharishi, Maharishi Mahesh Yogi, Sathya Sai Baba, Anandamayi Ma, and Ma Amritananda Mayi.

Deities

Hindu philosophy recognizes a supreme being (the ineffable Brahman) who is not limited by gender or number; classical rhetoric typically refers to 330 million 'gods'. Some sectarian traditions identify the supreme deity as Vishnu, some as Shiva, and some as a form of the Goddess. The supreme being may be understood as male, female, androgynous, or beyond gender.

Authoritative Texts

The Vedas are technically considered the most authoritative texts, though the epics (the *Ramayana* and the *Mahabharata*, including the *Bhagavad Gita*), the *Puranas*, and several works in regional languages have also been very important.

Noteworthy Teachings

In general, Hindus recognize a supreme being, but conceptions of this being vary widely. For some it is a personal deity; for others, an impersonal cosmic force. This supreme being is believed to also reside in the local temple. Most think of the human soul as immortal and believe that when it reaches liberation it will be freed from the shackles of karma and rebirth. Specific teachings vary depending on sectarian tradition, region, and community.

may represent an early form of the deity who came to be known as the Goddess. Some Western scholars believe that goddess worship is indicative of a society in which women enjoyed high status, but we have no hard evidence to support this thesis in the case of the Harappan civilization. And though goddesses have certainly been worshipped in the later Hindu tradition, women were not necessarily held in high esteem in all strata of society.

Another recurrent theme on the seals is that of a spirit emerging from a *pipal* tree and worshippers standing in front of it. The *pipal* tree has been a part of the Hindu tradition for at least 2,500 years. If it indeed had religious significance during the Indus Valley period, this has been one of the more enduring features of the religious tradition. On some seals a horned person is emerging from the *pipal* tree and a row of seven figures with long braids is standing in front of it; the notion of seven beings is important in later Hindu mythology. These figures have been identified both as seven holy men (*rishis*) and as seven goddesses of later Hindu myths.

Scholars are not yet sure how the people who lived in these cities disposed of their dead. Since the manner of disposal frequently reveals religious convictions, this is an important gap in our knowledge. No large burial sites have been found, though it is possible that some land used for this purpose was later flooded and now lies under water. The small number of graves that have been discovered are oriented on a north–south axis. In a few of them objects were buried with the bodies, perhaps to serve the dead in an afterlife.

Graves containing more than one body are more difficult to interpret. The additional remains may be those of attendants. It is supposed that most bodies were cremated around the river bank. However, some pots hold collections of bones, and it is possible that both cremation and burial were practised.

There is no agreement about what might have brought the Indus Valley civilization to an end. Some scholars think it was destroyed by migrating Indo-European people from Central Asia around or after 1750 BCE. Other theories centre on flooding or epidemics that might have driven the population farther east.

From the fragmentary evidence and clues found in the Indus Valley, as well as in other regions of India, we can tentatively say that some features of the Hindu religion as practised today go back before 1750 BCE to Mohenjo Daro and Harappa.

The Indo-Europeans

Who were the Indo-Europeans? This question is still debated. Scholars use the term 'Indo-European' (or 'Indo-Aryan') to refer to the family of languages of which Sanskrit is one. Western scholars in the nineteenth century noted the similarities between some Indian and European languages. For example, the Sanskrit word **jnana** is a cognate of the English word 'knowledge'; 'lack of knowledge' is *ajnana* in Sanskrit and 'ignorance' in English. There are hundreds of similar cognates, including the words for 'father' and 'mother'. The Indo-European languages also have many grammatical structures in common. Based on linguistic evidence, nineteenth-century scholars posited a theory of migration that would account for the resemblances. According to this theory, people from Central Asia began migrating to widely distant regions at some time between 2000 BCE and 1500 BCE.

Some moved west and north into what is now Europe, from Ireland to Scandinavia. Others headed south or east and settled in the region of Iran, where they called themselves Arya-s—a name that eventually acquired a class connotation, coming to mean 'noble ones'.

Many scholars believe that the Indo-Europeans originated in Central Asia and that the migration began around 2000 BCE. Others think the migrants originated in the general region of modern Turkey and began spreading out as much as four thousand years earlier. The latter suggest that it was a peaceful migration undertaken by a growing agricultural population in need of additional land.

Yet another school of thought holds that the original home of the Indo-Europeans was actually the Indian subcontinent. Proponents of this theory base their arguments on astronomical data and contradictory evidence concerning the great river Sarasvati, which is said to have flowed from the mountains to the sea in the region of the Harappan civilization. According to the ancient Hindu text called the *Rig Veda*, the Sarasvati had five Aryan tribes living on its banks; yet geologists have shown that the river had run dry by the time that the Aryans were supposed to have entered India (i.e., around 1750 BCE). If the Aryans were there before the Sarasvati dried up, the theory goes, their dates must be pushed back to the time of the Harappan civilization or even earlier.

None of the evidence is conclusive, and some of these theories are motivated by political, religious, and nationalist agendas. Evidence from many areas of study has been drawn into the debate: Vedic philology, comparative philology, linguistic paleontology, linguistics, archeology, astronomy, geography, and geology, as well as religious traditions.

What we know is that the Indo-Europeans composed many poems and, eventually, manuals on rituals and philosophy. They committed these traditions to memory using various mnemonic devices to ensure correct pronunciation, rhythm, and intonation, and they passed them from generation to generation by word of mouth.

The Vedas

The earliest surviving Indo-European compositions are the **Vedas** (from the Sanskrit for 'knowledge'); these are the works collectively known as *shruti* ('that which was heard'). The Vedic *rishis* 'saw' the mantras and transmitted them to their disciples, establishing an oral tradition that has continued to the present.

Traditionally regarded as revealed scripture, the Vedas are now generally thought to have been composed between roughly 1500 BCE (some scholars put the earliest date closer to 1750 BCE) and 600 BCE. There are four Vedic collections: *Rig*, *Sama*, *Yajur*, and *Atharva*. Each of these collections in turn consists of four sections: hymns (*Samhitas*; the earliest parts), directions for the performance of sacred rituals (*Brahmanas*), 'compositions for the forest' (*Aranyakas*), and philosophical works called the **Upanishads** ('sitting near [the teacher]').

The earliest section of the *Rig Veda* contains 1,028 hymns. The hymns of the *Sama Veda* and *Yajur Veda* are largely borrowed from the *Rig*, and the *Sama Veda* was meant to be sung. The *Upanishads* are the most recent sections of each collection.

Each *Veda* has its own *Upanishads*—philosophical works composed around 600 BCE. Thus the famous *Chandogya Upanishad* belongs to the *Sama Veda*, the *Brihadaranyaka* and

Map 6.1   Hinduism

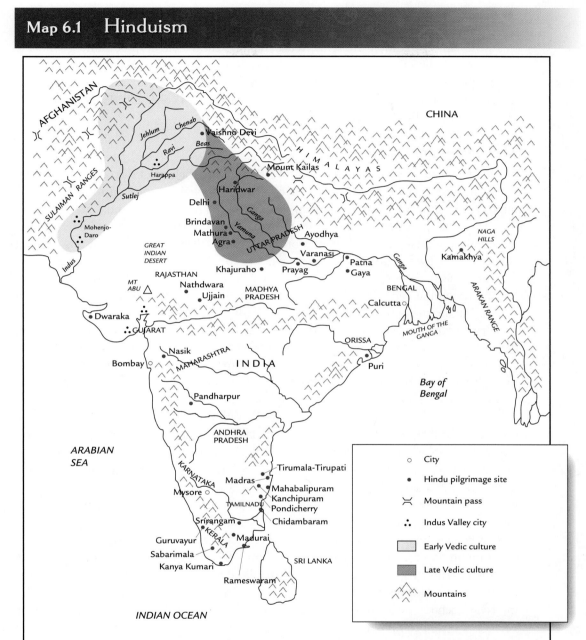

Source: Adapted from Nielsen et al. 1993: 85.

*Taittiriya Upanishad*s are affixed to the *Yajur Veda*, and the *Aitreya Upanishad* belongs to the *Rig Veda*.

The *Atharva Veda* differs from the other three Vedas in that it includes material that scholars consider non-Aryan, such as incantations and remedies to ward off illness and evil spirits. Unlike the hymns of the other Vedas, these chants were used for purposes other than sacrificial rituals. One verse (7.38) refers to the use of herbs to make a lover return, and another (7.50) requests luck in gambling.

In the Hindu tradition the term 'Vedas' denotes the whole corpus, starting with the hymns, continuing through the ritual treatises, and concluding with the texts of a more philosophical character. Many Orientalists and Western Indologists, however, have reserved the term for the hymns, the *samhita* portion of each collection. This narrower use of 'Veda' is generally not accepted by Hindus.

The Status of the Vedas

Almost all educated Hindus would describe the Vedas as their most sacred texts; yet most would be hard pressed to identify their contents. Although considered to be extremely important by all orthodox philosophers and theological treatises, the Vedas are not books that people keep in their homes. Rather, they are ritual texts that Hindus understand as representing eternal sound, eternal words passed on through the generations without change. A few hymns from them are recited regularly at home as well as in temple liturgies, and the philosophical sections have often been translated and commented upon, but the rest of the Vedas are known only to a handful of ritual specialists and to Sanskrit scholars familiar with the early Vedic form of the language.

For many centuries, acceptance as an orthodox member of the society we call Hindu depended on acceptance of the Vedas as authoritative. As custodians of the Vedas, the brahmins reserved for themselves the authority to study and teach these holy words. Though members of two other classes were technically 'allowed' to study the Vedas, in time this privilege was lost or, in some cases, abandoned.

Followers of the Nyaya ('logic') school of philosophy believed that God was the author of the Vedas and that, since God is perfect, the Vedas are infallible. Many other Hindu schools took different views. Two that continue to be influential, the Mimamsa and Vedanta schools, say that the Vedas are eternal and of non-human origin. The Vedic seers (*rishis*) 'saw' the mantras and transmitted them; they did not invent or compose them. The words have a fixed order that must be maintained by a tradition of recitation. The Vedic seers transmitted the words to their disciples, and the same oral tradition has come down to the present.

Not being composed by human beings, the Vedas are considered faultless, the perfect and supreme source of knowledge. From them we can learn about the Supreme Being, and their authority grants credibility to particular doctrines. But the Mimamsakas do not assume that any being, divine or otherwise, played a role in their composition. Except for the Nyaya school, orthodox Hindus have not necessarily attributed the perfection of the Vedas to a divine composer.

The Vedic collections have served as manuals of ritual for all the many strands of the Hindu tradition. Some sections have been recited and acted on without major changes for at least two thousand years. Interpretations have not been static, however. In every generation, specialists in Vedic hermeneutics have worked to make the texts' messages relevant to the particular time and place.

Several works have been more popular among Hindus generally, but the theoretical, ritual, and epistemological significance of the Vedas has been unquestioned. Thus the highest honour that could be given to any Hindu religious text was to describe it as the 'fifth Veda'.

The Vedic Hymns

The figures that were to become the principal Hindu deities—goddesses like Sri (Lakshmi) and gods like Narayana (Vishnu)—are rarely mentioned in the *samhitas*; only the later Vedic hymns address them directly. Rather, the earliest hymns of the Vedas speak of many deities who in time would be superseded, and many of the stories they allude to would not be familiar to most Hindus today.

Indra, for instance, is a warrior god who battles other cosmic powers. Agni is the god of fire who was believed to serve as a messenger, carrying to the deities the offerings that humans placed in the sacrificial fire. Soma is the name of a god identified with the moon, but also of a plant-based elixir, used for ritual purposes, that some modern scholars believe was derived from a hallucinogenic mushroom.

The early hymns typically offer praise to the gods; thus the river Indus is praised for giving cattle, children, horses, and food. But many of them also include petitions—not for salvation or eternal bliss (in fact, the idea of an afterlife is rarely mentioned) but for a good and happy life on this earth. Thus Agni is asked to protect those who praise him, and Indra is asked to crush the worshipper's enemies. A *rishi* named Sobhari simply requests 'all good things', but a woman poet named Ghosa specifically asks to be cured of her white-tinted skin, so that she may marry and live happily with her husband. Another woman poet, Apala, asks Indra for lush hair to grow on her head as well as her father's, and for crops to grow in her father's barren fields.

One of the dominant features of Vedic religious life was the ritual sacrifice (*yajna*), typically performed using fire. From simple domestic affairs to elaborate community events, these sacrifices were conducted by ritual specialists and priests who supervised the making of altars, the sacrifice of animals, and the recitation of hymns. Many rituals also involved the making, offering, and drinking of the *soma* elixir.

A connection was understood to exist between the rituals and the maintenance of cosmic and earthly order, or *rta*. *Rta* includes truth and justice, the rightness of things that makes harmony and peace possible on earth and in the heavens. Although it is an impersonal cosmic principle, it was upheld by Vedic gods like Varuna.

A number of hymns composed around 1000 BCE and included in the *Rig Veda* speculate on the origins of the universe. One, entitled 'The Creation Hymn', expresses wonder at the creation of the universe from nothing and ends with the suggestion that perhaps no one knows how it all came to be.

Another account, however, describes how the universe itself was created through the cosmic sacrifice of the primeval man (*Purusha*). This account, entitled the 'Hymn to the Supreme Person' (*Purusha Sukta*), is important even today in both domestic and temple rituals, and has figured continuously in the tradition for some three thousand years. Straining to capture infinity in words, the composer uses the notion of a 'thousand' to evoke what cannot be measured or perhaps even imagined:

(1)   The cosmic person has a thousand heads
        a thousand eyes and feet
        It covers the earth on all sides
        and extends ten finger-lengths beyond

(2)   The cosmic person is everything
    all that has been and will be . . . .

Various elements of the universe are said to have arisen from this sacrifice:

(13)   From his mind came the moon
    from his eye, the sun
    Indra and Agni from his mouth
    the wind came from his breath.
(14)   From his navel came space
    from his head, the sky
    from his feet, earth;
    from his ears, the four directions
    thus the worlds were created.

In this context an idea is introduced that was to change forever the religious and social countenance of the Hindu tradition:

(12)   From his mouth came the priestly class
    from his arms, the rulers.
    The producers came from his legs;
    from his feet came the servant class.

Thus the origins of the four classes (*varnas*) of Hindu society are traced to the initial cosmic sacrifice. Though this verse is the first explicit reference to what came to be called the caste system, it is likely that the stratification of society had already taken place long before this hymn was composed.

The Upanishads

By the time of the *Aranyakas* and *Upanishads*, in the seventh and sixth centuries BCE, the early Vedic emphasis on placating the gods through ritual sacrifice had given way to critical philosophical inquiry. This period—a little before and perhaps during the lives of Gautama Buddha and the Jaina teacher Mahavira—was a time of intellectual ferment, of questioning and rejecting authoritarian structures.

Yet the *Upanishads* do not totally reject the early hymns and sacrificial rituals. Instead, they rethink and reformulate them. Thus some rituals are interpreted allegorically, and the symbolic structures of the sacrifices are analyzed in some detail. Most of the *Upanishads* take the form of conversations—between a teacher and a student, between a husband and wife, or between fellow philosophers.

Karma and Samsara

It is in the *Upanishads* that we find the earliest discussions of several concepts central to the later Hindu tradition, among them the concept of **karma**. The literal meaning of 'karma' is 'action', especially ritual action, but in these books the word eventually comes to refer to a system of rewards and punishments attached to various actions. This system of cause and effect may require several lifetimes to work out. Thus the concept of karma implies a continuing cycle of death and rebirth or reincarnation called **samsara**. To achieve liberation (*moksha*) from this cycle, according to the *Upanishads*, requires a transforming experiential wisdom. Those who attain that wisdom become immortal (*a-mrta*, 'without death').

A frequent theme of the *Upanishads* is the quest for a unifying truth. This 'higher' knowledge is clearly distinguished from the 'lower' knowledge that can be conceptualized and expressed in words. Its nature cannot be explained or taught: it can only be evoked, as in this question posed by the seeker in the *Mundaka Upanishad*: 'What is it that, being known, all else becomes known?' (1.1.3). The *Brihadaranyaka Upanishad* of the *Yajur Veda* reflects the quest for enlightenment in these lines:

> Lead me from the unreal to reality
> Lead me from darkness to light
> Lead me from death to immortality
> *Om*, let there be peace, peace, peace.

Significantly, in later centuries the 'higher wisdom' is not connected with any Vedic or book learning or conceptual knowledge. It is only through the experience of enlightenment that one is freed from the birth-and-death cycle.

Atman and Brahman

At the heart of this wisdom is experiential knowledge of the relationship between the human soul (**Atman**) and the Supreme Being (**Brahman**). Brahman pervades and yet transcends not only human thought but the universe itself. Ultimately, Brahman cannot be described any more than infinity can be contained.

To know Brahman is to enter a new state of consciousness. The *Taittiriya Upanishad* associates Brahman with existence or truth (*satya*), knowledge (*jnana*), infinity (*ananta*), consciousness (*chit*), and bliss (*ananda*); elsewhere Brahman is described as the hidden, inner controller of the human soul and the frame over which the universe is woven.

Many passages of the *Upanishads* discuss the relationship between Atman and Brahman, but invariably they suggest rather than specify the connection between the two. In one famous conversation in the *Chandogya Upanishad*, a father asks his son to dissolve salt in water and says that Brahman and Atman are united in a similar manner. The father ends his teaching with a famous dictum—*tat tvam asi* ('you are that')—in which 'that' refers to Brahman and 'you' to Atman. More than a thousand years later, philosophers still differed in their interpretations of this passage. For Shankara in the eighth century, 'you are that' indicated that Brahman and Atman were identical; for Ramanuja in the eleventh century it meant that the two were inseparably united but not identical.

We learn more of the relationship between Brahman and Atman elsewhere in the *Upanishads*. In some passages, the sage Yajnavalkya refers to Brahman as the hidden, inner controller of the human soul (Atman); in others, as the frame and the substance of the universe. In the latter analogy the reference is to a weaving loom: the universe is said to be woven over Brahman.

The *Upanishads* represent the beginnings of Hindu philosophical thought; in the opinion of some, they also represent the best. The quest for a unifying knowledge or higher wisdom is a recurring theme in various systems of Hindu philosophical reasoning, and it continues to preoccupy thinkers today.

Women in the Vedas

The *Upanishads* identify a number of women who participated in the quest for ultimate truth. These women were among the teachers through whom the sacred knowledge was transmitted. In the *Brihadaranyaka Upanishad*, for instance, Maitreyi, the wife of the sage Yajnavalkya, questions him in depth about the nature of reality, and a woman philosopher named Gargi Vachaknavi challenges him in a public debate. When he does not answer to her satisfaction, Gargi presses the question, and eventually she pronounces a judgment about him to her fellow philosophers, saying that he is indeed wise. Apparently Gargi and Maitreyi were honoured and respected for their wisdom, as were dozens of other women whose names appear in the *Veda*s.

Each of the *Upanishads* contains a list of teachers. In many cases the father of the teacher is mentioned, but in the *Brihadaranyaka Upanishad* (VI.5.1) roughly 45 teachers are identified with their mothers' names instead. So, while it is clear that a male spiritual lineage is generally accepted (after all, it is the male teachers who are being named), it is possible that some teachers received spiritual instruction from their mothers.

❧ CRYSTALLIZATION

Classical Hinduism

The literature that was composed after the Vedas, starting around 500 BCE, was recognized to be of human origin and was loosely called **smrti** ('that which is remembered'). Though theoretically of lesser authority than the 'revealed' *shruti*, this material was nonetheless considered inspired, and it has played a far more important role in the lives of Hindus for the last 2,500 years. There are three types of *smrti*: epics (*itihasas*), ancient stories (**Puranas**), and codes of righteous action and ethics (*dharmashastras*). (The term *smrti* can also refer to the codes alone.)

For many Hindus the phrase 'sacred books' refers specifically to two epics, the **Ramayana** ('Story of Rama') and the *Mahabharata* ('Great [Epic of] India' or 'Great [Sons of] Bharata'). The best-known works in the Hindu tradition, these stories are told to children by their parents and invariably constitute their first and most lasting encounter with Hindu scripture.

The Ramayana

The *Ramayana* has been memorized, recited, sung, danced, enjoyed, and experienced emotionally, intellectually, and spiritually for 2,500 years. A source of inspiration for countless generations, it is performed as theatre and as dance in places of Hindu (and Buddhist) cultural influence throughout Southeast Asia, and its characters are well known as far away as Cambodia, Thailand, and Indonesia.

The hero of the *Ramayana* is the young prince Rama, whose father, Dasaratha, has decided to abdicate in favour of his son. On the eve of the coronation, however, a heart-broken Dasaratha is forced to exile Rama because of an earlier promise made to one of his wives. Rama accepts cheerfully and leaves for the forest, accompanied by his beautiful wife Sita, and his half-brother Lakshmana, who both refuse to be separated from him. Bharata, the brother who has now been named king, returns from a trip to discover that Rama has gone into exile and his father has died of grief. He finds Rama and begs him to return, but Rama refuses because he feels he must respect his father's decision to banish him. He asks Bharata to rule as his regent.

While in the forest, Sita is captured by the demon king Ravana. Rama sets out to search for her with the aid of his brother and a group of monkeys led by Hanuman, a monkey with divine ancestry. It is Hanuman who finds Sita and reports her whereabouts to Rama, who, with the monkeys' help, goes to war with Ravana. After a long battle, Rama kills Ravana and is reunited with Sita. They eventually return to the capital and are crowned. A paragon of virtue, Rama is considered such a just king that *Ram rajya* ('kingdom or rule of Rama') is the Hindu political ideal.

Rama is also regarded as the ideal son and husband, but Sita too has been idealized both for her own qualities and for her relationship with her husband. In a sequel to the *Ramayana*, however, Rama's subjects begin to doubt Sita's virtue following her captivity in Ravana's grove. Because there is no way of proving her innocence, Rama banishes her, even though she is now pregnant. (In later centuries, this episode was given an additional inter-pretation, according to which Rama did not want to create a legal precedent for excusing a wife who has spent time in another man's home.)

The exiled Sita gives birth to twin boys. Years pass, and it is only when her sons are preparing to meet Rama in battle that Sita tells them he is their father. There is a brief reunion. Rama asks Sita to prove her innocence in public by undergoing some ordeal, but Sita refuses and asks Mother Earth to take her back. She is then swallowed by the ground.

Many Hindus have seen Sita as the ideal wife because she follows her husband into the forest. Others see her as a model of strength and virtue in her own right. She complies with her husband as he does with her; their love is one worthy of emulation. Yet she is also a woman who stands her ground when asked by her husband to prove her virtue. On one occasion she acquiesces, but the second time she gently but firmly refuses and so rules out any possibility of a reunion. There have been other versions of this tale called *Sitayana*, which tell the story from Sita's viewpoint. Even conservative commentators agree with the time-honoured saying '*sitayas charitam mahat*' ('the deeds of Sita are indeed great'). In later centuries Rama himself came to be seen as an incarnation of Vishnu. Temples dedicated to Rama and Sita are found in many parts of the world.

The **Mahabharata** *and the* **Bhagavad Gita**

With approximately 100,000 verses, the *Mahabharata* is said to be the longest poem in the world. It is not found in many homes, but many people own copies of an extract from it called the **Bhagavad Gita**.

The *Mahabharata* is the story of the great (*maha*) struggle among the descendants of a king named Bharata. The main part of the story concerns a war between the Pandavas and the

Kauravas. Though they are cousins, the Kauravas try to cheat the Pandavas out of their share of the kingdom and will not accept peace. A battle ensues in which all the major kingdoms are forced to take sides. Among the supporters of the Pandavas is Krishna, an **avatara** (incarnation) of the god Vishnu who is among the most beloved figures in Hinduism. Though Krishna refuses to take up arms, he agrees to serve as charioteer for the warrior Arjuna, who in later centuries would come to be seen as symbolizing the human soul in quest of salvation.

Just as the war is about to begin, Arjuna, who has until now been portrayed as a hero, becomes distressed at the thought of fighting his own kin. Putting down his bow, he asks Krishna whether it is correct to fight a war in which many lives will be lost. Krishna replies that it is correct to fight for what is right; one must try peaceful means, but if they fail one must fight for righteousness ('dharma'). In the conversation that follows, which unfolds across the 18 chapters of the *Gita*, Krishna instructs Arjuna on the nature of God and the human soul, and how to reach liberation.

One of the holiest books in the Hindu tradition, the *Gita* teaches loving devotion to Krishna and the importance of selfless action. It was probably written sometime between 200 BCE and 200 CE, and for centuries people learned it by heart. In verses that are still recited at Hindu funerals, Krishna describes the soul as existing beyond the reach of the mind and the senses, unaffected by physical nature. Just as human beings exchange old clothes for new ones, so the human soul discards one body and puts on another through the ages, until it acquires the knowledge that will free it forever from the cycle of birth and death.

The Three Ways to Liberation

In the course of the *Gita* Krishna describes three ways (or three aspects of a single way) to liberation from the cycle of birth and death: (1) the way of action, (2) the way of knowledge, and (3) the way of devotion. Each way (*marga*) is also a discipline (*yoga*).

From the *Bhagavad Gita*

On the immortality of the soul:

Our bodies are known to end, but the embodied self is enduring, indestructible, and immeasurable; therefore, Arjuna, fight the battle!

He who thinks this self a killer and he who thinks it killed, both fail to understand it does not kill, nor is it killed.

It is not born, it does not die; having been, it will never not be; unborn, enduring, constant, and primordial, it is not killed when the body is killed. . . .

As a man discards worn-out clothes to put on new and different ones, so the embodied self discards its worn-out bodies to take on other new ones.

Weapons do not cut it, fire does not burn it, waters do not wet it, wind does not wither it. It cannot be cut or burned; it cannot be wet or withered; it is enduring, all-pervasive, fixed, immovable, and timeless. . . .

(Miller 1986: 32).

The way of action (*karma yoga*) is the path of unselfish duty performed neither in fear of punishment nor in hope of reward. Acting with the expectation of future reward leads to bondage and unhappiness. If our hopes are disappointed we may respond with anger or grief, and even if we do receive the expected reward, we will not be satisfied for long. Soon that goal will be replaced with another, leading to further action—and further accumulation of karma, which only leads to further rebirth.

Krishna also explains the way of knowledge (*jnana yoga*): through scriptural knowledge, one may achieve a transforming wisdom that destroys one's past karma. True knowledge is an insight into the real nature of the universe, divine power, and the human soul. Later philosophers say that when we hear scripture, ask questions, clarify doubts, and eventually meditate on this knowledge, we achieve liberation.

The third way to liberation—and the one emphasized most throughout the *Gita*—is the way of devotion (*bhakti yoga*). Ultimately, Krishna promises Arjuna that if we surrender to him in loving devotion, he will forgive all our sins (*Gita* 18:66).

The Deities of Classical Hinduism

The period of the Gupta empire (c. 320–540) saw major advances on many fronts. As commercial activity increased, so did contact with Greek and Roman trade missions from the Mediterranean. In mathematics the concept of zero was introduced, along with the decimal system. Around 499 Aryabhatta is said to have calculated, in an approximate form, the value of pi (3.14) and established the length of the solar year (365.3586 days); he also proposed that the earth is spherical and rotates on its axis.

The Gupta period also saw a surge in religious and literary activity. Temple construction was encouraged, pilgrimages were undertaken, and playwrights used religious themes in their dramas. Hindus, Jainas, and Buddhists all composed poems and plays that reveal a great deal about religious trends of the time. Temple architecture, literature, astronomy, and astrology received royal patronage.

Under the Guptas, Buddhist influences receded and Hinduism came to dominate India. Eventually, some Hindu texts would even assimilate Siddhartha Gautama, the Buddha, as one of the incarnations of Vishnu.

Starting around 300 BCE and continuing until a little after 1000 CE, numerous texts known as *Puranas* (from the Sanskrit for 'old') were composed that retold the 'old tales' or ancient lore of the Hindu tradition, shifting the emphasis away from the major Vedic gods and goddesses in favour of other deities. In the Hindu tradition nothing is ever really discarded. Older deities or concepts may be ignored for centuries, but eventually they are discovered afresh. As we have seen, a prototype for Shiva may have existed as long ago as the ancient Harappa culture, and Vishnu was mentioned as a minor figure in the early Vedic hymns. These gods moved to the forefront in the first millennium of the Common Era. In the process, the Hindu tradition as we know it today crystallized.

Vishnu

Vishnu ('the all-pervasive one') is portrayed as coming to Earth in various forms, animal and human, to rid the world of evil and establish dharma or righteousness. In the first of these incarnations (*avataras*) he appears as a fish who saves Manu, the primeval man. This story was originally part of the Vedic literature, but it is expanded in the *Puranas*.

While bathing in a lake, Manu finds a small fish in his hand. The fish speaks to him and asks him to take it home and put it in a jar. The next day it has expanded to fill the jar. Now Manu is asked to put the fish in a lake, which it outgrows overnight, then into a river, and finally the ocean. The fish, who is really Vishnu, then tells Manu that a great flood is coming, and that he must build a boat and put his family in it, along with the seven sages or *rishis*, and 'the seeds of all the animals'. Manu does as he is told. When the flood sweeps the earth, those on the ship survive. This story is sharply reminiscent of flood myths in other religious traditions.

Eventually, Vishnu will have ten incarnations in the present cycle of creation. Nine are said to have already happened, and Vaishnavas (followers of Vishnu) expect the tenth at the end of this present age. Vishnu's seventh incarnation was Rama, the hero of the epic, and according to some narratives the ninth was the Buddha, who may have diverted attention away from Hindu teachings but is praised by some interpreters for the emphasis he gave to non-violence. In other texts Vishnu's ninth incarnation is Krishna, whom we have already met in the *Bhagavad Gita*. The *Puranas* tell other stories from the life of Krishna: the delightful infant, the mischievous toddler who steals the butter he loves, the youth who steals the hearts of the cowherd girls and dances away the moonlit nights in their company. Some of the later *Puranas* celebrate the love of Krishna and his beloved Radha.

Vishnu and his consort Lakshmi in the interval between the destruction of one universe and the beginning of the next, when Brahma will emerge from the lotus flower to carry out the work of creation. A painting from the Punjab hills, c. 1870 (© Victoria and Albert Museum, London).

Shiva

Like Vishnu, Shiva emerged as a great god in the post-Upanishadic era. Unlike Vishnu, however, he did not reveal himself sequentially, through a series of incarnations. Instead, according to Shaivas (his followers), Shiva expresses the manifold aspects of his power by appearing simultaneously in paradoxical roles: as creator and destroyer, exuberant dancer and austere yogi. The wedding portrait of Shiva and his divine consort, Parvati, is an important part of his tradition, and his creative energy is often represented in the symbolic form of a **linga** (a conical or cylindrical stone column). Popular throughout India, stories of Shiva and his local manifestations—for instance, as Sundaresvara in the city of Madurai—are beloved by Hindus.

The Goddess

Of the many goddesses who appeared in the Vedas, none was all-powerful. Likewise, the epics and the early *Puranas* honoured many consort goddesses, but no supreme female deity. It is only in the later *Puranas* that we begin to see explicit references to worship of a goddess not just as an appendage to a male deity but as the ultimate power, the creator of the universe and the redeemer of human beings. She was sometimes considered to be the *shakti* or power of Shiva, but frequently her independence from the male deity was stressed.

The great Goddess, or Devi, appears in multiple forms, though the lines between them are not always clearly defined (Western scholars tend to emphasize the distinctions, while Hindus generally blur them). The most familiar manifestation of the Goddess is Parvati, the wife of Shiva, though in this benevolent aspect she may also be called Amba (mother). Durga is her warrior aspect, represented iconographically with a smiling countenance and a handful of weapons. As Kali, the Goddess is fierce and wild, a dark, dishevelled figure who wears a garland of skulls; yet even in this manifestation, her devotees call her 'mother'. In addition there are countless local goddesses with distinctive names and histories who are all manifestations of the same Goddess.

Festivals like the autumn celebration of **Navaratri** ('nine nights') are dedicated to the Goddess, and millions of Hindus offer her fervent devotions every day. The continuing importance of the Goddess is a distinctive characteristic of the Hindu tradition.

Sarasvati

In the *Puranas* the Vedic goddess Sarasvati becomes the goddess of learning. Although she is the consort of a creator god named **Brahma** (a minor deity, not to be confused with Brahman), their relationship is not celebrated iconographically, as those of Vishnu and Lakshmi or Shiva and Parvati are.

Rather, Sarasvati seems to enjoy a certain autonomy: portraits usually depict her alone, without any male god. Clad in a white sari and a golden crown over flowing hair, radiant with wisdom, she sits gracefully on a rock beside a river. She has four hands; two of them hold a stringed musical instrument called a *vina*, another holds a string of beads, and the last holds a manuscript. The *vina* symbolizes music and the manuscript learning, while the beads signify the counting and recitation of holy names, which leads to transformative knowledge or wisdom.

It seems that writing was associated with pollution until well into the Common Era. Yet Sarasvati's manuscript came to symbolize her mastery of writing and books, and by the thirteenth century a library was called *Sarasvati bhandaram*, or 'the storehouse of Sarasvati'. Some texts also portray Sarasvati as the source of the **devanagari** script used for writing the Sanskrit language. All these themes coalesce in later Hindu tradition, yielding the composite picture of Sarasvati as the patron goddess of arts and education, music and letters.

Other Deities

A number of other gods are also very popular. Ganesha, the elephant-headed son of Shiva and Parvati, is probably the most beloved god in all of Hinduism. Seen as a remover of all obstacles and hindrances, he is the god that people look to for help in difficult situations, and no new project or venture begins without a prayer or an offering for him. Murugan, another son of Shiva, is popular in the Tamil region of South India. And the monkey god Hanuman (also known as Maruti), a model devotee of Rama and Sita, is everyone's protector.

In South India the major deities Vishnu, Shiva, and Devi are frequently known by local names. Thus in the Tirupati hills and Srirangam Vishnu is known as Venkateshwara ('lord of the Venkata hill') or Ranganatha ('lord of the stage' or *ranga*). Each manifestation has a unique personality and a mythical history that links it with a particular place. These myths are recorded in books called *Sthala Puranas* ('*Puranas* about the place'). Local manifestation is extremely important in Hinduism. Every village has its own deity, and though most can be traced to one or another of the pan-Indian deities, it can take considerable effort to connect those deities with pan-Indian gods and goddesses.

Hindu gods and goddesses come to earth to intervene on behalf of human beings. Thus in one of her incarnations the gracious Parvati, the consort of Shiva, is a princess named Meenakshi who benefits her subjects by beginning a new dynasty (the Pandyas, who ruled a kingdom of the same name in South India in the first millennium CE).

Sri or Lakshmi, the consort of Vishnu, is known as the mother of all creation, the goddess of good fortune, the bestower of wisdom and salvation. Many teachers have composed hymns celebrating her compassion, and she is worshipped by Jainas as well as Hindus.

The Hindu 'Trinity'

The notion of the *trimurti* ('three forms') seems to have been part of the Hindu tradition since at least the fourth century.

In the symbolism of *trimurti*, the three gods Brahma, Vishnu, and Shiva are sometimes represented as equal and sometimes coalesce into a single form with three faces. This has sometimes been interpreted as implying a polytheistic belief in three gods: Brahma the creator, Vishnu the preserver, and Shiva the destroyer. This interpretation does effectively bring together the three great functions of a supreme god and distribute them among three distinct deities. But it is more misleading than informative in two ways.

First, it suggests that Hindus give equal importance to all three gods. In practice, most sectarian Hindu worshippers focus their devotions on only one deity, whether Shiva, Vishnu, the Goddess (in one of her multiple forms), or a local deity who may be unknown in other parts of India. Such devotees consider the other deities important but secondary to their own faith and practice. Furthermore, although Vishnu and Shiva are certainly popular, Brahma has not been worshipped as a supreme deity for more than two millennia (and perhaps never was). Though portrayed in mythology as the creator god, he is only the agent of the supreme deity who created him; that deity, at whose pleasure Brahma creates the universe, may be Vishnu, Shiva, or the Goddess, depending on the worshipper's sect.

Second, the 'polytheistic' interpretation of *trimurti* suggests that creation, preservation, and destruction are functions that can be performed separately. Yet followers of Vishnu or Shiva commonly understand creation, preservation, and destruction to be three parts of an integrated process for which their own particular supreme god is responsible. In this context, destruction is neither unplanned nor final: it is simply one phase in the ongoing evolution and devolution of the universe. All of creation temporarily becomes one with Vishnu or Shiva until a new cycle of creation begins. The cycle of creation will continue as long as there are souls caught up in the wheel of life and death. It is in this sense that devotees of Shiva, Vishnu, or the Goddess see their own chosen deity as the creator, the maintainer, and the destroyer of the universe.

Caste and the *Laws of Manu*

'Caste' is used as a shorthand term to refer to the thousands of social and occupational divisions that have developed from the simple fourfold structure laid out in the 'Hymn to the Supreme Person': priests, rulers, merchants, and servants. There are more than one thousand *jatis* ('birth groups') in India, and people routinely identify themselves by their *jati*. Underlying this hierarchical system is the idea that people are born with different spiritual propensities. Ritual practices, dietary rules, and sometimes dialects differ between castes, and until recently, inter-caste marriages were relatively rare. Although the modern word 'caste' signifies both the four broad *varnas* and the minutely divided *jatis*, Western scholars sometimes translate *varna* as 'class' and *jati* as 'caste'.

By the first centuries of the Common Era, many treatises had been written regarding the nature of righteousness, moral duty, and law. These *dharmashastras* are the foundations of later Hindu laws. The most famous of them is the *Laws of Manu* (*Manava Dharmashastra*), attributed to the primordial man whom Vishnu saved from the flood. This particular treatise was probably written around the first century, for it reflects the social norms of that time: women have slipped to an inferior position from the relatively high status they enjoyed in the period of the Vedas, and the caste system is firmly in place.

The *dharmashastras* set out the roles and duties of the four principal castes that make up Hindu society: brahmins (priests and teachers), **kshatriyas** (rulers and warriors), **vaishyas** (merchants), and **shudras** (servants). The brahmins were (and are still) the priestly class, the only group in Hindu society authorized to teach the Vedas. Although not all members of the brahmin community were priests, all enjoyed the power and prestige associated with spiritual learning.

The dharma of the kshatriya class, who were permitted to study but not to teach the Vedas, was to protect the people and the country. In the Hindu tradition, past and present, lines of descent are all-important. Thus many kings sought to confirm their legitimacy by tracing their ancestry to one of the primeval progenitors of humanity—either the sun (*surya vamsa*) or the moon (*chandra vamsa*)—and even usurpers of thrones invoked divine antecedents.

Members of the merchant class (vaishyas) were responsible for most commercial transactions, as well as agricultural work, including the raising of cattle. The power of wealth and economic decisions lay with the vaishyas, who were also permitted to study the Vedas but not to teach them. Members of all three upper classes were generally called 'twice born', in reference to the initiatory rite in which young males were spiritually reborn as sons of their religious teachers. This rite, the **upanayana**, marked a boy's initiation into studenthood.

Finally, the lowest caste identified in the *dharmashastras* is the shudras. According to the texts, it is their duty to serve the other classes and they would not be permitted to accumulate wealth even if they had the opportunity to do so.

In practice, however, the rules were not followed strictly in all regions of India, and the caste system was far more complex and flexible than the *dharmashastras* suggest. For example, the Vellalas of South India were wealthy landowners who wielded considerable economic and political power, even though the brahmins considered them to belong to the shudra caste. The *dharmashastra* prohibitions do not seem to have had any effect on their fortunes.

Manu tells us that it is better to fulfill one's own dharma obligations imperfectly than to fulfill another person's dharma well (the *Bhagavad Gita* makes the same point). However, the law books acknowledge that in times of adversity one may perform tasks assigned to other classes. While the texts emphasize the importance of marrying within one's own caste, they recognize that mixed marriage is not uncommon, and so they go on to list the various subcastes produced by different caste combinations.

The caste system is such a strong social force in India that even non-Hindu communities such as Jainas, Sikhs, and Christians adopted it and still tend to marry within the same caste. In Southeast Asia, inscriptions after the eighth century show that Manu was known, as were the *varna* and *jati* systems; brahmins were honoured and several held high positions. In other respects, however, the caste system bears little resemblance to the Indian model. The caste system still functions to a limited extent in some diaspora communities, but it has been significantly diluted in North America.

Becoming a Brahmin

Nahusha asked Yudhishthira:
'Who can be said to be a brahmin, O King?'
Yudhishthira replied:
'O lord of Serpents! The one who is truthful,
is generous, is patient, is virtuous, has empathy,
is tranquil, and has compassion—such a person is a brahmin'
    (*Mahabharata Vana Parva*, 177.15, trans. Vasudha Narayanan).

❦ DIFFERENTIATION

Vedanta

Six schools of philosophy are recognized within the Hindu tradition—Samkhya, Nyaya, Vaisheshika, Mimamsa, Yoga, and Vedanta—and elements of all six can be seen in modern Hinduism. Some features of Yoga have attracted a wide popular following in recent years, but as a philosophical school Vedanta is by far the most important. Vedanta ('end of the Vedas') has engaged Hindu thinkers for more than a thousand years. Although the term 'Vedanta' traditionally denoted the *Upanishads*, in popular usage it more often refers to systems of thought based on a coherent interpretation of the *Upanishads* together with the *Bhagavad Gita* and the *Brahma Sutras* (a collection of roughly five hundred aphorisms summarizing the teachings of those texts).

An important early interpreter of Vedanta was Shankara (fl. c. 800). For him, reality is non-dual (**advaita**): the only reality is Brahman, and this reality is indescribable, without attributes. Brahman and Atman (the human soul) are identical; Shankara interprets the Upanishadic phrase 'you are that' in a literal way and upholds the unity of what most people perceive as two distinct entities. Under the influence of *maya* we delude ourselves into believing that we are different from Brahman, but when the illusion is dispelled, the soul is liberated by the realization of its true nature. Liberation, therefore, is the removal of ignorance and the dispelling of illusion through the power of transforming knowledge. That goal can be reached in this life; human beings can achieve liberation while still embodied (*jivanmukti*). Those liberated in this life act without binding desire and help others to achieve liberation. Final release, however, will come only after the death of the body.

Shankara also posits three levels of reality. He recognizes that human beings believe life is real, but points out that when we are asleep we also believe that what happens in our dreams is real. Only when we wake up do we discover that what we dreamt was not real. So too in this cycle of life and death, we believe that all we experience is real. And it is— until we are liberated and wake up to the truth about our identity. One might argue that there is a difference: that the dream seems true only to the individual dreamer, whereas the phenomenal world seems real to millions who seem to share the same reality. But the school of Shankara would say that our limited reality is the result of ignorance and illusion. With the transformative knowledge that the *Upanishads* speak of, we recognize that we are in reality Brahman and are liberated from the cycle of life and death. But that cycle goes on for the other souls still caught in the snares of *maya*.

Shankara's philosophy was criticized by later philosophers like Ramanuja and Madhva. One of their principal objections is connected with the status of *maya*: if *maya* is real, then there are *two* realities: Brahman and *maya*. If *maya* were unreal, Shankara's critics argue, surely it could not be the cause of the cosmic delusion attributed to it. Shankara tries to circumvent this objection by saying that *maya* is indescribable, neither real nor unreal, and his followers would say that in the ultimate state of liberation, which is totally ineffable, such criticisms are not valid in any case.

Ramanuja (traditionally 1017–1137) was the most significant interpreter of theistic Vedanta for the Sri Vaishnava community—the devotees of Vishnu and his consorts Sri

(Lakshmi) and Bhu (the goddess Earth)—in South India. Ramanuja proclaims the supremacy of Vishnu–Narayana and emphasizes that devotion to Vishnu will lead to ultimate liberation. He challenges Shankara's interpretation of scripture, especially regarding *maya*, and his belief that the supreme reality (Brahman) is without attributes. For Ramanuja, Vishnu (whose name literally means 'all-pervasive') is immanent throughout the universe, pervading all souls and material substances, but also transcending them. Thus from one viewpoint there is a single reality, Brahman; but from another viewpoint Brahman is qualified by souls and matter. Since the human soul is the body and the servant of the Supreme Being, liberation is portrayed not as the realization that the two are the same, but rather as the intuitive, joyful, and total realization of the soul's relationship with the lord.

The Sri Vaishnava community differs from other Hindu traditions in that it reveres as sacred not only Sanskrit texts like the Vedas, the epics, and the *Purana*s but also the Tamil compositions of the **Alvars**: a group of 12 South Indian poet-saints who lived between the eighth and tenth centuries CE. The community also considers the 108 temples that the Alvars glorified in their poems to be heaven on earth.

Yoga

Yoga is the physical and mental discipline through which practitioners 'yoke' their spirit to the divine. Many Hindu texts have held it in high regard, and the word has had many meanings in the history of the Hindu tradition. Its origins are obscure, though some scholars have pointed out that seals from the Harappan culture portray a man sitting in what looks like a yogic position.

A crucial aspect of yoga practice is learning to control the body and the mind. Perfection in concentration (*dharana*) and meditation (*dhyana*) lead to *samadhi*: absorption into and experiential knowledge of the divine. There are various stages of *samadhi*, but the ultimate stage is complete emancipation from the cycle of life and death. This state is variously described as a coming together, uniting, and transcending of polarities; empty and full, neither life nor death, and yet both. In short, this final liberation cannot be adequately described in human language.

'Yoga' is often used in a general way to designate any form of meditation and in the broadest terms it may refer to any path that leads to final emancipation. Thus the *Bhagavad Gita* refers to the way of action as *karma yoga* and the way of devotion as *bhakti yoga*. In the popular understanding, the eight 'limbs' of classical yoga are not present; *bhakti yoga* simply comes to mean the way of devotion. Recent decades have seen increasing interest in the physical aspects of yoga, especially in the West, but that interest does not always extend to the psychological and theoretical foundations of the practice.

Tantra

The tantric component of the Hindu tradition is hard to define, partly because advocates and detractors portray it in very different lights. **Tantra** refers both to a body of ritual practices and to the texts prescribing and interpreting them, which are said to be independent of the Vedic tradition.

'Tantra' may be derived come from a root word meaning 'to stretch' or 'expand'. It began to gain importance in the Hindu and Buddhist traditions in about the fifth century. Some scholars believe it originated in the indigenous culture of the subcontinent and re-emerged more than a millennium after the Aryan migration. Others see it as a later development external (though not in opposition) to the Vedic tradition. A number of other movements within Hinduism, including Shaivism and Vaishnavism, incorporated elements of tantra in their own practice. For example, when images of deities are installed in temples, large geometric drawings (*mandalas*) representing gods or goddesses and the cosmos are drawn on the floor and used as objects of meditation and ritual.

Tantrism developed its own forms of yoga, and some tantra texts focus on practices connected with the *kundalini,* centred on the *shakti* or power of the Goddess, which is said to lie coiled like a serpent at the base of the spine. When awakened, this power rises through six chakras or 'wheels' within the body to reach the final chakra under the skull known as the thousand-petalled lotus.

The ultimate aim of this form of yoga is to awaken the power of the *kundalini* and allow it to unite with the divine which resides in the thousand-petalled lotus. When this union is achieved, the practitioner is granted visions and psychic powers that eventually lead to emancipation (*moksha*).

There are many forms of tantrism, but the main division is between the 'left-handed' and 'right-handed' schools. As the left hand was considered inauspicious, the term 'left-handed' was applied to movements that did not meet with the approval of the larger or more established schools. 'Left-handed' practices centred on the ritual performance of activities forbidden in everyday life, such as drinking liquor, eating fish and meat, and having sexual intercourse with a partner other than one's spouse. These activities were disapproved of in many other Hindu circles, so that to a large extent left-handed tantrism remained esoteric. The 'right-handed' school was more conservative and parts of it are integrated into domestic and temple rituals.

One may also see divisions in tantra along sectarian lines: the Shaiva, Shakta, and Vaishnava communities all have their own canons of texts called *tantras*.

Ayurvedic Medicine

Medicine made great progress in the Hindu world in the first millennium. One of the most important systems was called **Ayurveda**: the *veda* (knowledge) of enhancing life. The physician or *vaidya* ('one who is learned') promotes both longevity and quality of life. The prototype is a deity called Dhanavantari, sometimes identified as an incarnation of Vishnu. The South Indian parallel to Ayurveda is the Tamil system called Siddha.

At some time during or after the last three centuries BCE, the surgeon Sushruta and the physician Charaka presented theories that they claimed had been transmitted to them by the gods. These teachings reflected an understanding of illness as a lack of balance among three elements: air, phlegm, and bile. This analytic approach recalls Greek and Chinese medical theories of roughly the same period. The *Sushruta Samhita* begins by declaring that the physician's aim is 'to cure the diseases of the sick, to protect the healthy, to pro-long life', while the *Charaka Samhita* includes a detailed statement of the ethics required of a physician. In these respects, the ancient roots of Ayurvedic medicine seem strikingly modern.

Today in India, Ayurveda serves as a bridge between modern international medicine and traditional Indian religio-philosophical theories. Ayurvedic clinical practice relies on specific remedies and therapies, just as modern medicine does, while Ayurvedic theory draws on elements of tantra and yoga. It shares their outlook on life and the world, but puts greater emphasis on health than on spiritual attainment.

Hinduism in Southeast Asia

Hindu culture today is associated almost exclusively with the Indian peninsula, but its influence can still be found across Southeast Asia. Archeological evidence suggests that extensive trade links were established by the second century CE, and both Hindu and Buddhist texts in India refer to Southeast Asia as the land of gold (*suvarna bhumi*) and gems. Chinese texts from about the third century CE refer to kings of Funan (a kingdom in ancient Cambodia) with Indian names. Sanskrit inscriptions are seen in the Khmer empire beginning about the late fifth century CE. Until the fourteenth century, Hindu narratives and temple-building traditions were popular across much of Southeast Asia, especially in Cambodia.

Cultural connections between India and Southeast Asia were also widespread. Many Sanskrit inscriptions and thousands of icons and sculptures portraying Hindu deities indicate that Hindu influences were pervasive in Cambodia, Thailand, Laos, Vietnam, Java, Indonesia, and Bali. Most of the popular Hindu deities are seen in temple iconography all over Southeast Asia. While the features and clothing are distinctively local in texture, the attributes, weapons, and other iconographic signifiers clearly identify them as the Hindu deities. One of the largest Hindu temples in the world is Angkor Wat, built by King Suryavarman II in the twelfth century CE and dedicated to Vishnu. And kings and queens of Cambodia had names reminiscent of Indian–Hindu royalty—names such as Jayavarman, Indravarman, Mahendravarman, and Indira-Lakshmi.

One of the most widely worshipped deities across Southeast Asia was Shiva. In the *Puranas*, the river Ganga is said to reside in the hair of Shiva, but other narratives refer to the river itself as a deity, a consort of Shiva. Local rivers in Cambodia came to be considered holy, among them the rivers flowing from a hill called Phnom Kulen (near Siem Reap, Cambodia), to irrigate Angkor. The sacred nature of these rivers was proclaimed in carvings made on rocks on their banks, which emphasized their identification with the Ganga.

Carvings of Vishnu, in various incarnations, can also be found in temples across South and Southeast Asia. Endowments were made to Vishnu temples as early as the fifth century CE, when, according to inscriptions, Queen Kulaprabhavati made major donations in Cambodia. Knowledge of Indian Vaishnava texts, including the two epics, was widespread, at least among the elite, and even though Shaivism and other forms of Hinduism were largely displaced by Buddhism by the fifteenth century, the *Ramayana* continues to thrive through the performing arts. The Prambanan temple near Yogyakarta, Indonesia, is just one of many in the region whose walls are carved with scenes from the *Ramayana* and the *Puranas*.

The Prambanan temple also has shrines for Brahma and Vishnu, although the main shrine is dedicated to Shiva. In fact, most of the temples in Southeast Asia were home to more than one deity: Shiva, Vishnu, and Devi—the great goddess—were frequently worshipped in the same building. Sectarian affiliation and devotion to either Shiva or Vishnu seems to have been flexible within families as well.

A combination of Vishnu and Shiva named Hari-Hara was popular in Cambodia. Portrayed in relief in the Badami caves (c. sixth century CE, Karnataka) but otherwise little known, Hari-Hara appears in many Cambodian inscriptions after the seventh century; we also see him represented in many icons. In addition, icons of other deities including Brahma, Vishnu, Shiva, Ganesha, Murugan, Nandi (a bull sacred to Shiva), Garuda (the 'eagle mount' of Vishnu), and the nine planets worshipped by Hindus have been found all over Southeast Asia. A few inscriptions also refer to amalgamated deities such as Ardha-narisvara (a combination of Shiva and his consort Parvati).

We can also note the importance attributed to biological ancestry. Many inscriptions, especially in Cambodia, trace matrilineal as well as patrilineal descent. Particular pride was taken in brahmin ancestors who were learned in the Vedas; the title *vrahmana* (Sanskrit *brahmana*, a

A statuette of Ganesha from Malaysia (©Fred de Noyelle/ Godong/Corbis).

brahmin) is attached to some names in Khmer. Yet despite the great respect shown to the brahmins in Cambodian (as well as Thai) culture, the caste system as we know it in India did not exist in that region. It may be that the caste system in Cambodia was largely ceremonial, or of relevance only to brahmins and royalty.

There seems to have been a strong matrilineal tendency in Cambodia; whether this was a local phenomenon or imported from South India is impossible to say. The famous inscription called the Sdok Kak Thom (c. 1052), one of the most important sources of information about Cambodian culture, speaks of generations of kings and priests, some of whom inherited their offices through the maternal line. Many women seem to have held royal offices, and they certainly executed many pious and charitable works. Inscriptions refer to several queens—Indra-lakshmi, Kambuja-raja-lakshmi, and Jayaraja-devi—who apparently wielded considerable power. Claims to the throne seem to have been made by royal women as well as men.

Although Hinduism is not practised widely in Southeast Asia today, except in Indonesia and by immigrants in other places, cultural traditions associated with the tradition still linger. Dances with Indian themes, particularly stories connected with the *Ramayana* and Tamil works such as the *Manimekalai* (c. second to fifth centuries CE) are part of almost every cultural event, and names of Indian origin are still common among people in Indonesia, Thailand, and Cambodia.

South Indian Devotion (*Bhakti*)

The standard portrait of Vedic and classical Hinduism is based on the culture of the northern part of the Indian subcontinent. But South India—that is, the region south of the Vindhya mountains—had a flourishing cultural life of its own by 400 BCE and possibly earlier. It was here that an entirely new type of Hindu devotion (**bhakti**) emerged and spread throughout India.

A sophisticated body of literature in the Tamil language existed two thousand years ago. Its earliest components are several poems on secular themes that are thought to have been composed at the time of three great Tamil academies. Known as the *Sangam* (Academy) poems, they fall into two groups: one dealing with the outer (*puram*) world of warfare, the valour of kings, chivalry, and honour, the other with the inner (*akam*) world of love and romance, of secret meetings, anguished separation, and the overwhelming joy of union.

The Tamil language has a long history of sophisticated poetry, drama, and grammatical analysis. The earliest extant Tamil composition shows some undeniable similarities to Sanskrit literature, and the early poems of love and war include many words borrowed from Sanskrit. Tamil literature on the whole, however, is neither imitative of nor derived from early Sanskrit material.

The oldest collections of Tamil poems, known as the *Ettutokai* (Eight Anthologies) and the *Pattupattu* (Ten Songs) were probably composed between the first and the third centuries. Lost for more than a thousand years, they were rediscovered in the nineteenth century. Five basic situations or moods are associated with five distinct landscape settings (*tinai*). Thus in the *akam* poems the seashore represents separation between lovers, and a jasmine flower symbolizes a woman patiently waiting for her beloved. The underlying meaning of each poem would have been instantly clear to the audiences that heard it recited.

The *bhakti* movement represented a major shift in Hindu culture. It arose sometime around the sixth century, when poet-devotees of Vishnu and Shiva began travelling from temple to temple singing the praises of their chosen deity not in formal Sanskrit but in Tamil—the mother tongue of the people, the language of intimacy and powerful emotion. By the twelfth century, 75 of these devotees had been recognized as saints: 63 devotees of Shiva known as the Nayanmars ('masters') and 12 devotees of Vishnu known as the Alvars ('those "immersed deep" in the love of Vishnu').

Composed between the seventh and ninth centuries, the vernacular songs of the Alvars were introduced into the temple liturgy as early as the tenth century—contrary to orthodox claims that Sanskrit was the exclusive vehicle for revelation and theological communication. Moreover, brahmin theologians honoured their authors as ideal devotees. This response was extraordinarily significant, for some of the Alvars came from lower-caste (perhaps even outcaste) backgrounds and one of them—Andal—was a woman. Selections from their works, collected in the eleventh century as the *Nalayira Divya Prabandham*, or *Sacred Collect of Four Thousand Verses*, are recited daily in temples and in homes by the Sri Vaishnava community, which considers them the Tamil equivalents of the Sanskrit Vedas.

The poems of the Alvars follow the literary conventions of earlier Tamil poetry, incorporating the symbols of the *akam* and *puram* poems. Vishnu is seen as a lover and a king, both accessible and remote, gracious and grand. In their songs of devotion, the Alvars seek from Vishnu both the embrace of the beloved and the protection of the king.

Many incidents from the *Ramayana*, *Mahabharata*, and *Puranas* make their way into the Alvars' songs, along with some stories not found in any of these sources. Above all, the poets emphasize the supremacy of Vishnu-Narayana, whose incarnations—sometimes as Rama, sometimes as Krishna—attest both to his power and to his desire to save. Sometimes the Alvars identify themselves with characters from the epics or the *Puranas*, expressing their longing for Vishnu by speaking in the voice of one who is separated from Rama or Krishna. A royal devotee of Rama, Kulacekara Alvar imagines the grief felt by Dasaratha, the father of Rama, after banishing his son to the forest:

> Without hearing him call me 'Father' with pride and with love,
> Without clasping his chest adorned with gems to mine,
> Without embracing him, without smoothing his forehead,
> Without seeing his graceful gait, majestic like the elephant,
> Without seeing his face [glowing] like the lotus,
> I wretched one,
> having lost my son, my lord,
> Still live.
>   (*Perumal Tirumoli 9.6*)

Many of the Tamil saints, both Vaishnava and Shaiva, travelled all over South India and parts of the north, visiting temples in which their chosen deity was enshrined and 'present'. In this way pilgrimage became an important feature of the Hindu tradition, and as the character of Vishnu or Shiva varied from one region to another, individual places became associated with different stories of the lord himself.

Eventually, 108 sites came to be known as sacred places in which Vishnu abides, and the number was even higher for Shiva. However, followers of the Vira ('heroic') Shaiva tradition, which developed in what is now the state of Karnataka, in the twelfth century, rejected temple worship and expressed their devotion to Shiva symbolically, by carrying a small *linga*. The *vachanas*, or sayings, of the Vira Shaiva poet-saints—who included a woman, Akka Mahadevi—made explicit their contempt for the caste system.

Classical Carnatic Music

Music has been part of Hindu worship ever since the time of the *Vedas*. The mystical syllable *om* was considered the beginning of sound in the universe and a manifestation of the Supreme Being. Knowledge of the nature of sound and its proper expression was therefore considered to be religious knowledge. The *Vedas* specify the particular pitch and tone in which the verses were to be recited or—in the case of the *Sama Veda*—sung. The exalted status of the latter was probably a reflection of the musical quality of the melodies prescribed for its hymns.

Classical music was for the most part religious in nature. Treatises on music refer to a divine line of teachers, frequently beginning with the deities Shiva and Parvati, and

From the Songs of Andal

Andal ('she who rules') was an eighth-century Alvar who is worshipped in many South Indian temples dedicated to Vishnu. Her passionate poetry is still recited and sung by the Vaishnava community today, and is broadcast over every radio station in Tamilnadu and Karnataka in the month of December. Tradition says that she refused to marry and longed for union with Vishnu—a wish that her biographers claim was fulfilled. Thus in her life as well as her work Andal represents a radical alternative to Manu's view of women and their role. Icons of Andal are found in major temples throughout the South Indian diaspora.

A thousand elephants circle,
as Narana, Lord of virtues,
walks in front of me.
Golden jars brim with water;
Festive flags and pennants fly through this town,
eager to welcome him—
I saw this in a dream, my friend!
Drums beat happy sounds; conches were blown.
Under the canopy strung heavy with pearls,
Madhusuda, my love, filled with virtue,
came and clasped the palm of my hand
I saw this in a dream, my friend!
Those with eloquent mouths recited the good Vedas,
With mantras they placed
the green leaves and the grass in a circle.
The lord, strong as a raging elephant,
softly held my hand as we circled the fire.
I saw this in a dream, my friend!
    (*Nachchiyar Tirumoli* 1.1 and 1.6–7; trans. Vasudha Narayanan)

honour Sarasvati as the patron goddess of the fine arts. Bharata's *Natya Sastra*, a classical text on dance and mime composed around the beginning of the Common Era, speaks of the performing arts as a spiritual path to liberation. Some later *Puranas*, such as the *Brhaddharma*, say that Vishnu and Sri (Lakshmi) are manifested as Nada Brahman or the Supreme Being in the form of sound.

Properly controlled and articulated, sound itself could lead to mystical experience. Thus the sound of a hymn was considered no less important than the words. *Nadopasana*, meditation through sound, became a popular religious practice. The Alvars composed their poems to be sung and danced. Many devotional poet-composers addressed their songs to the deities.

What we know today as carnatic music—the classical music of South India—began to take its distinctive present form in the fifteenth century, when the musicians Purandaradasa and Annamacharya introduced a number of new *ragas* (musical modes based on specific scales) accompanied by particular rhythmic beats. As devotees of Vishnu in particular sacred places (Pandharpur in Maharashtra and Tirupati in Andhra Pradesh), they developed these new *ragas* to sing his praises.

This form of music was raised to new heights in the eighteenth century by three musicians who apparently never met one another, although they were all born in the same village in Tamilnadu at about the same time. Diksitar wrote in praise of Parvati, while Shyama Shastri composed some three hundred songs devoted mainly to the Goddess. The third, Tyagaraja (1767–1847), composed intensely moving songs in praise of Rama, became the most renowned poet-musician of South India, and is considered one of the world's greatest composers.

Tyagaraja became an ascetic towards the end of his life. In his songs, *bhakti* is the means by which the devotee seeks to approach Rama. Finally, though, the joy of the song and the experience of devotion become ends in themselves:

> Devotion steeped in the nectar
> of melodious tones and modes
> Is the celestial bliss,
> O my heart and soul
>   (Jackson 1991: 334).

Tyagaraja's music is still sung at wedding concerts, songfests, on radio and television broadcasts, and in many homes today; internet sites also carry a wide selection of his compositions. Every spring, South Indian Hindus in America hold music festivals in his honour.

North Indian *Bhakti*

The *bhakti* tradition that began in South India gradually spread to the north. Under the Islamic sultanate established in Delhi in the twelfth century, relations between Muslims and Hindus were sometimes hostile, and several Hindu temples were looted and razed to the ground. On the other hand, the synergy made possible by the coming together of cultural influences from the Middle East and India gave rise to extraordinary innovations in all the arts, from music and dance to poetry and architecture, under the patronage of both Muslim and Hindu rulers.

North Indian *bhakti* resembled its southern counterpart both in its use of vernacular languages and in the fact that it was open to people of every caste, from high to low. The two differed, however, in the focus of their devotion. South Indian *bhakti* was generally addressed to either Vishnu or Shiva in the particular form in which he manifests himself in a local temple, but in the north the object of devotion was often one of Vishnu's avataras—either Rama or Krishna—or even the divine being without a form. The sometimes synergistic relationship that developed between Hindus and Muslims in northern India was reflected in the delightful, sometimes poignant works composed in the vernacular by poet-singers of the Sant ('holy person' or 'truth') tradition.

Emphasizing the *nirguna* ('without attributes') Brahman of the *Upanishads*, the Sants held the divinity to be without form. Hence their worship had nothing to do with physical images, and—unlike the Tamil poet-saints, who travelled from temple to temple precisely in order to express their devotion to local manifestations of their chosen deity—they expressed their devotion either in poetry or in silent meditation. At the same time they rejected distinctions between religious communities. Among the most important Sant poets was Kabir, a Hindu weaver from Varanasi whose life is said to have spanned more than a hundred years (1398–1518). In his insistence that God is beyond the particularities of any religious community, Kabir had much in common with a Punjabi religious leader named Nanak (1469–1539) and a Sufi Muslim teacher named Dadu (1544–1603). All three men attracted followers but Nanak's disciples—the Sikhs—ultimately formed a separate community. Kabir was one of several Sant poets whose works became part of the Sikh scripture.

An early exponent of Krishna devotion was the twelfth-century poet Jayadeva, who is thought to have lived in the city of Puri on the Bay of Bengal. His Sanskrit work *Gita Govinda* ('Song of the Cowherd') extols the love of Radha and Krishna; it also contains a reference to the Buddha as an incarnation of Krishna–Vishnu, filled with compassion.

Two other important poets in North India were Surdas and Tulsidas. Surdas (c. 1483–1563), who settled just south of Delhi near Agra, was a blind singer and poet whose compositions are in a dialect of Hindi. In his *Sursagar,* Krishna is the mischievous butter thief, but also the irresistible flute player, and the verses celebrate Radha's affection for him as a model of *bhakti.* Tulsidas (1543?–1623) is perhaps best-known for his *Lake of the*

From Kabir

Go naked if you want,
Put on animal skins.
What does it matter till you see the inward Ram?
If the union yogis seek
Came from roaming about in the buff,
Every deer in the forest would be saved. . . .
Pundit, how can you be so dumb?
You're going to drown, along with all your kin
Unless you start speaking of Ram.
Vedas, Puranas—why read them?
It's like loading an ass with sandalwood!
Unless you catch on and learn how Ram's name goes,
How will you reach the end of the road?
You slaughter living beings and call it religion:
Hey brother, what would irreligion be?
'Great Saint'—that's how you love to greet each other:
Who then would you call a murderer?
Your mind is blind. You've no knowledge of yourselves.
Tell me, brother, how can you teach anyone else?
Wisdom is a thing you sell for worldly gain,
So there goes your human birth—in vain.
   (Hawley and Juergensmeyer 1988: 50–1)

Deeds of Rama, a retelling or translation of the ever-popular *Ramayana* in verses that have their own beauty and have inspired hundreds of traditional storytellers and millions of Rama devotees in Hindi-speaking areas. Large sections of this work are learned by heart: sidewalk vendors, shopkeepers, housewives, and learned people can all quote from it even today ,and this version became the basis for TV blockbuster in the late twentieth century.

Finally, a Bengali contemporary of Surdas was Chaitanya (1486–1583) who taught that the only way to liberation is through trusting devotion to a loving and gracious deity .

For Chaitanya, however, the ultimate goal was not liberation from attachment in the traditional sense but rather the active enjoyment of his intense spiritual love of Krishna—a passionate love like the one that the cowherd girls felt for him. Chaitanya is said to have led people through the streets, singing about his lord and urging others to join him in chanting Krishna's names. Eventually, many of his followers came to believe that Krishna and Radha were present in Chaitanya himself.

Chaitanya's movement had waned somewhat by the late nineteenth century, but it was revived by several teachers. Among them was Abhay Charan De (1896–1977), who took the name A.C. Bhaktivedanta and carried the lineage abroad, launching the International Society for Krishna Consciousness—better known as the Hare Krishna movement—in New York in 1966. Both its theology, locating divine grace in Krishna, and its practice, centred on devotional chanting, can be traced directly to Chaitanya.

What has been the legacy of the *bhakti* movement? With its spread, the message of the Sanskrit scriptures was reinforced by powerful devotional works, many of which have come to function as scripture themselves. Composed in vernacular languages, these poems and songs offer the faithful far more guidance, inspiration, consolation, hope, and wisdom than the Vedas have ever done. This is not to say that the vernacular literature of the poet-saints is at variance with the Vedas. Rather, it is perceived as making the message of the Vedas accessible to everyone, inspiring devotion and preparing devotees to receive the shower of divine grace.

Reform and Revival

It was the Portuguese explorer Vasco da Gama (1469–1524) who fulfilled Columbus' ambition of finding a sea route to India from Europe. When he landed in Calicut, on the western coast of India in 1498, he opened the way to the Indian subcontinent for a long line of traders, missionaries, and eventually rulers. Before long the Dutch, English, and French were also travelling to India and establishing settlements there. Early European scholarship in Indian languages, especially Sanskrit, led to speculation on the movements of the Indo-European people from Central Asia. Studies in comparative philology pioneered the theory of a common Indo-European ancestry. In time, the foreign powers became involved in local politics, and possession of territory became one of their goals. As the Mughal empire disintegrated in the early eighteenth century, many chieftains attempted to acquire parcels of land and to enlist English or French help in their efforts. Eventually large parts of the Indian subcontinent were loosely united under British control.

In the past, most Hindu and Muslim rulers had accepted a large degree of local autonomy, but the British felt a moral and political obligation to govern and impose sweeping changes without regard to local tradition or practice. At the same time, foreign missionaries were severely critical both of what they saw as Hindu 'idolatry' and of the caste system and practices such as *sati*. The foreigners were not the only ones to call for change, however. Some Hindu intellectuals were equally convinced of the need for reform. Among them was Ram Mohan Roy.

The Brahmo Samaj

Ram Mohan Roy (1772–1833), born in western Bengal, eventually joined the East India Company. He became familiar with Western social life and the Christian scriptures and formed close ties with members of the Unitarian movement. Roy rejected the Christian belief in Jesus as the son of God, but admired him as a compassionate human being, and in 1820 he published a book called *The Precepts of Jesus: The Guide to Peace and Happiness*, in which he emphasized the compatibility of Jesus' moral teachings with the Hindu tradition.

Roy believed that if Hindus could read their own scriptures they would recognize that practices such as **sati** were not part of classical Hinduism and had no place in Hindu society. Therefore he translated extracts from Sanskrit texts into Bengali and English and distributed his translations for free. In 1828 he established a society to hold regular discussions on the nature of Brahman as it appears in the *Upanishads*. This organization, which came to be called the Brahmo Samaj ('congregation of Brahman'), emphasized monotheism, rationalism, humanism, and social reform. Although Roy rejected most of the stories from the epics and the *Puranas* as myths that stood in the way of reason and social reform, he drew on the Vedas, particularly the *Upanishads*, to defend Hinduism against missionary attacks. At the same time, with the Unitarians, he accused the missionaries, who believed in the Christian Trinity, of straying away from monotheism. A pioneer in the area of women's rights, including the right to education, he fought to abolish *sati*, founded new periodicals, and established educational institutions.

The Brahmo Samaj has never become a 'mainstream' movement. Nevertheless, it revitalized Hinduism at a critical time in its history by calling attention both to inhumane practices and to the need for education and reform, and in so doing it played a major part in the modernization of Indian society.

The Arya Samaj

The Arya Samaj was established in 1875 by Dayananda Sarasvati (1824–83). Having left home to avoid an arranged marriage, he spent 15 years as a wandering yogi. Then he met and studied Sanskrit under a charismatic guru named Virajananda who believed that the only true Hindu scriptures were the early Vedas and rejected as false all later additions to Hindu tradition, including the worship of images. On leaving his teacher, Dayananda promised that he would work to reform Hinduism in accordance with the true teachings of the Vedas.

Dayananda believed that the Vedas were literally revealed by God, and that the vision of Hinduism they presented could be revived if later human accretions such as votive rituals were stripped away and young people were taught their true Vedic heritage. To that end, he founded many educational institutions. He also believed that the Vedic teachings were not at variance with science or reason. Rejecting an anthropomorphic vision of the divine, he believed that the human soul is in some way coeval with the deity. In his view, the ideal was not renunciation but a full, active life of service to other human beings: working to uplift humanity in itself would promote the welfare of both the body and the soul.

The Ramakrishna Movement

Ramakrishna Paramahamsa (1836–86; born Gadadhar Chatterjee) was a Bengali raised in the Vaishnava *bhakti* tradition, cultivating ecstatic trance experiences. In his early twenties he was employed as a priest by a wealthy widow who was building a temple to the goddess Kali; by his account, he experienced the Divine Mother as an ocean of love. From the age of 25 he took instruction in tantra as well as Vedanta. He concluded that all religions lead in the same direction and that all are equally true.

Following his death, his disciples in Calcutta formed the Ramakrishna Mission to spread his eclectic ideas. Among those disciples was Swami Vivekananda (Narendranath Datta, 1862–1902), a former member of the Brahmo Samaj who believed that Western science could help India make material progress, while Indian spirituality could help the West along the path to enlightenment. As a Hindu participant in the 1893 World's Parliament of Religions in Chicago, and subsequently as a lecturer in America and Europe, he presented an interpretation of Shankara's non-dualist (*advaita*) Vedanta in which Brahman is the only reality. As a consequence of the attention he attracted, it was this philosophy that the West generally came to consider the definitive form of Hinduism.

Under Vivekananda's leadership the movement established a monastic order and a philanthropic mission, both dedicated to humanitarian service. In keeping with Ramakrishna's ecumenical vision, it encouraged non-sectarian worship. It also ignored caste distinctions, opening hundreds of educational and medical institutions for the welfare of all. The Ramakrishna movement's introduction of a Hindu presence into this field of activity was particularly significant because until then most of India's new medical and educational institutions had been run by Christian missionaries.

The monastic wing of the movement maintains that renunciation promotes spiritual growth. Unlike other monastic orders, however, it insists that its members should not be isolated ascetics, but should live in and for the world, giving humanitarian service to others.

✣ PRACTICE

The Sacred Syllable *Om*

The word *om* is recited at the beginning and end of all Hindu and Jaina prayers and recitations of scripture; it is used by Buddhists as well, particularly in Tibetan Vajrayana. The word is understood to have three sounds, *a–u–m*, with the diphthong *au* producing an *o* sound. The sound of *om*, which begins deep in the body and ends at the lips, is considered auspicious. Its history in the Hindu tradition is ancient; the *Mandukya Upanishad* discusses its meaning and power. Hindu philosophers and sectarian communities all agree that *om* is the most sacred sound.

According to followers of the philosopher Shankara—that is, non-dualist interpreters of Vedanta—each of the three sounds *a*, *u*, and *m* has its own specific experiential meaning:

- *A* stands for the world that we see when we are awake, the person who is experiencing it, and the waking experience.
- *U* stands for the dream world, the dreamer, and the dream experience.
- *M* represents the sleep world, the sleeper, and the sleep experience.

In addition to these three states that we experience on earth, a fourth, unspoken syllable represents the state of liberation.

Some Vaishnava devotees, on the other hand, say that *a* represents Vishnu, *u* denotes the human being, and *m* represents the relationship between the two. Other Vaishnavas say that the sounds represent Vishnu, Sri, and the devotee. Thus Hindus agree that *om* is the most sacred sound, but they interpret it in multiple ways. In a sense, then, the sound of *om* is a whole greater than the sum of its parts, exceeding in significance the many meanings attributed to it.

Temple Worship

There is nothing in the Vedic literature to suggest that temples existed in that era, despite the evidence that the Harappa culture may have set some buildings apart for worship and treated some figures as icons. When exactly temples began to play a role in Hindu worship is uncertain. However, cave carvings of Vishnu and icons of Shiva found in Madhya Pradesh suggest that worship was taking place at public shrines by the early fifth century. Today temples are a common feature of the Indian landscape, with many regional variations in architecture and patterns of worship.

Deities in Hindu temples are treated like kings and queens. (The Tamil word for temple is *koil*, 'house of the king'.) The *murtis*—variously translated as 'idols', 'icons', 'forms', or 'objects to be worshipped'—are given ritual baths, adorned, carried in procession, and honoured with all the marks of hospitality offered to royal guests, including canopies to shelter them, fans to keep them cool, and music and dance to entertain them. Wedding rituals between the god and goddess are celebrated, and the Srirangam temple alone is the site of special festivities on 250 days of the year.

Devotees believe that the presence of the deity in the temple does not detract from his or her presence in heaven, immanence in the world, or presence in a human soul. The deity is always complete and whole, no matter how many forms he or she may be manifest in at any given time. Generally, in Hinduism, there is no tradition of congregational prayer in the style of Christian or Muslim worship. Rather, the priest prays on behalf of devotees, presents offerings of fruit, flowers, or coconut to the deity, and then gives back some of the blessed objects to the devotees. The food thus presented is considered ennobled because it is now *prasada* (literally 'clarity', but meaning 'divine favour'), a gift from the deity. Traditionally, Hindu priests have been primarily ritual specialists rather than counsellors, though they may be taking on a more pastoral role today in the Americas.

Because there are so many philosophical and sectarian traditions within Hinduism, understandings of the *murti* vary widely. Many Hindus believe that, once consecrated, the image in the temple becomes not a symbol but the actual deity, fully present and accessible to devotees. The image in the temple, then, is a direct analogue to the incarnation (*avatara*) of Vishnu as Rama or Krishna in times past. Others, however, believe that the image in a temple is only a symbol of a higher reality, and some—including members of the Brahmo Samaj and Vira Shaiva movements—have rejected images altogether. Adherents of Shankara's non-dual Vedanta believe that Brahman is identical to the human soul, Atman, and that it is transforming wisdom, not *bhakti*, that leads to liberation. Therefore Vedantins theoretically have no reason to worship in a temple. In practice, however, even they throng to shrines to express their devotion.

Temple festivals celebrate events portrayed in the local myths as well as more generic observances. At Madurai in Tamilnadu, for instance, the Meenakshi-Sundaresvara temple complex honours the goddess Parvati in her incarnation as the Pandyan princess Meenakshi. After a military career in which she is said to have conquered many chiefs, Meenakshi marries Sundaresvara, who is considered to be Shiva himself. The wedding of the god and goddess is celebrated with much pomp and joy every year at a festival attended by pilgrims in the hundreds of thousands.

Vishnu temples in South India also have large shrines for the goddess Sri or Lakshmi. Similarly, temples dedicated to a manifestation of Shiva or Parvati usually include a shrine for the deity's consort. The processional image of Vishnu in the inner shrine always shows him with his consorts Sri-Lakshmi and Bhu, the goddess of the earth. In Sri's own shrine, however, she is represented alone and is only occasionally accompanied by an image of Vishnu. In other words, while Vishnu is worshipped only in conjunction with Sri-Lakshmi, she herself may evidently be worshipped alone, and several festivals are celebrated for her exclusively.

Temples dedicated to Murugan, a son of Shiva and Parvati, are common in the Tamil region of South India, though not in the north. Hanuman, who figures in the story of Rama and Sita, is venerated both at temples and at home shrines. Many temples in South India and the diaspora also contain representations of the nine planets, which may cause harm if they are not propitiated. Especially dreaded is Shani (Saturn), who is said to wreak havoc unless he is appeased by appropriate prayers or rites.

Only a few temples are dedicated to the creator god Brahma or his consort Sarasvati, the goddess of learning. Karambanur or Uttamar koil, near Srirangam in Tamilnadu, is one: an early example of a syncretic temple, it contains separate shrines for Shiva, Parvati, Vishnu, Lakshmi, Brahma, and Sarasvati. Students often visit the shrine of Sarasvati, especially on the eve of an examination. She is also worshipped at a famous temple at Sringeri, Karnataka, where she is known as Sharada. Devotion to Sarasvati is most evident in the domestic setting, however. Children recite prayers to her daily, and students carry little pictures of her to school.

Although most of the temples in northern India today were built after the end of the Mughal period, architectural guides from as early as the fifth century suggest that at least some elements of temple design and construction have remained constant.

A temple has a correlation to the universe itself and to the body of divine beings, and is therefore planned with care. In the Sri Vaishnava community, the temple is said to be heaven on earth. An ideal temple has seven enclosures and is located near a body of water of some kind—whether the sea, a river, a pond, a spring, or an artificial pool (called a 'tank' in India)—which automatically becomes holy. Devotees making a formal pilgrimage from a faraway place sometimes bathe in the water before entering the temple. In South Indian temples, the enclosures have gateways over which stand large towers ; the tallest one in the Srirangam temple is approximately 83 metres (270 feet) high. The towers are an essential part of the religious landscape, and in popular religion even a vision of the temple tower is said to be enough to destroy one's sins.

Devotees frequently walk around the temple inside one of the enclosures; this 'circumambulation' of the deity is an essential part of the temple visit. They bow down before the deity and may also take part in an *archana* ('formal worship'), in which the priest praises the deity by reciting his or her names. Sometimes they will go to the temple kitchen for *prasada*. In some temples devotees must buy the *prasada*; in others it is provided at no charge, paid for by endowments made by patrons in the past. Such patrons frequently earmark their donations for particular charitable deeds or functions in the temple, and their donations are inscribed on stone plaques on the temple walls.

Women, especially those from royal families, were liberal benefactors of temples and other institutions. In the year 966, in Tiru Venkatam (Tirupati), a woman named Samavai donated money for the temple to celebrate some festivals and consecrate a silver processional image of Vishnu (known here as Venkateshwara). A record of her endowment, inscribed in stone, concludes with the phrase *Sri vaishnava rakshai* ('by the protection of the Sri Vaishnavas'). Within a short time Samavai also donated two parcels of land, totalling roughly 10 hectares (23 acres) and ordered that the revenues derived from them be used for major festivals. She also gave a large number of jewels to the temple for the adornment of the image of the lord. Today this temple has the largest endowments and revenues of any in India.

Studies by epigraphers and art historians show that Samavai was not an isolated example. We know, for instance, that queens of the South Indian Chola dynasty were enthusiastic patrons of Shiva temples and religious causes around the tenth century. At that time, a South Indian queen called Sembiyan Mahadevi gave major endowments to many Shiva temples.

The inscriptions recording endowments represent a tangible honour for the many patrons over the centuries who have generously donated funds. In addition, the large amounts of money received point to the temples' power as economic institutions. Inscriptions are an important source of information about a temple and the social life of the times. For example, the fact that a woman like Samavai was able to make such generous donations suggests a certain independence of lifestyle and income.

Hindu temples may have been built in Vietnam as early as the fourth or fifth century, and some of the largest temples dedicated Shiva and Vishnu are found in the region of the Khmer empire, which stretched from modern Cambodia to parts of Thailand and Laos. Although there are striking similarities to temples and iconographic styles in different parts of India, including the states along the eastern coast, the Southeast Asian buildings have their own architectural idiom. Shiva temples are shaped like mountains; the large mountain-temples at Bakheng and Bakong in the Siem Reap area of Cambodia look more like the Buddhist temple of Borubodur in Indonesia than those in India. The large Vishnu

The great temple of Angkor Wat, where the sun rises directly over the central tower at the time of the equinox in the spring and fall (Photo courtesy of Vasudhan Narayanan).

temple of Angkor Wat in Cambodia, like many temples in India (and Central America as well), is situated and constructed according to astronomical calculations: the sun rises directly behind the central tower at the time of the spring and autumn equinoxes. The Udayagiri cave complex may also reflect astronomical knowledge, since it is situated close to the latitude where the Tropic of Cancer—the northernmost point where the sun appears to stand directly overhead at noon on the summer solstice—would have been around 400 CE.

Some temples in India have minimal funds, but others are very well endowed. An example is the temple of Venkateshwara (Vishnu) at Tiru Venkatam (the Tirupati hills in Andhra Pradesh). Although it enjoyed royal patronage in the past, it is only in the last century that it began attracting large numbers of pilgrims and substantial revenues. The popularity of the temple is said to have increased dramatically after a major reconsecration in 1958.

Sculptural and Pictorial Symbolism

The Naga

One of the earliest symbols in the Hindu tradition may be the *naga* (serpent). In many villages (as well as quiet spots in large cities) there are sacred trees surrounded with small stone images of intertwined snakes, which are venerated with spots of red powder (the same kumkum powder that is used to adorn women's foreheads). Women come to

The dancing Shiva, carved in the sandstone of the Badami caves in northern Karnataka (Photo courtesy of Vasudhan Narayanan).

these open-air shrines to worship at particular times of the year, or when they want to make a wish regarding a matter such as childbirth. *Nagas* are also important in the iconography of Shiva and Vishnu.

In Cambodia balustrades in the form of large *nagas* are an integral part of both Hindu and Buddhist temple landscapes. Cambodian narratives trace the descent of the kingdom from a Hindu prince from India and a *naga* princess.

The Dance of Shiva

Iconographically, Shiva is often portrayed as a cosmic dancer known as Nataraja, the king of the dance. In this form Shiva is the archetype of both the dancer and the ascetic, symbolizing mastery over universal energy on the one hand and absolute inner tranquillity on the other.

In the classic Nataraja representation, Shiva has four hands. One of the right hands holds an hourglass-shaped drum, symbolizing sound—both speech and the divine truth heard through revelation. The other right hand is making a *mudra* (gesture) that grants fearlessness to the devotee. One of the left hands holds a flame, symbolizing the destruction of the world at the end of time. The feet grant salvation and are worshipped to obtain union with Shiva. The left foot, representing the refuge of the devotee, is raised, signifying liberation. The other left hand points to this foot.

Dancing through the creation and destruction of the cosmos, Shiva–Nataraja is the master of both *tandava*, the fierce, violent dance that gives rise to energy, and *lasya*, the gentle, lyric dance representing tenderness and grace. The entire universe shakes when he dances; Krishna sings for him, the snake around his neck sways, and drops of the Ganga River, held in his hair, fall to the earth.

The Linga

In temples Shiva is usually represented by a *linga:* an upright shaft, typically made of stone, placed in a receptacle called a *yoni,* which symbolizes the womb. Although *linga* is generally translated into English as 'phallus', and in Sanskrit *linga* means 'distinguishing symbol', Hindus do not normally think of it as a physical object. Rather, it serves as a reference point to the spiritual potential in all of creation, and specifically to the creative energies of Shiva. The union of the *yoni* and *linga* is a reminder that male and female forces are united in generating the universe. Although Shiva is stereotyped in some literature as the 'destroyer', his devotees think of him as the protector and creator who (a) destroys evil and (b) periodically annihilates the universe in order to create it anew.

Erotic Sculpture

People from other cultures have often been shocked by temple sculptures celebrating *kama*, sensual love. Probably the most famous examples of such art are found at Khajuraho (c. 1000 CE), in the state of Madhya Pradesh, southeast of Delhi, and Konarak (c. 1250), in the eastern coastal state of Orissa. Although many other temples also contain erotic sculptures, they are frequently kept in inconspicuous niches or corners.

Some art historians have speculated that such images may have been intended to serve an educational purpose for young men who as students were isolated from society, in order to prepare them for adult life in a world where *kama*—sensual enjoyment—of all kinds was considered a legitimate goal and spouses were expected to be partners in *kama* as well as dharma. Other scholars have suggested that such scenes illustrate passages from various myths and literary works such as the *Puranas*.

Forehead Marks

Perhaps the most common visual sign of Hindu culture is the forehead mark or *tilaka* ('small, like a *tila* or sesame seed'), especially the red dot (*bindi*) traditionally worn by married women. In many parts of India, male ascetics and priests also wear various forehead marks in the context of religious rituals. Like many elements in the Hindu traditions, a forehead mark may be interpreted in various ways, depending on the gender and marital status of the person wearing it, the occasion for which it is worn, the sectarian community that the wearer belongs to, and, occasionally, his or her caste.

At the simplest level the forehead mark is decorative. In this spirit, unmarried and Christian as well as married Hindu women today wear *bindis*, and the traditional dot of kumkum powder is increasingly replaced by stickers in a wide variety of shapes and colours. Thus many people today do not think of forehead marks as having anything to do with religion. Yet their value is more than cosmetic. Married women see the *bindi* as a symbol of the role that they play in society. Other marks indicate the wearer's sectarian affiliation. When worn correctly in ritual situations, the shape and colour indicate not only which god or goddess the person worships, but also the socio-religious community to which he or she belongs.

The materials used to create the mark depend on the wearer's sect and the purpose for which the mark is worn. Marks denoting affiliation to a particular deity may be made with white clay, sandalwood paste, flower petals, or ash. In general, followers of Vishnu, Krishna, and Lakshmi wear vertical marks; worshippers of Shiva and

A married woman wearing a *bindi* (© Steve Evans).

Parvati wear horizontal or slightly curved crescent marks made of ash or other substances with a red dot in the middle; and a combination of dots and crescents usually indicates a preference for the goddess (Devi) in one of her many manifestations. Other variations are instantly identifiable to those familiar with India's many philosophical traditions.

Domestic Worship

One of the most significant ways in which Hindus express their devotion to a deity or a spiritual teacher is through rituals performed in the home; such worship is usually called **puja**. Many Hindu households set aside some space—if only a cabinet shelf—for a shrine to hold pictures or small images of the revered figure, whether god or guru.

The rituals performed in the home are simplified versions of temple rituals, performed by family members rather than priests. In the home as in the temple, the deity is treated with all the hospitality that would be accorded to an honoured guest. Daily puja typically consists of simple acts in which all family members can take part, such as lighting oil lamps and incense sticks, reciting prayers, or offering food to the deity. More elaborate rituals, however—such as the puja offered to Satyanarayana (a particular manifestation of Vishnu) on full-moon days—may involve a priest or other specialist.

Significantly, a number of domestic rituals are specific to the women of the household. In many parts of India, women gather on certain days of the year to celebrate the goddess by fasting and feasting, and then perform what are called 'auspiciousness' rituals for the happiness of the entire family. Other women's rituals are found only in certain geographic regions. In northern India, during domestic festivals such as Navaratri (see below) young virgin girls are venerated by other women who believe that they are temporary manifestations of the goddess.

In the home as in the temple, worshippers participate in the myths associated with the various deities. At the same time, in speaking a prayer or singing a hymn, they take part in the passion of the composer. Thus in Sri Vaishnava worship, devotees who recite a verse of Andal's are to some extent participating in Andal's own devotion, and through this identification they link themselves with the devotional community extending through time.

The Significance of Food

The Hindu tradition is preoccupied with food: not just what kind of food we eat, where and when we do so, and how it is prepared, but who prepares it, who has the right to be offered it first, and who may be given the leftovers. Certain dates and lunar phases require either fasting or feasting. Furthermore, there are technical distinctions among fasts: some demand abstention from all food, others only from grain or rice. Some texts say that one can win liberation from the cycle of life and death simply by observing the right kinds of fast.

Contrary to a common Western stereotype, most Hindus are not vegetarians. Nor does vegetarianism for Hindus mean abstaining from dairy products. Generally speaking, vegetarianism is a matter of community, caste, and calendrical details. The strictest vegetarians are generally the Vaishnavas, who are found all over India. In addition, most brahmins are vegetarian—except in Bengal, Orissa, and Kashmir. Members of the Swaminarayan movement and ISKCON are strict vegetarians and even avoid certain vegetables that are thought to have negative properties, such as onions and garlic.

These dietary customs are based on the idea that food reflects the general qualities of nature: purity, energy, and inertia. Pure foods such as dairy products and many vegetables are thought to foster spiritual inclinations. By contrast, meat, poultry, and onions are believed to give rise to passion and action, while stale food and liquor are seen as encouraging sloth. Thus a strict vegetarian diet is prescribed for people who are expected to cultivate spiritual tranquillity.

In addition, the nature of a given food is thought to be influenced by the qualities of the person who cooks it. For this reason it was common even in the mid-twentieth century for strictly observant brahmins to eat only food prepared by people of their own caste.

A central element in temple rituals is the offering of food to the deity, after which the 'leftovers' are served to devotees as *prasada*. Inscriptions on the walls of medieval temples show that most endowments were intended for food offerings, and in the case of the temple at Tirupati they include detailed instructions for the preparation of offerings. Tirupati is one of several pilgrimage centres that eventually became famous for particular kinds of *prasada*. The cooking and distribution of *prasada* is now a multi-million-dollar industry at such temples.

The Annual Festival Cycle

In the Hindu tradition there is a festival of some kind almost every month of the year. The most popular are the birthdays of Rama, Krishna, and Ganesha; the precise dates for these celebrations vary from year to year with the lunar calendar, but they always fall within the same periods.

Some festivals are specific to certain regions. **Holi**, for instance, is a North Indian festival celebrated in March or April with bonfires to enact the destruction of evil, and exuberant throwing of coloured powder to symbolize the vibrant colours of spring. It commemorates Vishnu's fourth incarnation, in which he took the form of a man-lion in order to save the life of a devotee. His fifth incarnation, as a dwarf-brahmin, is celebrated in the state of Kerala in a late-summer festival called Onam. Other festivals, like Navaratri and **Deepavali** (known colloquially as Divali in some areas) are more or less pan-Hindu. A detailed discussion of Navaratri will give us an idea of the complexity of the variations in observance across the many Hindu communities.

Navaratri

The festival of Navaratri ('nine nights') begins on the new moon that appears between mid-September and mid-October. It is celebrated all over India, but in different ways and for different reasons.

In Tamilnadu, for instance, Navaratri is largely a festival for women. Exquisite dolls representing the goddesses Sarasvati, Lakshmi, and Durga are arranged in elaborate tableaux depicting scenes from the epics and *Puranas*. Every evening, women and children dressed in bright silks visit one another, admire the dolls, play musical instruments, and sing songs from the classical repertoire in praise of the goddesses. It is a joyous time of music and beauty, and a glorious celebration of womanhood. On the last two days—a special countrywide holiday—large pictures of Lakshmi and Sarasvati, draped with garlands of fresh flowers, are placed in front of the display of dolls and worshipped.

Celebrating Holi in Hyderabad (AP Photo/Mahesh Kumar A., 08032108952).

In the state of West Bengal, by contrast, the same nine or ten days are dedicated to a festival called Durga Puja, commemorating the goddess Durga's killing of the buffalo-demon Mahisa. Devotees make sumptuous statues of Durga for her spirit to inhabit; then, after nine nights, they immerse the statues in water to symbolize her return to the formless state.

Some Hindus believe that it was on the ninth day of Navaratri that Arjuna found a cache of weapons he had hidden a year before. Because of this story, they call the last two days *Ayudha Puja* ('veneration of weapons and machines'): cars and buses are draped with garlands, while computers and typewriters are blessed with sacred powders and given the day off work. The ninth day of the festival honours Sarasvati, the patron of learning and music. All the musical instruments in the house, any writing device, and selected textbooks are kept in front of her image, to be blessed by her for the rest of the year.

In many parts of India, the last day of the festival is dedicated to Lakshmi. This is a time for fresh starts: to begin new ventures and new account books, to learn new prayers and music, to acquire new knowledge, and to honour traditional teachers. On the last days of the Navaratri festival, the fortune of learning, the wealth of wisdom, and the joy of music are said to be given by the grace of the goddesses.

Deepavali

Deepa means 'lamp' and *vali* means 'necklace' or 'row'. Thus Deepavali (or Divali) means 'necklace of lights'. It is celebrated at the time of the new moon between 15 October and 14 November. Hindus all over the world decorate their houses with lights, set off firecrackers, and wear new clothes. In some parts of India, Deepavali marks the beginning of a new year, but that is only one of several reasons for the festival. As in the case of Navaratri, the significance of Deepavali varies from one region to another.

In South India, for instance, Deepavali celebrates the dawn when Krishna killed Narakasura, a demon from the nether world, thus ensuring the victory of light over darkness. In North India, however, Deepavali marks the return of Rama to Ayodhya and his coronation. And in Gujarat it is the beginning of the new year, when businesses open new account books and new clothes are worn. Presents are exchanged in some communities, and it is generally a time of feasting. In Tamilnadu, it is said that the river Ganga itself is present in all the waters on Deepavali day. People get up at three or four in the morning for a special purifying bath, and members of some communities greet one another by asking 'Have you had a bath in the river Ganga?'

Life-Cycle Rites

Every culture has its rites of passage: rituals that mark the transitions from one stage of life to another. In some of the *dharmashastra* texts the discussion of the life-cycle sacraments begins with the birth of a child. In others the first sacrament is marriage, for it is only in marriage that each new life should begin.

Two factors are important to note in discussing life-cycle rites. First, not all are pan-Hindu, and even those that are do not necessarily have the same importance in all communities. Second, many important rites, especially those involving girls or women, are not discussed in the classical texts—possibly because those texts were written by men. Women were considered merely as partners to males, who were the main focus of the books. It may also be that some of these rites developed after the texts were written. We shall discuss first the normative *dharmashastra* sacraments, and then look at a few rites of passage that have more localized regional importance.

The English word 'auspiciousness' has become the standard translation for a category of concepts for which Sanskrit uses several different terms including *kalyana, mangala, shubha,* and *sri*. Certain kinds of people, animals, rituals, smells, sounds, and foods are considered auspicious: that is, they are thought to have the power to bring about good fortune and a good quality of existence (*su asti*). Marriage is called 'the auspicious ceremony' in Tamil, and in some North Indian usage the word *shubha* ('auspicious') precedes the word *vivaha* ('marriage'). The most auspicious times for the performance of all sacraments depend on the horoscope of the person concerned, which is cast at birth.

The right hand is associated with auspicious activities, such as gift-giving, eating, and wedding rituals. The left hand is associated with the inauspicious and the impure: insults, bodily hygiene, funerals, rituals honouring ancestors.

Birth Rituals

The cycle of sacraments (*samskaras;* literally, 'perfecting') begins before birth. The time of conception, the rituals administered to the mother, and her behaviour during pregnancy were all thought to condition the personality of the child. Thus there was a ritual for proper conception of a child, and mantras were to be uttered before the man and woman came together. The *Upanishads* describe specific rituals that prospective parents could follow to ensure the conception of a learned daughter or a heroic son. Abortion has generally been considered sinful, but the texts apparently have little influence on modern Hindu life: abortion is legal in India today and is rarely a subject of debate in Hindu religious discourse.

Many communities in India also follow two other prenatal rites called *pumsavana* ('seeking a male offspring') and *simanta* ('hair parting'). Although they used to be performed in the fifth month of pregnancy, today they are performed closer to the delivery date, to ensure the safe birth of a son.

At the moment of birth, care is taken to note the exact time, to ensure an accurate horoscope. The first ceremony performed after the birth, called *jatakarma* ('birth action'), was supposed to precede the cutting of the umbilical cord, but it is now done much later. The *jatakarma* rites include *medhjanana* ('birth of intelligence'), in which the father prays for the intellectual well-being of the child, and *ayushya*, in which he prays for longevity for himself and for the child, saying, 'May we see a hundred autumns, may we hear a hundred autumns.' The ceremony ends with a request for the infant's physical well-being and strength.

Initiation Rituals

The *upanayana* ritual that initiates a young brahmin boy into the study of the Vedas is also known as *brahma upadesha*. *Upanayana* can mean either 'acquiring the extra eye of knowledge' or 'coming close to a teacher' to get knowledge while *brahma upadesha* refers to receipt of the sacred teaching (*upadesha*) concerning the Supreme Being (Brahman).

The *upanayana* ritual is traditionally performed around the age of eight and initiates the boy into the first stage of life, called *brahmacharya*—literally 'travelling on the path that will disclose the Supreme Being' (that is, studenthood). The boy is bathed in water into which the essence of all the sacred and life-giving waters has been invoked through the recitation of sacred verses from the Vedas. This ritual is called *udaga shanti* ('peace brought on the waters'), and in a larger sense it seeks peace on all the waters and lands of the earth. The verses end with repeated requests for *shanti* (peace): peace for the individual, for the soul, the body, the divine beings, the family, the community, and the entire earth. During the ritual the boy is given a sacred 'thread' or cord to wear over his left shoulder. The meaning of this cord is unclear. Some think it represents an upper garment that the student would wear when he was ready to perform a sacrifice. Others think it symbolizes a spiritual umbilical cord representing the boy's connection to his teacher—the spiritual parent through whom he will be reborn.

The central part of the ritual is the imparting of the sacred teaching. As the boy sits with his father and the priest sits under a silk cloth (perhaps symbolizing the spiritual womb) a sacred mantra is given to him that he will be expected to chant 108 times in succession, three times each day. Known as the *Gayatri* or sun mantra, it is very short—'I meditate on the brilliance of the sun; may it illumine my mind'—but it is considered the most important of all mantras.

Today very few young men undertake any Vedic studies and the initiation ceremony is rarely performed outside the brahmin community. Nevertheless, efforts are underway in some communities to create a similar initiation ceremony for girls.

Weddings

According to the *dharmashastra* codes of law and ethics, a man must have a wife in order to pay his debts to the gods and the ancestors. The debt to the gods is discharged through the correct performance of domestic and social rituals with his wife (and only with her); the debt to the ancestors, by having children. A wife is a man's partner in fulfilling dharma, and without her a man cannot fully meet his religious obligations.

Traditionally, most marriages were arranged. To find a suitable bridegroom, the parents of the prospective bride often relied on the help of friends and extended family. Ideally, he would come from the same geographic region, speak the same language, and belong to the same community and sub-community, though he had to belong to a different clan; he would also be compatible with the bride in education, appearance, age, and outlook, and the two families would be of similar socio-economic status.

When a potential husband was finally found, the family would have an astrologer analyze his horoscope and compare it with that of the bride. The purpose of this reading was not only to assess compatibility and character but also to balance the ups and downs in the partners' future lives. Although arranged marriages are less common today than they were in the era when young women were largely sheltered from the world outside the home, horoscopes can still play a part in the choice of a marriage partner.

However the bride and groom find one another, Hindus believe that the marriage ceremony must include several basic features if it is to be legal. These include the *kanya dana* (the gift of the maiden by the parents), *pani grahana* (the clasping of hands), *sapta padi* (taking seven steps together around fire, which is the eternal witness), and for some, though not all, communities, *mangalya dharana* (the giving of 'auspiciousness' to the bride). In addition, the bride and bridegroom usually exchange garlands.

Some weddings include lavish exchanges of presents with friends and extended family members, processions on horseback or in antique cars, feasting, entertainment, and fireworks. The festive atmosphere often recalls a fairground, with vibrant splashes of colour and plenty of noise. Everyone has a good time, and relatively little attention is paid to the bride and groom.

The ceremony itself lasts several hours and for the bride may involve several changes of elaborate clothing and jewels. Often the couple sits on a platform near a fire, to which offerings are made. The bride's parents have an active role to play, as do the groom's sister and the bride's brother and maternal uncle at particular moments in the ritual, but the hundreds of guests are free to come and go as they please. During the 'giving of the maiden', the bride's father quotes from the *Ramayana,* reciting the words spoken by the father of Sita as he gives her in marriage to Rama: 'This is Sita, my daughter; she will be your partner in dharma.'

The groom's family then presents the bride with the 'gift of auspiciousness': a gold necklace, a string of black beads, or a simple yellow thread carrying the insignia of the god the family worships (a conch and discus symbolizing Vishnu, for instance, or a *linga* symbolizing Shiva). In many communities in South India, the groom fastens the necklace or string around the bride's neck as her symbol of marriage (corresponding to a wedding ring in the West). She will wear it for the duration of her marriage. There is no equivalent symbol for the groom, although men who wear the sacred thread will wear a double set of threads after they marry.

In the central rite of the wedding, the bride and the bridegroom take seven steps around the fire together and the groom speaks:

Take the first step; Vishnu will follow you. You will not want for food for the rest of your life. Take the second step; Vishnu will guard your health. Take the third step; Vishnu will follow you and see that you may observe all religious rituals. Take the fourth step; Vishnu, following you, will grant you happiness. Take the fifth step; Vishnu will follow and grant you cattle and kine. Take the sixth step; let Vishnu follow you and let us enjoy the pleasures of the season. Take the seventh step; Vishnu will follow you. We shall worship together.

Then, clasping the bride's hand (*pani grahana*), the groom says:

You have taken seven steps with me; be my friend. We who have taken seven steps together have become companions. I have attained your friendship; I shall not forsake that friendship. Do not discard our relationship.

Let us live together; let us think together. We have come to a right and fitting stage of our lives; let us be happy and prosperous, thinking good thoughts.

Let there be no difference in our hopes and efforts; let us attain our desires. And so we join ourselves (our lives). Let us be of one mind, let us act together and enjoy through all our senses, without any difference.

You are the song (*Sama*), I am the lyric (*Rig*), I am *Sama*, you are *Rig*. I am the sky, you are the earth. I am the seed; you shall bear my seed. I am thought; you are speech. I am the song, you are the lyric. Be conformable to me; O lady of sweet unsullied words, O gem of a woman, come with me; let us have children and attain prosperity together.

Later in the evening the new husband and wife are taken outside for a ritual called *Arundhati darshana* ('the sighting of Arundhati'). In Indian astrology, the seven brightest stars of the Great Bear constellation (the Big Dipper) represent the seven sages, one of whom (Vasistha) is accompanied by a companion star identified as his wife, Arundhati—a symbol of fidelity throughout India. Just as the stars Vasistha and Arundhati remain close through the years, so the newlyweds are urged to stay together forever.

Funeral Rites

Funeral rites reflect different combinations of elements from the Vedas and the *Bhagavad Gita* with elements specific to individual regions and communities (Shaiva, Vaishnava, etc.). Except for infants and ascetics (who may be buried), cremation by fire is the final sacrament in most communities. No fire is to be lit or tended in the house where the death occurred until the cremation fire has been lit, and the family of the deceased is considered to live in a state of pollution for a period of time that varies from twelve days to almost a year after the death. Each religious community has its own list of scriptures to recite from. Although the funeral rituals for most Hindu communities would include portions of the Vedas and the *Bhagavad Gita*, many would also include recitations from texts sacred only to that specific community. The Sri Vaishnava community, for example, recites Nammalvar's *Tiruvaymoli*, in which the poet-saint expresses his longing to be united with Vishnu.

The funeral rituals are usually performed by the eldest son of the deceased. For the first few days the spirit of the deceased is a *preta* (ghost). To quench the thirst resulting from the body's fiery cremation, the spirit is offered water and balls of rice. Some of these rituals go back to the earliest Vedic times, when the dead were thought to need food for the journey to their dwelling place on the far side of the moon.

After a designated period of time, the length of which depends on the caste of the deceased, the injunctions relating to pollution are lifted in an 'adoption of auspiciousness' ceremony. On every new-moon day the departed soul is offered food in the form of libations with sesame seeds and water. After a year, the anniversary of the death is marked with further ceremonies, and the family is then freed from all constraints.

Women's Rituals

Most women's rituals are domestic, undertaken for earthly happiness and the welfare of the family, but a few are intended solely for personal salvation or liberation. Many practices, such as worship at home shrines or temples, pilgrimages, and the singing of devotional songs, are similar to those undertaken by men, but some are unique to married women whose husbands are alive. Underlying many of the rites is the notion that women are powerful and that the rites they perform have potency. Though many women's rituals share certain features, the differences among the many communities, castes, and regions are so great that generalizations should be avoided.

Early History

Some scholars believe that, in the ancient past, upper-caste girls may have been permitted to study the Vedas. The epics tell of women lighting and tending the sacrificial fire to make ritual offerings to the gods. They also refer to women ascetics, who would presumably have undergone renunciatory rites similar to those required of men. These privileges appear to have been withdrawn by the beginning of the Common Era, however.

Calendrical and Life-cycle Rituals Today

Many traditional women's rituals are no longer practised today, but a number of votive rituals are still observed on particular days during specific lunar months. These rituals involve the welfare of others—the husband, the extended family, or the community—and only unmarried women or married women whose husbands are alive may participate in them; widows are excluded. Although Sanskrit manuals say that performing these rites will enable a woman to attain final liberation from the cycle of birth and death, most participants ask only for more worldly rewards, such as marriage for themselves or a long life for their husbands.

After prayers to the family deity, the women may eat a meal together and distribute emblems of auspiciousness such as betel leaves, coconuts, and kumkum powder. The rituals may take anywhere between a few minutes and five days to complete, with periods of fasting alternating with communal eating.

In the upper castes the standard life-cycle rituals associated with childhood, marriage, and death are much the same for both sexes. There are many other sacraments associated with women, however, that have not received scriptural ratification. Some of these rites are specific to certain regions and communities. In the past, for instance, many communities would celebrate a young girl's first menstrual period, since this 'blossoming' meant

Karva Chauth is North Indian festival celebrating married women's devotion to their husbands. Participants observe a 24-hour fast, during which they pray for their husbands' well-being (REUTERS/ Ajay Verma).

that she was ready for marriage. Today urban people tend to consider this tradition old fashioned, but it is still practised in rural areas. The girl is showered with gifts of money or clothing by her family, and the ritual celebration often resembles a mini-wedding. Special rituals may also attend pregnancy, especially the first.

Attitudes towards Women

On the whole, the view of women expressed in the Hindu scriptures has been contradictory. Woman is portrayed—often by the same author—as servant and goddess, strumpet and saint, the protected daughter and the powerful matriarch, the shunned widow and the worshipped wife.

The *Laws of Manu* make it clear that the status of women at that time was far below that of men. For example: 'Though destitute of virtue, or seeking pleasure elsewhere, or devoid of good qualities, a husband must be constantly worshipped as a god by a faithful wife' (*Manu* 5.154). The text goes on to say that a wife is the goddess of fortune and auspiciousness (*Manu* 9.26) and that women must be honoured in order for religious rituals to prove beneficial (*Manu* 3.56). On balance, however, the negative statements outweigh the positive ones. Perhaps the most famous of *Manu's* pronouncements on women is the following:

> By a girl, by a young woman or even by an aged one, nothing must be done independently, even in her own house. In childhood a female must be subject to her father, in youth to her husband, when her lord is dead, to her sons; a woman must never be independent (*Manu* 5.147–8).

Such statements did much to influence Western notions of Hindu women. As influential as *Manu* has been in some communities, however, its dictates were not necessarily followed. Women in the Vedic age composed hymns and took part in philosophical debates. And medieval women were more than dutiful wives. As we have seen, they composed poetry, and endowed temples. Some gave religious advice and wrote scholarly works, including commentary on scripture. Far from being ostracized or condemned, those women were respected, honoured, and in some cases even venerated. Despite *Manu*, many women of the upper socio-economic groups enjoyed both religious and financial independence and made substantial contributions to literature and the fine arts.

Some of the contradictions in Hindu thinking about women can be traced to the concept of auspiciousness. Auspiciousness refers primarily to prosperity in this life—prosperity being associated above all with wealth and progeny. Thus cattle, elephants, kings, and married women with the potential to bear children are all said to be auspicious, as are birth and marriage rituals, because they are associated with the promotion of three human goals recognized by classical scriptures: dharma (duty), artha (prosperity), and kama (sensual pleasure).

There is also a second level of auspiciousness, however, that is related to the fourth and ultimate human goal: *moksha* (liberation). The two levels of auspiciousness have been implicit in Hindu religious literature and rituals. In many contexts, women have auspiciousness in different degrees, which determine the levels of their acceptance.

In the *Puranas*, which reflect codes of conduct dating back two thousand years, the dharma of a faithful wife was to worship and serve her husband as god. The ideal wife, according to a line from the *Padma Purana* (probably written after the eleventh century), would combine the qualities of a slave, a harlot, a mother, and a counsellor. It is paradoxical but consistent with the Hindu value system that the truly faithful wife, having surrendered all power over her own life to her husband, was said to gain virtually limitless power—power so great as to burn up the world and make the sun and the moon stand still. The *Puranas* and the oral tradition contain many stories about the power of such women to save lives and even perform miracles. Even *Manu* seems to recognize the necessity of treating women with due respect:

> Where women are honoured, there the gods are pleased; but where they are not
> honoured, no sacred rite yields rewards. Where the female relations live in grief,
> the family soon perishes; but that family where they are not unhappy ever prospers.
> The houses on which female relations, not being duly honoured, pronounce a
> curse, perish completely, as if destroyed by magic (*Manu* 3.56–8).

The virtuous dead are also believed to have significant power. *Sumangalis*—married women whose husbands are still alive—regularly perform rituals in honour of the family's past *sumangalis*. A female ancestor who died before her husband retains the power to influence the well-being of the family. When propitiated, she radiates auspiciousness; when offended, she has the power to curse. In this context she is held to be almost more powerful, morally, than the man, and she is just as worthy of worship as her husband.

In some circumstances even courtesans were traditionally considered auspicious, at least in principle. A *devadasi* ('servant of the god') was offered to a temple by her family, usually as a young child, and ritually married to its deity. Thereafter, in some cases, it was deemed to be her dharma to provide sexual services to the priests and others. Since the deity himself was immortal, such a woman could never be widowed, and therefore in theory was continually, eternally auspicious (*nitya sumangali*), even if in practice she was likely to be ostracized by the mainstream society.

As for adultery, attitudes changed over time. Before the time of *Manu* female infidelity was considered regrettable but was not absolutely condemned. Once an adulterous woman had performed the prescribed purification rituals, her menstrual cycle would erase her lapses and she would be allowed to resume a reasonably normal life. For *Manu*, however, an unfaithful wife was worse than a prostitute: a disloyal wife 'is censured among men, and [in her next life] is reborn in the womb of a jackal and tormented by diseases, the punishment of her sin'.

The only possible exception to the rule regarding extra-marital love is Radha, who—according to some sacred texts—was married before she met Krishna and left her husband for him. In this case, renunciation of the marriage vow symbolizes the depth of her love, and Radha herself represents the ideal human soul, willing to renounce everything to be with her lord. In short, her act of renunciation is interpreted in a spiritual rather than a social context.

For centuries, the practice of *sati* (self-immolation on the husband's cremation pyre) offered widows a way to retain their honoured status as *sumangalis* and to escape the misery of life as a widow. The British banned the practice as a form of homicide in 1829, but it has continued to resurface from time to time. In 1987, for instance, hundreds of witnesses watched a young woman named Roop Kanwar burn to death on her husband's funeral pyre.

Brahmin women did not generally practise *sati*, but after the fourteenth century (especially in northern India), widows of the kshatriya caste made it a point of honour to accompany their husbands in death. Although there were no injunctions for women in other castes to commit *sati*, they adopted the practice in emulation of the 'higher' classes.

Women and Pollution

With a few exceptions—notably among the Vira Shaivas—most Hindu communities traditionally regarded menstruation as physically polluting. Menstruating women were excluded from everyday life, and even though strict segregation is no longer widespread, vestiges of the old attitudes remain. Most communities still do not permit menstruating women to attend a place of worship or participate in any religious ritual, and even Vira Shaiva households may prohibit menstruating women from cooking. Virtually all Hindu women take a purifying ritual bath on the fourth day.

Krishna (known locally as Shyamasundara, 'the dark handsome one') and Radha are the presiding deities of the New Raman Reti temple in Alachua, Florida (Vasudha Narayanan).

The same concept of pollution extends to childbirth. Even though the birth of a child is a happy and auspicious occasion, it is thought to render the entire family ritually impure. For several days after the birth, the family cannot go to a temple or celebrate an auspicious event, and the mother, who may bleed for up to six weeks after giving birth, is treated as if she were menstruating.

🌺 INTERACTION AND ADAPTATION

Religious Leaders

For more than 20,000 years Hindus have venerated holy men and women. The *Taittiriya Upanishad* urges a departing student to consider his **acharya** (religious instructor) as a god, and there have been countless other gurus, ascetics, mediums, storytellers, and **sadhus** ('holy men') who have commanded anything from obedience to veneration. It would not be an exaggeration to say that for many Hindus, the primary religious experience is mediated by someone they believe to be in some way divine.

This is no less true of modern times than of the ancient past. Followers of Sri Sathya Sai Baba (Sathyanarayan Raju, 1926–2011), a charismatic teacher from the southern state of Andhra Pradesh, believed him to be an *avatara*.

Monasteries established by the philosopher Shankara in the eighth century continue to exercise considerable influence among educated urban people, as do a number of intellectual Vedantic commentators. In their interpretation of the ancient scriptures and their mediation of traditional values, we see the dynamic and adaptable nature of the Hindu tradition.

All *acharyas* are gurus, but not all gurus are *acharyas*. Most *acharyas* belong to a specific lineage and teach a particular sectarian tradition. Gurus, by contrast, are not necessarily connected to any particular tradition; they tend to emphasize more 'universal' and humanist messages, stressing the divinity in all human beings and encouraging their followers to transcend caste and community distinctions. Another difference is that *acharyas* are almost invariably male, while many women have been gurus. An example is Ma Amritananda Mayi ('Ammachi'), the leader of a movement that sponsors an international network of charitable, humanitarian, educational, and medical institutions. Known as the 'hugging guru', she is one of the most popular religious leaders in the world today.

Many charismatic teachers are called *swami* ('master') by their followers. Others take their titles from the ancient Vedic 'seers' known as *rishis*. An example is the founder of the Transcendental Meditation movement, popularly known in the west as TM. Maharishi ('great seer') Mahesh Yogi (1911?–2008) is probably one of the most influential teachers in the Western world.

Mohandas Karamchand Gandhi (1869–1948) is best known for his successful use of non-violent protest in the campaign to gain India's independence from British colonial rule. The title 'Mahatma' ('great soul') was given to him by Rabindranath Tagore, India's famed poet and Nobel laureate. Born in coastal Gujarat and trained as a barrister in England, Gandhi practised law in South Africa from 1893 to 1915. It was in response to the racial discrimination faced by the Indian minority there that he began experimenting with civil disobedience and passive resistance as vehicles for protest. After his return to

India, where he became the leader of the Indian National Congress in 1921, he combined the techniques he had developed in South Africa with practices drawn from India's Hindu and Jaina religious traditions and applied them to the campaign for India's freedom.

In particular, Gandhi emphasized the principle of non-violence (*ahimsa*) and developed a strategy of non-violent resistance called *satyagraha* ('truth-force'). Also borrowed from religious observances was his practice of fasting, which he used both as a means of 'self-purification' and as a psychological weapon. Gandhi's fasts drew attention to social injustices and the atrocities perpetuated by the British authorities. Faced with brutality, he refused to retaliate, saying that 'An eye for an eye makes the world blind.' Another major influence was the *Bhagavad Gita*, which he first became acquainted with as a student in England and understood as an allegory of the conflict between good and evil within human beings. It remained his guide throughout his life.

In addition to his political work, Gandhi promoted social reform, especially with respect to those most discriminated against by the caste system. He gave the generic name 'Harijan' ('children of God') to the outcaste communities. Although the latter today reject the name as patronizing, it drew attention to discriminatory practices within Hindu society.

Less successful were Gandhi's efforts to promote peace between Hindus and Muslims in 1947, when the subcontinent was partitioned to form the independent republics of India and Pakistan. For Gandhi, the violence that accompanied the achievement of independence from Britain represented a major failure. Within a few months, on 30 January 1948, he was assassinated by a Hindu incensed by what he perceived to be Gandhi's championing of Muslim causes. Since then, Gandhi's influence has made itself felt in many parts of the world, but perhaps most notably in the US movement for civil rights under the leadership of Martin Luther King, Jr.

The Hindu Diaspora

The first brahmins crossed the seas to Cambodia and Indonesia early in the first millennium CE. The second major wave of emigration came in the nineteenth century, when the British took large numbers of indentured workers from India to work on plantations in other parts of the world. The third wave began in the second half of the twentieth century and has included growing numbers of skilled, educated people embracing professional opportunities in the West as well as political refugees fleeing civil strife. The watershed year was 1965, when American immigration laws were relaxed, allowing engineers, physicians, and, towards the end of the century, software professionals to settle in the United States.

Hindu leaders were establishing places of worship as early as 1906 in the San Francisco area, but the first really ambitious attempt to reproduce the traditional architecture and atmosphere of a Vaishnava sacred place was the Sri Venkateshwara temple in Penn Hills, a suburb of Pittsburgh, Pennsylvania, which opened in 1976. The Penn Hills temple enshrines a manifestation of Vishnu as Venkateshwara, lord of the hill known as Venkata ('that which can burn sins') in the Andhra Pradesh. (Other Venkateshwara temples have been established in many parts of the world.) The Penn Hills temple was built with the help, backing, and blessing of one of the oldest, richest, and most popular temples in India, the Venkateshwara temple at Tiru Venkatam (also known as Tirumala-Tirupati).

Despite devotees' desire to maintain sacred traditions and remain faithful to the architectural forms common in India, some compromises and innovations have been necessary. As far as possible, for instance, the ritual calendar has been adapted to fit the American secular calendar, since many festival organizers live far from the temple and need a long weekend to travel there. Nevertheless, the land on which the temple is located is considered sacred and the devotees celebrate the significance of having Venkateshwara dwelling on American soil with his consort Sri (known locally as 'the lady of the lotus' or Padmavati).

There are many differences in architecture and modes of worship in diaspora temples, but at least two elements are quite common. First, most temples focus on *devotional* practices as opposed to meditation or yoga exercises. Second, many of them sponsor regular classes in classical Indian dance. The Bharata Natyam dance form has become one of the main vehicles for the transmission of Hindu culture to younger generations in the diaspora. Learning the dance forms and performing them at public events during festivals has become one of the main avenues for young girls to participate in the larger Hindu community. Another popular Hindu form is *garbha* (literally, 'the womb'; a reference to the creative and regenerative powers of the goddess) a dance from the state of Gujarat that has been introduced wherever the Gujarati presence is well established.

Contemporary Issues

Hinduism has been global in multiple ways. In addition to the sizeable numbers of Hindus who trace their roots to the Indian subcontinent there are people in many other parts of the world who have adopted teachers, doctrines, beliefs, or practices from various Hindu traditions. There are also numerous ideas and practices derived from Hindu traditions that have been decontextualized and incorporated into very different cultures. An example of the latter can be seen in the United States. From the early 1800s, when New England Transcendentalists such as Ralph Waldo Emerson and Henry David Thoreau began exploring Hindu scriptures, through to the twenty-first century, Americans have engaged with ideas and practices that originated in the Indian sub-continent but have rarely been identified as Hindu.

Influential works have included the Upanishads, the epic *Ramayana*, the *Puranas*, and many plays of the most famous Sanskrit playwright, Kalidasa (c. 400 CE). Perhaps the most influential of all, however, was the *Bhagavad Gita*, which was first published in English (in a translation by Charles Wilkins, under the direction of Warren Hastings, the Governor-General of India) in 1785 as *The Bhagvat Geeta, or Dialogues of Kreeshna and Arjoon*. Emerson's poem 'Brahma' bears some striking resemblances to passages from the second chapter of the *Gita*. And his 'Hamatreya' appears to be directly modelled on the *Vishnu Purana* (c. first–fourth century CE), with its poignant treatment of themes such as the impermanence of life and the futility of holding on to earthly possessions, land, wealth, or fame.

The dual stereotype of America as the home of scientific progress and material goods and India as the seat of a 'timeless' spiritual wisdom would be accepted and repeated by many gurus in later decades. Even Hindu teachers such as Vivekananda and Yogananda, who travelled to the United States in the years around the turn of the twentieth century, emphasized the 'timeless', 'universal' nature of concepts such as reincarnation, or the identification of the human soul with the divine, and practices such as meditation and yoga. It is only since the late 20th century, as India has emerged as a leader in information technology and the contributions of scientists who happen to be Hindus have been recognized, that these stereotypes have begun to fade.

With the rise of the internet has come a proliferation of web pages devoted to specific communities, sects, deities, philosophies, prayers, rituals, temples, and so on. In addition, almost every community and sub-community has an email list that people can subscribe to, as well as a website for those seeking suitable marriage partners. Whereas marriages in the past were arranged through extended family networks, today more and more people with specific requirements regarding caste, community, and language rely on the internet to find one another.

Hinduism and the Environment

The history of environmental activism in India has been traced as far back as the late fifteenth century, when a guru named Jambho-ji—inspired by the pastoral life of Krishna the cowherd—taught his followers to minimize harm to the natural world. The community he established took the name Bishnoi, after the 29 ('bish-noi') principles he taught, which included everything from vegetarianism to water conservation and the protection of trees. Based in Rajasthan, the Bishnoi have continued to follow those teachings for more than five hundred years.

Environmental responsibility is not confined to the Bishnoi, however. Today, growing numbers of Hindu leaders and institutions are drawing on the classic texts to encourage eco-activism. Visitors to the Venkateshwara temple in Tirumala-Tirupati, for instance, are greeted by billboards proclaiming *vriksho rakshati: rakshatah* ('Trees, when protected, protect us'), and the temple authorities often quote a line from the *Matsya Purana* in which the goddess Parvati declares that 'One tree is equal to ten sons.' In a culture where sons are so highly prized, the force of this statement is striking.

The Tirumala-Tirupati temple has also established a large nursery on the surrounding hills. In addition to plants of many varieties, it cultivates tree saplings, which pilgrims are given as *prasada* and are encouraged to plant at home. Apart from this consciousness-raising venture, the temple invites pilgrims to offer donations for the purchase and planting of trees and plants.

Activists are also mining religious narratives to clean up the rivers Ganga and Yamuna and plant more trees all over the country. Responsibility to the environment is seen and presented as religious duty or dharma, as honoring the Earth goddess, and as part of devotional praxis.

Religious teachers and institutions retrieve and re-envision the meaning of the Vedas by emphasizing the sections that speak of peace and harmony. The *Song of Peace* (shanti path), for example, composed about three millennia ago, has become a source of inspiration for environmental activists:

> May there be peace in the skies, peace in the atmosphere, peace on earth, peace in the waters. May the healing plants and trees bring peace; may there be peace [on and from] the world, the deity. May there be peace in the world, peace on peace. May that peace come to me! (*Yajur Veda* 36.17).

Modern Reproductive Technology

Of all the technological innovations developed in recent years, those associated with reproduction have been among the most controversial. Yet Hindus on the whole appear to accept intervention in this area. In the case of assisted reproduction, this acceptance is probably not surprising: the traditional teachings on dharma have always emphasized reproduction as a primary duty. Thus Hindus today do not object to in vitro fertilization or artificial insemination, although the husband is generally the only acceptable donor. Many well-known religious narratives tell of unusual means of conception. In the *Mahabharata*, for instance, a queen named Gandhari grows a hundred sons in jars. In other texts, an embryo is transplanted from one woman to another, Krishna's brother Balarama is transplanted into a different womb, and deities are invoked to 'fertilize' women whose husbands cannot give them children.

The ethical considerations become more complex where issues such as contraception and gender selection are concerned. For thousands of years, male children were more welcome than females, largely because of the traditional duty to the ancestors: in a patriarchal, patrilineal society, sons would continue the family line and could be counted on to look after their parents in old age, whereas daughters would be of benefit only to their husbands' families.

Today sonograms and amniocentesis are used by some women for the express purpose of learning the sex of the fetus early in pregnancy, so that females can be aborted. As a result, the number of female births has dropped dramatically in recent years.

The *dharmashastra* texts maintain that the unborn fetus has life; according to popular belief and stories from the *Puranas*, it is even capable of hearing and learning from the conversations that take place around it. Nevertheless, abortion is legal in India and is accepted without strong objections from religious leaders or even prolonged editorial, legislative, or judicial debate.

CONCLUSION

As diaspora communities face the challenges of raising a new generation in the faith, Hindus in many parts of the world are actively working to define Hinduism. The difficulty of doing so underscores the complexities of a religious tradition that has evolved through more than three thousand years of recorded history—five thousand if the Harappa culture is included.

The dynamism of the many Hindu traditions is unmistakable. Vedanta is continually being interpreted. People continue to experience possession by deities, to situate their homes in auspicious directions, and to choose religiously correct times for happy events. Temples continue to be built, consecrated, and preserved. The sacred words of the Vedas and the *smrti* literature are still broadcast widely. Manuscripts are being restored, edited, and published, and new technologies are making the literature more widely accessible; the tradition confining the sacred word to particular castes is gone forever. The airwaves are flooded with religious programs, horoscopes are cast and matched by computer, surgeries are scheduled for auspicious times. In short, Hinduism continues to adapt to new contexts and changing times.

Sacred Texts Table

Religion (Sect)	Text(s)	Composition/ Compilation	Compilation/ Revision	Use
Hinduism	Vedas (Sanskrit)	Composed between c. 1500 and 600 BCE		Considered the most authoritative of all texts. Parts of the Vedas were used in both domestic and temple rituals.
	Upanishads: the last section of the Vedas, focusing on philosophy (Sanskrit)	c. 6th century BCE.	Most Vedanta philosophers used these texts in commentaries or wrote commentaries on them. The commentarial tradition continues today.	Philosophical
	Ramayana (Sanskrit)	c. 5th century BCE–1st century CE Very approximate dates	Periodically rendered in local languages. Tulsidas' *Ramcharitmanas* in Hindi is very important.	Doctrinal, ritual, performative, inspirational, devotional, narrative. educational.
	Mahabharata (Sanskrit)	c. 5th century BCE–2nd century CE		Doctrinal, ritual, narrative, performative, inspirational, devotional, educational
	Bhagavad Gita (part of the *Mahabharata*; Sanskrit)	c. 2nd century BCE–2nd century CE	Extensive tradition of commentary.	Doctrinal, ritual, performative, devotional, inspirational, narrative, educational
	Puranas (Sanskrit)	1st millennium CE	Often recreated in local languages.	Doctrinal, ritual, devotional, narrative, inspirational, educational
(Vaishnava, specifically Gaudiya and ISKCON)	*Bhagavata Purana* (Sanskrit)	c. 1st millennium CE		Doctrinal, ritual, devotional, narrative, inspirational, educational
	Dharmasutras followed by the *Dharmashastras* Many texts, of which the *Manava Dharmashastra* ('Laws of Manu') is the most important (Sanskrit).	Dharmasutras composed in the 1st millennium BCE; dharmashastras in the 1st millennium CE.	Extensive tradition of commentary. Medathithi (c. 9th–11th centuries CE?) commented on *Manu*.	Ritual, moral, and legal prescriptions on all aspects of life: personal, domestic, and public; discussions of right behaviour.
	Yoga Sutras of Patanjali	c. 200 BCE–300 CE	Commentarial tradition.	Classical philosophical text for yoga

Sacred Texts Table (continued)

Religion (Sect)	Text(s)	Composition/ Compilation	Compilation/ Revision	Use
(Vaishnava, Tamil)	*Nalayira Divya Prabandham* Sacred Collect of 4000 verses by the Alvars (Tamil)	c. 8–10th centuries. CE; said to have been 'revealed' in 11th century.	Extensive commentarial tradition.	Doctrinal, ritual, performative, devotional, inspirational, narrative, educational use
(Saiva Tamil)	Tirumurai	c. 8th–12th centuries		Devotional and philosophical use
Vaishnava	Poems of Surdas (Hindi/ Braj Bhasha)	16th century		Doctrinal, ritual, performative, devotional, inspirational, narrative, educational use
Vaishnava (Marathi)	*Dnyaneshwari* or *Jnaneswari*	Composed by *Dnyaneshwar*, c. 13th century		Doctrinal, devotional, and educational use

Sites

Almost every village has a locally important temple, and countless hills, mountains, rivers, and groves are considered sacred. The following list offers a very small sample.

Badrinath, Uttaranchal An important pilgrimage site, high in the mountains, with a temple of Vishnu in the form of the sages Nara and Narayana; one of 108 sacred places for the Sri Vaishnava community.

Chidambaram, Tamilnadu The abode of Nataraja, the Dancing Shiva, a large temple complex with shrines to both Shiva and Vishnu.

Dwaraka, Gujarat One of the seven holiest places, according to some *Puranas*, and the home of Krishna in the latter part of his life. The ancient site of Dwaraka is now said to be submerged in the Arabian Sea but the place close to it is now the pilgrimage site.

Guruvayur, Kerala This temple dedicated to the youthful Krishna draws millions of pilgrims every year.

Haridwar, Uttaranchal One of seven holy sites identified in the *Puranas*. Located on the banks of the river Ganga, it is one of the cities where a great festival called Kumbha Mela is held.

Kamakhya, Assam One of the most important Shakti *peethas* (sites where the power of the Goddess is said to be palpably felt). The temple is dedicated to the goddess Kamakhya, a form of Shakti/ Parvati/Durga.

Kanchipuram, Tamilnadu A temple town important for at least two millennia, home to dozens of temples dedicated to Vishnu and Shiva.

Kanya Kumari, Tamilnadu A small temple town at the southernmost tip of the Indian peninsula, famous for its temple dedicated to Parvati.

Madurai, Tamilnadu A large city, important for more than two thousand years and home to dozens of temples including a famous complex dedicated to the goddess Meenakshi (a form of Parvati) and the god Sundaresvara (Shiva).

Mathura and Brindavan, Uttar Pradesh A city and a complex of pastoral and urban pilgrimage sites nearby, all associated with incidents in the early life of Krishna.

Mayapur, West Bengal Birthplace of Chaitanya Mahaprabhu and the current spiritual world headquarters of the International Society for Krishna Consciousness. A memorial for A.C. Bhaktivedanta Prabhupada, the founder of ISKCON, is located here, as is one of the largest temples for Radha-Krishna.

Mount Kailas An important peak in the Himalayan range, said to be the abode of Lord Shiva.

Nathdwara, Rajasthan Home of a celebrated temple to Krishna in the form of Srinathji, in which legend says he lifted up the mountain Govardhana. Located near Udaipur.

Pandharpur, Maharashtra Home of a temple to Vithoba or Vitthala (a form of Vishnu) and Rukmini (Lakshmi).

Prayag, Uttar Pradesh The holy site where the Ganga and Yamuna rivers are said to come together with a legendary subterranean river called Saraswati.

Puri, Orissa Site of a temple dedicated to Jagannath (a form of Vishnu), his brother Balabhadra, and their sister, Subhadra. Also the site of a famous festival (Ratha Yatra) in which Lord Jagannath (the origin of the English word 'juggernaut') is taken through the streets on a huge chariot.

Puttaparthi, Andhra Pradesh Hometown of Sathya Sai Baba and one of the newest pilgrimage sites in the Hindu tradition.

Sabarimala, Kerala A temple to Ayyappan, set in the hills of Kerala and site of an important pilgrimage where millions of pilgrims, almost all male, congregate every January. Women are ordinarily forbidden to make the pilgrimage.

Srirangam, Tamilnadu An island temple-town in the Kaveri river, where Vishnu, here called Ranganatha ('Lord of the stage'), reclines on the serpent Ananta ('infinity'); one of the most important pilgrimage sites for the followers of Vishnu, celebrated in the poems of the Alvars.

Tirumala-Tirupati (also known as **Tiruvenkatam**), **Andhra Pradesh** Probably one of the most important pilgrimage sites in India. The temple, located on seven hills, is dedicated to Venkateshwara (Vishnu) and is said to be the richest religious institution in the world next to the Vatican.

Vaishno Devi, Jammu and Kashmir Located at an elevation of more than 1,580 metres, this temple is dedicated to the Goddess Vaishno Devi, who is sometimes perceived as a form of Durga and sometimes as an amalgamation of all the major goddesses.

Varanasi, Uttar Pradesh Also known as Kasi or Banaras; one of the holiest cities in India, located on the banks of the river Ganga. After cremation, many Hindus' ashes are brought here to be ritually submerged in the waters.

Study Questions

1. What is the origin of the word 'Hindu'? What elements of the Harappa culture suggest connections with Hindu traditions?
2. Why are the *Ramayana* and the *Mahabharata* central to Hinduism?
3. What role do sacred texts play in Hinduism?
4. Identify some of the deities, major and minor, that Hindus worship. How is it that Hindus describe themselves as monotheistic?
5. Who is Brahman? What is the relationship between Brahman and deities such as Vishnu, Shiva, and the Goddess?
6. What is *bhakti*? What role does it play in Hinduism?
7. What are the three ways to liberation discussed in the *Bhagavad Gita*?
8. Describe some of the distinctive features of Hinduism as it developed in Southeast Asia.
9. What is the role of the performing arts in Hinduism?
10. What are the primary ways in which women historically contributed to various Hindu traditions?

Glossary

acharya The leading teacher of a sect or the head of a monastery.

advaita Shankara's school of philosophy, which holds that there is only one ultimate reality, the indescribable Brahman, with which the Atman or self is identical.

Alvars Twelve devotional poets in South India whose works are central to the *bhakti* tradition.

artha Wealth and power; one of the three classical aims in life.

ashramas Four stages in the life of an upper-class male: student, householder, forest-dweller, and ascetic.

Atman The individual self, held by Upanishadic and Vedantic thinkers to be identical with Brahman, the world-soul.

avatara A 'descent' or incarnation of a deity in earthly form.

Ayurveda A system of traditional medicine, understood as a teaching transmitted from the sages.

Bhagavad Gita A section of the *Mahabharata* epic recounting a conversation between Krishna and the warrior Arjuna, in which Krishna explains the nature of God and the human soul.

bhakti Loving devotion to a deity seen as a gracious being who enters the world for the benefit of humans.

Brahma A creator god; not to be confused with Brahman.

Brahman The world-soul, sometimes understood in impersonal terms.

Brahmanas The sections of the Vedas that concern ritual.

brahmin A member of the priestly class.

darshana Seeing and being seen by the deity in the temple or by a holy teacher; the experience of beholding with faith.

Deepavali (Divali) Festival of light in October–November, when lamps are lit.

devanagari The alphabet used to write Sanskrit and northern Indian vernacular languages such as Hindi and Bengali.

dharma Religious and social duty, including both righteousness and faith.

guru A spiritual teacher.

Holi Spring festival celebrated by throwing brightly coloured water or powder.

jnana Knowledge; along with action and devotion, one of the three avenues to liberation explained in the *Bhagavad Gita*.

kama Sensual (not merely sexual) pleasure; one of the three classical aims of life.

karma Action, good and bad, as it is believed to determine the quality of rebirth in future lives.

kshatriya A member of the warrior class in ancient Hindu society.

linga A conical or cylindrical stone column representing the creative energies of the god Shiva.

Mahabharata A very long epic poem, one section of which is the *Bhagavad Gita*.

mantra An expression of one or more syllables, chanted repeatedly as a focus of concentration in devotion.

moksha Liberation from the cycle of birth and death; one of the three classical aims in life.

murti A form or personification in which divinity is manifested.

Navaratri 'Nine nights'; an autumn festival honouring the Goddess.

om A syllable chanted in meditation, interpreted as representing ultimate reality, or the universe, or the relationship of the devotee to the deity.

prasada A gift from the deity, especially food that has been presented to the god's temple image for blessing and is then returned to the devotee.

puja Ritual household worship of the deity, commonly involving oil lamps, incense, prayers, and food offerings.

Puranas 'Old tales', stories about deities that became important after the Vedic period.

Ramayana An epic recounting the life of Lord Rama, an incarnation of the god Vishnu.

rishi A seer; the composers of the ancient Vedic hymns are viewed as *rishis*.

sadhu A holy man.

samsara The continuing cycle of re-births.

sati The self-sacrifice of a widow who throws herself onto her deceased husband's funeral pyre.

shruti 'What is heard'; the sacred literature of the Vedic and Upanishadic periods, recited and transmitted orally by the brahmin priests for many centuries before being written down.

shudra A member of the lowest of the four major classes, usually translated as 'servant', though some groups within the *shudra* class could be quite prosperous.

smrti 'What is remembered', a body of ancient Hindu literature, including the epics, *Puranas*, and law codes, formed after the *shruti* and passed down in written tradition.

tantra An esoteric school outside the Vedic and brahminical tradition, which emerged around the fifth century and centred on a number of controversial ritual practices, some of them sexual.

tilaka A dot or mark on the forehead made with coloured powder.

upanayana The initiation of a young brahmin boy into ritual responsibility, in which he is given a cord to wear over his left shoulder and a mantra to recite and is sent to beg for food for the day.

Upanishads Philosophical texts in the form of reported conversations on the theory of the Vedic ritual and the nature of knowledge, composed around the sixth century BCE.

vaishya A member of the third or merchant caste in the ancient fourfold class structure.

Vedas The four collections of hymns and ritual texts that constitute the oldest and most highly respected Hindu sacred literature.

yoga A practice and discipline that may involve a philosophical system and mental concentration as well as physical postures and exercises.

Further Reading

Baird, Robert D. 1993. *Religions and Law in Independent India*. New Delhi: Manohar. Takes up some problems of the status of various groups.

_____, ed. 1995. *Religion in Modern India*. 3rd ed. New Delhi: Manohar. Good individual chapters on nineteenth- and twentieth-century sectarian movements.

Basham, Arthur Llewellyn. 1954. *The Wonder That Was India*. London: Sidgwick & Jackson. Arguably still the definitive introduction to the early culture of the subcontinent.

Blurton, T. Richard. 1992. *Hindu Art*. London: British Museum Press; Cambridge: Harvard University Press. A good introductory survey.

Bryant, Edwin F. 2001. *The quest for the origins of Vedic culture: the Indo-Aryan migration debate*. Oxford England: Oxford University Press. A detailed analysis of the sources connected with the Indo-Aryan homeland debate.

_____.2007. *Krishna: a sourcebook*. Oxford: Oxford University Press. Annotated translations on Krishna from many regions of India.

Chapple, Christopher, and Mary Evelyn Tucker, eds. 2000. *Hinduism and Ecology: The Intersection of Earth, Sky, and Water*. Cambridge, MA: Center for the Study of World Religions, Harvard Divinity School. Part of an important series in which various traditions address current environmental issues.

Chatfield, Charles, ed. 1976. *The Americanization of Gandhi: Images of the Mahatma*. New York: Garland. Includes American applications of Gandhi's ideas concerning the struggle for racial justice.

Dimock, Edward C., Jr., and Denise Levertov, trans. 1967. *In Praise of Krishna: Songs from the Bengali*. Garden City, NY: Doubleday. Lyrical expressions of devotion in eastern India.

Eck, Diana L. 1981. *Darcan: Seeing the Divine Image in India*. Chambersburg, Penn.: Anima Books. Brief but authoritative, on the significance of coming into the presence of the deity.

Erndl, Kathleen M. 1993. *Victory to the Mother: The Hindu Goddess of Northwest India in Myth, Ritual, and Symbol*. New York: Oxford University Press. Well focused on one region.

Findly, Ellison B. 1985. 'Gargi at the King's Court: Women and Philosophic Innovation in Ancient India'. In Yvonne Y. Haddad and Ellison B. Findly, eds. *Women, Religion and Social Change*, 37–58. Albany: State University of New York Press. Shows that intellectual activity was not totally limited to males.

Flood, Gavin D. 2006. *The tantric body: the secret tradition of Hindu religion*. London: I.B. Tauris. Elaborates the different forms of Tantra and the many manifestations of Tantric ritual practice.

Hawley, John Stratton. 2005. *Three bhakti voices: Mirabai, Surdas, and Kabir in their time and ours*. New Delhi: Oxford University Press. Engaging study on Kabir, Mira, and Surdas.

———. 1996. *Devi: Goddesses of India*. Berkeley: University of California Press. A very useful work on feminine aspects of the Hindu tradition.

Hiriyanna, Mysore. 1985. *The Essentials of Indian Philosophy*. London: Allen and Unwin. A frequently consulted, accessible introduction.

Huntington, Susan L., and John C. Huntington. 1985. *The art of ancient India: Buddhist, Hindu, Jain*. New York: Weatherhill. Comprehensive survey of Indian art.

Jones, Kenneth W. 1976. *Arya Dharm: Hindu Consciousness in 19th-century Punjab*. Berkeley: University of California Press. Describes Dayananda Sarasvati's Arya Samaj and its legacy in modern India.

Leslie, Julia, ed. 1991. *Roles and Rituals for Hindu Women*. London: Pinter; Rutherford, NJ: Fairleigh Dickinson University Press. A coherent set of essays on the subject.

Lopez, Donald S., Jr., ed. 1995. *Religions of India in Practice*. Princeton: Princeton University Press. A sourcebook containing a fine range of material; strong on ritual.

Lubin, Timothy, Donald R. Davis, and Jayanth Krishnan,ed. 2010. *Hinduism and law: an introduction*. New York: Cambridge University Press. Essays focus from ancient to modern law connected with Hinduism.

Lutgendorf, Philip. 1991. *The life of a text performing the Rāmcaritmānas of Tulsidas*. Berkeley: University of California Press. An excellent study of one of the most popular versions of the Ramayana.

Marglin, Frédérique, and John B. Carman, eds. 1985. *Purity and Auspiciousness in Indian Society*. Leiden: E.J. Brill. A useful collection, in an anthropological series.

Michell, George. 1989. *The Penguin Guide to the Monuments of India*. Vol. 1. London: Penguin. Local maps, plans, and descriptions of pre-Mughal Indian temples and other sites.

Miller, Barbara Stoler, trans. 1977. *Love Song of the Dark Lord: Jayadeva's Gitagovinda*. New York: Columbia University Press. An important *bhakti* text.

Miller, Barbara Stoler, and Barry Moser, tr. 1986. *The Bhagavad-Gita: Krishna's counsel in time of war*. New York: Columbia University Press.

Mittal, Sushil, and Gene R. Thursby, ed. 2004. *The Hindu world*. New York: Routledge.

Mittal, Sushil, and Gene R. Thursby, ed. 2008. *Studying Hinduism: key concepts and methods*. London: Routledge. This and the earlier volume introduce concepts and practices central to Hinduism.

Narayan, R.K. 1972. *Ramayana: A Shortened Modern Prose Version of the Indian Epic*. New York: Viking. A useful point of access to this classic.

Narayanan, Vasudha. 1994. *The Vernacular Veda: Revelation, Recitation, and Ritual Practice*. Columbia: University of South Carolina Press. The ritual use of the *Tiruvaymoli* among India's scheduled castes as well as brahmins.

———. 1996. "'One Tree Is Equal to Ten Sons': Hindu Responses to the Problems of Ecology, Population, and Consumption'. *Journal of the American Academy of Religion* 65: 291–332. Discusses some classic resources for addressing concerns of today.

Nelson, Lance E. 1998. *Purifying the earthly body of God religion and ecology in Hindu India*. Albany, N.Y.: State University of New York Press. One of the best introductions to Hindu attitudes to the environment.

Olivelle, Patrick, trans. 1996. *Upanisads*. New York: Oxford University Press.

———, trans. 1997. *The Pancatantra: The Book of India's Folk Wisdom*. New York: Oxford University Press.

———, trans. 1999. *Dharmasutras: The Law Codes of Apastamba, Gautama, Baudhyayana, and Vasistha*. New York: Oxford University Press. This and the two foregoing items are lucid translations of influential texts.

Orr, Leslie C. 2000. *Donors, Devotees, and Daughters of God: Temple Women in Medieval Tamilnadu*. New York: Oxford University Press. Provides a useful corrective to prescriptive male writings in Sanskrit on Hindu women.

Patton, Laurie, ed. 2002. *Jewels of Authority: Women and Textual Tradition in Hindu India*. New York: Oxford University Press. Essays focus on women's initiatives in Hinduism.

Pechilis, Karen. 2004. *The graceful guru: Hindu female gurus in India and the United States*. New York: Oxford University Press. Showcases the impact of modern and some medieval women gurus in India and globally.

Pintchman, Tracy. 2007. *Women's lives, women's rituals in the Hindu tradition*. Oxford: Oxford University Press. Explores complex relationships between rituals, domesticity, and religious praxis.

Radhakrishnan, Sarvepalli, and Charles A. Moore, eds. 1957. *A Source Book in Indian Philosophy*. Princeton: Princeton University Press. Still the best anthology for philosophical texts.

Rajagopalachari, Chakravarti. 1953. *Mahabharata*. Bombay: Bharatiya Vidya Bhavan. A sampling from this vast epic.

Ramanujan, A.K., trans. 1981. *Hymns for the Drowning: Poems for Vishnu by Nammawvar*. Princeton: Princeton University Press. An excellent source for Tamil *bhakti*.

Richman, Paula, ed. 1991. *Many Ramayanas: The Diversity of a Narrative Tradition in South Asia*. Berkeley: University of California Press. Reflects the importance of the *Ramayana* in vernacular South Asian tradition.

———, ed. 2000. *Questioning Ramayanas: A South Asian Tradition*. Delhi: Oxford University Press.

Roy, Kumkum, ed. 1999. *Women in Early Indian Society*. Delhi: Manohar. A useful collection of articles on both Hindu and Buddhist women.

Snellgrove, David L. 2004. *Angkor-before and after: a cultural history of the Khmers*. Trumbull, CT: Weatherhill. Scholarly study of one of the largest Hindu temples outside of India and the Khmer culture.

Soneji, Davesh, ed. 2010. *Bharatanatyam: A Reader*. New York: Oxford University Press. Excellent collection highlighting role of the dance form in the larger Hindu cultural matrix.

Tharu, Susie J., and Ke Lalita. 1991. *Women writing in India: 600 B.C. to the present*. New York: Feminist Press at the City University of New York. Excellent sourcebook of translations.

von Stietencron, Heinrich. 1989. 'Hinduism: On the Proper Use of a Deceptive Term'. In Günther D. Sontheimer and Hermann Kulke, eds. *Hinduism Reconsidered*, 11–27. New Delhi: Manohar. One of the best discussions of the problem of viewing Hinduism as a single 'religion'.

Waghorne, Joanne P., Norman Cutler, and Vasudha Narayanan, eds. 1985. *Gods of Flesh, Gods of Stone: The Embodiment of Divinity in India*. New York: Columbia University Press. Explores a range of forms in which Hindus see deity manifested.

Williams, Raymond Brady, ed. 1992. *A Sacred Thread: Modern Transmission of Hindu Traditions in India and Abroad*. Chambersburg, PA: Anima. A good description of the diaspora in the 1970s and 1980s.

Wujastyk, Dominik, intro. and trans. 1998. *The Roots of Ayurveda: Selections from Sanskrit Medical Writings*. Delhi: Penguin. Useful for the relationship between traditional Indian medicine and religion.

Younger, Paul. 2010. *New homelands: Hindu communities in Mauritius, Guyana, Trinidad, South Africa, Fiji, and East Africa*. Oxford: Oxford University Press. Best introduction to global Hindu traditions.

Zimmer, Heinrich. 1946. *Myths and Symbols in Indian Art and Civilization*. New York: Pantheon. A classic study, still often cited.

Recommended Websites

www.sacred-texts.com/hin/index.htm   Free online translations (mostly late-nineteenth to early-twentieth century) of the Vedas, epics, *Puranas*, *Yoga Sutras*, *smrti* literature, etc.

www.sscnet.ucla.edu/southasia/   Very good links for South Asian culture, religions, and history.

www.wabashcenter.wabash.edu/resources/result_browse.aspx?topic=569&pid=361   A meta-site with links to many useful resources, including course syllabi.

www.columbia.edu/itc/mealac/pritchett/00 general-links/index.html   A good site with links to many resources on South Asia.

http://virtualvillage.wesleyan.edu/   An on-the-ground look at a 'virtual village' in North India.

www.veda.harekrsna.cz/encyclopedia/index.htm   Links to articles on various topics in Hinduism from an iskcon perspective.

www.sathyasai.org/   The official site of Sri Sathya Sai Baba, maintained by his devotees.

http://prapatti.com/   Texts and mp3 audios of several Tamil and Sanskrit Vaishnava prayers.

www.hindupedia.com/en/Main_Page   An online encyclopedia offering 'a traditional perspective' on the Hindu religion and way of life.

www.hinduismtoday.com/   A popular magazine based in Hawaii, rooted in the classical Shaiva tradition, but offering articles of interest to Hindus all over the world.

References

Hawley, John S., and Mark Juergensmeyer, trans. 1988. *Songs of the Saints of India*. New York: Oxford University Press.

Jackson, William J., trans. 1991. *Tyagaraja: Life and Lyrics*. Delhi: Oxford University Press.

Miller, Barbara Stoler, trans. 1986. *The Bhagavad-Gita: Krishna's Counsel in Time of War*. New York: Columbia University Press.

Nielsen, N.C., et al., eds. 1993. *Religions of the World*. 3rd ed. New York: St Martin's Press.

Radhakrishnan, Sarvepalli, trans. 1953. *The Principal Upanisads*. London: Allen and Unwin.

Chapter
7
Jaina Traditions

❧ Anne Vallely ❧

A frail monk sits cross-legged on a bed, leaning against the wall for support as his followers enter the room. Everyone knows this is the last time they will gather for *darshana*—to pay homage to their guru and receive his blessing—for he has taken the vow of *sallekhana* and the process is nearing its end. *Sallekhana* is the ritual death achieved at the end of a long fast. No Jaina is required to undertake such a fast; in fact, Jainas are expressly forbidden to cause harm to any living being, whether in thought, speech, or action. But the Jaina path is one of renunciation—of departure from life during life—and *sallekhana* is its logical end. Voluntary death is the most radical statement possible of detachment from the body and the world. A dispassionate death is a triumph for the eternal soul on its journey towards perfection.

OVERVIEW

Jainism confronts us with a simple yet extraordinary message: the path to happiness, truth, and self-realization is the path of restraint. Happiness is the product not of doing but of not-doing; not of embracing the world but of disengaging from it.

It is this emphasis on restraint that gives Jainism its distinctive ascetic character. To study the Jaina tradition, however, is to realize that it cannot be contained within such narrow bounds. For one thing, the Jaina community is equally well known for its business acumen, worldly success, and strong social identity—in other words, for its effective, dynamic engagement with the world.

Outsiders often perceive a paradoxical disjunction between the Jaina community's this-worldly achievements and its other-worldly ethos. But this seeming paradox reflects the spirit of the tradition: the path of renunciation is a path of transformative power. The power of renunciation lies not in opposing worldly power, but in transcending and subsuming it. Some of the most interesting dimensions of Jainism can be traced to this interplay between the worldly and the other-worldly, both in scripture and in lived practice. Ultimately, following the Jaina path means withdrawing from the world—not just from its sorrows but also from its ephemeral joys, from family and community, from pride and desire, even from one's own body. Conquering our attachment to the world is the most difficult of all battles, but for Jainas it is the only battle worth engaging. Such is the message of the **Jinas** ('victors' or 'conquerors'), the 24 ascetic–prophets who taught the path to eternal happiness. It was from the Sanskrit word *jina* that the term 'Jaina' was derived.

Jainism is a tradition that expresses itself ritually through the veneration and emulation of the Jinas (also known as '**Tirthankaras**'—builders of bridges across the ocean of birth and death, or *samsara*). The Jina is the highest expression of the Jaina ideal, and the focus

◄ Pilgrims pray at the feet of a colossal statue of Bahubali at Shravanabelgola (Raghu Rai/Magnum).

of the Jaina devotional apparatus. A commanding figure who could just as easily have been a worldly *chakravartin*—the ideal benevolent ruler, endowed with all the powers and possessions the world has to offer—the Jina 'conquers' the world by turning his back on it. Indeed, the Jina is venerated in both his potentialities: as the regal *chakravartin*, magnificently bejewelled and crowned, and as the unadorned ***Arhat***, deep in meditation, entirely detached from worldly concerns. World renouncer and world conqueror, though antithetical in their orientations, both trace their beginnings to the auspicious karma accrued from a life of non-violence. Restraint, self-discipline, and commitment not to harm are the starting points for the Jina and the *chakravartin* alike.

To grasp the vigorous, even forceful character of Jainism, we need to keep in mind that the Jaina path of renunciation is one not of retreat from the harshness of the world, but of

Timeline

c. 850 BCE	Parsavanath, the 23rd Tirthankara
599–527 BCE	Traditional dates of Mahavira
4th century BCE	Possible beginning of split within Jaina community with southward migration of one group
2nd century CE	Umasvati, Digambara author of the *Tatthvartha Sutra*
5th century CE	First Jaina temples
9th century CE	Jinasena, Svetambara philosopher
10th century CE	Colossal statue of Bahubali erected in Shravanabelagola, Karnataka
11th century CE	Dilwara temple complex in Rajasthan
12th century CE	Hemachandra, Svetambara philosopher
15th century CE	Lonkashaha initiates reform in the Svetambara tradition
16th century CE	Banarsidass initiates reform in the Digambara tradition
17th century CE	Beginning of Svetambara Sthanakvasi subsect
18th century CE	Beginning of Svetambara Terapanthi subsect
19th century CE	Emergence of modern Jaina reform groups, and the widespread publication of Jaina scriptures
20th century CE	Revitalization of the Bhattaraka tradition within the Digambara sect
1962	Consecration of Jain temple (Svetambara) in Mombasa, Kenya, the first to be built outside India
1966	Jain Centre of New York established
1981	Jain Federation of North America (JAINA) established
1983	Siddhachalam ashram founded in New Jersey by Acharya Sushul Kumarji; the first recognized Jaina pilgrimage site outside India, it is visited by both Svetambaras and Digambaras

triumph over it. The world surrenders its bounty spontaneously to those who conquer it through detachment—though of course the true renouncer is indifferent to such rewards.

For Jainas the highest possible value is non-violence. So central is this value that Jainas commonly express the essence of their tradition in three words: '*ahimsa paramo dharma*' ('non-violence is the supreme path'). This is not to say that Jainas seek to eradicate the

Traditions at a Glance

Numbers
Estimates range from five to eight million worldwide.

Distribution
Primarily India; smaller numbers in East Africa, England, and North America.

Principal Historical Periods

599–527 BCE	Traditional dates of Mahavira, the most recent of the Jinas
c. 310 BCE	Beginning of the split within the Jaina community
2nd century BCE	Possible composition of *Kalpa Sutra*
6th century CE	Crystallization of Svetambara and Digambara sect
17th century	Emergence of the Svetambara Sthanakvasi subsect
18th century	Emergence of the Svetambara Terapanthi subsect

Founders and Leaders
The 24 Jinas or Tirthankaras: a series of 'ford-builders' who achieved perfect enlightenment and serve as guides for other human beings. The most important Tirthankaras are the two most recent, Parsavanath and Mahavira.

Deities
None in philosophy; a few minor deities in popular practice; some Jainas also worship Hindu deities such as Lakshmi. Although the Tirthankaras are not gods, their images are revered by many Jainas.

Authoritative Texts
All Jainas agree that the earliest teachings (14 *Purvas*) were lost long ago. The Svetambara sect reveres a collection called the *Agama*, consisting of various treatises known as *Angas* and *Angabahyas* (which are believed to contain the essence of the lost Purvas), as well as the *Kalpa Sutra*, which contains the life stories of the Tirthankaras. The Digambara sect believes that the original *Angas* were lost as well and focus instead on a set of texts called the *Satkhandagama* and *Kasayaprabhrta*, which are believed to contain portions of the original *Purvas*.

Noteworthy Teachings
The soul is caught in karmic bondage as a result of violence, both intended and unintended, done to other beings. Non-violence is the most important principle, in thought, word, and deed. Freed from karma, the soul attains crystal purity.

violence of the world. In a universe where every life exists only at the expense of others, such a commitment would be futile; furthermore, any engagement with the world only causes us to sink deeper into its depths, generating ever more karma to fasten to our souls. Rather, the Jaina commitment to non-violence is a commitment to radical non-interference.

Jainas equate non-violence with renunciation because it is only through the total cessation of activity—of mind, speech, and body—that one can truly avoid harming others and, consequently, oneself.

We are surrounded by countless life forms, many of which are invisible to the eye. All possess an eternal soul (*jiva*), and none desires to be harmed. Yet the omnipresence of these forms means that we cannot perform any action without causing them harm. And in causing them harm, we harm ourselves, for every act of violence we perpetrate increases the negative karma attached to our souls, impeding our ability to know our true Self. Lack of intention to commit harm is an important mitigating factor. But even unintended acts of harm still result in some degree of karmic bondage—though that karma is less heavy, dark, and damaging than the kind created when the harm is intentional.

Jainism tells us that attachment to the world, our bodies, and the cultivation of our personalities comes at the expense of knowing our true Self. The Self has nothing to do with this world—not with its sounds, its colours, or its rhythms, nor with our own talents, aptitudes, or experiences, nor even with the relationships we forge with others. The worldly, social self that we construct with such care from the time of our birth is no more than an elaborate sand castle, washed away with each wave of the ocean of *samsara*.

The Self is fundamentally other. Its deep, silent tranquillity is indifferent to the cacophony of the world. And precisely because the soul does not lobby for the attention of our consciousness, its presence is easy to ignore amidst the endless distractions created by the demands of the body. Nevertheless, the soul is luminous, radiating peace, and on very rare occasions our conscious minds may catch a glimpse of its magnificence. Jainas call this momentary awakening **samyak darshan** ('right faith' or 'correct intuition' into the workings of the world), and it is the starting point of Jainism.

According to Jainas, there is only one path to emancipation: the path of self-discipline and non-harm. Yet this singular path leads to a remarkable range of Jaina communities, and the lived traditions of Jainism vary widely in both interpretation and practice. In fact, diversity is one of the distinguishing characteristics of Jainism.

The most fundamental distinction is the one between the two Jaina sects: **Digambara** (naked or 'sky-clad') and **Svetambara** (white-clad). This sectarian split occurred some two hundred years after the death of **Mahavira** (599–527 BCE) and was the product of enduring differences in views regarding ascetic practice, women's spiritual capacity, and the nature of the Jina, among other things.

Other issues that divide Jainas include the worship of images or idols, the use of 'living beings' such as flowers, water, and fire in worship, and the necessity of a guru to guide one's spiritual development. Despite the diversity of their interpretations, however, all Jainas share the commitment to renunciation and non-violence that is the heart of the tradition. The message of restraint is unambiguously conveyed by the 'sky-clad' ascetics who literally embody the principle of renunciation, but it is also present in the beliefs and practices of lay Jainas, including those who live in a context of plenty. Out of the clamorous diversity of Jaina expression emerges the unbroken and unvarying message that non-violence is the only path to liberation.

🦋 ORIGINS

Jainism appeared on the historical scene sometime between the ninth and sixth centuries BCE as part of the same *shramana* ('world-renouncing') movement that gave rise to Buddhism. The imprecise dating reflects the meagre data that historians have at their disposal. The later date is the more commonly accepted because the historicity of Mahavira (born Vardhamana Jnatrpura) has been widely established. The earlier date is associated with the twenty-third Tirthankara, Parsavanath, whose life is undocumented. (The only evidence for his existence is the occasional scriptural reference; for instance, Mahavira's parents were said to be devotees of the lineage of Parsavanath.)

United in their condemnation of the status quo, the *shramanas* also held similar views regarding the need for salvation from a meaningless cosmos. All regarded the cosmic order not as the creation of a transcendent, cosmic god—the existence of which they denied—but rather as a purposeless place of suffering that must be transcended. Finally, each *shramana* group claimed a unique insight into the workings of the cosmos, as well as a way to escape its confines and attain *moksha*/nirvana. Despite their similarities, therefore, the various *shramana* groups developed as distinct traditions and even rivals.

Digambara Jainas greet the saint Acharya Vidyasagar Maharaj with a procession (Ian Berry/Magnum).

Mahavira is said to have been born to a ruling family in the region of what is now Nepal or northeastern India. Our knowledge of his life is derived from very limited scriptural sources (Jaina texts and parts of the Buddhist Pali canon). Almost all that can be said with any certainty is that he was a historical personage whose teachings on restraint attracted a considerable number of disciples and lay followers.

Nevertheless, the Jaina tradition has many tales of the teacher they call Mahavira, or 'Great Hero', whose most recent incarnation is said to have begun with the miraculous transfer of his embryo from the womb of a brahmin woman named Devananda to that of Queen Trisala (which unequivocally established the supremacy of the kshatriya caste over the brahmins). Accounts of his life are retold and re-enacted throughout the year, but especially during the festival known to Svetambara Jainas as Paryushana and to Digambara Jainas as Daslakshana.

Jainas believe that the cycles of generation and degeneration produce predictable patterns in social, moral, and physical life. Thus within each cycle of generation and degeneration there are periods that favour the emergence of Jinas who teach the path of liberation. For Jainas, therefore, Mahavira—far from being the founder of Jainism—is merely the final Jina of the current degenerate time period. In the next cycle, which will be one of generation, another 24 Jinas will appear and preach the same wisdom. During the cycle of decline that will inevitably follow, yet another 24 will appear, and so on, in an unending cycle of decay and growth.

In this context, linear time carries very little weight. Jainas are both diachronically and synchronically oriented, moving easily between the understanding of time in terms of historical sequence and the understanding that past, present, and future are simultaneously 'present' or at hand. Most crucially, however, Jainas assert that Jainism—like the cosmos itself—has no point of origin. Just as the cosmos has existed from 'beginningless time', so too has the struggle for liberation from it—as well as the truth about how to attain salvation. 'Jainism' is simply the name we give to this path. By declaring the cosmos to be eternal, Jainism directs our attention away from the fruitless question of origins to the more pressing existential issue of our bondage in *samsara* (the cycle of birth and death).

Jainism is overwhelmingly concerned with conveying its message of restraint. This task is urgent because, even though the message is eternal, it is accessible only to one life form (the human) in one specific region of the cosmos (the *karmabhumi*, or realm of action) and, as noted above, within limited time periods. Thus we who are living in this world, at this moment, are privileged to be capable of receiving the message: we must not squander our chance to act on it.

CRYSTALLIZATION

Mahavira established Jainism as a four-fold community (**caturvidhyasangha**) made up of monks, nuns, laymen, and laywomen. His open acceptance of women in his sangha is noteworthy, particularly since the *shramana* groups generally regarded women as 'objects of desire', to be avoided lest they distract male ascetics from their path. (The Buddha's initial reluctance to permit women to join his order is well known.)

It is true that many Jaina scriptures suggest a mistrust of women, and that until recently nuns have never held positions of authority within the order. Even so, they have always been present in large numbers, and they have played an integral part in the sangha's operations. Mahavira's sanctioning of the involvement of women as well as men was crucial to the success of the developing community, as was his recognition of the interdependence between householders and mendicants.

For its first three decades the sangha was held together by the charismatic example of the living Jina. It is said that Mahavira's sangha grew to include 36,000 nuns and 14,000 monks, as well as 318,000 laywomen and 159,000 laymen (Jaini 1979: 37). The preponderance of nuns over monks—highly unusual for a religious order in India—has remained a distinguishing feature of Jainism throughout its history.

At the age of 72 Mahavira 'left his body' and attained *moksha*. For Jainas (as for Theravada Buddhists) *moksha* is a state of complete detachment from the world, a state from which communication with those still in the cycle of *samsara* is impossible. Thus Mahavira's followers were deprived of the sort of post-mortem cult typical of some other religious traditions, in which followers have sought to maintain contact with their central figures through prayer. Instead, the Jainas faced the enormous challenge of sustaining their tradition without any hope of spiritual guidance from the Jina.

Mahavira's disciples assumed leadership of the community, but the process of institutionalization soon gave rise to dissension. Within two centuries of Mahavira's death, the once cohesive Jaina community had begun to split into two discrete traditions, with two distinctive collections of scripture that were at variance with one another. The precise causes of the split remain unknown, but many sources suggest that the turning point came in the fourth century BCE, when one group moved south (possibly in response to a severe famine in the north). Thereafter the two groups developed in isolation. Differences inevitably arose, and in time each group came to see the other as deviating from the vision of Mahavira, and therefore as inauthentic.

That the northern group had abandoned Mahavira's principle of nudity and begun wearing white robes was a particular abomination to the southerners, for whom nudity was among the most elemental expressions of non-attachment and non-violence. The northerners argued that a simple garment had no bearing on spiritual progress. Nevertheless, the matter of clothing was such a central and visible difference that it

Marble footprints symbolize the departed Tirthankaras (Photo courtesy of Gabriel Jones).

became the basis for the two groups' self-identification. Eventually, in the early centuries of the Common Era, the northerners came to be known as the Svetambara (white-clad) and the southerners as the Digambara (sky-clad, or naked). The lay followers of both groups (including the fully clothed lay followers of the naked monks) likewise took on these appellations as markers of their religious identity.

This was not the only point of division, however. Another important disagreement involved women's eligibility for initiation into the order. The Digambaras' insistence on nudity meant that women were, *a priori*, disqualified from taking the vows of renunciation. The Svetambaras, by contrast, imposed no such condition and therefore did permit women to join them.

Both groups regard women's bodies as inferior to men's in that they are weaker by nature. Therefore the ascetic path is more difficult for them. For the Svetambaras, however, the female body is not an insurmountable obstacle; they permit women to take full initiation, and even maintain that the nineteenth Jina (Mallinath) was female. Digambaras vehemently disagree, arguing that asceticism requires a powerful, 'adamantine' body, which women lack (Jaini 1979: 39). They believe that rebirth in a male body is a prerequisite for full renunciation, but in the interim they permit women to become *aryikas* (noble women) and lead a life of semi-renunciation.

Finally, the nature of the Jina's omniscience when embodied (that is, while in life) came to be a point of contention between the two groups. According to the Digambaras, one who is omniscient must already have transcended bodily appetites and functions. Thus the Jina has no need of normal bodily activities such as sleep or the consumption and elimination of food, and does not preach: instead, he communicates via a divine, supernatural sound. The Svetambaras, by contrast, believe that all embodied beings are subject to bodily demands; therefore the omniscient Jina eats, sleeps, and communicates in the regular way through the spoken word.

Sacred Literature

The sacred literature of the Jainas is said to have been transmitted by the Jina Mahavira to his followers, but it is not believed to have originated with him. In our time cycle, the eternal teachings were first propounded by the Jina **Rsabha** and then promulgated anew by each succeeding prophet. Mahavira's teachings were committed to memory by his closest disciples, who then transmitted them orally to other disciples, who in turn passed them along down the generations. Thus the Jaina canon, the *Agama*, for many years existed as a purely oral tradition.

The *Agama* consists of three main branches: the *Purva* ('the ancient'), concerned with Jaina metaphysics, cosmology, and philosophy; the *Anga* ('the limbs'), which includes discussion of mendicant conduct, doctrine, karma, and religious narratives; and the *Angabahya* ('ancillary limbs'), a subsidiary collection of commentaries on the above topics, along with dialogues on subjects such as astrology and the cycles of time.

The canon was faithfully preserved and transmitted orally from generation to generation within the ascetic orders for more than two hundred years. In the early fourth century BCE, however, northern India was struck by a devastating famine that is said to have

From the *Bhaktamara Stotra*

The Bhaktamara Stotra *is one of the most beloved Jaina texts. It is addressed to Adinatha—another name for Rsabha, the first Tirthankara.*

In the fullness of faith
I bow
to the feet of the Jina,
shining as they reflect the gems in the crowns
of the gods
who bow down in devotion,
illuminating the darkness
of oppressive sin,
a refuge in the beginning of time
for all souls
lost in the ocean of birth (1)

. . .

Praising you
instantly destroys
the sinful karma that binds
embodied souls
to endless rebirth
just as the sun's rays
instantly shatter
the all-embracing
bee-black
endless dark night (7)

. . .

Gods like Hari and Hara
don't have your shining knowledge.
Light is glorious
in a glittering jewel
but not in a piece
of even the best glass.

I think it is good
that after seeing
Hari, Hara, and the rest of the gods
my heart is pleased

only with you.
I have gained so much in this world
by seeing you
o lord.
None other can steal my mind,
not even in my next life (20–1)

. . .

Praise to you,
o lord,
remover of the pain
of the three worlds.
Praise to you,
stainless ornament
of the earth's surface.
Praise to you,
supreme lord
of the triple world.
Praise to you,
o Jina,
you dry up
the ocean of rebirth (26)

. . .

O Jina King
Laksmi comes quickly to Manatunga,
who forever wears around his neck
your garland of praise,
woven from the qualities
of my bhakti
and adorned by the multihued flowers
of radiant color (44)

(*Bhaktamara Stotra*, Manatunga, 1, 7,
20–1, 26, 44; Cort 2005: 95–8).

continued for twelve years. The Jaina canon was nearly lost altogether as both the ascetics and the householders who were their only source of sustenance struggled to survive.

From this point on, what happened to the *Agama* becomes sketchy and contentious. The *Purvas*—the most ancient section, believed to contain the universal teachings of all the Jinas, from the first (Rsabha) to the twenty-fourth (Mahavira)—disappeared, although it is thought that much of the content was contained in the final section of the *Anga*, called the *Drstivada*. Unfortunately, the *Drstivada* as well was eventually lost, but Jainas believe that its essence was preserved through mnemonic allusions elsewhere: Svetambaras find it in one of the texts that make up the *Angabahya*; Digambaras, in the *Satkhandagama* and *Kasayaprabhrta*.

In addition to the *Agamas*, vast collections of post-canonical writing were produced by the learned *acharyas* (mendicant scholars) of both the Svetambara and Digambara sects. Known collectively as *Anuyogas* ('branches of scripture'), their writings achieved canonical status within their respective traditions and are today among the most celebrated works of ancient and medieval Indian philosophy.

Cosmology

Jainas believe that the entire cosmos (*loka*) is made up of six eternal substances called *dravya*, and that knowledge of these *dravya* is an important step towards self-perfection. These substances are classified in two broad categories: *jiva* (soul) and **ajiva** (non-soul). *Jiva* is an eternal substance with consciousness. Souls caught in the cycle of rebirth (*samsara*) are often referred to as *samsari jiva*, whereas those that are liberated are referred to as *muktatma*. *Ajiva* is a substance without consciousness and consists of five types: *pudgala* (pure matter), *kala* (time), *dharma* (principle of motion), *adharma* (principle of rest), and *akash* (space). The latter four—all variants of *pudgala*—are 'supportive' forms, without which existence would not be possible.

Pudgala is a concrete substance with the attributes of touch, taste, smell, and colour. Although it has no special function, in its most subtle form it is the basis of all matter and energy. All activities of the mind and body, including thought and speech, are considered to be *pudgala*. All worldly knowledge is acquired by means of *pudgala*—including the knowledge of how to free ourselves from it! Indeed, it is only through perception, which is also a form of *pudgala*, that we can know the cosmos and its contents.

Thus *pudgala* is not antithetical to *jiva*. It is neutral in this regard, although its natural tendency is to become attached both to other forms of matter and to *jiva*. This is an important point, because the renouncers typically speak of matter in highly negative terms (for example, referring to the world as vomit, or the body as a trap). Those terms are chosen largely for rhetorical impact, however, for *pudgala* is *jiva*'s friend as well as its foe. The effective omnipresence of *pudgala* makes this unavoidable. The worldly soul that seeks release from it is nevertheless utterly dependent on it.

The most fundamental existential problem, shared by all beings in the cosmos, is the fact that *jiva* and *ajiva* are thoroughly enmeshed. This is what prevents the soul from achieving a state of bliss, for bliss can be experienced only in a state of purity and separation from all that is not-soul. Jainas do not posit an original state of separation from which there was a 'fall'. Instead they assert that this state of entanglement is eternal, 'without beginning', and that we are constantly exacerbating it, since every activity of the mind as well as the body causes vibrations that create ever more particles of sticky, binding karma. These karmic particles come in two types—auspicious ('good karma', called **punya**) and inauspicious ('bad karma', called **paap**)—but ultimately all forms of karma must be purged. The forces behind those karma-creating activities, and hence the root causes of our bondage, are the passions.

This is the quandary from which the Jaina path of self-restraint offers a coherent way out. Through self-restraint, Jainas believe, we can discipline the passions and eventually quell them. By limiting—eventually, eliminating—the inflow of karma and cleansing the soul of all the karmic particles that have become encrusted on it through eternity, we can eliminate the cause of the soul's suffering. The process of purging is called *nirjara*, and it is the purpose behind most Jaina practices. Normally, karma dissolves when (after giving its pain or pleasure) it comes to fruition. But karma can be made to 'ripen' and vanish prematurely through the practice of certain austerities, and this is the aim of ascetic discipline. Among the austerities, or *tapas*, that cause karma to dissociate from the soul are fasting, study of the *Agamas*, and meditation.

The Jaina view of the soul's lonely, blundering voyage through endless time within a violent and purposeless cosmos is a harsh one, from which the only sensible response is escape. The tradition crystallized around ideas that explain our predicament, and practices that offer a way out.

❧ DIFFERENTIATION

As a tiny, heterodox minority within the vast Indian mosaic, Jainas have always been vulnerable to assimilation. How they have managed to differentiate themselves, expand, and thrive when other world-renouncing traditions have not is an interesting question. Paradoxically, the success of 'other-worldly' Jainism likely owes much to its 'this-worldly' know-how. The skills required to forge alliances with ruling elites and make inroads into established economic structures were key to its survival in the medieval period (from the fifth century through the seventeenth). The Jaina tradition developed those skills early on, in the first two centuries of its existence, when it enjoyed the patronage of the kshatriya rulers.

In the final centuries before the beginning of the Common Era, the fate of all the *shramana* groups, including the Buddhists as well as the Jainas, depended on their ability to secure royal patronage. The socio-political 'alliance' between the kshatriyas and the various *shramanas* was rooted in a shared ideological opposition to brahminic orthodoxy. The fact that Mahavira came from a kshatriya clan was a sign of the kshatriyas' social ascent. The alliance was mutually beneficial: the *shramanas* prospered with the economic support of the kshatriyas, while the latter gained in a myriad of ways through the extension of their popular support.

Jaina philosophy flourished over the following centuries. Among the *acharyas* who produced important treatises were the Digambaras Umasvati (the second-century author of the *Tatthvartha Sutra*), his contemporary Kundakunda, and Haribhadra in the seventh century, and the Svetambaras Jinasena in the ninth century and Hemachandra in the twelfth. Together, the philosophical works of the *acharyas* constitute an enormous and celebrated body of sacred literature.

The social organization of the Jaina community retained its 'fourfold' character throughout the medieval period, preserving the interdependence between householders and renouncers. Instead of establishing large monasteries, as the Buddhists did, the Jaina ascetics continued to rely directly on householders for sustenance. Rules of ascetic

Major Branches of Jainism

Svetambara:

Murtipujak (idol worshipping)
Sthanakvasi (non-idol worshipping)
Terapanthi (non-idol worshipping)

Digambara:

Terapantha (idol worshipping)
Bisapantha (idol worshipping)

practice placed severe restrictions on personal possessions and comforts. Householders were keenly aware of these rules, and because of their direct involvement in the lives of renouncers, they acted as unofficial enforcers of proper conduct.

Their influence may help to account for the fact that the Jainas did not establish large monasteries. It has been suggested that the Jainas resisted the wave of Hindu devotionalism, and the arrival of Islam, in the twelfth century far more successfully than the Buddhists did, precisely because of their social organization. The Buddhist monasteries also relied on the support of their lay followers, but never to the extent that the Jaina ascetics relied on Jaina householders, who provided mendicants with sustenance as often as three times a day. The latter played a central role in the perpetuation of Jaina tradition, and for that reason they may have been less vulnerable than their Buddhist counterparts to the rise of the Hindu *bhakti* (devotional) movement. Furthermore, whereas the concentration of the Buddhist monks and scriptures in large, wealthy monasteries made them easy targets for marauding armies, the Jainas were dispersed throughout the society and had no property to plunder. Thus the decentralized nature of Jaina groups may have inadvertently contributed to their survival.

REFORM

Idol (*murti*) veneration became an established feature of Jainism very early in its history (third century BCE), but the first Jaina temples did not appear until the early medieval period (c. fifth century CE)— an era of widespread temple construction. With time and growing affluence, the temples became the anchors of Jaina religious life, sites not only of devotion but of interaction between householders and the mendicants who gathered there.

Idol-veneration continues to be central religious activity for most Jainas. Today, however, the care and management of temples is almost exclusively the responsibility of the laity. The only exception to the rule of enforced itinerancy developed in the last century, with the revitalization of the Bhattaraka tradition within the Digambara sect; *bhattarakas* are semi-ascetics who control the religious community's assets and are involved in the administration of temples. The general absence of settled, temple-based communities of

Map 7.1   Origin and dispersion of Jainism

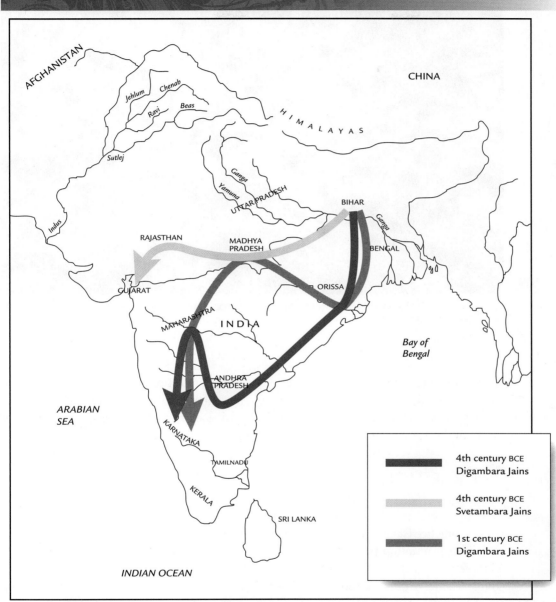

████	4th century BCE Digambara Jains
████	4th century BCE Svetambara Jains
████	1st century BCE Digambara Jains

Today, most Svetambara Jainas live in western India (Gujarat, Rajasthan, Madhya Pradesh, Uttar Pradesh) and most Digambara Jainas in the south, but communities of both sects can be found throughout India, as well as abroad.

mendicants today can be traced to a number of powerful reform movements that arose between the fifteenth and seventeenth centuries and reinvigorated the tradition of ascetic discipline among both Svetambara and Digambara Jainas.

The reformers saw a direct correlation between the proliferation of temples and what they considered to be a growing laxity on the part of many Jaina ascetics, who gradually

One of the five Dilwara temples at Mount Abu in Rajasthan, built between the eleventh and thirteenth centuries (Willard G. Oxtoby).

abandoned their itinerant way of life for the relative comfort of a settled life in and around the temples. Although murmurs of protest against the laxity and considerable wealth of these *caityavasis* (temple-dwellers) could be heard as early as the eleventh century, it was not until the 1400s that the practice of dwelling in temples was forcefully condemned.

PRACTICE

The importance that Jainism attaches to practice is one of the tradition's defining features. Correct practice (*samyak caritra*) constitutes one of the 'Three Jewels' of the tradition, along with correct intuition (*samyak darshan*) and correct knowledge (*samyak jnana*). Although all three are equally fundamental, correct practice tends to overshadow the others because so many of its features are so unusual—from the strict avoidance of certain very common foods to the Digambara ascetics' insistence on nudity. Before we look at specific practices, however, it is important to grasp the special significance that the concept of practice has in Jainism, and how it is grounded in Jaina metaphysics.

The Jaina emphasis on practice reflects an understanding of the world and human suffering as *real*—not illusory—and in need of active human intervention. This understanding stands in sharp contrast to that of Vedanta-Hinduism and Buddhism, which essentially see the world and human suffering as products of thought and perception, and therefore focus on changing consciousness as the way to freedom. While Jainas recognize that lack of right consciousness plays a key role in the problems of earthly existence, they also believe that earthly problems are caused by real physical (not just mental) activities and therefore must be dealt with through practices such as penance and fasting.

We have already described the Jaina view of the eternal soul (*jiva*) and matter (*ajiva*) as enmeshed in a web that will never be untangled without concrete action. Because our entrapment is real in a physical sense—not just an illusory state that can be dispelled through clearer thinking—our enlightenment hinges as much on our practice as it does on our worldview. Good intentions, for Jainas, can never be enough; action must always be the foremost consideration. It is for this reason that renouncers follow an ascetic discipline designed to heighten their awareness of how they move their bodies in and through space—how they walk, sit, lie down, speak, hold things, collect alms, sleep, go to the toilet, etc. It is no exaggeration to say that the focus on practice is a defining feature of the Jaina path.

The elaborate edifice of Jaina practice aims to cleanse the soul of the *pudgala* that clings to it. By shedding obstructive karma, the soul becomes free to manifest its true, radiant and powerful nature. Practices are of two types: defensive and offensive. Defensive strategies, such as inculcating detachment and mindfulness, impede the accumulation of new karma (a process called *samvara*), while practices such as fasting, meditation, and various forms of physical discipline 'burn off' old karma. Jainas call this process *nirjara*.

The Great Head Bathing Ceremony of Lord Bahubali (Frédéric Soltan/Sygma/Corbis). The second son of the first Jina, Lord Rishab, and the heir to half his father's kingdom, Bahubali chose not to resist when his elder brother sought to take his inheritance from him. Instead, Bahubali renounced violence and entered a state of deep meditation. He stood motionless, allowing creepers to grow on his body and birds to nest in his hair—the image that inspired the famous statue in Shravanabelgola. Eventually he attained *moksha*.

For renouncers and householders alike, the purpose of Jaina practice—ascetic discipline, dietary restrictions, fasting, **samayika** (state of equanimity), **pratikramana** (prayer of forgiveness), *sallekhana* (fast to death), even Jina puja (worship of the Jinas)—is purification of the soul through the dual processes of *samvara* and *nirjara*. The main difference between the paths of the renouncer and the householder lies in the degree of purification they permit; the renouncer's life is structured by a series of vows (**mahavratas**) that make it nearly impossible for new karma to develop, whereas the vows that householders live by (**anuvratas**) are less demanding, but more generative of karma.

Because renouncers are largely shielded from the risk of accumulating new karma, they can devote their time to whittling away the karmic load they carry. Householders, immersed as they are in worldly activities—working, raising families, preparing food—are awash in karmic influences. Nevertheless, they can limit the influx of negative karma (*paap*) through lay practices (*anuvratas*) such as fasting or limiting possessions, travel, cosmetics, and so on; many women in particular undertake these moderate exercises in restraint. What marks such activities as characteristically Jaina is that they all involve disengagement from the world. Even a devotional activity such as Jina puja, which outwardly resembles a Hindu form of worship, is understood from the Jaina perspective as a way of fostering worldly detachment.

Ideally, the vows that govern the lives of all Jainas, whether renouncers or householders, serve to limit worldly engagement, discipline the body, and help the soul develop the tools it will need for its eventual liberation. Thus Jainism is unequivocally a *shramana* or renouncer tradition even though the vast majority of Jainas at any given time have always been householders actively, and successfully, involved in worldly pursuits.

Jainism remains a *shramana* tradition because its defining framework is thoroughly ascetic in character. It creates and moulds religious identity by asking the faithful to accept increasingly restrictive boundaries. The main difference between the *mahavratas* of the mendicants and the *anuvratas* of the householders is the degree to which the vows restrict worldly engagement.

Ascetic Practice

The *mahavratas* are five 'great vows' accepted by everyone who takes up the life of a Jaina ascetic: *ahimsa* (non-harm), *satya* (truthfulness), *asteya* (non-stealing), *brahmacharya* (celibacy), and *aparigraha* (non-possession/non-attachment). It is said that Mahavira established celibacy as a separate vow, independent of the fourth vow of non-attachment under which it had been incorporated, during the time of Parsavanath.

Although the discourse of renunciation often refers to the poetic image of the solitary wanderer, initiation into the renouncer path is very much a collective endeavour. Aspiring ascetics must first seek and receive permission from their families (or spouses), as well as from the leader of a mendicant order.

In addition, the ascetic orders impose certain restrictions themselves. Neither sect accepts individuals who are physically, emotionally, or mentally fragile. The renouncer path was not designed as a refuge for those on the margins of conventional society; it is an arduous path suitable only for the courageous, committed, and stalwart. It is for this reason that the Digambara sect continues to claim that women's physical and emotional natures make them unsuitable for the ascetic life. The female body's 'femaleness'—determined as it is by karma—is seen as too great an impediment, making the already challenging life of mendicancy impossible. In other words, the renouncer path is to be undertaken only by those who have both the spiritual desire and the physical fortitude for a life of denial.

By drawing the Self back from worldly concerns, the vows create the conditions in which its true vitality and force can reveal themselves. The first vow (*ahimsa*) is the weightiest of the five; Jainas commonly say that it essentially encompasses all the others. In effect, *ahimsa* forbids all involvement with the world and ensures that no action is undertaken spontaneously, without restraint. Because the vow of *ahimsa* is total and unconditional in its application, renouncers must constantly strive to cause no harm—through speech,

From the *Acaranga Sutra* on Good Conduct

He who injures these (earth bodies) does not comprehend and renounce the sinful acts; he who does not injure these, comprehends and renounces the sinful acts. Knowing them, a wise man should not act sinfully towards the earth, nor cause others to act so, nor allow others to act so. He who knows these causes of sin relating to earth, is called a reward-knowing sage. Thus I say (Jacobi 1884: 10–11).

. . . the sage who walks the beaten track (to liberation), regards the world in a different way. 'Knowing thus (the nature of) acts in all regards, he does not kill,' he controls himself, he is not overbearing.

Comprehending that pleasure (and pain) are individual, advising kindness, he will not engage in any work in the whole world: keeping before him the one (great aim, liberation), and not turning aside, 'living humbly, unattached to any creature.' The rich in (control) who with a mind endowed with all penetration (recognizes) that a bad deed should not be done, will not go after it. What you acknowledge as righteousness, that you acknowledge as sagedom . . . ; what you acknowledge as sagedom, that you acknowledge as righteousness. It is inconsistent with weak, sinning, sensual, ill-conducted house-inhabiting men. 'A sage, acquiring sagedom, should subdue his body.' 'The heroes who look at everything with indifference, use mean and rough (food, &c.)'. Such a man is said to have crossed the flood (of life), to be a sage, to have passed over (the samsara) to be liberated, to have ceased (from acts). Thus I say (Jacobi 1884: 46–7).

action, or thought—even to 'one-sensed' beings (invisible air-bodied beings, water, fire, earth) as well as plants, insects, animals, and fellow human beings. Avoiding harm to humans and other animals is easy compared to avoiding harm to water and air and other minute forms of life, all of which are equally endowed with an eternal soul. This is a monumental challenge and is the main reason behind the Jaina insistence on correct practice.

Monks and nuns are not permitted to prepare their own food, since even harvesting plants or boiling water inevitably causes harm to living beings. Thus the ascetics depend entirely on the generosity of householders, and even so they must be vigilant to maintain their vow of *ahimsa*. They are permitted only a small portion of the householder's 'leftovers'; they cannot accept food that has been prepared expressly for them, as this would implicate them in whatever violence that preparation entailed; and the food and water they receive in their alms bowls must already have been cooked or (in the case of fruits) peeled, to ensure that it is *ajiv* (without life).

It is critical to understand the rationale underpinning these practices. The path of renunciation is open to all, irrespective of caste, gender, or social position. But it is extremely demanding, and Jainas know that very few will ever be able to take it. The overwhelming majority who remain householders therefore accept, implicitly or explicitly, that a certain amount of violence will be a regular part of their lives. For these people, support for the renouncers is both a duty and an honour—with the additional benefit of earning them karmic merit (*punya*). More important, it sustains a system in which the ideal of living without doing harm remains a genuine possibility for anyone with the required strength of character.

The Mahavratas

1. Non-violence (*ahimsa*)
2. Truth (*satya*)
3. Non-stealing (*asteya*)
4. Chastity (*brahmacharya*)
5. Non-possession/non-attachment (*aparigraha*)

The *mahavrata* of *ahimsa* prohibits outright many aspects of the renouncers' former householder lives, and no aspect of embodied existence escapes the framework of restraint. Eating, talking, sleeping, walking, defecating, urinating, thinking, even dreaming—every activity is subject to the discipline of non-harm. Renouncers must not walk on grass, for to do so would cause it harm; wherever they step they must look carefully to be sure they do not harm anything on the ground; they are forbidden to use electricity and flush toilets (which cause harm to fire-bodied and water-bodied beings respectively); and their thoughts are subject to continuous self-censure as they try to eliminate anger, jealousy, greed, and desire. Negative or aggressive thoughts are believed to accrue bad karma (*paap*) in much the same way that stepping on an insect would. The restrictions on speech, body, and thought contained within the principal vow of *ahimsa* are potentially limitless.

The subsidiary vows of non-attachment, truthfulness, non-stealing, and celibacy reinforce and enlarge the vow of *ahimsa*. The vows of truthfulness and non-stealing forbid false speech and the use of anything that has not been freely given. *Brahmacharya* is more than a vow of celibacy: it is a vow to renounce all desire. Even dreams of a 'carnal' nature have the power to attract karma and therefore require penance. The vow of *aparigraha* entails the renunciation not only of all possessions (home, clothing, money, etc.) but of all attachments, whether to places, people, things, or dogmatic ideas.

In addition to the *mahavratas*, which specify actions to be avoided, there are six 'obligatory actions' that renouncers are required to perform, some of which will be discussed in detail below. In brief, they are equanimity (*samayika*), praise to the Jinas (Jina puja), homage to teacher (*vandana*), repentance (*pratikramana*), body-abandonment (*kayotsarga*), and, finally, the more general pledge to renounce all transgressions (*pratyakhyana*).

Taken together, the *mahavratas* and obligatory actions can appear overwhelming. But it is important to bear in mind that the constraints they impose are not seen as barriers to freedom. Rather, they are understood as catalysts to self-realization, the means to the sublime state of unconditional freedom, permanent bliss, and omniscience. Furthermore, each step along the way to self-realization is believed to bring benefits for the community as well as the individual. For Jainas, the renouncers embody a spiritual power that can work miracles—though of course they are not supposed to use their powers for 'worldly' purposes.

The path to the very highest levels of self-realization has 14 stages. Householders rarely rise above the fifth step, and must fully renounce worldly life if they wish to go beyond it. Nevertheless, the householder path offers considerable opportunities for spiritual progress as well.

Householder Practice

The *anuvratas* are the 'small (or lesser) vows' that govern lay life and are normally taken without any formal ceremony. Modelled on the mendicant's *mahavratas*, they reflect the same aspiration to limit worldly engagement. They are identical in name and number to the *mahavratas*, but are interpreted and applied more leniently.

For instance, the *anuvrata* of *ahimsa* is partial, not total. It prohibits the consumption of certain foods, as well as eating after dark (when the risk of injury to insects is especially great). But it does not concern itself with one-sensed beings, accepting that harm to them is unavoidable for householders. Two of the subsidiary vows work in a similar manner: celibacy is redefined to mean chastity in marriage, and the *anuvrata* of *aparigraha*, instead of requiring householders to live without possessions, demands only that they scrutinize their psychological attachment to those possessions. The *anuvratas* of truthfulness and non-stealing, however, are much the same as the equivalent *mahavratas*. The *anuvratas* are seen as establishing a compromise between worldly existence and spiritual progress. They do not interfere with the householder's ability to lead a 'normal' existence. Quite the contrary: Jainas have long been among the wealthiest, most literate, and most accomplished communities in India. And from the Jaina perspective, there is a direct connection between their socio-economic success and their religious vows.

The Fast to Death

Jainas boast that whereas other traditions celebrate birth, they celebrate death. This statement is a powerful reminder that they trace their origins to the *shramana* tradition in which the highest goal was to escape embodied existence. A death that is 'celebrated' is one that has been accepted voluntarily and with equanimity, indicating total detachment from the body and the world. Again, the root of 'Jainism' is the *Jina*—the 'one who has conquered' his ego, greed, and attachment to the world, even his body.

For Jainas the ideal death is voluntary, achieved through the ritual fast called *sallekhana*. Although *sallekhana* is not the universal practice, it is not uncommon even among householders. It is seen as a fitting and highly auspicious conclusion to a life dedicated to self-discipline and detachment. To be able to 'discard the body' without pain or fear, and greet death with calmness and equanimity, is to reap the ultimate reward of a life lived in accordance with Jaina principles.

A Jaina ascetic who has taken the vow of *sallekhana* prays (Frédéric Soltan/Sygma/Corbis).

In addition, *sallekhana* is believed to be highly advantageous for the soul as it journeys forward. A dispassionate death results in a powerful expulsion of *paap* (bad karma) while attracting the *punya* (good karma) required to ensure a good rebirth either in a heavenly realm or in a spiritually advanced human state. Jainas believe that at the moment of physical death, the karma-saturated soul will be instantaneously propelled into a new incarnation, determined by its karma. (A soul free of all karma, instead of being reborn, would ascend to the realm of liberation, **siddha loka**; but that is not possible in the current time cycle.)

If the Jaina ideal is detachment, a progressive withdrawal from life during life, then *sallekhana* becomes its logical conclusion. The title of an essay on the subject by James Laidlaw captures this idea beautifully: 'A Life Worth Leaving' (2005). For Jainas, therefore, *sallekhana* is the natural culmination of a life dedicated to the discipline of detachment from the world; it is the ultimate embodiment of Jaina values, paradoxically achieved through a kind of dis-embodiment. Whether or not they choose *sallekhana*, Jainas endeavour to accept the inevitability of death with self-control and serene detachment.

Jina Worship

The objects of Jaina worship are the 24 perfected beings known as the Jinas. Temples are constructed to house icons of them, pilgrimages are made to places associated with them, and they are worshipped daily in prayer. Although four of the Jinas are especially revered (Mahavira, Parsavanath, Neminath, Rsabha), all receive regular devotions.

The main festivals celebrate events in the lives of the Jinas, especially Mahavira, as do the exquisite Jaina miniature paintings, while Jaina sculpture is devoted almost exclusively to portraits of the Jinas in meditation. Even in the two Svetambara sects that reject image worship—the Sthanakvasis and Terapanthis—the Jinas are ever-present in narrative and prayer. Clearly, then, to be a Jaina is to be a worshipper of the Jinas.

And yet the Jinas are profoundly absent. Having perfected themselves, they are indifferent to their worshippers, whose transient worldly concerns are literally 'beneath them'. The existence of a lively, emotional cult of devotion within a tradition centred on dispassionate renunciation of all attachments may seem paradoxical, but Jainas insist that the real purpose of devotion is self-transformation through surrender to the ideal that the Jina embodies.

What most Jainas mean by 'self-transformation' through Jina puja, however, is not terribly different from what we find in theistic traditions. Proper devotional practice leads to proper mental activity, which in turn leads to the elimination of negative karma and the attraction of good karma. In this way devotional practice produces karmic 'blessings' even if the Jina who is the ostensible object of that practice is indifferent to it. Again, one of the most fundamental tenets of the Jaina tradition is its rejection of the concept of a creator God who intervenes in human affairs. Here we see how the proper manipulation of karma makes such a figure superfluous.

The central prayer in Jainism, called the **Namokar Mantra**, suggests how the devotional cult operates. The first part begins by proclaiming homage to the Jinas ('Namo Arihantanum'), then to all liberated beings ('Namo Siddhanum'), to *acharyas*, ('Namo Ayariyanam'), to religious leaders ('Namo Uwajayahanum'), and finally to all renouncers everywhere ('Namo loe savva sahunam'). The second part consists of the statement 'This five-fold mantra destroys all sins and is the most powerful of all auspicious mantras.'

Terapanthis and Sthanakvasis are uncomfortable with the quasi-miraculous language of the latter section and therefore omit it. But most Jainas consider it an integral part of the prayer. As such, it provides insight into the way Jaina devotionalism parallels the devotionalism of theistic cults even though devotees expect nothing from the objects of their devotion. What is important is the power of the mantra itself to produce good karma.

Puja assists the devotee in two ways, helping him or her along the path of self-realization and at the same time bringing 'worldly' benefits. The beneficent power of good karma (*punya*), earned through devotional practice, makes a reciprocal relationship with a god unnecessary. It is important to add here that even though the Jaina devotional cult operates in a non-theistic framework, Jainas do venerate a number of gods and goddesses who are believed to reside in heavenly realms. These divinities (e.g., Padmavati, the female guardian deity of Parsavanath, or the Hindu god Ganesha) *are* capable of interceding on behalf of their followers. Jainas worship and pray to them for assistance in worldly matters, but not for assistance along the path of liberation.

The *Sakra Stava* (Hymn of Indra)

'Sakra' is an alternative name for the god Indra. This hymn, in which the god praises the Jinas, is recited by observant Jainas.

[Indra, the god of the celestial one, spoke thus]:
'My obeisance to my Lords, the Arhats, the prime ones, the Tirthankaras, the enlightened ones, the best of men, the lions among men, the exalted elephants among men, lotus among men.
Transcending the world they rule the world, think of the well-being of the world.
Illuminating all, they dispel fear, bestow vision, show the path, give shelter, life, enlightenment.
Obeisance to the bestowers of *dharma*, the teachers of *dharma*, the leaders of *dharma*, the charioteers of *dharma*, the monarchs of the four regions of *dharma*,
To them, who have uncovered the veil and have found unerring knowledge and vision, the islands in the ocean, the shelter, the goal, the support.
Obeisance to the Jinas—the victors—who have reached the goal and who help others reach it.
The enlightened ones, the free ones, who bestow freedom, the Jinas victorious over fear, who have known all and can reveal all, who have reached that supreme state which is unimpeded, eternal, cosmic and beatific, which is beyond disease and destruction, where the cycle of birth ceases; the goal, the fulfillment,
My obeisance to the *Sramana Bhagvan Mahavira*
The initiator, the ultimate Tirthankara, who has come to fulfill the promise of earlier Tirthankaras.
I bow to him who is there—in Devananda's womb from here—my place in heaven.
May he take cognizance of me.'
With these words, Indra paid his homage to *Sramana Bhagvan Mahavira* and, facing east, resumed his seat on the throne (*Kalpa Sutra* 2; Lath 1984: 29–33).

Festivals

The Jaina ritual calendar revolves around three major festivals, with many minor ones in between. The three are Divali, which coincides with the start of the New Year in November–December; **Mahavira Jayanti** in spring; and, most important, Paryushana/ Daslakshana, in August–September.

Although it is common to think of Divali as a Hindu or even pan-Indian festival of light, many Jainas believe it began as a Jaina commemoration of the *moksha* of Mahavira and over time was co-opted by other traditions. For Jainas, the 'light' that Divali celebrates is the light of omniscience. While Hindus celebrate the defeat of the evil King Ravana and the establishment of social and cosmic order with the return of Lord Rama, Jainas commemorate their Lord's transcendence of society and the cosmos altogether.

Even so, Jaina celebrations of Divali do not differ markedly from those of their Hindu neighbours. For example, because Divali coincides with the new year, the Hindu goddess of wealth, Sri Lakshmi, is enthusiastically worshipped by all. And because the festival marks the start of a new financial year, members of the business community (of which Jainas constitute an important segment) are especially fervent in showing their appreciation of the goddess. Of course, the ascetics are never far away to remind the Jainas that the greatest wealth is *moksha* itself. Once again it is important to remember that financial success, in itself, is not considered antithetical to the Jaina ideal: as long as one does not become covetous, the possession of wealth is regarded as an indicator of an auspicious life.

Mahavira Jayanti is a joyous festival held in the month of *caitra* (March–April). Celebrating the birth of Lord Mahavira, it is an occasion for great pageantry, with shops, streets, and temples all sumptuously decorated. Jainas enthusiastically undertake pilgrimages, listen to sermons, sing devotional hymns, and take part in pujas as well as ritual re-enactments of the wondrous events associated with Mahavira's birth. Ritual actors in heavenly costume play the roles of the adoring gods and goddesses, who descend from the heavens to pay the baby homage and carry him to the mythical Mount Meru, where he is ceremoniously given his first bath and his name. To perform the role of Indra, the king of the gods, or his queen Indrani is especially meritorious, and the right to do so is usually won at auctions that generate huge sums of money for various philanthropic and social service organizations.

A worshipper pours water on statues of Lord Mahavira as part of the Mahavira Jayanti celebration (Raj Patidar/ Reuters/Landov).

The most important of all Jaina festivals, however, is Paryushana/Daslakshana (the Svetambara and Digambara names for the festival, respectively). This festival is celebrated at the end of the summer rainy season—a four-month period of such lush fecundity that renouncers are forbidden to travel during it, lest they cause unnecessary violence to the innumerable sentient beings that the rains bring to life.

The literal meaning of Paryushana is 'abiding together'—a reference to the sustained interaction that takes place between householders and renouncers during the summer. Obliged to stay in one place, the renouncers must seek alms from the same local householders for several months, and the latter take advantage of this daily contact to seek the renouncers' advice on issues of all kinds, worldly as well as spiritual. Paryushana comes at a time of transition in the annual calendar, marking the end of the rains and the resumption of the renouncers' peripatetic rounds. It is the climax of a period of heightened religiosity.

Although Paryushana is a festival of restraint, it is celebrated with characteristic Jaina enthusiasm. The end of the eight-day festival, called Samvatsari Pratikraman, is a day of introspection, confession of sins, and fasting. The penultimate day is celebrated as the Day of Forgiveness (Kshamavani), when Jainas seek to wipe the slate clean with one another and with the world itself by asking and offering forgiveness for all harms.

Forgiveness is fundamental to social interaction and amity. For Jainas, however, it is equally important in the context of erasing the obligations that tie us to the world. Forgiveness—or, more accurately, 'detached forgiveness'—is essential to self-control and renunciation. To 'clean the slate' with all beings in the world, Jainas recite the universal prayer, *Micchami Dukkadam*:

> We forgive all living beings
> We seek pardon from all living beings
> We are friendly towards all living beings,
> And we seek enmity with none.

An interesting 'minor' festival is Astanika, celebrated three times a year, in spring, summer, and fall. It reveals the importance that Jaina cosmology attributes to human birth, for it is only during Astanika periods that the minor gods have the opportunity to worship the Jinas—an opportunity that humans enjoy throughout their lives. In Jaina cosmology, those minor gods are reaping the fruits of the good karma they earned in their previous human lives. When that karma is exhausted, however, their sojourn in the heavens will end. Then they will have to return to the earth and resume the human work of eliminating bad karma. During their time in the heavenly realms, they have no opportunity to purify their souls except during the Astanika intervals when they can travel to the legendary Nandishwara Island and worship the Jinas. Nandishwara Island is a unique plane within Jaina cosmography, home to 52 naturally formed Jaina temples and more than five thousand Jaina idols of liberated beings (*siddhas*). Humans have no access to Nandishwara Island, but celebrate Astanika by building replicas of the island and its temples, and performing puja before them. Jainas claim that this practice earns good karma and wins them worldly favours from the gods.

Going to Temple

While the Sthanakvasi and Terapanthi sects disapprove of temple construction and image veneration on the grounds that they constitute unnecessary violence, for most Jainas temple and puja rituals are an essential component of their devotional practice. Among the majority of Jainas who do worship idols, Svetambaras and Digambaras differ on some points of devotional practice (e.g., women are not permitted to touch or bathe idols within the Digambar tradition), but much is shared in common. Preparation for a visit to the temple begins at home, with bathing and the donning of freshly laundered clothes. At the temple, worshippers remove their shoes and then enter in a humbled posture, uttering the word 'nissihi' ('I renounce') to indicate their relinquishment of worldly concerns on entering the sacred space.

At the first sight of the Jina *murti*, the worshipper offers *pranam* (salutation) with folded hands and bowed body, and the greeting 'Namo Jinanam' ('I salute the Jina'). The idol is then circumambulated (clockwise) three times, symbolizing commitment to the three jewels of Jainism: right faith, right knowledge and right conduct. *Pranam* is offered a second time as the worshipper enters the inner sanctum containing the idols. Then a third and final *pranam* called *panchanga pranipat*) is offered by lowering oneself to the ground so that knees, hands, and forehead all touch the ground. Only now can puja (worship) be performed.

Jainas consider puja to be of two types, internal and external. *Bhav puja* is internal worship through the cultivation of the proper emotional states, and *dravya puja* is external worship through the devotional offering of material substances. The *dravya puja* ritual, for both Svetambara and Digambara Jainas, consists of the offering of eight substances (*asta dravya*) and symbolizes the giving up of worldly attachments and the strengthening one's resolve for liberation:

- water symbolizes the need to cleanse oneself of worldly attachments;
- sandalwood powder mixed in water symbolizes the need for quiescence and the desire for the end of suffering;
- de-husked white rice symbolizes the end of the cycle of rebirth (just as dehusked rice can never again germinate, a liberated soul will never again take birth);
- flowers (or saffron-coloured rice representing flowers) symbolize the worldly pleasures that must be renounced;
- coconut (or some kind of sweet) symbolizes pleasing food, for which our desires must be disciplined if we are to attain liberation;
- a flame (or saffron-coloured coconut representing a flame) symbolizes the light of knowledge that is needed to destroy the darkness of ignorance;
- incense (or cloves representing incense) symbolizes the destruction of all karmas; and
- fruit (or coconut representing fruit) symbolizes the final state of liberation, the ultimate goal of the Jain path.

The puja concludes with a recitation of the virtues of the Jinas, a prayer for peace, and finally a prayer requesting forgiveness for any mistakes made during the puja.

Almost all Jaina cultural expressions (art, ritual, iconography) are tied in one way or another to the Five Auspicious Events (*Panch Kalyanaka*) in the lives of the Jinas: conception, birth, renunciation, omniscience, and *moksha*. These five paradigmatic events are universally celebrated and powerfully inform the Jaina religious imagination. They are vividly represented in sculptures and miniature paintings, re-enacted in theatre and ritual, and devotedly described in narrative—most famously in the ancient *Kalpa Sutra* text. They are also closely associated with pilgrimages, since every *tirtha* (site of devotion) is linked with one or more of them.

The centrality of the Jinas in the cultural expressions of Jainism—in its rituals and iconography, and as ethical archetypes—is overwhelming. Ultimately, however, Jainism insists that the Jinas are irrelevant: self-realization does not depend on them, and since the Jinas have by definition passed out of this world into a state of liberation, any connection they might have had with life in this world is radically absent. Clearly, the Jina is not central to Jaina metaphysics in the way that God is central in theistic traditions. Nevertheless, the Jina is the bedrock on which the Jaina imagination has developed and around which Jaina devotional life revolves.

Asta dravya puja in Varanasi (Photo courtesy of Nika Kuchuk).

INTERACTION AND ADAPTATION

An important factor in the success of Jainism has been Jainas' ability to maintain good relations with their religious neighbours, particularly Hindus. Because Jainas have never made up more than a small proportion of the communities they live in, a capacity for effective interaction with non-Jainas has been essential.

Jainas themselves credit their adaptive success to their commitment to *ahimsa*: non-violence in thought, speech, and deed makes for easy friendship. Another factor encouraging broad-mindedness and compromise is the doctrine of *anekantavada*: literally meaning 'not one-sided', it teaches that all human truth claims are partial and context-bound, and that intolerance is the product of confusing those claims with truth.

Of course Jainism is not a relativist epistemology. It unequivocally affirms the existence of Truth, as well as its ultimate attainability, and it has strategically used this doctrine to dismiss the rival philosophies of Buddhism and Hindu Vedanta as *ekanta* (one-sided). At the same time it affirms that, among those who have not reached enlightenment, no one can claim more than partial understanding. Jainas maintain that this perspective fosters a general attitude of tolerance towards difference.

We have seen how Jainism's ethical principles—the restrictions it places on dietary practices, livelihoods, and so on—serve as 'fences' to keep the violence of worldly life at bay. Socially, however, Jainism has never erected fences to ensure religious purity. To insist on exclusion would likely have doomed such a small and vulnerable community. Instead, Jainas seek the closest possible integration with their neighbours, adopting local languages and customs while safeguarding their fundamental practices and beliefs.

According to Padmanabh Jaini (1979:287), a prominent scholar of Jainism and Buddhism, the Jaina *acharyas* were prescient when they recommended 'cautious integration' with neighbouring peoples and practices. Well aware of the risk of assimilation into Hindu culture, they also recognized the necessity of forging close social and economic ties with non-Jainas. The *acharya* Jinasena (ninth century CE) went the furthest in prescribing selective integration, and his ideas have been enormously influential.

Jinasena did this in two ways. First, he defined some Hindu practices as falling outside the sphere of religion and taught that Jainas should feel free to adopt any local custom that did not conflict with their basic tenets. Second, he 'Jaina-ized' other Hindu practices, re-interpreting them in terms of Jaina doctrine so that they could be adopted without fear of assimilation. So, for example, he developed a Jaina version of the age-old Hindu *samskaras* (life-cycle rituals), creating an interpretive overlay for Hindu rituals that had already been widely adopted by Jaina householders.

In addition, Jinasena redefined the caste system—an institution that Mahavira had soundly denounced—so as to rationalize it and ease social intercourse for Jainas living in a caste-bound society. Thus he argued that the caste system was not (as the brahmins claimed) divinely ordained, but simply a product of economic and political expediency. He also argued that 'brahmin' should be an honorific title reserved for those who lead righteous lives, not a status ascribed at birth. In this way Jinasena was able to argue that Jainas, because of their superior ethical conduct, were the true brahmins.

Perhaps because of its individualist ontology, emphasizing the solitary nature of the soul, Jainism is not inclined to question the 'authenticity' of its followers. So, for instance, Jainas rarely debate who is and who is not a 'true' Jaina. This is not necessarily the case with Jaina practices, however. The absorption of Hindu influences into Jainism (e.g., theistic elements, ritual practices) has gone on for a long time without becoming a cause for great concern. But in the current climate of religious revival, as the symbolic boundaries between traditions are hardening, the issue of authenticity in practice appears to be taking on increasing significance.

WOMEN

That a separate section on women's roles is required reflects the degree to which the various religious traditions have undervalued those roles in the past. This is as true of Jainism as it is of any other tradition, despite the importance of women's contributions throughout its long history. It is significant that women have never been disqualified from Jainism's renouncer path, as was common among other traditions, which considered the ascetic life to be reserved exclusively for men. Mahavira seems not to have shared the Buddha's doubts regarding women's capacity for the religious life, and the four sections of the order he established for his followers explicitly included two sections for women (renouncers and householders).

Renunciation—Jainism's most (perhaps only) truly venerated path—has been available to Jaina women and men alike. And since the time of Mahavira, the majority of those who have responded to its call have been women. This is highly unusual in the South Asian context, where asceticism has been, and remains, forcefully associated with maleness.

Women have always played a central role in Jaina asceticism, embodying its most venerable ideals. In so doing, they repudiated the 'feminine' obligations of wife- and motherhood. Nuns' writings form part of the philosophical tradition, and their roles are recognized in the narrative literature. Furthermore, most rules of ascetic discipline were applied to nuns in much the same way as they were to monks.

Nevertheless, women at no time came near a position of equality with men. Although women scholar-ascetics are known, they are few in number. And religious narratives often contain ambivalent messages extolling women for their piety and chastity, but condemning them as capricious and sexually predatory. While women were permitted to renounce marriage and motherhood for spiritual advancement, those belonging to the Digambara tradition are still not allowed to take the full vows of ascetic initiation. Furthermore, Digambaras hold that *moksha* is not achievable from within a female body. Svetambaras part company with the Digambara sect here, permitting women full entry into mendicancy and not considering the female body to be an obstacle to liberation. Yet even in the Svetambara sect, nuns do not possess an equal status to monks, and senior nuns are expected to demonstrate their ritually subordinate status through gestures of deference to junior monks. In addition, disciplinary scriptures such as the *Chedasutras*, which outline ascetic rules of conduct, are unambiguous in their insistence that nuns require additional regulations to protect them both from others and from their own weaknesses. Consider:

> A nun is not allowed to be alone. A nun is not allowed to enter alone the house of a layman for food or drink, or to go out from there alone. A nun is not allowed to enter alone a place to ease nature or a place to stay, or to go out from there alone. A nun is not allowed to wander about alone from one village to the other. A nun is not allowed to be without clothing. A nun is not allowed to be without superior. . . . (*Brhat-Kalpa-Sutra* 5.15-21: Shubring 1977, 31. Cited in Balbir, 1994:122).

Nonetheless, the numerical strength of nuns over monks—a phenomenon that has endured from the time of Mahavira—may to some extent have offset the ideological bias in favour of monks. In the contemporary period, it means that nuns are a regular presence in Jain communities, serving as role models and teachers, and they are able to operate with considerable autonomy. For instance, within the Terapanthi Svetambara order, the *pramukha* (female leader) has near-absolute control over the order of nuns. Although she remains formally subject to the ultimate authority of the *acharya* (male leader), she effectively governs nearly 600 nuns.

Svetambara nuns devoted to Lord Bahubali on the road to Shravanabelgola (Frédéric Soltan/Sygma/ Corbis).

Despite the numbers, vigor, and symbolic importance of Jaina nuns, they constitute a tiny portion of the overall Jaina population. The vast majority of Jaina women (and men) choose a far more 'worldly' life that includes family, career and community. Monks and nuns may be the religious heroes of Jainism, but they are utterly dependent on lay women and men for their existence. In defining itself as a four-fold community, Jainism explicitly acknowledges this dependence, and hence the religious importance of the laity. Renouncers could not set themselves apart from the violence of worldly existence if it were not for the householders who shield them from it. Lay Jainas willingly act as buffers between renouncers and the world, enabling the heroic endeavours of the ascetics to bear fruit and in the process creating good karma for themselves. Importantly, it is mainly women who daily provide the necessities of life to mendicants of both sexes. This role is so significant that the entire Jain infrastructure can be said to rest upon it.

It is only through the efforts of lay women that the institution of mendicancy exists: they are the ones who purchase fruits and vegetables, perform whatever predation is necessary to make them acceptable as food (i.e., without life), cutting, cooking, and finally follow the detailed rules governing giving. The sustenance they provide is the foundation that makes everything else possible: the tradition, knowledge, teachings, experience, living role models, and ascetic ideal itself. And the giving of food to ascetics produces highly auspicious karma that benefits not just the giver, but her entire family. Behind these activities of nurturing and reverence lie years of learning.

Young girls begin helping their mothers in the preparation and offering of food at an early age. They quickly learn the scriptural injunctions behind the prohibition of animal flesh, eggs and alcohol, root crops, honey, and unfiltered water. They attune themselves to the movement of the sun, to ensure that all food is prepared and consumed before sundown, as well as the phases of the moon, whose waxing and waning determine the periods of fasting. Perhaps because of women's close attention to the rules governing the preparation and donation of food, it is they who observe dietary restrictions most closely and faithfully. Fasting is Jainism's most archetypal religious act, and women are its most dedicated disciples.

Finally, as in all traditions, it is lay women who are primarily responsible for maintaining home and family, and for cultivating religious ideals. Children learn from their mothers the proper demeanour in prayer and puja, the bodily knowledge contained in the correct performance of rituals, the wondrous and instructive stories of the Jinas and their triumphs, the intricate nature of the Jaina cosmos and its karmic workings, the rhythms of the festival calendar, the centrality of *ahimsa*, the importance of discipline and food restrictions, and, most important, the sense of a meaningful world in which they can confidently live as Jainas.

🦋 CONTEMPORARY DEVELOPMENTS

Over the last century Jainism—like many of the world's religious traditions—has been undergoing a profound revitalization. This renewal is expressing itself in many ways: a growth in Jaina educational institutes, the wide dissemination of Jaina publications, including sacred texts, the emergence of nationwide Jaina organizations, a rise in the numbers of mendicants, a revival of naked mendicancy in the Digambara sect, the birth of a strong and vocal diaspora Jainism, and the development of a more muscular political identity. All these changes have had the effect of creating a Jainism that is more visible and self-conscious, and whose followers are increasingly concerned to define what is (and what isn't) 'correct' Jaina belief and practice.

The roots of these changes can be traced to India's turbulent colonial period (1857–1947), which saw the rise of reform movements seeking to modernize the Jaina tradition and give it a greater national presence alongside its Hindu, Muslim, and Christian counterparts. Reformers worked to move Jainism away from the narrow socio-cultural and spiritual concerns of particular communities of adherents. From the perspective of the reformers, the Jainism of their day was deeply conservative and defensive, under the control of insular mendicants whose obsession with purity limited access to the tradition's scriptures and condemned Jaina teachings to public obscurity. The reformers launched a two-pronged attack: they sought to have Jainism recognized as an essential part of India's national cultural heritage, integrated into its secular educational institutions; and they fought to combat the prejudice against those institutions within their own communities, which feared that secular education would endanger Jaina spiritual goals (Flügel, 2005). Their successes were swift and momentous: within a century Jainas would be among the most educated communities in India (their literacy levels second only to the tiny Parsi community); their cultural achievements would be recognized as part of India's national heritage (symbolized by the issuance of India's first 'Jainism stamp' in 1935); and their scriptures would be widely accessible.

The decades since Indian independence (1947) have witnessed simultaneous efforts to define more clearly the boundaries of Jaina identity and to gain recognition of Jainism as a world religion with universal appeal. Although these endeavours might seem contradictory—one constrictive and introverted, the other expansive and extroverted—both are fundamental characteristics of Jainism today. Indeed, far from being peculiar to Jainism, the tension between those two poles is characteristic of identity politics in all world religions today.

The effort to define Jaina identity took a more political turn in the second half of the twentieth century, focusing on the community's status as an explicit *minority*, distinct from and vulnerable to the overwhelmingly dominant Hindu majority. This was a new development, and must be seen as part of the trend towards pluralistic identity politics that can be seen in all of the world's religious and cultural traditions today. Communities devoted to the teachings of the Jinas over the last 2600 years have certainly not understood and defined themselves in the same way. Being 'a follower of the Jina' may or may not have been a significant marker of identity, and it was almost certainly not predicated on exclusion of non-Jaina ideas and practices. To the contrary, as was mentioned earlier, the Jaina community traditionally followed a strategy of 'cautious integration' in its relations with cultural others. This strategy effectively amounted to assimilation in most matters; the only exceptions were matters involving core principles such as non-violence. Thus meat-eating would forever be beyond the pale, but in other respects Jainas could readily embrace the customs of the surrounding community, including its language, styles of dress, and cultural festivals.

In recent decades, this strategy has become anachronistic for a sizeable number of Jainas. In an environment where Hindu, Muslim, and Sikh nationalisms find frequent and flamboyant public expression, Jainism's low-key strategy has been criticized as ineffective, insufficient to safeguard a robust identity. Reform-minded Jainas have gained momentum in their efforts to have Jainism recognized as an independent and historically discrete minority tradition in India, but so far the issue remains at an impasse.

While accepting that historical relations between Jainas and Hindus have been generally trouble-free, these contemporary reformers strongly object to the fact that Indian law places Jainism under the heading of 'Hinduism'. They demand recognition of fundamental differences between the two traditions: Jainas do not consider the Vedas to be sacred, for instance, nor do they believe in any creator God. But the desire to identify differences has made it necessary to distinguish ideas and practices that may be considered 'legitimately' Jaina from ideas and practices borrowed from Hinduism. Thus the veneration of Hindu deities such as Ganesha, Hanuman, and Sarasvati—a common practice among Jainas—has become suspect in some quarters, as has any Jain puja that suggests a transactional exchange between the worshipper and the object of worship (the Jina). This ideological shift toward differentiation has resulted in some striking changes in the way some segments of the Jaina community conceptualize, organize, and practise their religion.

On the other hand, the demand for minority status is by no means universally supported by Jainas themselves, and some Jaina organizations have spoken out against it. Stressing the overwhelming social fact of cultural integration (including marriage) between Jainas and Hindus, and the harmonious relations that have existed between the two groups throughout history, they see no reason to upset the status quo. Other critics see Jainism as a distinctive member within a family of distinctive members, all of which constitute variants of 'Hinduism'. The differences between 'members' notwithstanding, their shared geography and common culture (*sanskriti*) are emphasized. Some Jainas even express sympathy with the conservative ideology of the Hindutva movement, treating its claims regarding ancient greatness and its sense of historical victimization at the hands of 'foreign invaders' (especially Christians and Muslims) as their own. Those who oppose recognition of the Jaina community as an official minority within India do not deny that differences of a theological or religious nature exist between Jainas and Hindus; however, they consider the social, cultural and ideological commonalities between the two communities to supersede the differences.

Far less divisive for the Jaina community have been contemporary efforts to establish Jainism as a world religion. The co-existence of expansive with constrictive tendencies is not unique to Jainism; it is characteristic of all contemporary traditions, being an expression of modernity itself. To be 'modern' is to be simultaneously universal *and* distinctive; to be globally relevant *and* utterly singular. Interestingly, one factor that has bolstered both tendencies in Jainism has been the rise of the Jaina diaspora. There are now sizeable Jaina communities in England, the United States, and Canada that are forging their own understanding of what constitutes Jainism. The kind of Jainism that is taking root outside India—removed from the immediate influence of the mendicant tradition—is contributing to significant new developments.

Outside India, for example, the renunciatory ethos becomes harder to sustain, and seemingly less important for Jaina religious identity. Although Jainas everywhere retain their philosophical commitment to the *ahimsa* principle, in diaspora communities it is often expressed in the 'worldly' terms of animal rights, ecological health, and societal improvement; aspirations to self-purification and world transcendence seem to be less common. A similar shift is occurring with respect to dietary practices, which are no longer inextricably tied to the ideology of renunciation; the connection with the *ahimsa* principle remains close, however. What we seem to be witnessing is a redefinition of *ahimsa* and a de-coupling of the previously inseparable relationship between *ahimsa* and renunciation.

Diaspora Jainas are far less inclined to describe Jainism as an ascetic, renunciatory ideology than as one that is progressive, environmentally responsible, egalitarian, non-sectarian, and scientifically avant-garde. In the same way, the cosmological dimensions of Jainism have been eclipsed by its ethical dimensions. This shift marks Jainism's universalizing aspirations; its message of *ahimsa* as globally germane establishes its credentials as a world religion.

Finally, Jainism's sectarian differences are less salient in the diaspora, partly because the community's small numbers make them largely irrelevant. To identify oneself as 'Jaina' is already to identify with a sub-category within the general category of 'Indian', so for many (especially those of the second generation) additional identifiers carry little significance. The markers distinguishing the two Jaina sects may remain meaningful within families, but they carry little currency on the cultural or societal level. As a consequence, Jaina identity is increasingly emphasized, and this development in turn may play a role in the arena of identity politics in India.

Sacred Texts Table

Religion (Sect)	Text(s)	Composition/ Compilation	Compilation/ Revision	Use
Jainism (Svetambara and Digambara)	*Purva Agama*	Ancient and timeless 'universal truths' preached by all the Jinas, from the first (Rsabha) to the last (Mahavira). Communicated to disciples by Jina Mahavira and transmitted orally until the 3rd century BCE, when the verbatim recitation of teachings was no longer possible. Both Svetambara and Digambara accept that all the *Purvas* were eventually lost.	Reconstructed by monks mainly between the 5th and 11th centuries CE. Commentaries and narratives added by scholar-monks.	Object of study for metaphysics, cosmology, and philosophy.
Jainism (Svetambara)	*Anga Agama*	The 12 *Angas* were compiled by the principal disciples of Mahavira. Svetambaras believe that the 12th *Anga*, called the *Drstivada*, contained the teachings of lost *Purvas*. All were transmitted orally until the 3rd century BCE (see above).	Reconstructed by monks mainly between the 5th and 11th centuries CE. Commentaries and narratives were added by scholar-monks.	Object of study for rules of mendicant conduct, stories of renouncers, karma.
Jainism (Svetambara)	*Angabahya* (believed to contain the lost teachings of the *Purva* and *Anga Agamas*)	Compiled and orally transmitted by monks who succeeded the principal disciples of Mahavira. Contained the earliest commentaries on the *Purva* and *Anga*.	Reconstructed by monks mainly between the 5th and 11th centuries CE. Commentaries and narratives added by scholar-monks.	Object of study for specialized topics, story literature etc.
Jainism (Digambara)	*Satkhandagama* (contains parts of *Drstivada* canon, said to mnemonically contain the lost teachings of the *Purva* and *Anga Agamas*)	Orally transmitted until 2nd /1st century CE, when it was put in writing; the first Jaina scripture to be preserved in written form.	No substantial revisions, though commentaries are common.	Object of study for entire canon: metaphysics, cosmology, karma, and philosophy.
Jainism (Digambara)	*Kasayaprabhrta* (text based on *Drstivada*)	Written by Yati Vrasabha based on compilations of Gunadhara, 1st–2nd century CE.	No substantial revisions, though commentaries are common.	Studied for philosophy of detachment.
Jainism (Digambara)	*Nataktrayi* (*Samaysara*, *Pravanasara* and *Pancastikaya*)	Written by Kundakunda between 1st century BCE and 2nd century CE.	No substantial revisions, though commentaries are common.	Object of study for mysticism, doctrine / philosophy, and ontology. The most sacred Digambara author and texts.

Sacred Texts Table (continued)

Religion (Sect)	Text(s)	Composition/ Compilation	Compilation/ Revision	Use
Jainism (Svetambara and Digambara)	*Anuyogas* ('Expositions')	From 1st century BCE to 6th century CE.		Object of study for philosophy, etc.
Jainism (Svetambara and Digambara)	*Tatthvartha Sutra*	Written by Umasvati in 2nd century CE.	Many commentaries were written by Svetambaras between the 2nd and 8th centuries CE, but the process of commenting continues.	Object of study for doctrine, cosmology, ethics, philosophy, etc.
Jainism (Svetambara and Digambara)	*Bhaktamara Stotra*	Written by Acharya Mantunga in 3rd century CE.		Used in devotion.
Jainism (Svetambara)	*Kalpa Sutra* (life of Mahavira and doctrine)	3rd century CE		Used in devotion and ritually during Paryushana.
Jainism (Digambara)	*Adi Purana/ Mahapurana*	Written by Acharya Jinasena between 6th and 8th centuries CE.		Object of study for life stories of Tirthankaras and all Digambara rituals.

Sites

Dilwara Temples An exquisite complex of white marble temples on Mount Abu in Rajasthan, dating from the eleventh century.

Ranakpur Temples Another beautiful complex, also in Rajasthan, dating from the fifteenth century.

Palitana, Gujarat A major pilgrimage site with an extensive temple complex dating from the eleventh century.

Gwalior Fort, Madhya Pradesh Site of enormous rock-cut sculptures of Jinas.

Sammet Shikarji, Bihar An important pilgrimage site where it is claimed that 23 of the 24 Jinas achieved omniscience.

Shravanabelagola, Karnataka Home of the colossal (18-metre) statue of the renouncer Bahubali (also known as Gomateshwara), and the site of an enormous pilgrimage once every twelve years.

Jaina Centre, Leicester, England The first Jaina temple outside India, consecrated in 1980.

Jaina Center of Greater Boston The first such centre in North America.

Study Questions

1. Lay (householder) Jainas are integral to the tradition, which has always recognized the centrality of their role. Explain.
2. What are some of the major differences between Svetambara and Digambara Jainism?
3. What are the main reasons believed to be responsible for the split that gave rise to the Svetambara and Digambara sects?
4. How are women understood within Jainism? What are some of the main differences between Svetambaras and Digambaras in terms of female theology and women's religious roles?
5. Although Jainism envisions final liberation (*moksha*) as a purely spiritual state, it does not see the spiritual and the material in oppositional terms. Explain.
6. Karma is envisioned as *more* than a moral law of cause and effect in Jainism. Explain.
7. Non-violence (*ahimsa*) informs every aspect of Jainism, from cosmology to dietary practices and devotional rituals. Elaborate.
8. Jainas worship beings (Jinas) who they believe to be utterly removed from all worldly matters and unresponsive to their concerns. How do they understand their acts of devotion?
9. What is the significance of 'right faith' (*samyak darshan*) in Jainism?
10. How do Jainas understand the final state of liberation (*moksha*)?
11. What are some of the main ways in which diaspora expressions of Jainism differ from Jainism in India today?

Glossary

agama Canonical texts within Svetambara Jainism

ahimsa Literally, non-harm or non-violence. For Jainas it denotes a philosophy of life in which all living beings should be respected and, to the greatest degree possible, protected from harm.

ajiva Non-soul, non-consciousness; *ajiva* is also referred to as 'matter' or 'karma'.

anuvratas Five vows modelled on the great vows of the renouncers but modified to make them applicable to lay life: non-violence, truthfulness, non-stealing, non-attachment, and chastity.

caturvidhyasangha Literally, 'four-fold community'; the community consisting of monks, nuns, laymen, and laywomen.

Digambaras Early sectarian node within Jainism with its own sacred scriptures; identified by the male mendicant practice of nudity.

Jina Literally, 'conqueror'; name given to the 24 ascetic–prophets who conquered the world of desire and suffering, and taught the path to eternal happiness; alternatively called Tirthankara.

jiva Eternal soul/consciousness; all living beings are endowed with *jiva*.

Mahavira Literally, 'Great Hero'; epithet of the 24th and final Jina of our time cycle, born Vardhamana Jnatrpura in the sixth century BCE.

Mahavira Jayanti A joyous spring festival celebrating the birth of Mahavira.

mahavratas The five 'great vows' adopted by renouncers: absolute non-violence, truthfulness, non-stealing, non-attachment, and celibacy.

Namokar Mantra The central prayer in Jainism.

paap Karmic particles of an inauspicious nature ('bad karma').

pratikramana The ritual practice of repentance.

puja Ritual worship, usually of a Jina, for the purpose of self-purification.

punya Karmic particles of an auspicious nature ('good karma').

Rsabha The first Tirthankara of our current time cycle; also called Adinath.

sallekhana A voluntary fast to death, usually undertaken in old age.

samayika A desired state of equanimity achieved through ritual practice of meditation.

samyak darshan Right vision, faith, or intuition into the basic truth of the cosmos; spiritual growth is dependent on the attainment of *samyak darshan*.

siddha loka Final abode of the liberated *jiva*.

Svetambara One of the two early sectarian nodes within Jainism; mendicants wear simple white robes.

Tatthvartha Sutra An important philosophical text accepted by all Jaina sects, composed by Umasvati in the second century CE.

Tirthankara Literally, 'ford-maker'; epithet for the 24 Jinas who, through their teachings, created a ford across the ocean of *samsara*.

Further Reading

Babb, Lawrence A. 1996. *Absent Lord: Ascetics and Kings in a Jain Ritual Culture*. Berkeley: University of California Press.

Banks, Marcus. 1992. *Organizing Jainism in India and England*. Oxford: Clarendon.

Carrithers, Michael, and Caroline Humphrey, eds. 1991. *The Assembly of Listeners: Jains in Society*. Cambridge: Cambridge University Press.

Cort, John E. 2001. *Jains in the World: Religious Values and Ideology in India*. New York and Delhi: Oxford University Press.

Dundas, Paul. 2002. *The Jains*. 2nd ed. London: Routledge. A comprehensive overview of Jainism and an excellent introduction to the subject.

Granoff, Phyllis, 2006. *The Forest of Thieves and the Magic Garden*. Penguin Classics.

Jaini, Padmanabh S. 1979. *The Jaina Path of Purification*. Berkeley: University of California Press. The standard general study of Jainism.

Kelting, Whitney, 2009. *Heroic Wives: Rituals, Stories, and the Virtues of Jain Wifehood*. Oxford: Oxford University Press

Kelting, Whitney, 2001. *Singing to the Jinas: Jain Laywomen, Mandal Singing, and the Negotiations of Jain Devotion*. Oxford: Oxford University Press

Laidlaw, James. 1995. *Riches and Renunciation: Religion, Economy, and Society among the Jains*. Oxford: Oxford University Press.

Long, Jeffrey, 2009. *Jainism, an Introduction*. New York: I.B. Tauris & Co.

Recommended Websites

www.jaindharmonline.com A portal dedicated to Jainism and Jaina dharma, containing information and links to news articles.

www.jainstudies.org The International Summer School for Jain Studies.

www.jainworld.com Jainism Global Resource Center, USA.

http://pluralism.org/wrgb/traditions/jainism Resources from Harvard University's Pluralism Project.

References

Cort, John E. 2001. *Jains in the World: Religious Values and Ideology in India*. New York and Delhi: Oxford University Press.

———. 2005. 'Devotional Culture in Jainism: Manatunga and His *Bhaktamara Stotra*'. In James Blumenthal, ed. *Incompatible Visions: South Asian Religions in History and Culture*. Madison, WI: Center for South Asia, University of Wisconsin—Madison.

Gelra, M.R. 2007. *Science in Jainism*. Ladnun, Rajasthan: Jain Vishva Bharati Institute.

Jacobi, Hermann, trans. 1884. *Jaina Sutras*, Part I. In F. Max Müller, ed., *Sacred Books of the East*, 22. Oxford: Clarendon Press.

Jain, S.C. 2008. 'Jain Festivals'. Unpublished manuscript prepared for the International Summer School of Jain Studies.

Jaini, Padmanabh S. 1979. *The Jaina Path of Purification*. Berkeley: University of California Press.

———. 1990. 'Ahimsa'. Inaugural Roop Lal Jain Lecture, Centre for South Asian Studies, University of Toronto.

Laidlaw, James. 2005. 'A Life Worth Leaving: Fasting to Death as Telos of a Jain Religious Life'. *Economy and Society 34*, 2: 178–99.

Lath, M., trans. 1984. *Kalpa Sutra*. V. Sagar, ed. Jaipur: Prakrit Bharati.

Note

1. This text was compiled by Jinendra Varni and published by Sarva Seva Sangh Prakashan, India. It was translated into English in 1993 by T.K. Tukol and K.K. Dixit.

Chapter

8

Buddhist Traditions

❧ Roy C. Amore ❧

At the heart of Buddhism are three elements known as the 'Three Jewels' or the 'Triple Gem': the Buddha, the Dharma (teachings), and the Sangha (congregation). Buddhists express their faith in these elements by 'taking refuge' in them.

🦎 OVERVIEW

With his last words to his disciples—'Everything that arises also passes away, so strive for what has not arisen'—the Buddha passed into **nirvana** some 2,500 years ago. After a deep enlightenment experience at the age of 35, he had spent the remaining 45 years of his life teaching that all worldly phenomena are transient, caught up in a cycle of arising and passing away. He set the wheel of **dharma** (teaching) in motion, established a community (**sangha**) of disciples, and charged his followers to carry the dharma to all regions of the world. The missionary effort succeeded. Today there are Buddhists in nearly every country, and Buddhism is the dominant religion in parts of East, South, and Southeast Asia.

Buddhism has three main traditions or 'vehicles', all of which originated in India. The earliest is **Theravada** (also known as **Hinayana**), which spread to Sri Lanka and Southeast Asia; the second is **Mahayana**, which became the principal school in East Asia; and the third is **Vajrayana**, which developed out of Mahayana and became closely associated with the Himalayan region. All three traditions also have followers beyond Asia, especially in Europe and North America.

🦎 ORIGINS

Religious Life in Ancient India

Along the Ganges basin 2500 years ago there was a tension between the religion of the brahmins, now known as Hinduism, and another traditional system of beliefs and practices that we might call Ganges Spirituality. Its leaders, drawn from any social class, practised various forms of asceticism, or spiritual discipline. While the brahmin priests married and conducted the animal sacrifices central to their tradition, the ascetic masters—among them the Jaina master Mahavira and **Shakyamuni** Buddha— were celibate and—in keeping with their strict ethic of *ahimsa* (non-violence)—denounced the practice of sacrifice.

Another major difference between the brahmin and ascetic traditions had to do with the role of deities. In the former, the deities required regular praise and ritual offerings, and in return they would respond to devotees' requests for assistance. Some of the major deities were also recognized by the other ascetic traditions—especially the creator god Brahma and the storm god Indra. For the most part, though, deities played quite a small

◀ Theravada monks and novices at the Phu That stupa in Udomxai, Laos (Amanda Ahn\© dbimages Alamy).

Major Branches (Vehicles and Schools) of Buddhism

1. Theravada ('Way of the Elders', sometimes called Hinayana, 'Little Vehicle'), now dominant in Sri Lanka and Southeast Asia: the main survivor of the 18 sects that existed in the third century BCE

2. Mahayana ('Great Vehicle'), now dominant in East Asia and Vietnam:
   - Madhyamika in India, Sanlun in China
   - Yogacara in India, Faxiang in China
   - Tiantai in China, Tendai in Japan
   - Huayan in China, Kegon in Japan
   - Zhenyan in China, Shingon in Japan
   - Pure Land, Jingtu in China, Jodo in Japan
   - Chan in China, Son in Korea, Zen in Japan
     - Linji in China, Rinzai in Japan
     - Caodong in China, Soto in Japan
   - Nichiren in Japan

3. Vajrayana ('Diamond Vehicle'), now dominant in Tibet and the Himalayas:
   - Gelugpa ('Yellow Hats')
   - Kargyu ('Red Hats')
     - Karma Kargyu ('Black Hats'), a subsect of Kargyu
   - Sakyapa
   - Nyingma ('Ancient' school)

role in the non-brahminic traditions. Minor gods might provide practical help from time to time, but there was no question of asking the gods for assistance along the spiritual path.

The liberation that the ascetics sought could be achieved only through their own efforts. The spiritual masters led the way, but the disciples had to walk the path themselves, without any supernatural assistance. A verse of the *Dhammapada*, a collection that is a favourite of Buddhists everywhere, puts it this way: 'You must strive for yourselves. The Tathagatas [buddhas] are only your guides. Meditative persons who follow their path will overcome the bonds of **Mara** [death]' (*Dhammapada* no. 276).

It was in this environment that Buddhism originated. Some aspects of Buddhist thought were major innovations: the concept of the impermanence of the human self or soul, for instance, and the idea of social egalitarianism. But others—including the notions of **karma** and successive reincarnations, the ideal of ascetic withdrawal from the world, and the belief that gods, demons, and spirits play active roles in human life—were common to all the traditions of the Ganges region.

Among the students along the ancient Ganges was a prince from the small kingdom of the Shakya people in what is now southern Nepal. Named Siddhartha Gautama, he was to become known first as Shakyamuni—the 'Shakyan sage'—and eventually as the Buddha of the current age.

Timeline

c. 531 (or 589 or 413) BCE	Shakyamuni's enlightenment
c. 486 (or 544 or 368)	Shakyamuni's *parinirvana* or passing
c. 395	First Buddhist council
c. 273	Accession of King Ashoka
c. 225	Mahendra takes Theravada Buddhism to Sri Lanka
c. 67 CE	Buddhism takes root in China
c. 100	Emergence of Indian Mahayana
c. 200	Nagarjuna, Madhyamika philosopher
c. 350	Asanga and Vasubandhu, Yogacara philosophers
372	Buddhism introduced to Korea from China
c. 500	Emergence of tantra in India
538	Buddhism introduced to Japan from Korea
604	'Prince' Shotoku, Japanese regent and patron of Buddhism, issues Seventeen-Article Constitution
c. 750	Padmasambhava takes Vajrayana Buddhism to Tibet
806	Shingon (tantric) Buddhism introduced to Japan
845	Persecution of Buddhism in China
1173	Birth of Shinran, Japanese Pure Land thinker (d. 1262)
1222	Birth of Nichiren, founder of the Japanese sect devoted to the *Lotus Sutra* (d. 1282)
1603	Tokugawa regime takes power in Japan; Buddhism is put under strict state control
c. 1617	Dalai Lamas become rulers of Tibet
c. 1900	Beginnings of Buddhist missionary activity in the West
1956	B.R. Ambedkar converts to Buddhism, leading to the conversion of 380,000 other dalits and re-establishing Buddhism in India
1959	China takes over Tibet; the Dalai Lama and many other Tibetans flee to India
1963	Thich Quang Duc immolates himself in protest against the persecution of Buddhists in South Vietnam
2001	Taliban forces destroy colossal Buddhist statues along ancient trade route in Afghanistan
2008	Tibetan Buddhists protest treatment by China before Olympics.

Traditions at a Glance

Numbers
Most estimates range between 200 and 300 million.

Distribution
South, Southeast, and East Asia, plus minorities in Europe and North America.

Founder
Shakyamuni Buddha, who taught in northern India 2,500 years ago; believed to be the most recent in a long line of major buddhas.

Principal Historical Periods

5th to 1st century BCE	Early Indian Buddhism; the roots of the Theravada tradition, which eventually spread to Sri Lanka and Southeast Asia
1st century CE	Mahayana emerges and later spreads to Southeast, Central, and East Asia
5th century CE	Vajrayana emerges and begins spreading to the Himalayan region

Deities
The Buddha is not worshipped as a god: he is venerated as a fully enlightened human being. However, regional varieties of Buddhism have often incorporated local gods and spirits. Mahayana developed a theory of three bodies of the Buddha, linking the historic buddhas to a deity-like cosmic force. The bodhisattvas came to play a role similar to that of deities or saints in other religions, using their 'store of merit' to assist believers who asked for their help.

Authoritative Texts
Theravada has the *Tripitaka* ('Three Baskets'): *vinaya* (monastic rules), *sutras* (discourses), and *abhidharma* (systematic treatises). Mahayana has a great number of texts in various languages, including Chinese, Japanese, and Tibetan. Vajrayana has the Kanjur (the main 'translated' texts) and Tanjur (commentaries).

Noteworthy Teachings
The Three Characteristics of Existence are suffering, impermanence, and no-self. The Four Noble Truths are suffering, origin of suffering, cessation of suffering, and the Eightfold Path. Other notable teachings include karma, rebirth, and nirvana. In addition, the Mahayana and Vajrayana schools stress the emptiness (non-absoluteness) of all things. All schools emphasize non-violence and compassion for all living beings.

The First Gem: The Buddha

The Bodhisattva Vow and Previous Lives

Buddhism, like Hinduism and Jainism, understands the cosmos in terms of an endless succession of universes arising and passing away. Our current universe, having evolved millions of earthly years before the present, was already in the declining phase of its life cycle when Shakyamuni, the Buddha of the present age, was born. In every era, when the inevitable decline in morality and truth—that is, dharma—becomes severe, a highly developed being is born to become the buddha for that era. (In the same way, Hindu tradition maintains that the lord Krishna comes to save the earth when dharma has declined.)

Although many Buddhists believe in gods and spirits, no almighty god is needed to mastermind the arrival of a new buddha: such a highly developed being is aware of the state of the world and knows when the time has come. Buddhists tell the story of Shakyamuni, the Buddha for our era, with the understanding that there have been buddhas in previous eras and there will be buddhas in subsequent ones. Each era is believed to have only one fully enlightened, teaching buddha, but there are numerous other beings in every age who are thought to have achieved some degree of enlightenment. Among them are *pratyeka buddhas* (hermits who live in isolation from the world and do not teach), **Arhats** ('worthy ones', 'saints'), and **bodhisattvas** (those who have dedicated themselves to achieving buddhahood). All the Buddhist traditions agree that Shakyamuni lived to the age of 80, but scholars are not certain when he lived. Some Indian and Western Buddhologists who have correlated the Buddhist chronicles with Greek evidence believe he was born in 566 BCE; others argue for 563. In Sri Lanka and Southeast Asia, however, the standard birth date is several decades earlier (624 BCE), while Japanese scholars, relying on Chinese and Tibetan texts, have adopted a later date of 448 BCE.

It is significant that Shakyamuni achieves enlightenment through his own reflective and meditative efforts. However his 'mind of enlightenment' has already been nearly perfected through hundreds of previous lives as a bodhisattva. Unlike the Hindu *avatara* or the Christian god incarnate, the Buddha is not a god on earth; he is simply a human being who has fully realized the spiritual potential that all living creatures possess.

The story of the Buddha begins in earlier ages. During the lifetime of one previous buddha, a young man comes upon a crowd of people filling mud holes in the road in anticipation of the arrival of the buddha of that era. But when the buddha arrives before one of the holes has been filled, the young man puts himself into the hole to serve as a stepping-stone. Instead of stepping on him, the buddha announces that the young man will become a buddha himself in the distant future.

The young man takes the startling prophecy to heart and vows to work towards full enlightenment. To solemnly promise to work towards buddhahood is to take what is called a 'bodhisattva' vow. *Bodhi* means 'enlightenment' and *sattva* means 'being', as in 'human being'. After the young man in our story dies, his karma complex—the matrix of all his past actions—gives rise to a new being. In short, he is reborn, as are all living beings. Over many lives, he makes progress towards purifying his inner nature. Stories of more than five hundred of his lives are preserved in a collection called *Jataka* ('birth stories').

The best known and most beloved of the *Jataka* tales is the final one, which tells the story of the bodhisattva's last rebirth before he becomes the Buddha. Here the bodhisattva is reborn as a prince named Vessantara, who as a young boy bodhisattva takes a vow of perfect generosity: whenever he is asked for something, he will give it. The consequences of this promise are not terribly serious as long as he is a child, but eventually his father, following an old royal custom of India, retires and passes the throne to him.

No one complains much when Vessantara takes food and clothing from the public treasury to give to the poor, for his generosity is credited with bringing rains and prosperity to the kingdom. When he gives the kingdom's lucky white elephant to citizens of a rival kingdom, however, the people demand that his father resume the throne and banish Vessantara. Yet even in exile he continues to give away everything he is asked for, up to and including his wife and children. Finally his father intervenes, Vessantara is reunited with his family, and we learn that the gods have been guiding events so as to give him the opportunity to test his resolve. Vessantara's strict adherence to his vow serves as a model for Buddhist self-discipline.

Siddhartha's Birth and Childhood

After Vessantara dies, he is not reborn immediately. Rather, the new being generated by his karma complex waits in heaven until the time comes when the dharma of the previous buddha has been lost and a new 'wheel turner' is needed to set the wheel of dharma (the *dharmachakra*) in motion once again. Finally, when the world needs him, he chooses to be born into the ruling family of a small kingdom in what is now southern Nepal.

The story of the Buddha's birth and childhood varies to some extent among the Buddhist traditions. What follows is a very brief version, based on the early account preserved in the Theravada tradition. (Later versions tend to be longer and to include many more miracles.) According to this early account, the queen of the Shakya people, Mahamaya, is keeping a vow of sexual abstinence in observance of a festival. One afternoon she takes a nap and dreams she is carried by the four 'world protectors' to a pleasant grove of trees. (The world protectors are minor gods who look after the earth, one for each cardinal direction. Although Buddhists do not believe that enlightenment requires any kind of divine intervention, they do think that minor gods play an active role in the unfolding of events.)

In the grove, a spiritual being in the form of a sacred white elephant—albino elephants were associated with good fortune—descends from the heavens and miraculously enters through Mahamaya's side, where it becomes the embryo of the Buddha-to-be. After a pregnancy marked by supernatural signs—she can see the child in her womb—she sets out for her home city, intending to give birth there. While she stops to rest at a roadside park known as Lumbini, the baby is born through her side as she holds onto a tree branch for support. In later Buddhist accounts, the tree miraculously lowers its branch to assist her, flowers appear out of season, and streams of hot and cold water rain down from the sky to wash the baby.

In the Theravada tradition, the birth takes place on the full-moon day of the month called **Vaishakha** ('rains'), which usually falls in April or May of the Western calendar (East Asian Buddhists follow a different tradition). A bright light illuminates the world that night, to mark the holy event. In the ancient world, the birth of an extraordinary person was often thought to be marked by unusual astral events, such as a bright light or an auspicious alignment of the planets.

The infant bodhisattva is presented to the father, King Shuddhodana, who holds a naming festival. The name chosen for him, Siddhartha, can be translated as 'he who achieves success'. But Buddhists rarely use it, preferring the titles that refer to his spiritual role, such as Shakyamuni or (Lord) Buddha.

During the naming ceremony, various brahmins offer predictions based on their reading of his physical features. They declare that if he stays 'in the world', he will become a great emperor, but if he 'departs the world', he will achieve the highest possible goal for a monk, becoming a fully enlightened buddha.

His father, the king, wants Siddhartha to become a great emperor, so he orders that no evidence of sickness, old age, or death be allowed near the boy, so that knowledge of life's inevitable suffering will not lead him to renounce the world and become a monk. Evidently the early Buddhists who told this story shared the view of those modern scholars who see religion as a response to the adversities of life and suggest that, in the absence of adversity, humans would have little reason to pursue the spiritual path.

As the Buddha explained to his followers, his early life was that of a pampered prince:

> I was delicate, most delicate, supremely delicate. Lily pools were made for me at my father's house solely for my benefit. Blue lilies flowered in one, white lilies in another, red lilies in a third. I had three palaces; one for the Winter, one for the Summer and one for the Rains (*Anguttara Nikaya* iii.38; Nanamoli 1972: 8).

There are only a few stories of the bodhisattva's childhood. In the most significant of them, the boy is sitting in the shade of a rose-apple tree watching his father perform a spring ground-breaking ritual when he enters a meditational trance and the shadow of the tree miraculously stands still even though the sun moves. The memory of this wakeful meditation state will play a role in his eventual achievement of enlightenment.

The Four Sights and the Great Departure

Despite all King Shuddhodana's precautions, Siddhartha learns the bitter truth of life's sorrows around the time of his thirtieth birthday. By then he is happily married to Yasodhara and the father of a son named Rahula. Going for a chariot ride through the royal park, the prince happens to see four sights that will alter the course of his life. The first three are a sick man, a suffering old man, and a dead man. When he asks what is wrong with these men, his chariot driver answers honestly, revealing to him for the first time the harsh realities of life. The Buddha would later explain to his disciples what he learned from seeing the reality of sickness:

> When an untaught ordinary man, who is subject to sickness, not safe from sickness, sees another who is sick, he is shocked, humiliated and disgusted; for he forgets that he himself is no exception. But I too am subject to sickness, not safe from sickness, and so it cannot befit me to be shocked, humiliated and disgusted on seeing another who is sick. When I considered this, the vanity of health entirely left me (*Anguttara Nikaya* iii. 38; Nanamoli 1972: 8).

The fourth and final sight is a monk, whose aura of tranquil detachment from the world suggests that there is a way to overcome the suffering of life after all. To this day, Buddhist monks often say that they were first inspired to join the sangha when, as children, they saw the calmness and serenity of the older monks and nuns on their daily alms-seeking rounds.

On returning home, the bodhisattva ponders the four sights. That night, with the help of the four world protectors, he flees the palace, along with his horse and servant. Many Buddhist temples have murals depicting this event, known as the Great Departure.

From the *Dhammapada*

Many of the Buddhist sutras include one or more verses that sum up the teaching. These memory verses were eventually collected as a separate work called the Dhammapada, *'fundamentals of Dharma'. The verses from Chapter One concern the pure mind.*

1. The mind is the source of all mental actions [dharmas], mind is the chief of the mental actions, and they are made by the mind. If, by an impure mind, one speaks or acts, then suffering follows the mind as a cartwheel follows the footprint of the ox.
2. The mind is the source of all mental states, mind is their leader, and they are made by the mind. If, by a pure mind, one speaks or acts, then happiness follows the mind like a shadow.
3. 'I was abused.' 'I was beaten.' 'I was hurt.' 'I was robbed.' Those who dwell excessively on such thoughts never get out of their hating state of mind.
4. 'I was abused.' 'I was beaten.' 'I was hurt.' 'I was robbed.' Those who leave such thoughts behind get out of their hating state of mind.
5. In this world hatreds are never ended by more hating. Hatreds are only ended by loving kindness. This is an eternal truth [dharma].
6. Some people do not know that we must restrain ourselves. But others know this and settle their quarrels.
7. One who dwells on personal gratifications, overindulges the senses, overeats, is indolent and lazy, that person is overthrown by Mara [Death] like an old, weak tree in a windstorm.
8. One who dwells in meditation on the bodily impurities, keeps the senses under control, eats moderately, has faith and disciplined energy, that person stands against Mara like a rocky mountain.
9. Whoever puts on the ochre robe but lacks purity, self-control, and truthfulness, that person is not worthy of the robe.
10. Whoever puts on the ochre robe and is pure, self-controlled, and truthful, that person is truly worthy of the robe.
11. Mistaking the unessential for the important, and mistaking the essential for the unimportant, some persons, dwelling in wrong-mindedness, never realize that which is really essential.
12. Knowing the essential to be important, and knowing the unessential to be unimportant, other persons, dwelling in rightmindedness, reach that which is really essential.

Having departed the worldly life, the bodhisattva dismisses his servant and horse, exchanges his princely clothes for those of a poor hunter, obtains an alms bowl, and begins a new life as one of the wandering students seeking spiritual truth along the banks of the Ganges. Determined to learn all eight levels of classical yoga, he soon masters the six levels known to his first yoga teacher (*guru*). He then finds one who is able to teach him the seventh level as well, but even the deep tranquillity of the seventh level does not satisfy his desire for enlightenment.

Therefore, with five other students (*shramanas*), he embarks on an independent program of rigorous ascetic discipline. After six years he is subsisting on nothing more than one palmful of water and one of food per day. [He becomes so emaciated that he loses consciousness, but the four world protectors preserve him.]

Enlightenment

Now convinced that even the most extreme asceticism cannot bring about the enlightenment he seeks, the bodhisattva leaves the cave where he has been living and goes to a pleasant town now called Bodh Gaya ('bodh' is a short form of *bodhi*, enlightenment). There he resumes eating and drinking, but he still needs a method. Then he remembers the wakeful meditational trance he experienced spontaneously as a child:

> I thought of a time when my Sakyan father was working and I was sitting in the cool shade of a rose-apple tree: quite secluded from sensual desires, secluded from unprofitable things I had entered upon and abided in the first meditation, which is accompanied by thinking and exploring with happiness and pleasure born of seclusion. I thought: Might that be the way to enlightenment? Then, following up that memory there came the recognition that this was the way to enlightenment (*Majjhima Nikaya*; Nanamoli 1972: 21).

Choosing a pleasant spot beside a cool river, under a *pipal* tree (a large fig tree considered sacred in India at least as far back as the Harappa civilization, known thereafter to Buddhists as the Bodhi tree), he sits to meditate and vows that he will not get up until he has achieved nirvana.

According to some versions of the story, it is at this point, just before dusk on the evening of the full-moon day in the month of Vaishakha, that Mara, the lord of death, arrives. Mara plays a role in Buddhism similar in some ways to that of Satan in Christianity. His main function is to come for people at death and oversee their rebirth in an appropriate place. But he wants to exercise power over events in this world as well. Determined to thwart the bodhisattva's attempt to achieve enlightenment, Mara summons his daughters—whose names suggest greed, boredom, and desire—to tempt him. When that fails, Mara offers him any worldly wish, if only he will return home and live a life of good karma (merit) as a householder. The bodhisattva refuses.

Now Mara becomes violent. He sends in his sons—whose names suggest fear and anger—to assault the bodhisattva. But the bodhisattva's spiritual power is so great that it surrounds and protects him from attack like a force field.

Having failed in his efforts to tempt and threaten the bodhisattva, Mara challenges him to a debate. Mara himself claims to be the one worthy to sit on the Bodhi Seat—the place of enlightenment—on this auspicious night, and he accuses the bodhisattva of being unworthy. With his sons and daughters cheering him on, Mara thinks he has the upper hand. But the bodhisattva has the truth on his side. He responds that he has the merit of the generosity, courage, and wisdom perfected through countless previous lives, and he calls on the Earth herself to stand witness on his behalf. The resulting earthquake drives Mara away. Buddhists today understand this story as symbolizing the surfacing of the last remnants of the mind's deep impurities, which the bodhisattva must overcome before he can attain liberation.

Bodh Gaya, the place of the Buddha's enlightenment and a major pilgrimage site. The Bodhi tree is visible behind the small stupa in the foreground. Beyond that is a large modern temple (Photo courtesy of Roy C. Amore).

With Mara defeated, the bodhisattva begins to meditate in his own way—the reverse of the way taught by the yoga masters. A yogi seeks to move ever deeper into unconsciousness, drawing in the conscious mind as a turtle draws in its head and limbs, in effect shutting out the world. The bodhisattva, by contrast, meditates to become more conscious, more aware, more mindful.

The night passes in three stages. During the first stage, the bodhisattva remembers his own past lives; the ability to do this is considered one of the psychic powers that come with spiritual advancement, but it should not be a goal in itself. During the second, he acquires deeper insight into the working of karma, understanding how the past lives of various people have been reflected in later rebirths. During the third stage, he turns his awareness to the question of how to put an end to suffering and in due course arrives at what will become known as the Four Noble Truths.

Finally, just before dawn, the bodhisattva enters the state of complete awareness, of total insight into the nature of reality. After hundreds of lives, he has fulfilled his bodhisattva vow. He is no longer a being (*sattva*) striving for enlightenment (*bodhi*); he is now a buddha, a 'fully enlightened one': 'I had direct knowledge. Birth is exhausted, the Holy Life has been lived out, what was to be done is done, there is no more of this to come' (*Majjhima Nikaya*; Nanamoli 1972: 25).

Having completed his journey to full enlightenment, he has earned the title Tathagata ('thus-gone one'). It is this title that the Buddha will most often use to refer to himself. For example: 'Whatever a Tathagata utters, speaks, and proclaims between the day of his enlightenment and the day he dies, all that is factual, not otherwise, and that is why he is called "Tathagata"' (*Anguttara Nikaya* ii.22; Dhammika 1989: 50).

Another term for the state of enlightenment or *bodhi* that the Buddha has reached is 'nirvana' (*nibbana* in the vernacular Pali language). This state has two aspects, negative and positive. In its negative aspect, nirvana has the sense of 'putting out the fires' of greed, hatred, and delusion. In its positive aspect, it means ultimate bliss.

Setting the Wheel in Motion

Reflecting on his experience, the new Buddha concludes that the way to enlightenment can be taught. His first impulse is to share his knowledge with his two former yoga teachers, but his psychic powers tell him that they have died. Next he thinks of the five ascetics who were his companions through the years of ascetic discipline. Knowing that they can be found at a deer park known as Sarnath, near Varanasi (Banaras), he sets out.

On the way there he encounters two merchants who show their respect by offering him food. In a sense, this act marks the beginning of institutional Buddhism, which depends on the material support (food, clothing, financial donations) given by laypeople in return for the spiritual services offered by ordained Buddhists. This pattern of reciprocal giving remains central to all forms of Buddhism. On arriving at the deer park, the Buddha is at first shunned by his five friends because he has abandoned the rigorous discipline they so value, but when they see his aura they recognize that he has attained nirvana, and ask to know how he did it. He responds with his first **sutra** (discourse or sermon), often referred to as the 'Wheel Turning' *sutra* because it marked the moment when the wheel of true dharma was once again set in motion.

Another name for this first discourse is the 'Instruction on the Middle Path', for in it the Buddha encourages his former companions to follow a path of moderation between indulgence and asceticism. As long as he lived the life of a pampered prince he did not advance spiritually. Yet the years of ascetic discipline left him too weak to make any real progress. Only after he began to eat, drink, and sleep in moderation was he able to reach enlightenment. In time, this principle of moderation would be developed into a general ethic of the Middle Way, leading some to refer to Buddhism itself as 'the Middle Way'.

Having counselled the five to abandon the ascetic way of life, the Buddha explains the Four Noble Truths and the Eightfold Path for overcoming suffering. He ordains the five as his first disciples and sends them into the world to teach the dharma to others.

Shakyamuni and his five fellow ascetics in the deer park at Sarnath, the site of his first discourse (Photo courtesy of Roy C. Amore).

Entering Parinirvana

For the next 45 years the Buddha travels, ordaining disciples and teaching thousands of lay followers, including various local kings. He also ordains several members of his own family, one of whom—his cousin Devadatta—eventually leads a group of dissident disciples in revolt, and makes more than one attempt on the Buddha's life.

His body is becoming weak as he nears 80. Finally, one day he and his disciples are dining with the leader of a local tribal group when an odd-smelling dish is brought to the table. He asks his host to serve it only to him, not to his disciples. On eating the dish, he falls ill. When it becomes apparent that he is dying, the Compassionate One tells his disciples not to blame the host, who meant well. They ask whom they should follow if he dies, and he tells them to follow the dharma. Thus in Buddhism no individual has absolute authority, although there are senior authorities in particular traditions (the Dalai **Lama** in the Gelugpa sect of Vajrayana Buddhism, for example).

On his deathbed—in a grove of trees at Kushinagar—the Buddha meditates up through the eight yoga stages, back down through them, and finally back up through the first four. Then, at the moment of death, he experiences ***parinirvana***: the final end of the cycle of rebirth, the total cessation of suffering, the perfection of happiness. Until that moment he has been in the state known as nirvana 'with remainder'—the highest level of nirvana possible for one still living.

🌱 CRYSTALLIZATION

The crystallization of the Buddhist tradition began with the transformation of the Buddha's discourses into a set of doctrinal teachings (the dharma), and the movement towards an institutionalized monastic system. We will begin with the Dharma, the Second Gem, and then turn to the Third Gem, the Sangha.

The Second Gem: The Dharma

> Avoid doing all evil deeds,
> cultivate doing good deeds,
> and purify the mind—
> this is the teaching of all buddhas.
>   (*Dhammapada* 183)

To 'take refuge in the dharma' is to have confidence in the eternal truth of the Buddha's teachings. 'Dharma' (*dhamma* in Pali) is a central concept in Buddhist thought, and the range of its meanings and associations extends well beyond the meaning of 'dharma' in the Hindu context.

In classical Indian culture generally, the Sanskrit word *dharma* carries the sense of social and moral obligation. The *Bhagavad Gita*, for instance, assumes that each individual's dharma is the duty appropriate to the caste and the life situation into which he or she born. (Thus the law codes governing Hindu society came to be called the *dharmashastras*.)

From the *Itivuttaka*

The Itivuttaka *('So I heard') is a collection of the Buddha's teachings said to have been made by Khujjuttara, a lay woman of the servant class who used it to teach other women. Each section begins with the expression 'So I heard' ('Itivuttaka').*

Even if one should seize the hem of my robe and walk step by step behind me, if he is covetous in his desires, fierce in his longings, malevolent of heart, with corrupt mind, careless and unrestrained, noisy and distracted and with sense uncontrolled, he is far from me. And why? He does not see the Dhamma, and not seeing the Dhamma, he does not see me. Even if one lives a hundred miles away, if he is not covetous in his desires, not fierce in his longings, with a kind heart and pure mind, mindful, composed, calmed, one-pointed and with senses restrained, then indeed, he is near to me and I am near to him. And why? He sees the Dhamma, and seeing the Dhamma, sees me (Dhammika 1989: 49–50).

It is no surprise, then, that the 'dharma' referred to in Buddhist texts is sometimes translated as 'law'. Buddhist usage, however, reflects the root meaning of 'dharma' 'that which holds'. In fact, the Sanskrit *dharma* is related to the Latin word *firma*; thus in English we could understand 'dharma' to mean 'teachings that are firm'—that is, eternal truths. For Buddhists, these eternal truths include the laws of nature, the reality of spiritual forces such as karma, and the rules of moral conduct or duty. Believing the Buddha's understanding of those realities to be definitive, generations of thinkers studied and systematized his insights, creating a program of instruction that anyone seeking enlightenment could follow.

The Four Noble Truths

At the core of the Buddha's first sermon in the deer park were the Four Noble Truths about suffering (**duhkha**) and the Eightfold Path to overcoming it:

1. Noble Truth of Suffering: No living being can escape suffering. Birth, sickness, senility, and death are all occasions of suffering, whether physical or psychological.
2. Noble Truth of Origin: Suffering arises from excessive desire or craving.
3. Noble Truth of Cessation: Suffering will cease when desire ceases.
4. Noble Truth of the Eightfold Path: It is possible to put an end to desire, and hence to suffering, by following eight principles of self-improvement.

The Eightfold Path

The eight principles that make up the Eightfold Path are not sequential: they must work together, in concert, like the petals of a flower unfolding. They are right understanding (specifically of the Four Noble Truths), right thought (free of sensuous desire, ill-will, and cruelty), right speech, right conduct, right livelihood, right effort, right mindfulness, and right meditation.

The Three Characteristics of Existence

Existence has three characteristics, according to the Buddhist dharma: suffering, impermanence, and no-self. 'Suffering', as a characteristic of existence, refers to all the varieties of pain and deprivation, physical and psychological, that humans are subject to. 'Impermanence' is the passing nature of all things. Remember the last words of the Buddha: 'Everything that arises also passes away.' With the exceptions of empty space and nirvana, nothing in life is static: everything is in process. Some philosophies, both in India and in the West, treat change as a problem to be overcome and attribute permanence to what they value most highly; by contrast, Buddhist thought regards change as a reality of life.

Finally, the concept of no-self (anatman) draws attention to the psychological implications of that existential impermanence. The Sanskrit term anatman means 'without Atman': but what is Atman? The Hindu understanding at the time of Shakyamuni is reflected in the Upanishads, where Atman represents the eternal self or soul in humans and is related to Brahman, the underlying energy of the universe. The Buddha proposed that no such eternal, unchanging self exists. And in denying the existence of a self, he made the concept of ownership unsustainable for his followers: if there is no 'I', there can be no 'mine'.

On the other hand, the anatman concept does not mean that there is 'no person' or 'no personality'. Buddhism teaches that the person is composed of five bundles (complexes) called skandhas. The first skandha produces the physical body. The remaining four—sensation, perception, mental formations, and consciousness—together produce all of the individual's mental processes. But none of the skandhas incorporates any eternal element worthy of the term atman. This insight was developed into the Mahayana doctrine of emptiness (shunyata), according to which all phenomena, including humans, are devoid of anything permanent or eternal.

The Three Instructions, the Path of Purity and the Three Evil Roots

Morality, concentration, and wisdom are the Three Instructions. Morality (sila) is the essential foundation. Perfecting concentration (samadhia), means developing a mental state in which one is focused, tranquil, and alert. The third level, higher wisdom (prajna) is essential to attain nirvana. Buddhaghosa, the most important Theravada commentator on the Tripitaka, entitled his book on the three instructions The Path of Purity, suggesting that Buddhist dharma may be understood as a quest to purify the mind by eradicating the 'three evil roots': greed, hatred, and delusion.

The Twelve Stages of Dependent Origination

One of the central insights gained at that third level is the nature of causality, which underlies the theory of Dependent Origination: everything that arises does so in response to other factors, and will in turn cause changes in other things. Because early Buddhist teachers delivered the dharma teachings orally, they often used visual images and numbered lists to help fix them in listeners' minds. Thus Buddhist dharma uses the image of a wheel with twelve spokes (not to be confused with the eight-spoked wheel that symbolizes the Eightfold Path) to represent the view of life as a cycle of 12 interdependent stages or dimensions.

The 12 links that make up the chain of dependent origination may be further divided into three stages, reflecting the movement from a past life through the present one and on to the future:

Past
1. Ignorance, leading to
2. karma formations, leading to

Present
3. a new individual 'consciousness', leading to
4. a new body–mind complex, leading to
5. the bases of sensing, leading to
6. sense impressions, leading to
7. conscious feelings, leading to
8. craving, leading to
9. clinging to (grasping for) things, leading to
10. 'becoming' (the drive to be reborn), leading to

Future
11. rebirth, leading to
12. old age and death

The process does not stop with the twelfth link, of course, since old age and death lead to yet another birth, and so the wheel of rebirth turns on and on.

The Third Gem: The Sangha

The third part of the Triple Gem has two components: the monastic community of ordained men (**bhikshus**) and women (**bhikshunis**), and the broader community, the universal sangha of all who follow the Buddha's path.

Bhikshus and Bhikshunis

Shakyamuni began accepting disciples from the time of his first discourse in the deer park. Within a short time, an ordination ritual took shape in which the new disciples recited the Triple Refuge and took vows of chastity, poverty, obedience, and so on, and put on the distinctive saffron-coloured robes of a monk. Most Theravada monks still wear saffron robes, but in East Asia other colours were eventually adopted, such as red and brown. There is no special meaning to the colour, although all members of a particular branch of Buddhism wear the same one.

Ordained and Lay Women

Unlike many other religious traditions, Buddhism never defined women as the 'property' of men. Yet the early texts in particular indicate a profound ambiguity about the status of women in Buddhism. Shakyamuni himself is said to have cautioned the *bhikshus* against allowing themselves to be distracted by women.

Shakyamuni is also said to have at first resisted the formation of an order for women, and to have predicted that a *bhikshuni* sangha would be detrimental to the survival of his teachings. On the other hand, he did agree to its establishment, and he encouraged close relatives, including his stepmother, to join it. He taught that women were no less capable than men of becoming Arhats (saints), and that the way to nirvana was the same regardless of gender.

> And be it woman, be it man for whom
> Such chariot doth wait, by that same car
> Into Nirvana's presence shall they come.
> (Horner 1930: 104)

Other early Buddhist texts are similarly ambiguous about women. On the positive side, they describe approvingly the support provided to the early sangha by some wealthy women. And one book of the Pali canon, the Therigatha, contains poems by early *bhikshunis*. On the negative side, there was a significant difference in status between *bhikshus* and *bhikshunis*, who were forbidden to teach their male counterparts and never allowed complete independence. The Theravada bhikshuni order lasted for nearly a millennium in Sri Lanka, but died out after the population had been devastated by famine and too few senior monks or nuns survived to ordain new members. Although the king imported a party of senior *bhikshus* from Southeast Asia to ordain new monks, there was no equivalent group of nuns available to perform the same service for the female order.

A Theravada *bhikshu* with a palm-leaf umbrella (Photo courtesy of Roy C. Amore).

Ordination

Eventually, as Buddhism became more institutionalized novices were required to master the basics of dharma before ordination. Each novice was assigned both a rigorous, demanding teacher and a supportive spiritual guide.

The full ordination ritual can be performed only in certain designated areas, which some ordination traditions still mark off with 'boundary stones', as in ancient India. The ceremony takes several hours to complete. Friends and relatives of the candidates pay their respects to the new sangha members, who give presents to their teachers and counsellors in gratitude for their assistance. Because seniority plays a large role in monastic life, careful attention is paid to the exact date and time of the ordination ceremony.

The Lay Sangha

Lay Buddhists are considered members of the sangha in its wider sense. The sangha of all disciples has four levels: those who have entered the stream (to nirvana), those who have advanced far enough to return (be reborn) just once more, those who are so advanced that they will never return, and those who have advanced to the status of Arhats. At each of the four levels, a distinction is drawn between those who have just arrived and those who have nearly completed their sojourn there, making a total of eight classifications of noble persons.

All Buddhist traditions maintain that laypeople are capable of advancing towards nirvana. However, some expect lay members of the sangha to seek ordination eventually, so that they can devote themselves completely to the spiritual quest.

Tripitaka: The Three Baskets of Sacred Texts

Shakyamuni did not write down any of his teachings. For the first four centuries or so, members of the Buddhist sangha recited the teachings from memory. Thus one of the most important tasks at the early conferences of sangha members was to recite the teachings in their entirety. At the first council after Shakyamuni's death, *Bhikshu Ananda*, who had been his travelling companion, recited the discourses on dharma ascribed to Shakyamuni. *Bhikshu Upali* is credited with reciting the section on monastic rules. The systematic treatises (*abhidharma*) composed after Shakyamuni's *parinirvana* were recited at later meetings. The oral teachings were finally put into writing by the Theravada monks of Sri Lanka in the first century CE, after a famine had reduced the monks' numbers so drastically that the survival of the tradition was threatened. The fact that Theravada Buddhists refer to their scriptures as the *Tripitaka* ('three baskets') suggests that the manuscript copies of the three types of texts may have been stored in three baskets. The collection survives in the Pali language and is therefore referred to as the Pali canon.

Controversies, Councils, and Sects

In the fourth century BCE, trouble arose when a *bhikshu* visiting the city of Vaishali found that his colleagues there were accepting donations of gold and silver from the lay people. He criticized them publicly, and they demanded that he apologize in front of their lay supporters. As a consequence, a meeting of all the *bhikshus* in the area had to be convened. The meeting, called the Vaishali Council, decided that monastic discipline did indeed forbid the acceptance of gold and silver. Most of the Vaishali *bhikshus* agreed to abide by the ruling, but a schism soon developed when one dissident monk raised five points of controversy concerning the status of Arhats.

The issue was the level of spiritual attainment possible for Buddhists in this life. Most of the monks took a relatively liberal position, holding out the prospect of enlightenment for ordinary people, but many of the senior monks (the 'elders') disagreed, arguing that attaining the Arhat level was beyond the reach of all but a few. In this way a division arose between the majority group, who formed the Mahasanghika or 'Great Sangha' sect, and the Sthavira group, who formed the Sthaviravada or Theravada sect. This debate gave the *bhikshus* a foretaste of the split that would lead to the development of the Mahayana and Theravada schools as distinctly different forms of Buddhism.

By the time of King Ashoka, in the third century BCE, there were 18 sects, each with its own oral version of the Buddhist teachings. They all shared a similar ordination tradition and all followed more or less the same monastic rules.

King Ashoka's Conversion

The spread of Buddhism within India was quite remarkable. Unlike many reformers, Shakyamuni had succeeded in gaining converts across a broad social spectrum, from low caste to royalty. But the fact that some kings were converted in Shakyamuni's lifetime did not necessarily mean that their successors were Buddhists as well. There was a longstanding Indian tradition that the king had a duty to defend and support all the legitimate religious traditions of his kingdom. It seems that Buddhism became one of several legitimate dharma systems.

Approximately 150 years after the passing of Shakyamuni, in 326 BCE, northwestern India was invaded by Alexander the Great. As a result, the region came under Greek control, but the Greeks were soon driven out by an Indian king based in central India. When that king's grandson, Ashoka (r. c. 273–232 BCE), inherited the throne, he embarked on a series of wars to expand his kingdom to the south and east. Buddhist accounts claim that it was Ashoka's reflection on the horrible carnage of his bloody war with the kingdom of Kalinga on the eastern coast that led him to convert to Buddhism and begin promoting the ethic of non-violence. Under the patronage of Ashoka, Buddhism enjoyed its golden age in India. Buddhist accounts say that Ashoka turned from military conquest to dharma conquest.

To spread the dharma of non-violence, Ashoka ordered that large stones or pillars be erected at the principal crossroads throughout his empire, with messages carved on them for the moral instruction of his subjects. Some of these stones and pillars have been recovered by archaeologists, and the messages are still readable. He lays out his ideals for governing his new subjects, saying that he desires security, self-control, impartiality, and cheerfulness for all living creatures in his empire. Ashoka spells out his 'conquest by dharma' and claims that it is spreading not only within the Indian continent but westward among the various Alexandrian kingdoms. Ashoka states that satisfaction in ruling over people comes only from inducing them to follow dharma.

Ashoka's promotion of dharma became a model for later Buddhist rulers. Like 'Dharma-Ashoka', as Buddhists later called him, they were willing to sentence criminals (and rebels) to punishment, including death, but they remained committed to non-violence in other matters. Ashoka himself encouraged his subjects to become vegetarian and give up occupations such as hunting.

Buddhism and the State

From the time of Shakyamuni, Buddhism understood rulers to have special duties with regard to the dharma. Kings were expected both to provide for the physical welfare of their subjects (by providing food in times of need, for instance) and to promote dharma both by setting a good example and by sponsoring lectures, translations, and the distribution of literature. The king who promoted dharma would be a true successor to the Buddha, the definitive wheel-turner.

As Buddhism spread throughout Asia, so did its social and moral ideals regarding kingship. An East Asian Zen Buddhist story tells of a Chinese king named Wu who has dedicated himself to doing all the good works expected of a Buddhist king, probably with the goal of winning a long and pleasant rebirth in heaven. Wu summons the monk Bodhidharma to court and proudly shows him everything he has done: the altar he has had built for daily worship, the rice kitchens he has established to feed the poor, the rooms filled with scribes translating and copying the sacred Buddhist texts that will be read aloud and explained to the people at Buddhist festivals.

After the tour, the king asks Bodhidharma, 'How much merit do you think I have made from all this?' 'None whatsoever!' is the famous response. Bodhidharma proceeds to explain that true merit comes only from activities that increase one's wisdom and purify one's mind. It seems that the emperor has been doing all the right things, but for the wrong reason. With regard to Buddhism and the state, what this story tells us is that although the rulers were encouraged to support the sangha and actively promote dharma

Map 5.1　The spread of Buddhism

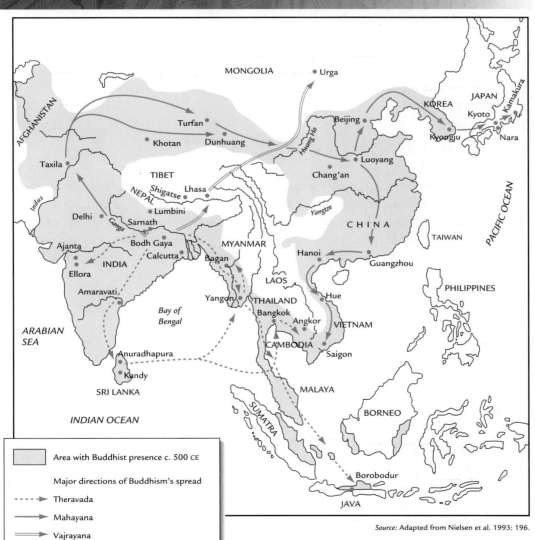

Source: Adapted from Nielsen et al. 1993: 196.

in their realms, the ultimate goal was the ruler's own spiritual advancement. This helps to explain why Buddhist kings sometimes abdicated at a fairly early age in order to take ordination as *bhikshus*.

Non-violence as a Public Ethic

One characteristic of Buddhist political rule, at least ideally, was promotion of non-violence. Unnecessarily harsh punishments were forbidden, and kings were expected to release prisoners during Buddhist festivals. Justice was to be administered not just fairly, regardless of the social status of the accused, but quickly. A particularly pious king of ancient Sri Lanka is remembered for instructing his staff to wake him even in the middle of the night if a citizen came seeking justice. At the same time, the Buddhist king was expected to maintain an army and a police force, to defend the public against criminals and foreign enemies. There is no such thing in Buddhist scripture as a 'just war' of aggression, but many Buddhists have believed that a defensive war is not against dharma, and that the state may use force as necessary to maintain law and order.

With very few exceptions, Buddhism spread by missionary conversion rather than force. However, there were territorial wars among various Buddhist kingdoms of Southeast Asia, and in Sri Lanka the conflict between the Buddhist Sinhalese and Hindu Tamils has a long history.

🦌 DIFFERENTIATION

After the time of Ashoka all but one of Buddhism's 18 sects gradually declined. One survivor, Theravada, represents one of the three major divisions of Buddhism that exist today. The second major school, which emerged around the first century CE, called itself Mahayana, 'Great Vehicle', in contrast to what it called the Hinayana, 'Lesser Vehicle', of Theravada and its contemporaries. The third division, Vajrayana, emerged some five hundred years later in what its followers considered the third turning of the wheel of dharma.

Theravada

We know very little about the early history of the 'Way of the Elders', but it appears to have been widespread in India by the time of Ashoka in the third century BCE. We do know that the Theravada tradition was conservative, as its name suggests. Rejecting all scriptures composed after the formation of the *Tripitaka*, it considers itself the preserver of Buddhism in its original form.

Theravada in Sri Lanka

Theravada Buddhism is said to have been taken to Sri Lanka in the third century BCE by a monk named Mahinda (Mahendra in Sanskrit), who was Ashoka's son. The legend says that Mahinda and his assistant monks travelled through the air, using psychic powers, and arrived on a large hill near the island's capital, Anuradhapura. There they were discovered by the king of Sri Lanka and his hunting party, all of whom soon became followers of the

Buddha's dharma. The next day, Mahinda entered the capital and taught dharma to the members of the king's court, who in turn were also converted. On the following day the biggest hall available—the royal elephant stable—was put into service as a hall of dharma instruction, whereupon all the remaining Sri Lankans were converted. The king ordered the building of a proper temple, dharma hall, and **stupa** (a mound-like structure built to hold cremation ashes or a sacred relic). The temple grounds were made complete with the arrival of a Bodhi tree sapling brought from India by the *bhikshuni* Sanghamitta, Mahinda's sister.

Theravada in Southeast Asia

The spread of Buddhism into Southeast Asia took place in stages over many centuries. Today Buddhist culture remains dominant in much of mainland Southeast Asia, including Cambodia, Thailand, and Myanmar. It was also influential in the Indonesian islands and the Malay Peninsula, although Islamic religion and culture eventually became dominant there.

The history of Buddhism in mainland Southeast Asia may be summarized along the following lines. Before 1000, various early Buddhist sects competed among themselves as well as with Mahayana and Vajrayana sects, but by the fifteenth century the rulers of all the region's major kingdoms had embraced Theravada and imported senior *bhikshus* from Sri Lanka to re-ordain the indigenous monks in the Theravada lineage. Other forms of Buddhism gradually died out across most of Southeast Asia, and Theravada flourished under royal patronage in Burma, Thailand, Laos, and Cambodia.

Mahayana, The Second Vehicle

The Mahayana ('Greater Vehicle') movement appears to have emerged around the first century CE. Although its origins are unclear, we know that its members were dismissing older forms of Buddhism as Hinayana ('Lesser Vehicle') by the third or fourth century. Around the same time it was becoming the dominant form of Buddhism across the region traversed by the Silk Road, from Central Asia to northern China. It remains the main form of Buddhism in China, Korea, and Japan.

Mahayana differed from Theravada in everything from the doctrines and scriptures it emphasized to its rituals and meditation practices. Whereas Theravada saw the discipline of the *bhikshu* as a precondition for enlightenment and liberation, Mahayana offered laypeople the opportunity to strive for those goals as well. Whereas Theravada focused on the historical Shakyamuni, Mahayana developed a framework in which he represented only one manifestation of buddhahood. Furthermore, whereas Theravada emphasized that the only way to enlightenment and liberation was through personal effort—that there was no supernatural force on which human beings could call—Mahayana populated the heavens with bodhisattvas dedicated to helping all those who prayed to them for assistance.

How did all these differences arise? It seems likely that Mahayana Buddhism emerged in southern India as part of a movement towards more liberal interpretation that spread across several of the early Indian sects. Despite their differences, Mahayana and the earlier forms of Buddhism share a common core of values and moral teachings, practices (such as meditation, chanting, scripture study, and veneration of relics), and forms of monastic life and buildings. In short, Theravada and Mahayana are different vehicles (*yanas*) for travelling the same path to enlightenment.

Mahayana Doctrine

The Lay Sangha

The practice of venerating Shakyamuni at the stupas enshrining his relics had begun soon after his death. In time, many lay people began making pilgrimages to stupas with major relics, and new ones were built in all Mahayana countries. (The veneration of sacred relics was an important part of several religions in this period, including Hinduism and Christianity.) Lay Buddhists came to believe that they could earn valuable karmic merit by making a pilgrimage.

This development marked a major shift away from early Buddhism, in which laypeople had no role beyond providing material support for the sangha and only limited prospects for progress along the spiritual path. Anyone who wished to seek enlightenment more seriously was expected to 'depart the world' and join a monastic order. Mahayana Buddhism, by contrast, offered laypeople the possibility of pursuing spiritual development and even attaining enlightenment while living in the world.

Doctrine of the Three Bodies (Trikaya)

To account for the various ways in which one could experience or refer to buddhahood, Mahayana developed a doctrine of 'three bodies' (*trikaya*). The earthly manifestation body of a buddha is called the Appearance Body or Transformation Body. The heavenly body of a buddha that presides over a buddha-realm and is an object of devotion for Mahayana Buddhists is called the Body of Bliss. These are supported by the buddha as the absolute essence of the universe, called the Dharma Body (*dharmakaya*).

The Three Bodies doctrine calls attention not only to the oneness of all the buddhas that have appeared on earth, but also to the unity of the buddha-nature or buddha-potential in all its forms. That is, the *trikaya* doctrine envisions one cosmic reality (Dharma Body) that manifests itself in the form both of heavenly beings (Body of Bliss) and of humans such as Shakyamuni (Appearance Body). By connecting the earthly Buddha to the Dharma Body or Absolute, the doctrine of the three bodies also moved Mahayana Buddhism in the direction of theistic religion—in sharp contrast to the Theravada school, which continued to revere the Buddha not as a deity but as an exceptional human being.

Teaching by 'Skillful Means': The Parable of the Burning House

The Sanskrit word *upaya* forms part of an expression frequently translated as 'skill in means' or 'skillful means'. Shakyamuni's teachings were practical, even pragmatic, and he seems to have tailored his presentation of them to suit his audience's capacity to grasp them.

A Mahayana text that places a strong emphasis on *upaya* is the *Lotus Sutra*, which explains many Buddhist teachings as steps towards a more complete understanding. As an illustration of this perspective, the *Lotus Sutra* tells a story about a father whose children are inside a burning house, so absorbed in their play that they pay no attention when they are told to come out. Only when he tells them he has special toy carts outside for them to play with are they willing to leave the house. In fact the carts don't exist, but the lie serves an important purpose. Similarly, those just starting on the path are not taught the ultimate truth: instead, they are taught temporary formulations that will allow them to advance to a point where they will be able to see the purpose of the earlier stages. By treating earlier teachings as temporary expedients or 'skillful means', Mahayana thinkers were able to incorporate new elements such as celestial buddha figures into a tradition that originally did not include them.

Bodhisattvas

Early Buddhism taught that there was no supernatural source of grace. The Mahayana school, however, envisioned a multitude of spiritually advanced beings prepared to help anyone who prays for assistance.

Bodhisattvas were not unknown in early Indian Buddhism: in a previous life Shakyamuni himself had become a bodhisattva when he vowed to attain buddhahood one day, and he remained a bodhisattva until the night of his enlightenment. For most Theravada Buddhists, however, the highest goal was to reach the status of an Arhat. The Mahayana school criticized this goal as self-centred, focused solely on achieving personal liberation. It argued that those who take bodhisattva vows are dedicating themselves first and foremost to the salvation of all living beings. All Mahayana Buddhists were therefore encouraged to take the bodhisattva vow, pledging not only to attain buddhahood themselves but also to work towards the liberation of all beings.

The corollary of this innovation in Buddhist thought was the idea that humans could appeal to the bodhisattvas for assistance. Early Indian Buddhism had considered Shakyamuni, after his *parinirvana*, to be beyond the realm of direct involvement with human lives; therefore it had no tradition of praying to him for help. In some forms of Mahayana Buddhism, by contrast, worshippers not only venerate the bodhisattvas but petition them for blessings.

Merit Transfer

Early Buddhism taught that merit—that is, good karma—is made solely by the individual, not by any external agent such as a saint or a god. However, individuals could transfer merit made by themselves for the benefit of their dead relatives and the welfare of all beings (as in the Theravada **dana** ritual described later in this chapter). In Mahayana, by contrast, the buddhas and bodhisattvas are believed to be capable of transferring merit from themselves to human beings. Thus devotees can appeal to their chosen bodhisattvas for assistance in the same way that Christians can pray to their chosen saints for intercession.

Meditation and Visualization

The Mahayana belief in various buddhas and bodhisattvas, each with his or her own heaven, gave rise to a practice known as 'vision meditation', in which the meditator would focus intensely on his or her chosen bodhisattva or buddha in the hope of being granted a vision of that figure. In this way practitioners sought to achieve a heightened state of consciousness and develop a special rapport with the object of their devotion. Such visualization would eventually become a central element in Vajrayana Buddhism.

Mahayana Schools in India

The above overview suggests some substantial differences between Mahayana and Theravada Buddhism, especially regarding scriptures, the nature of the Buddha, and the efficacy of prayer. But the various schools that developed within the Mahayana tradition, first in India and eventually across East Asia, also vary significantly among themselves. The **Chan** (**Zen**) school has more in common with Theravada and its emphasis on the personal achievement of enlightenment than it does with the Pure Land school, in which salvation is achieved by placing one's trust in Amida Buddha.

Madhyamika

Early Buddhism taught that there were six types of perfection. The sixth and most important of these was the perfection of the particular wisdom known as *prajna*. This wisdom is accessible only to those with a highly developed consciousness or awareness. Mahayana thinkers wrote a number of texts on the development of *prajna* (most notably the *Heart Sutra* and the *Diamond Cutter Sutra*), emphasizing that the key to the highest spiritual wisdom is awareness of the emptiness (**shunyata**) of all things.

Sometime during the latter part of the second century, a brahmin from southern India converted to Buddhism and took the ordination name Nagarjuna. His philosophical position is called the 'Middle Way' (Madhyamika) because it refuses either to affirm or to deny any statement about reality on the ground that no such statement can ever express ultimate truth. All realities (dharmas) are equally 'empty' of absolute truth or 'self-essence'. According to Nagarjuna's doctrine of Emptiness, everything in the phenomenal world is ultimately unreal. By a process of paradoxical logic he concludes that Emptiness itself is unreal, although it may be experienced directly in meditation.

Nagarjuna summed up this paradox in a famous eightfold negation:

> Nothing comes into being,
> Nor does anything disappear.
> Nothing is eternal,
> Nor has anything an end.
> Nothing is identical,
> Or differentiated,
> Nothing moves hither,
> Nor moves anything thither.
>   (Chen 1964: 84)

For Madhyamika and the later Mahayana schools that developed under its influence, including Chan/Zen, enlightenment demands recognition of the emptiness of all dharmas.

Of course Nagarjuna recognized that his own thinking was no less empty than any other. Thus he made it his philosophical 'position' to refrain from taking any dogmatic position. Through his paradoxical logic, Nagarjuna asserts that nirvana is dialectically identical to *samsara*, or the phenomenal world. In other words, each is present in the other. This is the most characteristic Madhyamika teaching and also the most puzzling. Early Indian Buddhism had taken the two to be opposites, *samsara* being the temporal, worldly process of 'coming to be and passing away' and nirvana being the eternal, unchanging goal of the spiritual quest. Yet Madhyamika holds that '*samsara* is nirvana, and nirvana is *samsara*'. From the standpoint of conventional wisdom the two may be distinguished, but ultimately the distinction is not tenable.

Yogacara or 'Consciousness Only'

In the late fourth century, three Indian thinkers named Maitreyanatha, Asanga, and Vasubandhu founded a new Mahayana school that is usually known as Yogacara ('Practice of Yoga') because it emphasizes meditation and uses a text by that name. Its alternative name, 'Consciousness Only', reflects its argument that what most of us assume to be realities are in fact merely ideas and images from a 'storehouse consciousness' shaped by past karmic actions and attachments. As a consequence, we can never truly know either the external world or ourselves.

For Yogacara, the universe itself exists only in the perception of it; the same is true of the perceivers, our 'selves', and our karma. All are merely reifications of momentary awareness. Sensory impressions are 'seeds' that lead to acts or thoughts:

> A seed produces a manifestation,
> A manifestation perfumes a seed.
> The three elements (seed, manifestation, and perfume) turn on and on,
> The cause and effect occur at the same time.
> (Chen 1964: 323)

According to this theory, the only way to avoid false substantialization is to exhaust the consciousness, through yoga and spiritual cultivation, to the point that it becomes identical to the ultimate reality called 'thusness' (*tathata*), which corresponds to the 'emptiness' of Madhyamika. Critics from rival schools argued that the concept of the storehouse consciousness seemed to contradict the traditional Buddhist doctrine of no-self (*anatman*) and come close to affirming the Hindu notion of Atman that the Buddha had rejected. The Yogacara writers, however, were careful to point out that even though the storehouse consciousness, like the Atman in Hinduism, transmigrates from birth to birth, unlike the Atman it has no eternal, unchanging substance.

Pure Land Buddhism

Another Mahayana school developed around the veneration of a celestial buddha of 'infinite life' and 'infinite light' known in Sanskrit as Amitayus or Amitabha, in Chinese as Omitofo, and in Japanese as Amida (the Japanese spelling is the one most commonly used in English). This school most likely began to take shape around the first century, some five hundred years after Shakyamuni's *parinirvana*.

According to an account attributed to Shakyamuni himself, Amitabha was a buddha of a previous age who in an earlier life, as a young prince named Dharmakara, took 48 bodhisattva vows detailing his intention to strive for enlightenment and help others in specific ways. In one of the most important vows Amitabha promised to establish a heavenly region—the 'Pure Land' or 'Western Paradise'—into which all beings who so desired could be reborn. No extraordinary effort would be required to earn rebirth in that land: admission would be free to all who had faith in Amitabha's compassionate power and who made their desire for rebirth in his heaven known by thinking of him:

> If, after my obtaining Buddhahood, all beings in the ten quarters should not desire in sincerity and trustfulness to be born in my country, and if they should not be born by only thinking of me for ten times, except those who have committed the five grave offences and those who are abusive of the true Dharma, may I not attain the Highest Enlightenment (Bloom 1965: 2–3).

In short, Dharmakara vowed that he would strive to become a completely enlightened buddha on the condition that thereafter he could continue to help all living beings towards liberation.

Suffering, old age, and death would be unknown in the Pure Land. There would be food, drink, and music for all; the streets and buildings would be made of jewels; and the buddha's followers would be so uplifted by his merit that their progress towards *nirvana* would be certain.

This notion of the 'Pure Land' marked a remarkable transformation in the Buddhist idea of heaven. In early Buddhism, meritorious individuals could hope to be reborn in some kind of paradise, but as long as they were there, they would be unable either to 'make' any new merit or to develop their higher wisdom. There was no path leading from heaven to nirvana: once the inhabitants' store of merit was exhausted, they would have to return to earth, be reborn in human form, and resume the work of earning enlightenment. The Pure Land, by contrast, offered the ideal conditions for spiritual progress: therefore rebirth on earth would no longer be necessary.

A second text, the *Shorter Sutra on the Pure Land*, explained that, in order to benefit from Amitabha's merit, one needed only to recollect and repeat his name before dying; then, after death, one would be reborn in his Pure Land. Rebirth in the Pure Land was a gift made available through the infinite merits of the buddha Amitabha. (The concept of salvation through faith in divine grace is a Christian parallel.)

A third text of early Pure Land Buddhism, the *Meditation on Amitayus Sutra*, offered detailed instruction in vision meditation. For those unable to undertake the rigorous training required to achieve a vision, however, it also offered an easier path. This was the formula that was to become central to Pure Land Buddhism: 'Homage to Amitabha Buddha'. Even the meritless or wicked could gain rebirth in the Pure Land through sincere repetition of the sacred formula.

The Pure Land school introduced into Buddhism a path to salvation based solely on faith. The *Shorter Sutra on the Pure Land* teaches that the only condition for rebirth in the Pure Land is faith in the infinite compassion of Amitabha, shown through prayerful and meditative repetition of his name. This reliance on an external 'other-power' stands in sharp contrast to the self-reliance emphasized in early Buddhism. Over the centuries that followed, Pure Land Buddhism spread from India to China and from there to Japan. In the process, the basic concept was refined to the point that the Indian thinkers who first developed it came to be seen more as forerunners than as founders. Pure Land became the most popular of all Buddhist schools in East Asia, and it remains the most popular school today.

Mahayana in China

The major Mahayana schools spread along the trade routes from India to Central Asia and on to China in the early centuries of the Common Era. Once there, they tended to take on forms of thought, social norms, and architecture more reflective of Chinese culture.

Sanlun: Chinese Madhyamika

The Sanlun ('Three Treatises') school is the Chinese extension of Nagarjuna's Madhyamika ('Middle Doctrine'). The monk Kumarajiva, famous as a translator of Buddhist texts into Chinese, introduced this teaching into China with his translation of two treatises by Nagarjuna and a third by Nagarjuna's disciple Aryadeva (or Deva, c. 300). These three works became the foundation of the Sanlun school. Essentially a restatement of Nagarjuna's ideas, the chief teaching of the Sanlun school was that everything is empty (*shunya*), because nothing has any independent reality or self-nature. In this unreal world we function as in a dream, making distinctions between subject and object, *samsara* and nirvana, but higher wisdom understands all entities to be empty of absolute reality.

Faxiang: Chinese Yogacara

The Chinese version of the Yogacara or 'Consciousness Only' school also has two names, Weishi ('Consciousness Only') and Faxiang ('Dharma Character'). First introduced into China in the sixth century, the school developed around a text by Asanga entitled *Compendium of Mahayana*. It was his perplexity over the meaning of this work that spurred a monk named Xuanzang to set out for India in search of more scriptures; on his return, the Big Wild Goose Pagoda was built in Xian (the Chinese terminus of the silk route) to house the manuscripts he brought back. This temple, along with its smaller companion the Little Wild Goose Pagoda, remains an important centre of Buddhism in this historic city. (The story of Xuanzang's perilous journey to India is celebrated in Chinese Buddhist art and inspired the famous novel *Journey to the West*, best known in English under the title *Monkey: A Folk-Tale of China*.)

Tiantai: The Lotus School

The Tiantai school—named after its place of origin on a mountain in southeastern China—is also called the Lotus school. Its founder, Zhikai or Zhiyi (538–97), proclaimed himself a practitioner of meditation rather than a philosopher, but he left behind a important attempt to reconcile and harmonize all Buddhist teachings.

According to Zhiyi, doctrinal inconsistencies within Buddhism reflect the fact that the Buddha taught different things at different times. Moreover, each of the *sutras* speaks on several different levels because each is addressing a different audience. So he distinguishes among five approaches in the Buddha's life of preaching, four methods of teaching (sudden, gradual, secret indeterminate, and explicit indeterminate), and four modes of doctrine (Hinayana, the teaching of Emptiness, Yogacara, and the perfect teaching of the *Lotus Sutra*).

Tiantai Buddhism thus represents an attempt to establish a great eclectic school that recognizes all forms of Buddhism and gives a place to all their scriptures by looking at them as products of a gradual process. It is an example of the Chinese propensity for asserting the harmony of opposites, but the synthesis it achieved was founded on the belief that the *Lotus Sutra* represents the culmination of the Buddha's teaching.

Jodo: Chinese Pure Land

In China, Pure Land is known as Jingtu and Amitabha Buddha as Omitofo. He is assisted by two bodhisattvas (*pusa* in Chinese), one of whom is Guanyin, the bodhisattva of compassion.

During the recitation of praise to Omitofo, devotees typically use a string of 27 (the traditional 108 divided by 4 to make it a more manageable size) beads to count the repetitions; some practitioners will recite thousands of repetitions every day. Thus Pure Land Buddhism offers several parallels with some Christian traditions: a God-figure (Amida), a mediator (Guanyin), a doctrine of faith and grace, and a devotional practice not unlike the recitation of the rosary.

In China, Pure Land Buddhism has had a special appeal for the masses of people who seek not only ultimate salvation but also a power that will assist them in everyday life. Guanyin is particularly important in this respect, especially for women. The fact that she came to be seen as the 'giver of children' points to the more worldly focus of Chinese Buddhism, compared with its Indian counterpart.

Chan

Chan Buddhism is better known in the West by its Japanese name, Zen. Its founder was Bodhidharma—the same sixth-century Indian monk who told King Wu that all his good

The Bodhisattva of Compassion

The bodhisattva of compassion originated in India as Avalokiteshvara ('the Lord who looks down'). He was often depicted with multiple heads and arms, signifying his infinite capacity to see and help those who are suffering, and he was said to be able to take whatever form might be necessary in order to benefit believers.

That shape-shifting ability was eventually confirmed in East Asia, where Avalokiteshvara is known as Guanyin in China and Kannon in Japan. Although early sculptures and paintings represented the compassionate bodhisattva in male form, over time those images began to show increasingly feminine features, until the bodhisattva took on the feminine form now evident in Mahayana. She is usually depicted holding a lotus, a water sprinkler, and a rosary with 108 beads representing the number of 'passions' she helps devotees to overcome.

Guanyin is the most widely venerated of all the bodhisattvas: the protector of women, children, and sailors, among many others, who grants children to those who long for them and takes care of infants who die (as well as aborted fetuses). Because many images show her holding a child, Westerners in particular often describe her as the 'Virgin Mary of East Asia'. In China she is associated with the medieval legend of the princess Miaoshan, who was killed by her parents to prevent her from becoming a nun.

Guanyin, the bodhisattva of compassion, in heaven, seated on her lotus throne and holding the jar of water she uses to bestow blessings. Other figures in this scene (displayed behind glass at a temple in Xian, central China) include Amida Buddha (above Guanyin) and various attendants (Photo courtesy of Roy C. Amore).

works had earned him no merit at all. In sharp contrast to the Pure Land sect, with its emphasis on 'other-power', Chan emphasizes 'self-power' and the rigorous practice of meditation, to clear the mind in preparation for the experience of enlightenment.

The Flower Sermon

Chan Buddhism traces its origins to a day late in the life of Shakyamuni when the disciples are said to have asked him for a dharma talk. He agreed, but having taken his seat on the teaching throne, he did not speak: instead, he simply held up a white lotus flower. All but one of the disciples were dumbfounded. The exception was Kashyapa, who in that moment experienced an intuitive flash of enlightenment. For this reason Kashyapa the Great (Mahakashyapa) came to be considered the first patriarch of the tradition that Bodhidharma carried to China. The Chan school took its name from the Chinese rendering of the Sanskrit word *dhyana*—the term for the deep meditative state of mind that the young Shakyamuni reached while sitting under the rose-apple tree.

Just as the Buddha relied on a single enigmatic gesture to deliver his 'flower sermon', so Bodhidharma and his successors relied on means other than logic or reason to bring about the state of mind known in the West by the Japanese term *satori*. One master twisted a disciple's nose so hard that the pain and indignity led to a breakthrough. One simply held up a single finger. Another held up one hand and demanded to be told what sound it made: this was the origin of the familiar question 'What is the sound of one hand clapping?' Since there is no logical answer to such a question, the correct response can only come from some place other than the rational mind.

Bodhidharma's teaching is summed up in four phrases attributed to him:

> A special transmission outside of doctrines. Not setting up the written word as an authority. Pointing directly at the human heart. Seeing one's nature and becoming a buddha (Robinson 1959: 332).

This formula puts into words Kashyapa's 'flower sermon' experience of enlightenment through direct contact between master and disciple, without texts, doctrines, or rational argumentation.

Chan and the Martial Arts

Bodhidharma settled into a cave in the mountains above the village of Shaolin, and the monastery in the valley below became a centre of Chan training not only in meditation but in martial arts, which Bodhidharma is said to have begun teaching as an antidote to the long hours of sitting meditation. All the East Asian martial arts traditions trace their roots to the Shaolin monastery. Today the small mountain town of Shaolin remains a centre of martial arts training, with dozens of elementary and high schools (mostly for boys) that combine academic instruction with martial arts training.

The Lineage of Patriarchs

One winter day a Chinese man arrived at Bodhidharma's cave, hoping to study under the master. But no such invitation was forthcoming. He waited, shivering in the snow, all night. Finally he cut off his left arm and presented it to Bodhidharma as proof of his resolve. The master accepted him as a disciple. The one-armed man took the name Huike, and after Bodhidharma's death he went on to become the first **Han** Chinese patriarch. There is a small temple dedicated to Huike at the monastery in Shaolin, with a statue of him standing in the snow just outside.

The lineage of patriarchs continued and the Chan school gradually spread to other areas. Most Chan monasteries in China, Korea, and Japan were located part-way up a mountain, where the cool, dry atmosphere was thought to optimize the chances of a spiritual breakthrough. For this reason Chan Buddhism has been called the 'mountain school.'

Huineng and the Poetry Contest

During the era of the fifth Chan patriarch, in the late seventh century, a young boy from southern China named Huineng arrived at the Chan monastery at Shaolin, seeking admission as a novice. He was not accepted, perhaps because he spoke a southern dialect that was difficult for the northerners to understand. But Huineng stayed to work in the kitchen, pounding rice and helping to cook for the monks.

Huineng had made the long journey because he had learned that the monastery taught a radical new form of Buddhism that offered the possibility of a direct breakthrough to a higher level of consciousness, without undue dependence on knowledge of scriptures or the performance of rituals. He understood the essence of Buddhism to involve an intuitive, mystical experience, the 'direct pointing of the mind' that Bodhidarma had taught.

When it came time for the aging fifth patriarch to choose his successor, candidates were asked to compose a poem expressing their state of enlightenment. The most senior disciple wrote this verse on the wall:

> This body is the Bodhi-tree;
> The soul is like the mirror bright;
> Take heed to keep it always clean,
> And let no dust collect upon it.
> (Suzuki 1991)

This poem captures much of the Chan point of view. Instead of practising ritual veneration of the Buddha who was enlightened under the Bodhi tree long ago in a distant land, one should think of one's own body, here and now, as the place of enlightenment. And Mahayana Buddhism had a long tradition of comparing the mind to a mirror that must be kept perfectly clean in order to truly reflect reality. Thus the senior disciple's poem encourages regular meditation to keep the mind clear and pure. That night, however, Huineng wrote a counter-poem on the wall nearby:

> The Bodhi (True Wisdom) is not like the tree;
> The mirror bright is nowhere shining:
> As there is nothing from the first,
> Where does the dust itself collect?
> (Suzuki 1991)

Huineng's poem reveals a deeper understanding of Chan enlightenment. In denying the validity of the other poem's imagery, it implies that the truly pure mind corresponds to the state of emptiness central to the Mahayana tradition.

The fifth patriarch called Huineng into his room, acknowledged his deep understanding, and awarded him the robe and staff of the patriarch—but with the advice that he should return to the South. In this way, even though he was still a layman Huineng took the Chan message to the masses in southern China, from where it was eventually taken first to Korea (where it came to known as Son) and then to Japan (where it came to be known as Zen). Eventually he was ordained and recognized as the true sixth patriarch.

Caodong and Linji: Gradual and Sudden Enlightenment

Two subsects of southern Chan focused on practical matters of spirituality, but differed on whether enlightenment comes suddenly or gradually. The Caodong sect, which proposed a gradual transformation of life and character, sought 'silent enlightenment' through sitting meditation (in Chinese, *zuochan*; in Japanese, *zazen*). It considered silence to represent the primal stillness of the enlightened mind, and compared the effort of silent meditation to that of 'the bird hatching the egg'.

Chan Buddhism

The following extracts are from the Platform Sutra, *an important scripture attributed to the sixth Chan patriarch, Huineng, and compiled by one of his disciples in the early 700s.*

Meditation and Wisdom
Good friends, how then are meditation and wisdom alike? They are like the lamp and the light it gives forth. If there is a lamp there is light; if there is no lamp there is no light. The lamp is the substance of light; the light is the function of the lamp. Thus, although they have two names, in substance they are not two. Meditation and wisdom are like this (*The Platform Sutra of the Sixth Patriarch*, sec. 15; Yampolsky 1976: 137).

Sudden and Gradual Enlightenment
Good friends, in the Dharma there is no sudden or gradual [enlightenment], but among people some are keen and others dull. The deluded commend the gradual method; the enlightened practice the sudden teaching. To understand the original mind of yourself is to see into your own original nature. Once enlightened, there is from the outset no distinction between these two methods; those who are not enlightened will for long kalpas be caught in the cycle of transmigration (*The Platform Sutra of the Sixth Patriarch*, sec. 16; Yampolsky 1976: 137).

The Linji sect, which had a much wider following, aimed for sudden enlightenment through the use of shouting, beating, and paradox. These are considered aids in provoking mystical experience, for which no slow preparation is necessary or possible.

A story traces the Linji sect's use of hitting, shouting, and paradox to its founder and namesake, Linji (in Japanese, Rinzai) (d. 867), who is said to have entered training as a shy young boy. After training diligently for more than a year, he met with the master, Huangbo. When the master asked why he had come, Linji humbly requested instruction in enlightenment, whereupon the master hit him hard with his stick.

When Linji told his teacher what had happened, he was advised to try again, which led to a second beating. After three such beatings, Linji thought he was not worthy of further training and requested permission to leave. The master agreed, but asked that he first visit an old hermit monk who lived farther up the mountain. The hermit, after hearing Linji describe what had happened, exclaimed, 'Poor old Huangbo, he must have nearly exhausted himself hitting you.' This lack of sympathy so shocked and angered Linji that he experienced a breakthrough and burst out laughing. 'Why the sudden change?' demanded the hermit. 'There's not so much to old Huangbo's Zen after all' was the reply. Upon returning to Huangbo, Linji threatened to hit the master with his own stick. 'Just get back to your training,' said the master.

When Huangbo died, Linji succeeded him as master and gave his name to a new ordination lineage or sect focused on exactly the kind of 'sudden enlightenment'—*satori*—that Linji experienced in response to Huangbo's apparently irrational behaviour. Subsequent masters discovered that one of the best ways to break down students' mental resistance and stimulate a breakthrough to Chan consciousness was to confound their expectations.

Central to this approach is the *gongan* (**koan** in Japanese): a paradoxical thought exercise designed to defy rational understanding and force the student out of normal 'heady' (reason- or word-centred) mode into a more intuitive, body-centred state of mind. The typical koan retells an incident in which, by doing something unexpected, a master sparked an enlightenment experience in his student. The point of the telling the anecdote is to evoke the same experience in successive generations of disciples. We will return to the subject of koan training in the Practice section below.

Mahayana in Korea

Physical proximity created close links between China and Korea. The Han dynasty conquered the northern part of the peninsula in the late second century BCE and Buddhism was introduced roughly two centuries later, spreading from the northern kingdom of Koguryo first to Paekche in the southwest and then to Silla in the southeast. It became most influential after Silla conquered the other two kingdoms and united the country (668–935).

The new religion expanded on an unprecedented scale during the Silla period. Among the major schools of Buddhism introduced from China were the Flower Garland or Huayan (Hwaom in Korean), and the Faxiang (Yogacara) school. The most influential school, however, was Son (Chan), introduced in the early seventh century. Nine Son monasteries, known as the Nine Mountains, were eventually established. In the late twelfth century, all those streams were united by a charismatic monk named Chinul to create the Chogye sect, which became the orthodox form of Buddhism in Korea and remains the largest denomination today. Chinul introduced the use of the paradoxical *gongan* (*gong'an* in Korean) into Korean practice.

The institutional form that survived, the Chogye sect, encompasses all the common forms of Buddhist practice in South Korea today. In a single monastery, individual monks may worship the buddha Amitabha of the Pure Land, recite *sutras*, or practise Son meditation, according to their own inclinations.

Mahayana in Japan

Buddhism was introduced to Japan from Korea in the sixth century CE—roughly a thousand years after the time of Shakyamuni. Today Japanese Buddhism is mainly Mahayana, but it reflects influences from other forms as well. A landmark in the process of gaining a foothold in Japan came in 604, when the regent, 'Prince' Shotoku, issued the 'Seventeen-Article Constitution': a set of moral guidelines for the ruling class that urged reverence for the Three Gems. Welcoming Buddhism (as well as Confucianism) for its civilizing influence, Shotoku became the centre of a Buddhist cult that still endures. The state even built Buddhist temples, and Japanese monks travelled to China to pursue further studies.

It was during the Nara period (710–94), under the influence of Buddhism, that Japanese culture experienced its first golden age. Eventually, however, the monks' close ties with the court led to increasing secularization, in some cases even political intrigue and corruption. The state responded by limiting the number of monks and forbidding them from proselytizing among the general populace. As a result, the practice of Buddhism was for a time mainly restricted to the aristocracy.

Tendai

The most influential Buddhist sect during the Heian period (794–1185) was Tendai, founded by a monk named Saicho. Having gone to China to study Tiantai (Tendai in Japanese), Saicho returned home in 805 determined to reform Japanese Buddhism. He broke with the increasingly secularized older sects established in the Nara period and made Mount Hiei, northeast of the new capital of Kyoto, his base of operations. The temple complex on Mount Hiei eventually became a kind of fortress with its own monk-soldiers.

Like Tiantai, Tendai took particular inspiration from the *Lotus Sutra*, taught that anyone can attain buddhahood or salvation, and promoted the harmonization of Buddhist teachings. Unlike Tiantai, however, Tendai incorporated a variety of esoteric elements from the **tantric** Buddhism of Tibet and Mongolia.

Shingon

A second Japanese sect to incorporate tantric elements into its practice was Shingon, based on a Chinese sect called Zhenyan whose devotees sought to identify themselves with the buddhas and bodhisattvas. Zhenyan died out in China but was taken to Japan by the monk Kukai soon after Saicho introduced Tendai there.

Both Shingon and Tendai taught the universal attainment of buddhahood and affirmed life in this world. Both sought the favour of the court and the support of the nobility, and both practised magical rites aimed at assuring material prosperity and earthly happiness. These two sects became the prototypes of all later Japanese Buddhist sects.

Zen

The two main Zen sects in Japan today are Rinzai and Soto, based on Chinese Linji and Caodong respectively. While Rinzai, introduced to Japan by a former Tendai monk named Eisai, emphasizes the use of koans to facilitate spontaneous enlightenment, the Soto school, introduced to Japan by Dogen (1200–53), prefers gradual spiritual cultivation through sitting meditation (**zazen**). Neither sect is exclusive in its practice, however. Both use koans and *zazen*; the differences lie mainly in emphasis and tradition.

Jodo: Japanese Pure Land

In Japan Pure Land Buddhism is called Jodo (from Chinese Jingtu), its Buddha is called Amida (from Omitofo), and the bodhisattva of compassion is called Kannon (from Guanyin). The Pure Land school was introduced to Japan in the twelfth century by a monk named Honen, who wanted to provide a simpler way to salvation for those who were unable to undertake the demanding program prescribed in the *Meditation on Amitayus Sutra*. The devotional practice that he taught required nothing but faith in Amida's power of salvation, as expressed in the words 'Homage to Amida Buddha'. Repeated chanting of this phrase, called the *nenbutsu* in Japanese, leads to a spiritual state of consciousness. During services, the chanting often starts slowly and then quickens to a feverish pace.

Honen's disciple Shinran further developed Japanese Pure Land, underlining the need for the 'other-power' of Amida's grace in a 'degenerate' age when Buddhist dharma was believed to be in decline. Condemning the magical and syncretic tendencies that he saw in other schools, Shinran taught the *nenbutsu* as an act of faith and thanksgiving. In a moving passage about the salvation of the wicked, Shinran says:

> If even a good man can be reborn in the Pure Land, how much more so a wicked man! People generally think, however, that if even a wicked man can be reborn in the Pure Land, how much more so a good man! This latter view may at first sight seem reasonable, but it is not in accord with the purpose of the Original Vow, with faith in the Power of Another. The reason for this is that he who, relying on his own power, undertakes to perform meritorious deeds, has no intention of relying on the Power of Another and is not the object of the Original Vow of Amida. Should he, however, abandon his reliance on his own power and put his trust in the Power of Another, he can be born in the True Land of Recompense. . . Amida made his Vow with the intention of bringing wicked men to Buddhahood. Therefore the wicked man who depends on the Power of Another is the prime object of salvation (Tannisho; Tsunoda 1958:217).

Shinran founded a new sect called Jodo Shinshu ('True Pure Land', sometimes known as Shin Buddhism). He also broke from Buddhist tradition in openly choosing to marry (he maintained that husband and wife were to each other as the bodhisattva Kannon was to the believer). Today most Buddhist priests in Japan are married, and temples are usually passed down through their families; the oldest son is called the 'temple son' and is expected to train for the priesthood and continue the family tradition.

Nichiren

Nichiren Buddhism was founded in the thirteenth century by a controversial monk with the religious name Nichiren ('Sun and Lotus'). He had studied on Mount Hiei but left because he believed that Tendai had abandoned the teachings of its central scripture, the *Lotus Sutra*. His own message was very simple. Whereas the Pure Land school placed its trust in Amida, Nichiren placed his in the power of the *Lotus Sutra* itself.

Like the Pure Land Buddhists who invoked the power of Amida simply by calling on his name, Nichiren invoked the power of the *Lotus Sutra* by chanting the words '*Namu Myoho renge kyo*' ('Homage to the *Lotus Sutra*'). Nichiren inscribed this formula, called the Daimoku, on a calligraphic scroll known as the Gohonzon. Today each disciple has a small Gohonzon for personal devotional use.

Nichiren believed that the *Lotus Sutra* was the key to the salvation of Japan itself, and he was aggressive in attacking other Buddhist sects, especially Pure Land and Zen. For this he was sentenced to death, but the execution was called off when an apparent miracle intervened. Instead he was exiled to an island, where he wrote extensively.

Vajrayana, The Third Vehicle

'Vajrayana'—from *vajra*, meaning both 'diamond' and 'thunderbolt'—is just one of several names for the third vehicle of Buddhism. The image of the diamond suggests something so hard that it cannot be broken or split, while the thunderbolt suggests a very particular kind of power. Hand-held Vajra wands are used regularly in rituals. The curved prongs represent

A large *vajra* in the courtyard of the Swayambhunath temple in Kathmandu makes a comfortable perch for people-watching (Photo courtesy of Roy C. Amore).

various buddhas, and the wand symbolizes the power of the enlightened awareness—itself unbreakable, but capable of shattering spiritual obstacles such as ignorance, greed, or hatred. It remains a central symbol in the principal Vajrayana school today, Tibetan Buddhism.

Followers of Vajrayana refer to it as the 'third turning of the wheel of dharma', the culmination of the two earlier vehicles, Theravada and Mahayana. This is exemplified in a system of Vajrayana training with three stages named after the three vehicles. In the 'Hinayana' phase of practice, beginners concentrate on basic moral discipline. In the 'Mahayana' stage, they receive instruction in basic Mahayana doctrines. And in the third and highest stage, the Vajrayana, they learn the doctrines and practices that Vajrayana itself considers the most advanced.

The view of Vajrayana as the third turning of the wheel also makes sense in historical terms, for it dates from a later period than Theravada and Mahayana. Arising in India during or after the third century, it was subsequently taken to virtually all parts of the Buddhist world. In many of these regions Vajrayana either died out or remained a minor influence, but it became the dominant religion in the region of Nepal and Bhutan, and across the Himalayas in Tibet and Mongolia. For this reason Vajrayana is sometimes referred to as 'northern' Buddhism (as opposed to 'southern' Theravada and 'eastern' Mahayana).

Vajrayana incorporates numerous elements that originated in Indian Hindu and Buddhist practice, but often gives its own emphasis to them. An example is its use of **mantras**: sacred syllables or phrases that are believed to bring great spiritual blessings when properly spoken or chanted. A Vajrayana mantra was a closely guarded secret, passed only from master to initiated pupil. For this reason the Vajrayana tradition is sometimes described as 'esoteric' Buddhism.

Finally, Vajrayana is also known as tantric Buddhism. Like Hindu tantrism, Buddhist tantrism envisions cosmic reality as the interplay of male and female forces and teaches a set of practical techniques for tapping into the spiritual energy produced by that interplay. The image of a male figure in sexual embrace with his female consort is common in Vajrayana art. Known in Tibetan as the *yab-yum* (father–mother), this union of male and female symbolizes the coming together of complementary elements (such as compassion and wisdom) that is essential to enlightenment.

Thus a central component of tantric Buddhism is the concept of sexual union. Some tantric texts suggest that since the world is bound by lust, it must be released by lust. While the 'right-hand' school understood this symbolically, the 'left-hand' school understood it in a more literal fashion, practising ritual unions in which a man and woman visualized themselves as divine beings. Such practices, properly undertaken, would confront lust, defeat it, and transcend it. The texts that lay out such techniques are called tantras. The Tibetan canon includes a vast library of sutras and tantras under the heading Kanjur and various commentaries under the heading Tanjur.

The Vajrayana tantras classify the many buddhas and bodhisattvas in various families, which are often depicted in a sacred geometric design called a **mandala**. For example, the head of the family will occupy the place of honour in the centre of the design, surrounded by the other family members, each of whom occupies a specific position.

Practitioners meditate on a particular buddha or bodhisattva in order to achieve a vision that will help them along the path to enlightenment. The Vajrayana guru initiates the disciple into the symbolic meanings of the various members of the family and their relationships, as well as the rituals required to develop inner wisdom.

Having built up a visualization, practitioners begin to identify with their chosen figures and tap into their energies. In this way practitioners become aware of the centres of power (*chakras*) in their own bodies and may perceive themselves to be at the centre of a sacred space defined by a mandala. At the culmination of this process of gradual enlightenment, initiates aspire to dissolve slowly into emptiness (*shunyata*), liberated from ego attachment.

A classic mandala pattern reflects tantric Buddhism's emphasis on the *Mahavairocana* ('Great Sun') *Sutra*. For example, a mandala might centre on Mahavairocana, surrounded by the buddhas of the four directions, all of whom together represent the various emanations of buddhahood itself. It is also characteristic of tantric Buddhism to give female counterparts not only to the buddhas but to the bodhisattvas who accompany them; as a result, mandalas often include numerous figures.

These deities have both pacific and angry aspects, depending on their functions (e.g., to assist in beneficial activities or to repel evil forces). The union of wisdom and compassion, considered the key to enlightenment, is represented by the father–mother image evoked by the embrace of deities and their consorts.

Vajrayana in Tibet

Shakyamuni had been born near the foothills of the Himalayas, and he had converted his home region (now part of Nepal) in the early years after his enlightenment. But the high

Himalayan plateau was so difficult to reach that Buddhism made little headway there for the first 1,200 years of its history. It was not until the late eighth century that a few Buddhist texts and missionaries found their way to Tibet at the invitation of Tibetan kings.

Vajrayana is said to have been established in Tibet by a *bhikshu* named Padmasambhava. Revered as Guru **Rinpoche** ('precious teacher'), he combined instruction in dharma with magical practices involving the world of the spirits. The figure of Padmasambhava is particularly identified with a school of Tibetan Buddhism known as the Nyingma, the 'ancient' school that dates back to his time.

The indigenous religion of the region when Buddhism arrived is known as Bon (a name meaning 'truth' or 'reality'). Little is known of Bon belief and practice in that era, but most scholars agree that its ritual objectives included the safe conduct of the soul to an existence in a land beyond death. To get the soul to that realm, the Bon priests would sacrifice an animal such as a yak, a horse, or a sheep during the funeral ritual. Kings were buried in large funeral mounds that resemble Chinese tomb mounds.

The Bon religion appears to have combined and interacted with Buddhism in Tibet, but elements of it have survived to the present day. One element that distinguishes Bon from Buddhism is the claim that it originated not in India but in a mythical region west of Tibet named Ta-zig (from the same root as 'Tajikistan') or Shambhala. Today some Tibetans still identify themselves with Bon rather than, or alongside, Buddhism.

Tibetan Buddhism is divided among several ordination lineages or orders. The best-known, the Gelugpa, was founded in the late fourteenth century by the reformer Tsongkhapa. Members of the Gelugpa wear large yellow hats on ritual occasions, whereas the Kargyu lamas wear red hats, and the Karma Kargyu subsect is called the black hats because their leader, the Karmapa, wears a black hat. The ceremonial hats and robes of past masters are preserved in some monasteries.

PRACTICE

Shakyamuni himself disapproved of the rituals conducted by the brahmins of his day, especially those involving animal sacrifice. He also recognized the potential for ritual and doctrine to become objects of attachment, and he warned his followers against becoming dependent on them. To make his point, he told a parable about a man who builds a raft to cross a flooded river during the rainy season and then, because it has been so useful, decides to carry it with him over dry land. Doctrine and rituals, he said, are like rafts: they can be useful, but should not become a burden on the journey towards mental purification and nirvana.

Despite the Buddha's teachings, however, all forms of Buddhism soon developed their own rituals. There were no specific Buddhist rituals for life-cycle events such as the naming of an infant, coming of age, marriage, or death, but 'blessing' rituals centring on the chanting of sacred texts developed throughout the Buddhist world to mark these occasions. Participating in these rituals came to be seen as a way of earning merit, as did the building of stupas, the painting of Buddhist scenes, the creation of Buddha images, the copying of scriptures, and the releasing of captive birds during important Buddhist festivals (eventually, young people would catch birds specifically in order to sell them to pious Buddhists hoping to earn merit by releasing them).

Four places associated with Shakyamuni himself became important pilgrimage sites—Lumbini (birth), Bodh Gaya (enlightenment), Sarnath (first sermon), and Kushinagar (*parinirvana*)—and as Buddhism spread, a number of places in other countries also became pilgrimage destinations.

Theravada Practice

The most common Theravada ritual is the Buddha-puja. Typically, when visiting a temple, Buddhists pay respect to the guardian spirit at the entrance and place flowers on altars near the stupa and Bodhi tree before proceeding into the temple to place flowers on the altar(s) there. They may also put coins into an offering box. Then they say prayers expressing their dedication to living according to the dharma. In front of the main altar, they perform the Buddha-puja, chanting praise to the Buddha and vowing to observe the 'five precepts'. Unlike the 'commandments' of the Judeo-Christian tradition, these precepts are moral rules that Buddhists voluntarily undertake to follow. The Buddhist vows to refrain from:

- taking life
- taking that which is not given
- sensual misconduct (sexual immorality)
- wrong speech (lying, slander and the like) and
- intoxicants leading to the loss of mindfulness.

On holy days lay Buddhists may undertake to observe additional precepts.

Theravadins also perform a number of more elaborate 'merit-making' rituals specifically designed to produce good karma. Of these, three of the most important are almsgiving, the *dana* ritual, and the Buddha Day (Vaishakha) festival.

Almsgiving

Traditionally, members of the sangha would leave the monastery early each morning carrying bowls to collect their daily food. As they moved slowly through the streets without speaking, their eyes downcast to maintain a tranquil, composed state of mind, laypeople would come out of their houses, put cooked food into the alms bowls, and then bow low or prostrate themselves as a sign of respect.

The practice of going for alms is increasingly rare today. It is still common in Thailand, however, and efforts have been made to revive it in Sri Lanka. In other countries, such as Malaysia, the ritual is performed in the vicinity of the temple on important Buddhist occasions. People bring rice and food packets from home and put their offerings in the alms bowls as the *bhikshus* proceed along the road near the temple.

The Dana Ritual

The practice of giving food and other necessities to the sangha has developed into a ritual called ***dana***, from the Sanskrit word for 'giving'. A *dana* might be held at a temple or a pilgrimage site, but is often held by a family in their home to celebrate some important occasion. The following description of a *dana* ceremony in a Sri Lankan home offers a glimpse of several other Buddhist rituals as well.

As the monks arrive at the door, their feet are washed by the men of the family. (If the guests were *bikshunis*, this hospitality ritual would be performed by the women of the family.) On entering the home, the *bhikshus* first bow before the Buddha altar. Then they seat themselves on the floor around the room and conduct a Buddha-puja, after which they chant from a collection of scriptures called *paritta*.

Preparations for the next ritual are made before the chanting begins and involve running a string from the Buddha image on the home altar to a pot containing water, then to the monks, and finally to all the laypeople. The monks and laypeople hold the string in their right hands during the chanting and dharma talk. The water and the string become sacred objects through the power of the chanting. The chanting is followed by a merit-transfer ritual, in which the merit made by all present through their participation is transferred 'to all living beings': 'May the merit made by me now or at some other time be shared among all beings here infinite, immeasurable; those dear to me and virtuous as mothers or as fathers are, . . . to others neutral, hostile too. . . .'

In some respects merit transfer resembles the old Roman Catholic traditions of performing penance or purchasing 'indulgences' for the benefit of deceased relatives; the Buddhist merit transfer is intended to help one's ancestors, and others, in the afterlife. Although the practice might seem to violate the early Buddhist principle that all of us must make our own karma, the scriptures say that Shakyamuni himself advocated it.

After the merit-transfer ritual, the *bhikshus* cut the string into short pieces, which they tie around the right wrist of each male. A layperson ties a string around the wrists of the women, because monks are not supposed to come into contact with members of the opposite sex. The string is left on the wrist until it falls off.

Vesak, the Buddha Day Festival

Many Buddhist festivals developed out of earlier seasonal festivals, and there are variations from country to country. However, Buddhists in most countries celebrate the day of the full moon in the 'rains' month. This is the day on which three major events in the life of Shakyamuni are said to have occurred: his birth, his enlightenment, and his *parinirvana*. Known in Theravada countries as Vesak (Sanskrit Vaishakha) , this festival is often called 'Buddha Day' in English.

A rock inscription from 259 BCE states that King Ashoka organized a procession to be held annually on Vaishakha day. In contemporary Sri Lanka, Buddhists travel from place to place to see special paintings depicting scenes from the life of the Buddha. Talks are given on Shakyamuni's life, and special Buddha-pujas are performed.

Life-cycle and Death Rituals

Early Indian Buddhists continued to follow the life-cycle rituals of what we now call Hinduism, and as Buddhism spread, converts in other regions continued to mark those events in their traditional ways. Thus there are no specifically Buddhist wedding or childhood rituals. It is in part for this reason that Buddhism has co-existed with the traditional belief systems of each country where it has established itself. Sri Lankan Buddhists still observe Indian rituals; Thai Buddhists still worship traditional spirits; and Japanese Buddhists still visit Shinto shrines.

There is a Theravada funeral ritual, however, based on the ancient Indian cremation ceremony. The funeral includes a procession, prayers, a water-pouring ritual, and a communal meal, but the pattern varies from country to country, and cremation is replaced by burial in regions where wood is not easily available.

A traditional Buddhist funeral in Sri Lanka illustrates the principal features of the ceremony. The corpse is taken in a procession to the cemetery along a route prepared in advance by filling in potholes, cutting the weeds beside the road, and placing flowers along the way. These preparations reflect traditions that have parallels in many parts of the ancient world (Christians may recall the preparations made for Jesus' procession into Jerusalem on Palm Sunday).

At the cemetery the body is placed in a temporary wooden structure above a funeral pyre. A brief service is then held that includes chants, prayers, and a ritual in which family members and friends take turns pouring holy water from one container into another while a long prayer is chanted. After the service the pyre is lit, ideally by the eldest son of the deceased. In the event that a crematorium is used instead of a funeral pyre, some aspects of the traditional ceremony, such as the water-pouring ritual, are postponed until the *dana* held on the seventh day after the death, but one or more *bhikshus* will still come to recite prayers over the body.

The loss of a loved one is always a difficult experience, but Buddhists prepare for it through years of prayer and meditation on the inevitability of death. One of Buddhism's strengths is the way it helps its followers develop a realistic view of the end of life by reminding them that all things pass away.

Buddhist death rituals do not end with the burial. On the sixth night after the death, a dharma-preaching service is held at the home, followed by a *dana* on the morning of the seventh day. Other memorial *dana* rituals are held at the home of the deceased after three months and on the first anniversary. Family members and friends who live too far away to attend the funeral itself are able to participate in these memorials. After the passage of time has lessened the pain (*duhkha*) of losing a loved one, the memorial services provide an occasion for family and friends to remember happy times with the deceased and to enjoy a family reunion.

Vipassana Meditation

Theravada Buddhists practise a simple form of meditation called **vipassana** ('insight' or 'mindfulness'). While sitting in a meditational posture, practitioners concentrate on their breathing, focusing either on the sensation of air passing through the nostrils or on the rising and falling of the abdomen. Although the breaths are usually counted (in cycles of ten), the point is not to keep track of the number but to focus the mind. Unlike some forms of yoga, *vipassana* does not require practitioners to slow down their breathing. Practitioners may also cultivate mindfulness of other parts of the body, personal emotions, or relationships with others. The goal is to live in a totally mindful way.

Mahayana Practice

The Bodhisattva Practice

Many of the most important features of Mahayana practice, as we have seen, centre on the bodhisattvas who share their merit with all beings. Mahayana cosmology envisions many spiritually advanced bodhisattvas, each presiding over a heavenly region.

Bodhisattva Vows

In early Buddhism, Shakyamuni's 'bodhisattva vow' was understood as a special case. Few Buddhists dared to think that they themselves might be destined to become the buddha of some future era: they were content to hope that in some future life they might achieve the status of Arhat. By contrast, Mahayana Buddhists—male and female, lay and monastic—were encouraged to take the bodhisattva vows declaring their intention to become buddhas someday, while actively working to help liberate all beings.

Veneration of Bodhisattvas

Only a few individual bodhisattvas are venerated by name, and each of them has a special function. Bodhisattva Manjusri is the guardian of Buddhist wisdom, and novices entering training often call on him to guide and inspire them. Bodhisattva Maitreya, the 'Friendly One', is destined to be the next buddha. He will come after the dharma wheel set in motion by Shakyamuni has stopped turning and the world needs a new fully enlightened buddha to teach dharma. Some people pray to Maitreya, requesting that they be reborn when that time comes, because it will be so much easier to reach enlightenment when there is a living buddha to follow. And, as we have seen, Guanyin is closely associated with children.

With the emergence of Mahayana Buddhism, the distinction between the buddha who enters nirvana and the bodhisattva who has earned entry but chooses to forgo it almost disappears. The bodhisattvas have had enormous appeal as saviour figures. In their compassionate self-sacrifice, they have been compared to the Christian Jesus.

Meditation

Meditation is an important practice in all forms of Buddhism. Monastic training involves careful attention to the posture of the body and the method of concentration. The goals include the quieting of the mind and the heightening of mental alertness. The ultimate goal is to break through into a state of pure mind known as the buddha-mind or emptiness (*shunyata*). In some Mahayana schools, terms such as 'buddha-nature' and 'buddha-mind' became virtual synonyms for 'enlightenment'.

The practice of meditation is particularly intense among Soto Zen monks. One famous Soto monk kept his seat cushion in the sleeve pocket of his robe so that he could practise sitting meditation (*zazen*) whenever he had a moment of free time. When *zazen* is practised in a group, the leader signals the beginning of the session by striking a bell. Typically, after half an hour of sitting meditation during which attention is focused on breathing, the bell is rung again, signalling that it is time to stand and practise walking meditation—focused on the slow lifting of the feet high off the ground—for a similar length of time. Then another bell signals that it is time to return to sitting meditation.

Koan Training and Sudden Enlightenment

The use of koans is especially closely associated with the Rinzai Zen sect, which uses a standard collection of 48 koans called the Mumonkan in training. The first koan presented to disciples is known as 'Joshu's *Mu*'. It tells of a time when the ancient master Joshu and a disciple were walking through the monastery grounds and saw one of the stray dogs that lived there. The disciple asks Joshu, 'Does a dog have buddha-nature?' Joshu replies '*mu*' ('no'; *wu* in the Chinese original). There are many layers to this reply. On the surface, we might say that the standard Buddhist answer to the question would be 'yes', since all living beings have buddha-nature. Yet Joshu seems to deny that fundamental doctrine. The correct response to the koan lies not so much in a rational explanation as in the experience of intuitively breaking through the confines of the rational mind. It is the master's task to reject all false responses to the koan until a proper response is achieved.

Relic and Stupa Veneration

In Mahayana countries, the Buddha's birth, enlightenment, and *parinirvana* are remembered on separate days, determined by the lunar calendar. Festivals honouring other buddhas and bodhisattvas are also observed, especially Guanyin's birthday.

Under the influence of the ancestor cults of China and Japan, the dead are honoured by an 'all souls' day'. In China this day is celebrated by burning imitation money (drawn on the 'Bank of Hell') and releasing paper boats to free the *preta* ('hungry ghosts') who have perished in violence. In Japan, at the feast called Obon, two altars are built, one for offerings to the dead ancestors and the other for the 'ghosts'. Traditionally, Chinese Buddhists avoided non-essential outside activity during the 'ghosts' month', to lessen the risk of encountering a ghost.

Buddhism has also adopted local customs surrounding occasions such as New Year. In China pilgrimages are made to four sacred mountains, each dedicated to a different bodhisattva. In Japan the temple gong is struck 108 times on New Year's Eve, symbolizing forgiveness of the 108 kinds of bad deeds. Many Japanese gather at temples before midnight to hear the striking of the gong, but many more watch television coverage of the ceremony broadcast from a major monastery.

Mantra Repetition

Practice in the Pure Land tradition focuses on opening oneself to the grace of the bodhisattva Amida (Amitabha). In this tradition rebirth is not earned by meritorious works and wisdom, as was the case with the path laid down by Shakyamuni: it is granted through Amida's grace. The *Meditation on Amitayus Sutra* promises that whoever achieves a vision of Amida will be reborn in the Pure Land and explains 16 ways of meditating to achieve such a vision.

Vajrayana Practice

The use of mandalas in Vajrayana meditation has already been outlined. In addition, this tradition makes ritual use of mantras, as well as various gestures. Mantras need not be spoken to be effective; they can be written on banners or slips of paper and hung on trees or lines, or rotated in cylindrical containers called prayer wheels.

The best-known Vajrayana mantra is the Sanskrit phrase *Om mani padme hum*, which may be interpreted in various ways. The words are Sanskrit: *om* and *hum* are sacred syllables, not words per se; *mani* means 'jewel'; and *padme* is 'lotus'. So in English we might say 'O the jewel in the lotus', or simply 'Om jewel lotus hum'. But Vajrayana Buddhists offer several interpretations. Some see the jewel and lotus as symbolic of the male and female principles, and understand their union to represent the harmony of the male and female cosmic forces. Others understand it to refer to the bodhisattva Avalokiteshvara in feminine form as the 'jewelled-lotus lady'. Some believe its six syllables refer to six realms of rebirth or six spiritual perfections. Whatever the interpretation, the mantra evokes a cosmic harmony.

A unique feature of Tibetan Buddhism is the text called the Bardo Thodol ('Liberation by Hearing on the After-Death Plane'), better known as The Tibetan Book of the Dead. A set of written instructions concerning the afterlife, the Bardo Thodol is read aloud to the dying in order to help them achieve liberation as they pass through the *bardo* state between death and subsequent rebirth.

During the first *bardo* stage the dying person loses consciousness, experiences a transitional time of darkness, and then emerges into a world filled with strange objects unknown on the earthly plane. A brilliant light then appears. Anyone who recognizes the light as the Dharma Body of Buddha will attain liberation and experience nirvana rather than rebirth. More often, however, bad karma prevents recognition of the light's true nature and the person turns away in fear. Thus most people then pass on to a second *bardo* stage in which some consciousness of objects is regained. One may be aware of one's own funeral, for

Buddhist nuns during morning chanting service in Lhasa, Tibet (J. Essex).

example. Peaceful deities appear for seven days, then wrathful deities appear for seven more days. These are all the Buddha in the Body of Bliss form, and those who meditate on them as such will experience liberation. Those who do not recognize them will gradually assume a new bodily form within a few weeks of death. Liberation is possible right up to the moment of rebirth, but karma keeps most people in the grip of *samsara*, the wheel of death and rebirth. In the third stage the individual's karma is judged and the appropriate rebirth is determined.

Choosing a New Dalai Lama

Considered to be a manifestation of the bodhisattva Avalokiteshvara, each Dalai Lama is said to be the reincarnation of the previous one. When a Dalai Lama dies, a complicated search is undertaken to find a young boy who shows signs of being his reincarnation. The candidate must display intellectual qualities and personality characteristics similar to those of the deceased, and he is shown a variety of objects to see if he recognizes any that belonged to the latter. Finally, the State Oracle enters a trance state in order to contact the spirits to confirm the selection. The current Dalai Lama was chosen in this way from a family of Tibetan descent living in China. A senior monk's vision played a key role in locating the boy.

❦ CULTURAL EXPRESSIONS

Because Buddhism has been the principal religion of many Asian countries, cultural expressions of its influence are widespread.

Stupas and Pagodas

After the Buddha's *parinirvana*, several kings requested the honour of enshrining his cremated remains in their kingdoms. This created a problem that the disciple in charge of funeral arrangements solved by dividing the remains into seven portions. The urn that had held the remains and the cloth that had covered it were also given the status of primary relics, and so nine memorial stupas were built over the nine relics. But as Buddhism spread to other parts of India, additional sacred objects were needed to establish sites for Buddhist rituals. Thus some stupas were built over the cremated remains of the Buddha's major disciples, or even portions of the Buddhist scriptures.

The architecture of these memorials has a rich history. When asked before his death about the disposal of his remains, the Buddha was said to have answered that a Tathagata's remains should be enshrined in a memorial stupa like that of a great ruler. The funeral itself lasted seven days, during which the mourners walked ceremonially around the mound and placed food, water, and flower offerings on the altars. Circumambulation is always clockwise, the devotee keeping the shrine to his or her right, a much more auspicious side than the left in Indian tradition. For the same reason, monks' robes keep the right shoulder bare while covering the left.

The cremated remains were placed in small caskets, about the size of shoe boxes, richly decorated with jewels, each of which was interred in a crypt made of stone slabs.

The crypt was then covered over with a large mound of earth and a layer or two of bricks, which were plastered and finally whitewashed. Then the builders erected a pole, which was fixed in a square frame on top of the mound and positioned over the crypt.

The pole represents Mount Meru, a cosmic mountain that in Indian mythology reaches from earth up towards the pole star, and around whose axis the world is thought to turn. The part of the pole that extends above its support base symbolizes the upper reaches of the heavens. The pole runs through disks of wood that symbolize the layers of heaven. (The European parallel would be the notion of 'heavenly spheres'.) There are usually nine such layers, in keeping with Indian cosmology, which envisions nine layers of heaven and nine orbiting planetary bodies. The frame, the pole, and its planes later came to be built of stone because wood was difficult to maintain.

There are several names for these memorial structures. The Sanskrit term *stupa* and its Pali equivalent, *thupa*, are cognate with the English word 'tomb'. Another name is *caitya*, meaning 'shrine'. The term used throughout East Asian Buddhism is **pagoda**, which derives from a Sanskrit word for a monument. Whatever the name, nearly every Buddhist temple precinct in the world has one of these structures, and the relics they enshrine are often the subject of elaborate legends.

In addition to the large main stupa, a temple complex will often include smaller ones commemorating important local Buddhists. In popular piety, Buddhists sometimes strew flower petals at such locations and vow that they too will achieve nirvana someday.

Bodhanath, a Tibetan-style stupa with prayer flags in Kathmandu, Nepal. The eyes towards the top of the stupa are characteristic of Nepali temples (Photo courtesy of Roy C. Amore).

Building small stupas has been especially popular as a merit-making act of devotion in Myanmar, where thousands of devotional stupas have been built over the centuries. Some were built to last, such as the ones located near the ancient Burmese city of Pagan, but most were not. In fact, devout Buddhists often build stupas of sand at the shore. The merit comes not from the structure itself, but from the purification of the mind that takes place while the builder is working.

In East Asia, pagodas eventually developed into elegant towers that devotees could either climb up or circumambulate. The multiple storeys represent the multiple levels of the heavens symbolized by the wooden disks of the original Indian stupas.

Temples

Buddhist monasteries grew out of the simple refuges in which early monks lived during the rainy season—usually a collection of thatched huts located on the outskirts of a city. Wealthy devotees would earn merit by paying for the construction of permanent buildings, and over time a temple complex would take shape consisting of living quarters, a small shrine, and a meeting hall. Eventually, to accommodate large numbers of lay worshippers, the small shrine developed into a large temple housing images of the Buddha. Today, besides the stupa and temple, the grounds usually contain a Bodhi tree, dharma hall, monastery, library, and refectory, and are typically surrounded by an ornamental wall with elaborate entrances. The temple area often contains pieces of paper on which prayers have been written, and the area may be decorated with colourful strips of cloth known as **prayer flags**, which often have symbols, mantras, and prayers printed on them.

There are some similarities among temples in different parts of the ancient world. Most are rectangular buildings that are entered through one of the shorter sides, although in East Asian temples, access is through one of the longer sides. Entering through a tall portico, worshippers come into an outer chamber that in some cases is open to the air and can hold large numbers of people. At the far end of the building is an image of the revered figure flanked by attendant deities, angels, or supernatural animals. Often there is an altar in front of the image where flowers and other offerings are placed. Songs of praise are sung, and oil lamps and incense are lit. Ritual attendants bring food and water to the image, and in hot weather may even wave fans to keep it cool. In every way the image is treated like royalty. Although early Buddhists did not consider the Buddha to be a god, they adopted the local temple customs, and modern Buddhists continue to follow those customs today. In some regions of India, cave complexes were developed that included all the essentials of a temple complex, including separate caves for shrines, living areas, and even large dharma halls. Similar complexes can be found in various other places, including China (the Longmen caves) and Afghanistan (the largest complex is at Bamiyan, the site where the Taliban's destruction of two colossal bodhisattva images in 2001 helped to gain the American public's support for the US-led invasion).

In China, the rectangular wooden buddha hall reflected the influence of the tile-roofed imperial hall of state, with the buddha statue enshrined in the posture of an emperor. This style was the one that made its way to Japan, the best-known example being the Todaiji, the Great East Monastery in Nara, which houses a bronze image of Vairocana, the cosmic buddha, more than 16 metres (52 feet) high.

Images of the Buddha

The earliest known image of the Buddha was not created until almost five hundred years after his *parinirvana*. Until then, it was apparently assumed that no physical form could or should depict him. Instead, the Buddha and his teaching were represented by symbols such as his footprint, the Wheel of the Law, the Bodhi tree, or an empty seat. These forms played an important role in the decoration of the stone fences around ancient stupas.

The first representations of the Buddha himself date from the first century CE—the time when Mahayana devotions were becoming increasingly popular. They take the form of sculpted reliefs or statues showing Shakyamuni standing, sitting in the lotus position of meditation, seated on a throne, or reclining, either in sleep or at the moment of the *parinirvana*. These have remained the classic postures for Buddhist iconography.

A number of hand gestures (**mudras**) are possible, but most representations of the Buddha show some combination of the following five:

- 'Touching the earth': the fingers of the right hand are extended down, 'calling the earth to witness' his enlightenment, as during the encounter with Mara;
- 'Teaching': one hand raised with open palm and thumb touching index finger;
- 'Meditation': hand(s) resting in the lap, palm up;
- 'Granting protection': right hand raised, palm out; usually combined with;
- 'Fulfilling a wish': left hand extended down, palm out.

Buddhist iconography also includes the 32 major signs of Shakyamuni's status, the most obvious of which are elongated ear lobes and a protuberance on the top of his head that was supposed to be the locus of his supernatural wisdom. Some art historians think that these features were associated with royalty (earlobes stretched by heavy earrings, elaborate hair styles), but Buddhists see them as signs of Shakyamuni's supernatural nature. Other signs include wheel images on the soles of his feet and fingers that are all the same length.

Buddhist iconography in China typically shows the Buddha in the centre of his company like an emperor surrounded by his court. The Buddha is seated in a serene posture, flanked by his disciples Kashyapa and Ananda. Nearby stand the bodhisattvas and stern-looking Arhats. The Four World Protectors often stand guard at the entrance or along the sides of the entrance hall. Each of the four is associated with one of the cardinal directions, and each one holds a characteristic object.

Story Illustrations

Buddhist art, especially painting and relief carving, often illustrates scenes either from the life of Shakyamuni or from the *Jataka* ('birth story') collections that recount his previous lives. The walls of temples are often lined with such art so that visitors can see the story of the Buddha's life unfold as they circumambulate the structure.

In ancient India, stupas located away from temple grounds were surrounded by ornamental fences carved with similar scenes. The great stupa in the complex at Sanchi, in central India, offers the most important example of such art. The fences that survive today are all made of stone, but the prototypes would have been carved in wood. The narrative illustration panels in temples continue the ancient pattern.

As Buddhism spread, other cultures developed their own distinctive iconography. In China, images of Shakyamuni gradually took on a more Chinese appearance, and the figure of Guanyin developed into the graceful, standing feminine form found throughout East Asia. There is a distinctive Korean representation of Maitreya as a pensive prince with one leg crossed over the other knee. This kind of image also spread to Japan at the time of 'Prince' Shotoku. An example is the famous wooden statue of Maitreya—the greatest of all national treasures—in Kyoto's Koryuji temple, founded in 622 for the repose of Shotoku.

Zen Art and the Tea Ceremony

The highly ritualized tea ceremony was introduced by Zen monks and spread from monasteries to become one of the most familiar symbols of Japanese culture, expressed in everything from special tea bowls to distinctive tea houses. The Zen influence is also reflected in the minimalism of Japanese painting, in which empty space plays a central role, and the raked-sand gardens (the space accented only by the occasional boulder) typically found in the courtyards of Zen temples such as Ryoanji in Kyoto. Another cultural expression of Zen values is the Japanese art of flower arranging, which originated in the practice of creating floral offerings for altars and special ceremonies.

Interaction and Adaptation

China

In China the Buddhist concept of the afterlife was adapted to conform to local tradition. Chinese Buddhists extended the vague notion of the underworld and a home with their ancestors into a system of many-layered heavens and hells, with a variety of saviour figures that included Guanyin and the bodhisattva Dizang ('earth-store'; Jizo in Japanese), who relieves the suffering of those reborn in hell. Buddhism in turn had some influence on Chinese Daoism and folk religion, which incorporated the Buddhist idea of rebirth on a higher or lower level of life into the traditional system of retribution for good and evil.

Buddhist monasticism, however, did not fit well in a social system based on kinship and veneration of ancestors. Not only did the practice of celibacy put the family lineage in jeopardy, but endowments and donations enabled the monasteries to acquire large tracts of land that were worked by serf labour. Whereas Indian society respected the monks who relied on donations for their living, Chinese society looked down on those who did not support themselves. In time, therefore, Chan monks in particular incorporated labour into their discipline, growing their own food. As the eighth-century Chan master Baizhang Huaihai proclaimed, 'A day without work is a day without eating.'

Chinese imperial officials saw Buddhism as a direct threat to the state's authority, as this seventh-century memorial addressed to the first Tang emperor shows:

> Thus people were made disloyal and unfilial, shaving their heads and discarding their sovereign and parents, becoming men without occupation and without means of subsistence, by which means they avoided the payment of rents and taxes. . . . I maintain

that poverty and wealth, high station and low, are the products of a man's own efforts, but these ignorant Buddhist monks deceive people, saying with one voice that these things come from the Buddha. Thus they defraud the sovereign of his authority and usurp his power of reforming the people (Hughes and Hughes 1950: 77).

Two centuries later, in 845, the Chinese state launched a campaign of persecution against Buddhism that led to the destruction of more than forty thousand temples and the laicization of nearly three hundred thousand monks and nuns.

Meanwhile, the image of Maitreya underwent a transformation not unlike that of the Indian Avalokiteshvara into the Chinese Guanyin. Before the seventh century, Maitreya was a heroic bodhisattva figure, but he reappeared in the fifteenth century as Milo, a laughing monk with a pot-belly who carries a hemp bag and is often accompanied by small children. With his happy-go-lucky nature (*maitri* means 'friendly' in Sanskrit), his large belly, and his affinity for children, the 'Happy Buddha' reflects the importance that Chinese culture attached both to children and to worldly prosperity. His image is still popular today on altars and as a decorative motif, especially in restaurants.

Korea

In Korea as in other countries, new cults emerged that owed their inspiration to Buddhist teachings. The best-known is Won Buddhism, founded in the early twentieth century. This new religion seeks to modernize the old religion by translating the *sutras* into modern Korean, emphasizing social service, especially in the cities, and permitting monks to marry. Its meditation object is an image of a black circle on a white background, representing the cosmic body of the Buddha, the *dharmakaya*.

Japan

Dual Shinto

The introduction of Buddhism did not oblige the Japanese to choose between competing systems of beliefs and rituals. Instead, a syncretistic system developed, sometimes called Dual Shinto, combining elements of both traditions.

Shinto shrines were built within Buddhist temples, and Buddhist *sutras* were chanted at Shinto shrines. Eventually a 'shrine–temple' system emerged in which a Buddhist temple would be located within a larger Shinto shrine. The famous red gateways called *torii* were erected at the entrances to Buddhist temples as well as Shinto shrines. Shinto gods were worshipped alongside buddhas and bodhisattvas as their Japanese 'incarnations'. A rationale for this fusion was the concept of *honji suijaku* in which the Buddhist deities were regarded as the true or original entities (*honji*) and the Shinto deities as their local manifestations (*suijaku*).

Tokugawa 'Temple Buddhism'

By the late sixteenth century, its great monasteries and armed warrior-monks had made Japanese Buddhism a sufficiently important political and military force to represent a challenge to the shoguns. Although the Tokugawa shogunate (1603–1867) preferred

Confucianism as a source of ideological guidance, it eventually required that each household be registered with a Buddhist temple, partly to discourage the spread of Christianity.

Following the restoration of imperial rule in 1867–8, Buddhism again fell out of favour, partly because of its institutional identification with the shogunate and partly because of its foreign origins. The Meiji government strongly supported Shinto, and it ordered that Buddhist images be removed from Shinto shrines.

India and Sri Lanka

Buddhism's intellectual and institutional influence within India lasted for several centuries after the third-century reign of Ashoka. It was only in the seventh century CE that it began to decline.

The support that Buddhism had enjoyed in the past gradually disappeared as its royal patrons were replaced by Muslim rulers in northwestern India. Meanwhile, Muslim armies overran and destroyed many Buddhist universities. The scholar-monks and their students were under pressure to convert to Islam or face death. Some scholars fled to Tibet or elsewhere. With its centres of learning gone and the population converting to Islam, Buddhism dwindled.

B.R. Ambedkar and the Mass Conversion of Dalits

Only in the twentieth century did Buddhism begin to find new adherents in India. One catalyst was Dr Bhimrao R. Ambedkar (1891–1956), the lead author of the Indian constitution. He was born into the 'untouchable' dalit class in a time when dalits were banned from educational institutions, but his keen intelligence caught the attention of a brahmin teacher named Ambedkar, who formally adopted the boy so that he could have a name that would allow him to compete on a level playing field when he went for higher education. With the help of that teacher and the local Muslim ruler, the young Ambedkar earned an undergraduate degree in India and eventually a doctorate from the London School of Economics. On his return to India he became an active advocate for dalit rights at a time when his older contemporary M.K. Gandhi was pursuing the same goal. The two disagreed, however, on the best way to that goal.

Ambedkar blamed Hinduism for the discrimination that dalits faced and foresaw that entrenched social and economic interests would make substantial reform impossible. Therefore he turned his back on Hinduism and looked instead to Buddhism as a religion that was compatible with Indian cultural values, but that had always spoken out in favour of the equality of all humans, regardless of birth status. The history of Buddhism supports Ambedkar's view. The Buddha accepted both lay and ordained members into his movement without any regard for their caste. The Buddha also criticized the brahmin priests, and early Buddhist stories made fun of pompous brahmins who exploited the lower classes.

In 1956, at a large rally in the historic city of Nagpur, in the heart of Hindu India, Ambedkar and his wife publicly took the Three Refuges and Five Precepts from a Buddhist monk and thousands of dalits followed their example. Since then, many more dalits have converted to Buddhism as well.

Buddhism in Sri Lanka's Civil War

Since independence in 1948, Theravada Buddhism has had considerable influence on the policies of Sri Lanka's ruling parties, which draw support from the Sinhalese Buddhist majority. This has led to feelings of oppression among members of the Hindu minority, most of whom are Tamils—descendants of people from Tamilnadu in South India who migrated to the island at various times over the past two millennia. (The Sinhalese came from North India.) Conflict between the government and the Tamil separatists seeking an independent homeland in the northern part of the island led to more than two decades of bloodshed, although Hinduism and Buddhism alike teach non-violence. The civil war finally came to an end in 2009, but relations between the two communities are still severely strained.

Southeast Asia

Theravada also remains the most important vehicle across most of mainland Southeast Asia, although the Mahayana traditions of East Asia are dominant in Vietnam, Malaysia, and Singapore.

The end of Burmese kingship in the late nineteenth century, the years of British rule, and long periods of military rule since independence have weakened the traditional political influence of the Burmese sangha. Lately, Myanmar's economy has remained out of the mainstream of modernization and industrialization, and over the past few decades its sangha has been cut off from significant contact with other Buddhist countries. Its people are poor and its temples have fallen into disrepair, but its *bhikshus* are still important in the traditional village-centred society.

Similarly in modern Cambodia, the overthrow of Prince Norodom Sihanouk in the mid-1950s brought an end to the tradition of Buddhist kingship in which the ruler was expected to provide the basic human needs for all citizens. Since then, the Cambodian sangha's political influence has been limited. In the 1970s many *bhikshus* were among the innocents slaughtered in the 'killing fields' by the communist Khmer Rouge. Yet by the late 1980s, the newsletter of the coalition of movements opposed to the new pro-Vietnamese government proudly pictured Khmer Rouge soldiers and *bhikshus* working together on village projects. Today most laypeople of all political stripes remain Buddhists, and all factions appeal to Buddhist values to help legitimate their claims to power. At the village level, Buddhism continues to play its traditional role.

In Thailand Buddhism retains some political influence. The tradition of monastic training for the king continues, and members of the royal family take part in Buddhist ceremonial occasions. The most important ritual is the one in which the king, at the beginning of each season, changes the clothing on the Buddha image in the famous Temple of the Emerald Buddha in Bangkok and gives the Buddha image a ceremonial bath. These rituals symbolize the close ties between Thai Buddhism, the Thai monarchy, and Thai nationalism.

In Laos—under communist rule since the 1960s—Buddhism has lost the governmental support that it had traditionally enjoyed throughout Southeast Asia. The traditional relationship of *bhikshus* and laity continues in the villages, however.

The West

Knowledge of Buddhism in Europe and North America was almost non-existent before the middle of the nineteenth century, but in 1879 a book entitled *The Light of Asia*—a moving poetic account of the life of the Buddha, by Edwin Arnold—attracted wide public attention.

Even so, it was not until the beginning of the twentieth century that a few Western seekers began to publish first-hand accounts of Buddhist meditational practice. By the 1930s, Buddhist societies had been established in Great Britain, France, and Germany.

Mahayana Buddhism in the West

Buddhist influences in North America have tended to come more from the Mahayana tradition than the Theravada. This has been the case ever since the World's Parliament of Religions conference in Chicago in 1893. Among the delegates was a Zen monk named Shaku Soyen, who later returned to America to spread Buddhism. His young translator, Daisetsu T. Suzuki, became the most influential Buddhist writer in North America.

Suzuki made two extended visits to the United States, and wrote many popular books sprinkled with stories of Zen masters and the koans with which they challenged their disciples. Especially as popularized by Alan Watts, these writings caught the attention of Westerners looking for alternatives to the personal theism or the institutional structures of Christianity.

Some Westerners have considered Zen a form of mysticism. Others have argued against this view on the grounds that there is no experience of union with a personal god in Zen.

On the other hand, if 'mysticism' is understood to refer to transformative spiritual experience, beyond the bounds of rational consciousness, then Zen practitioners may well share some experience in common with mystics from other traditions, such as Sufi Muslims, Jewish Kabbalists, or contemplative Christians. Many Westerners have been interested in Zen meditational practice as well. Catholic missionaries and theologians, coming from a long contemplative tradition, have sought to learn from Zen insights and techniques. Zen has also attracted the attention of experts in depth psychology. It was also the first form of Buddhism to make significant numbers of converts in North America.

Vajrayana (Tibetan) Buddhism in the West

Since the 1960s, several lineages of Vajrayana or Tibetan Buddhism have also gained converts in North America. The Kargyu lineage, headed by the Karmapa lama, has established centres in many of the larger cities in Canada and the US; these centres often incorporate the word 'Shambala'—the name of a mythical Himalayan paradise—in their names. Chogyam Trungpa Rinpoche, having trained in both the Kagyu and Nyingma lineages, fled the Chinese takeover of Tibet in 1959 and, after further studies at Oxford, went to the US. The Naropa Institute (now Naropa University), which he founded in 1974 in Boulder, Colorado, has spawned other centres throughout the USA and Canada. The Dalai Lama heads the Gelugpa lineage from his home in exile, the Mamgyal Monastery in Dharmsala, India, but his followers have taken their lineage's traditions to North America as well. One of the earliest Western Gelugpa institutions was the Lamaist Buddhist Monastery of America (later the Tibetan Buddhist Learning Center), established in New Jersey in the late 1950s.

Ethnic Buddhist Congregations

Existing alongside and independent of the converts to Buddhism in the West are ethnic East Asian Buddhists. Beginning in the late 1880s, Chinese and Japanese immigrants settled along the west coast of North America, especially in places like Hawaii, California, and British Columbia, and gradually found the financial resources to build temples similar to those in their homelands. In ritual and teaching, these congregations represented many branches of Buddhism.

The most popular form of Buddhism in East Asia is Pure Land, and that popularity was reflected among early Buddhist immigrants to North America. Over time, some ethnic Buddhists have adopted Christian styles of worship, with pews, hymnals, and leaders who have taken on many the roles performed by North American clergy. Buddhist Sunday schools were founded, Buddhist cemeteries have been consecrated, and Buddhist wedding rituals have been brought under the supervision of a *bhikshu*, now sometimes called a 'priest'.

In North America, ethnic Buddhists use their temples not just as places of worship but as community centres. Although visitors are welcome, the emphasis on community affairs tends to limit congregation membership to people from the same ethnic community. Buddhist meditation centres, on the other hand, have attracted many Western converts. Umbrella organizations such as the Buddhist Council of Canada are helping to bring Western 'meditation Buddhists' into closer contact with the ethnic Buddhist congregations. Estimates are that approximately one per cent of Canadians and slightly under one per cent of Americans identify themselves as Buddhists.

Buddhist Meditation in the West

The influence of Buddhist meditation and doctrine has been greater than the relatively small numbers of Western converts to Buddhism might suggest. Without necessarily becoming Buddhists, many people in the West have adopted modified versions of Buddhist meditational practice in order to calm their minds or to concentrate before athletic or artistic performances. In addition, Buddhist (and Hindu and Jaina) values such as non-violence and concepts such as rebirth and karma have spread well beyond the traditional religious context.

❧ CONTEMPORARY ISSUES

Monasticism and the Female Sangha

Today, the rules governing Buddhist clergy vary widely. Even the basic practice of celibacy is not universal: as we have seen, although Buddhism has historically been a monastic tradition, in Japan the majority of Buddhist priests (who are always male) are married.

As we noted earlier, the Theravada women's sangha eventually disappeared, but efforts to revive it are underway. In Sri Lanka an order of females observing ten precepts was started 1905 with the help of women from Burma. A new order of *bhikshunis*, adhering to all the precepts, was started in 1996 with the help of *bhikshus* from Sri Lanka and Korea. The Ayya Khema International hostel for Nuns and Women is under construction in Colombo, Sri Lanka, as a centre for bhikshuni and lay female training as well as community social service.

Even without ordination, however, many Theravada women pursue a very active religious life, both at home and in the temples. In Thailand Buddhist laywomen can take vows of poverty and service similar to those taken by Roman Catholic nuns. Some of these women say they would not seek ordination even if it were available because they feel they have more freedom to serve others if they are not bound by the *vinaya* rules. In modern times,

Theravada has also moved towards greater acceptance of women's capacity for high religious achievement. A Thai poet named Upasika Kee Nanayon (1901–79), for instance, was revered by men and women alike for her mastery of meditation and her instructional talks.

The status of women in the Mahayana tradition tended to be higher from the beginning. Certainly Mahayana took a more sympathetic view of lay people in general than earlier forms of Buddhism did. The fact that Mahayana encouraged women as well as men to take the bodhisattva vow indicates that it considered women capable of enlightenment in a way that Theravada did not.

There is a continuing order of Mahayana nuns following a disciple (*vinaya*) of the Dharmagupta sect in China and Taiwan, and some of their *bhikshunis* may now be found in many countries. The Rinzai sect of Zen has nuns and female masters, but they are not as numerous as monks and male masters. Dogen taught males and females, but - during the Tokugawa period the nuns of the Soto Zen sect were not allowed to teach, become masters, reside in the temple compounds, or conduct funeral rituals. By the late medieval period the tradition of Soto convents died out. In North America and other locations outside Japan, both Rinzai and Soto trained Zen masters give equal status to male and female practitioners.

Tibetan Buddhism has a long tradition of ordained women, several of whom have been in the forefront of the struggle of Tibetans against Chinese dominance. Ani Pachen ('Great Courage') came to be known as the Joan of Arc of Tibet after she led her clan in a rebellion against the Chinese takeover of Tibet in 1949. She was imprisoned and tortured, but refused to denounce Buddhism or her loyalty to the Dalai Lama. On release from prison in 1981, she again played a leading role in Tibetan demonstrations against Hanification before escaping to Dhamsala, India to live among the Tibetans in exile.

The Controversy over Tibet

To understand the office of the Dalai Lama and the controversial Chinese claim that Tibet is a part of China, we need to understand the historic relationship between Tibet and the Mongols who ruled China from 1222 to 1368. The Mongols did not invade Tibet, but they did appoint the head of the Shakya monastery, the headquarters of the Sakya sect, to serve as their viceroy for the region. Some two centuries later, a Gelugpa missionary named

Jewel Brocade

In The Sutra of Sagara, the Naga King, *which was translated into Chinese in the third century, a princess named Jewel Brocade cleverly uses the Mahayana doctrine of the emptiness of all things to refute a male disciple who represents the stereotypical patriarchal position. No distinction between male and female spiritual abilities is valid, she argues, because all distinctions are ultimately invalid:*

You have said: 'One cannot attain Buddhahood within a woman's body.' Then, one cannot attain it within a man's body either. What is the reason? Because only the virtuous have eyes of Emptiness. The one who perceives through Emptiness is neither male nor female. The ears, nose, mouth, body, and mind are also Empty (Paul 1979: 236).

Sonam Gyatso went to Mongolia and converted its ruler, Altan Khan, who created the title Dalai Lama ('Ocean of Wisdom') and bestowed it posthumously on Gyatso's two predecessors, designating Gyatso the third in the succession. With the sponsorship of the Mongol princes, the Gelugpas soon became the dominant sect in both Mongolia and Tibet.

The first Dalai Lama to become the temporal as well as the spiritual leader of Tibet was the fifth, Ngawang Lobsang Gyatso (1617–82). With Mongol aid he subdued the challenge of the rival Karma-pa lineage and constructed the famous Potala palace in Lhasa. He recognized his teacher, Lobsang Chogye Gyaltsen, as an incarnation of the bodhisattva Amida and gave him the title Panchen Lama. That office still exists, but has been a matter of controversy since 1995, when the Dalai Lama and the Chinese government disagreed on the identity of the legitimate successor to the tenth Panchen Lama, who died in 1989.

The fifth Dalai Lama also established diplomatic relations with the Manchu (Qing) dynasty, which came to power in China in 1644. As a result, Tibet became a protectorate of China in the eighteenth century. These historic ties are the basis of modern China's claim to Tibet, which is now divided into three provinces known collectively as the Tibetan Autonomous Region (TAR).

The government of China considers the Dalai Lama to be the leader of a separatist movement whose goal is to split the TAR from the motherland. It offers incentives for Han Chinese to relocate in the TAR. Critics outside China sometimes refer to this policy as 'Hanification'.

The Fourteenth Dalai Lama

Born: 6 July 1935, in a peasant farming village northeast of Lhasa. His name was Lhamo Thondup.

Signs: After the death of the thirteenth Dalai Lama, in 1933, the head of his corpse turned to the northeast, and a senior monk had a vision that included a monastery and a house with distinctive guttering. When the party searching for his reincarnation finally found the house, in 1938, the three-year-old boy who lived there called one member of the party by name, and picked out the toys and other objects associated with the 13th Dalai Lama. He was then taken from his family to the monastery to begin training.

Instruction: After eighteen months the boy was reunited with his family, who moved with him to Lhasa. In 1940 he was ordained as a novice and installed as the spiritual leader of Tibet under the religious name Tenzin Gyatso. A long course of Buddhist studies followed.

High office: An earthquake and threats of invasion from China prompted his installation as the political leader of Tibet in 1950, at age 15.

Exile: By 1959 the Chinese had taken over Tibet. To avoid arrest or worse, the Dalai Lama crossed the Himalayas to Dharmsala in northern India, where he continues to lead a government in exile.

Writings: The Dalai Lama has travelled extensively and written numerous books on Tibetan Buddhism, meditation, and philosophy as well as an autobiography, *Freedom in Exile*.

Politics: The Dalai Lama continues to use non-violent means to advocate for the well-being of the Tibetan people. Negotiations with the Chinese government have so far not been fruitful.

Buddhism and the Modern World

In the 1920s—a time when Chinese intellectuals were calling for intellectual pluralism and greater openness to Western ideas—a Chan monk named Taixu ('Great Emptiness') sought to bring Buddhism into the modern world. Under his leadership, prominent lay Buddhists devoted themselves to social work and popular education. Such activism has become part of the Buddhist mission in many countries.

Similarly in Thailand, the Theravada reformer Bhikshu Buddhadasa (1906–93) severely criticized the Thai Buddhists, both lay and ordained, who he believed had grown too comfortable with the superficial rituals and routines of temple life, to the detriment of the true Buddhist goals of purifying the mind and helping others. Many monks spend time at the monastery in southern Thailand where he encouraged the development of what has been called 'engaged Buddhism'. Sulak Sivaraksa (b. 1932), influenced in part by Buddhadasa, has argued effectively for a Buddhist vision of society in which the means of development are harnessed for the good of everyone rather than the profit of a few capitalists. He has founded several organizations dedicated to that goal, including the Asian Cultural Forum on Development and the International Network of Engaged Buddhists.

In Vietnam, Buddhist activism became explicitly political in the 1960s, after the Roman Catholic president of what was then South Vietnam, Ngo Dinh Diem, imposed a number of restrictions on the (predominantly Mahayana) Buddhist majority. It was in protest against these restrictions that, in May 1963, an elderly monk named Thich Quang Duc assumed the cross-legged lotus position on a busy street in Saigon, had gasoline poured over himself, then calmly struck a match and became a human torch. A number of monks and nuns followed his example, attracting worldwide attention and contributing to the fall of the Diem government.

These self-immolations led Buddhists to examine the dharma concerning suicide. Shakyamuni himself forbade it: '[Monks], let no one destroy himself, and whosoever would destroy himself, let him be dealt with according to law' (Warren 1896: 437). According to the *Lotus Sutra*, however, the Medicine bodhisattva offered his own body to heal human beings:

> . . . he wrapped his body in a garment adorned with divine jewels, anointed himself with fragrant oils, with the force of supernatural penetration took a vow, and then burnt his body. The glow gave light all around to the world-spheres equal in number to the sands of eighty millions of Ganges rivers. Within them the Buddhas all at once praised him (Hurvitz 1976:294–5).

Thus the Mahayana tradition appears to accept suicide when it is committed for a good cause.

More recently, Buddhist leaders have been asked to consider the issue of same-sex marriage. The scriptures do not specifically address homosexuality. In taking the Five Precepts, Buddhists promise not to engage in sexual misconduct, but what might constitute misconduct is not defined: there is no list of activities to be avoided. What is clear is that Buddhism condemns any act, sexual or otherwise, that brings harm to others. Homosexual activity was traditionally frowned on in Buddhist countries, but this had more to do with prevailing cultural norms than with any specific Buddhist teaching. Some Buddhist leaders now take the position that since homosexual unions are not condemned by scripture, they are permissible as long as the relationship is consensual and does no harm.

Finally, a problematic area for Buddhism, as for other traditions, is abortion. The ethic of non-violence would seem to speak strongly against it. Yet the ethic of compassion urges empathy and support for those who have found it necessary to terminate a pregnancy. In Japan some Buddhist temples even offer grieving parents the opportunity to memorialize their aborted fetuses.

Prospects for the Future

According to the Buddhist understanding of long-term historical cycles, Shakyamuni began a new era by setting the wheel of dharma in motion again after a period of decline. Eventually the dharma will again go into decline, until a new buddha emerges to start the wheel turning again. This somewhat pessimistic view of the future stands in sharp contrast to the views of many other religions, including Christianity. Yet the idea that Buddhist teachings will eventually fall into decline does not in any way diminish Buddhists' zeal or sense of mission.

In a sense, the many volunteer associations promoting Buddhist solutions to modern problems are performing the same function as the Buddhist kings of the past who provided leadership for their people in education and social values. Thus meditation retreat centres offer help with modern problems such as stress and overdependence on material possessions by offering instruction in basic meditational posture and breathing techniques that promote calmness, mental focus, and insight into dharma truths. Most of them emphasize the importance of breaking through the normal bonds of ego, self-centredness, and the assumption of permanence. *Bhikshu* Buddhadasa identified the fundamental problem as the attitude of 'me and mine'. This attitude may be part of the human condition, but Buddhists believe that it is made worse by the materialistic and individualistic values of the contemporary world.

Another problem currently being addressed by some Buddhist organizations is the need for alternative approaches to economic development. Not surprisingly, they condemn projects that serve to make the rich richer and the poor poorer. Instead they advocate a middle path, favouring low-tech, local-level, people-oriented projects that will benefit all concerned.

There is a growing spirit of co-operation among the branches of Buddhism in most countries. Many people now identify themselves first as Buddhists and only secondarily as followers of a particular tradition such as Zen or Theravada. This tendency is strengthened by the fact that growing numbers of Buddhist periodicals and Internet sites are now publishing articles by writers from a variety of Buddhist traditions.

The sense of common purpose among Buddhists has been strengthened by the international presence of the Dalai Lama. Tenzin Gyatso is the spiritual head of just one Tibetan order, but Buddhists everywhere consider him their spokesperson in a sense, by virtue of his high office and his outstanding personal qualities. However great a loss his forced exile is for Tibet, in putting him on the international stage it may have given Buddhism the boost it needed to regain its place as one of the world's most vigorous religious traditions.

In the two and half thousand years that have passed since the time of Shakyamuni, the tradition he founded has spread far beyond the land of its origin, enlisting the dedication, challenging the intellect, and stimulating the imaginations of millions of people. There have been setbacks. In India it was eclipsed by Hinduism and Islam. In Sri Lanka and Southeast Asia it was undermined by the Western values introduced during the period of colonial domination. And political change in most of the Buddhist countries of southern Asia has meant the loss of the royal support system that helped to sustain it for many centuries. Like other religions, Buddhism has also been called into question by modern, secular ways of life. Buddhists today do not consider the scientific world view to represent a serious challenge, since Shakyamuni himself taught that everything is subject to causation. Still, the concepts of karma and rebirth do not fit comfortably into the standard scientific world view.

It is also true that *bhikshus* are no longer the main educators, social workers, dispute settlers, and advisers in Buddhist countries, especially in the major cities; their roles have been reduced to those of ritual leaders and directors of religious education. Yet Buddhists are not converting in any significant numbers to other religions, and most make some effort to live according to Buddhist values.

What gives Buddhism its energy? What makes it work for so many people in so many different cultures? The answer may lie in the power of the Triple Gem to shape people's spiritual lives. Buddhists feel confident 'taking refuge' in the Buddha, not as a god but as a great human being; in the dharma as a set of living teachings that go to the heart of reality; and in the sangha as a community committed to following the Buddha's path as closely as possible. They also feel confident that, in the distant future, when the wheel of dharma set in motion by Shakyamuni ceases to turn, Maitreya will arrive and turn the wheel yet again for the benefit of the next era.

Sacred Texts Table

Religion	Texts	Composition/ Compilation	Compilation/ Revision	Use
Buddhism: Theravada	*Tripitaka: Vinaya* (discipline), *Sutras* (sermons), and *Abhidharma* (further dharma)	Each of the various early sects had its own collection of texts, which were transmitted orally for several centuries before they were first written down in the 1st century BCE, in Sri Lanka.	Only the Theravada versions of the texts survive in full; commentaries include Buddhaghosa's *The Path of Purification* (5th century).	Study and discussion; selections called *Parittas* are chanted as blessings in various rituals; and verses from the *Dhammapada* (part of the *Sutra* collection) often used for guidance in everyday life.
Buddhism: Mahayana	*Lotus* and *Heart Sutras*, as well as hundreds of other sutras and commentaries.	Some written in early 1st century CE; others said to have been recovered from hiding.	Commentaries written on many major sutras.	Chanted for study or blessing rituals; different Mahayana schools had their own favourite texts.

(continued)

Sacred Texts Table (continued)

Religion	Texts	Composition/ Compilation	Compilation/ Revision	Use
Buddhism: Mahayana, Pure Land	*Sukhavati* (Pure Land) *Sutras*, of various lengths	Composed during early centuries of CE.	Commentaries written by major thinkers.	Studied and chanted; the source of the Bodhisattva vows that Pure Land practitioners take.
Buddhism: Mahayana, Chan	*Platform* and *Lankavatara Sutras*, among others; Mumonkan (koan collection).	Favourite Mahayana scriptures, plus stories of masters unique to Chan tradition.	Numerous translations of teachings, updated frequently over time.	Doctrinal, ritual, inspirational, educational; it can take years for students to work their way through the 48 koans of the Mumonkan.
Buddhism: Vajrayana	Kanjur (sutras and tantras).	Includes many Tibetan translations of Mahayana sutras.	Commentaries called Tanjur expanded on the Kanjur texts.	Study, chanting, rituals.

Sites

Lumbini Park in southern Nepal preserves the sacred area where the Buddha was born, with old stupas, the pond where Mahamaya bathed, a Bodhi tree, and a park surrounded by monasteries for visiting monks. This is the first of the four major pilgrimage sites of India/Nepal.

Kathmandu There are two great Buddhist temples in the Kathmandu area. Swayambhunath, nicknamed the 'monkey temple', sits high on a hill, its Nepali-style 'eyes' overlooking the countryside. Bodhanath is a Tibetan-style stupa surrounded by shops and cafés.

Bodh Gaya in northeastern India preserves the area where the Buddha was enlightened. There is the huge Bodhi tree, a temple, and a park surrounded by temples and monasteries representing different schools of Buddhism. Many Tibetans come here in the winter for a festival that is usually attended by the Dalai Lama. This is the second of the four great pilgrimage sites of India/Nepal.

Sarnath, the third of the four great pilgrimage sites of India/Nepal, is the deer park near Varanasi in northern India where the Buddha preached his first sermon. Sights include a new temple, several old stupas and temples, and a museum.

Kushinagar It was in a grove of trees near this town in northeastern India that the Buddha is said to have entered *parinirvana*. It is the fourth great pilgrimage site of India/Nepal.

Maharashtra state in west central India has two famous cave complexes. The Ajanta Caves, carved into a long, curving cliffside, filled with sculpture and paintings. Some caves were temples, carved and painted to look like traditional temples constructed of wood. Others were monasteries. Similar caves are found at Ellora.

Kandy The Temple of the Tooth in Kandy is the most important Buddhist site in Sri Lanka. The midsummer Perahera festival is a spectacular parade of elephants, musicians, and dancers. Both Buddhist and Hindu temples participate in the parade.

Bangkok On the grounds of the Grand Palace is the temple housing a famous jade sculpture known as the Emerald Buddha. Murals depicting scenes from the life of the Buddha are painted on walls surrounding one part of the palace grounds. The nearby Wat Pho is filled with interesting temples, including one with a 46-metre-long reclining Buddha image. Across the river is the picturesque Wat Arun, the Temple of the Dawn, whose tall pagoda sparkles at dawn and sunset.

Angkor Thom in Cambodia is one of the world's great Buddhist temples. Nearby is the Hindu temple called Angkor Wat.

Lhasa is the site of the Potala Palace, the traditional home of the Dalai Lamas before the Chinese occupation of Tibet drove the fourteenth Dalai Lama to relocate his headquarters in Dharmsala, India. Other important Buddhist sites in Lhasa include the Jokhang temple, the surrounding Barkhor pilgrimage circuit, huge monasteries, and an active nunnery.

Shaolin, in central China, is the home of both Zen Buddhism and the martial arts. The monastery has many buildings and statues of the early Zen patriarchs, and the town has dozens of martial-arts high schools. A two-hour hike up a mountain path will take you to Bodhidharma's cave.

Nara, Japan's first capital, has beautiful wooden temples set in a deer park. Todaiji is a tall wooden temple housing a huge bronze Buddha statue.

Kyoto, Japan's second capital, has many famous temples as well, including the 'rock gardens' at Zen temples such as Ryoanji.

Study Questions

1. Compare the life of the Buddha with that of a spiritual leader from a different tradition.
2. How was Shakyamuni's rejection of the authority of the Hindu Brahmin priests reflected in the development of Buddhism?
3. What role (if any) do deities play in Buddhism?
4. A verse from the *Dhammapada* sums up the dharma in three instructions, the last of which is to 'purify the mind'. What does this mean?
5. What is the status of Tibetan Buddhist culture in contemporary China?
6. Why does the Chinese government object when Western political leaders meet with the Dalai Lama?
7. Why does the *bhikshuni* sangha no longer exist in several Buddhist countries? What efforts are being made to revive it?
8. What does the term 'engaged Buddhism' refer to?
9. Why did Dr Ambedkar and many other dalits convert from Hinduism to Buddhism?
10. Is it fair to describe Buddhism as a system of self-development rather than a religion?

Glossary

anatman 'No-soul', the doctrine that the human person is impermanent, a changing combination of components.

Arhat A worthy one or saint, someone who has realized the ideal of spiritual perfection.

bhikshu, bhikshuni An ordained Buddhist monk and nun, respectively.

bodhi The word for enlightenment when used as the first part of a compound, as in 'Bodhi Tree', 'Bodhi Seat', Bodhidharma, or 'bodhisattva'.

bodhisattva In Theravada, a being who is on the way to enlightenment or buddhahood but has not yet achieved it; in Mahayana, a celestial being who forgoes nirvana in order to save others.

Chan/Son/Zen A tradition centred on the practice of meditation and the teaching that ultimate reality is not expressible in words or logic, but must be grasped through direct intuition; see also **koan** and **zazen**.

dana A 'giving' ritual, in which Theravada families present gifts of food, at their homes or a temple, to *bhikshus* who conduct rituals including chanting and merit-transfer.

dharma In Buddhist usage, teaching or truth concerning the ultimate nature of things.

dukkha The suffering, psychological as well as physical, that characterizes human life.

Han, Han Chinese The name for the majority people of China, as opposed to 'ethnic minorities' such as Tibetans.

Hinayana 'Lesser Vehicle'; the pejorative name given by the Mahayana ('Greater Vehicle') school to earlier Buddhist sects, of which Theravada became the most important.

karma The energy of the individual's past thoughts and actions, good or bad; it determines rebirth within the 'wheel' of samsara or cycle of rebirth that ends only when *parinirvana* is achieved. Good karma is also called 'merit'.

koan/gongan A paradoxical thought exercise used in the Chan–Zen tradition to provoke a breakthrough in understanding by forcing students past the limitations of verbal formulations and logic.

lama 'Wise teacher'; a title given to advanced teachers as well as the heads of various Tibetan ordination lineages.

Mahayana 'Greater Vehicle'; the form of Buddhism that emerged in India around the first century and spread first to China and then to Korea and Japan.

mandala A chart-like representation of cosmic Buddha figures that often serves as a focus of meditation and devotion in the Mahayana and Vajrayana traditions.

Mara The 'Lord of Death' who presides over the afterlife and tried to tempt Shakyamuni on the eve of his enlightenment.

mudra A pose or gesture in artistic representations of Buddha figures; by convention, each *mudra* has a specific symbolic meaning.

nirvana The state of bliss associated with final enlightenment; nirvana 'with remainder' is the highest level possible in this life, and nirvana 'without remainder' is the ultimate state. See also *parinirvana*.

pagoda A multi-storey tower, characteristic of Southeast and East Asian Buddhism, that developed out of the South Asian mound or stupa.

parinirvana The ultimate perfection of bliss, achievable only on departing this life, as distinct from the nirvana with 'remainder' achievable in the present existence.

prajna The spiritual wisdom or insight necessary for enlightenment.

Pure Land The comfortable realm in the western heavens that is reserved for those who put their trust in its lord, the celestial buddha Amitabha (Amida).

rinpoche A title of respect for Tibetan teachers or leading monks.

samadhi A higher state of consciousness, achieved through meditation.

sangha The 'congregation' or community of Buddhist monks and nuns; in some contexts the congregation of lay persons may also be referred to as a sangha.

Shakyamuni 'Sage of the Shakya clan', a title used to refer to the historical Siddhartha Gautama, the Buddha.

shunyata The Emptiness that is held to be ultimately characteristic of all things, stressed especially by the Madhyamika school.

stupa Originally a hemispherical mound built to contain cremation ashes or a sacred relic; in East Asia the stupa developed into the tower-like pagoda.

sutra A discourse or sermon attributed either to Shakyamuni himself or to an important disciple.

tantrism The esoteric element in some branches of Buddhism, especially Vajrayana and Shingon; a tantra is a tantric text.

Theravada 'Teaching of the Elders', the dominant form of Buddhism in Sri Lanka and Southeast Asia.

Tripitaka 'Three baskets'; the collection of early sacred writings whose three sections consist of discourses attributed to the Buddha, rules of monastic discipline, and treatises on doctrine.

Vaishakha/Vesak A Theravada festival held at the full moon around early May, marking Shakyamuni's birth, enlightenment, and *parinirvana*.

Vajrayana The tantric branch of Buddhism, which became established in Tibet and the Himalayan region and later spread to Mongolia and, eventually, India.

vinaya The rules of practice and conduct for monks; a section of the Pali canon.

vipassana 'Insight' or 'mindfulness' meditation practised by Theravada Buddhists.

zazen Sitting meditation in the Chan–Zen tradition.

Zen See **Chan**.

Further Reading

Amore, Roy C. 1978. *Two Masters, One Message*. Nashville: Abingdon. Compares and contrasts the figures of Buddha and Jesus.

Batchelor, Martine. 2006. *Women in Korean Zen: Lives and Practices*. Syracuse: Syracuse University Press. A good account based on ten years of Zen practice in Korea.

Dalai Lama. 1990. *Freedom in Exile: The Autobiography of the Dalai Lama*. New York: HarperCollins.

Dalai Lama, His Holiness The. 2002. *How to Practice: The Way to a Meaningful Life*. Trans. and ed. by Jeffrey Hopkins. New York: Pocket Books.

Fisher, Robert E. 1993. *Buddhist Art and Architecture*. London: Thames & Hudson. An overview of South and East Asian developments.

Gross, Rita M. 1993. *Buddhism after Patriarchy: A Feminist History, Analysis, and Reconstruction of Buddhism*. Albany: State University of New York Press. Material for provocative debate.

Kyabgon, Traleg. 2011. *The Essence of Buddhism: An Introduction to Its Philosophy and Practice*. Boston: Shambhala Publications. Inc. An introduction from a Tibetan Buddhist point of view.

Lopez, Donald S., Jr. 2002. *The Story of Buddhism: A Concise Guide to Its History and Teachings*. New York: HarperCollins.

Queen, Christopher S., and Sallie B. King, eds. 1996. *Engaged Buddhism: Liberation Movements in Asia*. Albany: State University of New York Press. Twentieth-century activism from India and Thailand to Tibet and Japan.

Seager, Richard Hughes. 2000. *Buddhism in America*. New York: Columbia University Press.

Shaw, Ronald D.M., trans. 1961. *The Blue Cliff Records: The Hekigan Roku [Pi yen lu] Containing One Hundred Stories of Zen Masters of Ancient China*. London: M. Joseph. Koans especially prized by the Japanese.

Sivaraksa, Sulak. 2005. *Conflict, Culture, Change: Engaged Buddhism in a Globalizing World*. Somerville, MA: Wisdom Publications. A book by an important Thai Buddhist social critic.

Yifa, Venerable. 2011. *Stories from the Sutras*. New York: Lantern Books. A Chinese nun from Taiwan uses stories to illustrate Buddhist teachings such as karma, impermanence, and suffering.

Recommended Websites

http://lhamo.tripod.com/   A site focusing on women in Buddhism.

www.americanbuddhist.net   Offers a broad overview of Buddhism, including Buddhist activism.

www.buddhamind.info   A site of interest to Buddhist families.

www.buddhanet.net   A comprehensive site, including a e-zine with cartoons, pictures, and much more.

www.dharmanet.org   Another comprehensive site, including video links.

www.buddhanet.net/e-learning/buddhistworld/china-txt.htm   A useful overview of the history and varieties of Buddhism in China, but does not address current issues.

www.dhamma.org   A good source on Theravada-style *vipassana* meditation.

www.freetibet.org   Site of the Free Tibet Campaign, a movement started by Tibetans in exile and their supporters.

References

Bloom, Alfred. 1965. *Shinran's Gospel of Pure Grace*. Tucson: University of Arizona Press.

Chen, Kenneth. 1964. *Buddhism in China: A Historical Survey*. Princeton: Princeton University Press.

Dhammika, Sravasti, ed. 1989. *Buddha Vacana*. Singapore: Buddha Dhamma Mandala Society.

Horner, I.B. 1930. *Women under Primitive Buddhism: Laywomen and Almswomen*. New York: Dutton.

Hughes, Ernest R., and K. Hughes. 1950. *Religion in China*. London: Hutchinson.

Hurvitz, Leon. 1976. *Scripture of the Lotus Blossom of the Fine Dharma*. New York: Columbia University Press.

Nanamoli [formerly Osborne Moore], trans. 1972. *The Life of the Buddha as It Appears in the Pali Canon, the Oldest Authentic Record*. Kandy: Buddhist Publication Society.

Nielsen, N.C., et al., eds. 1993. *Religions of the World*. 3rd ed. New York: St Martin's Press.

Paul, Diana Y., ed. 1979. *Women in Buddhism: Images of the Feminine in Mahayana Tradition*. Berkeley: Asian Humanities Press.

Robinson, Richard H. 1959. 'Buddhism: In China and Japan'. In R.C. Zaehner, ed., *The Concise Encyclopedia of Living Faiths*, 321–47. London: Joseph.

Suzuki, D.T. 1991. *An Introduction to Zen Buddhism*. New York: Grove Press.

Tsunoda, Ryusaku. 1958. *Sources of Japanese Tradition*. New York: Columbia University Press.

Yampolsky, Philip, trans. 1976. *The Platform Sutra of the Sixth Patriarch*. New York: Columbia University Press.

Chapter

9

Sikh Traditions

✺ Pashaura Singh ✺

The Punjabi word *Sikh* means 'disciple'. People who identify themselves as Sikhs are disciples of Akal Purakh ('Timeless Being', God), the ten Sikh Gurus, and the sacred scripture called the Adi Granth ('Original Book'). The youngest of India's indigenous religions, Sikhism emerged in the Punjab approximately five centuries ago and quickly distinguished itself from the region's other religious traditions in its doctrines, practices, and orientation—away from ascetic renunciation and towards active engagement with the world.

❧ ORIGINS

The religious environment of the fifteenth-century Punjab was suffused with the thought of the North Indian **Sants**. The founder of the Sikh tradition, Guru Nanak (1469–1539), shared both the mystic and the iconoclastic tendencies of 'poet-saints' such as Kabir, Ravidas, and Namdev. Nevertheless, Nanak declared his independence from the prevailing thought forms of his day and sought to kindle the fire of independence in his disciples.

The foundation of the tradition he created was his belief in the possibility of achieving spiritual liberation in a single lifetime through meditation on the divine Name (**nam**) and the living of an ethical life in the world. The interaction of this ideology with two environmental factors—the rural base of Punjabi society and the historical circumstances of the period during which Nanak's successors built on the foundations he laid—determined the historical development of Sikhism. About two-thirds of the Sikh population has always come from a rural background.

The name Punjab (literally, 'five waters') refers to the five rivers (Jehlum, Chenab, Ravi, Beas, and Sutlej) that define the region, all of which are tributaries of the Indus. The central Punjab has a rich layer of fertile soil resulting from the changing course of rivers and heavy rainfall. Historically, this region has been primarily agricultural, but it has also been a geographical crossroads where the cultures of the Middle East, Central Asia, and India have interacted in various ways, and through which a series of Muslim invaders—Afghans, Arabs, Iranians, Turks—had made forays into the region since at least the eighth century CE.

Sufi Islam had already become established in the Punjab by the eleventh century, and with the establishment of the Delhi Sultanate, in the thirteenth century, three Sufi orders from Iraq and Persia moved into northern India. By the fifteenth century the Buddhists had disappeared from the Punjab, although a few Jaina ascetics had survived. There were also three distinct Hindu communities devoted to Shiva, Vishnu, and Devi (the Goddess) respectively, along with a cluster of tantra-influenced yogic sects known collectively as the Nath tradition. It is only in the context of this diverse religious universe that the development of the Sikh tradition can be understood, for it compelled the Sikhs to define themselves in an ongoing process of interaction and lively debate.

◀ The Golden Temple, illuminated in celebration of Guru Granth Sahib's anniversary (Munish Sharma/ Reuters/Landov).

Timeline

1469 CE	Birth of Guru Nanak, the founder of the Sikh tradition
1499	Guru Nanak's mystical experience in the Vein River
1519	Establishment of the first Sikh community at Kartarpur
1539	Guru Nanak is succeeded by Guru Angad
1577	Guru Ram Das establishes the town of Ramdaspur (Amritsar)
1604	The Adi Granth is compiled under Guru Arjan's supervision
1606	Guru Arjan's martyrdom by order of Emperor Jahangir
1675	Guru Tegh Bahadur's martyrdom by order of Emperor Aurangzeb
1699	Guru Gobind Singh organizes the Khalsa
1708	Succession of personal Gurus ends with the death of Guru Gobind Singh; from now on the scripture is the Guru, revered as the Guru Granth Sahib
1765	Sikhs capture Lahore
1799	Punjab united under Maharaja Ranjit Singh
1849	Annexation of the Punjab by the British
1865	Publication of the first printed edition of the Guru Granth Sahib
1873	Singh Sabha movement is established
1892	Singh Sabha establishes Khalsa College in Amritsar
1920	Shiromani Gurdwara Prabandhak Committee (SGPC) is established
1925	Sikh Gurdwara Act gives the SGPC legal authority over all gurdwaras
1947	Punjab partitioned between India and Pakistan
1973	Beginning of Sikh ethno-nationalist movement
1984	Indian army attacks the Golden Temple and other gurdwaras in the Punjab
1985	Bombing of Air India Flight 182
1999	Sikhs celebrate the tri-centenary of the Khalsa
2004	Manmohan Singh is elected the first Sikh prime minister of India
2008	Tri-centenary celebration of the installation as Guru of the Guru Granth Sahib
2010	Tri-centenary celebration of Sikh rule established by Banda Singh Bahadur in 1710

Guru Nanak

Guru Nanak was born in 1469 to an upper-caste professional khatri ('merchant') family in the village of Talwandi (Nankana Sahib), not far from what is now Lahore, Pakistan. At the time of his birth, much of northern India, including the Punjab, had been under Muslim control for more than two centuries. By 1526, when the Delhi Sultanate was overthrown

Traditions at a Glance

Numbers
25 million around the world.

Distribution
Primarily northern India, especially Punjab, Haryana, and Delhi, with minorities in other provinces of India and many other countries, including Canada, the United States (especially California), and Britain.

Founders and Leaders
Founded by Guru Nanak c. 1500 CE, and developed over the following two centuries by a succession of nine other inspired teachers, the last of whom, Guru Gobind Singh, died in 1708.

Deity
The Supreme Being is considered to be One and without form. Guru Nanak refers to the deity as Akal Purakh ('Timeless Person'), Kartar ('Creator'), and Nirankar ('Formless'), among many other names.

Authoritative Texts
The Adi Granth (also known as Guru Granth Sahib) is a compilation of divinely inspired hymns by six Gurus, 15 poet-saints, and 15 Sikh bards. The Dasam Granth, a collection of hymns made in the time of the tenth Guru, is also revered as a secondary scripture.

Noteworthy Teachings
There is One Supreme Reality, never incarnated. In addition to reverence for the Gurus and the sacred scriptures, Sikhs emphasize egalitarianism, tolerance, service to others, and righteous life in this world as the way to ultimate liberation from the cycle of rebirth.

by the first Mughal emperor, Babur, Guru Nanak had already established a community of his followers in the village of Kartarpur ('The Creator's Abode'). For the next two centuries the Sikh tradition evolved in the historical context of Mughal rule in India.

The young Nanak was employed as a steward by a local Muslim nobleman, but his mind was preoccupied with spiritual matters, and he spent long hours at the beginning and end of each day absorbed in meditation and devotional singing. Early one morning, while bathing in the Vein River, he disappeared without a trace. Family members gave him up for dead, but three days later, following a profound mystical experience, he stepped out of the water and proclaimed: 'There is no Hindu, there is no Muslim.'

The significance of this statement becomes clear in the context of a religious culture divided between the conflicting truth claims of the Islamic and Hindu traditions. Nanak pointed the way towards the common humanity underlying the external divisions. After his three-day immersion in the waters—a metaphor of dissolution, transformation, and

Map 9.1   The Punjab

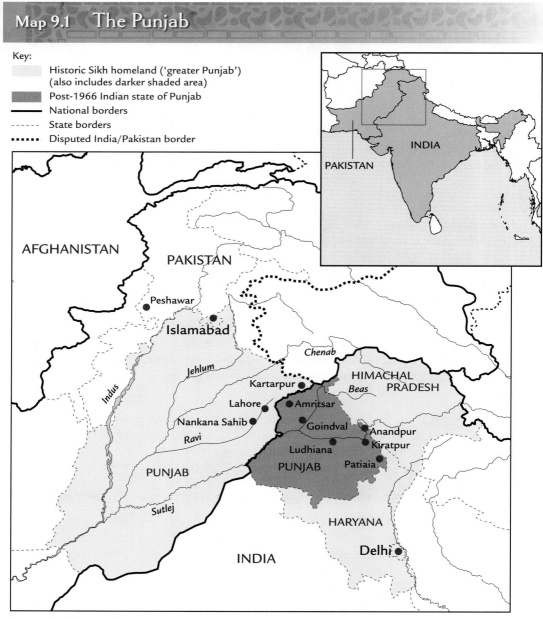

Key:

▓ (light)	Historic Sikh homeland ('greater Punjab') (also includes darker shaded area)
▓ (dark)	Post-1966 Indian state of Punjab
——	National borders
- - - -	State borders
•••••	Disputed India/Pakistan border

Source: **Adapted from Nesbitt 2005: 9.**

spiritual perfection—Nanak was ready to proclaim a new vision. One of his own hymns describes his mystical experience:

> I was a minstrel out of work; the Lord assigned me the task of singing the Divine Word day and night. He summoned me to his Court and bestowed on me the robe of honour for singing his praises. On me he bestowed the Divine Nectar (*amrit*)

in a cup, the nectar of his true and holy Name. (M1, *Var Majh* 27, Adi Granth / AG 150).[1]

This hymn is intensely autobiographical, explicitly pointing out Guru Nanak's own understanding of his divine mission and marking the beginning of his ministry. When he began to preach the message of the divine Name, Nanak was 30 years of age, had been married for more than a decade, and was the father of two young sons. Yet he left his family behind to set out on a series of journeys to both Hindu and Muslim places of pilgrimage in India and abroad. In the course of his travels he encountered the leaders of different religious persuasions and tested the veracity of his own ideas through dialogue with them.

Guru Nanak's Message to Different Audiences

Guru Nanak addressed Muslims as follows:

Make mercy your mosque and devotion your prayer mat,
Righteousness your Qur'an;
Meekness your circumcising, goodness your fasting;
For thus the true Muslim expresses his faith.
Make good works your Ka`bah, take truth as your Pir ['Guide']
Compassion your creed and your prayer.
Let service to God be the beads which you tell
And God will exalt you to glory.
(M1, *Var Majh*, AG 140–1)

To the 'twice-born' Hindus, he said:

Make compassion the cotton, contentment the thread,
Continence the knot, and truth the twist.
This is the sacred thread of the soul,
If you possess it, O Brahmin, then place it on me.
It does not break or become soiled with filth.
This can neither be burnt, nor lost.
Blessed are the mortals, O Nanak,
Who wear such a thread round their neck.
(M1, *Var Asa*, AG 471)

And he spoke to the Nath yogis in their own terms:

Make contentment your earrings, modesty your begging-bowl and wallet,
And meditation on the Lord your ashes.
Let the fear of death be your patched garment;
Be chaste like a virgin; make faith in God, your staff.
Your great Yogic sect (*ai panthi*) should be universal brotherhood,
And self-control the conquest of the world.
(M1, *Japu 28*, AG 6)

Foundation of the Sikh Panth

At the end of his spiritual travels Guru Nanak purchased a parcel of land on the right bank of the Ravi River in central Punjab, where he founded the village of Kartarpur in 1519. There he lived for the rest of his life as the 'spiritual guide' of a new religious community. His charismatic personality and teaching won him many disciples, who received the message of liberation through religious hymns of unique genius and notable beauty. They began to use these hymns in devotional singing (**kirtan**) as part of congregational worship. The first Sikh families who gathered around Guru Nanak at Kartarpur formed the nucleus of the Nanak-**Panth** (Path of Nanak), the community who followed his path to liberation. In his role as what the sociologist Max Weber called an 'ethical prophet', Nanak called for a decisive break with existing formulations and laid the groundwork for a new, rational model of human behaviour based on divine authority.

Guru Nanak rightly understood that his listeners would comprehend his message more clearly if it was expressed in the language of their own religious heritage. Thus he reached out to his Muslim audience by using Islamic concepts and used Nath terminology with the

Guru Nanak on Women

Guru Nanak's campaign for egalitarian reform was not limited to the caste system. He spoke out clearly against the inferior position assigned to women in Punjabi society, as the following verse from his celebrated Asa Ki Var ('Ballad in the Asa mode') shows:

From women born, shaped in the womb,
To woman betrothed and wed;
We are bound to women by ties of affection,
On women man's future depends.
If one woman dies he seeks another;
With a woman he orders his life.
Why then should one speak evil of women,
They who give birth to kings?
Women also are born from women;
None takes birth except from a woman.
Only the True One [Akal Purakh/God], Nanak [Guru Nanak often addresses himself], needs no
    help from a woman.
Blessed are they, both men and women,
Who endlessly praise their Lord.
Blessed are they in the True One's court,
There shall their faces shine.
(M1, *Var Asa*, AG 473; McLeod 1997: 241–2)

Nanak's egalitarian ideas about women set him far apart from the medieval poet-saints of North India, particularly Kabir, who described woman as 'a black cobra', 'the pit of hell', and 'the refuse of the world' (Kabir Granthavali: 30.2, 30.16, and 30.20).

yogis. The message in each case, however, reflected Guru Nanak's own understanding of the divine truth.

Guru Nanak, as founder, was the central authority for the Kartarpur community. He prescribed the daily routine, in which communal devotions—Nanak's *Japji* ('Honoured Recitation') was recited in the early hours of the morning, and *So Dar* ('That Door') and *Arti* ('Adoration') were sung in the evening—were balanced with agricultural work for sustenance. He defined the ideal person as a *Gurmukh* ('one oriented towards the Guru') who practised the threefold discipline of *nam dan ishnan*, 'the divine Name, charity, and purity' (AG 942). Corresponding to the cognitive, the communal, and the personal aspects of the evolving Sikh identity, these three features—*nam* (relation to the Divine), *dan* (relation to the society), and *ishnan* (relation to self)—established a balance between the development of the individual and the society. For Guru Nanak, the true spiritual life required that 'one should live on what one has earned through hard work and share with others the fruit of one's exertion' (AG 1245). Service, self-respect, truthful living, humility, sweetness of the tongue, and taking only one's rightful share were among the virtues most highly prized in the pursuit of liberation.

Guru Nanak's spiritual message found expression at Kartarpur through three key institutions: the *sangat* ('holy fellowship') in which all felt that they belonged to one large spiritual fraternity; the *dharamsala*, the original form of the Sikh place of worship; and the **langar**: the communal meal, prepared as a community service by members of the *sangat*, that is served to everyone attending the **gurdwara** (the Sikh place of worship) and that requires people of all castes and conditions to sit side-by-side in status-free rows—female next to male, socially high next to socially low, ritually pure next to ritually impure—and share the same food. This was the first practical expression of Guru Nanak's spiritual mission to reform society. The institution of the *langar* promoted egalitarianism, community service, unity, and belonging while striking down a major aspect of the caste system. In so doing it marked a major step in the process of defining a distinctive Sikh identity.

Lineage of Gurus

Finally, Guru Nanak created the institution of the Guru, who became the central authority in community life. Before his death in 1539, he designated his disciple Lehna as his successor by renaming him Angad, meaning my 'own limb'. Thus a lineage was established that would continue from the appointment of Guru Angad (1504–52) to the death of Guru Gobind Singh (1666–1708), the tenth and the last human Guru of the Sikhs.

Sikh women worshipping at Jalandhar (Reuters/Munish Sharma/Landov).

The Ten Gurus

Guru Nanak's decision regarding the succession was the most significant step in the development of the early Sikh Panth, for he not only promoted Angad to the status of 'Guru' within his own lifetime, but bowed before his own successor, becoming a disciple himself. In this act of humility, Guru Nanak clearly asserted both the primacy of the message over the messenger and the objective independence of the power behind divine revelation. In this way he gave the office of Guru charismatic authority and established that the Guru is 'one', whatever form the occupant of the office may take.

Guru Angad refined the **Gurmukhi** ('from the Guru's mouth') script in which the Guru's hymns were recorded. The original Gurmukhi script was a systematization of the business shorthand that Guru Nanak had used to write the Punjabi language as a young man. Apparently the early Gurus had no objection to the idea of an overlap between everyday life and the life of the spirit. Thus the use of the Gurmukhi script signals the early Sikhs' emphatic rejection of the hegemonic authority attributed to Sanskrit, Arabic, and Persian in the scholarly circles of that era. At the same time, the use of Gurmukhi reinforced the distinct identity of the Sikhs. In fact, language has been the single most important factor in the preservation of the Sikh cultural heritage. For Punjabis, the idea that spiritual truth could be inscribed in their own native language created a sense of empowerment that had been conspicuously absent.

The third Guru, Amar Das (1479–1574), introduced a variety of institutional innovations that helped to reinforce the cohesion and unity of the ever-growing Sikh Panth. In addition to founding the town of Goindval (southeast of Amritsar on the river Beas), he established two annual festivals (Divali and Baisakhi) that provided regular opportunities for the growing community to get together and meet the Guru; introduced a system of 22 **manjis** (seats of authority) as bases for missionaries seeking to attract new converts, and oversaw the preparation of the Goindval **pothis** ('volumes'): the initial collection of the compositions of the first three Gurus and some of the medieval poet-saints.

The reforms that Guru Amar Das instituted regarding women were very significant. He abolished not only the wearing of the veil but the practice of **sati** ('self-immolation by the wife at the funeral pyre of her dead husband'), and permitted widows to remarry. He also appointed women as missionaries (roughly half of the original twenty-two **manjis** were held by women) and gave all Sikh women equal rights with men to conduct prayers and other ceremonies in the congregational setting.

The fourth Guru, Ram Das (1534–81), established a town called Ramdaspur in 1577 and ordered the construction of a large bathing pool there. (After the pool was completed, the town was renamed Amritsar, 'nectar of immortality'.) He also contributed 679 new hymns to the collection that made up the Sikh scripture, and expanded the number of melodies (ragas) specified for their singing from 19 to 30. Together, the musicality and the emotional appeal of his hymns had a tremendous impact. The liturgical requirement not only to recite but to sing the sacred Word became part of the very definition of Sikhism, and contributed significantly to Sikhs' self-image as a distinct and cohesive community. Indeed, the process of distinguishing between 'us' and 'them' was effectively completed during the period of Guru Ram Das, who proclaimed the 'loyal Sikhs of the Gurus (gursikhs)' to be spiritually greater than the 'Bhagats [devotees], Sants [saints], and Sadhs [holy persons]' (AG 649).

The fifth Guru, Arjan (1563–1606), inherited a vibrant religious community. His 25 years as Guru were marked by several far-reaching institutional developments. First, he built the Darbar Sahib ('Divine Court', also known as Harimandir Sahib and, later, as the 'Golden Temple') in the sacred pool of Amritsar, a shining monument that remains the central symbol of the Sikh faith to this day. Its foundation was laid in January 1589 and the construction was completed in a decade. Second, he took it on himself to organize the scriptural corpus he had inherited into the Adi Granth, the definitive statement of Sikhism's unique spiritual stance. Third, by the end of the sixteenth century the Sikh Panth had developed a strong sense of independent identity: as Guru Arjan asserted, 'We are neither Hindu nor Musalman' (AG 1136). Finally, the period of Guru Arjan saw the founding of three new Sikh settlements that attracted converts among local Jats (peasants). The fact that conflict between the Sikh Panth and the Mughal authorities soon began to increase may be attributed at least in part to the militant traditions of the Jats.

Rise of Sikh–Mughal Conflict

To a large extent, the peaceful growth of the Sikh Panth through the sixteenth century can be attributed to the liberal policy of Emperor Akbar. Yet within eight months of Akbar's death in 1605, Guru Arjan himself was dead, executed at Lahore by order of the new emperor, Jahangir. This 'first martyrdom' was a turning point in Sikh history, pushing the community in the direction of self-consciousness, separatism, and militancy. In short, Guru Arjan's martyrdom became the decisive factor in the crystallization of the Sikh Panth.

The sixth Guru, Hargobind (1595–1644), signalled this new direction when, at his investiture, he donned two swords, one symbolizing spiritual (*piri*) and the other temporal

Bathing in the Pool of Nectar (Raghu Rai/Magnum).

(*miri*) authority. One symbol of this new temporal authority was Hargobind's construction, in 1609, of the Akal Takhat ('Throne of the Timeless Being') facing the Golden Temple, to resolve internal disputes within the community. Under his direct leadership the Sikh Panth took up arms to defend itself against Mughal hostility. The new emphasis on worldly affairs did not mean that the Sikhs had abandoned their spiritual base. As the writer and scholar Bhai ('Brother') Gurdas (c. 1558–1637) explained, in adopting a martial orientation the Guru was simply 'hedging the orchard of the Sikh faith with the hardy and thorny *kikar* tree'. After four skirmishes with Mughal troops, Guru Hargobind withdrew from Amritsar to the Shivalik hills—beyond the jurisdiction of the Mughal state—and Kiratpur became the new centre of the mainstream Sikh tradition.

Relations with the Mughal authorities eased under the seventh and eighth Gurus, Har Rai (1630–61) and Harkrishan (1655–64), although the Gurus held court to adjudicate on temporal issues within the Panth and kept a regular force of Sikh horsemen. But in the 1670s, the increasing strength of the Sikh movement in the Malwa region under the ninth Guru, Tegh Bahadur (1621–75) once again attracted Mughal attention. Guru Tegh Bahadur encouraged his followers to be fearless in their pursuit of a just society: 'He who holds none in fear, nor is afraid of anyone, is acknowledged as a man of true wisdom' (AG 1427). In so doing, he posed a direct challenge to Emperor Aurangzeb, who was determined to impose Islam on all his non-Muslim subjects. When a group of Hindu pandits (scholars) from Kashmir asked for the Guru's help against Aurangzeb's oppressive measures, he agreed to do whatever was necessary to defend their rights. A message was sent to the emperor saying that if Guru Tegh Bahadur could be persuaded to accept Islam, the Hindus would convert as well. Accordingly, the Guru was summoned to Delhi, and when he refused to abandon his faith he was publicly executed on 11 November 1675. If the martyrdom of Guru Arjan had helped to bring the Sikh Panth together, this second martyrdom helped to make human rights and freedom of conscience central to its identity.

Creation of the Khalsa

Tradition holds that the Sikhs who were present at Guru Tegh Bahadur's execution concealed their identity for fear of meeting a similar fate. His son and successor as Guru, Gobind Singh, therefore resolved to create a special order within the Panth for the most loyal Sikhs and to impose on its members a common identity and discipline (**rahit**) that would make them instantly recognizable. Thus on **Baisakhi** Day 1699 he gathered the Sikhs together and announced that he needed one of them to step forward and sacrifice his life. He took the first volunteer into a tent, from which he emerged holding a blood-covered sword and asked for a second volunteer. Only after three more Sikhs had offered their lives did the Guru open the tent to reveal that all five were alive and well. The volunteers became the nucleus of the **Khalsa** ('pure') and are commemorated as the 'Cherished Five' (*Panj Piare*).

To this day, the Khalsa initiation ceremony follows the pattern established in 1699: initiates drink sweet 'nectar' (**amrit sanskar**) that has been stirred with a two-edged sword and sanctified by the recitation of five liturgical prayers. Instructively, it was Guru Gobind Singh's wife Sundri who is remembered in Sikh lore for adding sugar-crystals to sweeten the *amrit* with which the members of the Khalsa were initiated in the original ceremony.

In so doing, she gave the Khalsa a feminine dimension that reflects the unique balance between the martial and the spiritual aspects of the institution.

The launch of the Khalsa was the culmination of the formative period in the development of Sikhism. But it was only one in a series of major reforms introduced by Guru Gobind Singh. After adding a collection of the works of his father, Guru Tegh Bahadur, to the Adi Granth, he closed the Sikh canon. And before he passed away in 1708, he brought to an end the succession of human Gurus. Thereafter, the authority of the Guru would be invested not in an individual but in the scripture (Guru-Granth) and the community (Guru-Panth). Together, Guru-Granth and Guru-Panth would continue the process of consolidating the Sikh tradition through the eighteenth century.

❦ CRYSTALLIZATION

The Sacred Scriptures

The Adi Granth is the primary scripture of the Sikhs. It includes the works of the first five Gurus and of the ninth, plus material by four bards (Satta, Balvand, Sundar, and Mardana), 11 Bhatts ('court poets' who composed and recited panegyrics in praise of the Gurus), and 15 Bhagats ('devotees' of the Sant, Sufi, and Bhakti traditions, including the medieval poets Kabir, Namdev, Ravidas, and Shaikh Farid)—a total of 36 contributors stretching historically from the twelfth century to the seventeenth. The standard version of the Adi Granth contains 1,430 pages, and every copy is identical in terms of the material printed on individual pages.

The text of Adi Granth is divided into three major sections. The introductory section includes three liturgical prayers. The middle section, which contains the bulk of the material, is divided into 31 major *ragas*, or musical patterns. The final section is a kind of epilogue consisting of miscellaneous works.

The second sacred collection, the Dasam Granth, is attributed to the tenth (*dasam*) Guru, Gobind Singh, but it is generally believed to include the writings of others as well. Mani Singh compiled the collection early in the eighteenth century. Its 1,428 pages offer four major types of compositions: devotional texts, autobiographical works, miscellaneous writings, and a collection of mythical narratives and popular anecdotes.

The third category of sacred literature consists of works by Bhai

The sword is one of the most important symbols of the Sikh identity (Reuters/Landov).

From the Sacred Writings of the Sikhs

Guru Nanak exalts the divine Name:

If in this life I should live to eternity, nourished by nothing save air;
If I should dwell in the darkest of dungeons, sense never resting in sleep;
Yet must your glory transcend all my striving; no words can encompass the Name.
(*Refrain*) He who is truly the Spirit Eternal, immanent, blissful, serene;
Only by grace can we learn of our Master, only by grace can we tell.
If I were slain and my body dismembered, pressed in a hand-mill and ground;
If I were burnt in a fire all-consuming, mingled with ashes and dust;
Yet must your glory transcend all my striving, no words can encompass the Name.
If as a bird I could soar to the heavens, a hundred such realms in my reach;
If I could change so that none might perceive me and live without food, without drink;
Yet must your glory transcend all my striving; no words can encompass the Name.
If I could read with the eye of intelligence paper of infinite weight;
If I could with the winds everlasting, pens dipped in oceans of ink;
Yet must your glory transcend all my striving; no words can encompass the Name.
(M1, *Siri Ragu* 2, AG 14–15; McLeod 1984: 41)

Gurdas and Bhai Nand Lal Goya (1633–1715). Along with the sacred compositions of the Gurus, their works are approved in the official manual of the *Sikh Rahit Maryada* ('Sikh Code of Conduct') for singing in the gurdwara.

The last category of Sikh literature is made up of three distinct genres. The *janam-sakhis* ('birth narratives') are hagiographical accounts of Guru Nanak's life dating from the seventeenth century but based on earlier oral traditions. The *rahit-namas* ('manuals of code of conduct') provide rare insight into the evolution of the Khalsa code in the course of the eighteenth and nineteenth centuries. And the *gur-bilas* ('splendour of the Guru') literature of the eighteenth and nineteenth centuries praises the mighty deeds of the two great warrior Gurus, Hargobind and Gobind Singh, in particular.

Finally, it is important to emphasize that the Adi Granth is set apart from other Sikh texts not only by the richness and semantic density of its content, but because it is inextricably embedded in daily life. For Sikhs, the scripture is not merely to be read or studied but to be appropriated and interiorized, to be practised and lived.

Institution of the Khalsa

Three aspects of the institution created by Guru Gobind Singh on Baisakhi Day 1699 are particularly significant. First, it was understood that, in undergoing the *amrit* ceremony, the Khalsa initiates were 'reborn' in the house of the Guru. From that day forward, Guru Gobind Singh would be their spiritual father and his wife, Sahib Kaur, their spiritual mother. As part of their new identity, male members of the Khalsa were given the surname *Singh* ('lion') and female initiates were given the surname *Kaur* ('princess'). Their birthplace became Kesgarh Sahib (the gurdwara that commemorates the founding of the Khalsa) and their home Anandpur Sahib (the town where Kesgarh Sahib is situated). The new collective identity conferred on the Khalsa initiates gave them a powerful sense of belonging.

Second, the Guru himself received the nectar of the double-edged sword from the hands of the Cherished Five, becoming part of the Khalsa Panth, subject to its collective will. In so doing, he symbolically transferred his spiritual authority to the Five and paved the way for the termination of personal Guruship. Finally, it was at the inauguration of the Khalsa that Guru Gobind Singh delivered the fundamentals of what would become the order's *Rahit* ('Code of Conduct'). To ensure that Khalsa members would never seek to conceal their identity as Sikhs, he made five physical symbols mandatory:

1. *Kes*, unshorn hair, symbolizing spirituality and saintliness;
2. *Kangha*, a wooden comb, signifying order and discipline in life;
3. *Kirpan*, a miniature sword, symbolizing divine grace, dignity, and courage;
4. *Kara*, a steel 'wrist-ring', signifying responsibility and allegiance to the Guru; and
5. *Kachh*, a pair of short breeches, symbolizing moral restraint.

Known (from their Punjabi names) as the **Five Ks** (*panj kakke*), these outward symbols of the divine Word imply a direct correlation between *bani* ('divine utterance') and *bana* ('Khalsa dress'). Every morning, in putting on the various items of dress (including the turban in the case of male Sikhs) while reciting prayers, Khalsa Sikhs dress themselves in the word of God; their minds are purified and inspired, and their bodies are girded to do battle with the day's temptations.

In addition to cutting the hair, four other sins are specifically prohibited: using tobacco (this injunction was later expanded to include all intoxicants); committing adultery; eating meat that has not come from an animal killed with a single blow; and the practice (common among some Punjabi clans) of female infanticide; in fact, Sikhs were expressly forbidden even to associate with 'sinners against girls'.

Sikh Doctrine

The primary source of Sikh doctrine is the Adi Granth. Its first words are Guru Nanak's invocation of One God (*1-Oankar*) in the **Mul Mantar** ('Seed Formula'). This succinct expression of the nature of the Ultimate Reality is the fundamental statement of Sikh belief:

There is One ('1') Supreme Being, the Eternal Reality, the Creator, without fear and devoid of enmity, immortal, never incarnated, self-existent, known by grace through the Guru. The Eternal One, from the beginning, through all time, present now, the Everlasting Reality (AG 1).

By beginning with 'One' (the original Punjabi text uses the numeral rather than the word), Guru Nanak emphasizes the singularity of the divine; as he put it in a later hymn, the Supreme Being has 'no relatives, no mother, no father, no wife, no son, no rival who may become a potential contender' (AG 597). At the same time he draws attention to the unity of Akal Purakh, the Eternal One, the source as well as the goal of all that exists. The Mul Mantar illuminates the way Sikh doctrine understands a Divine Reality that is at once transcendent and immanent, a personal God of grace for his humblest devotee. The vital expression of the One is through the many, through the infinite plurality of creation. This understanding of the One distinguishes the Sikh interpretation of 'monotheism' from its interpretation in the Abrahamic traditions.

Creation

According to Guru Nanak's cosmology hymn, the universe was brought into being by the divine order, will, or command (**hukam**). This *hukam* is an all-embracing principle, the sum total of all divinely instituted laws, and it is a revelation of the nature of God:

> For endless eons, there was only darkness.
> Nothing except the divine order existed.
> No day or night, no moon or sun.
> The Creator alone was absorbed in a primal state of contemplation . . .
> When the Creator so willed, creation came into being . . .
> The Un-manifest One revealed itself in the Creation.
> (AG 1035–6)

Elsewhere Guru Nanak describes how 'From the True One came air and from air came water; from water he created the three worlds [sky, earth, and netherworld] and infused in every heart his own light' (AG 19). In Sikh cosmology, the world is divinely inspired, the place that provides human beings with the opportunity to perform their duty and achieve union with Akal Purakh. Since 'all of us carry the fruits of our deeds', the actions we take during our earthly existence are important (AG 4).

Karam, Sansar, and Divine Grace

The notions of *karam* (/karma, 'actions', the principle of moral cause and effect) and *sansar* (/samsara, 'reincarnation') are fundamental to all religious traditions originating in India. In other Indian religions, karma is popularly understood as an inexorable, impersonal law. In Sikh doctrine, however, *karam* is not inexorable, not absolute, since it is subject to the 'divine order' (*hukam*) and therefore can be overridden in the name of justice by Akal Purakh's omnipotent grace. In fact, divine grace always takes precedence over the law of *karam* in the Sikh teachings, and can even break the chain of adverse *karam*.

Divine Revelation

Guru Nanak used three key terms to describe the nature of divine revelation in its totality: *nam* ('divine Name'), *shabad* ('divine Word'), and *guru* ('divine Preceptor'). *Nam* refers to the divine presence that is manifest everywhere around and within us, though most people fail to perceive it because of the self-centred desire for personal gratification. This self-centred-ness (*haumai*, meaning 'I, I' or 'me, mine') separates us from Akal Purakh, and is the reason we continue to suffer within the cycle of rebirth (*sansar*). But Akal Purakh looks graciously on human suffering. Thus he reveals himself through the Guru by uttering the *shabad* ('divine Word') that will communicate a sufficient understanding of the *nam* ('divine Name') to those who are able to 'hear' it. The *shabad* is the utterance that, once heard, awakens the hearer to the reality of the divine Name, immanent in all that lies around and within.

Remembering the Divine Name

Traditionally, *haumai* is the source of five evil impulses: lust, anger, covetousness, attachment to worldly things and pride. Under its influence humans become 'self-willed' (*manmukh*), so attached to worldly pleasures that they forget the divine Name and waste their lives in evil and suffering. To achieve spiritual liberation within one's lifetime it is necessary to transcend the influence of *haumai* by adopting the strictly interior discipline of **nam-simaran**, 'remembering the divine Name'.

There are three levels to this discipline, ranging from the repetition of a sacred word, usually *Vahiguru* ('Praise to the Eternal Guru'), through the devotional singing of hymns with the congregation, to sophisticated meditation on the nature of Akal Purakh. The first and the third levels are undertaken in private, while the second is a public, communal activity. The main purpose of *nam-simaran* is to bring practitioners into harmony with the divine order (*hukam*). Ever-growing wonder in spiritual life ultimately leads to a condition of blissful 'equanimity' (*sahaj*), when the spirit ascends to the 'realm of Truth': the fifth and the last stage, in which the soul finds mystical union with Akal Purakh.

The primacy of divine grace over personal effort is fundamental to Guru Nanak's theology. Yet there is neither fatalism nor passive acceptance in this view of life. Personal effort in the form of good actions is seen as an integral part of spiritual discipline: 'With your own hands carve out your own destiny' (AG 474). By teaching his followers to see their own 'free' will as part of Akal Purakh's will, Guru Nanak encouraged them to create their own destinies. The necessity of balance between meditative worship and righteous life in the world is summed up in the following triple commandment: earn your living through honest labour, adore the divine Name, and share the fruits of your labour with others.

Four Notions of Guruship

In Indic traditions the guru is a human teacher who communicates divine knowledge and guides disciples along the path to liberation. In Sikhism, however, the term 'guru' has evolved over time to encompass four types of spiritual authority: the eternal Guru, the personal Guru, Guru-Granth, and Guru-Panth.

God as Guru

Guru Nanak uses the term Guru in three basic senses: to refer to Akal Purakh himself, to the voice of Akal Purakh, and to the Word, the Truth of Akal Purakh. To experience the eternal Guru is to experience divine guidance. Guru Nanak himself acknowledges Akal Purakh as his Guru: 'He who is the infinite, supreme God is the Guru whom Nanak has met' (AG 599). In Sikh usage, therefore, the Guru is the voice of Akal Purakh, mystically uttered within the human heart, mind, and soul (*man*).

Akal Purakh is often characterized as *Nirankar*, 'the One without Form'. Guru Arjan states explicitly that 'The True Guru is *Niranjan* [the One who is wholly apart from all that is darkness and untruth—hence the 'One who is himself Truth', God]. Do not believe that he is in the form of a human being' (AG 895).

Sikhs evoke the absolute knowledge and power of the divine Name by chanting '*Vahiguru! Vahiguru!*' ('Hail the Guru'). The sound vibrations of this phrase are believed to be supremely powerful.

The Teacher as Guru

In Sikh doctrine, a theory of spiritual succession known as 'the unity of the office of the Guru' meant that there was no difference between the founder and the successors: all represented one and the same light, just as a single flame ignites a series of torches. The same principle can be seen in the Adi Granth, where all the Gurus sign their compositions 'Nanak' and each is identified by the codeword *Mahala* ('King') with an appropriate number. Thus the compositions labeled 'Mahala 1' (M 1) are by Guru Nanak, while those labeled M 2, 3, 4, 5, and 9 are by Guru Angad, Guru Amar Das, Guru Ram Das, Guru Arjan, and Guru Tegh Bahadur, respectively (the sixth, seventh, and eighth Gurus did not contribute any hymns to the corpus).

The Scripture as Guru

Sikhs normally refer to the Adi Granth as the Guru Granth Sahib ('Honourable Scripture Guru'). In so doing, they acknowledge their faith in the scripture as the successor to Guru Gobind Singh, with the same status, authority, and functions, in terms both of personal piety and of collective identity, as any of the ten personal Gurus. The Adi Granth has become the perennial source of divine guidance for Sikhs, and it is treated with the most profound respect.

The Adi Granth is more authoritative than the Dasam Granth. It is also the basis of the most important Sikh doctrines, rituals, and social and ethical positions. Simply to be in the presence of the Guru Granth Sahib, or to hear a sentence read aloud from it, makes Sikhs feel that they are on sacred ground.

The Community as Guru

The phrase 'Guru-Panth' is employed in two senses: one, 'the Panth *of* the Guru', refers to the Sikh community; the other, 'the Panth *as* the Guru', refers to the Guru-Panth doctrine, which developed from the earlier idea that the Guru is mystically present in the congregation. At the inauguration of the Khalsa in 1699, Guru Gobind Singh symbolically

The *Panj Piare* (Cherished Five) leading a Khalsa Day parade in Surrey, BC (THE CANADIAN PRESS/Darryl Dyck).

transferred his authority to the 'Cherished Five' when he received initiation from their hands. Sainapati, the author of *Gur Sobha* (1711 CE), recorded that Guru Gobind Singh designated the Khalsa as the collective embodiment of his divine mandate:

> Upon the Khalsa which I have created I shall bestow the succession. The Khalsa is my physical form and I am one with the Khalsa. To all eternity I am manifest in the Khalsa. Those whose hearts are purged of falsehood will be known as the true Khalsa; and the Khalsa, freed from error and illusion, will be my true Guru.

As the elite group within the Panth, the Khalsa has always claimed the authority to speak on behalf of the whole, although at times non-Khalsa Sikhs have interpreted the doctrine of Guru-Panth as conferring authority on the broader community. In practice, consensus is achieved by following democratic traditions.

Sikh Ethics

The Adi Granth opens with a composition of Guru Nanak's known as the *Japji*, in which a fundamental question is raised: 'How is Truth to be attained, how the veil of falsehood torn aside?' The Guru answers his own question: 'Nanak, thus it is written: Submit to the divine Order [*hukam*], walk in its way' (AG 1). In other words, truth is obtained not by intellectual effort or cunning, but by personal commitment alone. To know truth, one must live it. The seeker of the divine Truth must live an ethical life. In this context Guru Nanak explicitly says: 'Truth is the highest virtue, but higher still is truthful living' (AG 62). Indeed, truthful conduct is at the heart of Guru Nanak's message. Cultivating virtues such as wisdom, contentment, justice, humility, truthfulness, temperance, love, forgiveness, charity, purity, and fear of Akal Purakh not only enriches personal life but also promotes social responsibility, hard work, and sharing. In contrast to the Hindu tradition, in which holy men live by begging alms, Sikhism rejects both begging and withdrawal from social participation.

Service

The key to a righteous life is to render service to others. Such service must be voluntary and undertaken without any desire for self-glorification. Nor should the one who gives aid sit in judgment on those who receive it. The Sikh Prayer (*Ardas*) emphasizes the importance of 'seeing but not judging', urging the faithful to reflect on the merit of those 'who magnanimously pardoned the faults of others'. The ideals are social equality and human brotherhood. Therefore any kind of discrimination based on caste or gender is expressly rejected. The Gurus also emphasized the importance of optimism in the face of adversity, and preferred moderate living and disciplined worldliness to asceticism and self-mortification.

Justice

Guru Nanak held justice to be the primary duty of the ruler and the administrator. Thus he condemned the Muslim jurists of his day who were believed to take bribes and have no concern for truth: 'To deprive others of their rights must be avoided as scrupulously as Muslims avoid the pork and the Hindus consider beef as a taboo' (AG 141). In short, the violation of human rights was a serious moral offence.

The Sikh view of justice is based on two principles: respect for the rights of others and non-exploitation of others. To treat everyone's right as sacred is a necessary constituent of justice. Those who are truly just will not exploit others even if they have the means and opportunity to do so.

Guru Gobind Singh taught that, in the pursuit of justice, peaceful negotiation must always be the first course of action. Only when all such efforts have failed does the use of force become legitimate. A famous verse from the *Zafarnama* ('Letter of Victory')—a long poem written by Guru Gobind Singh and sent to Emperor Aurangzeb after the latter had sent his forces against the Sikhs without any attempt at negotiation—makes this point explicitly: 'When all other methods have been explored and all other means have been tried, then may the sword be drawn from the scabbard, then may the sword be used' (*Zafarnama*, verse 22). The use of force is allowed in Sikh doctrine, but only in defence of justice and then only as a last resort. Moreover, no sacrifice is too great in the face of tyranny: 'It does not matter if my four sons have been killed; the Khalsa is still there at my back' (verse 78). For the Sikhs of the Khalsa, the quest for justice is the primary ethical duty.

Oneness of Humankind and Religion

Sikhism is committed to the ideal of universal brotherhood, the defence of human rights, and resistance against injustice. It strives to eliminate poverty and to help the less privileged. In a celebrated passage from the *Akal Ustat* ('Praise of the Immortal One'), Guru Gobind Singh declares that 'humankind is one, and all people belong to a single humanity' (verse 85). Here it is important to underline the Guru's role as a conciliator who tried to persuade the Mughals to walk the ways of peace. Even though he had to spend the greater part of his life fighting battles forced on him by Mughal authorities and the Hindu rulers of various small hill states, a longing to transcend divisions is clear in this passage from the *Akal Ustat*:

> Allah is the same as the God of the Hindus, Purana and Qur'an are the same. All are the same, none is separate; a single form, a single creation (McLeod 1984: 57).

The above verses emphasize the belief that the differences between communities are in reality meaningless. In fact, all people are fundamentally the same because all are the creations of the same Supreme Being. To this day, Sikhs conclude their morning and evening prayers with the words 'in thy will, O Lord, may peace and prosperity come to one and all.'

🌼 PRACTICE

Prayer

Devout Sikhs rise during the 'ambrosial hours' (*amritvela*, the last watch of the night, between 3 a.m. and 6 a.m.) and begin their daily routine with approximately an hour of devotions, beginning with meditation on the divine Name and continuing with recitation of five liturgical prayers, including Guru Nanak's *Japji* ('Honoured Recitation') and Guru Gobind Singh's *Jap Sahib* ('Master Recitation'). Evening prayers are selected from a collection of hymns entitled *Sodar Rahiras* ('Supplication at That Door'), and the *Kirtan Sohila*

('Song of Praise') is recited before retiring for the night. These prayers are learnt by heart in childhood and recited from memory every day. Thus they are always available to provide guidance. In fact, knowing the *gurbani* ('Guru's utterances') by heart is often compared with having a supply of cash on hand and ready for use whenever it may be needed.

Congregational Worship

In every gurdwara a large copy of the Guru Granth Sahib is reverently wrapped in expensive cloth and installed ceremoniously every morning on a cushioned, canopied stand called the *palki* ('palanquin'). There is a broad aisle leading from the main entrance to the Guru Granth Sahib at the opposite end of the hall. All who enter the

Daily Routine of Liturgical Prayers
The Early Morning Order (3–6 a.m.)
1. *Japji* ('Honoured Recitation')
2. *Jap Sahib* ('Master Recitation')
3. The Ten *Savayyas* ('Ten Panegyrics')
4. *Benati Chaupai* ('Verses of Petition')
5. *Anand Sahib* ('Song of Bliss')
The Evening Prayer
Sodar Rahiras ('Supplication at That Door')
The Bedtime Prayer
Kirtan Sohila ('Song of Praise')

gurdwara are expected to cover their heads, remove their shoes, and bow before the sacred volume, touching the floor with their foreheads. Worshippers sit on the floor, and it is the Punjabi custom for men to sit on the right side of the hall and women on the left, although this is not mandatory.

Sikhism has no ordained priesthood. Instead, every gurdwara has a *granthi* ('reader') who, in addition to reading from the Guru Granth Sahib, takes care of the book and serves as custodian of the gurdwara. The office is open to men and women alike, though in practice most *granthis* are men.

Worship consists mainly of *kirtan*—the congregational singing of devotional hymns, led and accompanied by musicians (*ragis*) playing harmoniums and the small drums called *tabla*. Through *kirtan* the devotees attune themselves to the divine Word and vibrate in harmony with it. Many Sikhs today believe that this traditional practice helps them cope with the additional obstacles that a modern technological society puts in the way of their spiritual life.

At some time during the service, either the *granthi* or a traditional Sikh scholar may deliver a homily based on a particular hymn or scriptural passage appropriate to the occasion. Then all present will join in reciting the *Ardas* ('Petition', often called the Sikh Prayer), which invokes divine grace and recalls the rich heritage of the community.

The Sikh understanding of the Adi Granth as living Guru is most evident in the practice known as 'taking the Guru's Word' or 'seeking a divine command'. As a mark of respect, a ceremonial fan (*chauri*) is waved over the Guru Granth Sahib. Then the book is opened at random and the first hymn on the left-hand page is read aloud in its entirety (beginning on the previous page if necessary). In this way the congregation hears the Guru's **Vak** ('Saying') for that particular moment or occasion. Taken in the morning, the Vak is the divine lesson that will serve as the inspiration for personal meditation throughout the day; taken in the evening, it brings the day to a close with a new perspective on its particular joys and sorrows. The whole *sangat* (congregation) receives the Vak at the conclusion of different ceremonies.

The *granthi* reads from the Guru Granth Sahib inside the Golden Temple of Amritsar (Willard G. Oxtoby).

The reading of the Vak is followed by the distribution of **karah prashad**—a sweet, rich paste of flour, sugar, and butter that has been 'sanctified' during its preparation by the recitation of prayers and then by resting next to the scripture during the service. Symbolically, *karah prashad* represents the bestowal of divine blessings on all who receive it. At the end of congregational worship everyone shares in the *langar* prepared and served by volunteers as part of the community service expected of all Sikhs. All present, Sikhs and non-Sikhs alike, sit together to share a traditional vegetarian meal—usually flat bread, bean stew, and curry. This custom is a powerful reminder of the egalitarian spirit that is so central to Sikhism.

The Annual Festival Cycle

The most important festival day in the Sikh calendar is Baisakhi (Vaisakhi) Day, which usually falls on 13 April. Celebrated throughout India as New Year's Day, it has been considered the birthday of the Sikh community ever since Guru Gobind Singh inaugurated the Khalsa on Baisakhi Day in 1699. Sikhs also celebrate the autumn festival of lights, Divali, as the day when Guru Hargobind was released from imprisonment under the Mughal emperor Jahangir. Harimandir Sahib (the Golden Temple) in Amritsar is illuminated for the occasion. These two seasonal festivals were introduced by the third Guru, Amar Das, and Guru Gobind Singh added a third: Hola Mahalla, the day after the Hindu festival of Holi (March/April), is celebrated with military exercises and various athletic and literary contests.

The anniversaries of the births and deaths of the Gurus are marked by the 'unbroken reading' (*akhand path*) of the entire Sikh scripture by a team of readers over a period of roughly 48 hours. Such occasions are called *Gurpurbs* ('holidays associated with the Gurus'). The birthdays of Guru Nanak (usually in November) and Guru Gobind Singh (December/January) and the martyrdom days of Guru Arjan (May/June) and Guru Tegh Bahadur (November/December) in particular are celebrated around the world.

Life-Cycle Rituals

At the centre of every important life-cycle ritual is the Guru Granth Sahib.

Naming a Child

When a child is to be named, family members take the baby to the gurdwara and present it to the Guru Granth Sahib, along with the *karah prashad* that will be distributed after the

Langar at a Toronto gurdwara (Stephen Epstein/Ponkawonka.com).

ceremony. After various prayers of thanks and a recitation of *Ardas*, the Guru Granth Sahib is opened at random and the first letter of the first composition on the left-hand page is noted; then a name beginning with the same letter is chosen. In this way the child takes his or her identity from the Guru's word and begins life as a Sikh. Then a boy is given the second name *Singh* and a girl the second name *Kaur*. *Amrit* is applied to the eyes and head; the infant is given a sip of the sweetened water to drink; and the first five stanzas of Guru Nanak's *Japji* are recited.

Marriage

'They are not said to be husband and wife, who merely sit together. Rather, they alone are called husband and wife who have one soul in two bodies' (AG 788). This proclamation of the third Guru, Amar Das, has become the basis of the Sikh view of marriage, which emphasizes the necessity of spiritual compatibility between the spouses. In a traditional society where the family is more important than the individual, the fact that Sikh marriages have traditionally been arranged is consistent with that principle.

To be legal, a Sikh wedding must take place in the presence of the Guru Granth Sahib. The bride and groom circumambulate the sacred scripture four times, once for each of their four vows:

1. to lead an action-oriented life based on righteousness and never to shun obligations of family and society;
2. to maintain bonds of reverence and dignity between one another;

3. to keep enthusiasm for life alive in the face of adverse circumstances and to remain detached from worldly attachments; and

4. to cultivate a balanced approach in life, avoiding all extremes.

The circular movement around the scripture symbolizes the primordial cycle of life in which there is no beginning and no end, while the four marital vows reflect the ideals that the Sikh tradition considers the keys to a blissful life.

Khalsa Initiation

The Khalsa initiation ceremony (*amrit sanskar*) must also take place in the presence of the Guru Granth Sahib. There is no fixed age for initiation: all that is required is that the candidate be willing and able to accept the Khalsa discipline. Five Khalsa Sikhs, representing the original Cherished Five, conduct the ceremony. Each recites from memory one of the five liturgical prayers while stirring the sweet *amrit* with a double-edged sword.

The novices then drink the *amrit* five times so that their bodies are purified of five vices (lust, anger, greed, attachment, and pride), and five times the *amrit* is sprinkled on their eyes to transform their outlook towards life. Finally, the *amrit* is poured on their heads five times, sanctifying their hair so that they will preserve its natural form and listen to the voice of conscience. At each stage of the ceremony, the initiates repeat the words *Vahiguru Ji Ka Khalsa! Vahiguru Ji Ki Fateh!* ('Khalsa belongs to the Wonderful Lord! Victory belongs to the Wonderful Lord!'). Thus a person becomes a Khalsa Sikh through the transforming power of the sacred word and the sacred nectar. At the conclusion of the ceremony, a Vak is read aloud and *karah prashad* is distributed.

Death

For a dedicated Sikh (*Gurmukh*), death is a joy to be welcomed when it comes, for it means the perfecting of his or her union with Akal Purakh and final release from the cycle of rebirth. For a self-willed person (*Manmukh*), by contrast, death means the culmination of his or her separation from the Divine and continuation of the cycle of reincarnation.

Hymns from the Guru Granth Sahib are sung both in the period preceding the cremation and in the post-cremation rites. In India, the body of the deceased is bathed, dressed in new clothes, and placed on a pyre for cremation. The ashes are then disposed of in a nearby stream or river. In the diaspora, however, the rituals associated with death have had to be modified. Family and friends gather around the body at a funeral home with the necessary facilities for cremation. The body is placed in a casket, into which mourners may scatter flower petals as a tribute. Following devotional singing and eulogy, *Ardas* is offered by the *granthi*. Then the casket is pushed on a trolley to the cremation furnace, usually accompanied by family and friends. While the casket is burning, the congregation recites the late-evening prayer, *Kirtan Sohila*.

In addition, a reading of the entire scripture takes place either at home or in a gurdwara—a process that may take up to ten days to complete. At the conclusion of the reading a 'completion' ceremony is held, during which the final prayers are offered in the memory of the deceased.

From Sikh Hymns and Prayers

Despite his militancy, Guru Gobind Singh shares with Guru Nanak a sense that religious boundaries are irrelevant to God:

There is no difference between a temple and a mosque, nor between the prayers of a Hindu and a Muslim. Though differences seem to mark and distinguish, all men/women are in reality the same.

Gods and demons, celestial beings, men called Muslims and others called Hindus—such differences are trivial, inconsequential, the outward results of locality and dress.

With eyes the same, the ears and body, all possessing a common form—all are in fact a single creation, the elements of nature in a uniform blend.

Allah is the same as the God of the Hindus, Purana and Qur'an are the same. All are the same, none is separate; a single form, a single creation (*Akal Ustat, Dasam Granth*, 19–20; McLeod 1984: 57).

Martyrdom is a frequent theme in Sikh history, motivating Sikhs to persevere in struggles today:

These loyal members of the Khalsa who gave their heads for their faith; who were hacked limb from limb, scalped, broken on the wheel, or sawn asunder, who sacrificed their lives for the protection of hallowed gurdwaras never forsaking their faith; and who were steadfast in their loyalty to the uncut hair of the true Sikh: reflect on their merits, O Khalsa, and call on God, saying, *Vahiguru!* (*Ardas*; McLeod 1984: 104).

DIFFERENTIATION

Encounter with Modernity

The Khalsa spent most of its first century fighting the armies of Mughals and Afghan invaders. Finally, in 1799, Ranjit Singh (1780–1839) succeeded in unifying the Punjab, taking control of Lahore and declaring himself Maharaja. For the next four decades the Sikh community enjoyed more settled political conditions, and with territorial expansion as far as Peshawar in the west, people of different cultural and religious backgrounds were attracted into the fold of Sikhism. The appearance of the Golden Temple today owes a great deal to the generous patronage of the Maharaja, who also employed scribes to make beautiful copies of the Sikh scripture that were sent as gifts to the Sikh *Takhats* ('Thrones', the traditional seats of authority at Amritsar, Anandpur, Patna, and Nander) and other major gurdwaras.

Although Maharaja Ranjit Singh himself was a Khalsa member, his rule was marked by religious diversity within the Sikh Panth. Khalsa Sikhs, in their drive to carve out an empire for themselves, recognized that for their project to succeed they needed allies both inside and outside the Panth. Therefore they forged an internal alliance with the **Sehaj-dharis** or 'gradualists': Sikhs who live as members of the Nanak Panth but have not accepted the Khalsa code of conduct. The Khalsa conceded the religious culture of the *Sehaj-dharis* to be legitimate even though, in keeping with the inclusive approach of the

Maharaja, they revered Hindu scriptures as well as the Guru Granth Sahib and the Dasam Granth, and in some cases even worshipped Hindu images.

Sikh Reform Movements

After the death of Maharaja Ranjit Singh in 1839, his successors were unable to withstand the pressure exerted by the advancing British forces. After two Anglo–Sikh wars, in 1846 and 1849, the Sikh kingdom was annexed to the British Empire. With the loss of the Punjab's independence the Sikhs were no longer the masters of their own kingdom. It was in this context that three reform movements emerged in the second half of the nineteenth century, each of which sought to restore a distinct spiritual identity to a people whose religious tradition was now just one among a vast array of traditions encompassed within colonial India.

The Singh Sabha Movement

Among the most important contributions to the modernization of the Sikh tradition were the educational initiatives of the **Singh Sabha** ('Society of the Singhs'). Established in 1873 by four prominent Sikh reformers, the Singh Sabha sought to reaffirm Sikh identity in the face of two threats: the casual reversion to Hindu practices during the period of Punjabi independence under Maharaja Ranjit Singh and the active proselytizing efforts of the Hindu Arya Samaj and of Christian missionaries.

By the end of the nineteenth century the Tat ('Pure' or 'True') Khalsa, the dominant wing of the Singh Sabha, had eradicated the last traces of religious diversity within the Sikh Panth and established clear norms of belief and practice. In effect, they made the Khalsa tradition the standard of orthodoxy for all Sikhs.

In the twentieth century the Tat Khalsa reformers also contributed to two important legal changes. First they obtained legal recognition of the distinctive Sikh wedding ritual in the Anand Marriage Act (1909). Then in the 1920s they helped to re-establish direct Khalsa control of the major historical gurdwaras, many of which had fallen into the hands of corrupt *mahants* ('custodians') supported by the British. Inspired by the Tat Khalsa ideal, the Akali movement of the 1920s eventually secured British assent to the Sikh Gurdwara Act (1925), under which control of all gurdwaras passed to the Shiromani Gurdwara Prabandhak Committee (SGPC; 'Chief Management Committee of Sikh Shrines'). The Akalis were the forerunners of the modern political party known as the Akali Dal ('army of the immortal').

SGPC Rahit Manual

Control of the gurdwaras gave the SGPC enormous political and economic influence. By 1950 it had established itself as the central authority on all questions of religious discipline, and in that year it published a manual entitled *Sikh Rahit Maryada*, which has ever since been regarded as the authoritative guide to orthodox Sikh doctrine and behaviour.

Based on the teachings of the Guru Granth Sahib, supplemented with teachings from revered Sikh leaders, the *Sikh Rahit Maryada* enjoins Sikhs to attune their daily lives to the will of God, to cultivate a pure and pious inner spirituality, to abstain from four cardinal sins (hair-cutting, adultery, the use of intoxicants, and the eating of meat from improperly slaughtered animals), and to adopt the Five Ks as external signs of internal virtue.

The manual encourages the worship of God and meditation on his name, acceptance of Khalsa initiation, and attendance at divine services. It also calls on Sikhs to earn a living honestly and truthfully, to share selflessly with the needy and less fortunate in order to further the well-being of all, to nurture virtues such as compassion, honesty, generosity, patience, perseverance, and humility, and to avoid superstitions, idols, and images. Yet it urges tolerance of those who stray as well as those who, although they follow the teachings of Guru Granth Sahib, have not yet accepted the full discipline of the Khalsa; instead of condemning these *Sehaj-dharis*, it assumes that in time they will progress to the point where they will join the Khalsa.

The most significant aspect of the *Sikh Rahit Maryada* relates to gender equality, stressing that Sikhism requires men and women alike to obey the same rules. It explicitly states that women should not be veiled in the congregation, that they may sit in attendance on the Guru Granth Sahib, that they may be initiated into the Khalsa Order and may also be members of the 'Cherished Five' (*Panj Piare*) who administer initiation.

The only code of conduct sanctioned by the Akal Takhat—the highest seat of religious and temporal authority among Sikhs—the *Sikh Rahit Maryada* is distributed free of charge by the SGPC, and is now available in Hindi and English as well as Punjabi, in acknowledgement of the needs of Sikhs living outside their historical homeland.

Variations in Modern Sikhism

Although the *Sikh Rahit Maryada* tends to represent Sikhism as a single coherent orthodoxy, at the popular level the Sikh Panth today encompasses a number of variations. For instance, the Khalsa itself includes a distinctive order called the Nihangs, who are rigorous in the observance of the Khalsa *Rahit* and, having renounced all fear of death, are ready to die for their faith at any time. Their garments are always blue, with some saffron and white, and on their heads they wear a high turban surmounted by a piece of cloth called a *pharhara* ('standard' or 'flag'). In North America, some Sikhs wear Nihang dress on special occasions such as Baisakhi Day.

Another group within the Khalsa calls itself the Akhand Kirtani Jatha ('continuous singing of the Sikh scriptures'). Its members follow their own special discipline, which includes an entirely vegetarian diet. Female members wear a small turban.

In fact, the Sikh Panth has never been monolithic or homogeneous, and in recent years the Internet has allowed many groups to claim that they represent the 'true' Panth. Of the 25 million Sikhs in the world today, only about 20 per cent are orthodox **Amrit-dharis** ('initiated'). But many other Sikhs follow most of the Khalsa code even though they have not been initiated. (Those who 'retain their hair' are known as **Kes-dharis**.)

Less conspicuous are the many Sikhs (especially in North America and the United Kingdom) who do cut their hair but use the Khalsa names 'Singh' and 'Kaur' and do not consider themselves to be 'lesser Sikhs' in any way. In fact, they are the majority in the diaspora, and they play active roles both in the community's ritual life and in the management of the gurdwaras.

These semi-observant Sikhs are often confused with the *Sehaj-dharis*, who practise *nam-simaran* and follow the teachings of the Adi Granth but do not observe any of the Khalsa rules of conduct. The number of *Sehaj-dharis* has declined in the last few decades, but they certainly have not disappeared completely.

Finally, there are Khalsa Sikhs—especially in the diaspora—who have committed one or more of the four sins after initiation. These lapsed *Amrit-dharis* are known as 'Patit Sikhs' ('Apostates'). It should be emphasized that none of these categories is necessarily permanent. Individuals go through different stages in life, and their status within the Panth changes accordingly. In short, there is no single way of being a Sikh.

CULTURAL EXPRESSIONS

Cultural Norms of Family and Society

Caste has never been one of the defining criteria of Sikh identity. In fact, rejection of caste-based discrimination was a fundamental feature of Sikhism from the beginning, and the *Sikh Rahit Maryada* explicitly states that 'No account should be taken of caste' in the selection of a marriage partner. This is the ideal, however. In practice, most Sikhs still marry within their own caste group, though inter-caste marriages are becoming more common among urban professionals, in India and elsewhere.

In Punjabi society, marriage creates a connection not just between two individuals but, more important, between two groups of kin. It is in this context that the concept of honour (*izzat*) continues to play a significant role in family relationships.

The Sikh Gurus approached issues of gender within the parameters of a traditional patriarchal society. Thus despite their egalitarian principles and efforts to foster respect for womanhood, their ideas about women were inseparable from their ideas about family: in their view, the ideal woman was defined by her conduct in the context of family life, as a good daughter, a good sister, a good wife and mother. They condemned men as well as women who did not observe the cultural norms of modesty and honour in their lives. There was no tolerance for any kind of premarital or extramarital sexual activity, and rape was regarded as a particularly serious violation, for the dishonour it brought to the families of both the victim and the rapist meant the loss of social standing in the community. Furthermore, the rules governing the Khalsa are clearly egalitarian in principle. Those who seek initiation cannot be accepted without their spouses; hence the proportions of male and female initiates are roughly equal. And Khalsa women wear all of the Five Ks. Thus the involvement of both men and women has always been crucial to the success of the developing Sikh community.

A number of women are remembered for their contributions to the Panth, some but not all of them the sisters, wives, and daughters of the Gurus. Guru Nanak's older sister Nanaki, for instance, was unfailing in her love for her brother and supported his journeys to various centres, while his wife Sulakhani raised their two children through his long absences from home. Mata Khivi, the wife of the second Guru, is praised in the Guru Granth Sahib for her contributions to the development of the *langar* tradition. In 1705, when the forces of Guru Gobind Singh had abandoned him in battle, a brave woman named Mai Bhago persuaded them to return and fight. And after the Guru's death in 1708, his wife Sundri played a major role in guiding the destiny of the Khalsa. She appointed Bhai Mani Singh to compile the Dasam Granth, and a number of the edicts (*hukam-namas*) she issued to various Sikh congregations survive, reflecting her deep concern for the welfare of the Panth.

In modern times, Bibi Jagir Kaur became the first woman to be elected president of the SGPC twice, in 1999 and 2004—a sign of real progress towards equality. Other exceptional women include the mystic Bibi Nihal Kaur; Bibi Balwant Kaur, who established both a gurdwara and a women's group in honour of Bebe Nanaki in Birmingham (UK); and Bibi Jasbir Kaur Khalsa, who devoted her life to the promotion of Sikh music and established a Chair for its study at the Punjabi University in Patiala (India). Female musicians often perform in the gurdwaras. Women have also played important roles in the operations of the Akhand Kirtani Jatha and the Healthy, Happy, Holy Organization (3HO; now known as Sikh Dharma).

In practice, however, most Sikh institutions are still dominated by males, and many Sikh women continue to live in a society based on patriarchal cultural assumptions. In this respect they differ little from their counterparts in any of India's major religious communities.

Music, Art, and Literature

Sikhism is the only world religion in which song has been the primary medium for the founder's message. Sacred music has been at the heart of the Sikh devotional experience from the beginning. In specifying the *ragas* (melodies) to which the hymns were to be sung, Guru Nanak and his successors sought to promote harmony and balance in the minds of listeners and performers. Any *raga* likely to arouse passion was either excluded altogether or adapted to produce a gentler effect.

Graphic Art

The earliest examples of Sikh graphic art are illuminated scriptures dating from the late sixteenth and early seventeenth centuries. Sikh scribes followed the Qur'anic tradition of decorating the margins and the opening pages of the text with abstract designs and floral motifs. The earliest extant paintings of Guru Nanak appear in a ***janam-sakhi*** (birth-narrative from the mid-1600s).

Both fine and applied arts flourished under the patronage of Maharaja Ranjit Singh. In addition to painting, sculpture, armour, brassware, jewellery, and textiles, a distinctive Sikh architecture developed at the Sikh court in the first half of the nineteenth century. Murals and frescoes depicting major events from Sikh history can still be seen at historic gurdwaras including the Golden Temple in Amritsar.

More recently, Amrit and Rabindra Kaur Singh—twin sisters, born in England in 1966—apply the styles and

Nineteen Eighty-Four, by The Singh Twins, 1998 (© The Singh Twins: www.singhtwins.co.uk).

techniques of the classic Indian miniature tradition to contemporary themes. Their painting *Nineteen Eighty-Four*, inspired by the storming of the Golden Temple by Indian government forces in that year, is a powerful reflection not only on the event itself but on the responses it evoked in the Sikh diaspora.[2]

Literature

A rich literary tradition began with the introduction of the Gurmukhi script used to record the hymns of the Gurus. The influence of the Adi Granth is clear in the works of early poets such as Bhai Gurdas. The first Punjabi prose form was the *janam-sakhi*, which remained the dominant literary genre before the emergence of the twentieth-century novel. It is easy to see the impact of Sikh devotional literature on the writings of celebrated early modern authors such as Kahn Singh Nabha (1861–1938), the poet Bhai Vir Singh (1872–1957), and Mohan Singh Vaid (1881–1936), who wrote stories, novels, and plays as well as many works of non-fiction. All these writers emphasized optimism, resolute determination, faith, and love towards fellow human beings. Max Arthur Macauliffe (1837–1913) was an administrator in the British colonial government who became interested in Sikhism in the 1860s and devoted his life to the translation of the Sikh scriptures. Writers such as these were among the leaders of the Singh Sabha reform movement. Although much contemporary Punjabi literature reflects Western influences, Sikh devotional literature is still a source of inspiration for the passionate lyricism of some more recent writers, such as the poet Harinder Singh Mehboob (1937–2010).

🌿 INTERACTION AND ADAPTATION

Twentieth-Century India

Doctrinal Authority

By 1950, as we have seen, the Shiromani Gurdwara Prabandhak Committee had become the principal voice of authority in both religious and political affairs for the worldwide Sikh community. Although it has often been challenged by Sikhs living outside the Punjab, the SGPC is a democratic institution that claims to speak on behalf of the majority of Sikhs and hence to represent the authority of the Guru-Panth.

The ultimate authority, however, is the Akal Takhat in Amritsar. The most important of the five *Takhats*, the Akal Takhat may issue edicts (*hukam-namas*) that provide guidance or clarification on any aspect of Sikh doctrine or practice. It may punish any Sikh charged with a violation of religious discipline or with activity 'prejudicial' to Sikh interests and unity; it may also recognize individuals who have performed outstanding service or made sacrifices for the Sikh cause.

The Partition of India

In 1947 the British withdrew from India and the subcontinent was partitioned to create the independent republics of India and Pakistan. Partition was especially hard for Sikhs because it split the Punjab into two. Most of the 2.5 million Sikhs living on the Pakistani side fled as refugees; though many settled in the new Indian state of Punjab, some moved on to major cities elsewhere in India.

Since 1976 the Constitution of India has defined the republic as a secular state, and Article 25 guarantees the right to freedom of religion. However, a sub-clause of the same Article states that 'persons professing the Sikh, Jaina, or Buddhist religion' will be considered to fall within the general category of Hinduism. When the original Constitution was drafted, the Sikh members of the Constituent Assembly refused to sign the document because it did not recognize the Sikhs as a group with an independent identity. Since that time, Sikh and Hindu politicians alike have deliberately stirred up popular resentment on both sides for political purposes.

In 2002 the National Commission to Review the Constitution recommended that the wording of Article 25 be amended to refer specifically to the three religious groups—Sikhs, Jainas, and Buddhists—that are currently covered under the default term 'Hindu'. To date, however, this amendment has not been enacted.

The Events of 1984

In 1973 Sikh ethno-nationalists began demanding greater autonomy for all the states of India. Over the following years, relations with the Indian government became increasingly strained. In the spring of 1984 a group of armed radicals led by a charismatic young militant named Jarnail Singh Bhindranwale (1947–84) decided to provoke a confrontation with the government by occupying the Akal Takhat building inside the Golden Temple complex. The government responded by sending in the army. The assault that followed—code-named 'Operation Blue Star'—resulted in the deaths of many Sikhs, including Bhindranwale, as well as the destruction of the Akal Takhat and severe damage to the Golden Temple itself.

A few months later, on 31 October 1984, Prime Minister Indira Gandhi was assassinated by her own Sikh bodyguards. For several days unchecked Hindu mobs in Delhi and elsewhere killed thousands of Sikhs. As a consequence of these events, 1984 became a turning point in the history of the Sikhs, precipitating an identity crisis within the Panth and dividing Sikhs around the world into two camps, liberal and fundamentalist.

The Sikh Diaspora

Over the last century more than one million Sikhs have left India for foreign lands. Wherever they have settled—in Singapore, Malaysia, Thailand, Hong Kong, Australia, New Zealand, East Africa, and the United Kingdom, as well as Canada and the United States—they have carried their sacred scripture with them and established their own places of worship. Today there are more than five hundred gurdwaras in North America and the United Kingdom alone.

Although the institution of the gurdwara serves as a rallying point and an integrative force for the Sikh community, the management of its affairs can become a bone of contention within the community. This happens because members of the gurdwara committee often use their position to enhance their own image in the wider society. In most cases factional politics in gurdwara affairs have more to do with personalities than with issues. Paradoxically, this factionalism can strengthen community solidarity in the long term, because it tends to draws new people into community affairs. It may also lead to the establishment of new gurdwaras to serve different factions. In the short term, however, such factionalism can seriously weaken the community's ability to work towards common goals. New cultural environments have required some adaptation. In diaspora gurdwaras, for instance, congregational services are usually held on Sunday, not because it is the holy day—in India there is no specific day for worship—but because it is the only day when most Sikhs are free to attend services.

Western societies have also presented Sikh spirituality with serious challenges. Turban-wearing Sikhs have frequently faced discrimination by prospective employers, and Khalsa Sikhs have had to negotiate with various institutions, including education authorities, for permission to wear the *kirpan* as a religious symbol. At the same time, a gradual loss of fluency in the Punjabi language means that younger Sikhs are at growing risk of theological illiteracy. Diaspora Sikhs, fully aware that assimilation is making steady progress among the second and third generations, have responded with concerted efforts to revive interest in Sikh traditions and identity.

To meet the challenges of life in Western societies, many gurdwaras now hold 'Sunday school' classes for children, and many Sikh families now worship at home—in both Punjabi and English—as well as at the gurdwara. Another innovative response has been to organize Sikh Youth Camps offering intensive exposure to Sikh spirituality, values, and traditions.

Punjabi Sikhs and White Sikhs

Around 1970 a number of yoga students in Toronto and Los Angeles were inspired by their teacher, a Sikh named Harbhajan Singh Puri (Yogi Bhajan), to convert to the Sikh faith and join his Healthy, Happy, Holy Organization ('3HO'). Eventually renamed Sikh Dharma, the organization has since established chapters or *ashrams* in various North American cities.

All members of this organization—male and female—wear the same costume of white turbans, tunics, and tight trousers, and for this reason they have come to be known as 'White Sikhs'. They live and raise families in communal houses, spending long hours in meditation and chanting as well as yoga practice.

Punjabi Sikhs in general praise the strict Khalsa-style discipline of the White Sikhs. In other respects, however, they see the White Sikh culture as quite alien. In the Punjab, for instance—as in India as a whole—white clothing is normally a sign of mourning; only Namdhari Sikhs (a particularly austere sect) dress entirely in white. And the only Sikh women who wear turbans are members of the Akhand Kirtani Jatha. Finally, the concept of *izzat* ('prestige' or 'honour'), which plays such an important part in Punjabi culture and society, is irrelevant to the White Sikhs. Even in North America, therefore, Punjabi Sikhs have tended to distance themselves from the White Sikhs.

❧ CONTEMPORARY ISSUES

Religious Pluralism

The beginning of the third millennium has brought the issue of religious pluralism into sharper focus. The co-existence, in a single society, of multiple religious worldviews, some of which may be incompatible with one another, has always been a fact of life. But awareness of that fact has increased sharply in recent times with increasing urbanization, mass education, international migration, and advances in communications. Especially in democratic states that do not attempt to impose a single worldview, people of different faiths must learn how to live together harmoniously.

Acceptance of religious pluralism is a condition of religious tolerance. The fact that religious pluralism requires dialogue and interaction provides opportunities for spiritual reflection and growth. It is in this context that Sikhism emphasizes the importance of keeping an open mind and being willing to learn from other traditions, while preserving the integrity of one's own tradition. The Sikh Gurus strongly opposed any claim, by any tradition, to sole possession of the sole religious truth. A spirit of accommodation has always been an integral part of the Sikh attitude toward other traditions.

Sikhs are enthusiastic participants in inter-religious dialogue. The fact that the Adi Granth includes works by 15 non-Sikh poet-saints suggests a four-part theory of religious pluralism. First, participants in interreligious dialogue must recognize that the religious commitments of others are no less absolute than their own. Thus the quest for a universal religion must be abandoned, along with any attempt to place one religious tradition above others. Second, doctrinal differences must be respected. Third, interreligious dialogue requires an open mind, that allows for recognition of the points on which different traditions agree, but also disagreement on crucial points of doctrine. Finally, one must be willing to let the 'other' become in some sense oneself. In this way the experience of dialogue can enrich one's own spiritual life.

Sikh Militancy in Politics

Another issue confronting Sikhs around the world is the tendency to associate their tradition with violence. The use of warrior imagery to evoke the valour of the Sikhs has been standard since colonial times. Relatively little attention has been directed to the other, perhaps more demanding, dimensions of Sikhism. What is expected of the Sikh warriors is not violence but militancy in the sense that they are prepared to take an active and passionate stand on behalf of their faith.

In Canada the association between Sikhs and violence was underlined by the 1985 bombing of Air India Flight 182, 1985, in which 329 people—most of them Canadian citizens—were killed. This happened in the highly volatile context of the Indian army's assault on the Golden Temple in 1984. Nearly two decades passed before the two Vancouver men suspected of masterminding the attack were brought to trial, and in the end they were acquitted. It took more than 20 years and several government inquiries for the Canadian public in general to recognize that the bombing was a Canadian tragedy, the result of a Canadian plot and the failure of Canadian security officials—a conclusion that was made luminously clear by former Supreme Court Justice John Major in his 2010 report on the investigation into the attack.

In India separatist violence was contained within a decade and the main Sikh political party (Akali Dal) reasserted its right to work within the democratic system for greater justice and transparency. In the long run, peaceful public demonstrations and engagement in the political process have proved more effective than violent struggle.

Sexuality and Bioethical Issues

The official Sikh response to same-sex marriage has been negative and the Akal Takhat has issued a decree forbidding the performance of any such marriage in the gurdwara. As we have seen, the Gurus explicitly prohibited female infanticide. Thus Sikhism does not condone abortion for the purpose of sex selection; however, it does permit medical abortion when the mother's life is in danger, or in cases of incest or rape.

In the diaspora setting Sikhs are beginning to formulate responses to issues such as organ donation, genetic engineering, surrogacy, and the use of embryos in medical research. Sikhs often refer to the martyrdom of Guru Tegh Bahadur, who sacrificed himself to protect the rights of the Hindus, as an example that should encourage families to donate the organs of their deceased loved ones to save the lives of others.

Environmental Issues

Guru Nanak himself spoke of the natural world with great tenderness: 'Air is the Guru, water the Father and earth the mighty Mother of all. Day and night are the caring guardians, fondly nurturing all creation' (AG 8). Today environmental issues are coming into prominence both in the Punjab and in the diaspora. The celebration of Guru Har Rai's birthday in March has been fixed as 'Sikh Environment Day'. And in recent years the environmentalist Balbir Singh Seechewal has made it his mission to spread ecological awareness. He singlehandedly organized the restoration of the river associated with Guru Nanak's mystical experience, and he encourages Sikh congregations across the Punjab to plant trees in every available space.

CONCLUDING REMARKS

On 15 September 2001, an American Sikh became the first victim of the racial backlash that followed the 9/11 terrorist attacks. Balbir Singh Sodhi was shot dead in Phoenix, Arizona, by a self-described 'patriot' who mistook him for a Muslim. Even today it is painfully clear that too many people in the West simply do not know who Sikhs are.

The situation is somewhat better in academic circles. The first North American conference on Sikh studies was held in 1976 at the University of California, Berkeley. Participants at that conference generally felt that Sikhism was indeed 'the forgotten tradition' among scholarly circles in North America. This is no longer the case. In the last two decades the scholarly literature on Sikhism has grown steadily, and the mistaken notion that Sikhism represents a synthesis of Hindu and Muslim ideas has been almost entirely abandoned. Today there are eight endowed chairs in Sikh studies in North America, and Sikhism is increasingly recognized in undergraduate academic programs.

The Sikh community has been involved in a process of 'renewal and redefinition' throughout its history, and that process has only intensified in recent years. Today, the question 'Who is a Sikh?' is a subject of often acrimonious debate in online discussion forums. Each generation of Sikhs has to answer this question in the light of new historical circumstances. Not surprisingly, diaspora Sikhs approach issues of belief and practice from different perspectives, depending on the cultural and political contexts in which they live.

In many cases it is through interaction with other religious and ethnic communities that they discover their own religious identity. New challenges demand new responses, especially in a postmodern world where traditional authority is subject to constant questioning. Thus the process of Sikh identity formation is a dynamic and ongoing phenomenon.

Sacred Texts Table

Religion	Sacred Text	Compilation	Revision	Use
Sikhism	The Adi Granth / Guru Granth Sahib; the primary scripture	The first collection of Guru Nanak's hymns was compiled in the 1530s. This *pothi* ('sacred book') was expanded by the succeeding Gurus. A four-volume collection produced in 1570, under Guru Amar Das, came to be known as the Goindval Pothis.	The fifth Guru, Arjan, produced a prototype of the Adi Granth in 1604. The tenth Guru, Gobind Singh, added the works of his father and closed the canon in the 1680s. Before he passed away in 1708, he installed the Adi Granth as Guru Granth Sahib.	In worship, the hymns of the Guru Granth Sahib are sung in melodic measures (*ragas*), while prayers are recited. The sacred text also plays a pivotal role in all Sikh ceremonies, including life-cycle rituals, and is the central authority regarding both personal piety and the corporate identity of the Sikh community.
Sikhism	The Dasam Granth; the secondary scripture	The first collection of works attributed to the tenth Guru, Gobind Singh, dates to the 1690s.	18th–19th centuries: subsequent collections added the *Zafarnama* of Guru Gobind Singh and fixed the sequence of compositions.	Portions of the Dasam Granth are used as liturgical texts in the daily routine of the Sikhs and the Khalsa initiation ceremony.

Sites

Amritsar, Punjab The holiest of all places for Sikhs, Amritsar is the site of the Golden Temple and was named for the 'pool of nectar' that surrounds the shrine. Facing the Temple and connected to it by a causeway is the Akal Takhat ('Eternal Throne'), the most important of five seats of authority within the Sikh world.

Anandpur, Punjab The birthplace of the Khalsa; the Takhat Sri Kesgarh Sahib stands on the spot where Guru Gobind Singh is said to have created the 'Cherished Five' (*Panj Piare*) in 1699.

Talwandi Sabo, Punjab Guru Gobind Singh stayed here for several months c. 1705; site of the Takhat Sri Damdama Sahib.

Patna, Bihar The birthplace of Guru Gobind Singh and the site of the Takhat Sri Patna Sahib.

Nanded, Maharashtra The place where Guru Gobind Singh died and the site of the Takhat Sri Hazur Sahib.

Study Questions

1. Do you think that Guru Nanak intended to establish a new religion, independent of Hindu and Muslim traditions? What is the evidence in his works?
2. How did Sikhism evolve in response to changing historical circumstances during the time of the ten Gurus?
3. How did the martyrdoms of Guru Arjan and Guru Tegh Bahadur contribute to the emergence of militancy as a core tradition within the Panth?
4. How did modern Sikhism come into being? What role did the Singh Sabha reform movement play in defining Sikh doctrine and practice?
5. What is the role of the Guru Granth Sahib in Sikh life?
6. Why is the practice of *kirtan* ('devotional singing') central to Sikh congregational worship?
7. What role has the institution of the gurdwara played in the Sikh diaspora?

Glossary

Adi Granth Literally, 'original book'; first compiled by Guru Arjan in 1604 and invested with supreme authority as the Guru Granth Sahib after the death of the tenth Guru, Gobind Singh, in 1708.

Akal Purakh 'The One Beyond Time', God.

Amrit-dhari 'Nectar-bearer'; an initiated member of the Khalsa.

Baisakhi An Indian new year's holiday in mid-April, when Sikhs celebrate the founding of the Khalsa.

five Ks The five marks of Khalsa identity: *kes* (uncut hair), *kangha* (wooden comb), *kirpan* (sword), *kara* (wrist ring), and *kachh* (short breeches).

gurdwara Literally, 'Guru's door'; the Sikh place of worship.

Guru 'Teacher'; either a spiritual person or the divine inner voice.

Guru Granth Sahib See **Adi Granth**

hukam 'Divine order, will, or command'; an all-embracing principle, the sum total of all divinely instituted laws; a revelation of the nature of God.

janam-sakhis 'Birth testimonies'; traditional accounts of the life of Guru Nanak.

karah prashad A sweet pudding or paste of flour, sugar, and butter that is prepared in an iron (*karah*) bowl with prayers, placed in the presence of the Sikh scripture during worship, and then distributed to the congregation.

Kes-dhari Literally, 'hair-bearer'; a Sikh who affirms his or her identity by wearing unshorn hair.

Khalsa Literally, 'pure': the order of initiated Sikhs bound by common identity and discipline.

kirtan The singing of hymns from the scriptures in worship.

langar The term for both the community kitchen and the meal that is prepared there and served to all present in the congregation.

miri-piri The doctrine that the Guru possesses temporal (*miri*) as well as spiritual (*piri*) authority.

Mul Mantar Literally, 'Basic Formula'; the opening creedal statement of the Adi Granth, declaring the eternity and transcendence of God, the creator.

nam 'The divine Name'.

nam-simaran 'Remembrance of the divine Name', especially the devotional practice of meditating on the divine Name.

Panth Literally, 'path'; hence the Sikh community.

Rahit The code of conduct for the Khalsa.

Sahib 'Lord', an honorific used frequently when referring to holy scripture, but also to places of worship.

sangat 'Holy fellowship', referring to a Sikh congregation.

Sants Ascetic poets who believed divinity to exist beyond all forms or description. They were known for their knowledge of 'Truth'. They were not canonized as 'saints' by any ecclesiastic authority (as in the Roman Catholic Church), but came to be venerated as 'saints' because of their piety and understanding of reality.

Sehaj-dhari Literally, a 'gradualist'; a Sikh who follows the teachings of the Gurus but has not accepted the Khalsa discipline.

Singh Sabha Literally, 'Society of Singhs'; a revival movement established in 1873 that redefined the norms of Sikh doctrine and practice.

Takhat 'Throne'; any of the five principal seats of authority in the Sikh tradition.

vak 'saying'; a passage from the Guru Granth Sahib that is chosen at random and read aloud to the congregation as the lesson of the day.

Further Reading

Dusenbery, Verne A. 2008. *Sikhs at Large: Religion, Culture, and Politics*. New Delhi: Oxford University Press. A collection of essays bringing together different perspectives on the cultural and political dimensions of the Sikh diaspora and of Sikhism as a global religion.

Fenech, Louis E. 2008. *The Darbar of the Sikh Gurus: The Court of God in the World of Men*. New Delhi: Oxford University Press. Traces the evolution of the Sikh Gurus' court in the broader historical context of Indo-Persian courtly traditions.

Grewal, J.S. 1991. *The New Cambridge History of India: The Sikhs of the Punjab*. Cambridge: Cambridge University Press. A classic chronological study of Sikh history from the beginnings to the present day.

Jakobsh, Doris R. 2003. *Relocating Gender in Sikh History: Transformation, Meaning and Identity*. New Delhi: Oxford University Press. A recent study examining the development of gender ideals under the Sikh Gurus, and their adaptation and in some cases transformation by the new intellectual elite of the Singh Sabha during the colonial period.

Mandair, Arvind-pal S. 2010. *Religion and the Specter of the West: Sikhism, India, Postcoloniality, and the Politics of Translation*. New York: Columbia University Press. A recent study on the Sikh tradition from a postcolonial perspective.

McLeod, W.H. 1984. *Textual Sources for the Study of Sikhism*. Manchester: Manchester University Press. An anthology of selections covering all aspects of Sikh belief, worship, and practice.

———. 1999. *Sikhs and Sikhism*. New Delhi: Oxford University Press. An omnibus edition of four classic studies on the history and evolution of Sikhs and Sikhism by one of the field's leading scholars.

———. 2002. *The Sikhs of the Khalsa*. New Delhi: Oxford University Press. A study of how the *Rahit* or 'the code of belief and conduct' came into being, how it developed in response to historical circumstances, and why it still retains an unchallenged hold over all who consider themselves Khalsa Sikhs.

Nesbitt, Eleanor. 2005. *Sikhism: A Very Short Introduction*. Oxford: Oxford University Press. An ethnographic introduction to Sikhism, its teachings, practices, rituals, and festivals.

Oberoi, Harjot. 1994. *Construction of Religious Boundaries*. New Delhi: Oxford University Press. A major reinterpretation of Sikh religion and society during the colonial period.

Singh, Harbans, ed. 1992–8. *The Encyclopaedia of Sikhism*, 4 vols. Patiala: Punjabi University. A four-volume reference work covering Sikh life and letters, history and philosophy, customs and rituals, social and religious movements, art and architecture, and locales and shrines.

Singh, Nikky-Guninder Kaur. 2005. *The Birth of the Khalsa: A Feminist Re-Memory of Sikh Identity*. Albany: State University of New York Press. Examines the institution of the Khalsa from a feminist perspective, exploring the ways in which Sikh tradition has constructed a hyper-masculine Sikh identity.

Singh, Pashaura. 2006. *Life and Work of Guru Arjan: History, Memory and Biography in the Sikh Tradition*. New Delhi: Oxford University Press. A reconstruction of the life and work of the fifth Guru, based on history, collective memory, tradition, and mythic representation.

Recommended Websites

www.columbia.edu/itc/mealac/pritchett/ 00generallinks/ index.html   A good site with links to many resources on South Asia.

www.sikhs.org   The Sikhism Home Page, Brampton, Ontario, Canada.

www.sikhnet.com   SikhNet, Espanola, New Mexico, USA.

www.sgpc.net   Shiromani Gurdwara Parbandhak Committee, Amritsar, Punjab, India.

www.sikhchic.com   Online magazine: journey through the Sikh universe.

References

McLeod, W.H. 1984. *Textual Sources for the Study of Sikhism*. Manchester: Manchester University Press.

———. 1989. *Who Is a Sikh? Problem of Sikh Identity*. Oxford: Clarendon Press.

———. 1997. *Sikhism*. London: Penguin Books.

Singh, Pashaura. 2006. *Life and Work of Guru Arjan: History, Memory and Biography in the Sikh Tradition*. New Delhi: Oxford University Press.

Notes

This chapter is dedicated to the memory of my teacher, Professor Willard G. Oxtoby.

1. This reference means that the passage quoted comes from the 27th stanza of the ballad (1. *Var*) in the musical measure *Majh*, by Guru Nanak (M1), on page 150 of the Adi Granth (AG).

2. For a discussion of this work by the artists themselves, see http://www.sikhchic.com/article-detail.php?cat=21&id=747. *Nineteen Eighty-Four and the Via Dolorosa Project* (2009) is a semi-autobiographical documentary film in which the artists draw parallels with the Christian faith.

Chapter
10
Chinese & Korean Traditions

❧ Terry Tak-ling Woo ❧

Next time you go to a restaurant in Chinatown, take a look around and see if there is a shrine at the door, or perhaps the back of the sitting area. Chances are good that you will see a red shrine with three incense sticks in a censer, a small plate of fruit at the front, a candle on each side, and at least one figure standing in the centre. If the figure is holding a halberd, it will represent Guan Gong, who symbolizes the Confucian virtues of integrity and or loyalty (*zhong*) and the sense of what is right (*yi*). A traditional cap and a flowing beard signify the Daoist lineage ancestor Lu Dongbin, while a female figure will usually represent Guanyin, the Buddhist bodhisattva of compassion who sees and hears the suffering of all sentient beings. If there is no figure, the back panel of the shrine will often carry a verse of thanksgiving addressed to the local earth god.

OVERVIEW

When the Chinese talk about *sanjiao*, they are talking about the three (*san*) teachings, philosophies, or religions (*jiao*) of Confucianism, Daoism, and Buddhism. Collectively, these are sometimes described as the elite tradition. A much more diffuse fourth tradition, often described as folk or popular religion, honours an assortment of spirits that varies from place to place. These four traditions have coexisted, largely in peace, for millennia.

Many ordinary people do not hesitate to consult specialists from across the religious spectrum—Confucian teachers, Daoist priests, Buddhist monks, spirit mediums, astrologers, *fengshui* practitioners—although specialists in the elite traditions tend to be exclusive in their allegiances. Scholars have often noted that Chinese religions are more interested in right action than right belief. As varied as the three elite traditions are in their doctrines and goals, they all agree on the special importance of right action. A shared desire to avoid conflict and chaos has encouraged a shared commitment to maintaining harmonious relations.

This emphasis on harmony reflects a common recognition that human temperaments and capacities vary. Thus the Confucian Xunzi talks about the different ways in which different people might understand various religious rites. The Daoist *Daodejing* (*Classic of the Way and Power or Virtue*, also known as the *Laozi*) speaks of the universal, all-encompassing Way (**Dao**) as indefinable, beyond words, since any definition would necessarily be incomplete. And Buddhism uses its theory of 'skillful means' or 'doctrinal' categorization to reconcile different, even contradictory teachings.

◀ Incense coils at the Man Mo Temple in Hong Kong (© Jon Arnold Images Ltd / Alamy).

Timeline

c. 2350 BCE	Time of China's Sage kings Yao, Shun and Yu; some accounts place Dangun, the mythical founder of Old Joseon (Korea), in the same period
c. 2200–1750	Xia dynasty (China)
c. 1750–1040	Shang (Yin) dynasty (China)
c. 1040–256	Zhou dynasty (China)
722–479	Spring and Autumn period
551	Birth of Confucius (d. 479); some accounts place Laozi around the same time, some place him earlier, and others say that he never existed
479–221	Warring States period
c. 400–100	Huang–Lao school
c. 343	Birth of Mencius (d. 289); Zhuangzi (369?–286?) was a slightly older contemporary
c. 310	Birth of Xunzi (d. 219), who witnesses the carnage of the late Zhou period
c. 300	Old Joseon (Korea)
221–206	Qin dynasty (China); Confucian texts destroyed
202 BCE–9 CE	Former (i.e., early) Han period; Confucian texts reconstructed and edited
9–23	Interregnum
25–220	Latter Han
124	First state college for Confucian teachings established; first state examinations follow
c. 50 BCE–668 CE	Three Kingdoms of Goguryeo, Baekje, and Silla (Korea)
c. 48 CE	Birth of Ban Zhao (d. 112), who advocates education for women
142	Zhang Daoling founds the Daoist Celestial Masters (renamed 'Orthodox Unity' c. 400)
220–589	Period of North–South disunion or Six Dynasties (China)
317	Northern China falls to invaders from North and Central Asia
618–907	Tang dynasty (China)
600s	Tang rulers send Daoist priests, texts, and images to Goguryeo
647	The second Tang emperor orders the construction of Confucian temples with tablets commemorating 22 orthodox Confucians
668–936	Kingdom of United Silla (Korea)
682	United Silla establishes the National Confucian College
824	Death of Han Yu, who criticized Daoism and Buddhism and laid the groundwork for the renewal of Confucianism
890–936	Later Three Kingdoms (Korea)
960–1279	Song dynasty (China)

1368–1644	Ming dynasty (China)
1400s	Both China's Empress Xu and Joseon's Queen Sohye write texts entitled *Instructions for the Inner Quarters*; the former becomes one of the Four Books for Women
1500s	Joseon Neo-Confucianism thrives
1529	Death of Wang Yangming, who challenged Zhu Xi's orthodox Confucianism with his School of Heart-Mind
1644–1911	Qing (Manchu) dynasty (China)
1839	Lin Zexu, a Confucian minister of the Qing regime, writes an open letter to Queen Victoria protesting Britain's selling of opium in China; the Opium War and the beginning of China's Westernization follow
1850–64	Taiping Rebellion
1900s	East Asia reconfigured in response to Western challenges; new religions are established and traditional ones renewed
1910–1945	Japanese occupation of Korea
1911	Qing dynasty falls and China becomes a republic
1945	Korea divided between Democratic People's Republic (North) and Republic (South)
1949	People's Republic of China (PRC)
1950s	New Confucian movement finds a home in Hong Kong; Korean New Confucian Gim (Kim) Chungnyol travels to Taiwan to study with Fang Dongmei
1966-76	'Great Proletarian Cultural Revolution': Mao Zedong's campaign to eradicate traditional Chinese values and practices
1980s	Revival of Daoism in China after more than a century of persecution
1989	Confucius' birthday officially celebrated in the PRC for the first time since 1949 after student demonstrations at Tiananmen Square
2004	The first Confucius Institute opens in Seoul
2006	First World Buddhist Forum—the first government-sponsored religious conference held in China since 1949—opens in Hangzhou

Confucianism

Origins

Not all of the philosophy that the West calls Confucianism originated with Kongzi (c. 551–479 BCE[1]): the man whose name was latinized as **Confucius**. Some of its seminal ideas can be found in a collection of writings that we know as the Five Classics: the *Classic or Book of Changes* (Yijing), the *Classic of Documents or Book of History* (Shujing), the *Classic of Odes or*

Portrait of a Korean Confucian, attributed to Yi Che-gwan (1783–1837) (© The Trustees of the British Museum/Art Resource, NY).

Book of Poetry (*Shijing*), the *Records or Book of Rites* (*Liji*), and the *Spring and Autumn Annals* (*Chunqiu*). (A sixth work, the *Classic of Music* [*Yueji*], is now lost.) Some parts of these works may predate Confucius himself and others appear to have been written after his time. Nevertheless, Confucius is revered as the first of China's three foremost philosophers in the classical (i.e. Confucian) tradition, the other two being **Mencius** (c. 343–289 BCE) and **Xunzi** (c. 310–219 BCE).

Originating during the Zhou dynasty (c. 1040–256 BCE), the Classics were first standardized during the Han dynasty (202 BCE–220 CE) and they have formed a substantial part of the state examination curriculum since the establishment of the first state college in 124 BCE. The world they describe is the same one that shaped Daoist thought, as well as later folk beliefs and practices.

Historically, the Five Classics provided both the ideology that informed government policy and the framework in which that policy was implemented for some 2,000 years. They have also served as blueprints for good conduct within families, and as guidelines for individual moral and spiritual transformation.

The classics record a society in transition. During the Shang era (c. 1750–1040 BCE) the world was understood to be under the control of anthropomorphic deities, ghosts, and spirits. In the Zhou era this 'supernatural' worldview was gradually replaced by an increasingly humanized ethos and a new understanding that the world operated according to natural, impersonal principles. The content of the Five Classics therefore ranges from descriptions of deities, ghosts, and spirits, and the rites (**li**) performed for them, to philosophical explanations of the natural principles underlying those rites. The primary source of those explanations, the *Book of Rites*, also explains how the rites serve the ultimate goal of Confucianism: the creation of a harmonious society through careful self-cultivation not for the sake of the self, but for the sake of the society. Over time, the Five Classics were reinterpreted more than once with this goal in mind.

Confucian Concerns

The concerns addressed in the Five Classics can be categorized in four broad areas: political, familial, individual, and cosmic. The first duty of the exemplary Confucian (*junzi*) is to understand how to achieve and maintain peace, prosperity, and harmony.

The Classics make it clear that political harmony cannot be achieved by men alone, for there can be no harmony in the state without harmony in the private realm of family—and the family is the responsibility of the Confucian woman. They also explain how sacrifices and rituals give symbolic expression to the relationship between the outer world of politics and

Traditions at a Glance

Numbers

Confucianism: Estimates range from 6 to 8 million, but because most of the East Asian world does not consider Confucianism to be a religion, the true number is impossible to gauge.

Daoism: Estimates range from 2.5 to 3.5 million.

Chinese folk or popular religion includes numerous movements and sects whose devotees may consider their traditions to be more cultural than religious. Estimates range from 385 to 405 million.

Korean shamanism and popular religion: Estimates range from 1 to 7 million.

Distribution

Confucians and Daoists live mainly in East and Southeast Asia, Australia, New Zealand, northwestern Europe, and North America. Adherents of popular religions remain primarily in East Asia, with small pockets in diasporic communities in North America and Europe.

Founders and Teachers

Mythological founders and heroes include Yao, Shun, and Yu in China, and Dangun in Korea. Famous first teachers—some mythical, some historic—include the Yellow Emperor, Confucius, and Laozi in China, and Choe Chung in Korea.

Deities

For Confucians, the place of a deity is filled either by Heaven or by Heaven and Earth together. For some Daoists, the Way functions as a deity; others look to what is in effect a bureaucracy of deities. Popular religions, both Korean and Chinese, include deities from various traditions.

Authoritative Texts

For Confucians, the Classics from the Zhou and Han are the foundational texts. For Daoists, the *Daodejing* (or *Laozi*) is fundamental; other important scriptures vary from sect to sect. Popular and shamanistic religions tend not to be textually oriented.

Noteworthy Teachings

None of the East Asian traditions are exclusive. Daoism and Confucianism share cultural and social space with each other as well as popular religions, even if they differ doctrinally. The two elite religions share a utopian view of a peaceful and harmonious society whose members are devoted to self-cultivation and discipline, live frugally, serve the community, and try to be good.

the inner world of the family. The essential function of rituals, ancestor rituals in particular, was to define, frame, and encourage right relationships, especially between men and women.

Confucian Exemplars and Sages

The prototypes of the Confucian sage are three mythical 'sage kings' named Yao, Shun, and Yu, whose stories are told in the first chapters of the *Classic of Documents.* The virtues they embody are civil, familial, and filial rather than military, and their stories are interpreted as implicitly criticizing rulers who govern by force. For this reason, the Confucian scholars who took the sage kings as their models came to be known as the 'weak or soft ones'.

Yao's reign was considered a success because he brought harmony to his domain and, most important, made sure that the common people he served were well fed and prosperous. In the simple agrarian society of his day, Yao's exemplary virtue was said to have radiated throughout the land.

The *Classic of Documents* recounts how, when it came time for him to retire, Yao recognized that his own son was not virtuous enough to be a good ruler. He asked his ministers to find a more appropriate successor, and they unanimously recommended a man of humble status named Shun. When Yao asked them why Shun would make a good king, they answered that he had managed to transcend his circumstances, living in harmony with his family and fulfilling his filial duties, even though his father was blind (literally and figuratively) and stupid, his stepmother deceitful, and his half-brother arrogant. In other words, Shun had not allowed his situation to overcome him, but had triumphed over adversity. Accordingly, Yao married his two daughters to Shun, observed his conduct for three years, and then offered him the throne.

Among Shun's religious duties as king was the performance of rituals to the foremost deity, Shangdi (the Lord-on-High) and six 'venerables' who are thought to have symbolized various exemplary historical figures and political (as opposed to blood) ancestors. Shun's secular duties included setting common standards for units of measure, determining political boundaries for the land, and overseeing public works such as the deepening of rivers in anticipation of the inevitable floods.

The last sage king, Yu, is associated with the largely legendary Xia dynasty—the predecessors of the Shang. Yu's father was said to have thrown the natural cycle into chaos by building dams to contain the floodwater, but Yu dug deep canals to channel the water away. According to a chapter in the *Documents* entitled 'The Grand Model', this story was told to King Wu, the first king of Zhou, as a lesson in governance. Regarded as a blueprint for an equitable, prosperous, and harmonious society, the Grand Model was said to have been revealed to Yu as his reward for taking the 'right action' to prevent disaster, working with nature (by channelling the water) rather than against it.

Divination and the Pantheon of Spirits

At least two related elements from the stories of the sage kings survived into the Shang dynasty: an intense interest in 'right' governance and a belief in divine intervention through revelation to the king. We know, for instance, that the Shang kings practised divination: in fact, they were generally the only ones with the power to interpret the results of divination and forecast the future. By taking on the role of a shaman, in direct communication with the spirits that were believed to hold the real power over the land he ruled, the king optimized his understanding and control of affairs. Religious ritual was thus an indispensable part of governance in ancient China.

The Shang pantheon of spirits included human souls as well as natural elements and supernatural beings. At its apex, far above the natural realm, sat the Lord-on-High Shangdi. Thought to be the ancestor-god of the Shang clan, he was the sky god, the only one who could command natural elements such as the rain, thunder, and wind. Below the Lord-on-High were the nature spirits believed to animate natural phenomena such as rivers and mountains; then the celestial spirits like the sun and moon; then the 'venerables' (or 'Former Lords') who were associated with the Shang but were not royal clan members; and, finally, direct ancestors, both male and female. Together, the cult of ancestors and the royal practice of divination cloaked the Shang kings in an aura of sacredness.

Divination entailed reading the cracks created by pressing a hot brand or poker onto bone (typically cattle scapula) or the ventral part of a tortoise shell. Subjects of inquiry ranged from the king's health to the prospects for a successful harvest or military campaign to the interpretation of dreams. The king might also ask approval for his plans, suggesting that one function of divination was to legitimate the king's activities and, by extension, his rule. Traces of these ancient traditions—the belief in spirits, divination, the need to communicate with the supernatural world—survive today in folk beliefs and customs including the creation of shrines such as the ones described at the beginning of this chapter.

The Mandate of Heaven

After more than 700 years in power, the Shang dynasty fell to the Zhou about 1040 BCE. It was in the context of this power shift that the concept of the **Mandate of Heaven** (tian-ming) was developed.

When the first Zhou ruler, King Wu, died within a few years of taking the throne, his brother the Duke of Zhou served as regent for his young nephew. But the duke returned the throne to the boy once he was old enough to rule. Such loyalty was revered in the early Confucian tradition, and the Duke's popularity rivalled that of Confucius himself. An exemplary Confucian sage, the personification of restraint, humility, and willingness to listen to advice, the Duke declared that Heaven had withdrawn the Mandate of Heaven from the Shang because their later kings had failed to provide for the people.

In this way moral character became the primary determinant of the right to rule. The idea that good governance was a duty to Heaven reflected the Zhou belief in a moral force or supreme deity that ruled the world and took an interest in human affairs. How to

On the Mandate of Heaven

The Mandate of Heaven appears in the Classic of Documents *in the form of a public announcement legitimating the Zhou overthrow of the Yin (an alternative name for the Shang):*

Heaven has rejected and ended the Mandate of this great state of Yin. Thus, although Yin has many former wise kings in Heaven, when their successor kings and successor people undertook their Mandate, in the end wise and good men lived in misery. Knowing that they must care for and sustain their wives and children, they then called out in anguish to Heaven and fled to places where they could not be caught. Ah! Heaven too grieved for the people of all the lands, wanting, with affection, in giving its Mandate to employ those who are deeply committed. The king should have reverent care for his virtue (D. Nivison in de Bary and Bloom 1999: 36).

encourage a king to rule ethically became a central concern for Confucians. In the *Classic of Odes*, King Wen (the father of Wu) is imagined addressing the last Shang king:

> King Wen said, Woe!
> Woe upon you, Yin and Shang!
> You have been the harsh oppressor,
> you have been grasping and crushing.
> You have been in the places of power,
> you have held the functions.
> Heaven sent recklessness down in you,
> and you rise by acts of force (Owen 1996: 20).

Thus the mandate to rule was taken away from the cruel and negligent Shang and passed to the virtuous Zhou. In this political transition, the term 'god' (*di*) became increasingly associated with the earthly political ruler, while Heaven came to be portrayed as an impartial universal being or power, an intelligent cosmic moral force that cares for human welfare and so gives the people a wise and good king.

Humanization: The Transition from Shang to Zhou

With the establishment of the Zhou dynasty, the concept of Heaven gained ascendancy over the more personal 'Lord on High' of the Shang. Although the interest in divination continued, the methods and materials used for the purpose changed over time, reflecting a change in understanding of the universe. Eventually, shell and bone were replaced by

The Naturalist School

Members of the Naturalist or yin-yang school believed that those who followed the laws of nature would flourish while those who did not would perish. Yin-yang theory was later combined with the five 'elements', 'agents', or 'phases' (*wuxing*)—metal, wood, earth, water, and fire—to produce a theory of cyclic generation and 'overcoming' in which metal generates water, water generates wood, wood generates fire, fire generates earth, and earth generates metal, while water overcomes fire, metal overcomes wood, and so on. This cosmology suggests that there is nothing in the world that cannot be overcome, while at the same time there is no destruction from which growth cannot come.

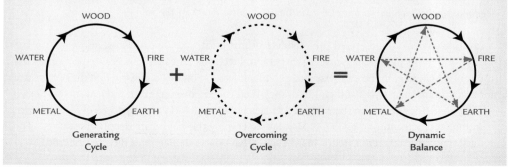

the plant stalks used for divination in the *Classic of Changes*—a change that reflected a conceptual shift away from an enchanted universe towards a more rational and impersonal one. This shift did not mean that the ancient belief disappeared. The understanding that the world as controlled by ghosts, nature spirits, and celestial beings remains an integral part of Chinese religion, especially in folk traditions. Nevertheless, many Zhou thinkers diverged from their Shang predecessors in this regard. A number of schools developed and thrived. Legalists stressed the power of law in the advancement of human security and well-being; Naturalists concentrated on natural elements and processes (see box); and Confucians emphasized human relationships, beginning with familial affection. Philosophers came to see the world as regulated by impersonal processes, which they sought to understand in order to use them as models for human society.

The quest to understand natural processes was driven in part by the desire to find a natural—hence 'right'—foundation on which to structure a harmonious human society. The 64 hexagrams that are the basis of the *Classic of Changes*, a divination text originating in the early Zhou dynasty (c. 1000 BCE), were said to capture the metaphysical structure, transformations, and 'Way' of the universe, providing both a general blueprint and a specific guide to correct behaviour for humans facing a cosmos in continual change.

Rites: Performance and Principles

The section on 'Principles of Sacrifice' in the *Records of Rites* explains that a ruler must have a wife as a helpmate in both state and familial duties. The principle of complementarity is reflected in the division of labour between king and queen, in the realms of activity prescribed for each, and in their gender differentiated roles in ritual performance. The king and queen were together responsible for making offerings at the ancestral temple representing the imperial family; in this way they symbolically attended to their different duties in the outer and inner realms of male and female responsibilities, respectively.

According to the *Rites*, it was the role of the Son of Heaven and his lords to provide grain for the sacrificial rites by ploughing and the role of the queen and the wives of the lords to provide silk for ritual vestments by raising silkworms. These activities were not meant to be understood literally; rather, they were symbolic expressions of sincerity, good faith, and the royal couple's particular responsibility to encourage both Heaven and Earth to treat the state and its people with benevolence.

Before the start of any state ritual, the royal couple had to observe a ten-day vigil; the king fasted and performed purification rituals outside the palace, while the queen carried out her ritual obligations inside the palace. This vigil symbolized the complementary differences between men and women, the separateness of the outer and inner quarters, and the ideal of the husband and wife working side by side in their separate realms.

The balance of yin (the shady side of the mountain) and yang (the sunny side) is reinforced by the first two trigrams in the *Classic of Changes*. Qian, Heaven and the creative, is represented by three solid lines:

≡

while *kun*, Earth and the receptive, is represented by three broken lines:

⚏.

The 64 trigrams that make up the *Changes* were understood to capture various transformations in the universe. The first two trigrams symbolized the generative forces that set the world in motion. It is not surprising that the yin–yang, male–female complementarity extended even to the foods offered to the spirits; they too had to be chosen so as to balance the forces of yin and yang.

The rituals described in the *Rites* evolved over time, as did the understanding of their place in the lives of the individual, the state, and the society. Belief in their magico-religious efficacy was gradually replaced by a sense of their value in terms of discipline, education, and moral development. The deeply religious culture of the Shang was humanized by the philosophers of the later Zhou, Confucius in particular. In *Master Tso's Commentary on the Spring and Autumn Annals*, for example, a duke is reprimanded when he remarks that the spirits will protect him because his sacrificial offerings are 'bountiful and pure':

> It is not simply that ghosts and spirits are attracted to human beings: it is virtue that attracts them. Hence . . . the *Book of History* says, 'August heaven has no partial affections; it supports only the virtuous.' It also says, 'It is not the millet that is fragrant; it is bright virtue that is fragrant' (adapted from J. Legge in Sommer 1995: 25).

The shift from reliance on the supernatural efficacy of rituals to reliance on moral behaviour finds support in another story from the same text, in which a marquis is rebuked for requesting an exorcism to ward off the evil threatened by the appearance of a comet in the sky: 'If your virtue is not unclean, then why this exorcism? . . . Do not transgress against virtue, and people from all quarters will come to you' (ibid., 26).

CRYSTALLIZATION

Confucius

Confucius spoke of himself as a transmitter of tradition rather than an innovator. On the connection between goodness and ritual, he famously said:

> Respect without ritual becomes tiresome, circumspection without ritual becomes timidity, bold fortitude without ritual becomes unruly, and directness without ritual becomes twisted (Sommer 1995: 46).

Confucius used the word *li* ('rites' or 'ritual') to mean not only religious ritual but also the rules of social etiquette and everyday courtesy. He believed that the *li* embodied the wisdom of the earliest Zhou tradition. He encouraged his students to practise them in all of the five fundamental relationships (between emperor and minister, father and son, elder and younger brother, husband and wife, and, finally, friends). At the same time he urged his students to seek the meaning, spirit, and principles behind the rites. Central to the Confucian understanding of history were the stories of the sage kings and the perfection they achieved by governing in accordance with the Way. According to 'The Evolution of Rites' (*Liyun*), Confucius believed that the time of the sage kings was preceded by a utopian age:

When the Great Way was practised, the world was shared by all alike. The worthy and the able were promoted to office and men practised good faith and lived in affection. Therefore they did not regard as parents only their own parents, or as sons only their own sons. The aged found a fitting close to their lives, the robust their proper employment; the young were provided with an upbringing, and the widow and widower, the orphaned and the sick, with proper care. Men had their tasks and women their hearths. They hated to see goods lying about in waste, yet they did not hoard them for themselves; they disliked the thought that their energies were not fully used, yet they used them not for private ends. Therefore all evil plotting was prevented and thieves and rebels did not arise, so that the people could leave their outer gates unbolted. This was the age of Grand Commonality [*Datong*] (B. Watson in de Bary and Bloom 1999: 342–3).

In time, greed and selfishness put an end to the Grand Commonality, ushering in the period of Lesser Prosperity. It was during this potentially chaotic era that the sage kings emerged as exemplars of correct, ethical governance. The primary source of Confucius' teachings on how to govern in such a period is the collection known as the *Analects* (*Lunyu*).

At the core of Confucius' ideal was the *junzi* (translated variously as 'gentleman' or 'noble'; the 'authoritative', 'exemplary', or 'superior person'). The standard meaning of *junzi* was 'son of a lord', indicating inherited social nobility, but in the *Analects* the word takes on a new meaning: this gentleman is a person of noble character, committed to the development of *de*—another word that underwent a shift in meaning with Confucius. Originally referring to a kind of magical charismatic power, in the *Analects* it signifies a moral power derived from virtuous, ethical behaviour.

The fact that Confucius used these words in non-traditional ways did not mean that the meanings he gave them were new; as we noted above, he saw himself as a transmitter, not an innovator. The socio-political ideals he promoted were already present in the classic texts (*Odes, Documents, Spring and Autumn Annals*, and *Changes*). Confucius used the single word **ren**— 'humaneness', 'benevolence', 'compassion', 'goodness'—to capture virtues such as respect, liberality, trustworthiness, earnestness, and kindness. He believed that the most effective way to cultivate *ren* was through careful observance of *li*.

Above all, Confucius emphasized the importance of filial piety or devotion. The 'Principles of Sacrifice' chapter of the *Rites* explains filial devotion as 'caring for' one's parents according to the Way (*Dao*): that is, to the greatest extent possible without neglecting one's responsibilities in other relationships (8.2.1). But it could include everything from looking after one's own health to protecting family members even when they had committed a crime. Confucius understood that ritual observance was essential to the maintenance of harmony:

Let there be no discord. . . . When one's parents are alive, one serves them in accordance with the rites; when they are dead, one buries them in accordance with the rites and sacrifices to them in accordance with the rites (2:5).

He also suggests that those who treat their parents and brothers with the proper respect will be equally loyal to a government ruling with the Mandate of Heaven. Thus Confucius explains that the 'noble person concerns himself with the root; when the root

A rock carving (c. 1127–1279) from the cave complex at Dazu, in Sichuan, depicts a loving son. Although the Dazu complex was mainly Buddhist in orientation, the ideal of filial piety transcended religious boundaries (© Pierre Colombel/CORBIS).

is established, the way is born. Being filial and fraternal—is this not the root of humaneness?' (1:2).

Above all, humaneness is reflected in two characteristics: loyalty and empathetic understanding or reciprocity (4:15). Refining this idea, Confucius encapsulates his teachings in the 'silver rule': 'What you would not want for yourself, do not do to others' (15:23). The noble person is the one who puts the self aside and 'relinquishes arrogance, boasting, resentment, and covetousness' (14:2).

Who can be a noble person? Anyone: all human beings are by nature similar. But there is a catch: Confucius also teaches that individuals are set apart by through their habits and actions (17:2). Thus even as he democratizes the idea of nobility, he creates a hierarchy of character based on moral cultivation. This hierarchy is all about the mastery of self:

> Through mastering oneself and returning to ritual one becomes humane. If for a single day one can master oneself and return to ritual, the whole world will return to humaneness. . . . Look at nothing contrary to ritual; listen to nothing contrary to ritual; say nothing contrary to ritual; do nothing contrary to ritual (12:1).

Confucius believed that if the ruler wants goodness, the people will be good: 'The virtue (*de*) of the exemplary (or noble) person is like the wind, and the virtue of small people is like grass: When the wind blows over the grass, the grass must bend' (12:19). To recreate the Grand Commonality, therefore, good, wise, and humane people must rule over the small-minded and morally inferior.

The Confucian mandate is to limit the negative consequences of ignoble behaviour. When a recluse describes Confucius as 'a scholar who withdraws from particular men' and suggests that instead he should withdraw from society, Confucius sighs and responds: 'If the Way prevailed in the world, [I] would not be trying to change it' (18:6). Personal goodness alone is not enough: ethical nobility must be reflected in action.

Mencius

The second most prominent classical thinker after Confucius is Meng Ke, whose name was latinized as Mencius. He lived more than a century after Confucius, in the fourth century BCE. By that time large conscript armies had replaced the elite chariot forces on which feudal rulers had relied in the past, resulting in a horrific increase in the human cost of war.

In an effort to stop the carnage, Mencius travelled from state to state meeting with rulers and trying to persuade them to act in the interest of their people. He deplored the consequences of war:

> In wars to gain land, the dead fill the plains; in wars to gain cities, the dead fill the cities. This is known as showing the land the way to devour human flesh. Death is too light a punishment for such men. Hence those skilled in war should suffer the most severe punishments . . . (4.A.14 Lau 1970: 124).

At the same time he tried to persuade rulers of the practical value of humaneness (ren), expanding on Confucius' understanding and placing the moral sense of what is right (yi) beside ren.

The book *Mencius* is a collection of conversations between Mencius and his disciples, his opponents in debate, and the rulers of the various feudal states. Prominent among the issues discussed are human nature and government. Wishing to 'follow in the footsteps of the three sages [King Yu of Xia, the Duke of Zhou, and Confucius] in rectifying the hearts of men, laying heresies to rest, opposing extreme action, and banishing excessive views' (ibid., 115), Mencius traced many of the problems of his day to the human 'heart-mind' (xin), of which he identified four types. The heart-mind of compassion yields benevolence; that of shame leads to observance of rites; that of respect moves people to duty or right behaviour; and that of right and wrong brings wisdom (6.A.6 ibid., 163).

Mencius taught that sensitivity to others' suffering is innate, but that this predisposition must be consciously developed if a ruler is to govern compassionately, as the ancient kings did. In later times, a great man—teacher, scholar-official, or imperial minister—was needed to encourage the ruler to cultivate that mature heart-mind; then, when the prince had become benevolent, dutiful, and correct, everyone else would seek to emulate him.

In contrast to the scenario described by Confucius, however, for Mencius the effect of the prince's character on the people was not automatic or magical. He believed that even though human nature was essentially good, the common people needed supervision and discipline: otherwise, once their bellies were full and their bodies warmly clothed, they would degenerate to the level of animals driven only by material needs and desires, with no higher consciousness. The best way of nurturing the heart-mind of the people, Mencius taught, was neither to deprive them nor to give them more than they needed to survive, but to teach them to reduce their desires.

Mencius's belief in the ability of the mature heart-mind to arrive at sound conclusions allowed him to take some unconventional positions. Thus he rejected the notion that filial piety demanded blind obedience. Once, when someone suggested that Shun, the son-in-law of King Yao, had defied the rule of filial piety by failing to inform his parents of his marriage to Yao's two daughters, Mencius defended Shun on the grounds that his parents' heart-minds were not sufficiently developed for them to consent to his marriage. Shun's own heart-mind, by contrast, was so well developed that he was justified in acting independently, according to his own conscience.

Similarly, Mencius argued against blind obedience to the rule that unrelated men and women should not touch one another, pointing out that it would be inhuman for a man not to rescue his sister-in-law if she were drowning. On another occasion he remarked that if everything in the *Documents* had to be accepted without critical thought, it would be better if the text had never been written. Most famously, he drew on the concept of the Mandate of Heaven to argue that rebellion is justified when the ruler is causing the people to suffer. In short, for Mencius it is not enough simply to follow the classical teachings: we must use our heart-minds to determine the morally correct course of action.

But Mencius was not only a political thinker. He is sometimes described as a mystic because of his emphasis on *qi* (or *ch'i*): the flood-like vital force, spirit, or energy that appears simultaneously to give substance to virtue and to be nourished by it:

> This is a *ch'i* which is, in the highest degree vast and unyielding. Nourish it with integrity and place no obstacle in its path and it will fill the space between Heaven and Earth. It is a *ch'i* which unites rightness and the Way. Deprive it of these and it will collapse. It is born of accumulated rightness and cannot be appropriated by anyone through a sporadic show of rightness. Whenever one acts in a way that falls below the standard set in one's heart, it will collapse (2.A.2; ibid., 77–8).

Virtue cannot be forced: it can be given substance only by following the heart-mind, behaving with integrity, and practising right action. Mencius suggests that nourishing this vital force through constant practice in both public and private life is what permits human beings to achieve cosmic oneness and harmony.

Xunzi

Xun Kuang or Xun Qing (c. 310–219 BCE), better known as Master Xun or Xunzi, was a generation younger than Mencius. Living at the end of the horrendously violent Warring States period, he likely witnessed the bloody conflict that ended in the conquest of the last feudal states by the first emperor, Qin. So perhaps it is not surprising that Xunzi did not agree with Mencius on the innate goodness of human beings: he believed that human nature was evil, and that 'goodness was the result of conscious activity' (Watson 1963: 157). Nevertheless, he did share the core Confucian belief in the possibility of sagehood and the value of culture and learning.

Xunzi believed that education and ritual were essential to the maintenance of the hierarchy required for a society to function in an orderly fashion. But he was not blind to the misuse of Confucian values by some corrupt men who called themselves Confucians. Like Mencius, who followed Confucius in criticizing the 'village worthy' as someone who performed all the right actions but was insincere, Xunzi spoke out against 'rotten Confucians' and people who 'stole a reputation for virtue'.

The collection known as the *Xunzi* was compiled and edited more than a century after Xunzi's time, during the Han dynasty. Its form marks a major departure from the recorded conversations of the *Analects* and *Mencius*: it consists mainly of essays in which Xunzi reflects on topics such as the original nature of human beings, learning, self-cultivation, government, and military affairs. The first chapter, 'Encouraging Learning', underlines the necessity of effort to achieve moral progress:

> Learning should never cease. Blue comes from the indigo plant but is bluer than the plant itself. Ice is made of water but is colder than water ever is. A piece of wood as straight as a plumb line may be bent into a circle as true as any drawn with a compass and, even after the wood has dried, it will not straighten out again (Watson 1963: 15).

The reason human beings need 'straightening out' is that they are bent with innate desires that spark feelings of envy and hate, and if these impulses are not curbed, competition for the scarce objects of desire will lead to chaos. This is what Xunzi meant when he said that human beings are 'evil' by nature and must seek transformation through the guidance of sages and observance of ritual principles: only then can they cultivate courtesy and humility. Together, Xunzi's belief that the rituals were created by the ancient sages specifically to prevent chaos and his focus on human effort mark a definitive break from the supernatural notion of divine revelation illustrated in the story of King Yu and the Grand Model.

In his chapter 'A Discussion of Heaven', Xunzi continues Confucius' effort to humanize the Zhou tradition, rejecting the supernatural in favour of the rational and natural. He sees Heaven, Earth, and humanity as forming a trinity in which each component has its own role. As human beings, even sages do not seek to understand Heaven, let alone to take over its 'godlike' role. Rather, humans should focus on the activities necessary for humans to live well and prosper. The noble person cherishes the power allotted to him and does not try to usurp the power of Heaven:

> When the work of Heaven has been established and its accomplishments brought to completion, when the form of man is whole and his spirit is born, then love and hate, delight and anger, sorrow and joy find lodging in him. These are called his heavenly emotions. Ears, eyes, nose, mouth, and body . . . are called the heavenly faculties. The heart (*xin*) dwells in the centre and governs the five faculties, and hence it is called the heavenly lord (Watson 1963: 80–1).

Even though Xunzi understood the world to operate without supernatural intervention, he supported the performance of traditional rituals addressed to Heaven because he believed that they had been perfected by the ancient kings. Only a sage can fully understand the rites, he said; but the noble person finds comfort in performing them as a part of human culture, while the common person accepts them as a reflection of the reality of the spirit world. Xunzi takes ritual and music out of the realm of magic by interpreting their functions in practical terms. Thus the purpose of teaching the rites (*li jiao*, another name for Confucianism) is to cultivate virtues such as courtesy and humility, which discourage aggression and promote harmony. Similarly, even if the performance of rituals does not 'satisfy fully the desire of the mouth and the stomach, the ears and the eyes', it can still produce satisfaction by 'teach[ing] people to moderate their likes and dislikes and return to the proper human Way [*rendao*]' (de Bary and Bloom 1999: 344).

❧ DIFFERENTIATION

Han Confucianism

The victory of the Qin brought an end to the carnage and unified the Warring States. To minimize dissent, however, the first emperor ordered the destruction of almost all the scholarly books that might encourage independent thought, among them the Confucian classics. Only one copy of each work was preserved in the imperial library. Thus when the Han dynasty (202 BCE–220 CE) replaced the short-lived Qin, a great many works had to be reconstructed.

The political and intellectual changes that took place under the Han would shape imperial ideology as well as religious beliefs and practices for the next two thousand years. To the four virtues identified by Mencius—humaneness, right action, ritual appropriateness, and wisdom—was added a fifth: trustworthiness. The notions that Heaven, Earth, and humankind form a trinity and that the celestial and terrestrial powers will respond to human entreaty were central to Han ideology. Han Confucian thinkers reflected the influence both of Xunzi and of a chapter in the *Rites* called 'Centrality and Equilibrium' (*Zhongyong*; also translated as 'Centrality and Harmony' or 'The Doctrine of the Mean'): they believed that humans who were sincere in their efforts to bring about peace and harmony could share in the creative, transformative powers of Heaven and Earth.

Echoing Mencius and Xunzi, Han Confucians identified economic welfare as the basis of morality. The government, in particular the emperor, was obliged to provide both the physical sustenance and the moral education necessary for the people to lead secure and happy lives. Following Xunzi, Han Confucians also promoted moral education through ritual, music, and literature.

It was during the Han that the idea of a Confucian canon in the form of the Five Classics was first proposed and political or state Confucianism was established. Philosophers seeking a holistic account of the universe and humankind's place in it tried to syncretize the Confucian tradition with other philosophies. The result was a Confucianism that blended ideas from traditional texts with those of thinkers such as the masters of technical methods, who sought to manipulate the cosmos; and the Naturalists, who developed the notions of *qi*, yin-yang, and five phases. It was also during the Han that a number of influential non-canonical texts were written or compiled and edited, among them the *Biographies of Exemplary* (or *Virtuous*) *Women* (*Lienu zhuan*), *Admonitions* (or *Lessons*) *for Women* (*Nu jie*), and the *Classic of Filiality* (*Xiaojing*). *Exemplary Women* and *Admonitions* in particular defined what was expected of women and formed the foundation of a specifically female Confucian tradition.

The Compilation of the Five Classics

Han Confucians believed that Confucius himself had transmitted the Zhou tradition through the canonical texts and that he had had a hand in the selection, compilation, and editing of all five Classics. However, later scholars have shown that a good portion of their content originated after Confucius' time.

The first classic, the *Changes*, which survived in the form it had taken over the course of the Zhou dynasty, assumed particular importance under the Han. As we have noted, it was thought to embody the metaphysical structure and the Way of the universe. It is divided into two parts: a series of short passages interpreting the 64 hexagrams, and ten appendices or 'wings' that elaborate on those interpretations. Traditionally, the ten wings were attributed to Confucius.

Confucius is also said to have edited or written a short introduction to each section of the second classic, the *Documents.* Although some of the content is now thought to date from as late as the fourth century CE, historically this volume was considered to be an accurate account of China's ancient rulers, from the sage kings to the early Zhou, offering examples of good and bad qualities in numerous governments and institutions.

The third classic, the *Odes*, consists of roughly three hundred poems that predate Confucius, mostly from the early Zhou, that he is believed to have chosen and edited. They include folk songs from various states as well as songs associated with the aristocracy; both types were often interpreted politically as expressions of popular sentiment, praising virtuous rulers and criticizing bad ones.

The fourth classic, the *Rites,* consists of three separate texts: *Rites of Etiquette and Ceremonials* (*Yili*) for minor officials, *Rites* (or *Institutions*) *of Zhou* (*Zhou li* or *Zhou guan*), and the *Records or Book of Rites* (*Liji*), which explores the principles behind particular rites. The contents likely date from between the mid- to late Zhou and the early Han and took their current form over time. Confucius is credited with the compilation and editing of some of these ritual texts, whose contents range from minutely detailed advice on how to live daily life to broad philosophical discussions of the meaning of state rituals and ceremonies.

The fifth and last classic, the *Spring and Autumn Annals,* is a terse chronicle of events in Confucius' native state of Lu from 722 to 481 BCE. Confucius is said to have compiled it from archival materials in order to express his judgments of past events. It was therefore used as a guide to moral laws and principles in the management of human affairs. Because the historical text is so brief, it is usually read with the help of commentaries.

The adoption of Confucianism as state orthodoxy was by no means a foregone conclusion, as competing religious–philosophical groups and ideas continued to develop throughout the Han. It was the text-focused Confucians who were hardest hit by the Qin emperor's book burning. And it was the Confucian literati who, more than any other group, took up the enormous task of retrieving and reassembling the lost texts in the third and second centuries BCE. They compiled, edited, and annotated dictionaries and great works of history belonging to other schools as well as their own.

The early 'books' were written on strips of bamboo bound together by cords or thongs, but over the centuries the cords decayed and the original order of their contents was lost. When they were recovered, it was difficult to determine which version was authoritative, and different arrangements of the recovered material gave rise to different interpretations. There were also texts written in different scripts. One legend has it that copies were found in the wall of Confucius' home in the state of Lu; these became known as the Old Text edition because, unlike the New Text copies, they were written in the archaic characters of the Zhou period rather than the standardized characters of the Qin and Han.

There was a private Old Text group based in the region of the old state of Lu, and one of its most famous scholars was a direct descendant of Confucius, Kong Anguo (156?–74? BCE). The most influential Confucian at court, however, was an older contemporary of Kong named **Dong Zhongshu** (195?–105? BCE).

Dong Zhongshu

It was Dong, the leading official proponent of the New Text School, who was largely responsible for persuading Emperor Wu to adopt Confucianism as state orthodoxy. Like many during the Han, Dong promoted a 'natural model' of the way the world works, based on the idea of correlation between the macrocosm of Heaven and Earth and the microcosm of the human body.

Dong set out to integrate Confucian thought with the supernatural thinking of court diviners, the correlative thinking of the Huang–Lao movement (see the section on Daoism), and the yin–yang thinking of the Naturalist school. Tracing the Confucian interest in human nature and emotion through Mencius and Xunzi, Dong took ideas from both and then combined them with the Naturalist concept of vital force (*qi*) operating through the dynamics of yin and yang.

Dong encouraged the establishment of a state college that would foster Confucian scholarship. Established in 124 BCE, it had some 3000 students by the end of that century, and by the end of the Han (220 CE) it had probably trained ten times that number. In this way the civil service came to be filled with men trained in the official Confucian curriculum, which included not only the Five Classics but the 'six arts' of 'ritual observance, music performance, archery, charioteering, calligraphy, and mathematics' (Kwok in de Bary and Bloom 1999:287). As these men steeped in Confucianism gradually replaced the feudal aristocracy of the Zhou in government, the Confucian vision of nobility as a matter of character and merit rather than birth moved closer to reality.

Some scholars have suggested that Emperor Wu chose Confucianism as the state orthodoxy because the Confucian idea of the Mandate of Heaven served to legitimate his authority. In fact, the Confucian model assumes that the emperor's authority would be circumscribed by ministers who would counsel restraint and discourage extravagance. According to the tradition, it was both the right and the duty of ministers to restrain the ruler's power by insisting on ministerial consultation. It is here that the significance of Dong's emphasis on yin-yang complementarity becomes clear. If the emperor and his ministers were not in harmony, as Heaven and Earth are, there would be chaos in the state. According to Han Confucianism, therefore, harmony requires that the emperor heed the counsel of his ministers, and that the husband heed the counsel of his wife.

At the close of the Han, two Old Text scholars named Yang Xiong and Wang Chong deconstructed Dong's system of correlation, separating classical Confucian teachings from the yin-yang–five phases–notions that Dong had associated with them, and cleared away some of the more extravagant aspects of his theory.

The Classic of Filiality

The importance of the minister's role was especially clear in the *Classic of Filiality* (*Xiaojing*). According to tradition, this influential text comes from the school traced to Confucius' disciple Zengzi. By the Latter Han, *Filiality* and the *Analects* of Confucius were added to the list of Classics. Presented in the form of a conversation (probably apocryphal) between Zengzi and Confucius, the *Classic of Filiality* broadens the definition of filial devotion outlined in the *Rites*, extends the notion of continuity between the human and spirit worlds through the veneration of ancestors, and connects filial piety to the idea of the

Map 10.1   Indigenous Chinese Religions

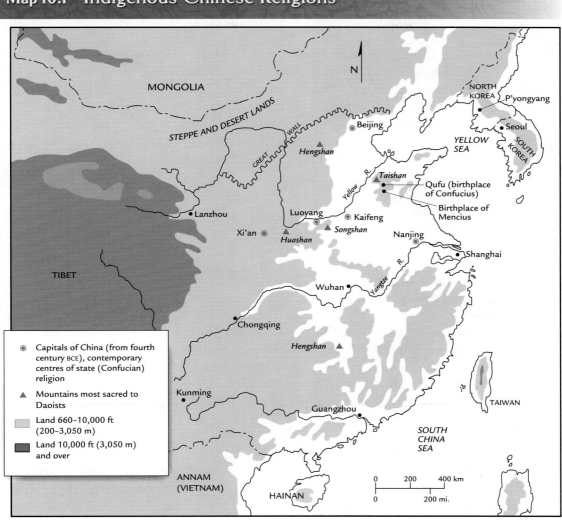

Source: Adapted from al Faruqi and Sopher 1974: 111.

triad formed by Heaven, Earth, and human beings. Following the *Rites*, the work clearly establishes filiality as the foundation of all virtues and the basis of public morality:

> The Master [Confucius] said, 'Loving one's parents, one dare not hate others. Revering one's parents, one dare not be contemptuous of others. When his love and reverence are perfected in service to parents, [the ruler's] moral influence is shed on all the people and his good example shines in all directions. . . .'
>
> The Master said, 'Filiality is the ordering principle of Heaven, the rightness of the Earth, and the norm of human conduct. This ordering of Heaven and Earth is what people should follow; illumined by the brightness of Heaven and benefited

by the resources of the Earth, all-under-Heaven (that is, the whole world) are thus harmonized. . . .' (W.T. de Bary in de Bary and Bloom 1999: 326–27).

Women

According to the *History of the Former Han Dynasty* (*Han shu*), Liu Xiang wrote the *Biographies of Exemplary Women* because he believed that women had a critical, albeit indirect and informal, role to play in government. To Liu's mind, the emperor would necessarily reflect the influence of his closest private counsellors, beginning with the empress. From the *Odes* and *Documents* Liu selected seven types of women, six of which had contributed to the peace and prosperity of their countries and the good reputation of their families, and one of which had brought about the downfall of dynasties (Raphals 1998: 19):

1. Maternal Rectitude,
2. Sage Intelligence,
3. Benevolent Wisdom,
4. Chaste and Obedient,
5. Chaste and Righteous,
6. Skill in Argument, and
7. Vicious and Depraved.

Under 'Maternal Rectitude' he tells the famous story of Mengmu, the widowed mother of Mencius. She is said to have moved three times, finally settling next to a school in order to facilitate her son's studies. The focus on education is strong. On one occasion, when Mengmu asked how his day at school had gone and Mencius answered nonchalantly 'As usual', she took a knife and destroyed the cloth she had been weaving. The purpose of this dramatic gesture was to teach him that a man who does not take learning seriously is like a woman who neglects her responsibility to provide for her family. Mencius' mother is said to have been a motivating force in his life.

Another story in *Exemplary Women*, presented under the heading 'Skill in Argument', tells of a girl of twelve who, against her mother's wishes, was determined to reprove the king (her uncle by marriage) for his dissolute ways. She intercepted his chariot and accused him of 'three calamities and five evils: dissipation, extravagance, the exhaustion of the country, starvation of the common people, and wicked ministers' (ibid., 45–6). The king responded by marrying her and turning over a new leaf. Both stories illustrate the influence that a woman could exercise through intelligence and wisdom, despite her yin nature and junior status in relation to her husband.

Ban Zhao

Like a man's moral development, a woman's cultivation began at home, in the family. Self-cultivation was especially important for women because the Han Chinese believed that the cultivation of proper behaviour in a child should begin before birth, while the fetus was still in the womb.

As children mature, according to the *Rites*, boys and girls should be separated: they should no longer sit on the same mat or eat together after reaching the age of seven. At the age of ten, boys were sent out to study with teachers and girls were discouraged from leaving the house. While boys learnt the six arts, girls were taught the domestic skills they would need as providers of material comfort, emotional stability, and moral guidance for their families.

In addition to learning how to weave, sew, and prepare food, girls were taught etiquette—the conventions of social behaviour required for harmonious relations—and how to perform the rituals, including the sacrifices required to express filial piety and keep peace with the ancestors. At the age of 15 a girl's hair was pinned up as a ceremonial rite of passage signalling that she was ready for marriage.

Ban Zhao (c. 48–112 CE) said that she wrote *Admonitions for Women* out of concern for her daughters who had not had the benefit of systematic training in their roles either as wives or as daughters- and sisters-in-law in their husbands' families. Ban did not want her daughters' lack of good manners to bring shame to their ancestors, family, and clan.

Born into a leading scholarly family, Ban was said to have taken over the compilation of the *History of the Former Han* after the deaths of her father and brother. According to one later history, she worked in the imperial libraries and supervised the writing of treatises on astronomy and the chronological tables of nobles. Recognizing Ban's erudition, the emperor appointed her as tutor to the women at court, and she later served as an advisor to Empress Deng, who became regent in 106 CE and remained in power for 15 years.

Well-educated, socially prominent, and politically influential, Ban Zhao was typical of aristocratic women in Han society. *Admonitions* is divided into seven chapters:

1. Humility
2. Husband and Wife
3. Respect and Caution
4. Womanly Qualifications
5. Whole-hearted Devotion
6. Implicit Obedience
7. Harmony with Younger Brothers- and Sisters-in-law.

Deferring to tradition, Ban describes three ritual customs performed at the birth of a girl and then explains the principles behind them. First, whereas a baby boy was placed on the bed, a girl was placed below it, to signify that she was lowly and weak and must humble herself before others; second, she was given potsherds (broken pieces of pottery) to play with because she must work hard; and third, her birth was announced to the ancestors to mark the importance of her future role in the veneration of ancestors.

Ban belongs in the Confucian lineage because she draws on the classical tradition, Mencius, and Dong Zhongshu. She believed that relationships are founded on the cosmic principles of yin and yang, and Heaven and Earth. Because yang is distinctive in its rigidity, a man was honoured for his strength; and because yin is characteristically yielding, a woman was considered beautiful for her gentleness. Over time, the name Ban Zhao became synonymous with womanly erudition. Some four hundred years after the Han, she was included in a list of exemplary women venerated in state sacrifices. And more than a millennium after her death, *Admonitions* was included in a collection called the Four Books for Women.

❧ INTERACTION AND ADAPTATION

Period of Disunion (220–589)

In 220 the Han fell and China entered a period of instability that was to last for almost four centuries. This was the Six Dynasties period, during which China experienced repeated invasions from the peoples of Central Asia. Confucianism lost the state support it had enjoyed under the Han and receded to the periphery, while those seeking personal well-being, political unity, and social harmony increasingly looked to Daoism and Buddhism instead.

Among the literati who turned to Daoist texts like the *Daodejing* and *Zhuangzi* were a group known as the Seven Sages of the Bamboo Grove (discussed later). Another prominent and precocious thinker of this period was Wang Bi, who wrote extensive commentaries not only on the *Laozi*, but on the *Analects* and *Changes* (a text revered by Daoists as well as Confucians). He was interested in the meaning and relevance of many issues discussed in Daoist texts, including being and nothingness, naturalness, the relationship of symbols and language to reality, and the nature of a sage. Above all, Wang emphasized principle (**li**).

This *li* (written differently in Chinese from the *li* meaning rites) traditionally referred to the pattern in natural materials like wood and stone, but Wang used it to refer to the order and processes found in the universe. Echoing the Han-era concern with the correspondences between human virtue and the ultimate nature of things, this notion of principle would be picked up by the Song Confucians and become a central idea in Neo-Confucianism. When asked why only Laozi talked about nothingness and Confucius seemed unwilling to speak about it, Wang answered:

> The Sage (Confucius) embodied nothing (*wu*), so he also knew that it could not be explained in words. Thus he did not talk about it. Master Lao, by contrast, operated on the level of being (*you*). This is why he constantly discussed nothingness; he had to, for what he said about it always fell short (R.J. Lynn in de Bary and Bloom 1999: 385).

Reflecting the syncretic ethos of the time, Wang saw Confucius in Daoist terms, as a sage who implicitly reflected Daoist principles.

Criticism of Buddhism

As Daoism and Confucianism drew closer together, both of them criticized Buddhism for its emphasis on ascetic detachment from emotions and desires and its rejection of the family and worldly service in favour of the monastic life. Chinese criticism focused on four aspects of the imported tradition: Buddhism's lack of authority, its unfilial practices, its social values, and its assumptions about the world, both material and spiritual (W.T. de Bary and L. Hurvitz in de Bary 1972: 125–38).

On the first point, Buddhism was perceived to lack authority because it did not originate in Chinese antiquity. If Buddhist teachings were important, why were they not mentioned in the Five Classics? There were also questions about Buddhist practices. To shave one's head, for instance, was construed as an act of gross disrespect, since it amounted to harming the body given by one's parents and ancestors. Leaving the family home to become an itinerant monk meant abandoning the duties of filial piety and ancestor veneration. And monastic celibacy struck at the heart of Confucianism, for to produce no offspring was the most unfilial act of all. As for social values, industrious Confucians interpreted Buddhist monks' ascetic withdrawal from productive work as a shirking of responsibility, and the tradition of begging for food as parasitism. Furthermore, the Buddhist renunciation of worldly pleasures went far beyond the Confucian ideal of moderation, effectively denying the value that Confucianism attributed to life in the world.

Finally, there was what seemed to be the extreme, even irrational nature of some Buddhist teachings. According to the *Disposition of Error*, Confucians were baffled by the Buddhist practice of reflecting on the impurity of the body:

> The ascetic engages in contemplation of himself and observes that all the noxious seepage of his internal body is impure. Hair, skin, skull and flesh; tears from the blinking of the eyes and spittle; veins, arteries, sinew and marrow; liver, lungs, intestines and stomach; feces, urine, mucus and blood: such a mass of filth when combined produces a man. . . . awakened to the detestability of the body, concentrating his mind, he gains *dhyana* (ibid., 129).

Then there were the Buddhist concepts of cause and effect (karma) and rebirth. While karma might find a parallel in the Confucian idea of the Mandate of Heaven, the idea that an ancestor might be reborn as a rat, or as his own grandchild, would have seemed preposterous to many Chinese. Even more troublesome was the idea that monastics who had transcended the dirty, polluted world did not pay obeisance to the emperor. Refusal to recognize the emperor as the apex of human society, the Son of Heaven, and the primary link between Heaven and Earth cut to the heart of the Confucian world view.

These conflicts notwithstanding, Buddhist ideas did attract Chinese followers, and as those ideas began to permeate Chinese society, different spheres were allocated to each religion. While Buddhism operated in the realm of the spirit, Confucianism continued to play an important role in family life despite its loss of official status and support. It survived over the next four hundred years not only through individual study of the Five Classics, the *Analects*, and the *Classic of Filiality*, but also in family handbooks offering practical advice on everyday matters; one famous example was entitled *Family Instructions of Mr Yan* (*Yanshi jiaxun*).

China Reunited (589–907)

In 589 China was reunited for the first time since the fall of the Han nearly four hundred years earlier, and in 618 the Tang came to power. Both Daoism and Buddhism were to reach new heights of popularity over the following centuries, but Confucianism also experienced an important revival. In the 600s the second Tang emperor, Taizhong, established an academy for scholar-officials where the curriculum was based on the classic Confucian texts, the students venerated Confucius alongside the Duke of Zhou, and—for the first time in Chinese history—it became possible for a commoner to work his way into officialdom. Taizhong also ordered all prefectures and districts to build Confucian temples for sacrifices to be performed by the literati. In 647 he installed in each temple 22 tablets commemorating orthodox Confucians of the Han era. A century later, in 739, the title 'King of Manifest Culture' was bestowed on Confucius, who now displaced the Duke of Zhou as the 'uncrowned king' of Chinese civilization.

One of the responsibilities of the Confucian officials was to oversee rituals. Four new types of worship that drew on earlier ritual systems were established at the royal clan temples during the Tang dynasty: honouring Earth (through the gods of the land and harvest), Heaven, Confucius, and imperial ancestors. Within a century the Confucian temples began to display carved images of honoured figures, similar to the images in Buddhist temples representing buddhas, enlightened beings, and Arhats. Among the figures so honoured were Confucius himself, Yan Hui (his favourite disciple, who died young), his 72 disciples, and 10 historical figures admired by Confucians and known as the 'Wise Ones'. These images remained in the temples for seven or eight hundred years, but—in an effort to differentiate Confucian temples from Buddhist ones—were eventually replaced by portraits.

In time, the Confucian curriculum for bureaucrats was expanded to include a total of 12 works, among them the *Analects* and the *Classic of Filiality*. The revival of interest in Confucian thought was reflected in three writers of particular interest to us here. Madame Zheng, author of the late seventh-century *Classic of Filiality for Women* (*Nu xiaojing*); **Han**

Ritual vessels and tablets on display at China's second-largest Confucius temple, in Jianshui, Yunnan (Alamy).

Yu (768–824), a prominent scholar-official intent on reintroducing Confucianism to the people; and Han's contemporary Song Ruozhao, the daughter of an official, who wrote the *Analects for Women* (*Nu lunyu*) in the early ninth century.

Madame Zheng and the Classic of Filiality for Women

The wife of a government official, Madame Zheng set out to create a female Confucian tradition starting from Ban Zhao. She emphasizes the importance of purity or chastity, filial piety, intelligence, and wisdom, so that women may guide their husbands by example. Zheng imagines Ban Zhao teaching a group of women acolytes that a wife should encourage her husband in good behaviour and guide him with 'modesty and deference, [so that] he will refrain from being contentious' (ibid., 826). Such a wife will use music and rites—in the broad sense that includes everything from formal courtesy in the household to religious ritual—to moderate his emotions, so that he will be pleasant and easy to get along with. When the women ask if they must obey their husbands' every command, Madame Zheng has Ban respond indignantly—'What kind of talk is that!' Then, echoing the original *Filiality*, Ban cites numerous historical examples of wives who corrected or criticized their husbands and explains:

> If a husband has a remonstrating wife, then he won't fall into evil ways. Therefore, if a husband transgresses against the Way, you must correct him. How could it be that to obey your husband in everything would make you a virtuous person? (ibid., 827)

Han Yu and the Critique of Buddhism and Daoism

Han Yu marks a point of renewal that is especially important in the history of Confucianism. He spoke for the tradition in a period when Daoism and Buddhism were flourishing, the former as the state religion and the latter as the religion of choice among both the elite and the masses. Although Confucian principles had been reintroduced into government, they had little popular currency. In an effort to bring Confucian teaching back to the centre of Chinese life after nearly six centuries on the periphery, Han Yu wrote *Essentials of the Moral Way* (*Yuandao lun*). In it he answers the question 'What is the teaching of the former kings?' as follows:

> To love largely is called a sense of humaneness; to act according to what should be done is called rightness. To proceed from these principles is called the moral Way; to be sufficient unto oneself without relying on externals is called inner power. . . . Its methods are the rites, music, chastisement, and government. Its classes of people are scholars, peasants, craftsmen, and merchants. . . . (C. Hartman in de Bary and Bloom 1999: 569)

Song Ruozhao and the Analects for Women

Analects for Women (*Nu lunyu*) is usually attributed to Song Ruozhao, though some say that her sister Ruohua actually wrote the text. Like Ban Zhao, Song came from a scholarly family. She was appointed to the court as scholar, and was assigned to teach the imperial princesses. Focusing on emotional restraint and self-cultivation as the basis for good familial relationships and efficient household management, her treatise consists of eight sections:

1. Establishing Oneself as a Person
2. Learning How to Work
3. Ritual Decorum: Learning Proper Etiquette
4. Rising Early to Begin Household Work
5. Serving One's Parents-in-Law
6. Serving a Husband
7. Instructing Sons and Daughters
8. Managing the Household.

Early Song Confucianism

Towards the end of the Tang, Daoist priests persuaded the Emperor Wuzong to put an end to the spread of Buddhism in China. In 845 he issued an edict summarizing the charges that defenders of China's indigenous social values laid against the foreign religion:

> . . . up through the Three Dynasties [Xia, Shang, and Zhou] the Buddha was never spoken of. It was only from the Han and Wei on that the religion of idols gradually came to prominence. So in this latter age it has transmitted its strange ways, instilling its infection with every opportunity, spreading like a luxuriant vine, until it has poisoned the customs of our nation. . . .
>
> Now if even one man fails to work the fields, someone must go hungry; if one woman does not tend her silkworms, someone will be cold. At present there are an inestimable number of monks and nuns in the empire, each of them waiting for the farmers to feed him and the silkworms to clothe him, while the public temples and private chapels have reached boundless number, all with soaring towers and elegant ornamentation sufficient to outshine the imperial palace itself . . . (B. Watson in de Bary and Bloom 1999: 585–6).

After the fall of the Tang, however, Daoism too was brought low. It was stripped of its status as the state religion, while the ongoing development of Confucianism culminated in the emergence of a new school known in the West as Neo-Confucianism. This development reached its apex with **Zhu Xi** (1130–1200), but much of his work drew on thinkers from the preceding century, among them Zhou Dunyi, Zhang Zai, and the brothers Cheng Yi and Hao, who studied with Zhou. Although the Neo-Confucians traced the roots of their philosophy to the ancient writings, much of their thinking reflected Buddhist and Daoist influences. Thus Zhou Dunyi advocated what he called 'quiet sitting'—a practice clearly modelled on Daoist and Buddhist meditation—and he based his most important work, 'An Explanation of the Diagram of the Great Ultimate', on a Daoist representation of the creation of the material world. With that work Confucianism took a definitive step away from its original humanism and towards a more metaphysical, recognizably religious orientation.

For Zhou, the Great Ultimate and the Ultimate Non-being are identical. Through movement, yang is generated from the Ultimate Non-being/Great Ultimate. When its limit

From Zhou Dunyi, 'An Explanation of the Diagram of the Great Ultimate'

The Ultimate of Non-being and also the Great Ultimate! The Great Ultimate through movement generates yang. When its activity reaches its limit, it becomes tranquil. Through tranquillity the Great Ultimate generates yin. When tranquillity reaches its limit, activity begins again. So movement and tranquillity alternate and become the root of each other, giving rise to the distinction of yin and yang, and the two modes are established (W.T. Chan in Sommer 1995: 185).

is reached, it becomes quiet and yin is generated. When yin reaches its limit, then activity, or yang, begins again. Thus the alternation between stillness and movement produces yin and yang, which in turn give rise to the five vital forces— fire, water, earth, metal, and wood—each of which has its own specific nature. When Ultimate Non-being interacts with the essences of yin-yang and the five elements, a mysterious union occurs, from which Heaven and Earth come into being.

Zhu Xi and the School of Principle

Working with this cosmology, the School of Principle (*Lixue*) explicitly linked *li*, the principles or patterns of nature, to human relationships and theories about education and government. Zhu Xi, considered the founder of this new school, synthesized the ideas of the early Song thinkers and gave Confucianism a metaphysical bent while drawing authority from classical Confucian writings.

Zhu focused on the nature, place, and function of self in the Great Ultimate. His thinking on this subject was not new. Like other Chinese philosophers, he understood human beings to be part of the fabric of the universe. Although he, like Zhou, was interested in Buddhist-style 'quiet sitting', Zhu was quintessentially Confucian in his emphasis on self-cultivation, social and political engagement, and the ancient *Book of Rites*. Zhu commented on 'Centrality and Equilibrium' and 'The Great Learning' (*Daxue*), another chapter from the *Rites*, in which

From 'The Great Learning' in the *Book of Rites*

Among the passages from 'The Great Learning' to which Zhu drew new attention was this one, which argues that proper self-cultivation begins with the acquisition of knowledge.

In antiquity, those who wanted to clarify their bright virtue throughout the entire realm first had to govern their states well. Those who wanted to govern their states well first had to manage their own families, and those who wanted to manage their families first had to develop their own selves. Those who wanted to develop themselves first rectified their own minds, and those who wanted to rectify their minds first made their thoughts sincere. Those who wanted to make their thoughts sincere first extended their knowledge. Those who wanted to extend their knowledge first had to investigate things (Sommer 1995: 39).

Zhu Xi on Human Nature

Following Zhou Dunyi, Zhu Xi believed human beings—like everything else in the universe—to be the product of the interaction between heavenly 'principle' and the material forces of yin-yang and the five elements. Thus human beings possessed both principle and material force. Like Mencius, Zhu Xi believed human nature to be the expression of heaven-given principle and therefore intrinsically good. Yet human action was not necessarily good. Zhu Xi attributed this apparent contradiction to the effects (or lack thereof) of material force on the three aspects of human personality: heavenly nature (i.e., principle), human feelings, and mind. Reflecting Zhou's cosmology, Zhu wrote that 'Nature is the state before activity begins and feelings are the state when activity has started, and the mind includes both of these states' (W.T. Chan in Sommer 1995: 192). Nature, being Heaven–given, is always good; but feelings can be good or bad, while the mind is the master and 'unites and apprehends both nature and the feelings, but it is not united with them' (ibid.). The mind brings nature and feelings together but remains a separate entity.

self-discipline or self-cultivation is the first link in a chain that extends from the individual through the family to the state and recalls the ideal of the Grand Commonality.

Confucianism into the Contemporary Era

Neo-Confucianism continued to thrive from the Song through to the Ming dynasty (1368–1644). When the Ming fell to the Qing—foreign invaders from Manchuria, beyond the Great Wall—the latter in turn would rely on the indigenous teaching to legitimate their rule over the Han Chinese.

The education of women received renewed attention during the Ming. Empress Xu, the wife of the third Ming emperor, wrote *Instructions for the Inner Quarters* (*Neixun*) under the inspirational influence of Empress Ma, her mother-in-law. The latter had often challenged her cruel, hot-tempered husband, believing it was her duty to serve as inner counsellor and Mother of the people. Empress Xu's *Instructions* reflects the same sense of a woman's broader responsibility. When a set of 'Four Books for Women' (*Nu sishu*) was compiled during the Ming, Empress Xu's work was one of them, along with Ban Zhao's *Admonitions*, Song Ruozhao's *Analects*, and Madame Zheng's *Filiality*.

Meanwhile, Neo-Confucianism continued to develop. Approximately three centuries after Zhu Xi's death, **Wang Yangming** (1472–1529) challenged his view that the process of self-cultivation must begin with studying the classical texts and learning about the outside world. He argued that the moral sense or intuition of the good is innate in the heart-mind of every human, and that cultivation of this internal conscience is more important than any external learning. Wang Yangming's school of thought became known as *Xinxue*, the School of the Heart-Mind.

The Qing Dynasty and the Need for Reform

In the mid-1600s, a Confucian scholar at the Qing court dared to question the traditional reliance on the virtue of the emperor, the son of Heaven, to ensure good governance.

Huang Zongxi argued for reform, including the introduction of constitutional law to constrain the absolute authority of the ruler. In his concern for the people, Huang echoed all Confucians, but especially Mencius, who wrote that 'The people are of supreme importance; the altars to the gods of earth and grain come next; last comes the ruler' (Lau 1970: 196). For ministers simply to counsel the emperor was not enough: they must be prepared to act against him when he acted against the interest of the people. In other words, ministers should take their role as agents of Heaven seriously, upholding or rescinding the Mandate of Heaven as circumstances required.

Huang's call for reform was rejected and the following century was one of prosperity and relative peace. In the late 1700s, however, the British began selling opium to the Chinese in an effort to balance their trade deficit with China. The consequences would be profound.

In 1838 the emperor appointed Lin Zexu to put an end to the opium trade. In addition to confiscating and destroying vast quantities of the drug, Lin composed an open letter of protest to Queen Victoria:

> The wealth of China is used to profit the barbarians [the British]. . . . By what right do they then in return use the poisonous drug [opium] to injure the Chinese people? Let us ask, where is your conscience? I have heard that the smoking of opium is very strictly forbidden by your country; that is because the harm caused by opium is clearly understood. Since it is not permitted to do harm to your own country, then even less should you let it be passed on to the harm of other countries—how much less to China! (S.Y. Teng and J. Fairbank in deBary and Lufrano 2000: 203).

A true Confucian, Lin framed his argument in moral terms: the fact that opium was outlawed in Britain made it all the more reprehensible for the British to sell it to the Chinese.

The British responded to this high-minded appeal with the first Opium War (1839–42; a second war would follow in 1856–60). The defeat of the hopelessly outgunned Chinese was a watershed in East Asian history, presaging the end of the dynastic system and ultimately leading to a profound reassessment of the traditional Confucian way of thinking. The final military nail in the coffin was Japan's victory in the Sino-Japanese War of 1894–5. The fact that Japan—a former vassal state—had been able not only to modernize itself along Western lines but to defeat China meant that radical reform was necessary. Some reformers urged the abandonment of all traditions; others argued that certain aspects of China's cultural heritage should be preserved. Among the latter was Kang Youwei (1858–1927), who believed that Japan's adoption of Shinto as its state religion had contributed to its modernization by reducing the stultifying influence of Buddhism and giving the country a strong national identity. But his argument that Confucianism could play a similar role for China went nowhere, and the ancient teaching continued to lose ground.

Post-dynastic China: The 'New Confucians'

Sun Yatsen, the founding father of modern republican China, found precedents for democracy in Confucian philosophers, specifically Mencius and the Neo-Confucian Cheng Yi. He identified three principles as fundamental to democracy—nationalism, citizen rights, and the welfare of human beings—and argued that they represented 'a completion of the development of . . . three thousand years of Chinese ideas about how to govern and maintain a peaceful world' (Bell and Hahm 2003: 9).

Sun Yatsen's insights notwithstanding, state Confucianism was disestablished following the fall of the Qing and the formation of the Chinese Republic in 1911. Over the next twenty years, the would-be modernizers of the New Culture Movement came to describe Confucianism as a teaching that 'cannibalizes' people. But scholar-teachers such as Fang Dongmei—a professor of Chinese philosophy who settled in Taiwan after the communist takeover of the mainland—encouraged the ongoing development of Confucianism in the diaspora. And in 1958 a group of 'New Confucians' based in Hong Kong responded to Western critics of China with an English-language 'Manifesto for a Reappraisal of Sinology and the Reconstruction of Chinese Culture'.

Following a discussion of what the West could learn from Eastern thought, the authors conclude with 'a few remarks' on the direction of the future 'intellectual development of China and of the world'. First, since 'The expansion of Western civilization has brought the peoples of the world into close contact and unfortunately has also produced much friction,' they call for the cultivation of 'an attitude of respect and sympathy toward other cultures'. Second, since 'scientific learning is inadequate' to that end, they call for 'a different kind of learning, one that treats [Man] as a conscious, existential being [and] applies understanding to conduct, by which one may transcend existence to attain spiritual enlightenment'.

Finally, in their third and last point, they suggest that the end product of that new learning would be 'a moral being that . . . can truly embrace God' (quoted by J. Berthrong in de Bary and Lufrano 2000: 559). Even though they clearly identified themselves with the Confucian tradition, the authors' use of the Christian term 'God' shows their willingness to adopt foreign concepts—not unlike those Confucians, centuries earlier, who integrated

Children at a private kindergarten in Wuhan, in the central province of Hubei, learn the Confucian classics (© ZHOU CHOA/epa/Corbis).

Daoist and Buddhist ideas into their thought. Their influence is evident in the work of contemporary scholars such as Du Weiming (Tu Weiming) of Harvard and John Berthrong of Boston University. It also inspired Lee Kuan Yew, the first President of Singapore, who tried (unsuccessfully) to encourage identification with the Confucian tradition following independence (1965).

🌿 CONTEMPORARY ISSUES

The first two generations of New Confucians wrote from the cultural margins—Hong Kong, Taiwan, Singapore, Boston—during the period when China was mired in poverty and political unrest and lagging substantially behind the West developmentally. Yet by the late 1970s—less than three decades after the formation of the People's Republic—it was clear that communism had failed to improve the conditions of life for the people. Thus in 1978 a process of economic and political reform began and a new constitution was adopted. Rapid industrial and economic growth followed: half a billion people were lifted out of poverty between 1981 and 2004, and by 2010 China had achieved exceptional economic stability. Despite (or because of) this remarkable success on the level of basic material security, some long-standing problems remained and some new ones surfaced: social alienation, ecological degradation, lack of spiritual direction, and continuing infractions of human rights.

Aspirations to prosperity were accompanied by wariness of full-scale Westernization. Confucian values—goodness, integrity, right action, and trustworthiness; love and respect for family and community; belief in the unity of human beings with the cosmos—were recommended by political and academic leaders as antidotes to the perceived poisons of market capitalism and liberalism. The cultivation of Confucian ideals became integral to China's efforts to combat corruption, promote ethical conduct, build strong familial and communal relationships, discourage rabid consumerism, and mitigate the effects of radical individualism.

The New Confucianism that developed in the diaspora gained state support and helped to neutralize international fears that rapid economic growth would propel China into superpower status. In 1984, just six years after the process of economic and political reform began, the state-supported China Confucius Foundation (CCF) was created with the explicit mandate to expand the influence of Confucianism both internally and internationally, through study and cultural exchanges. Ten years later, the International Confucian Association (ICA) was inaugurated with a mandate to study and advance Confucianism so as to promote freedom, equality, peaceful development, and prosperity around the world.

Designed to promote Chinese language and culture globally, the first Confucius Institute was established in Seoul, South Korea, in 2004. By 2007 there were close to 200 Institutes around the globe, supported by the Chinese government. The Confucius Institute/Classroom website offers a cyber-classroom with information on teaching materials, tests, teachers, and scholarships.

None of this activity is explicitly 'religious' in the Western sense. Yet the Chinese government's emphasis on education, both inside and outside China, clearly recalls the Confucian emphasis on self-cultivation as the key to moral development and a peaceful society. The contemporary need for stability and security, the failure of communism, the distrust of capitalism, and the ultimate goal of prosperity have in the twenty-first century given rise to a secular Confucianism with spiritual overtones.

🌿 Daoism

Introduction

Historically, Daoism was understood to have two branches, philosophical and religious. Daoist philosophy traced its origins to the third and fourth centuries BCE, but Daoist religion was not thought to have emerged until the second century CE, with the formation of two millenarian groups (the Celestial Masters and Yellow Kerchiefs). Only in recent decades has research revealed that philosophers at the Jixia Academy in the northeastern state of Qi were discussing ideas related to both philosophical and religious Daoism as early as the Warring States period, in the fourth century BCE.

The literature of that time does not use the term 'Daoist'. However, it does refer to a school of thought whose teachings correspond roughly to what we now consider philosophical Daoism. Named for the mythical 'Yellow Emperor' Huangdi and the legendary (historically dubious) philosopher Laozi, the Huang–Lao school came into being in the early fourth century, when King Xuan of Qi offered sinecures at the Jixia Academy to scholars from various states, north and south, in the hope that they would discuss the problems of the day and find solutions to them. Among those scholars were Mencius, Xunzi, the Naturalist Zou Yan, and a student of the Huang–Lao teachings named Huan Yuan.

Philosophical Daoism

The term 'Philosophical Daoism' refers to a prototypical early form of Daoism that was concerned with matters such as the nature of virtue, cultivation of the heart-mind, and attainment of good governance. Its early history has conventionally been associated with two main sources: the *Daodejing* (*Classic of the Way and Power*), a multi-layered, multi-authored verse text that is traditionally attributed to Laozi (the 'old master'); and the **Zhuangzi**, named for the thinker whose ideas it purports to represent. In fact, both works are collections of disparate texts written at different times by different authors.

This conventional view is changing, however. At least three new sources have proved helpful in reconstructing the early development of philosophical Daoism. Two of them are found in the *Guanzi*, a collection of writings traditionally attributed to a very early (seventh century BCE) figure named Guan Zhong, although it more likely originated during the fourth century and took its current form during the first century BCE. The *Guanzi* was categorized as Daoist during the Han era but was later reclassified as Legalist. For this reason it was neglected by students of Daoism, but recent research has found that two of its sections, both dealing with mental discipline, are directly relevant to them.

The first, *Techniques of the Mind I* (*Xinshu, Shang*), is written in verse but includes prose commentaries and addresses the broader concerns of government as well as methods of self-cultivation. The second, *Inward Training* (*Nei-yeh*), focuses exclusively on spiritual cultivation; it is written in verse and clearly bridges the streams of philosophical and religious Daoism.

The third new textual source for the study of classical Daoist development is a bundle of silk manuscripts, discovered in Hunan province in 1973, that contains the teachings of the Huang–Lao group. Including both verse and prose, the *Huang–Lao Silk Manuscripts* (*Huang–Lao boshu*) were also written and compiled over time. Our knowledge of classical Daoism in both its philosophical and religious aspects will undoubtedly improve as scholars continue to study these and other rediscovered texts.

Religious Daoism

Religious Daoism is widely associated with colourful rituals; belief in deities, ghosts, and spirits; and the pursuit of immortality or transcendence. Thus it may appear to be diametrically opposed to philosophical Daoism. Yet in fact the two streams do share a number of fundamental elements: the practice of self-discipline, the quest for transcendence of the ordinary self, the ideal of not-doing (**wuwei**), the assumption that religion and politics are embedded in one another.

What makes it difficult to recognize these common elements is the fact that religious Daoism also incorporates two traditions that are clearly not philosophical: a southern tradition of shamanism and a northern tradition known as the 'way of magic and immortality' (*fangxian dao*). Quite unlike the (northern) divinatory shamanism of the Shang and Zhou eras, this southern shamanism was distinctly non-philosophical and resolutely religious. Its character can be seen in a collection called *Songs of the South or Songs of Qu* (*Quchi*), which features lavish descriptions of gods and goddesses, 'serpentine cloud banners', 'soaring phoenixes', and fabulous unions between humans and gods. The northern 'way of magic and immortality', for its part, centred on a quest for an elixir of everlasting life conducted by such 'masters of technical methods' as magicians, doctors, diviners, geomancers, astrologists, and exorcists. The integration of these very different traditions only adds to the difficulty of understanding the early history of what came to be called religious Daoism.

Origins

Early Developments

The conjunction of the Daoist philosophical texts with the southern shamanistic tradition and the northern tradition of the masters of magic and immortality produced not just two but several distinctive streams in early Daoism. Three recurring elements have been identified in the classical texts: the concept of the Dao as the One, the primary force in the universe; the need for inner discipline to empty the heart-mind of distractions and reach the deep tranquillity that is necessary to experience unity with the One; and finally, the use of the first two elements to achieve benevolent government.

In light of these elements, it has been suggested that the concerns of the classical texts can be classified in three groups: Individualist, Primitivist, and Syncretist. The Individualist stream is mystical, concerned mainly with inner cultivation and the experience of union with the cosmos; it is basic to all six of the classical texts. The second stream takes the basic Individualist perspective and adds an appeal for a simple agrarian way of life. This Primitivist stream can be seen in the *Daodejing* as well as in several chapters of the *Zhuangzi* (8–10 and the first part of 11). The third and last stream combines teachings of Laozi and Zhuangzi with those of other schools and is found in the later chapters of the *Zhuangzi, Techniques of the Mind I*, and the *Huang–Lao* manuscripts. This Syncretist stream appears to have developed some time after the first two, likely during the early Han.

The exact chronology of the various writings is not known, but the *Daodejing* and *Inward Training* are generally considered to be the earliest. Anecdotes in the *Zhuangzi* that describe encounters between Confucius and Laozi would make the two men contemporaries, although the historical authenticity of the stories is questionable. The first seven chapters of the *Zhuangzi*, if they were in fact composed by Zhuang Zhou (known as Zhuangzi; 369?–286? BCE) are also of some antiquity.

Finally, the *Songs of the South* are traditionally attributed in part to Qu Yuan, the famously righteous minister remembered in the Dragon Boat festival, but most of them were probably written about a century after his death in 278 BCE. Thus the poems are likely of a slightly later period than the other texts. Brief descriptions of the six sources follow.

Inward Training *in Daoist and Confucian Contexts*

This short text is embedded in the *Guanzi*, a miscellany that was until recently neglected in the study of classical Chinese religions. It is important for us because it serves as a bridge between philosophical and religious Daoism and provides clear examples of the cultural beliefs and practices from the Zhou era that Confucians and Daoists shared.

Inward Training deals with the cultivation of the heart-mind. The focus on self-cultivation, as we noted at the start of this chapter, is common to all three of China's elite religious traditions. The theme of inner cultivation is evident in the Dacist emphasis on a type of meditation known as 'holding fast to the One', which can be found in the *Daodejing, Zhuangzi, Techniques of the Mind I*, and *Huang–Lao* sources. Other themes from *Inward Training*, however—notably the concepts of the vital essence (*jing*), vital energy or breath (*qi*), and the numinous or the spirit (*shen*)—are uncommon in the philosophical texts. Yet they became core features of religious Daoism, in which the integration of these three elements through meditation and dietary practices was believed to confer longevity and even physical immortality or spiritual transcendence.

Inward Training recalls early Confucianism when it suggests that the virtue of an exemplary person has a kind of magical, mystical efficacy. The emperor in particular was believed to be capable of 'righting' conditions in the empire without expending any vital energy, simply by virtue of the harmony that he has attained. Section 9 uses the same terms that the Confucians do to describe the noble or exemplary person (*junzi*) who cultivates this power-virtue (*de*):

> Only exemplary persons who hold fast to the One are able to do this.
> Hold fast to the One; do not lose it,
> And you will be able to master the myriad things.
> Exemplary persons act upon things,
> And are not acted upon by them,
> Because they grasp the guiding principle of the One (ibid., 62).

Like the ideal Confucian ruler, the ideal Daoist possesses a virtue-power that is capable of influencing lesser persons just as the wind causes the grass to bend.

Whereas Laozi and Zhuangzi suggest some antipathy towards Confucians, *Inward Training* does not. In fact, it hints at a shared desire for tranquillity and recovery of the individual's original or Heavenly nature. Later forms of Daoism, however, did include beliefs and practices that some later Confucians found abhorrent: for example, the use of esoteric sexual practices in religious ritual, the ingestion of cinnabar (a poisonous substance) to attain immortality, and the practice of mental discipline with the goal of escaping or transcending this mundane world.

Laozi and the *Daodejing*

If the apparent incongruity of such practices seems puzzling, it may be helpful to remember the famous first line of the *Daodejing*: 'The way that can be spoken is not the constant Way.' The dynamism and fluidity implied by this holy ineffability are characteristic of Daoism.

Unlike the authors (or editors) of *Inward Training*, Laozi takes a dim view of Confucian rites: 'The rites are the wearing thin of loyalty and good faith / And the beginning of disorder' (Lau 1963: 99). Yet, like the Confucians, he wants to ensure that 'the offering of sacrifice by descendants will never come to an end' (ibid., 115). The sage of the *Daodejing* shares with Confucius the ideal of discipline: the only difference is that he seeks to achieve it not through human-created rites but through the all-embracing cosmic Way.

The term *de* in the *Daodejing* refers to virtue-power, but this is no ordinary virtue. It embodies the mystic inner power attained through integrity and alignment with the unseen world, the power that allows a sage ruler to infuse his realm with the harmony he has achieved by 'doing nothing'. It's important not to take this phrase literally: in this context, 'doing nothing', or *wuwei*, refers to a state of mind or being in which one can be so permeated by the Way that one acts in concert with it, free of self, intention, or ulterior motives.

The Daoist sage models himself on the Dao, inviting it to dwell in him by making himself as empty as the hub of a wheel, the hollow of a cup, or the space in a room. Soft as the water that flows over and around rocks yet in time wears them down, and that occupies ravines and valleys, benefiting all things, he is spare in his desires. Overturning convention, he knows the honoured male but keeps to the traditionally subservient and humble female. He knows the symbolic goodness of white but keeps to the 'hoodwinking', unenlightened black (ibid., 127). He embraces the One and remains an uncarved block, transcending dichotomies. He refuses to be sculpted with conventional virtues—though Laozi makes it clear that he also teaches conventional values:

> What others teach I also teach.
> 'The violent will not come to a natural end.'
> I shall take this as my precept
>   (Lau 1963: 103).

Yet even as the *Daodejing* counsels against violence—just as the Confucian sages did in their time—it criticizes as 'false adornments' the Confucian concepts of the wise sage and righteous benevolence. It also finds fault with profit, ingenuity, and learning, declaring that they should be abolished. Simplicity, the Daoist sage suggests, should replace false values:

> These three [the Confucian sage, benevolence, and ingenuity], being false adorn-
> ments, are not enough
> And the people must have something to which they can attach themselves:
> Exhibit the unadorned and embrace the uncarved block,
> Have little thought of self and as few desires as possible (Lau 1963: 75).

Unlike the Confucian who deals mainly with the good and virtuous, the Daoist sage 'abandons no one' (ibid., 84). He is said to have three treasures: compassion, frugality, and 'not daring to take the lead in the empire' (ibid., 129). He is 'drowsy', 'muddled', 'foolish', and 'uncouth' (ibid., 77). He is inconspicuous and does not consider his own way to be the right one; he does not brag, boast, or contend with others (ibid., 79). He is self-effacing and 'avoids excess, extravagance, and arrogance' (ibid., 87). Such a sage is capable of surviving even the tumult of the Warring States.

Zhuangzi

The current working copy of the *Zhuangzi* comes from an edition by Guo Xiang (d. c. 312 CE). Unlike the sage of the *Daodejing*, the sage of the *Zhuangzi* shuns politics. Even more strikingly, in the *Zhuangzi* great sages, mythical rulers, and deities are not the only ones endowed with wisdom: a humble cook may also be wise. The fanciful and the historical exist side by side like black and white, or female and male.

The aspiration to transcend dichotomies can also be found in Zhuangzi:

> Everything has its 'that', everything has its 'this'. From the point of view of 'that' you cannot see it, but through understanding you can know it. . . . [The sage] illuminates all in the light of Heaven. He too recognizes a 'this', but a 'this' which is also 'that', a 'that' which is also 'this'. His 'that' has both a right and a wrong in it; his 'this' too has both a right and a wrong in it (Watson 1968: 39).

The sage allows his mind to wander in simplicity, blending with the vastness that is the Way. He follows things as they are and makes no room for personal views. In contrast to Laozi, with his 'doing nothing', Zhuangzi describes a state of 'self-so-ness' or spontaneity. Although the principle is not inconsistent with the Confucians' ideal of following the pattern in nature, it is expressed in remarkably different terms. The story of Cook Ding illustrates the Daoist position: when the prince asks the cook for advice on governing his empire, Ding counsels him to take the same approach to governance that he would to carving an ox. Instead of simply hacking at the animal, he would look for the hollows of the joints: in the same way, the ruler should not govern on the basis of preconceived rules and principles, but should examine the empire to determine where the hollows are.

The state in which it is possible to make a clear assessment, whether of an ox or an empire, is that of Oneness through emptiness (*xu*). In *Inward Training*, this empti-ness is achieved by using the body to discipline the heart-mind. Here Zhuangzi adds an unexpected non-sectarian, perhaps cheeky, twist, setting Confucius up with his favourite disciple, Yan Hui. When the latter asks about the meaning of fasting, Confucius replies:

> Make your will one! Don't listen with your ears, listen with your mind. No, don't listen with your mind, but listen with your spirit. Listening stops with the ears, the mind stops with recognition, but spirit is empty and waits on all things. The Way gathers in emptiness alone. Emptiness is the fasting of the mind (ibid., 57–8).

In his attention to the spirit, the sage in *Zhuangzi* takes an approach more reminiscent of *Inward Training* than of the practically focused Confucius and Laozi. This other-worldly orientation is confirmed in the image of the Holy Man who lives on Gushe Mountain, far away from human society. This is the sage as spiritual and cosmic healer. The themes of health, long life, and immortality are introduced in the *Zhuangzi* through reference to the mythical Yellow Emperor, who does not appear in either *Inward Training or the Daodejing*. This sage-emperor is the putative author of the medical text *Inner Canon of the Yellow Emperor* (*Huangdi neijing*).

Women and the Feminine in the Classical Texts

The subject of women is not addressed in either *Inward Training* or the *Daodejing*, although the latter does talk abstractly about the 'mother' and the 'spirit of the valley', which it describes as both the 'root of heaven and earth' and the 'mysterious female' that never dies (Lau 1963: 62). Nor does Zhuangzi concern himself much with women. Wives are mentioned only in passing as companions in life who are then grieved in death. The yin-yang dichotomy seems to have been generally accepted and was clearly reflected in the division of labour and social roles. Women are seen as weavers, working in the domestic realm, while men are farmers, working outside the home.

'This' and 'that'—representing subject and object, self and other—were also applied to the realm of the conventional and unconventional in the relations between women and

---

From the *Zhuangzi*

One chapter attributed to Zhuangzi is entitled 'Fit for Emperors and Kings'. It concludes with a little story about the damage that the imposition of sameness and conformity, even with the best intentions, can do.

The emperor of the South Sea was called Shu [Brief], the emperor of the North sea was called Hu [Sudden], and the emperor of the central region was called Hun-tun [Chaos]. Shu and Hu from time to time came together for a meeting in the territory of Hun-tun, and Hun-tun treated them very generously. Shu and Hu discussed how they could repay his kindness. 'All men,' they said, 'have seven openings so they can see, hear, eat, and breathe. But Hun-tun alone doesn't have any. Let's try boring him some!'

Every day they bored another hole, and on the seventh day Hun-tun died (Watson 1968: 97).

men. The Daoist Liezi is described as taking over the domestic realm of the feminine after he attains mature spiritual understanding:

> He went home and for three years did not go out. He replaced his wife at the stove, fed the pigs as though he were feeding people, and showed no preferences in the things he did. He got rid of the carving and polishing and returned to plainness, letting his body stand alone like a clod. In the midst of entanglement he remained sealed, and in this oneness he ended his life. (Watson 1968: 97)

This association of sacred oneness with animals and the feminine is not surprising. Nor is Zhuangzi's implied criticism of Confucian-style 'carving and polishing', given the Daoist preference for non-action and the natural. The theme of men seeking union with the feminine, and women with the masculine, becomes prominent in the poems of the south. Images of female power and divinity in themselves—without reference to men—appear only in the chapter entitled 'The Great and Venerable Teacher', which mentions a teacher called the Woman Crookback and a Queen Mother of the West who heads the pantheon of goddesses. These are mythical characters, however: unlike the Confucian classics, the *Zhuangzi* does not celebrate any historical woman.

The Songs of the South, Huang–Lao Silk Manuscripts, *and* Techniques of the Mind I

The *Songs of the South*, *Techniques of the Mind I*, and *Huang–Lao Silk Manuscripts* were likely compiled through the late Zhou, Qin, and early Han periods (between the fourth century BCE and the second century CE). The last two are syncretic and similar to the *Daodejing* and *Zhuangzi* in various ways, but the *Songs* are distinctive in their literary quality and their descriptions of love between deities and humans.

The *Huang–Lao Silk Manuscripts* were sealed in a tomb in 168 BCE. The ideas they record are drawn from a variety of schools, but their underlying theme is said to be Laozi's ideal of the tranquil sage king who governs through non-action. Like Dong Zhongshu and the New Text Confucians, the Huang–Lao Daoist scholars believed in the triad of Heaven, Earth, and humanity. They went further than the Confucians, imagining that the macrocosm of the universe was reflected in the microcosm of human society or even the individual human body, and discerning correspondences between Heaven, Earth, and human beings. They were active at court during the first 60 years of the Han dynasty (second century BCE), but seem to have disappeared after Emperor Wu made Confucianism the state religion. Until these manuscripts were excavated in 1973, none of the writings they contain were known.

Like the Huang–Lao teachings, *Techniques of the Mind I* reflects the Daoist concerns outlined in *Inward Training*, the *Daodejing*, and the **Zhuangzi**. Echoing the *Daodejing*, it seeks to explain how self-cultivation—specifically, the practice of restraining desire and emptying the mind—can help an enlightened ruler attain the tranquillity necessary to respond harmoniously to any situation in its 'self-so-ness'. The text has two parts: one written in verse and tentatively dated to the mid-200s BCE and the other a line-by-line prose commentary dated to 180 BCE.

Crystallization

Han Dynasty Daoism and Confucianism

Huang–Lao thinkers were influential at the early Han court. In 139 BCE Liu An, King of Huainan, presented to Emperor Wu (his nephew) a copy of the *Huainanzi*—a collection of 21 essays on topics ranging from cosmology and astrology to inner cultivation and political thought. A comprehensive guide to just and effective governance, it emphasizes the ruler's need to still his passions and rid himself of prejudice so that he can respond appropriately to all situations.

The essays are generally believed to have been composed by Daoist adepts and scholars under the direction of Liu An, although some historians have suggested that they were actually Huang–Lao texts and were presented to the emperor in an effort to thwart the rise of Confucianism. In any event, the account of Daoism in the discourse 'On the Six Lineages of Thought', by the court historian Sima Tan (d. 110 BCE), corresponds closely to the contents of the *Huainanzi*.

Sima, a follower of the Huang–Lao school, describes the Daoists approvingly as 'permit[ting] the numinous essence within people to be concentrated and unified', 'mov[ing] in unison with the Formless and provid[ing] adequately for all living things' (H. Roth and S. Queen in de Bary and Bloom 1999: 279). By contrast, he describes the ascendant New Text Confucians as 'erudite yet lack[ing] the essentials. They labour much yet achieve little. This is why their doctrines are difficult to follow completely' (ibid.). In short, Sima Tan distanced himself from purposeful 'right' action and made clear his preference for the Daoists in his 'On the Six Lineages':

> The essentials of the Great Way are simply a matter of discarding strength and avarice and casting aside perception and intellect. One relinquishes these and relies on the techniques [of self-cultivation]. When the numen (*shen*, 'spirit') is used excessively it becomes depleted; when the physical form labours excessively it becomes worn out. It is unheard of for one whose physical form and numen are agitated and disturbed to hope to attain the longevity of Heaven and Earth (H. Roth and S. Queen in de Bary and Bloom 1999: 279–80).

The concern for health and longevity in this account is typical of Daoism. And while Confucians would agree on the importance of renouncing avarice, they would argue in favour of strength (especially for men), perception, and intellect. Thus even though Daoists and Confucians alike talk about the universal Way and the welfare of others, their approaches to self-cultivation are quite different. The fact that the Confucians focus on ritual performance in the social and political realms while the Daoists focus on the fasting of the mind in the personal realm clearly reflects their contrasting priorities and visions of the world.

Nevertheless, underlying both traditions is a fundamental emphasis on self-cultivation for the sake of harmony in the universe. Both Confucians and Daoists seek to control the heart-mind, especially the passions, in order to attain the tranquillity necessary to achieve union with the Way. Both believe that oneness with the Way and, consequently, with Heaven and Earth allows us to transcend our ordinary selves in order that we may serve others. Universal harmony is the ideal for Confucians and Daoists alike, and both believe that it is the role of human beings to mediate between Heaven and Earth.

Beliefs, Meditation and Worship

Daoist practice continued to develop through the Han. The goal of Daoist meditation, according to the classical texts, was to return vital essence, vital energy, and the numinous spirit to the wholeness in which they existed before they were broken and scattered by worldly activity and the disruptive awareness of things as divided and separate from each other. Practitioners seek to return to the Dao by reversing those processes—as if they were sculptures 'unsculpting' themselves to recover their original unity and become once again the blocks from which they were carved. Devotees seek to move from form to essence, from essence to vitality or vital energy, from vitality to spirit, and from spirit to emptiness or the Void.

This ultimate Void is formless, but it can be visualized as the highest deity: the Great One, Supreme Unity, or Supreme Oneness (Taiyi). Classical texts suggest various ways of achieving (or maintaining) this original unity: by 'holding fast to the One' (shouyi); 'sitting and forgetting'; visualizing the cosmos within one's body; and following the internal circulation of vital energy. During the Han, it was thought that a long period of inward concentration would lead to the formation of an embryo containing or representing the True Self, which could develop into an immortal. Harking back to **Inward Training**, this True Self was said to be born when the spirit has been purified, united with and indistinguishable from vital energy and essence. This Self was referred to by various names: the Spirit Embryo, Holy Embryo, Golden Embryo, Golden Elixir, the True Person Cinnabar of the North, the Golden Pill, the Pearl.

The Celestial Masters and Yellow Kerchiefs

Over time, the Confucian underpinnings of the Han regime were challenged by a combination of political corruption, natural disaster, and military turbulence. The resulting economic and social turmoil provoked uprisings across the empire, some of which reflected a significant Daoist influence. At the same time, a text (now lost) called the *Classic of the Great Peace* (*Taipingjing*) was circulating that prophesied the coming of a celestial master who would bring peace to a time of surging chaos.

The Great Peace likely influenced both of the millenarian movements that in the past were believed to represent the beginning of religious Daoism: the Celestial Masters and the Yellow Kerchiefs (*Taiping Dao*, 'Way of Taiping'). Founded in 142 CE, the Celestial Masters (later renamed Orthodox Unity) sect traced its origins to a deified Laozi who was said to have appeared to **Zhang Daoling**, revealed the teachings of Orthodox Unity, and given him a covenant establishing a new relationship between the gods and humans. A central feature of this covenant was the abolition of the traditional blood sacrifice. No longer would the gods be influenced by animal offerings. Instead, they would come to operate as a kind of celestial bureaucracy to whom believers could present their appeals just as they did to state bureaucrats in ordinary life. Priests were expected to provide their services without monetary reward; for subsistence they relied on the devotees, who were required to donate five bushels of rice each year (for this reason the group is sometimes referred to as Five Bushels of Rice).

Initiates of the Celestial Masters gained access to esoteric sacred texts. Practices included chanting and meditation, and the *Daodejing* was used in liturgy. Purity chambers were provided for the cultivation of the Spirit Embryo. Talismans drawn on paper and offered to the gods and goddesses served as contracts with the deities, guaranteeing the faithful their protection. The sect established a theocracy in the state of Shu (in what is now Sichuan) and eventually became the state religion of the Wei kingdom. The Wei later dispersed the Celestial Masters across northern China, unintentionally aiding the spread of Daoism.

The Yellow Kerchiefs movement, based in Shandong in northeastern China, was established by three brothers named Zhang (Jue, Liang, and Bao) with the express purpose of challenging the Han regime in the name of the Yellow Emperor. They wore yellow kerchiefs (or 'turbans'—a common mistranslation) because, according to calculations based on the Naturalist yin-yang–five phases system, a new dynasty associated with the colour yellow and the element earth would overthrow the Han (associated with blue, green, and wood). Like the Celestial Masters, the Yellow Kerchiefs practised confession, repentance of sins, meditation, and chanting, they also believed in inherited guilt, passed on from ancestors to descendants. They attracted a massive following, but their success was short-lived. When the Yellow Kerchiefs rose in rebellion in the year 184 (the beginning of a new 60-year cycle in the Chinese calendar), they were crushed and the movement disappeared.

Differentiation

Six Dynasties Period (220–589)

In 220, as we have seen, northern China fell to the first in a series of invasions from Central Asia. Amid the chaos of this era, state Confucianism lost its central place as the state religion, Buddhism gained a foothold, and Daoism took a variety of directions.

Cultivation of stillness remained a focal point, as did the quest for transcendence. But that quest took two distinctly different forms. For some practitioners it meant the pursuit of spiritual transcendence through meditation; for others it meant the pursuit of physical immortality through the ingestion of substances such as cinnabar (mercuric sulphide).

Meanwhile, the influence of Buddhism led Daoists to begin reinterpreting their doctrine in terms of karma and rebirth (*samsara*), designing community rituals to ameliorate the prospects for the next rebirth, and moving towards the establishment of formal institutions: the first Daoist temple would be constructed in the fifth century. Daoist leaders remained active politically, but others began to turn inward, focusing more on individual cultivation.

Among the latter were the Seven Sages of the Bamboo Grove who gathered in the third century after the fall of the Han. Inspired by Zhuangzi's notions of spontaneity, spiritual freedom, and non-attachment to convention, they gained a reputation for eccentric behaviour (one of them was said to roam around naked in his hermitage). Having fled the turmoil of northern China for the south, the Seven Sages engaged in 'pure' or 'light conversation' on metaphysical rather than political topics and (as we have seen) reflected Confucian and Buddhist as well as Daoist influences.

It was likely sometime in the 300s that the *Liezi*—the third most important Daoist 'philosophical' text, after the *Daodejing* and *Zhuangzi*—was compiled, bringing together stories about one of the Daoist thinkers mentioned in the *Zhuangzi*. A less important but still

From the chapter 'Nourishing Life', in Ge Hong's *Baopu zi*

In a chapter entitled 'Nourishing Life', Ge Hong highlights what he sees as the main reason for failure to achieve one's aim in the study of the Dao: inflexible preference for one type of practice. He lists a variety of physical disciplines aimed at everything from preventing aging to achieving transcendence and suggests that adepts of any single approach have a tendency to become too attached to it.

. . . the danger is that those who devote themselves to one of these practices trust only their discipline of choice. Those who know the arts of the Mysterious Woman and the Pure Woman say that one can transcend the world only through the arts of the bedchamber. Those who are expert in breathing say that one can extend the number of years only through circulation of breath. Those who know the methods for bending and stretching [the body] say that one can avoid aging only through *daoyin* [sometimes translated as 'Daoist yoga']. Those who know the methods based on herbs and plants say that one can surpass any limit only through medicines and pills. When the study of the Dao does not bear fruit, it is because of biases like these (*Baopu zi* in Pregadio 2006:134–5).

informative text, probably written in the 320s, was Ge Hong's *Baopu zi* ('The master who embraces spontaneous nature'): a collection of essays on classic Daoist themes, including methods of driving away harmful spirits, reaching the gods, and gaining immortality.

Two new Daoist schools emerged in the latter part of the same century. The Highest Clarity (Shangqing) school was formed by a medium and shaman named Yang Xi, who claimed to have received scriptures from the immortal Lady Wei of the Heaven of Highest Clarity. Yang and his followers sought to become 'true beings', transcendents or 'perfected persons' through practices that included the use of external alchemy to facilitate flights of ecstasy to the star deities who controlled human destiny. Highest Clarity devotees ate very little, believing that fasting would make their bodies light and radiant in their ascent to the heavens.

The second new school, Numinous Treasure, was founded a few decades later by a grandnephew of Ge Hong. Ge Chaofu claimed to have received from his clan ancestors a series of revelations involving the Buddhist concepts of karma, rebirth, and *kalpa* (cycles of time). Whereas the focus in the Highest Clarity sect was on the individual, followers of the Numinous Treasure looked outward to the community and beyond, to all of humanity, suggesting a synthesis of Daoist and Buddhist ideas.

One of this sect's texts, the *Scripture for the Salvation of Humanity* (*Durenjing*), describes a great cosmic deity who is so concerned for the salvation of human beings that he sends an emissary from the Dao itself to reveal the teaching. This emissary serves a function similar to that of Amitabha, the Buddha of the Pure Land. Numinous Treasure focused especially on two kinds of ritual: purification (*zhai*) and communal renewal (*jiao*). These two categories continue to define the broad aims of Daoist practice today.

The goals of the purification rituals were typical of this era: preventing disease, warding off natural calamities, and ensuring the salvation of ancestors. They were performed around a temporary altar and started with a cleansing of the body through bathing and fasting and purification of the heart-mind through the confession of sins. Then a communal feast was held to celebrate the reinstatement of harmony between the gods and human beings. In community renewal rituals still practised today, deities were invited down into the altar, incense was offered, and the faithful who sponsored the rituals were granted audiences with the gods, during which they would request favours for their communities.

Creating a Canon

The first effort to establish a Daoist canon dates to the fifth century, when Lu Xiujing organized the existing texts into groups known as the 'Three Caverns' (paralleling the 'Three Baskets' of Theravada Buddhism). The Caverns of Perfection and Mystery held the writings of the Highest Clarity and Numinous Treasure sects respectively, while the Cavern of Spirit held images of talismans and explanations of their functions. Writings of the Celestial Masters were gathered in supplements, and three more supplements were eventually created, one each for the *Daodejing*, the *Scripture of Great Peace*, and writings from a Han-era alchemical tradition called Great Purity (*Taiqing*), which is no longer extant. A few years later Yang Xi's revelations were collected and edited by Tao Hongjing under the title *Pronouncements of the Perfected* (*Zhen Gao*; c. 500).

Meanwhile, the practice of meditation continued. The sixth-century *Secret Instructions of the Holy Lord on the Scripture of Great Peace* harked back to the teachings of the *Inward Training* and taught that to 'pursue long life you must love energy, venerate spirit, and value essence'. By 'holding fast to the One', practitioners of meditation could 'go beyond the world and ascend to heaven!' (Kohn in Sommer 1995: 147).

Interaction and Adaptation

The Tang Dynasty (618–907)

The founder of the Tang dynasty, Li Yuan, claimed descent from Laozi, and under his family's rule Daoism once again became the state religion. Some Highest Clarity patriarchs held government posts; others were invited to the capital, Chang'an (now known as Xi'an), to attend the emperors. One of the most famous patriarchs of the period, Sima Chengzhen (647–735), emphasized the personal practice of inner alchemy, meditation, and longevity techniques in two essays, 'On the Essential Meaning of the Absorption of Energy' (*Fuqi jingyi lun*) and 'On Sitting in Oblivion' (*Zuowang lun*).

In the eighth century the 'Brilliant Emperor' Xuanzhong wrote a commentary on the *Daodejing* and invited the Highest Clarity patriarch Sima Chengzen to court; princesses were ordained Daoist priestesses, performing state rituals for the protection of the empire; colleges of Daoism were established; and the *Daodejing* was briefly included in state examinations. By 739 there were 1,137 abbeys for male Daoists and 550 for women. In fact, classical Daoism reached the height of its power and popularity during the Tang, but it did not undergo any substantial new development.

From the Song Era (960–1279) to the Present

Daoism, like the other religions, experienced great changes during the Song dynasty. Confucianism reasserted itself at the state level and the Meditation (Chan) and Pure Land (Jingtu) Buddhist schools continued to thrive among all social classes. Daoism acculturated to this political and spiritual ethos under Wang Chongyang, who formally integrated Confucian and Buddhist teachings, focused less on supernatural elements, and instituted monasticism for the first time.

Complete Truth School

The school of Complete Truth (*Quanzhen*; also translated as Perfect Realization, Perfect Truth, or Complete Perfection), like Orthodox Unity, is still active today and is distinctive in its monasticism. It is associated with the White Cloud Abbey in Beijing, whose twelfth-century founder, Wang Chongyang, taught a more down-to-earth understanding of transcendence or immortality:

> Leaving the world does not mean that the body departs. . . . When you realize the Tao, your body will be in the sphere of the ordinary, but your mind will be in the realm of the sages. Nowadays, people want to avoid death forever and at the same time leave the ordinary world. They are very foolish, indeed, and have not even glimpsed the true principle of the Tao (Kirkland 2004: 188).

In addition to discouraging supernatural expectations, Wang urged his disciples to read across all three of the major traditions: the Confucian *Classic of Filiality* and the Mahayana Buddhist *Heart Sutra* (*Xinjing*) as well as the *Daodejing*. His 'Fifteen Precepts for Establishing the Teaching' includes practical recommendations alongside more elevated principles. For example, he advises that to achieve the ideal of harmony in spirit and vital energy, the body must be well rested. He also recommends the use of herbs for healing, living a simple life, and maintaining good Daoist friends. The 'basic motif of the art of self-cultivation', he wrote, is the 'search for the hidden meaning of Nature and mind' (Sommer 1995: 202).

Women

Where Confucians have Ban Zhao, the Daoists have Sun Buer (1119–83). The wife of Wang Chongyang's disciple Ma Danyang, she became the only woman among Wang's 'Seven Perfected' disciples. The following story is likely apocryphal, but it highlights the difficulties that women of her time faced in their search for enlightenment.

One day Sun heard Wang say that an immortal was expected to emerge in the city of Loyang, far from her home in Shandong. She told Wang that she wished to go and cultivate transcendence there, but he withheld permission, telling her that her beauty would arouse men's desire, that she would be molested, and that the shame would kill her.

Undeterred, Sun went to her kitchen and asked the servants to leave her alone. Then she heated some oil, poured cold water into it, and stood over the wok as the boiling oil spattered over her face. When Wang saw her scars, he recognized her sincerity and agreed to teach her the methods of inner alchemy, but he advised her to hide her knowledge even from her husband. To ensure that she would be left alone, Sun pretended to be insane. When her husband told Wang, the latter replied that she could not otherwise become an immortal. Eventually, Sun slipped out of the house and travelled to Loyang, where she continued to behave like a madwoman. Most of the townspeople left her alone, but—as Wang had anticipated—she was finally accosted by two men. When a rain of enormous hailstones allowed her to evade them, the men recognized her special nature and told the tale of her escape. Left in peace for twelve years, Sun attained her goal and became the only female master among the famed seven masters of the Complete Truth school.

Revival of Orthodox Unity

Daoism continued to thrive until the twelfth century, when Kublai Khan, the Mongolian ruler, extended his rule to the south. There he consolidated his control over religious life by giving exclusive authority to the Orthodox Unity sect, renamed (c. 400) for the revelations given to the Celestial Masters, which had survived through the dominance of Highest Clarity and Numinous Treasure. After the Mongols were overthrown, Orthodox Unity retained its position of authority, and its leader was entrusted with the compilation of the Daoist canon (*Daozang*), which was printed in 1445.

Stress and Recovery

Even as Neo-Confucianism became entrenched during the Qing dynasty (1644–1911), Daoism continued to inspire popular morality books and a variety of practices from meditation to **qigong** (breath exercises that help the movement of vital energy through the body) and **taiji** (the slow-motion movements known in the West as Tai Chi). It suffered enormous setbacks, however, in the period that followed the Opium Wars, when Western-inspired reformers began to attack traditional beliefs and practices.

Advocates of change or modernization, from the Christian-inspired Heavenly Kingdom of Great Peace (Taiping) movement to the Chinese Communist party, were particularly critical of Daoism, which they perceived as superstitious and hostile to progress. The deadliest period was the time of the Cultural Revolution (1966–76), during which temples and shrines of all traditions—folk, Daoist, Confucian, Buddhist—were attacked and sometimes destroyed. Daoism is now reestablishing itself in China and spreading around the world. It is especially popular in Europe and North America, where both its philosophical teachings promoting balance and simplicity and its physical practices promoting health and longevity are increasingly valued.

Contemporary Issues

Daoism has been popular in the West in a way that Confucianism has not. The *Daodejing* is one of the most translated books in the world. Daoist teachings were integral to the counterculture movement of the 1960s, and many young Westerners continue to cherish Daoist values.

The 'Eight Immortals' of Daoism; a sculpture on display in Singapore as part of New Year's celebrations. Representing men and women of different ages and stations in life, the Immortals serve as patrons of various groups and trades (© Kevin R. Morris/CORBIS).

Daoism has also been used to encourage 'green' ecological thinking in Taiwan. Ironically, while the tradition has been kept alive in Taiwan, Hong Kong, and diasporic communities in the West, it has only recently begun to receive state support in China. Its emphasis on nurturing simplicity and stillness in oneself, and harmony both with one's immediate environment and ultimately with the cosmos, are now seen as important antidotes to a frenzied modernity.

🦎 POPULAR RELIGION

Popular religion in China can be characterized as a loose collection of beliefs and practices centred on the power of deities, ghosts, and spirits. It is non-institutional and draws various elements from the more established traditions: Confucianism, Daoism, Buddhism, and, more recently, Christianity and Islam. Practitioners' goals can include anything from success on a test or conception of a son to happiness or prosperity to political change.

Two streams of popular religion can thus be identified: personal religiosity and political activism. One important element in personal religiosity is the belief that the spirits or souls of the deceased continue to intervene in the human world, and that their potentially malevolent power can be harnessed for the benefit of the living. This belief finds everyday expression in family shrines and altars dedicated to ancestor veneration as well as the kind of restaurant shrine described at the beginning of this chapter. Devotees also believe that numerous Daoist perfected beings as well as Buddhas bodhisattvas stand ready to help them deal with life's challenges.

But popular religion can also be externalized in a less individual, more dogmatic and partisan way. When ideas such as the Mandate of Heaven and messianic figures such as Milo (Maitreya), the Buddha of the future, are incorporated into popular religion, they can give rise to politically charged millenarian organizations such as the White Lotus Society and the Heavenly Kingdom movement.

The White Lotus Society

The White Lotus Society is thought to have originated in the eleventh or twelfth century as a lay movement dedicated to Amida Buddha. Over time it incorporated a variety of other elements, including Daoist longevity practices and millenarian expectations involving the messianic Future Buddha Milo. Its clergy married, it offered the kind of social services normally provided by family, and its unorthodox vernacular scriptures featured motifs such as apocalyptic change and the attainment of paradise. Its members played a substantial role in the overthrow of the Mongolian Yuan dynasty (1269–1368) and the establishment of the native Ming. Nevertheless, the first Ming emperor feared its power and sought to suppress it. By the early 1600s the name 'White Lotus' had become a kind of general pejorative used by officials to refer to any religious group they considered suspect, including the Christians who had recently arrived on Chinese soil.

The Taiping Rebellion

Five hundred years after the White Lotus Society helped to overthrow the Mongolian Yuan, the movement for the Heavenly Kingdom of Great Peace (*Taiping tianguo*) (1850–64) played a similar role, promoting rebellion against the Manchurian Qing regime. It came into being after the Opium War, when the Chinese government was shaken by the concessions demanded in the Treaty of Nanjing (1842). The founder of the Taiping movement, Hong Xiuquan, claimed to be the younger brother of Jesus, sent to establish an egalitarian kingdom that reflected influences from the Daoist past as well as the Christian present. In its enthusiasm for establishing the True Teaching, it set out to eradicate all others. The rebellion that erupted in 1850 continued until 1864, killing as many as 30 million people and destroying thousands of Daoist and Buddhist temples in southern China.

Practice and Cultural Expressions

In spite of the animus directed against traditional beliefs and practices over the last hundred and fifty years, Confucian, Daoist and folk practices have experienced a minor renaissance since the 1980s. In 2004, for instance, the government of the People's Republic of China for the first time celebrated the sage's birthday as a state holiday (Taiwan has always done so). Renewed interest in Confucian values is also reflected in some elementary schools, which have integrated the study of classical literature, rites, and ethics into the lives of their students. Furthermore, several elements of the Chinese government's recent rhetoric and policy recall Confucian concerns: for example, its emphasis on a 'harmonious society', non-interference in foreign policy, soft diplomacy, the establishment of Confucius Institutes outside China, and the development of online educational sites for Chinese language and culture. None of these elements is overtly religious, however: for that we must turn to Daoism.

Over the centuries, the quest for longevity and transcendence has led Daoists to experiment with a range of practices that includes everything from chanting, prayer, and meditation to the use of talismans, esoteric sexual practices (what Ge Hong called the 'arts of the bedchamber') and both kinds of alchemy (internal and external). Meanwhile, the quest for social stability and cosmic harmony has produced the two broad types of communal Daoist ritual noted earlier: both purification (*zhai*) and communal renewal (*jiao*) rituals are still performed today.

Through these rituals, Daoism has had a tremendous influence on material culture, aesthetic theory, and medicine. While Daoist community rituals feature beautifully woven and embroidered textiles and 'celestial' music, the disciplines of calligraphy and painting have had a profound impact on aesthetic theory, particularly in the use of empty space. And the Daoist interest in alchemy has contributed immeasurably to pharmaceutical and medical knowledge.

Banners, altar coverings, and ritual vestments all point to Daoism's enchantment with the beauty of this world. Flowing silk robes dyed in luminous yellow, red, blue, and green are often elaborately embroidered with the yin-yang symbol, totemic dragons, cranes and bats for longevity. Other popular design elements include auspicious objects associated with the Eight Immortals: hardwood clapper, fan, crutch, flute, sword, bottle gourd, whisk, and flower basket. These sumptuous garments offer a sharp contrast to the relatively simple orange, brown and yellow coloured robes typically worn by Buddhist monastics. Daoist liturgical music, variously used for praise of the immortals, prayer to the deities, release of the dead from hell, advancing the pursuit of longevity, and cultivation of equanimity, can be traced as far back as the Celestial Masters, whose dispersion carried their music across the empire. Music remains an integral part of Daoist practice to this day.

In the sphere of medicine, Daoist influence can be seen in the foundational assumption that the mind, emotions, and physical condition of the body are all closely connected. Traditional remedies for illness and dietary habits aimed at health have also benefited from knowledge gained through Daoist alchemical experiments. The contemporary body cultivation movement in China is rooted in aspects of internal alchemy and reflects the influence of disciplines such as *taiji* and *qigong* that promote physical flexibility and agility. Groups organized around these exercises are often associated with Daoism.

But Daoism does not exist in isolation: it shares the religious commons with a secular Confucianism, a devoutly committed Buddhism, and a pervasive folk religiosity. Adherents of all these traditions may take part in community activities such as going to the temple or organizing processions to celebrate the birthdays of local spirits, gods and goddesses, 'perfected persons', Buddhas and bodhisattvas. The fact that these figures often receive supplications and are celebrated as a group illustrates the syncretic nature of Chinese spirituality.

In the same way, major annual festivals are seldom confined to one religion, although the different communities may hold their own celebrations. The most important celebrations—the lunar New Year (or Spring Festival), Qingming (Clear and Bright), the Dragon Boat Festival, the Ghost Festival, and the Mid-Autumn Festival—are pan-Chinese. Today they have more to do with culture than with religion.

Family looms large in all these holidays. The lunar New Year celebration, which falls sometime between late January and mid-February, is above all a familial affair. Offerings are made to ancestors and gods on New Year's Eve at the family shrine or altar before the family sits down to dinner. On New Year's Day and through the next few days, red packets of 'lucky money' are given to children and 'junior' (younger) people go to visit 'senior' family members and friends.

A spring festival that is celebrated on the third day of the third month, Clear and Bright (Qingming) or 'Tomb Sweeping Day' is also family-oriented. On this day, the extended family gathers at the cemetery where the most recently deceased ancestor is buried, and the descendants pay their respects by cleaning and sweeping the gravesite.

The Dragon Boat Festival (Duanwu), celebrated on the fifth day of the fifth month, commemorates the poet Qu Yuan for his loyalty as a minister to King Huai of Chu in the third century BCE. Sent into exile after the king had refused his counsel, Qu drowned himself when he realized that he had failed to save the kingdom from ruin. Such loyalty was a classic Confucian virtue, but Qu is also considered a Daoist worthy. Today, long boats carved and painted as dragons represent the boats used by the local people to find Qu's body; and small packages of steamed rice wrapped in leaves are thrown into the water in memory of the people's efforts to appease the river god and prevent the fish from desecrating his remains.

During the seventh month the gates of hell are said to open, releasing ghosts to mingle with the living. The central event is the Ghost Festival, held on the fifteenth day of the month, when the living make offerings to the dead. Special ritual offerings are made to comfort and appease the dead who have no descendants to care for them in the afterlife. Though Buddhist in origin, the Ghost Festival is now an integral part of the Chinese religious landscape. Daoists as well as Buddhists perform all the rites, and one of the festival's central stories is a classic expression of Confucian filiality: when a disciple of the Buddha named Mulian, deep in meditation, sees his mother suffering in hell, he goes into the netherworld to save her.

The last major festival of the year is the mid-autumn festival, a celebration of the autumn harvest, on the fifteenth day of the eighth month. Second only to the New Year in importance, this is the time when the whole family comes together to enjoy the full, bright, low-hanging moon, eat moon-cake, and make elaborate lanterns for the children.

Conclusion

The ancient popular beliefs and practices at the roots of China's elite religions came from many different places and cultures. Yet all these diverse traditions share a single aspiration to harmony: individual and communal, earthly and cosmic. Furthermore, all see the achievement of harmony as depending on the disciplined transcendence of self. Although individual groups have varied in their specific goals and methods, they have all tended to believe that basic human desires—for material well-being, health, familial joy, personal security, social stability, spiritual maturity and release—should be harnessed and directed towards the care of family, friends, community, and state.

🦎 Korean Religions

Introduction

This section will concentrate on the historical development of religions on the Korean peninsula, although it will also take a brief look at the rapidly changing non-traditional religious culture of contemporary South Korea. North Korea will not be discussed, since the Communist government's antipathy towards religion makes it impossible to know anything about contemporary beliefs and practices.

In the early 2000s, census data showed that nearly half of South Korea's population professed to have no religion. Those who did claim an institutional affiliation were almost equally divided between Buddhism and Christianity (mainly Protestant, especially Pentecostal). Other unspecified affiliations accounted for less than 1 per cent of the population, while Confucianism came last at a negligible 0.3 per cent and the indigenous shamanic folk tradition was statistically invisible. The apparent lack of institutional affiliation and personal dedication to either shamanism or Confucianism is striking. Yet both these traditions still seem pervasive in contemporary Korean life.

Theoretically, traditional Korean religiosity can be classified as non-theistic at the elite level and polytheistic at the popular level. In practice, though, it (like its Chinese counterpart) tends to be syncretic. Thus neither of these categories necessarily excludes the other. It is even possible to identify a quasi-monotheistic belief in a purposeful and creative Way (or Heaven, or Heaven-and-Earth) co-existing with both the polytheistic belief in ancestral spirits and nature deities and the non-theistic belief in an impersonal natural Way.

Korea and China: A Shared History

Ancient Korean culture shows traces of influences both from continental East Asia and from Central Asia. Migration from China to the Korean peninsula was underway as early as the Zhou dynasty, and political relations between the two populations have from the beginning reflected a mixture of kinship and antipathy, relatedness and differentiation. The earliest written records of Korea are Chinese. Sima Qian's *Records of the Grand Historian* describes Wiman, one of the later kings of the proto-state of Old Joseon (Choson), as a refugee from northern China who ruled over Chinese refugees and indigenous inhabitants at Wanggeom (Wanggom) (present-day Pyongyang) in the sixth and fifth centuries BCE. And the sixth-century *History of the Wei Dynasty* tells how the mythical king Dangun (Tangun) founded Old Joseon during the time of China's legendary sage king Yao. The fact that the Wu family shrine in the Chinese coastal province of Shandong, built in 147 CE, is engraved with the myth of Dangun is another illustration of the connection between these ancient peoples.

Foundation Myths

Old Joseon

An early Korean source, now lost, started with Dangun's divine ancestors, his grandfather Hwanin and father Hwanung. Hwanin knew that his son wanted to descend from heaven and live in the world of human beings, so he settled Hwanung in a cave in one of the highest mountains, Mount Taebaek.

But Hwanung was not alone in the cave: a bear and a tiger were also living there, and they asked him to transform them into human beings. So Hwanung gave them a bundle of sacred mugworts and 20 cloves of garlic, with instructions to eat these foods and avoid the sunlight. After 21 days the bear became a woman, but the tiger had failed to avoid the light and therefore was not transformed. The woman remained alone, unable to find a husband, so she prayed for a child. In response to her prayers, Hwanung transformed himself, lay with her, and gave her a son, Dangun Wanggeom.

This foundation myth became a marker of national identity in the thirteenth century, when Korea faced a series of Mongol invasions (1231–1270). According to the *Memorabilia of the Three Kingdoms* (*Samguk yusa*), compiled during that period by the monk Iryeon (Iryon), the god Hwanung descended into the human world and married a she-bear who gave birth to Dangun (a bear cult is still current among the Ainu people of Japan as well as some Siberian tribes in Russia). Yi Suenghyu (Yi Sunghyu) in his *Songs or Rhymed Record of Emperors and Kings* (*Chewang ungi*; 1287) gives a variant account in which the great king Hwanung gave medicine to his granddaughter to change her into a human being; she then married a tree god and bore Dangun (a tree cult was prevalent in the southern portion of the Korean peninsula). Interestingly, there is no reference to Dangun in the official *History of the Three Kingdoms* (*Samguk sagi*), compiled a century earlier, under Confucian inspiration, by Gim Busik (Kim Pusik).

The Three Kingdoms

The proto-state of Old Joseon was followed by the Three Kingdoms (c. 50 BCE–668 CE) of Goguryeo (Koguryo), Baekje (Paekche), and Silla. Goguryeo's foundation myth (found in a collection from the thirteenth century) tells how its founder Jumong (Chumong), who eventually took the title King Dongmyeong (Tongmyong), was born from an egg after the sun—Haemosu, the Son of Heaven—shone on the breast of his mother, the eldest

The Lay of King Dongmyeong (Tongmyong)

From the Collected Works of Minister I (Yi) of Korea

In early summer, when the Great Bear
   stood in the Snake,
Haemosu came to Korea,
A true Son of Heaven.
He came down through the air
In a five-dragon chariot,
With a retinue of hundreds,
Robes streaming, riding on swans,
The atmosphere echoed with chiming music.
Banners floated on the tinted clouds.
. . .
North of the capital was the Green River,

Where the River Earl's three beautiful daughters
Rose from the drake-neck's green waves
To play in the Bear's Heart Pool.
Their jade ornaments tinkled.
Their flowerlike beauty was modest—
They might have been fairies of the Han River banks,
Or goddesses of the Lo River islets.
The king, out hunting, espied them,
Was fascinated and lost his heart.
Not from lust for girls,
But from eager desire for an heir.
   (Lee et al. 1993: 24)

daughter of the River Earl. In both style and content, this poem recalls the *Songs of the South*. After ruling for 19 years, Dongmyeong forsook his throne and rose to heaven. The founder of Baekje, King Onjo, is said to have been his son.

Silla's foundation myth, like Old Joseon's, was recorded in Iryeon's *Memorabilia*. Like King Dongmyeong, King Hyeokgeose (Hyokkose) ('Bright'), the founder, was born from an egg, a red one in this case. His birth was announced by an eerie lightning-like emanation from a well. When the people cracked open the egg, they found inside it a beautiful boy. When they bathed him he emitted light; the 'birds and beasts danced for joy, heaven and earth shook, and the sun and the moon became bright' (Lee et al. 1993: 33). Soon after, a dragon appeared near a well and brought an infant girl from under her left rib. The child's features were lovely except for a beak-like lip, which fell off after she was bathed in the river. When the two reached the age of 13, they married and became king and queen.

Indigenous Traditions

Korea's indigenous shamanistic traditions are deeply animist. Each village has its own deity: a local mountain god or goddess in inland regions and a dragon king by the sea. Two spirit-generals, one female and one male, are responsible for all activities below and above the earth respectively. Traditional household deities include the gods of the hearth, the roof beam (in the main room where guests were received and family corpses laid out), and the outhouse.

While there were both male and female shamans in traditional Korea, most contemporary shamans are women. Some shamans (**_mudang_**) choose their vocations, and others are born into it. Active everywhere, they are summoned in cases of demonic disturbance at home, at work, or out on the streets, and regularly perform exorcisms. Shamans also allow spirits to possess and use them to communicate with the living: family, friends, and foes. They also perform auspicious rituals at community celebrations and ceremonies of thanksgiving, and act as shaman-diviners who offer inspired advice to their clients by discerning signs from the spirits.

Daoism in Korea

With its focus on deities, ghosts, and spirits, Daoism found deep resonance in Korea's foundation myths that contain several elements reminiscent of the shamanist stream in Daoism, including nature deities (the River Earl), marriage between gods and human beings (Hwanung and the bear-woman), and ascension into heaven (King Dongmyeong). In Silla, the people believed in the Holy Mother, a mountain goddess who was the guardian of the country. She was said to live on a mountain to the west of the capital, recalling the Queen Mother of the West in the *Zhuangzi*.

These apparently Daoist elements have led some scholars to suggest that the cult of the Holy Mother was a composite of an indigenous mountain deity and a Daoist immortality cult. In the *Memorabilia* there is an account of the Holy Mother appearing to a Buddhist nun who was seeking to repair a Buddha Hall. This 'immortal fairy', who had learned 'the art of the immortals', is said to be the daughter of a Chinese emperor. After settling in Korea, she had given birth to a holy man who became the first ruler of Silla; the story suggests that 'perhaps' this was Hyeokgeose.

This mythological syncretism is reinforced in Silla's history. In the 700s Gim Jiseong (Kim Chisong), a vice-minister of state, kept one image each of Amitabha, the Buddha of the West, and Maitreya, the Buddha of the Future. He read Mahayana literature but also enjoyed Laozi and the first chapter of the *Zhuangzi*, 'Free and Easy Wandering'. Echoes of Daoist scripture continued into the 1400s, during the staunchly Neo-Confucian Joseon or I (Yi) dynasty, when one minister, disappointed in his ruler, left the court to spend the

The Holy Mother of Mount Fairy Peach

The phrases 'art of the immortals' and 'art of longevity' refer to Daoism: by emphasizing that the Holy Mother embraced both Daoism and Buddhism, the passage underlines the syncretic nature of Korean religion.

During the reign of King Chinpyong [579–632], a nun . . . wished to repair a hall for the Buddha . . . but could not carry out her desire. A beautiful immortal fairy, her hair adorned with ornaments, appeared in the nun's dreams and consoled her: 'I'm the holy goddess mother of Mount Fairy Peach [Mount West], and I am pleased that you would repair the Buddha Hall. I offer you ten *kun* of gold . . .' The holy mother, originally the daughter of a Chinese emperor, was named Saso. Early in her life she learned the art of the immortals . . . . When Saso first came to Chinhan, she gave birth to a holy man who became the first ruler of Silla—perhaps he was Hyokkose. . . . Saso donated gold to make a Buddha image, lighted incense for the living beings, and initiated a religion. How could she be merely one who learned the art of longevity and became a prisoner in the boundless mist? (Lee et al. 1993: 94) rest of his life wandering as a monk, writing poetry and telling stories, and other literary men (much like the Seven Sages of the Bamboo Grove) retired from official life to engage in metaphysical conversation.

Murals in Goguryeo tombs suggest that the Daoist cult of immortality merged with local Korean beliefs in prognostication. At the start of the dynasty, the Tang court sent a memorial asking about Daoism in Korea, along with an adept and seven other envoys, plus a copy of the *Daodejing*. In the same period, a Buddhist monastery in the region of what is now the border between North Korea and China was converted into a Daoist

A female shaman performs a prayer for peace at a festival in Seoul marking the first full moon of the lunar year (© JEON HEON-KYUN/epa/Corbis).

temple; and in 643, at the request of the Goguryeo king, eight Daoist priests were sent there from China. By 650, the Daoist influence at the Goguryeo court was so strong that a monk who opposed the state's adoption of Daoism fled and sought refuge in Baekje.

Confucianism in Korea

Korea has the largest network of Confucian shrines in the world today. The process of Confucianization started during the Three Kingdoms period and stretched over a millennium. After the Ming dynasty fell to the Manchurians in 1644, Korea prided itself on being the world's only true Confucian nation.

Three Kingdoms, United Silla, and Goryeo

It was during the Goryeo (Koryo) period, when Buddhism was at its height in Korea, that Confucianism became firmly rooted there. King Taejo ('Ultimate Ancestor'), who defeated Silla and founded Goryeo in 918, was an ardent Buddhist, but he also encouraged Confucian learning. Thus he rejected Silla's tradition of governance by a hereditary aristocracy and adopted instead the examination-based bureaucratic system of the Tang. In addition, Taejo is said to have left for his successors a list of 'Ten Injunctions' that reflected his syncretic approach, bringing together Buddhist, Confucian, and indigenous perspectives. The first injunction, for example, clearly honours the Buddhist tradition:

> The success of the great enterprise of founding our dynasty is entirely owing to the protective powers of the many Buddhas. We therefore must build temples for both Son [Meditation] and Kyo (Textual) Schools and appoint abbots, that they may perform the proper ceremonies and themselves cultivate the way (Lee 1985: 132).

But the third injunction pays tribute to the Confucian tradition:

> . . . if the eldest son is not worthy of the crown, let the second eldest succeed to the throne. If the second eldest, too, is unworthy, choose the brother the people consider the best qualified for the throne.

And the fourth injunction emphasizes the primacy of indigenous traditions:

> In the past we have always had a deep attachment for the ways of China and all of our institutions have been modelled upon those of Tang. But our country occupies a different geographical location and our people's character is different from that of the Chinese. Hence, there is no reason to strain ourselves unreasonably to copy the Chinese way . . . (H. Kang in Lee 1993: 263).

Soon after this period, the influence of Confucianism in Korea was further reinforced when Choe Chung (984–1068) established a private Confucian academy.

Joseon (1392–1910)

Antipathy to Buddhism

By the late fourteenth century Buddhism's influence had increased to the point that a second Taejo, the founder of the Joseon dynasty, banned the building of new Buddhist temples and stopped the growth of the monastic population. His son Taejong continued the effort to bring Buddhism under control. Many temples were disestablished and their estates and workers, including slaves, were confiscated; certain rituals were prohibited; and Buddhist activities were confined to specific areas.

Around the same time, Buddhist funerals and memorial rituals were discontinued and families began installing shrines for ancestral tablets in their homes. The responsibility for performing the ancestor veneration rites was eventually entrusted to the first son, who became the only one with the right of inheritance. This system of primogeniture put an end to the Goryeo system, under which female as well as male offspring were entitled to inherit property and couples could hold property jointly.

Korean Neo-Confucianism

In the early 1500s, the philosopher Jo Gwangjo (Cho Kwang-jo) continued the process of Confucianization by rooting out superstitions considered incompatible with it. He encouraged government by moral suasion and instituted a system of local self-government based on the idea of a village code, outlined by the Chinese Neo-Confucian Zhu Xi in a work entitled *Lu Family Compact with Additions and Deletions*. At the heart of this system was a notion of reciprocity expressed in mutual encouragement of morality, mutual supervision of conduct, mutual decorum in social relations, and mutual aid in times of hardship or disaster.

Zhu Xi's influence extended beyond the world of practical politics into the metaphysical realm. His understanding of human nature, rooted in the classical literature, was particularly influential. He believed that human beings have in them both the principle or pattern of Nature, which is wholly good, and a vital or material force that can be good when the desires and emotions through which it is expressed are in appropriate balance, but is bad when balance is lacking. This view inspired a famous exchange of letters between the Korean philosophers I Hwang (Yi Hwang or Toegye) and I I (Yi I or Yulgok) in the mid-1500s.

At the centre of this exchange, known as the 'Four–Seven Debate', was the relationship between the four heart-minds—which, according to Mencius, reflect the fundamental goodness of human nature—and the seven emotions (happiness, anger, sorrow, fear, love, hate, and desire), which, according to 'Centrality and Equilibrium', cause some human actions to be less than good when they are extreme and not expressed in correct proportion.

Both taking Zhu Xi as their starting-point, I Hwang and I I arrived at different conclusions. I Hwang argued that principle or pattern in nature (*i*) rises and material force (**ki**) follows, implying that human nature is mixed from the beginning. I I, on the other hand, argued that if principle pervades everything, is uniform and undifferentiated, then it must be material force that initiates action, implying that human nature is originally wholly good. Behind the philosophers' quest for a deeper understanding of human nature was the commitment to psychological–moral transformation of the self—the Neo-Confucian equivalent of the self-cultivation emphasized in classic Confucianism.

The search for efficacious methods of self-improvement was not limited to men. In early Joseon Korea, as in Ming China, women's education became a focal point. Three prominent publications written by or for women were: Queen Sohye's *Instructions for the Inner Quarters* (*Naehun*; 1475); a letter written by the seventeenth-century Confucian Song Siyol on the occasion of his daughter's marriage, emphasizing the importance of a mother's influence on her children; and a letter from Lady Hyegyeong (Hyegyong, 1735–1815) to her nephew in which she sought to impress on him the importance of Confucian virtues: being honest and conscientious, respectful of elders, affectionate and filial at home, and compassionate to paternal aunts.

As Neo-Confucianism became increasingly entrenched at the state level and Daoism was gradually assimilated into Joseon culture, Buddhist monastics argued for reconciliation of the various religions—in effect, syncretism. As the sixteenth-century monk Hyujeong (Hyujong) wrote in his *Mirror of Three Religions* (*Samga kwigam*): 'An ancient man said: "Confucianists plant the root, Taoists grow the root, and Buddhists harvest the root"' (Lee et al. 1993: 662). Nevertheless, Confucianism retained its dominant position.

1897 to the Present

Korean responses to the increasingly politically dominant and culturally influential West varied. One of the few English-speaking politicians of time, Yun Chiho (1864-1945), favoured wholesale Westernization and an end to the relationship with a radically weakened and defeated China, which by the late nineteenth century was known as the 'sick man of East Asia'. Yet Korea was still implicitly expected to play the subordinate role. Yun, like his contemporaries in China, considered Confucianism to be both regressive and oppressive: if Koreans were poor and oppressed, Korean women degraded, Korean families weak, and Korean officials cruel, in his view it was the fault of Confucianism. Another reason for Yun's antipathy was Japan's use of Confucianism as an instrument of control during its occupation of Korea from 1910 to 1945.

Contemporary Issues

Other Korean scholars agreed that Korea's adherence to the conservative teachings of Zhu Xi, which focused on maintenance of the status quo, had held it back. However, like the Chinese New Confucians, they believed that a renewed transnational Confucianism based on the traditional values of filial piety, chastity, and frugality could help to bring peace, security and stability to the whole world. Among those scholars was Bak Eunsik (Pak Unsik, 1859–1925), who preferred the Confucianism of Wang Yangming. For Bak, Wang's emphasis on human beings' 'innate knowledge of the good' offered hope. He was not alone in his choice of Wang's Confucianism as a response to modernity.

Gim Chungnyol (Kim Chungnyol), a professor of East Asian philosophy who studied with the New Confucian Fang Dongmei in the 1950s and 1960s, was an activist in the Korean democracy movement during the 1970s and 1980s. He believed that Confucianism could serve as an antidote to the excesses of capitalist industrialization. But the movement for the revival of Confucianism in Korea is not monolithic.

In the 1980s and '90s, for instance, So Chonggi was critical of authoritarianism of any kind, including Confucian. Nevertheless, like Pak, he believed that Confucianism could be good for Korea. Differentiating between 'royal', 'official', and 'scholar' Confucianisms, he criticized all three for their narrow focus on 'ethical politics', 'ritual politics', and 'eremitic politics', respectively. In their place he proposed a Confucianism of the people, based on their moral purity and creative capacities.

The recent establishment of an Institute of Confucian Cultural Studies as part of a nationwide network—headquartered at Sungkyunkwan University's Academy of East Asian Studies—suggests a revival of scholarly interest in the Confucian tradition. However, recent census data indicate that this interest has not spread beyond the academy: popular support for Confucianism as a religion is not strong.

NEW RELIGIONS

Today there are more than two hundred new religions in South Korea. The syncretic nature of their beliefs and practices demonstrates well the pluralism of Korean spirituality, combining elements from ancient indigenous shamanism, well-established foreign traditions (Confucianism, Daoism, and Buddhism), and more recent arrivals, notably Christianity.

Some modern progressives call for revival of Korea's shamanism-steeped folk traditions as a way of reclaiming the national culture. Others see shamanism as mere superstition and urge that it be rooted out. A sampling of new religious movements shows that Korean religious responses to modernity are diverse.

The Religion of the Heavenly Way or Cheondogyo (Chondogyo is the oldest of Korea's new religions. Founded in 1860, it began as a reaction to Catholic Christianity; one of the early names it used for God was Cheonju (Ch'onju) or 'Lord of Heaven', a name coined by the Catholics. It combines Christian monotheism and belief in the equality of all human beings with the broadly East Asian, and more particularly Confucian, vision of humans living in harmony with the universe. As Cheondogyo evolved, it came to understand Hanullim (God) as the all-pervasive animating force of the universe—a force, not unlike *ki*, that can be experienced as Ultimate Energy when we ask it to fill our hearts.

Another response to the dominance of Western culture and growing globalization is the Religion of the Great Ancestors (Daejonggyo), which sees itself as a revival of ancient Korean shamanism. Although it denies any foreign influence, it has clearly drawn a few central ideas from Shinto and Christianity. Founded in 1910 by Na Chol, it depicts God as Korean (in the same way that Shinto depicts Amaterasu as Japanese), while presenting the heavenly triad of indigenous ancestors (Hwanin, Hwanung, and Dangun) as an alternative to the Christian Trinity. It is the only indigenous religion that worships a Christian Trinitarian God and at the same time mimics the Shinto myth about the divinity of the Japanese royal family: Daejonggyo teaches that Dangun is the divine founder of both the Korean state and the Korean people.

Daoist internal alchemy aimed at longevity and spiritual transcendence continues to influence new religions as well. It lives on in a controversial organization called Dahn World, which operates internationally under various names and teaches a form of meditation that it calls 'brain respiration'. It claims that if enough people were to practise its techniques, they could bring about a worldwide 'enlightenment revolution'.

Practice and Cultural Expression

Many of the festivals celebrated in Korea today originated in antiquity among the ancestors of the Goguryeo people but were eventually aligned with the Chinese holiday calendar; a few even came to share the same name. These ancient rituals were passed on to later dynasties and performed alongside new rites for new gods. During Goryeo, rituals for ancestors were added, and the Buddhist festivals of the Lotus Lantern and Eight Vows, derived from Goguryeo agricultural festivals, were sanctioned by the state. By Joseon, state rites were performed for indigenous gods of nature and local village guardian deities. These traditional practices continue today: nature spirits and guardian deities are still worshipped in villages; rituals are still conducted at ancestors' graves and at family shrines or altars on New Year's; Dano is celebrated on the fifth day of the fifth month like the Chinese Duanwu; and Chuseok, like the Chinese mid-harvest festival, is a major harvest festival held on the fifteenth day of the eighth month.

Koreans and Chinese alike celebrate the lunar New Year by paying their respects to ancestors, visiting family and friends, and celebrating community. However, the festivals they celebrate on the fifth day of the fifth month—the date of China's Dragon Boat Festival (Duanwu)—are very different. The Korean Dano has nothing to do with either boats or national heroes. Instead, it is a spring festival that is believed to have

Students wearing traditional costumes perform during one of the regular celebrations of Confucius held at Sungkyunkwan University in Seoul (© Seoul Shinmun/epa/Corbis).

originated in efforts to ward off infectious diseases during the rainy season. Medicinal plants are woven into tiger dolls and placed over the entrance to the home, while the main room of the home is hung with printed paper talismans designed to keep out disease and bad luck.

Conclusion

Korea's religious culture has undergone significant transformations over the last fifteen hundred years, incorporating new influences—from Daoism to Christianity—without abandoning its indigenous shamanistic traditions. Today it remains pluralistic and syncretic. Which of the many new religions will survive and how they will interact with one another remains to be seen.

Sacred Texts Table

Religion	Texts	Composition/ Compilation	Revision	Use
Confucianism (Texts are 'classics' attributed to sages and are not considered 'sacred')	The *Classics* (or *Books*) of *Music, Poetry, History, Changes, Rites*, and the *Spring and Autumn Annals*	5th to 3rd century BCE	175 CE The Five Classics were engraved in stone after they had been reconstructed following the great book-burning of 213 BCE. The *Classic of Music* is lost.	Educational; initially used for individual study, but eventually became the core of the curriculum for state scholar-officials
Confucianism	*Classic of Filial Piety, The Analects, Er Ya* (the earliest Chinese dictionary), three commentaries on the *Spring and Autumn Annals*, and the *Rites*	7th to 10th century	The Five Classics are gradually increased to Twelve	As above
Confucianism	Zhu Xi organizes the standard texts into the *Four Books: The Great Learning and Centrality and Equilibrium* (both from the *Book of Rites*); *Mencius; The Analects*, and the *Five Classics* from ancient times	10th to 13th century	With the addition of *Mencius*, the Twelve Classics become Thirteen	As above
Confucianism	First text written specifically for women: *Admonitions for Women*	1st to 2nd century	7th to 18th century saw three new additions: *Filial Piety for Women* in the 7th century, *Analects for Women* in the 9th, and *Instructions for the Inner Quarter* in the 15th; *Filial Piety* was replaced by a *Handy Record of Rules for Women* c. 1700	Women's education

Sacred Texts Table (continued)

Religion	Texts	Composition/ Compilation	Revision	Use
Daoism (early texts attributed primarily to sages)	*Daodejing*	Contested; possibly early 3rd century BCE	3rd century CE: Wang Bi commentary	Liturgical
Daoism	*Zhuangzi*	First seven chapters attributed to 'Zhuangzi' (4th–3rd century BCE)	Guo Xiang (d. 312) is thought to have compiled the current text	Educational (known as the Classic of South China)
Daoism	*Techniques of the Mind and Inward Training*	4th century BCE	Both were lost to the main tradition and recently 'found' in the Legalist *Guanzi*	Likely used as meditation manual
Daoism	*Classic of the Great Peace*	1st century CE	Destroyed in 3rd century and reconstructed in 6th	Ritual and instructional
Daoism	*Master Who Embraces Spontaneous Nature or Simplicity*	320s	14th century: 'inner' and 'outer' sections combined to form the current text	Used as manual for external alchemy
Daoism	Highest Clarity scriptures	Revealed 364 to 379	Edited into Pronouncements of the Perfected by Tao Hongjing	Doctrinal and ritual
Daoism	*Scripture for the Salvation of Humanity* of the Lingbao school	Revealed 4th century	12th century: 61-chapter version presented to Song emperor	Used in recitation (Liturgical)
Daoism	*Fifteen Precepts for the Establishing of the Teaching*	12th century	Collected as part of Wang Chongyang's writings	Doctrinal for Complete Truth school
Popular tradition	Countless handbooks of religious rituals and devotion	Throughout history	New movements produce new writings	Instructional and ritual

Sites

CHINA

Beijing The Imperial Palace complex, also known as the Forbidden City, includes the Tiantan (Altar or Temple of Heaven), where the Ming and Qing emperors performed the grandest sacrifices. The city is also home to the Taimiao, the ancestral temple of both dynasties; a Confucian temple dedicated to scholar-officials; various Daoist and Buddhist temples; and the tombs of the later Ming emperors.

Nanjing The first capital city of the Ming, whose first emperor, Hongwu, is buried here in the Xiaoling Tomb. Scholar-officials were trained at the Confucian Academy in this thriving ancient metropolis. The Jinghai Temple is dedicated to the goddess of the sea, in honour of China's great seafarer of the early 1400s, the Muslim admiral Zhenghe.

Qufu The complex of monuments in the birthplace of Confucius, in Shandong, includes a temple, a family mansion, and a cemetery containing Confucius' tomb and the remains of more than 100,000 of his descendants.

Wudangshan Mount Wudang in Hubei is known for its many Daoist monasteries. It is also home to an organized complex of palaces and temples; most were built during the Ming, but some of its Daoist buildings date from as early as the seventh century. The complex contains some of the finest examples of Chinese art and architecture.

Xian The capital for numerous dynasties, the city and its environs are home to the famous terracotta warrior guardians; numerous Daoist and Buddhist temples; and Huashan, one of the five sacred mountains of Daoism.

KOREA

Seoul The Changdeokgung Palace (Palace of Prospering Virtue) complex was established by Taejong, the first king of the Joseon dynasty. It includes Jongmyo, the oldest and most authentic of the surviving Confucian royal shrines, which are dedicated to the ancestors of Joseon. It houses tablets bearing teachings of the royal family.

Study Questions

1. How does the popular shrine described at the beginning of this chapter illustrate the syncretic nature of Chinese religion?
2. What assumptions and values do Confucianism and Daoism share? What sets them apart?
3. How would you characterize Confucianism's treatment of women?
4. What are some of the core spiritual concerns in the early prototypical Daoist texts? How did they influence the goals, methods of cultivation, and institutional development of religious Daoism?
5. Compare and contrast classical and Neo-Confucianism. What accounts for the differences?
6. What allows for such disparate groups as the Seven Sages of the Bamboo Grove and Complete Truth to coexist under the umbrella of Daoism? What makes them both Daoist?
7. Who are the 'New Confucians'? What issues are they tackling? What are their goals?

8. Recall the Korean foundation myths outlined in this chapter. What do they suggest about the nature of Korean culture and religiosity?

9. Explain briefly the relationship between the elite and folk shamanistic traditions in China and Korea. What are the similarities and differences?

10. In this book, the religions of East Asia have been organized geographically in two groups: 'China and Korea' and 'Japan'. Would a different organization, based on the various traditions—(shamanism, Daoism, Confucianism, and East Asian Buddhism—be more appropriate or less so? Why?

Glossary

Ban Zhao (c. 48–112 CE) An influential female Confucian scholar who wrote *Admonitions* (or *Lessons*) *for Women*.

Confucius (551–479 BCE) The first teacher of Confucianism, known in Chinese as Kongzi.

Dao/dao Either the 'Way' in the sense of the Ultimate or the 'way' in the sense of the path taken by followers of a particular tradition.

Datong The Grand Commonality; an age of complete harmony, in which all people are as they should be: faithful, trustworthy, loving, conscientious, and cared for.

Dong Zhongshu (195?–105? BCE) The most prominent Confucian of the New Text school, who helped establish Confucianism as the state religion.

five phases The generative and destructive cycles based on the relationships between the five elements (metal, wood, water, fire, and water). 'Phases' may also be translated as 'agents' or 'elements' depending on the context. See also *wuxing*.

Han Yu (768–824) Played a pivotal role in the revival of Confucianism in a period when it was overshadowed by Daoism and Buddhism.

i Transliteration of the Korean pronunciation of **li** ('principle').

junzi A person of exemplary or authoritative behaviour, especially in Confucianism; traditionally translated in English as 'gentleman', implying the virtues of the upper class; a superior person, or one of virtue and exceptional character.

ki Transliteration of the Korean pronunciation of *qi* (see *qigong*).

Laozi The 'Old Master'; the putative patriarch of Daoism and author of the *Daodejing* who may or may not have been a real historical figure.

li The single English transliteration used for two different Chinese words. *Li* in the first sense refers to ritual practice and decorum and is usually translated as 'rites'. *Li* in the second sense refers to the pattern in natural materials such as wood or stone; it was used by the Neo-Confucians to designate the force that pervades the cosmos and is translated as 'principle'.

Mencius (c. 343–289 BCE) The second most prominent Confucian thinker, known in Chinese as Meng Ke, Master Meng, and Mengzi; he believed that human nature is inherently good.

mudang Korean female shaman.

qi Material force or vital energy.

qigong A 'breath' discipline or set of exercises used to enhance health and spiritual well-being; also the vital or material energy or force that animates everything in the universe.

ren The central Confucian virtue, usually translated as 'humaneness', 'benevolence', 'goodness', or 'compassion'.

taiji The 'Great Ultimate', understood to coexist with the Ultimate of Non-being; also the term for the slow-motion exercise widely known in English as Tai Chi.

tianming The Mandate of Heaven.

Wang Yangming (1472–1529) The Ming Confucian who challenged Zhu Xi's understanding of self-cultivation and established the Neo-Confucian School of Mind.

wuwei 'Not-doing' as a way of being in the world: a state not of 'doing nothing' but of acting without intention or self-interest; an ideal for both Daoists and Confucians, though most prominently associated with the former.

wuxing Five agents, elements and or phases. See **five phases**.

xin The single English transliteration used for two different Chinese characters. The first, translated throughout this chapter as 'heart-mind', is associated with both the thinking and feeling capacities; the second means trustworthiness, a quality valued by Confucians and Daoists alike.

Xunzi (c. 310–219 BCE) The third most important classical Confucian thinker, Xunzi believed that human nature is evil and that conscious effort is required to develop goodness.

yi A moral sense of what is right, what is required and appropriate for a situation; most often used in conjunction with *ren*.

yin-yang wuxing 'Yin' and 'yang' originally referred to the shady and sunny sides of a mountain, but in time they came to be associated with female and male qualities and, more broadly, complementary forces in the universe. *Wu* means 'five' and *xing* can be translated as 'element', 'agent', 'force', or 'phase'. Together, these terms specify the dynamic nature of the universe—a concept integral to the Naturalist school of thought, which was popular during the Han dynasty.

Zhang Daoling Founder of the oldest surviving Daoist school; according to tradition, he established the Way of the Celestial Masters after Laozi appeared to him in a vision in 142 CE.

zhong Integrity or being true to oneself; also the loyalty expected of everyone but especially junior partners in the five relationships: minister, son, younger brother, wife, and younger or less experienced friend.

Zhuangzi (369?–286?) The second most important early Daoist thinker, after Laozi; also the title of the book attributed to him.

Zhu Xi (1130–1200) The systematizer who was the most important member of the Neo-Confucian School of Principle.

Further Reading

Bell, Daniel A., and Chaibong Hahm, eds. 2003. *Confucianism for the Modern World*. Cambridge: Cambridge University Press. Draws from Chinese, Korean, and Japanese texts and histories to argue that Confucianism is relevant to our world.

Buswell, Robert E., ed. 2007. *Religions of Korea in Practice*. Princeton: Princeton University Press. Contains primary-source selections regarding ordinary devotional beliefs and practices together with critical analyses; also includes a helpful introductory essay by Don Baker.

Elman, Benjamin A., ed. 2002. *Rethinking Confucianism: Past and Present in China, Japan, Korea, and Vietnam*. Los Angeles: UCLA Asian Pacific Monograph Series. Explores issues of gender and national variations, and asks who represents Confucianism.

Kirkland, Russell. 2004. *Taoism: The Enduring Tradition*. London: Routledge. An introductory text by an author who believes Daoism has been misrepresented and seeks to offer a new perspective.

Kohn, Livia, ed. 1993. *The Taoist Experience: An Anthology*. Albany: SUNY Press. Primary sources (with brief notes) for a range of philosophical, liturgical, and alchemical texts, mostly from medieval Daoism.

Lopez, Donald S., ed. 1996. *Religions of China in Practice*. Princeton: Princeton University Press. Includes essays on the religious practices of ethnic minorities such as the Manchus and Yi; Stephen Teiser's introductory essay provides a helpful overview.

Miller, James. 2003. *Daoism: A Short Introduction*. Oxford: Oneworld. Covers the historical development, political involvement, and physical practices of Daoism as well as its understanding of nature.

Rainey, Lee Dian. 2010. *Confucius and Confucianism: The Essentials*. London: Wiley-Blackwell. A delightfully accessible introduction to the origins and development of Confucianism, with an account of its contemporary relevance.

Robinet, Isabelle. 1993. *Taoist Meditation: The Mao-Shan Tradition of Great Purity*. Julian F. Pas and Norman J. Giradot, trans. Albany: SUNY Press. A detailed study of the Shangqing (Highest Clarity) tradition.

Wu, Ch'eng-en. 1970 [1943]. *Monkey*. Arthur Waley, trans. New York: Grove Press. A fictional look at popular religious beliefs and practices in medieval China.

Yao, Xinzhong. 2000. *An Introduction to Confucianism*. Cambridge: Cambridge University Press. Focuses on China; Korea and Japan are dealt with very briefly.

Yu, Anthony. 2005. *State and Religion in China*. Chicago and La Salle, IL: Open Court. Argues persuasively that religions in China have always been closely involved with worldly politics.

Recommended Websites

www.orientalarchitecture.com Asian Historical Architecture offers photographs of numerous religious sites in China, Korea, and other countries in Asia, with brief historical notes and descriptions of how the buildings are used.

www.clickkorea.org/ A general-interest site, sponsored by the Korea Foundation; to access essays on Korean religions, select the main category 'Thought & Religion' and then choose from six subcategories.

www.stanford.edu/~pregadio/index.html 'The Golden Elixir: Taoism and Chinese Alchemy' is hosted by Fabrizio Pregadio of Stanford University, who gives a concise introduction to Daoism and includes an impressive list of sources on alchemical beliefs and practices in Daoism.

eng.taoism.org.hk The Taoist Culture and Information Centre offers an insider's view of Daoism's history and place in the world today. The site is sponsored by a

Daoist temple in Hong Kong and maintained with the help of scholars from North America, Europe, and China.

afpc.asso.fr/wengu/wg/wengu.php?l=bienvenue
'*Wengu zhixin*' ('review the old, learn the new') is hosted by the Association Française des Professeurs de Chinois and contains several original Chinese texts with English and French translations. The scholarship is traditional, but the site offers convenient access to texts.

www.chinakongzi.org   The Chinese-language site of the China Confucius Foundation (CCF). Established in 1984, the CCF dedicated to promoting the teachings of Confucius.

www.ica.org.cn   The mandate of the International Confucian Association is to advance the study of Confucianism in order to promote peace and prosperity around the world. Its site is also available in Chinese.

http://english.hanban.org/node_10971.htm   The English-language site of the Confucius Institute/ Classroom offers information on teaching materials, tests, teachers, and scholarships.

http://college.chinese.cn/en   The Confucius Institute Online; the contents of this site are available in many languages, including Chinese, French, German, Russian, Korean, Spanish, Japanese and Arabic.

References

al-Faruqi, I., and D.E. Sopher, eds. 1974. *Historical Atlas of the Religions of the World*. New York: Macmillan.

de Bary, Theodore, ed. 1972. *The Buddhist Tradition in India, China and Japan*. New York: Vintage Books.

Bell, Daniel A., and Chaibong Hahm, eds. 2003. *Confucianism for the Modern World*. Cambridge: Cambridge University Press.

Ch'oe, Yongcho, Peter Lee, and W. Theodore de Bary, eds. 2000. *Sources of Korean Tradition*. Vol. II. New York: Columbia University Press.

Cleary, Thomas. 1989. *Immortal Sisters: Secret Teachings of Taoist Women*. Berkeley: North Atlantic Books.

———, and Irene Bloom, comp. 1999. *Sources of Chinese Tradition*, 2nd edn. Vol. 1. New York: Columbia University Press.

———, and Richard Lufrano, comp. 1999. *Sources of Chinese Tradition*, 2nd edn. Vol. 2. New York: Columbia University Press.

Fung, Yu-lan. 1934/1953. *A History of Chinese Philosophy*. Vol. 2. Derk Bodde, trans. Princeton: Princeton University Press.

Jochim, Christian. 1986. *Chinese Religions: A Cultural Perspective*. Englewood Cliffs, NJ: Prentice-Hall.

Kirkland, Russell. 2004. *Taoism: The Enduring Tradition*. New York and London: Routledge.

Lau, D.C., trans. 1970. *Mencius*. Middlesex and New York: Penguin.

———, trans. 1963. *Lao Tzu: Tao Te Ching*. Middlesex and New York: Penguin.

Lee, Ki-Baik. 1985. *A New History of Korea*. Edward Wagner, trans. Cambridge, MA: Harvard University Press.

Lee, Peter H., et al., eds. 1993. *Sourcebook of Korean Civilization*. Vol. I. New York: Columbia University Press.

Little, Reg. 1995. 'Confucius in Beijing: The Conference of the International Confucian Foundation'. *Culture Mandala: The Bulletin of the Centre for East-West Cultural and Economic Studies*. Vol. 1, issue 2, article 4. Available at http://epublications.bond.edu.au/cm/vol1/iss2/4.

Owen, Stephen, ed. and trans. 1996. *An Anthology of Chinese Literature*. New York, London: W.W. Norton.

Pregadio, Fabrizio. 2006. *Great Clarity: Daoism and Alchemy in Medieval China*. Stanford: Stanford University Press.

Raphals, Lisa. 1998. *Sharing the Light: Representations of Women and Virtue in Early China*. Albany: SUNY Press.

Roetz, Heiner. 2008. 'Confucianism between Tradition and Modernity, Religion, and Secularization: Questions to Tu Weiming', *Dao* 7: 367-380.

Roth, Harold D. 1999. *Original Tao: Inward Training and the Foundations of Taoist Mysticism*. New York: Columbia University Press.

Sommer, Deborah, ed. 1995. *Chinese Religion: An Anthology of Sources*. New York, Oxford: Oxford University Press.

Watson, Burton, trans. 1968. *The Complete Works of Chuang Tzu*. New York: Columbia University Press.

———. 1963. *Xunzi: Basic Writings*. New York: Columbia University Press.

Note

1. Some scholars prefer 552 BCE, based on scientific dating of an eclipse mentioned in the records of the time.

Chapter

11

Japanese Traditions

❧ John K. Nelson ❧

As a way to introduce Japanese religious traditions, let's start with a little comparison. Remember what you were doing last year on New Year's eve? If you don't, maybe it's because so many Western cultures promote drinking yourself silly as the way to mark the end of one year and the start of the next. The Japanese New Year celebration is quite different. A mixture of religious rituals from the country's major religious traditions, it offers the pragmatic benefits of atonement, purification, and revitalization. And if that sounds overly solemn, those benefits are enjoyed in a festive public setting, alongside hundreds and sometimes thousands of people.

A typical New Year's eve would begin at a local Buddhist temple with a large hanging bell that, over the course of the evening, will be struck exactly 108 times. Each ring of the bell represents atonement for one of the 'defilements' (such as greed or hatred) that prevent humans from attaining spiritual awakening and liberation, though hardly anyone can identify all 108 of them.

The next stop is a Shinto shrine for rituals of purification and revitalization. After rinsing their hands and mouths at a special water basin, visitors wait in long lines for the sound of the drum that will signal the start of the new year. At precisely midnight, an excited (but orderly) rush begins as people move forward to throw coins into a vast coffer and offer prayers to the shrine's deities requesting an auspicious year. Many will then purchase a paper fortune or a magical arrow that is thought to ward off evil spirits and bring good luck (a tradition with origins in shamanism and Chinese Daoism).

If all that makes you think that the Japanese are overly religious, think again. A majority of the individuals who buy charms to ward off evil and who mark the new year by taking part in religious rituals would probably tell you that they have no religion at all.

◀ Shinto shrine attendants at a multi-faith ceremony in Nagasaki commemorating the victims of the 1945 atomic bomb (© Franck Robichon/epa/Corbis).

Timeline

c. 8000 BCE	Hunter-gatherers produce sophisticated cord-pattern pottery, arrowheads, and human figures with possible religious significance
c. 450 BCE–250 CE	Immigration from north Asia introduces new technology, cultural forms, language, religious rituals, and other cultural expressions
c. 250–600	Kofun period; rulers interred in massive burial mounds (*kofun*), with grave goods and clay models of attendants that indicate complex local hierarchies in this life and the next
538	Introduction of Buddhism; Yamato clan establishes its dominance over other clans
594	'Prince' Shotoku (*Shotoku taishi*) promotes Confucian principles alongside Buddhism; later considered the patron saint of Buddhism in Japan
600s	Early temple-building; ruler referred to as 'heavenly sovereign' (*tenno*)
710–794	Nara period; capital city, Heijokyo, is located on the site of present-day Nara
712, 720	Compilation of two key texts (*Kojiki, Nihon Shoki*) used to legitimate imperial rule and aristocratic privileges; more than a thousand years later, these texts would be used in the campaign to revitalize 'Shinto'
752	Dedication of Todaiji temple and completion of its Great Buddha image
785	Saicho, founder of Tendai sect, establishes a temple on Mount Hiei
794–1184	Heian period; capital city, Heiankyo, moved to what is now Kyoto
834	Kukai, founder of Shingon sect, establishes a monastery on Mount Koya
985	Genshin produces the text *Essentials of Salvation* that begins Buddhist 'pure land' belief and practice in Japan
1039	Tendai monks attack monasteries of rival Buddhist sects
1052	Beginning of the 'Final Decline of the Buddhist Dharma' (age of *mappo*) marked by fires, famines, earthquakes, wars, pestilence, etc.
1175	Honen begins propagating 'Pure Land' Buddhism
1185–1333	Kamakura period, characterized by dominance of the samurai class; capital moved to Kamakura
1200	Eisai establishes Rinzai Zen school with support of the samurai
1233	Dogen establishes Soto Zen school
1253	Nichiren forms a sect centred on recitation of the *Lotus Sutra*
1254	Honen's disciple Shinran introduces True Pure Land Buddhism
1274, 1281	Attempted invasions by Mongol armies are thwarted when violent storms, called 'divine winds' (*kamikaze*), sink many of their ships
1430–1500	Major fires, famine, epidemics, social disorder; Onin War (1467) devastates Kyoto and marks start of regional power struggles
1474–1550	True Pure Land peasant protest movement spreads throughout the country

1542	Systematization of Shinto shrines, priestly certification via Yoshida clan
1549	Christianity enters Japan with the Jesuit Francis Xavier
1573–1602	Gradual centralization of political power; Oda Nobunaga, Toyotomi Hideyoshi, and Tokugawa Ieyasu establish military regimes that subdue regional lords
1603–1867	Edo Period; Tokugawa clan dominates all political, military, and bureaucratic activity; country closed to outside trade in 1633
1638	Shimabara rebellion; Christianity banned
1644–1860	Rise of Neo-Confucian teachings as challenge to Buddhist dominance
1705	First major pilgrimage of commoners to Ise
1812	Beginning of movement to revitalize Shinto
1853–1867	Commodore Matthew Perry arrives in Japan and demands open ports; Christian missionaries return; regional wars between feudal and imperial forces end with defeat of Tokugawa shogunate
1868	New Meiji government orders separation of *kami* and buddhas, resulting in destruction of many temples and religious art throughout the country
1879	Establishment of Yasukuni Shrine, where the spirits of military dead are venerated
1890–1944	State campaign to establish ideology centered on notions of imperial divinity, Japan as a sacred country, and military conquest
1936–1945	War in the Pacific, ending in the systematic destruction of most major and many minor Japanese cities
1945–1953	Allied occupation of Japan; emperor renounces divinity; disestablishment of Shinto as state religion
1953-1975	The postwar period and a new constitution guarantees religious freedom. Many new religions (such as Soka Gakkai, Tenrikyo, and Omotokyo) grow rapidly, especially in urban areas
1995	Aum Shinrikyo attack on Tokyo subways; government passes new laws regulating religion organizations and activity
2010	Nara commemorates 1,300 years of history, beginning with its role as the capital of Japan from 710 to 794
2011	Pure Land (Jodoshu) and True Pure Land (Jodo shinshu) celebrate their founding, 800 and 750 years ago, respectively

❧ INTRODUCTION

Over the five centuries since Martin Luther launched the Protestant Reformation, most Westerners have come to think of religion as a matter of personal belief, based on individual experience and spiritual needs. A poll conducted in the US in 2010 discovered that 42 per cent of those who reported a religious affiliation had chosen a different religion from the one in which they were raised. We often ask in casual conversation, 'So what religion

Traditions at a Glance

Numbers

(All membership numbers are based on self-assessment by various religious groups. Because most Japanese religions are complementary rather than exclusive, the numbers of adherents reported by various sects may reflect periodic participation rather than ongoing membership.)

Shinto: Estimates range from 3.5 million self-described adherents to more than 100 million if annual New Year's visits to shrines are counted as indicating 'Shinto' affiliation.

Buddhism: Estimates range from 85.1 million, based on a 1999 government assessment of membership in the major denominations, to more than 100 million.

'New' religions: Estimates range from 10 to 30 million worldwide.

Christianity: Generally estimated at a little under 1 million nationwide.

Distribution

Buddhism, Shinto, and 'new' religions are practised in every part of Japan, as well as in overseas communities. Japan itself counts approximately 75,000 Buddhist temples and more than 80,000 Shinto shrines, although many of the latter do not have resident priests.

Founders

Shinto is an ethnic religion, with no founder, that developed through the clans, ancestors, and political affiliations of Japanese leaders and subjects. Important founders of new Buddhist schools include Saicho (Tendai), Kukai (Shingon), Eisai (Rinzai Zen), Dogen (Soto Zen), Honen (Pure Land), Shinran (True Pure Land), and Nichiren (Nichiren).

Deities

Shinto has a vast number of deities known as *kami*, many of which are specific to local communities. Since the late 1800s, the Sun Goddess, Amaterasu, has been promoted as the supreme deity because of her association with the imperial household. The imperial state also actively promoted Hachiman, associated with military valour, in the late nineteenth and early twentieth centuries.

The primary deities in Japanese Buddhism include the Medicine Buddha, the Cosmic Buddha, and Amida, the Buddha of the Pure Land, along with various bodhisattvas associated with compassion, healing, and deliverance from a variety of hells.

Authoritative Texts

Since the nineteenth century the primary texts for Shinto have been the *Kojiki: Record of Ancient Matters* and the *Nihon Shoki*. Individual Buddhist denominations and 'new' religions all have their own primary texts.

Noteworthy Teachings

Shinto leaders and scholars today emphasize harmony with nature, sincerity, and ritual purity. Each Buddhist denomination (Tendai, Shingon, Rinzai Zen, Soto Zen, Pure Land, True Pure Land, and Nichiren) and 'new' religion (Tenrikyo, Omotokyo, Rissho Koseikai, etc.) likewise emphasizes key points of doctrine to differentiate itself from competing sects. These doctrinal matters range from secret teachings about the nature of reality, to faith in the Buddha of the Pure Land, to an absolute reliance on the *Lotus Sutra*, to the importance of memorial rites for ancestral spirits, and so on.

do you believe in?' and we usually respond to almost any answer with a certain degree of respect. After all, to most people belief is a personal matter, and a mature democracy is supposed to honour every citizen's right to freedom of religion.

Contrast this perspective with that of a typical middle-aged Japanese woman who finds it quite natural to ring a bell at a Buddhist temple late on the evening of 31 December and then visit a Shinto shrine in the first minutes of the new year. Religion in Japan is still personal. But it is also pluralistic, and belief is less important than social propriety and cultural conventions.

Over the previous year, the same woman probably celebrated Christmas and Valentine's Day, though the nature of the celebrations would have been distinctly Japanese (at Christmas the emphasis is on special sweets, and women give chocolate to men for Valentine's) and may well have made a nod to Halloween by sending out greeting cards or buying some special food. She almost certainly took part in the more traditional festivals associated with Buddhism, such as **Obon**, when the spirits of the departed are honoured. Now she may be looking forward to a friend's Christian-style wedding, followed by a Shinto-style sharing of sake (rice wine). At the end of her life she may choose to be interred either in the family plot at the local Buddhist temple or in a communal grave for women only. She regularly consults the online horoscopes and occasionally has her palm read. If asked what religion she believes in, she might very well answer 'none'.

In fact, the Japanese language had no equivalent to the word 'religion' until the 1880s, when, as part of a state-directed modernization campaign, the characters meaning 'teachings' (kyo) and 'sect' (shu) were combined to form shukyo. Lack of specific 'religion', however, does not necessarily mean that religious beliefs, feelings, or orientations are lacking (Pye 2004). Japan has no fewer than seven major and 16 minor schools of Buddhism; countless 'new religions', most of them founded in the wake of the government modernization campaign; and what are conventionally said to be more than eight million different **kami**—the individual spirits associated with specific natural phenomena, powers, and places. So it's not surprising that people might feel confused when asked whether they adhere to the teachings of one particular sect. Most Japanese people have no trouble tolerating doctrinal diversity at the popular level. Nor do most religious traditions demand exclusivity.

It should be clear by now that, in Japan, religious belief is generally less important than religious activity. Taking some kind of action—if only to purchase an amulet from a Shinto shrine or a Buddhist temple—may significantly reduce anxiety about an upcoming exam, a relationship problem, or a health condition. Whether someone in need of a blessing gets it at a shrine or a temple depends in part on the nature of the blessing requested and in part on local custom, family tradition, or the recommendations of friends and neighbours, based on their own experience.

In the past, a textbook introduction to Japanese religions would typically emphasize the most important doctrines, institutions, incidents, and leaders associated with each of the three major traditions: Buddhism, Confucianism, and Shinto. This chapter will certainly touch on all of these. However, recent scholarship has questioned the validity of this approach. Scholars now generally agree that for much of Japanese history, these grand religious traditions—one of which did not exist as such until the late nineteenth century—were not discrete or autonomous entities. Specific doctrines and ritual practices have been less important than the benefits they offer for more than a thousand years.

Seeking Benefits

Central to most religious practices in Japan is the pragmatic desire to secure various benefits, either in this world or in the next. It matters little to the average person whether a sanctuary is devoted to the Buddha or to a particular local *kami*. What matters is the efficacy of prayers offered there in helping the petitioner recover from an illness, win a contest, start a new business, pass an examination, find a marriage partner, or conceive a child. A person may visit both temples and shrines, engage priests to perform rituals, and make regular offerings until the desired outcome is obtained—or until it seems clear that those efforts have failed. Then he or she may well have little to do with any organized religion until the next problem arises. 'Turning to the gods in a time of trouble' is a well-known expression that summarizes the pragmatic attitude of the average person in Japan towards religious institutions and beliefs.

To those who identify themselves religiously as Christians, Jews, or Muslims, this behaviour may seem to have more to do with self-interest than spiritual sincerity. Where are the moral codes, the commandments, the sacred texts that guide all aspects of life? Where is the congregation of fellow believers with whom the faithful can share their sorrows and joys? How is it possible to draw from multiple religious traditions without violating at least some 'sacred' principles?

One way to understand the diversity of religion in Japan is to imagine religious life as a marketplace in which consumers decide which shops to patronize on the basis of the products they offer, their quality, and their cost. Variables of time, place, and occasion also enter into consumers' calculations. Thus a religious 'product' appropriate for the end of summer—for example, the ritual that is required to protect the ripening rice crop from insects, typhoons, or fire—is not the same ritual required to protect one's business from financial trouble or one's soul from the flames of hell. Just as consumers know which stores carry the particular goods they want to buy, so Japan's religious consumers know which traditions offer the appropriate assistance for the situation at hand.

Religious and Spiritual Agents: The *Kami*

One of the most fundamental themes of Japanese culture and civilization has been the idea that there is a kind of life-energy that circulates throughout the phenomenal world, and that humans can align themselves with it through worship of the *kami*. Highly mobile, fluid, and capable of entering any object useful for exercising their power, *kami* can be found in flowing water, rain, mountains, clouds, fire, earth, and wind, as well as certain animals that serve as their agents, messengers, and avatars. Their peaceful side helps humans prosper, while their destructive side can only be endured and appeased through rituals.

Mythology

We can see these dynamics at work in the myths explaining the origins of what would become 'Japan'. The basic contours of Japan's creation myth first took shape in the **Kojiki**, a collection of regional stories compiled in 712 CE to legitimate the dominance of the Yamato clan by associating it with the divine origins of Japan. However, these stories were not widely known until the nineteenth or even the twentieth century, when they were circulated as part of the nation-building campaign to create a cultural heritage that citizens of the new nation could share.

The positive and peaceful side of the primordial *kami* couple, Izanagi and his 'wife' Izanami, can be seen in their creation of the islands and the primary elements of the phenomenal world. After a false start produces a 'leech baby', which must be cast aside, the two successfully create all the dimensions of the natural world: seas, straits, winds, trees, mountains, plains. Then suddenly, with neither warning nor rationale, Izanami gives birth to the deity of fire and in the process is fatally burned. As her grieving partner consigns

Map 11.1   Japan: Major cities and religious sites

Source: Adapted from W.A. Young, *The World's Religions*
(Englewood Cliffs: Prentice-Hall, 1995):211.

her body to the land of the dead, he laments: 'Alas, I have given my beloved spouse in exchange for a mere child!' (Philipi 1985: 57).

The destructive side of the *kami* is then revealed in several examples. First, the enraged Izanagi kills the newly-born fire deity and journeys to the gates of Yomi (the netherworld) to beseech his wife to return so that they can continue creating the world. Although she has eaten from the hearth of Yomi, she agrees to negotiate with the gods of the underworld on the condition that Izanagi does not look at her. Of course he cannot resist taking a peek and is shocked to see her corpse covered with 'squirming and roaring maggots' (ibid., 62). As he attempts to flee the underworld, she cries out, 'He has shamed me!' and, furious at this betrayal of trust, sends her 'hags' to stop him. After several narrow escapes, Izanagi leaves the land of the dead and uses a huge boulder to block the opening. As a final example of a *kami*'s vengeful side, Izanami vows that she will cause 1,000 of Izanagi's subjects to die each day, but he counters that he will cause 1,500 to be born.

Izanagi then bathes in a river to purify himself after this ghastly encounter with death and its defilements. As he does so, the female *kami* of the sun, **Amaterasu**, is born from his left eye; she will become the primary deity associated with the imperial family. She is followed by the male moon *kami*, which springs from Izanagi's right eye; then the last imperial *kami*, associated with the land, issues from his nose. Izanagi rejoices: 'I have borne child after child, and finally . . . have obtained three noble children' (ibid., p. 71).

What we learn from this myth is that the *kami* are constantly at work in the natural world, and that they are responsible for both its blessings and its afflictions. *Kami* may also enter into human beings, enabling them to perform heroic tasks, such as unifying warring clans or chiselling a tunnel through solid rock to give a riverside community access to a road. Whenever the well-being of individuals, families, and communities is threatened, the *kami* will be petitioned for help.

ORIGINS

Japan itself has no written records from the first four centuries of the Common Era. However, Chinese histories from the fourth century say that 'the land of Wa' (Japan) was ruled by a female queen who used 'black magic and witchcraft' to control the *kami* and thus maintain power. The belief that early kings and 'emperors' (second to fifth century CE) embodied the *kami* gave their rule legitimacy as a function of divine will.

When these rulers died, earthen mounds (*kofun*) of all sizes and shapes— more than ten thousand in all—were built to house their tombs, into which were deposited various items that they would need in the netherworld. Unlike their counterparts in Egypt and China, however, the Japanese did not sacrifice human beings to accompany their masters to the next life. Instead, they relied on clay models called *haniwa* to provide the servants, musicians, shamans, and soldiers that the ruler would require for life in the next world. These early rulers became guardian spirits of the clans, communities, and regions they once ruled, assuming positions alongside the local *kami*. We can still visit some of their ancient burial sites: at Mount Miwa near Nara (in central Japan) and Yoshigaoka (in northwestern Kyushu), at Asuka and Sakai (both in central Japan; their construction would have required almost as many slave labourers as the Great Pyramid of Cheops), and near Miyazaki (in eastern Kyushu).

From the *Nihon Shoki*

Japan's second oldest book after the Kojiki *(712), the* Nihon Shoki *('Chronicles of Japan', 720) combines origin myths with accounts of the reigns of early emperors. The following extract purports to be from the Korean document recommending Buddhism to the Japanese king.*

This Dharma is superior to all others. It is difficult to grasp and difficult to attain. Neither the Duke of Zhou nor Confucius was able to comprehend it. It can give rise to immeasurable, limitless merit and fruits of action, leading to the attainment of supreme enlightenment. The treasure of this marvelous Dharma is such that it is as if one owned a wish-fulfilling gem that granted every desire. Every prayer is granted and nothing is wanting. Moreover, from distant India to the three kingdoms of Korea, all receive these teachings and there is none who does not revere and honor them (Bowring, 2006: 15).

These traditions changed dramatically after 538 CE, when (according to the chronicle known as the **Nihon Shoki**) the ruler of what is today western Korea wrote to the Japanese king praising the Buddhist dharma as 'superior to all others'. Buddhism offered a whole new set of deities and rituals that could be petitioned to protect the ruler and maintain the status quo. The clans especially devoted to *kami* worship did not simply roll over and submit to this foreign religion, however. There was prolonged contention and conflict over how to accommodate new foreign influences within the existing local orders.

The Great Buddha (Vairocana) that overlooks the interior of Todaiji temple in Nara is nearly 15 metres (50 feet) in height (John K. Nelson).

For its first 150 years in Japan, Buddhism was sustained mainly by clans with ties to Korean immigrants from earlier centuries. But in time its new rituals, its promises of 'liberation' and 'salvation', and its unique teachings attracted state patronage. Meanwhile, a steady stream of refugees from ongoing wars in southern China and the Korean peninsula was arriving in Japan, bringing cultural knowledge—in architecture, philosophy, astrology, divination, courtly protocol—that contributed significantly to the development of the fledgling state.

Japan's first Buddhist temple was constructed in 596 CE with the assistance of Korean builders, and the first Buddhist rituals were conducted there by specialists (both men and women) from the Korean kingdom of Paekche. Remarkably, temples established in those early years are still in existence at places like Shitennoji (in Osaka), Horyuji (in Nara, which incidentally houses the world's oldest wooden building, from the early seventh century), and Todaiji (also in Nara).

Other Spiritual Agents

The role of the **bodhisattva** in Mahayana Buddhist traditions was discussed at some length in Chapter 8. In Mahayana thought, a bodhisattva is an enlightened being who chooses to delay entry into nirvana in order to help all the living beings that have not yet been released from worldly suffering.

The bodhisattva with the greatest reputation for intervening in human affairs is undoubtedly the one known in India as Avalokiteshvara, in China as Guanyin, and in Japan as Kannon. The fact that the bodhisattva of compassion eventually came to be depicted with feminine features may have something to do with the common tendency to associate qualities such as caring and sympathy with women rather than men. Today Kannon is usually depicted as female.

In Japan, Kannon is committed to alleviating the suffering she perceives (*kan*) and hears (*on*). Countless tales of 'miracles' testify to her powers of intercession, especially in desperate situations, when people are facing calamity and death. She was very popular with the warrior class, since one of the gifts she confers is fearlessness in the midst of terror and trouble. But as a female deity, she was considered to be especially receptive to the needs of women in what were, for many, extremely difficult lives. From the terrors of childbirth to maladies of all sorts, and from economic setbacks to the final payoff of religious salvation, Kannon was the 'go-to' bodhisattva when a situation seemed hopeless. Significantly, Kannon is one of the two bodhisattvas shown flanking the Amida Buddha in the sculptures on temple altars and in countless paintings.

Another bodhisattva who has provided comfort to millions of Japanese is known as Jizo (Ksitigarbha in Sanskrit), or, more respectfully and affectionately, Ojizo-sama. Known for his ability to descend into hell and free tormented souls, he also protects children and travellers. With his shaved head, staff, and wish-fulfilling jewel (which lights the darkness), Jizo is an easily recognizable figure, and statues of him can often be seen standing at crossroads or near main thoroughfares. We will encounter Jizo in his most recent role at the end of this chapter.

Unsettled Spirits

The tradition of the 'unsettled spirit' has complex roots, combining native Japanese, Korean, and Chinese folk beliefs and practices with Daoist dynamics and Buddhist demonology. In ancient times, the spirits of people who had lost their lives to powers beyond their control were thought to become angry and very possibly vengeful. In order to calm these spirits, periodic rituals of acknowledgment and pacification were necessary. This belief appears to have been in place since prehistoric times, and it permeates Japanese attitudes towards death even today. One of Japan's most respected scholars of death and dying, Shigeru Gorai, believes that all Japanese funeral and memorial rites reference this tradition, in which the spirits of the dead must be placated before they can become benevolent ancestral influences (Gorai 1994: 105).

Before Buddhism was imported in the early sixth century, spirit appeasement had been the exclusive domain of shamans who venerated the *kami*. Yet even after the aristocracy had begun to adopt Buddhism, the task of calming and controlling potentially vengeful spirits (especially those of assassinated rivals or powerful enemies killed in battle) remained high on the list of state-sponsored ritual activities. To neglect or ignore these spirits was to invite retribution in any number of forms: storms, earthquakes, droughts, infertility, sickness. Accordingly, controlling unsettled spirits has been an enduring responsibility for all of Japan's religious traditions.

A second set of influences that Japanese culture absorbed from the mainland consisted of various concepts and practices that we now associate with religious Daoism. The need to control and exorcise spirits is only one part of this cultural and religious heritage. Attention was clearly paid to the movement of the stars: the constellations painted on the ceilings of imperial tombs help to link the Japanese court to its counterparts in Korea and China, where the same constellations can be found. Stories about magical peaches ('Momotaro') and time-travel ('Urashima Taro') also contain themes that can be traced to Daoist ideas about immortality and alchemy. Even elements of the material culture associated with the imperial household—the mirror, sword, and jewel, as well as the colour purple—have roots in continental Daoist practices, which themselves were influenced by the older traditions of shamanism (Senda 1988: 133–8).

🌱 MOMENTS OF CRYSTALLIZATION

The fluid, richly syncretic nature of Japanese religious traditions makes it impossible to isolate a single moment of 'crystallization'. At best we can identify a series of crystallizing moments occurring over a period of nearly 1,500 years.

Perhaps the first of those moments came during the formative Nara period (710–794). In 701, the government had set up a ministry to manage the shrines of the *kami*. At the same time, a council of senior Buddhist priests formed the Sangha Office to oversee the behaviour, training, and duties of Buddhist monks. The growing Buddhist organization was represented through various bureaus (library, textiles, art and architecture) within the Ministry of Central Management.

This administrative control and oversight helped to set the stage for the Nara and Heian periods. The same basic administrative structure would remain in place for nearly 350 years, reasserting itself whenever a strong centralized government took charge. Knowledge of Chinese history made the early Japanese rulers well aware of the potential of religious organizations and ideas to undermine the state. All religious appointments and construction projects were carefully monitored, and none was permitted to proceed without bureaucratic supervision.

Tendai and Shingon

For roughly three centuries, from its introduction in 538 until the late ninth century, Buddhism was the preserve of the Nara elite, who commissioned Buddhist temples dedicated to their ancestors, consigned their second or third sons to Buddhist monasteries, and sponsored Buddhist art as a way to cultivate religious merit, even as they continued to worship the local *kami* responsible for such crucial matters as weather and agricultural production.

In 804, however, two monks named Saicho (767–822) and Kukai (774–835) travelled separately to China in order to study the dominant forms of Buddhist practice at the time. They would return to 'the land of the rising sun' with some important new perspectives, one of which emphasized the written word. Specifically, they were both impressed with the text known as the *Lotus Sutra*, which had originated in north India, been translated into Chinese (in 209 and again in 406 CE), and was thought to be a vehicle for enlightenment and salvation simultaneously. The *Lotus Sutra* taught that there is only one vehicle to salvation—the body in which we live here and now—and that we all have the potential to become buddhas ourselves. The priests who had mastered the teachings of the *Lotus Sutra* saw themselves as instrumental to the welfare of the state.

When Saicho and Kukai returned from China, in 805 and 806 respectively, they brought with them volumes of teachings and commentaries, paintings, mandalas, and ritual implements, as well as letters from Chinese masters certifying their grasp of the powerful traditions they had studied. It might sound like little more than a wholesale borrowing of the religious 'software' from another culture, but the sects founded by these two monks—Tendai by Saicho and Shingon by Kukai—helped to domesticate Buddhist teachings and rituals in very pragmatic ways.

For one thing, both Tendai and Shingon taught a kind of short-cut approach that put the possibility of enlightenment and salvation within the reach of the common person: anyone could actually *become* a buddha in this lifetime. Though a combination of incantation, ritual gestures, meditation, visualization, and austerities, individuals could connect with and obtain benefits from deities in other spheres of existence. Whereas earlier schools of Buddhism had viewed the human body as highly problematic because of its fragility, desires, and impermanence, the new doctrines, which we now identify as 'tantric' or 'esoteric', attributed a spiritual value to the physical body: much as geothermal steam and seismic activity can be transformed into electricity, bodily desires could be harnessed through ritual and directed towards the quest for salvation and enlightenment.

Another moment of crystallization was the consolidation of the relationship between Buddhism and *kami* worship suggested by the concept of **honji suijaku** (the phrase comes from the *Lotus Sutra*). *Honji*, the 'original ground', refers to the fundamental reality and power of a given buddha or bodhisattva, while *suijaku* refers to the 'trace' or particular form in which the deity chooses to manifest him- or herself in Japan. Thus the *kami* of a particular mountain or a powerful clan came to be seen as the 'provisional manifestation' (*gongen*) of a particular buddha or bodhisattva. Today Buddhist and Shinto deities are clearly differentiated, but for many centuries the *honji suijaku* principle made them essentially interdependent.

The powerful Fujiwara clan established both a shrine honouring its principal *kami* (the Kasuga Grand Shrine in Nara, c. 768) and a major Buddhist temple (Kofukuji), where rituals were performed to memorialize ancestors, heal illness, exorcise spirits, and so forth. Each of the Kasuga *kami* had a specific domain and function, either in sustaining the legitimacy of the Fujiwara regime or in controlling forces and events (insurrections, diseases, earthquakes, etc.) that might threaten the clan's power.

A young *bugaku* dancer performs on the grounds of Osaka's Shitennoji temple, established in 593 CE. An ancient dance form associated with the imperial court, *bugaku* is traditionally performed outdoors (John K. Nelson).

As Buddhism expanded from the ninth century onward, it increasingly overshadowed the traditional ritual practices centred on *kami*. The *honji suijaku* principle was applied to local shrines as a way both to incorporate their *kami* and to give these deities a way to achieve salvation along more obviously Buddhist lines. The four main *kami* of Kasuga—two associated with agriculture and two with war—were linked to Buddhist counterparts: Shakyamuni Buddha, Kannon the bodhisattva of compassion, the Medicine Buddha, and the Buddha of the future.

Taboo Words at the Ise Shrine

To preserve the purity of the Grand Shrine of Amaterasu at Ise, regulations forbade the use of certain terms in the presence of the 'consecrated princess' who served as the imperial family's representative there. In place of the taboo words a special code was used: illness became 'slumber', death 'getting well', and a tomb a 'clod of earth'. In addition to these (presumably) unlucky words, a number of specifically Buddhist terms were forbidden: thus Shakyamuni Buddha was the 'Central One' and a temple a 'tiled roof'; *sutras* were 'dyed paper' and Buddhist monks, with their shaved heads, became 'long hairs'(Felicia Bock, cited in Bowring 2005: 191).

A number of rituals honouring *kami* and buddhas could be performed by priests of either tradition. We are fortunate to have the early eleventh-century diary of a high-ranking noblewoman who served as the chief spiritual medium at the Kamo Shrine in Kyoto, a shrine ranked second in importance only to the Grand Shrine of Amaterasu at Ise (pronounced *ee-say*). A devout Buddhist who aspired to salvation in the Pure Land (see below), she nonetheless served in a ritual capacity for the Kamo deities for nearly four decades (Kamens 1990).

🦎 DIFFERENTIATION

New Sects in the Kamakura and Muromachi Periods

Around the world, people deeply affected by changing political, economic, and cultural conditions have often been open to innovations in religious belief or practice that promise to help them cope with challenging new circumstances. In Japan, not just one but three new types of Buddhist practice emerged during the Kamakura period (1185–1333): Pure Land, Nichiren, and Zen. Significantly, these are the three principal forms of Buddhism still practised in Japan today. It was during the same period that innovations in *kami* worship were laying the foundations for what would eventually come to be known as 'Shinto'.

The relative stability of the Heian period ended in a war that overthrew the courtly families in power since the early days of Japanese civilization and resulted in the destruction of numerous temples, including the magnificent Todaiji. Once the imperial capital of Kyoto was under the control of the new regime, which drew its power from the warrior elite that we call **samurai**, they promptly shifted the centre of political power north to Kamakura, near what is today Tokyo. For the aristocrats, priests, doctors, and merchants still living in the Kyoto region, this was an unmitigated disaster. Yet they knew that conflict, corruption, and vice would be the order of the day because a popular Buddhist teaching had predicted that the year 1052 would mark the beginning of the degenerate age known as **mappo**, during which the Buddhist dharma would decline.

Pure Land Salvation

It is no wonder, then, that a new interpretation of Buddhism promising salvation in a Pure Land gained widespread acceptance at every level of Japanese society. Prior to this development, Buddhism had been almost exclusively the faith of aristocrats. There had been individual monks who worked with the common people—men like Gyoki (668–749), renowned as a bodhisattva for his charity and public works, and Kuya (903–972), who used song and dance to convey the dharma to the lower classes—but it was not until Genshin (942–1017) organized Pure Land beliefs into a coherent system that Buddhism began to attract wide public attention. To make the doctrine of salvation more compelling, his *Essentials of Salvation* (*Ojo yoshu*, completed in 985), described in graphic, often terrifying detail the six realms of existence (hell, hungry ghosts, demonic beings, animals, human beings, and heavenly beings) through which every living creature must pass, in multiple incarnations, before reaching the perfection of the Pure Land.

For the first time in Japan, groups of Buddhist monks began to concern themselves with the salvation of the ordinary person, but it took another two hundred years before a new institutional form emerged that gave practical expression to their concern. It was a Tendai monk, frustrated by his sect's preoccupation with politics and the profits it took from its vast landholdings, who developed Pure Land Buddhism as we know it today. Honen (1133–1212) believed it was impossible for people in an age of *mappo* to attain salvation by traditional means (following the precepts, chanting *sutras*, meditating, worshipping the Buddhist deities), so he emphasized repeated recitation of the **nenbutsu**. Honen argued that the saving grace of **Amida Buddha** did not discriminate according to social rank, past karma, or present activity: sincere faith and repeated recitation of '*Namu Amida Butsu*' alone were enough. In this way Honen opened the door to what was then the radical notion of universal salvation.

In 1207 Honen was banished from the Kyoto region. Also banished was his disciple Shinran (1173–1262). Earlier that year, Shinran had scandalized both temple and courtly communities by marrying—a 'degenerate' practice that was fairly common among monks (as was keeping a concubine) but was *never* made public. Shinran reasoned that if the power of Amida Buddha was great enough to save even those of the lowest social status, mere marriage could not be a serious impediment to achieving salvation.

Honen's exile lasted only four years, but Shinran was banished for seven. According to popular biographies, he used this time to preach and organize among farmers and fishermen, refining his 'True Pure Land' doctrine to the point of maintaining that a *single* sincere repetition of the *nenbutsu* would secure salvation. Shinran believed human beings

The Amida Hall of the Isshinji temple in Osaka is dedicated to the Buddha of the Pure Land (John K. Nelson).

to be incapable of mustering the disciplined 'self-power' (*jiriki*) necessary for attaining salvation: therefore we must rely on 'other-power' (*tariki*) for deliverance from suffering.

In the tumultuous disorder of the Kamakura period (and beyond), Pure Land teachings gained wide popular support, but detractors were still powerful. In 1227, monks from the Tendai temples on Mount Hiei desecrated Honen's grave and burned copies of his major works. Pure Land was spread via small groups devoted to *nenbutsu* practice. Around 1450, the eighth hereditary leader of the True Pure Land movement, Rennyo, began to systematize the teachings and organize the scattered True Pure Land communities into a well-disciplined religious group. Taking advantage of a time of widespread civil unrest, he drew on the existing networks of True Pure Land followers to create a kind of militant security force dedicated to protecting the sect's Honganji temple (in what is today the city of Osaka).

The result was a new development in Japanese Buddhism: bands of armed peasants and low-ranking samurai loyal to the True Pure Land tradition rose up against those they saw as oppressors. These were not the first Buddhists to take aggressive action: as early as 1039, Tendai 'monk warriors' from Mount Hiei had attacked rival sects and temples, and even challenged the legitimacy of the imperial court itself. Four centuries later, however, the True Pure Land insurrection was led by masterless samurai and common people. With nothing to lose and salvation guaranteed through their faith in Amida Buddha, fearless True Pure Land militias were able to hold their own against experienced armies and sometimes even overwhelm them. By 1500 they controlled several provinces as well as what is today the city of Osaka. Although their fortress temple in that city was never breached, they were finally defeated and brought at least partially under control by the warlord Oda Nobunaga in the 1580s.

Rinzai Zen and Kamakura Culture

Zen Buddhism established itself in Japanese society in much the same way as Pure Land, but with an important difference: Zen was imported directly from China, and its development benefited from the leadership of Chinese masters who immigrated to Japan in the thirteenth century. Although the seeds of Zen can be found in Tendai doctrines as early as the ninth century (when a meditation practice referred to as 'constantly sitting' was introduced), it was not until the latter part of the twelfth century that the tradition took root, imported by a Japanese monk who had encountered it during a visit to China in 1168.

The word 'zen' is the Japanese version of the Chinese word *chan*, which is itself a translation of the Sanskrit term for meditation, *dhyana*. Whereas the Pure Land traditions focused directly on securing salvation through simple recitation of the name of Amida Buddha, the Chan/Zen tradition saw salvation as a distant goal, to be attained only at the end of a long and rigorous quest for enlightenment through the disciplined practice of seated meditation.

The cultural exchanges that had led to the introduction of the Tendai and Shingon sects to Japan four hundred years earlier—along with many other cultural innovations in areas from architecture and music to medicine and astrology—had been terminated in the ninth century, after the Japanese government learned of the Tang dynasty's persecution of Buddhism. The next time Japanese monks and bureaucrats ventured to China was in 1168, after Japan had experienced its own political upheaval.

Among the religious members of the 1168 delegation was a Tendai monk named Eisai (1141–1215) who went to China expecting to explore the traditions from which Tendai and Shingon had developed in the ninth century. Instead he discovered Chan. The state persecution campaign of 845 had targeted the esoteric traditions because of their lavish wealth, landholdings, political meddling, and 'parasitic' monks and nuns who did nothing for society. Chan temples, however, were located mostly in rural areas, where their monks worked with their hands and displayed none of the elaborate trappings that had become attached to other traditions. Although it too suffered persecution, Chan was better positioned than the other schools to survive, and by the twelfth century it was the dominant Buddhist tradition in China.

Eisai stayed in China for only six months, but he studied Chan doctrines for the next 20 years while continuing to fulfill his duties as a Tendai priest. A second trip to China in 1187 gave him the opportunity to study with an eminent Chan master in the Linji (Rinzai in Japanese) tradition, who certified his enlightenment before he returned to Japan in 1191. In addition to his knowledge of Chan, Eisai imported other Buddhist and Confucian teachings—as well as a plant from which a hot drink could be made to keep sleepy monks awake during meditation. His work 'Drink Tea and Prolong Life' is credited with promoting tea in Japan; and the tea ceremony (developed a century later) was deeply influenced by Zen aesthetics and symbolism.

Soto Zen, the Gradual Path

The other major Zen school, also based on a Chinese tradition, promotes 'gradual enlightenment' through the practice of 'just sitting' without any conceptual or metaphoric stimulation.

According to the Soto school, its founder, Dogen (1200–53) began his studies at the Tendai monastery on Mount Hiei, but was troubled by a persistent question: if humans are born with an innate Buddha-nature, as the Tendai school maintained, why should it take so much effort to achieve enlightenment? After studying at Kenninji with Eisai's successor, the young monk somehow gained a place with an official mission to China in 1223, in the course of which he encountered a Chan tradition known as Caodong. Its emphasis on integrating body and mind through activity became central to Dogen's concept of

Dogen and the Cook

As a young monk travelling in China, the founder of the Soto Zen school, Dogen, encountered an old priest who was serving in the office of *tenzo* (head cook). Dogen felt the *tenzo* was working too hard for a person of his age, so he asked him, 'Reverend sir, why don't you do *zazen* or read the ancient texts? What is the use of working so hard as a cook, drying these mushrooms in the blazing sun?' The *tenzo* laughed for a long time and then he said, 'My foreign friend, it seems you don't really understand Zen practice or the words of the ancients.'

Hearing the elder monk's words, Dogen felt ashamed and surprised. He asked, 'What is practice? What are words?' The *tenzo* said, 'One, two, three, four, five.' Dogen asked again, 'What is practice?' and the *tenzo* replied, 'Everywhere, nothing is hidden' (adapted from Dogen 1996).

Inside the hall for visitors to Eiheiji, a hand-painted map shows the layout of the main Soto Zen monastery, established far from the center of political power by the priest Dogen in 1246 (John K. Nelson).

liberation. Supposedly, a conversation with a monastery cook helped him understand the importance of 'enlightened activity' and led to his own spiritual awakening.

On his return to Kyoto in 1227, it became apparent to Dogen that his Soto Zen could not hope to compete with the increasingly influential Rinzai school. Leaving the capital voluntarily, he discovered local aristocrats and wealthy landowners outside the cities who were more receptive to his message than the samurai had been. The Eiheiji monastery he founded (near present-day Fukui city) is still the headquarters of the Soto denomination, and continues Dogen's emphasis on 'just sitting' *zazen* coupled with rigorous study and physical labour.

Nichiren

The last new Buddhist sect of the Kamakura period was founded by a charismatic priest who drew on the Tendai tradition of reciting mantras but believed that the only path to salvation, for the individual and for the nation, lay in the teachings of the *Lotus Sutra*. Convinced that it provided an all-encompassing guide to both secular and spiritual affairs, Nichiren (1222–82) instructed his followers to study its teachings and chant the mantra '*Namu myoho renge kyo*' ('Hail the marvellous teaching of the *Lotus Sutra*!'). To Nichiren, other types of Buddhism were merely provisional, introductory teachings, irrelevant in the final, degenerate age of *mappo*.

After being expelled from his monastery in Kyoto, he travelled to Kamakura where he preached on street corners the radical message that 'the *nenbutsu* is hell, Zen is a devil, and Shingon is the nation's ruin.' He was exiled twice for subversive teaching and was even sentenced to death—a fate he was spared only because (according to his account) the executioner's sword was shattered by divine intervention as it was about to fall on his neck. Nichiren's 1260 work, 'On Establishing the True Dharma to Bring Peace to the Nation' (*Ankoku-ron*), established him as a pioneer in politicizing religion. If the nation suffered invasions, plagues, and social disorder, he argued, it was the fault of the ruler who had not adopted the *Lotus Sutra* as his guide to sound governance.

When Japan actually was invaded by the Mongol dynasty in 1274, Nichiren's warnings were seen as a kind of prophecy, and he was pardoned. Weary of continual confrontation, he accepted an offer of land at Mount Minobu, not far from Mount Fuji. The temple he established there became both a memorial to his teachings and a training facility for the next generation of disciples. Devoted students such as Niko, Nissho, and Nichiko proselytized widely, and though they were harassed by the authorities and ostracized by other Buddhist sects, they succeeded in establishing a network of temples throughout central Japan. However, each had different ideas about what should be emphasized, leading to centuries of factionalism. It's important to note that some of Japan's most prominent 'new religions'—Nichiren Shoshu, Soka Gakkai (which has branches all over the world and counts a number of Hollywood celebrities among its adherents), Rissho Koseikai—trace their roots to one or another of these sectarian denominations.

Confucianism and the Beginnings of Shinto

In the thirteenth century, when Japanese Tendai monks were once again travelling to China and returning with new teachings and texts, and Chinese Chan masters were coming to

Major Branches of Buddhism in Japan

First-time visitors to Japan may be tempted to think that if they've seen one temple, they've seen them all. While older temples do tend to resemble one another in architectural style (modelled on Chinese temple designs), there is actually wide variation among the many Buddhist denominations in Japan.

The oldest traditions are found in the Nara region (central Japan). The **Hosso**, **Ritsu**, and **Kegon** schools (among others) were introduced in the years around 600 CE and have remained quite close to their Chinese roots. The next stage of development began in the ninth century with the founding of the **Tendai** and **Shingon** schools, which took on a more distinctly Japanese character. Several hundred years later, during a long period of political change and instability that stretched from the twelfth century to the fifteenth, a number of new sects appeared. These included two types of **Zen** (**Rinzai** and **Soto**) and two of Pure Land (**Jodo** and **Jodo shinshu**). Finally, the same period produced the Nichiren school, with its exclusive emphasis on the *Lotus Sutra*.

When scholars discuss the dominant types of Buddhism in Japan today, the focus tends to be on the seven denominations that developed after the eighth century. Of these seven, the ones with the greatest numbers of temples are Jodo Shinshu and Soto Zen.

Japan to head Rinzai Zen temples, the teachings of Confucius also made the journey from China. Although Confucian ideas (dating from the fifth century BCE) had been present at the very beginning of Japanese civilization in the sixth century CE, they had not developed into a distinct body of knowledge or ritual practices. During the political and social disruptions of the Kamakura and Muromachi periods, however, Japan's ruling classes began to take a new interest in religions and philosophies that promoted order in society.

Confucian values, as interpreted by the scholar Zhu Xi, laid out the 'Way' that every member of society—ruler, minister, parent, friend, child—should follow, as determined by his or her position in that society. Awareness of the responsibilities in each relationship would promote reciprocity between superiors and subordinates, which in turn would foster a stable and harmonious society. Zen monks found that these teachings resonated with their own monastic and religious traditions, and so they were taught within the 'Five Mountain' system of Zen temples and monasteries in Japan, and were recommended to rulers by their Buddhist advisers for nearly four hundred years.

The Emergence of 'Shinto'

And what of the older tradition based on the ritual veneration of natural and human spirits called *kami*? Recent scholarship has demonstrated that it was only in the medieval period that 'Shinto' began to take form as a distinct and self-conscious organization. With the replacement of the imperial court by the shogunate after 1185, the Ise Grand Shrines, dedicated to the sun goddess Amaterasu, lost their main source of financial support, and by the early fifteenth century they were in obvious decline. Fearful of further decay, their priests had to devise new strategies to attract support.

Since the early eleventh century, the imperial household had made regular pilgrimages to the Kumano shrines some 80 kilometres to the west, rather than Ise. Therefore the priests opened up Ise to visits from samurai and lower-ranking officials and developed new rituals for them. Purification was of primary importance, but now, in recognition of the institutional power of Tendai and Shingon and the doctrine of *honji suijaku*, Ise ritual practices were coupled with Buddhist notions of enlightenment so that, instead of competing, the two traditions complemented one another. At one time there were more than three hundred Buddhist temples on the Ise shrine grounds.

With its emphasis on rituals rather than texts, the 'way of the *kami*' had always lacked the kind of conceptual structure that was so highly developed in Buddhism. Now the Ise priests set out to reverse the *honji suijaku* principle that the *kami* were lesser manifestations of the original buddhas and bodhisattvas. They argued that *kami* were indigenous to the land of Japan, and that although they could have Buddhist counterparts, they were not subordinate to Buddhist deities. With new doctrines in place, pilgrimages at an all-time high, and increasing interest in the power of Ise's main deities to provide benefits even for common people, a foundation was in place for the *kami* tradition to assume a new importance in the life of the nation. An organized system began to emerge in 1542, when the central government granted the powerful Yoshida clan the authority to appoint and demote shrine priests outside of Ise. Today, in part because of Ise's appeal as a source of Japanese cultural identity and its association with imperial mythology, the Ise Grand Shrines receive more than five million visitors annually.

Torii gateways, each one donated by an individual or organization, line the ascent of the sacred mountain of Fushimi Inari Shrine in Kyoto. Inari is the *kami* of rice, business, and prosperity (John K. Nelson).

❧ PRACTICE

The variety of benefits (*riyaku*) that worshippers may seek is almost endless: from good health and financial prosperity to individual salvation in the afterlife, fertility and beneficial weather to enlightened governance. Equally diverse are the religious practices believed to help bring about these conditions. Here are just a few examples:

- Individuals, families, businesses, entire communities, or even political leaders can contract religious specialists to conduct rituals at a temple or shrine. In most cases, petitioners address their requests to a particular spiritual agent (buddha, bodhisattva, or *kami*) believed capable of exerting a beneficial influence on the situation in question.
- Undertaking a pilgrimage to a sacred place is another way of accessing benefits in this world and beyond. Even today, the 88 sacred temples of the island of Shikoku are regularly visited by more than 100,000 pilgrims a year. Some walk the entire 1,400 km route at once, but most take buses or private transportation and complete the journey in segments, as time permits. Smaller, less demanding pilgrimage routes exist all over Japan, each of which is believed to provide pilgrims with some kind of spiritual benefit.
- Grand festivals (**matsuri**) involving the entire community generate benefits not only for those who participate but even for those who do not. Although many

Buddhist temples have also adopted this practice, it is especially common for Shinto shrines to periodically remove their central object of worship and place it in a portable shrine that can be paraded through the community. In large communities, the *matsuri* can be a major annual event commanding a staggering degree of financial, personal, and administrative commitment.

A second widespread religious practice is the veneration and memorialization of spirits. Unlike Western traditions, in which the spirits of the deceased have no lingering engagement with this world, the religious traditions of East Asia and Japan in particular maintain that the spirits of the dead continue to play an active part in the lives of the living. Whoever the deceased may have been in life—a religious leader, a soldier killed in war, the sweetest grandmother in the world—his or her spirit may become angry or vengeful in death. Therefore periodic rituals are performed long after the funeral to ensure that this does not happen. If the spirits are satisfied, they can become benign and beneficial allies to those who show them the proper respect.

❦ Cultural Expressions

From painting and sculpture, architecture and landscape design, to ritual attire and habits of personal hygiene derived from purification rituals, countless elements of Japanese culture reflect the influence of religion. Let's consider just a few of the things that a visitor to Japan would likely encounter in the course of a week.

Even before leaving the international airport, a visitor might see an example of *ikebana*, the Japanese art of flower arranging. Having developed in Buddhist temples, where the spare, deceptively simple arrangements were used in memorial services, the practice of *ikebana* eventually filtered through all social classes. Today there are many different styles of *ikebana*, but most still share a few basic features, including organic materials (not necessarily flowers—stems and leaves are at least as important), sensitivity to the season, balanced composition, and poetic or religious symbolism (a classic three-part arrangement, for instance, is likely to symbolize heaven, earth, and humanity).

A similar combination of natural materials, restrained composition, and religious symbolism is found in the Japanese garden. The art of garden design also developed first at temples, where a few artfully placed rocks in a bed of gravel might symbolize islands

Barrels of sake are often presented as offerings to the resident deities at both temples and shrines. After the ritual presentations have finished, the contents are distributed to parishioners and priests (Liba Taylor/Corbis).

in the sea of eternity. Gardens were later constructed in imperial palaces and, as the centuries passed, on the estates of wealthy aristocrats, samurai, and merchants. Today even the most humble residence will often have a carefully tended garden that evokes ancient cultural values. The temple has also been a major influence on architecture. The sweeping roof lines, overhanging eaves, and verandas of the classic temple have consti-tuted the dominant paradigm for builders for more than a thousand years. Inside the traditional Japanese house, one room would typically be modelled on the abbot's quarters in a temple, with a scroll painting hanging in an alcove, an *ikebana* arrangement, and open space conveying a calming sense of space in harmony with form. Even many ultramodern high-rise condominiums still try to incorporate the alcove into their designs.

The influence of Japan's religious traditions can also be seen in both literature and popular culture. The minimalism of image and language in the *haiku*, for example, is said to reflect Zen's emphasis on penetrating to the essence of reality. In its 17 syllables, the *haiku* typically offers both sharply defined detail and a connection to a wider universe. The following *haiku* was composed in the late 1600s by one of Japan's most noted poets, Matsuo Basho (1644–94):

The sea darkens;
the plaintive calls of the wild ducks
are faintly white.

One final example of the way ancient religious traditions are reflected in contemporary Japan concerns the major holiday season at the end of one year and beginning of the next. We saw at the beginning of this chapter how Buddhist and Shinto ritual practices work hand-in-hand to give the transition special significance. More than 70 per cent of Japan's roughly 120 million people take part in these customs. On returning home from the shrines and temples it's common to enjoy a bowl of buckwheat *soba* noodles, not only because they taste good but also because their length symbolizes a long life and abundant new year. For individuals unable (or, because of the sizeable crowds, unwilling) to visit a shrine on New Year's eve, the next five days are considered equally auspicious, and some people visit more than one shrine. Western observers might assume that Japanese Christians would not take part in these customs, but in fact many Christians will attend a midnight church service and then visit a shrine sometime during the next five days. It is a festival, after all, and religious beliefs are less important than participation in a central expression of Japanese culture.

INTERACTION AND ADAPTATION

Christianity, New Religions, and Native Learning

In the fifteenth century, while Japan was embroiled in a series of wars over local territory, European powers such as Spain, Portugal, the Netherlands, and England were navigating the globe, claiming new territory for their kings and new souls for the Christian church.

The first Europeans to reach Japan were some shipwrecked Portuguese sailors who arrived there in 1543, but they were soon followed by Jesuit missionaries under the leadership of Francis Xavier (1549). The Jesuit strategy for missionary work was to take advantage of the Portuguese ships travelling between Macao (near what is today Hong Kong), India, Mozambique, and Europe for transport and use the lucrative incentive of trade as leverage to gain access to ports and rulers.

Christianity's Rise and Fall

Had Japan not been in a state of ongoing internal conflict, it is doubtful that the Jesuits would have been permitted to enter Japan at all. Yet because of a unique convergence of social and political factors, they were able to broker agreements with a number of local warlords. It was also a stroke of luck that the first Europeans arrived during the rise to power of Japan's first military unifier, Oda Nobunaga. Highly distrustful of the Tendai warrior-monks as well as the True Pure Land militias, Nobunaga tolerated Christianity for its potential to undermine the strength of Buddhism in Japan. He also tolerated the missionaries because he profited handsomely from the trading opportunities that came with them.

Although Nobunaga was assassinated in 1582 by one of his own vassals, his chief aide quickly established himself as a visionary leader and patron of religion. Toyotomi Hideyoshi continued the unification effort that Nobunaga had begun, but he also embarked on a building and consolidation campaign among Buddhist and Shinto sects that led to the construction of many of the temples and shrines we see today. So great were his economic resources that he even tried twice to take the Korean peninsula in preparation for an invasion of China (neither attempt succeeded).

Hideyoshi's tolerance extended beyond Buddhism to Christianity, which by 1590 may have acquired as many as 100,000 converts. Not all the conversions were voluntary: some were forced by local warlords seeking to facilitate trade first with the Portuguese and later with the Spanish and Dutch. New legal restrictions were imposed on Christian missionaries, however, after a Spanish ship ran aground in Shikoku in 1596 and its captain threatened military reprisals to be delivered by an armada stationed in the Philippines. A number of European missionaries and Japanese converts were expelled and some were put to death.

The third of Japan's great unifiers, Tokugawa Ieyasu, at first tolerated Christianity (because of the lucrative trade), but in time he came to see its priests as meddlesome and disruptive of the social order. His successors in the 1620s cracked down hard, requiring all adults to register at the local Buddhist temple; those who resisted or refused to step on an image of Jesus or Mary were arrested and threatened with torture if they did not recant their Christian faith.

In 1637 an estimated 25,000 oppressed peasants and rogue samurai warriors took over an abandoned castle in Shimabara, Kyushu, and tried to mount an armed insurrection. Using Christian symbols on their flags, this rag-tag army held off the government's forces for nearly seven months. Dutch ships were called in to bombard the rebel fortifications, but with little effect. It was only when the rebels ran out of food and gunpowder that an army of more than 125,000 was able to storm the fortifications and kill all those inside, effectively ending the last resistance to the Tokugawa regime.

With the defeat of the Shimabara rebels, Japan closed the door not only on Christianity but on Europe. From 1641 to 1853, the only port open to the outside world was Dejima, a small artificial island near Nagasaki, and it was rigidly controlled. Christianity did not entirely disappear, however. Rather, it went into hiding in remote valleys and on far-flung islands. Believers adopted Buddhist practices but continued reciting mass and worshipping images of the Virgin Mary disguised as the bodhisattva Kannon.

Unification and Stability

As part of its effort to impose stability after half a century of political turmoil, the Tokugawa shogunate set out to restructure Japanese society into four distinct classes: samurai, farmers, artisans, and merchants. This structure (like the temple registration law) was inspired by the Confucian doctrines introduced to Japan by Chinese Chan priests some four hundred years earlier. In addition, a number of newer Confucian texts discovered in Korea during Hideyoshi's attempted invasions were now re-interpreted in ways that would promote the regulation of society above all other values.

Each social class was given specific guidelines regarding occupation, travel, and civic duties, with infractions punishable by the confiscation of property, imprisonment, or execution. Likewise, the central government imposed regulations on both Buddhist and Shinto institutions, requiring them to adopt a hierarchical organizational model that held both sect leaders and branch priests accountable for adhering to the rules. The Tokugawa **shoguns** had Zen priests as some of their closest advisers in the seventeenth and early eighteenth centuries. Buddhist priests continued to provide counsel, but as the regime tightened its control over the nation, it also sought advice from Neo-Confucian scholars.

The overall mood of society was changing as well. During the medieval period, Buddhism had flourished because its doctrines of salvation in the next life offered hope to people whose prospects in this life were bleak. Now, with growing economic prosperity in the cities and order imposed by a police state (although heavy taxes and famines still sparked periodic rebellions in the countryside) Neo-Confucianism became more relevant to Japan. Scholars and intellectuals developed ideologies that were critical of Buddhism and emphasized what they considered to be truly 'Japanese' qualities.

New Religious Expressions

Scholars in particular were eager for new philosophies that would explain the meaning of life and the individual's purpose in society from a perspective less fatalistic than the one that Buddhism offered. The first wave of Neo-Confucian thought, beginning in the late 1500s, promoted a vision of harmony between the basic principles of the universe (purity, honesty, sincerity, moderation) and the role of the individual, whose true inner nature was said to demand acceptance of his or her place in the social order. No wonder these new applications of Confucian principles appealed to the authorities of the time! Disseminated through essays, teaching academies, and government policies, Neo-Confucian ideas encouraged the development of inner constraints based on the individual's intellect, reason, morals, and sense of propriety. Government officials produced almanacs and calendars promoting Neo-Confucian principles of social regulation, and counselled village head men accordingly. Hayashi Razan and Yamazaki Ansai were key figures in this movement, as was Yamaga Soko, the seventeenth-century scholar who codified samurai ethics to create the 'way of the warrior' known as **bushido**.

The next movement, beginning in the late 1600s, was 'Native Learning' or *Kokugaku* (literally, 'study of one's country'). Its advocates argued for the superiority of all things Japanese over their foreign counterparts, including the superiority of native spiritual traditions over Buddhism and Confucianism. Some scholars believed that for convincing evidence of Japan's superiority, one needed only to consider the story of Noah and the flood, which Japan had survived untouched. Likewise, the reason Japan had not produced medical breakthroughs was that it was essentially pure and less polluted than other countries (Jansen 2000: 208). Scholars like Motoori Norinaga used ancient texts like the *Kojiki* (which contains the highly dramatic foundation myth of Izanagi and Izanami) to suggest the will of the *kami* regarding the roles of a ruler and his subjects. In so doing, they implied that the solution to the country's growing political problems and the threats it faced from abroad lay in direct imperial rule—although to voice this opinion publicly would surely have led to charges of treason.

In 1825, during the last decades of the 250-year-old shogunate, the scholar and samurai Aizawa Seishisai argued for the unification of religion and the state on the model of the colonial powers from Europe that were slowly encircling and threatening Japan's sovereignty. He urged the adoption of Shinto as the national faith and the sun deity Amaterasu as the primary *kami* as a way to enhance national polity (*kokutai*). These ideas created controversy at the time, but they later became central to the leaders of samurai clans in the far west and south.

While emphasizing the role of Neo-Confucian and nativist thinking on political affairs at this time, we should not lose sight of the consequences for the religious life of commoners. By and large, the Tokugawa period of nearly 250 years saw society stabilize into distinct classes, each with specific attributes, obligations, and regulations governing their activities. There was very little upward mobility except among an increasingly powerful merchant class whose money could purchase rank, whose daughters could marry impoverished samurai or aristocrats, and whose patronage was crucial to the stability of local and regional religious institutions.

Japanese society became even more patriarchal and stratified during this period as Chinese-Confucian models of superior/subordinate relationships affected not only social relations but also courtship and marriage. With so few paths open to their personal and intellectual development, many women turned to religion as a refuge from the stifling restrictions of social life. One of the few ways they could leave home for brief periods of time without public censure was to embark on a short pilgrimage, or to spend part of a day visiting local religious sites. It would take an actual revolution and a change of political regime to improve their position.

In 1868, following a brief but bloody civil war, samurai clans from Japan's western region overthrew the Tokugawa state. Well aware of how far behind Japan had fallen during its period of isolation, and fearing colonization by European and American powers, the new government embarked on an unprecedented program of industrialization, militarization, and nation-building. Legitimized by a new emphasis on the emperor's status as a direct descendent of the *kami* (exactly as Aizawa had recommended four decades earlier), this agenda would dramatically alter Japan and the Asian region in both positive and negative ways.

🦁 JAPANESE RELIGIONS IN RECENT HISTORY

How does a government create a nation of citizens where only feudal loyalties had existed before? This was the daunting challenge that faced the social architects of the Meiji government (1868–1911). Whereas the previous regime had been named after the dominant clan, the new government named itself after the emperor Meiji, in acknowledgement of the 'divine' authority that legitimated the policies of the state. In its effort to promote a kind of national cult based on the emperor and his associations with various *kami* and Shinto precedents, the state subjected Buddhism to a brief but dramatic period of persecution, in part because it had served the Tokugawa military government so well.

Institutions that had been fully syncretic—combining Buddhist and *kami* worship— were now split apart. Their ritual specialists were either forced into lay life or re-educated as government-certified Shinto priests. Even more extreme was the destruction promoted by over-zealous officials and carried out by mobs. Temple grounds all over Japan are still scattered with the remains of Buddhist statues decapitated during this period.

The government embarked on ambitious programs of education, industrialization, and militarization modelled on Western precedents. Shinto was designated the official religion of the state, although adherence to it was described by the state as a matter of 'civic duty' rather than religious conviction. Not everyone supported these policies, of course. However, a series of wars with China (1894–95), Russia (1904–05), and Korea (1910)—which cost the lives of some 80,000 young men while gaining Japan overseas resources that it would use to expand its manufacturing base—inspired a general patriotic fervour that drowned out opposition voices.

It was during this period that the government sponsored the establishment of a shrine dedicated to the veneration of the spirits of soldiers who had died in the service of the nation. Although Shinto shrines had traditionally avoided association with the impurity of death, the Yasukuni Shrine in Tokyo combined Shinto-style rituals with Buddhist ancestor worship and shamanic traditions of spirit appeasement and control. As young men cut down in the prime of life, Japan's military dead were at high risk of becoming unsettled and vengeful spirits. The emperor and his household, high-ranking government officials, and leading businessmen, intellectuals, and even Buddhist priests all visited the shrine regularly to pay their respects during the Second World War.

Shrines throughout the country were coerced into participating in a 'spirit-cycle' that saw ancient local festivals appropriated for the purposes of civic and national unity. There was no greater glory (according to the government and educational curriculum) than to die for the nation and be enshrined at Yasukuni. An imperial edict on education instructed the youth of Japan that, 'should emergency arise', they were expected to

offer [themselves] courageously to the State; and thus guard and maintain the prosperity of Our Imperial Throne coeval with heaven and earth' (Hardacre 1989: 122).

The 'divine wind' (*kamikaze*) missions undertaken in desperation at the end of the Second World War to attack American naval vessels in the Pacific were extreme expressions of this ideology.

After Japan's devastating defeat in 1945, a period of occupation by the Allied forces laid the groundwork for its transformation into a stable democracy. The emperor was obliged to renounce his divinity and Shinto was stripped of its status as the *de facto* state religion. In the spiritual void that followed a war in which so much had been lost, constitutional guarantees of religious freedom encouraged a proliferation of new religious movements. Among them were Soka Gakkai and Rissho Koseikai (both based on the *Lotus Sutra*), Shinnyo-en (derived from Shingon), and others such as Mahikari (True Light) and Perfect Liberty Kyodan (Obaku Zen), each of which claims more a million followers today.

Women in post-war Japan

Compared to previous periods of Japanese social history, the post-war period was liberating for women. Not only did they join new religions—where personal belief blended with self-help and personal empowerment—in very high numbers, they also sought more participation in the affairs of local temples and shrines. Nearly every religious institution in Japan now has a 'women's group' in which women from the neighborhood meet to discuss topics of interest, hear guest speakers, and find ways to volunteer their services for the temple or shrine. They do this not because they are coerced into service, as was the case before the war, but because they find significance in the spiritual merit (as well as the social capital) that their efforts produce.

This is not to say that there is no need for greater equality with men in Japan's religious worlds. It is very rare for a Shinto shrine to have a woman as its head priest: appointment to that position almost always depends more on heredity than on individual skill or qualifications. In Buddhism as well, women have been discriminated against for centuries regardless of the principle that all sentient beings possess the same capacity for enlightenment.

The True Pure Land (Jodo shinshu) tradition has been the most accommodating of Japan's Buddhist denominations, perhaps because its founder, Shinran, dared to marry and have a family. There are more female priests in Jodo shinshu than in any other tradition. But it would be a mistake to focus on women-as-priests and ignore the influential roles that women play as wives to head priests. A priest's wife is expected to produce a male heir who will inherit the temple from his father. However, she is also a partner in the administration of the temple, and serves as the main liaison between priest and parishioners, who may come to the temple at any time of day or night.

❧ CONTEMPORARY ISSUES

Today, religious institutions of all sizes and persuasions, many originating in the feudal period (or before), are trying to adapt to a society that is now part of a transnational economic order. Their traditions offer little guidance for dealing with the social complexities that have accompanied globalization. Priests may still look to the doctrines and hierarchies of their denominations, but the autonomy to run their temples and shrines as they see fit means that their effectiveness depends largely on their own initiatives. They are being forced to adopt a more experimental approach to their traditions in order to accommodate incremental yet significant changes in worldviews, technology, demographics, and culture.

Four dynamics common to liberal democracies around the globe are reshaping not only Japan's cultural, social, and religious traditions, but the consciousness of its citizens. The first trend is a growing social and political tolerance for pluralism and diversity, framed by the democratic principles of human rights and freedom of religion in a context where no single religious or political organization has a monopoly on 'truth'.

A second dynamic affecting religious practices around the world involves new communication technologies. Religious teachings, appeals, and activities can now reach a global audience on the worldwide web, but they must compete in a noisy forum of diverse approaches, as well as challenges, to religious belief and practice. Meanwhile, the rise of digital publishing and networking has helped to de-centralize authority and control of information. Major denominations still have doctrinal authority, of course, but the world has 'flattened' so that anyone with rudimentary computer skills has at least the technological capacity to challenge that authority. Many religious organizations and institutions in Japan, as elsewhere, now have sophisticated websites full of information about their history, teachings, and so forth. Likewise, growing numbers of priests are using social networking systems to advance their ideas and communicate with people who may have no connection with their temples.

A third worldwide trend that has affected religions in Japan, as elsewhere, is the corporate restructuring and downsizing that has cost so many workers their jobs. Although people who have been adversely affected by economic change may still petition deities for support or inspiration, they are not likely to consider donations to religious institutions more important than the financial welfare of their families. Retaining the services of a full-time priest is therefore becoming increasingly difficult for many temples and shrines.

The final global dynamic is perhaps the most consequential for religions in Japan: a growing sense of personal agency that encourages people to reject the traditional identities grounded in family, community, and occupation and determine their own 'unique' life course. In Japan as in the West, the grip of class, gender, religion, and local culture has loosened to the point that contemporary individuals find themselves in an continuing struggle with the questions 'Who am I?' and 'What do I want?'

Many people and organizations have reacted strongly against the speed of change. They want to preserve what they feel are essential values from the threats they perceive globalization and pluralism to represent. As a result, the globalizing forces that have reinforced class divisions based on wealth have also fostered the growth of new forms of nationalism, racism, religious fundamentalism, and sexism as defensive reactions to forces that many fear are beyond their control. Aum Shinrikyo—the new religious movement responsible for the sarin gas attacks on the Tokyo subway system that killed 13 and injured more than a thousand people in 1995—was a prime example of the power a charismatic 'holy man' with an apocalyptic message can exert over disaffected young people.

When we consider the interaction between these four global dynamics and religion in contemporary Japan, we begin to see a number of cause and effect relationships between local and global trends. Growing tolerance for pluralism and diversity, combined with increasing access to information, higher education, travel, and new ideas generally, has empowered individuals to explore a range of religious possibilities (or, of course, to avoid religion altogether). Consumers are now able to invest their time and money in the religious services that *they*, not their parents or their local priest, consider to offer the optimal benefits. This tendency has weakened the financial foundations of many temples and shrines, as parishioners who leave or pass away are not replaced. But greater personal choice has also aided those temples that have been able to use innovation and activism to attract new members. Now that nearly every temple or shrine has a homepage, there is a more market-driven model for choosing religious services.

For most educated people, Japan's religious traditions no longer provide credible explanations for the events that shape their lives: the task of constructing meaningful narratives out of those events is now left largely to the individual. This freedom has been especially important to women who now have the economic clout to decide for themselves what religious practices are meaningful, regardless of what their husbands or in-laws may think.

Women have played a particularly important role in the development of new options for mortuary rituals and commemoration practices. Traditionally, a woman would become part of her husband's family upon death. However, since women today usually outlive their husbands, they now have the opportunity to consider where and how they want to be memorialized. Many women today are choosing to have their ashes interred in communal rather than family graves, in many cases because of strained relations with husbands and relatives. As a result, a number of temples have established burial societies that give their members the chance to meet and develop relationships based on mutual interests rather than family obligation. This might be one of the few times in a woman's life when she can firmly assert her independence, choosing to be interred separately from her husband (and his family) in an individual space. On the other hand, if she and her husband get along well, they may choose a location other than his family's traditional gravesite in order to be closer to their children. Whatever the arrangement, making their own interment plans can afford people considerable peace of mind while they are still alive.

It might be surprising to learn that issues such as abortion, same-sex marriage, bioethics, and stem-cell research that have both asserted and complicated the role of religion in Western societies influenced by Christianity do not receive the same kind of attention in Japan. There are very few religious lobby groups that have taken up these issues. When topics such as bioethics or abortion

Jizo figures at a temple in Osaka (John K. Nelson). The bodhisattva Jizo is thought to comfort the souls of children who died in infancy, or were still-born or aborted, and to assist them in their passage away from darkness to the Pure Land paradise.

are raised in the media, they are discussed without anything like the contention and passion they typically arouse in the West. Emphasizing religious practice over dogma and teachings, most Japanese wear their beliefs lightly.

A prime example of this tendency to use religion for pragmatic rather than ideological or political purposes can be seen in a practice that developed during Japan's 'economic miracle' of the 1970s and 1980s. For many people aspiring to make the most of the boom, an unexpected pregnancy represented a setback, and so abortion became quite common among working women in particular. To help them deal with the anguish and guilt of giving up a child (and to capitalize on this new social reality), many temples began to offer memorials for the spirits of aborted fetuses, watched over by the popular bodhisattva **Jizo**.

A woman who might otherwise have had to endure her loss in isolation could now take comfort in sponsoring a little Jizo figure to represent her 'water baby' (*mizuko*) and receive the prayers offered by temple priests for its well-being in the afterlife. While some people continue to commemorate their water babies far into the future, most do not. After a set number of years, their memorial Jizos are placed with tens of thousands of others in a communal chamber where the departed spirits become undifferentiated but benevolent ancestors. In this way an ancient religious tradition has been adapted to serve contemporary spiritual, psychological, and social needs.

Concluding Remarks

Today the religious traditions of Japan appear to be entering a new and somewhat experimental phase. Ancient shrines and temples still attract many visitors, but most of the latter are more interested in history and art than religious experience. A number of younger Buddhist priests are encouraging their temples to engage more directly with the problems of society, offering community services, providing sanctuary for victims of domestic violence, working to protect the environment, and opposing unnecessary development. In urban areas, local festivals mounted by Shinto shrines continue to attract broad-based participation, especially among women who in the past were barred simply because of their gender. In many rural areas, however, it is becoming difficult to find enough people even to carry the portable shrine. New religions continue to develop on the strength of savvy public relations, charismatic leaders, and the social support offered by a community of like-minded believers. Meanwhile, there is an increasing tendency to move away from traditional religious affiliations and especially the financial demands they impose.

It is predicted that, as Japan's baby-boomers age and pass away, their funeral rituals will become less identifiably Buddhist and more like the eclectic services typical of North America and Europe. Increasing numbers of rural Buddhist temples no longer have resident priests and have been forced to sell land and buildings. Although young people are distrustful of organized religion in general, partly because of financial scandals and partly because of the Aum terror attack, many still seem interested in more individual spiritual pursuits. The fact that books related to the occult, fortune-telling, and the spirit world continue to sell well suggests that the most ancient of all Japan's religious traditions— 'turning to the gods in times of trouble'—remains a guiding paradigm.

Sacred Texts Table

Religion	Text	Compilation	Revision	Uses
Shinto	*Kojiki*	8th century; compiled by O no Yasumaro at emperor's request	13th, 15th, 19th, 20th century versions	Legitimates imperial rule; provides myth for founding of Japan; select parts used in ritual purification; ideological use
Shinto	*Nihon Shoki*	8th century; Prince Toneri; O no Yasumaro	13th, 15th, 19th, 20th century versions	More historical than the *Kojiki*, it has been more useful to scholars researching the origins of Japanese civilization
Tendai Buddhism	*Lotus Sutra*; writings of founder, Saicho; other esoteric Buddhist texts	3rd century China, brought to Japan in early 9th century	Translations are updated; commentaries added periodically	Ritual, doctrinal, and ideological
Shingon Buddhism	Mahavairocana and Vajrasekhara *sutras*	7th century (India)	Periodic updates, new translations, and commentaries	Doctrinal, ritual, inspirational, educational
Rinzai Zen	Various *sutras*, including the *Lankavatara*; apocryphal stories of enlightened masters; koans	12th century (and earlier)	Numerous translations of teachings, updated frequently over time	Doctrinal, ritual, inspirational, educational
Soto Zen	*Heart*, *Diamond*, and *Lankavatara Sutras*; writings of Dogen	13th, 16th, 18th century texts and commentaries	Periodic updates, new translations, and commentaries	Doctrinal, ritual, inspirational, educational
Pure Land	'Infinite Life' Sutra	3rd century	Periodic updates, new translations, and commentaries	Doctrinal, ritual, inspirational, educational
True Pure Land	*Tannisho*, sayings of Shinran the founder	13th century version	Periodic updates and commentaries	Doctrinal, ritual, inspirational, educational
Nichiren	*Lotus Sutra*; writings of founder, Nichiren	13th century version	Translations are updated; commentaries added periodically	Doctrinal, ritual, inspirational, educational

Sites

Neighbourhood temples and shrines. One of the easiest ways to become acquainted with Japanese religious traditions is to visit local (Buddhist) temples and (Shinto) shrines. They are usually open to the public and at festival time may offer opportunities for direct participation.

Nara The Nara region is believed to be the cradle of Japanese civilization, beginning in the fifth century. Japan's capital from 710 to 784, the city of Nara is the site of many famous buildings. The **Todaiji**

Temple, said to be the world's largest wooden building, houses a colossal Buddha image. Both **Kofukuji** and **Horyuji Temples** feature ancient five-storied pagodas, and the latter is home to the world's oldest wooden building. **Kasuga (Shinto) Shrine** hosts a famous lantern festival in late summer. There is even a festival dedicated to the deer that roam through Nara Park.

Kyoto   The Kyoto region was the political and religious centre of Japan for almost a thousand years, from 794 to 1869. The city abounds in temples and shrines. **Toji** is a Buddhist temple with Japan's tallest pagoda. **Ryoanji** is a Zen temple with a world-renowned rock and sand garden. The picturesque (but tourist-thronged) **Kinkakuji**, or **Golden Pavilion**, was built as a shogun's palace and is now part of a Zen temple. Japan's first Zen temple (**Kenninji**), its second most important Shinto shrine (**Kamigamo**), and the famous **Kiyomizu Temple**, built on the side of a mountain overlooking the city, are also worth seeing, along with the **Imperial Palace** and **Nijo Castle**.

Ise Shrines   The ancient shrines dedicated to the imperial *kami* Amaterasu now receive more than five million visitors a year.

Izumo Shrine   Located in Shimane prefecture on the Japan Sea coast, Izumo Shrine is one of Japan's oldest, mentioned in several myths and ancient accounts of the founding of the nation.

Kamakura   In 1185 a samurai-led army from the north seized power and moved the capital from Kyoto to Kamakura, a fishing port some 50 km southwest of Tokyo. In less than 150 years, the village became home to grand temples, shrines, palaces, and one of the most famous Buddha statues in the world.

Nikko   Nikko's religious architecture and dramatic mountain setting, north of Tokyo, have become major tourist attractions. **Rinnoji** is a Buddhist temple founded in the eighth century by the monk Shonin, who also established the nearby **Futarasan Shrine**, dedicated to the *kami* of the surrounding mountains. The **Toshogu**, the tomb of first Tokugawa shogun, is open to visitors. Look for the beautiful ceremonial bridge and the famous carving of the three monkeys who 'see no evil, hear no evil, and speak no evil'.

Mount Fuji and Mount Koya   are two of at least ten high mountains that are sacred to several of Japan's religious traditions.

Study Questions

1. Why is it not unusual for contemporary Japanese to visit Buddhist temples, purchase amulets at Shinto shrines, and yet say they are 'not religious'?
2. What are several of the principal spiritual agents in Japan that interact with human beings and the natural world?
3. Identify two of Japan's most popular bodhisattvas. How do they help human beings in trouble?
4. How did the monks Saicho and Kukai help to domesticate Buddhism in Japan?
5. What were the three new sects of Buddhism that emerged during the Kamakura period? What were their distinguishing features?
6. What are some of the aesthetic contributions of Zen Buddhism to Japanese culture?
7. Why are spiritual benefits (*riyaku*) more important for Japanese people than the teachings of any particular religious denomination?
8. What role did religion play in the creation of a 'modern Japan' between the mid-nineteenth century and the beginning of the Second World War?

Glossary

Amaterasu Female deity of the sun, born from the eye of the primordial deity Izanagi following his purification; enshrined at Ise as the patron deity of the imperial family.

Amida Buddha The 'celestial Buddha' of Japan's Pure Land traditions (Jodoshu and Jodo shinshu). During a lifetime as the bodhisattva Dharmakara, he vowed that anyone reciting his name would be reborn into the Pure Land. Today Amida is the principal object of worship in tens of thousands of Pure Land temples.

bodhisattva A Buddhist 'saint' who has achieved spiritual liberation but chooses to remain in this world to help alleviate the suffering of all sentient beings.

bushido Literally, the 'way of the warrior'; an ethical code that combined a Confucian-style emphasis on loyalty with the discipline of Zen.

honji suijaku Literally, 'manifestation from the original state'; the concept that *kami* are local manifestations of buddhas or bodhisattvas.

jiriki Literally, 'self-power'; the principle that people can attain liberation through their own efforts, without any external assistance from buddhas or bodhisattvas. ties and devotional activities.

Jizo One of the most popular of all Japanese bodhisattvas, Jizo eases the suffering of departed spirits and delivers the faithful into the western paradise of Amida Buddha. He receives prayers and petitions for good health, success, and the welfare of children.

kami The spirits that animate all living things, natural phenomena, and natural forces. Shinto shrines were built to accommodate their presence during rituals.

Kojiki A collection of stories commissioned to legitimate the imperial regime by linking it with Japan's mythical origins; published in 712 CE but largely forgotten until it was taken up by the Kokugaku movement in the eighteenth century.

Kokugaku Literally, 'learning about one's country'; the intellectual movement of the eighteenth and nineteenth centuries that privileged Japanese culture and ideas over those from abroad.

mappo The period of 'decline of the (Buddhist) dharma', thought to have begun in 1052; a time of social disorder during which humans were believed incapable of achieving liberation without the aid of buddhas and bodhisattvas.

mizuko Literally 'water baby'; the term for an aborted fetus that is memorialized at a temple. This practice became especially widespread in the 1970s and 1980s.

nenbutsu The key prayer of the Pure Land traditions: *Namu Amida Butsu* ('praise to the Amida Buddha').

Nihon Shoki An ancient text (c. 720 CE; also called *Nihongi*) commissioned to present a more positive and systematic account of the Yamato clan's rise to power than the one set out in the earlier *Kojiki*.

obon Often described as a 'festival' of 'all souls', this annual Buddhist commemoration of the spirits of the dead incorporates both entertainment (dancing, aerial fireworks) and solemn rituals at temples, ancestral graves, and household altars. It has become one of the two occasions each year (the other being New Year's) for family reunions. Local traditions determine the date (from mid-July to mid-August) and nature of *bon* celebrations.

samurai A popular term for the *bushi* ('warrior'), who served regional warlords in various capacities; samurai made up the top 5 per cent of society during the Edo period (1603–1867).

shogun The supreme military commander of Japan, appointed by the emperor and effectively ruling in his name.

tariki The 'other-power' offered by buddhas and bodhisattvas, without which people living in the age of *mappo* would be unable to achieve liberation.

Further Reading

Bowring, Richard. 2006. *The Religious Traditions of Japan, 500–1600*. Cambridge: Cambridge University Press. A comprehensive and highly readable account of Japanese religious history covering more than 1,000 years.

Covell, Stephen. 2005. *Japanese Temple Buddhism: Worldliness in a Religion of Renunciation*. Honolulu: University of Hawaii Press. A rare examination of contemporary temple Buddhism, with an emphasis on the Tendai sect.

Jaffe, Richard. 2002. *Neither Monk nor Layman: Clerical Marriage in Modern Japanese Buddhism*. Princeton: Princeton University Press. An engaging analysis of the tension between the historical image of Buddhist priests as monks and the modern reality that they are expected to have families and run their temples like businesses.

Meeks, Lori. 2010. *Hokkeji and the Reemergence of Female Monastic Orders in Premodern Japan*. Honolulu: University of Hawaii Press. A wide-ranging study of issues surrounding women's engagement with Buddhism at a major convent temple during a time when the status of women within Buddhism was undergoing significant change.

Nelson, John. 1996. *A Year in the Life of a Shinto Shrine*. Honolulu: University of Hawaii Press. An ethnographic and historical study of what goes on behind the scenes at a major Shinto shrine in the city of Nagasaki. This is the first book to present the actual voices of Shinto priests, as well as shrine attendants and parishioners.

———. 2005. *Spirits of the State: Japan's Yasukuni Shrine*. 28 min. Documentary film, distributed by Films for the Humanities (www.films.com). A documentary, made for university audiences, about the controversy surrounding the Yasukuni Shrine, where the spirits of the military dead are enshrined and venerated by the state.

Nelson, John, and Inken Prohl, eds. Forthcoming. *The Handbook of Contemporary Japanese Religions*. Leiden: Brill Publications. A multi-author volume covering a wide range of topics focused on the interaction between religious traditions and post-war Japanese society, set within a global context.

Reader, Ian. 2005. *Making Pilgrimages: Meaning and Practice in Shikoku*. Honolulu: University of Hawaii Press. A detailed study of the Shikoku pilgrimage, including the religious significance of the 88 sacred temples that make up the route.

Rowe, Mark. 2011. *Bonds of the Dead: Temples, Burials, and the Transformation of Contemporary Japanese Buddhism*. Chicago: University of Chicago Press. A highly contemporary account of one of the major forces driving Japanese religious practices.

Schnell, Scott. 1999. *The Rousing Drum: Ritual Practice in a Japanese Community*. Honolulu: University of Hawaii Press. An insider's look at a major festival in a small mountain city and what it means to the cultural identity of the local people.

Swanson, Paul, and Clark Chilson, eds. 2006. *The Nanzan Guide to Japanese Religions*. Honolulu: University of Hawaii Press. The most recent compilation of scholarly articles on many topics related to Japanese religions.

Tanabe, George J., ed. 1999. *Religions of Japan in Practice*. Princeton: Princeton University Press. A valuable collection of documents from all historical periods that lets readers hear the voices of religious practitioners through time.

Thal, Sarah. 2006. *Rearranging the Landscape of the Gods: The Politics of a Pilgrimage Site in Japan, 1573–1912*. Chicago: University of Chicago Press. A comprehensive history of the wrenching changes forced on a formerly Buddhist temple, now converted to a major Shinto shrine.

Watsky, Andrew. 2004. *Chikubushima: Deploying the Sacred Arts in Momoyama Japan*. Honolulu: University of Hawaii Press. One of the best studies of the artistic, architectural, and aesthetic contributions of the sixteenth-century Toyotomi regime to the religious landscape of Japan.

Williams, Duncan. 2005. *The Other Side of Zen: A Social History of Soto Zen in Tokugawa Japan*. Princeton: Princeton University Press. Surprising and often shocking in its account of corruption and exploitation among priests from the sixteenth to the nineteenth centuries, this study reveals the 'dark' side of institutional Zen, which dominated Japanese society for more than 250 years.

Recommended Websites

www.nanzan-u.ac.jp/SHUBUNKEN/publications/jjrs/jjrsMain.htm A semi-annual journal dedicated to the academic study of Japanese religions.

www2.kokugakuin.ac.jp/ijcc The English-language website of the Institute of Japanese Culture and Classics at Kokugakuin University, specializing in Shinto studies. Many online publications.

global.sotozen-net.or.jp/eng/index.html The English-language website of the Soto Zen school introduces key teachings and practices, and a comic or two!

(Each Buddhist denomination has a similar site; many temples also have their own websites.)

www.jodo.org An English-language website offering a variety of resources on Pure Land Buddhism.

www.onmarkproductions.com/html/buddhism.shtml A vast photo library devoted to artwork, especially sculpture, depicting Buddhist and Shinto deities in Japan.

www.japanese-religions.jp/index.html A scholarly website full of resources for research sponsored by the National Christian Council Center for the Study of (all) Japanese Religions (office in Kyoto).

References

Bowring, Richard. 2005. *The Religious Traditions of Japan: 500–1600*. Cambridge: Cambridge University Press.

Dogen, Eihei. 1996. 'Tenzo kyokun: Instructions for the Tenzo'. Yasuda Hoshu and Anzan Hoshin, trans. White Wind Zen Community. Accessed 8 Feb. 2011 at http://www.wwzc.org/translations/tenzokyokun.htm.

Hardacre, Helen. 1989. *Shinto and the State: 1868–1945*. Princeton: Princeton University Press.

Jansen, Marius. 2000. *The Making of Modern Japan*. Boston: Harvard University Press.

Kamens, Edward. 1990. *The Buddhist Poetry of the Great Kamo Priestess: Daisaiin Senshi and Hosshin Wakashu*. Ann Arbor: University of Michigan Press.

Philipi, Donald L. 1985. *The Kojiki*. Tokyo: Tokyo University Press.

Pye, Michael. 2004. 'The Structure of Religious Systems in Contemporary Japan: Shinto Variations on Buddhist Pilgrimage'. Occasional Paper No. 30, Centre for Japanese Studies. University of Marburg.

Senda, Minoru. 1988. 'Taoist Roots in Japanese Culture'. *Japan Quarterly* 35, 2.

Shigeru, Gorai. 1994. *Nihonjin no shiseikan* ('Japanese views of death'). Tokyo: Kadokawa Shoten.

Chapter

12

New Religious Movements

≈ Roy C. Amore ≈

The youngest of the traditions we have examined so far has existed for more than five hundred years, but innovations in religion did not end with Sikhism. The early nineteenth century saw the emergence of many new faiths, and more have developed since then. This chapter explores a selection of those newer religious movements. First, though, we need to consider what distinguishes a 'religion' from a 'sect' or a 'cult'.

🌿 DEFINING NEW RELIGIONS, SECTS, AND CULTS

What is a 'new religion'? The question might be easier to answer if scholars could agree on what constitutes a religion. But there are hundreds, if not thousands, of ideas on that subject. Even a definition as seemingly basic as 'belief in a god or goddess' would not take into account non-theistic traditions such as Buddhism and Jainism. Fortunately, it is not our task here to define religion, but to understand what is meant by the terms 'sect' and 'cult', and how those terms are applied to new religious movements.

Sociologists of religion such as Max Weber, writing in the early 1900s, used the word '**sect**' to refer to Christian splinter groups: new institutionalized movements that had broken away from mainstream denominations, usually in order to practise what they considered to be a purer form of the faith. Often the breakaway group would denounce the parent institution and adopt stricter rules, new modes of worship, or distinctive clothing to set itself apart. With the passage of time, most sectarian movements have either faded away or moved back towards the mainstream. In other words, new movements would begin as sects (or sectarian movements) and evolve into churches (new denominations). A similar process can be seen in the history of many other religions.

As for '**cult**', it was originally a neutral term, used as a synonym for 'worship' or even 'religion'. Yet today its connotations—at least in the popular media—are almost always negative: a cult is generally assumed to be a small group under the control of a charismatic leader who is suspected of brainwashing followers (especially young people) and promoting self-destructive, illegal, or immoral behaviour.

A movement that is accepted by outsiders as a 'new religion' will enjoy all the constitutional protections and tax exemptions afforded to established religions. One that gets labelled a cult is likely to attract scrutiny, if not harassment, from legal authorities and taxation officials. In divorce cases where custody of the children is in dispute, it is not unusual for one parent to use the other parent's association with a 'cult' to argue that he or she is unfit. And in the 1994 race for the California Senate, one candidate received damaging media attention because his wife was thought to be associated with a cult (Lewis 2003: 208).

In fact, the definitional lines between a cult and a sect (or new religion) are quite vague. By the usual definitions, for example, the **Hare Krishna** movement was a sect of

◀ At the Pagan Pride Parade in London, UK, May 2010 (David Hoffman / Alamy).

Timeline

1830 CE	Church of Jesus Christ of Latter-day Saints (United States)
1844	Baha'i (Iran)
1929	Nation of Islam (United States)
1930	Soka Gakkai (Japan)
1940s	Wicca (England)
1954	The Church of Scientology (United States)
1965	International Society for Krishna Consciousness (ISKCON) (United States)
1965	The Kabbalah Centre (United States)
1974	Raëlian Movement (France)
1990	Falun Dafa (China)
2006	Richard Dawkins, *The God Delusion*

Hinduism in India, but in the West its members' unusual practice and dress soon led to their branding as a cult. This suggests that the 'cult' label has less to do with the nature of the movement itself than with how sharply it differs from the mainstream religious culture. In that sense, one person's religion is often another person's cult.

Yet it is possible to identify several traits that many cults seem to share. Cults typically claim to have some special knowledge or insight, perhaps based on a new interpretation of an old scripture, or revealed through contact with spirits (sometimes even aliens). Their practice often includes rituals designed to promote ecstatic experiences, and they tend to focus more on individual spiritual experience than institutional organization (see Dawson 2006: 28–9).

Perhaps the most widely shared characteristic, however, is a charismatic individual leader who demands extreme loyalty. Adherents may be required to work long hours for little or no pay, cut ties with family and friends from the past, denounce former religious beliefs and practices, or even submit sexually to the leader. In extreme cases, leaders may go so far as to demand that followers be willing to die for the cause. The mass suicide (coerced or voluntary) of more than 900 members of the Peoples Temple at Jonestown, Guyana, in 1978 is one famous example. Others include the succession of murders and suicides in the mid-1990s associated with the Solar Temple cult, in which more than 70 people in Switzerland, France, and Canada died; the suicides of 37 Heaven's Gate adherents in California in 1997, and the murder–suicide of 780 members of a breakaway Catholic cult called the Movement for the Restoration of the Ten Commandments in Uganda in 2000 (Dawson 2006: 13). The 1993 murder–suicide of 80 people at the Branch Davidian compound near Waco, Texas, was somewhat different in that it was precipitated by an assault on the compound by law enforcement officers. In most of these cases the underlying belief was that the current world order was about to end and be replaced by a new order in which the cult's members would be rewarded for their loyalty. In other words, these movements had a **millenarian** belief in an imminent 'End of Time' leading to the dawning of a 'New Age'.

What gives rise to new religious movements? It has often been noted that new religions tend to appear at times of serious cultural disruption or change. The indigenous prophetic movements discussed in Chapter 2 are classic examples, emerging in societies whose traditional cultures were breaking down under the pressure of European colonization. Similarly, the massive cultural changes of the 1960s gave rise to several new religions in North America.

Hundreds of new religions and movements have emerged over the past two centuries. This chapter will focus on a small selection of the ones that have been most successful or have attracted the most attention in the West. We will discuss them in three groups, organized according to their spiritual roots: traditional Asian religions, Abrahamic traditions, and other forms of spirituality.

NEW RELIGIONS FROM THE EAST

Soka Gakkai

Soka Gakkai was founded in Japan in the years leading up to the Second World War and emerged as an important force after 1945, in a period that saw a flowering of new Japanese religions. But its roots lie deep in Buddhist history, in the tradition of the controversial thirteenth-century monk Nichiren.

The dominant tradition of Nichiren's day was the Pure Land school of Mahayana Buddhism, which taught its followers to trust in the saving power of Amida Buddha. Nichiren, however, believed that a Mahayana scripture called the *Lotus Sutra* represented the culmination of all Buddhist truths, and he warned that Japan would be doomed if the people ignored its teachings. At the same time he became increasingly critical of the Pure Land sects of his day, so angering their leaders that they persuaded the emperor to exile him to a remote island. While in exile, he continued to write tracts criticizing other Buddhist sects and promoting his own.

Nichiren's prophecies of impending doom seemed to come true when the Mongols attempted to invade Japan in 1274. Thus he was allowed to return from exile and, with his followers, establish a sect based on his teachings, together with the *Lotus Sutra*. It is to this sect, eventually known as Nichiren Shoshu, 'True Nichiren', that Soka Gakkai traces its roots.

Soka Gakkai ('Association for Creating Values') was established in 1930 as a lay organization within Nichiren Shoshu. Its founder, Makiguchi Tsunesaburo, was a reform-minded schoolteacher who wanted to promote moral values among young people. Many of its leading figures were imprisoned during the Second World War because they refused to recognize the divinity of the Emperor as required by the officially Shinto Japanese state, and Makiguchi himself died in prison before the war ended.

The organization's new leader, Toda Josei, adopted an aggressive recruitment strategy based on an ancient Buddhist missionary principle. To break down resistance to their message, Soka Gakkai members might gather outside the home of a potential convert and chant all day and all night, or point out to shop-owners that conversion would benefit their business because Soka Gakkai members would shop at their stores. Although critics complained that these tactics amounted to harassment and coercion, the approach was effective, and Soka Gakkai grew exponentially under Toda's leadership. Meanwhile, small groups of practitioners began to establish themselves throughout much of Asia, Europe, and the Americas. Often the leaders of these local groups were ethnic Japanese, but the majority of the members were not. As usual with new religious movements, young people made up the majority of the converts.

Today Soka Gakkai International (SGI)— founded in 1975 as a worldwide organization under the umbrella of Soka Gakkai in Japan—claims 12 million members. Most 'new religions' in Japan promise this-worldly happiness, and Soka Gakkai is no exception. In particular, it stresses the benefits of chanting for passing tests, getting promotions, and improving one's outlook on life. Soka Gakkai is also active in youth activities and the enjoyment of nature, sponsoring summer camps designed to give urban youth a taste of Japan's natural beauty and a chance to experience life in a more traditional setting.

At the core of Soka Gakkai is the belief that, through the practice of Nichiren Buddhism, a personal transformation or 'human revolution' can be achieved that will empower the individual to take effective action towards the goals of peace, justice, social harmony, and economic prosperity. An example of the organization's economic perspective can be seen in a 2008 speech by SGI President Daisaku Ikeda in which he called for 'humanitarian competition' in a new economic order that would avoid both the excessive greed of capitalism and the lack of competition historically associated with socialism (Ikeda 2008).

An emphasis on social engagement had been a central feature of Soka Gakkai from the beginning, and in 1964 it led some prominent members to form a political party. Known as **Komeito**, the new party was not officially affiliated with Soka Gakkai, but its unofficial association with the organization was well recognized. It had socialist leanings, took a strong stand against corruption in Japanese politics, and worked with several other parties in opposition to the long-ruling Liberal Democratic Party (LDP). Finally, in 1993, the LDP government was replaced by a short-lived centre–left coalition of which Komeito was part. When the coalition fell apart, however, the LDP returned to power and Komeito itself soon fragmented as well. The New Komeito party, formed in 1998 through a union with the New Peace party, is more conservative than its predecessor, with a platform of reducing the size of central government, increasing transparency, and promoting world peace through nuclear disarmament.

Meanwhile, Nichiren Shoshu had officially severed its links with Soka Gakkai in 1991. It was the most dramatic event in recent Japanese religious history, and the climax of a long dispute between the conservative clergy and the reform-minded lay organization. Following the split, the priests of Nichiren Shoshu even tore down the Grand Hall that Soka Gakkai had built on the grounds of the main Nichiren temple.

The profile of Soka Gakkai in Japan has been somewhat diminished because of the split. But the international organization has continued to grow, even establishing a university in California in 1995, and the split has not affected Soka Gakkai's practice. Members continue to follow the religious teachings of Nichiren Shoshu, studying the *Lotus Sutra* and chanting the sacred mantra *namu-myoho renge-kyo*: 'homage to the Lotus Sutra'.

Falun Dafa (Falun Gong)

Falun Dafa ('Energy of the Wheel of Law'), popularly known as Falun Gong, arose out of a Buddhist Qigong tradition in China in the early 1990s. The term *qi* (pronounced 'chi' and often spelled *chi* in the older transliteration system) refers to unseen energy flowing through the body, while *qigong* refers to various techniques of breathing and movement designed to permit energy to flow properly through the body, promoting healing, health, and long life. Although Western science has been reluctant to incorporate the flow of energy into its worldview, the belief in *qi* and the various ways to strengthen it have been part of Chinese and other East Asian cultures for centuries. In addition to exercise techniques designed to enhance the flow of *qi*, the Chinese have developed eating patterns that are thought to maintain the proper balance between the *yin* (feminine, cold, wet, dark) and *yang* (masculine, warm, dry, light) forces in the body. Even skeptics have trouble explaining why acupuncturists are able to anesthetize patients by inserting needles at various energy points in the body.

A man named Li Hongzhi brought Falun Dafa to prominence in China in 1992. He explains it as a system of Buddhist cultivation passed down through the centuries, and he considers himself only the most recent in a long line of teachers. The system's Buddhist roots are reflected in its name, for the *falun* or Dharma Wheel and its symbols, among them the swastika, are auspicious symbols in Buddhism. Li's teachings of compassion and self-development are based on Buddhist principles and he uses Buddhist symbols and terms, but Falun Dafa is not officially recognized as a traditional school of Chinese Buddhism. As a consequence, the Chinese government has been able to outlaw Falun Dafa without contravening its policy on the five religions it does recognize.

Although Falun Dafa has traditional roots, Li Hongzhi was the first to turn it into a popular practice adapted to everyday life, and the practice spread quickly among the Chinese, for whom it was simply a new variation on a familiar theme. Unfortunately, its rapid growth in popularity attracted the attention of the Communist Party, which in 1999 counted a total party membership of just over 63 million. With as many as 70 million members in that year, Falun Dafa was seen as a threat to the party, and the fact that it was increasingly popular among younger party members and their children was particularly disturbing. When some senior party officials began expressing alarm over Falun Dafa in 1998 and early 1999, the movement's leaders made a fateful decision. They organized a demonstration in April 1999 in the section of Beijing where the

The Falun Dafa symbol (Courtesy of Falun Dafa Association). Note the Daoist *yin–yang* (*taiji*) symbols and Buddhist rotating swastikas. The outer symbols rotate individually, and together they rotate around the central swastika, first in one direction and then in the other. The colours are said to vary depending on the level of visions experienced by the practitioner.

top government officials live and work. Sitting silently in orderly rows, without banners or placards, they intended to show that Falun Dafa posed no threat either to the government or to the social order. But their silent demonstration had the opposite effect. The government was alarmed by the sudden presence of so large a gathering in the heart of Beijing.

Government officials persuaded the Falun Dafa leaders to send the demonstrators home. Then, three months later, the organization was banned on the grounds that it was an unregistered religion and had the effect of discouraging people from seeking proper medical attention. Falun Dafa members throughout China were arrested, fired, imprisoned, sent to prison camps, tortured, or killed.

Under pressure from the government, Li Hongzhi had left China two years before the ban was imposed. He now lives in New York City, which has become the base of a worldwide organization claiming more than a hundred million followers in over a hundred countries. Its literature has been translated into more than forty languages.

Practice

Whereas some people practise *qigong* purely for its physiological benefits, Falun Dafa practitioners seek both physical and spiritual purification through meditation and *qigong* exercises. The organization describes Falun Dafa as 'a high-level cultivation practice guided by the characteristics of the universe—Truthfulness, Benevolence, and Forbearance' ('Introduction'). And Li Hongzhi himself refers to it specifically as a 'buddhist practice' (Li 2000).

Practitioners are said to develop a *falun* or 'law wheel' in the abdomen. This is not the same as the *qi*, which is naturally present in everyone. Once acquired, the *falun* spins in synchrony with the rotation of the planets, the Milky Way, and other objects in the universe. When rotating clockwise, the *falun* absorbs and transforms energy from the universe, and when rotating counter-clockwise, it dispenses salvation not only to the practitioner but to others and to the universe. According to Li, healing comes not from the *qi* but from the *falun* when it is rotating counter-clockwise. The *falun* changes its rotational direction according to its own dynamics, and it continues to rotate even when one is not actually practising the Dafa exercises. Li writes that this feature of Dafa practice sets it apart from other cultivation systems. The energy cluster emitted by the *falun* is called *gong*—hence the alternative name Falun Gong—and is said to glow like light.

In 2001 Falun Dafa held a candlelight vigil in Washington, DC, to mark the second anniversary of the Chinese government's crackdown (Alex Wong/Getty Images). Members spelled out both the organization's name and the Chinese characters for their three guiding principles: Truthfulness, Benevolence, and Forbearance.

Li divides Falun Gong practices into five sets of exercises with names such as 'Buddha showing a thousand hands' (the foundational set). It is repeated three times and is meant to open the body's energy channels. When it is performed properly, the body will feel warm; this is said to indicate that the energies have been unblocked and that energy is being absorbed from the universe.

Reflecting its Buddhist background, Falun Dafa teaches non-violence, and one of its goals is to cultivate 'mind-nature' (*xinxing*); that is, to build a character that is kinder, more honest, and more patient. Yet practitioners have faced serious persecution in China, and therefore it is regularly denounced as an evil cult working against the good of the people. Curiously, the organization has not been banned in Hong Kong, which has been a part of China since 1997; but when it wanted to hold a major international rally there in 2007, Beijing blocked the event by refusing to grant visas to Falun Dafa members from abroad.

Outside China, Falun Dafa is openly practised and has mounted a campaign of severe criticism of the Chinese government. It claims that many practitioners are imprisoned in long-term work camps, where they are used as what amounts to slave labour to produce various goods that are sold in the West. The organization also claims that organs are involuntarily removed from prisoners to be used for transplants. Organizations such as Amnesty International have lent some credence to these accusations (Amnesty International).

INTERNATIONAL SOCIETY FOR KRISHNA CONSCIOUSNESS (ISKCON)

In September 1965 a 70-year-old Hindu holy man arrived by freighter in New York City with virtually nothing but a short list of contacts. A few weeks later, he sat under a now famous tree in Tompkins Square Park and began to chant:

Hare Krishna Hare Krishna,
Krishna Krishna Hare Hare,
Hare Rama Hare Rama,
Rama Rama Hare Hare.

He had learned this *Maha Mantra*, 'great mantra', from his guru in India, who learned it from his guru, and so on—it was said—all the way back to the sixteenth-century Hindu mystic Chaitanya, who was reputed to enter a state of mystical ecstasy while chanting the three names of the god: Krishna, Hare, Rama. Within a year of his arrival, A.C. Bhaktivedanta Swami Prabhupada had established the International Society for Krishna Consciousness (ISKCON) and the 'Hare Krishna' movement was beginning to take root in America.

The Hare Krishna movement was new to the West, but it was hardly a new religion. It was simply a Western mission of **Vaishnava** Hinduism, the school that emphasizes devotion to Vishnu. Traditional Vaishnavas worship Vishnu both as the Supreme Godhead and in the forms of his ten major avatars—the animal or human forms he has assumed at different times to 'come down' to earth to save humanity. In this system Krishna, 'the dark-complexioned one', is the eighth avatar. However, Prabhupada belonged to a regional

Hare Krishna devotees in New York's Central Park in May 1978 (Ernst Haas/Hulton Archive/Getty Images).

(Bengali) variant known as Gaudiya Vaishnava, in which the Cowherd (Gopala) Krishna is the Supreme Godhead—the source of everything, including other divine forces. As the Supreme Personality, Krishna is understood to encourage a very personal relationship between the devotee and himself. Like other forms of Hinduism, ISKCON teaches that the soul is eternal and subject to reincarnation according to the individual's karma; however, those who practise loving devotion to Krishna will go to his heaven when they die and thus escape from the cycle of rebirth. The movement's fundamental texts are the Bhagavad Gita and a collection of stories about Krishna's life called the *Srimad Bhagavatam*.

Between the founding of ISKCON in 1966 and his death only 11 years later, Srila Prabhupada carried the fundamental beliefs and practices of his version of Hinduism around the world. Soon the Hare Krishna movement was establishing centres in cities across North America and abroad. Schools were started to educate the children of devotees in Vedic culture, and some devotees studied 'Vedic architecture'. Each centre included a temple with an altar area featuring images of Krishna and his consort Radha, as the male and female aspects of the divine, as well as pictures of the guru, Prabhupada. In addition to the temples, located mostly in large cities, farms were established that undertook to work the land in traditional ways consistent with Vedic (ancient Hindu) ways.

It is not uncommon for new religions to undergo a difficult period of adjustment after the death of the charismatic founder/leader. Following Prabhupada's death, ISKCON vested authority not in a new guru, but in a Governing Body Commission (GBC). Eleven devotees who had risen to high positions under Prabhupada's leadership were recognized by the GBC as gurus, each of whom was authorized to ordain recruits and oversee operations in one

From Swami Prahupada

On the potential for God-consciousness in all:

This love of God is now in a dormant state in everyone's heart. And, there, love of God is manifested in different ways, but it is contaminated by the material association. Now the material association has to be purified, and that dormant, natural love for Krishna has to be revived. That is the whole process (Prahupada 1972:606).

On the ethical ideals of Krishna Consciousness:

A person in Krishna Consciousness, fully devoted in the transcendental loving service of the Lord, develops many good qualities. . . . Lord Chaitanya described only some of them to Sanatan Goswami: A devotee of the Lord is always kind to everyone. He does not pick a quarrel with anyone. He takes the essence of life, spiritual life. He is equal to everyone. Nobody can find fault in a devotee. His magnanimous mind is always fresh and clean and without any material obsessions. He is a benefactor to all living entities. He is peaceful and always surrendered to Krishna. He has no material desire. He is very humble and is fixed in his directions. He is victorious over the six material qualities such as lust and anger. He does not eat more than what he needs. He is always sane. He is respectful to others; but for himself he does not require any respect. He is grave. He is merciful. He is friendly. He is a poet. He is an expert. And he is silent. (Prahupada 196:104).

of 11 regional zones. Some of the 11 got into trouble with the law over matters including illegal guns, drugs, child abuse, and murder, and by the 1980s six of the original group had either quit or been removed from office by the GBC. Those who were following in the tradition of Prabhupada had to deal with the bad publicity attracted by those who were not.

Practice

In the *Gita*, Krishna is the charioteer for a heroic royal leader named Arjuna. On the eve of a great battle between two factions of the royal family, Arjuna is troubled at the thought of fighting his own kin. His charioteer counsels him, and in the course of their conversation he reveals his identity. He tells Arjuna that he, Krishna, is the highest of all gods, and informs him that although the yoga (spiritual practice) of good karma actions and the yoga of spiritual wisdom are both valid, the best and highest path is **bhakti** yoga: loving devotion to Krishna.

These ideas, combined with the practice (introduced by Chaitanya) of chanting the praises of Krishna while dancing in ecstasy, are at the heart of the tradition that Prabhupada introduced to the West. Rituals (*pujas*) honouring Krishna are performed several times a day. One devotee (male or female) stands near the altar and makes offerings of fire and vegetarian food to the images on the altar (representing Krishna, his consort Radha, and his brother Balarama) while the other devotees play music and chant. As the pace of the chanting builds, the music becomes louder and the devotees raise their arms over their heads while dancing feverishly. As the chanting reaches its crescendo, many devotees jump high into the air.

Devotees are given a Sanskrit name by the guru. They wear saffron-coloured robes and show their devotion to Krishna by adorning their bodies with painted marks called *tilaka*, made of cream-coloured clay from the banks of a holy lake in India that is associated with the life of Krishna. Two vertical marks represent his feet, or the walls of a temple, and below them is a leaf representing the sacred *tulasi* (basil) plant. The diet is strictly vegetarian, including neither fish nor eggs. Recreational drugs of all kinds, including alcohol and caffeine, are shunned.

Great effort is put into keeping the temple clean, and every activity is to be performed 'for Krishna', as an act of devotion. In this way the mental state known as Krishna consciousness is developed. Some devotees live and work in the general community, attending the temple only for worship. Others work full-time for the movement and live in or near the temple. Since sexual activity is allowed only within marriage, for the purpose of procreation, living quarters for single devotees are strictly separated by gender.

Most temple-based male devotees shave their heads except for a pigtail at the back of the head. Women are required to dress very modestly. Devotees carry a small bag containing a string of 108 chanting beads, similar to a Christian rosary, made from the *tulasi* plant. (The number 108 is sacred in India partly because it represents the multiple of the 12 zodiac houses and 9 planetary bodies as understood in Indian astrology.) Devotees chant the Hare Krishna mantra hundreds of times throughout the day, using the beads if their hands are free. In addition to observing all the standard Hindu holidays, ISKCON celebrates the Gita Jayanti in December–January, commemorating the conversation between Krishna and Arjuna. Lavish festival parades in India and elsewhere follow the style of traditional Indian religious processions.

The Hare Krishna movement has provoked strong reactions, both positive and negative. On the positive side was the enthusiasm shown by celebrities like George Harrison of the Beatles. Harrison's 1970 song 'My Sweet Lord' contributed greatly to the acceptance of the movement. But there have been many negative reactions as well, especially in the early years. One reason was simply that the movement was so foreign to Western culture and that its members were so keen to adopt Indian styles of dress, music, and worship. The practice of chanting in public places such as airports while trying to raise money generated bad publicity. Another reason was the fact that in the early years the organization discouraged devotees from making contact with their families and former friends. As a consequence, the media quickly branded the movement a 'cult', and concerned parents hired 'deprogrammers' to kidnap their offspring and hold them for several days in an effort to break the 'cult program' that had been 'brainwashed' into them. Sometimes these interventions succeeded, but many young people returned to the Hare Krishnas as soon as they were free to do so.

The schools operated by ISKCON for children of devotees have also generated controversy, first from concerned outsiders and eventually from former students. Efforts were made to correct the problems and address the concerns of former students. But in 2000 a class action suit was filed in Dallas, Texas, by a group of 44 former students who claimed to have been victims of physical, emotional, and sexual abuse in ISKCON-operated schools in the US and India. Although the case was initially dismissed on technical grounds, it was

Indian ISKCON devotees celebrate Ratha Yatra, the festival of chariots, in Hyderabad (Noah Seelam/afp/ Getty Images).

refiled in another court. By the time a settlement was reached, hundreds of others had joined the list of plaintiffs and ISKCON had been forced to seek bankruptcy protection. The claims, totalling $20 million, were finally settled in 2008.

ISKCON now runs approximately 350 temples and centres worldwide. It has been especially successful in the former states of the Soviet Union, including Russia, and South America has also proven receptive. The (re)introduction of ISKCON to India has been particularly interesting. After starting his mission in America, Prabphupada frequently returned to India, where he established temples in Mumbai as well as various places associated with either Krishna or Chaitanya. Today Indian devotees now may outnumber Western ones.

RELIGIONS ARISING FROM THE ABRAHAMIC LINEAGE

We now turn our attention to some new religions arising from the three Abrahamic religions. The Church of Latter-day Saints can be classed either as a branch of Protestant Christianity or as a new religion developing out of Christianity. Our second example, the Baha'i Faith, originated in Iran in the context of Shi'i Islam. The Kabbalah Centre draws on a Jewish mystical tradition that is centuries old, while the Nation of Islam was established in the United States by leaders raised in the Christian tradition.

Church of Jesus Christ of Latter-day Saints (Mormons)

The founder of the Church of Jesus Christ of Latter-day Saints, Joseph Smith, Jr (1805–44), claimed that in 1820, as a boy in upstate New York, he had experienced a vision of God and Jesus in which he was told not to join any of the existing denominations. In subsequent visions, he said, an angel of God named Moroni persuaded him that he had been divinely chosen to restore the true Church of Christ. The new Church was founded in 1830.

From *The Book of Mormon*, Chapter 1

Here the prophet-historian named Mormon explains how he was instructed to recover the texts hidden by Ammaron, a record-keeper among the Nephites—one of four groups said to have migrated from Jerusalem to the Western hemisphere more than five centuries before the time of Jesus.

1. And now I, Mormon, make a record of the things which I have both seen and heard, and call it the Book of Mormon.

2. And about the time that Ammaron hid up the records unto the Lord, he came unto me, (I being about ten years of age, and I began to be learned somewhat after the manner of the learning of my people) and Ammaron said unto me: I perceive that thou art a sober child, and art quick to observe;

3. Therefore, when ye are about twenty and four years old I would that ye should remember the things that ye have observed concerning this people; and when ye are of that age go to the land Antum, unto a hill which shall be called Shim; and there have I deposited unto the Lord all the sacred engravings concerning this people.

4. And behold, ye shall take the plates of Nephi unto yourself, and the remainder shall ye leave in the place where they are; and ye shall engrave on the plates of Nephi all the things that ye have observed concerning this people.

5. And I, Mormon, being a descendent of Nephi, (and my father's name was Mormon) I remembered the things which Ammaron commanded me.

15. And I, being fifteen years of age and being somewhat of a sober mind, therefore I was visited of the Lord, and tasted and knew of the goodness of Jesus.

. . .

Chapter 4

22. And it came to pass that the Nephites did again flee from before them, taking all the inhabitants with them, both in towns and villages.

23. And now I, Mormon, seeing that the Lamanites were about to overthrow the land, therefore I did go to the hill Shim, and did take up all the records which Ammaron had hid up unto the Lord.

The Book of Mormon. 1961. Salt Lake City. The Church of Jesus Christ of Latter-day Saints. 460–7.

As a textual basis for the enterprise, Smith published the *Book of Mormon*, which he said he had translated from gold plates inscribed in 'reformed Egyptian' that had been entrusted to him by Moroni during a hilltop meeting near Palmyra, New York. Though subsequent editions referred to Smith as the 'translator', the title page of the 1830 first edition declared him 'author and proprietor'. He said that he was aided in translating the *Book* by two special stones he called 'Urim and Thummin'—the names given in the Old Testament to two unidentified objects used by the Hebrew high priests to determine the will of God.

The *Book of Mormon* uses the style of the 1611 King James translation of the Bible to tell the previously unknown (and otherwise undocumented) story of two groups, both descended from one of the lost tribes of Israel, that supposedly migrated from the Near East to the New World around 600 BCE and became the ancestors of the indigenous peoples of the Americas. Including accounts of visitations by Christ some time after his crucifixion, the book is understood by **Mormons** to be a scriptural account of God's activity in the Americas, parallel with the Bible and its account of divine events in the ancient Middle East.

Also scriptural for Mormons are Smith's *The Pearl of Great Price*, a book of revelations and translations, and *Doctrine and Covenants*, a collection of his revelatory declarations. Passages in the latter work address specific moments in the Church's early years. General reflection is interspersed with passages of guidance regarding particular issues, in a manner that recalls the letters of Paul or certain *surahs* of the Qur'an.

Facing ridicule and persecution from mainstream Christians in New York, Smith led his small band of followers westward in search of a safer place. They established settlements in Ohio and Missouri, and, when driven out of Missouri in 1839, moved on to Nauvoo, Illinois, on the Mississippi River. By now the Mormons were calling themselves the Church of Jesus Christ of Latter-day Saints. It was in Nauvoo that Smith secretly introduced 'plural marriage' (polygamy), rumours of which added to the suspicions of outsiders. He also declared himself a candidate for the American presidency in the 1844 elections, advocating a blend of democracy and religious authority he called 'theodemocracy'. Some of these innovations caused strife between factions of the Latter-day Saints. In 1844 Smith and his brother were killed by an anti-Mormon mob.

A number of the traditionalist, anti-polygamy Mormons stayed in the Midwest as the Reorganized Church of Latter-day Saints, with headquarters in Independence, Missouri. For years this branch of the Mormons was led by descendants of Smith, and they prided themselves on remaining true to his legacy. In 2001 they renamed themselves the Community of Christ. Although relatively small in numbers, the Community of Christ is very active in spreading its message around the world. It continues to regard the *Book of Mormon* and the *Doctrine and Covenants* as scripture, but emphasizes the Bible and its teachings about Jesus. It sees itself not as a 'new religion', but as a branch of Christianity in the line running from the Hebrew prophets through Jesus to Joseph Smith.

The larger branch of the Mormons, the Church of Jesus Christ of Latter-day Saints, has a separate history. In 1847 most of them moved to Utah under the leadership of Brigham Young, who had been president of an inner council of twelve that Smith had organized on the pattern of the apostolic Church and who continued to lead the Mormons for the next thirty years. Although they were unsuccessful in their bid to make Utah a Mormon state, they dominated the region and Young was chosen by the US government to serve as governor of the Utah Territory.

Practice

The Mormons set their community apart with a code of behaviour that includes a rigid sexual morality outside marriage, strict abstinence from tea and coffee as well as alcohol and tobacco, and a strong pro-life stance (although abortion is permitted in cases where the health of the mother is at risk or the pregnancy is the result of rape). They are respected for their strong family bonds.

Young adults are expected to serve as volunteer missionaries for two years after completing high school—a practice that has helped spread awareness of the faith and attract new members around the world. Distinctive Mormon doctrines include the notion that God is increasing in perfection as human beings improve. Distinctive practices include the augmentation of the spiritual community through baptism by proxy of the deceased; because of this practice, Utah has become a world centre for genealogical research. Mormons have also taken a keen interest in Western-hemisphere archaeology, in the hope that physical evidence of the events described by the *Book of Mormon* will be found.

The most controversial Mormon practice, however, was plural marriage, which was officially adopted in 1852 and officially dropped in 1890 after the federal government threatened to abolish it. The practice soon faded among mainstream LDS members. But a few congregations refused to accept the change and broke away from the Church of Jesus

The Tabernacle in Salt Lake City, Utah, home to the famous Mormon Tabernacle Choir, is renowned for its acoustics (Jed Jacobsohn/Getty Images).

Christ of Latter-day Saints to form independent sects known collectively as 'Fundamentalist Mormons'. The largest of these sects, the Fundamentalist Church of Jesus Christ of Latter-day Saints (FLDS) in particular is known for allowing its male leaders to have multiple wives. Because the women involved are often quite young, FLDS congregations have come under intense scrutiny by government officials and women's organizations. In 2007 FLDS leader Warren Jeffs was sentenced to ten years in prison for being an accomplice to rape.

Another issue that generated a great deal of controversy was the traditional Mormon view of Africans. It had been the Mormon teaching that the dark skin of people with African ancestry reflected 'the pharaoh's curse' put on one of the peoples mentioned in the Book of Mormon, which was interpreted to mean that Blacks were cursed by God. For this reason it was the policy of the Church to refuse admission to the priesthood to people of African ancestry (although they could be lay members). In addition, it was alleged that Black students at Brigham Young University were discriminated against, and the church tended to send missionaries only to non-black populations in Africa. During the civil rights era in the 1960s, these policies and allegations attracted negative publicity. Some universities refused to schedule games with Brigham Young University; the NCAAP brought a suit against the Boy Scouts of America, alleging that it allowed Mormon troops to discriminate against Black children; and several Black clergy organized a boycott of the Mormon Tabernacle Choir's planned concert tour of New England (Embry, 1994: 169). Perhaps in response to these actions, in 1978 LDS President Kimball announced a revelation changing Mormon policy so that all humans were fully eligible for the priesthood, and its discriminatory practices disappeared almost overnight.

Whether the Mormons constitute a new religion or merely a new denomination of Christianity is open to question. Joseph Smith saw himself as reforming the Christian Church, and the fact that Mormons treat the Bible as scripture argues for inclusion under the umbrella of Christianity. On the other hand, the Mormons' belief in new scriptures, revelations, and modes of worship (e.g., using water rather than wine for the communion sacrament) suggests a new religion. This issue came into focus during the lead-up to the 2000 electoral primaries, when Massachusetts governor Mitt Romney was seeking nomination as the Republican party's candidate for president. Some conservative Christians who admired his strong family values were nevertheless reluctant to support his candidacy because of his Mormon faith.

Baha'i

Baha'i developed out of Islam in the mid-nineteenth century, when Islam was already more than 1,200 years old. Although it has many elements in common with Islam, it gives those elements a new and more nearly universal configuration. The main point of divergence is that Baha'is believe that their leader, Baha'u'llah, was a new prophet, whereas Muslims believe there can never be another prophet after Muhammad.

The roots of Baha'i lie in the particular eschatology of Iranian Shi'ism. Ever since the last imam disappeared in 874, Twelver Shi'a had been waiting for a figure known as the **Bab** ('gateway') to appear and reopen communication with the hidden imam. After ten centuries, most people no longer expected this to happen anytime soon. But seeds of messianic expectation germinated in the soil of political unrest.

Thus in 1844 Sayyid 'Ali Muhammad declared himself to be the Bab, the gateway to a new prophetic revelation. Although he himself was imprisoned in 1845, his followers, the Babis, were not discouraged. They repudiated the Islamic *shari'ah* law and in 1848 the Bab proclaimed himself the hidden Imam. He was executed by a firing squad in 1850, but he left behind a number of writings that have been considered scriptural.

The leadership momentum passed to Mirza Husayn 'Ali Nuri (1817–92), whose religious name was Baha'u'llah, 'Glory of God'. He had not met the Bab personally, but had a profound experience of divine support while imprisoned in Tehran in 1852. On his release the following year he was banished from Iran to Baghdad in Turkish-controlled Iraq, where he became a spiritual leader of Babis in exile. Then, since he was still near enough to Iran to be considered a threat, in 1863 he was moved to Istanbul. Before leaving, he declared himself to be 'the one whom God shall manifest' as foretold by the Bab. He also claimed to have had a 'transforming' twelve-day mystical experience in 1862.

This transfer to the Mediterranean world expanded the sphere of Baha'u'llah's spiritual activity well beyond the horizons of Iranian Shi'ism. Now he was in a position to address the entire Ottoman Empire. Although he was banished to Acre in Palestine a few years later, his following continued to grow. Nearby Haifa, today in Israel, remains the world headquarters of the Baha'i Faith today.

Baha'u'llah wrote prolifically throughout his years in Acre, producing more than a hundred texts. Baha'is believe his writings to be God's inspired revelation for this age. Among the most important are *Kitab-i Aqdas* ('The Most Holy Book', 1873), containing Baha'i laws; *Kitab-i Iqan* ('The Book of Certitude', 1861), the principal doctrinal work; and *Hidden Words* (1858), a discourse on ethics. *The Seven Valleys* (1856), a mystical treatise, enumerates seven spiritual stages: search, love, knowledge, unity, contentment, wonderment, and true poverty and absolute nothingness.

For 65 years after Baha'u'llah's death in 1892, authority in interpretation of the tradition was passed on to family heirs. His son Abdu'l-Baha (born 'Abbas Effendi) was considered an infallible interpreter of his father's writings, and on his death the mantle of infallibility was bequeathed to his grandson, Shoghi Effendi Rabbani. Shoghi Effendi appointed an International Baha'i Council, and from 1963 leadership was vested in an elected body of representatives called the Universal House of Justice.

Baha'i teachings are based on Baha'u'llah's writings. The soul is believed to be eternal, a mystery that is independent both of the body and of space and time, but becomes individuated at the moment of the human being's conception.

The Baha'i notion of prophethood is in line with the Abrahamic religions. Prophets are sent by God to diagnose spiritual and moral disorder and to prescribe the appropriate remedy. Islam holds that God sent prophets to various peoples before Muhammad with a message to each. Similarly, the Baha'i faith affirms that the world has known a sequence of prophets. Baha'is do not believe the prophets' messages to have been community-specific, however: instead, they understand the prophets to speak to the entire world. They also believe that the series remains open; according to their doctrine of 'progressive revelation', more prophets will come in future ages.

It may well be their ideal of world community that has done the most to energize Baha'is and make their tradition attractive to serious searchers. Baha'u'llah himself wrote that he came to 'unify the world', and Baha'is have asserted the unity of religions. Over a doorway to one Baha'i house of worship is the inscription, 'All the Prophets of God proclaim the same Faith.' Various religions are seen as corroborating the Baha'i faith itself.

But there is more to unity than doctrinal teaching. Baha'is actively advocate economic, sexual, and racial equality. Extremes of poverty and wealth are to be eliminated, and slavery rooted out—along with priesthood and monasticism. Women are to enjoy rights and opportunities equal to men's, marriage is to be strictly monogamous, and divorce is frowned on. The Baha'i Faith has consultative status with the United Nations as an official NGO (non-governmental organization). World peace is to be achieved through disarmament, democracy, and the rule of law, along with the promotion of international education and human rights. Although these goals are clearly compatible with modern secular values, they have a spiritual quality for Baha'is, who cite Baha'u'llah as saying that human well-being is unattainable until unity is firmly established, and Shoghi Effendi as saying that 'Nothing short of the transmuting spirit of God, working through His chosen Mouthpiece [Baha'u'llah], can bring it about.'

Unity of the races in the human family is actively proclaimed, and interracial marriage is welcomed. In recent decades this emphasis has been a major factor in the appeal of the Baha'i Faith to African-Americans. Some Baha'is say that the United States will be the spiritual leader of the world once it has eliminated its own racism.

Practice

Baha'is strive to live a peaceful and ethical life. Personal spiritual cultivation is encouraged, and recreational drugs and alcohol are forbidden. Since the Baha'i Faith sees itself as the fulfillment of other religions, Baha'is are unusually open to dialogue with other faiths.

Baha'is follow a distinctive calendar in which the number 19 plays an important role. Beginning with the spring equinox, Iran's traditional time for the new year, there are 19 months of 19 days each, with four additional days (five in leap years) to keep up with the solar year. Local Baha'i societies assemble for a community feast on the first day of each month, and the final month, in early March, is devoted to dawn-to-dusk fasting, as in the Muslim observance of Ramadan.

Although the 19-day calendar does not recognize the seven-day week, Sunday gatherings for study and reflection have become common among Baha'is in the West. Important days in the annual cycle are essentially historical, marking events in the founding of the religion: several days in April and May are associated with Baha'u'llah's mission, for instance. In addition, the Bab's birth, mission, and martyrdom are commemorated, as are the birth and passing (or ascension) of Baha'u'llah.

Devotions at the monthly feasts feature a cappella singing but no instrumental music. Prayers are in Farsi (Persian), Arabic, or the local language. Readings are mainly from

Baha'i Prayer

A prayer, composed by 'Abdu'l-Bahá, reflecting the Baha'i belief that the oneness of humankind overrides any religious, racial or national divisions.

Oh kind Lord! Thou Who art generous and merciful! We are the servants of Thy threshold and we are under the protection of Thy mercy. The Sun of Thy providence is shining upon all and the clouds of Thy mercy shower upon all. Thy gifts encompass all, Thy providence sustains all, Thy protection overshadows all and the glances of Thy favour illumine all. O Lord! Grant unto us Thine infinite bestowals and let Thy light of guidance shine. Illumine the eyes, make joyous the souls and confer a new spirit upon the hearts. Give them eternal life. Open the doors of Thy knowledge; let the light of faith shine. Unite and bring mankind into one shelter beneath the banner of Thy protection, so that they may become as waves of one sea, as leaves and branches of one tree, and may assemble beneath the shadow of the same tent. May they drink from the same fountain. May they be refreshed by the same breezes. May they obtain illumination from the same source of light and life. Thou art the Giver, the Merciful! (*Baha'i Prayers*, 1969: 43–4).

scripture composed by Baha'u'llah or the Bab, but they may be supplemented with devotional readings from other traditions. Life-cycle rituals include a simple naming ceremony, and many who grow up as Baha'is may make a personal profession of faith at the age of 15. Converts simply sign a declaration card. Baha'i weddings reflect the tastes of the couple, but always include the declaration 'We will all, truly, abide by the will of God.' At funerals there is a standard prayer for the departed, which is virtually the only Baha'i prayer recited in unison. Personal devotions are similar to Islamic practice. The faithful wash their hands and faces before praying. Set prayers are said at five times of the day. Also reminiscent of Islam is the practice of repeating the phrase *Allahu-'l Abha* ('God is the most glorious').

Conclusion

Its similarities with Islam notwithstanding, the Baha'i Faith has gone its own way. Its revelation does not conclude with the Qur'an, and its ideals for society depart from those reflected in the *shari'ah*. There have also been political tensions with Islam. Muslims have tended to see the Baha'is as Israeli sympathizers, and in Iran the Baha'i community suffered serious losses in lives and property after the Islamic revolution of 1979.

Since the end of the nineteenth century, the Baha'i Faith has spread around the world. It now claims some 7 million adherents in 235 countries. These include 750,000 in North America and several times that number in India. More than one-quarter of local councils are in Africa and a similar number in Asia. The southwestern Pacific region has nearly as many Baha'i councils as Europe.

The Nation of Islam

It has been estimated that at least 20 per cent of the Africans taken as slaves to the Americas were Muslims. One early promoter of Islam—or a version of it—among African-Americans was Noble Drew Ali, who in 1913 founded the Moorish Science Temple of America in Newark, New Jersey. By the time of his death in 1929, major congregations had been established in cities including Chicago, Detroit, and Philadelphia.

Whether Wallace D. Fard was ever associated with the Temple is unclear; his followers say he wasn't. But the idea that Islam was the appropriate religion for African Americans was in the air when Fard established the Nation of Islam (NOI) in Detroit in 1930. His version of Islam bore little resemblance to either the Sunni or the Shi'i tradition. For Muslims, who understand Allah to be a purely spiritual entity, the most fundamental difference lay in the NOI's claim that Allah took human form in the person of Fard himself. In fact, Fard was identified as the second coming of Jesus as well. These claims may have originated in Fard's first encounter with Elijah Poole, a young man who had felt called to a religious mission of some kind, but did not think of it as a Christian one and had stopped attending church before his fateful 1923 meeting with Fard. He later described the meeting:

> when I got to him I . . . told him that I
> recognized who he is and he held his head
> down close to my face and he said to me,
> 'Yes, Brother.' I said to him: 'You are that one
> we read in the Bible that he would come

in the last day under the name Jesus.' . . .
finally he said; 'Yes, I am the one that you
have been looking for in the last two thousand
years' (quoted in Sahib 1951: 91–2).

Fard was so impressed with the young man—who later changed his name to Elijah Muhammad—that he authorized him to teach Islam with his blessing. Elijah quickly became Fard's favourite disciple.

The men who developed the theology of the Nation of Islam were more familiar with the Bible than the Qur'an, but the story they told was no more familiar to mainstream Christians than it was to Muslims. They maintained that all humans were originally black and had lived in harmony as one tribe called Shabazz for millions of years, until an evil man named Yakub rebelled and left Egypt for an island where he created a white race by killing all dark babies. Eventually, the evil white race returned to Egypt and subjugated the blacks, bringing oppression and disunity to humankind. God sent Moses to try to redeem them, but that effort failed. Now the blacks needed to undergo a 'resurrection' and recognize themselves as proud members of the Shabazz people who once had a great and peaceful society.

Martha Lee has argued that the Nation of Islam is a millenarian movement (1996: 3). In its version of history, white rule has lasted more than six thousand years and is approaching the 'end time', when the Mother of Planes—a huge aircraft base in the sky—will destroy the 'white devils'. The 'Fall of America' is to be expected soon. In fact, Elijah Muhammad originally prophesied that the fall would occur in the mid-1960s. When that prediction failed to come true, NOI thinking about the 'end time' became less literal.

An economic as well as a religious movement, the NOI advocates black economic self-sufficiency and teaches a strict ethical way of life. It follows the Islamic prohibitions on pork and alcohol, but does not practise Friday prayers (services are generally held on Sunday) and does not follow the *shari'ah* law. Although Elijah Muhammad called for a separate state, such a demand was too impractical to pursue seriously.

The Nation of Islam came to the attention of the authorities in Detroit when it was rumoured that Fard had promised life in heaven for anyone who killed four whites. This was most likely not true, although he was known to have preached that anyone who killed four devils would go to heaven. In any event, Fard disappeared after he was arrested and expelled from Detroit in 1933. Elijah Muhammad took over the leadership but the movement fragmented, and some factions were quite hostile to him. Leaving Detroit in 1935, he settled in Washington, DC, where he preached under the name Elijah Rasool (Lee 1996: 26).

In 1942, he was convicted of sedition for counselling his followers not to register for the draft. He spent four years in prison, but his wife, Clara, directed the organization in his absence, and after his release in 1946 the NOI's numbers soon began to grow. Much of the credit for the movement's expansion in the 1950s has been given to a convert named Malcolm X.

Malcolm X

Malcolm Little (1925–65) was born in Nebraska but spent much of his childhood in Lansing, Michigan. When he was 6 his father was run over by a streetcar; the coroner ruled it a suicide, but the Little family believed he had been killed by a white supremacist group. After his father's death the family was impoverished and his mother suffered a nervous breakdown, so the children were put in foster care. Later, Malcolm moved to Boston and became involved with criminals. It was while he was serving time for theft that he was encouraged by his brother to join the NOI. He read widely and after release in 1952, he became a key disciple of Elijah Muhammad. Like other converts at that time, he took the surname X to mark the absence of an African name and recall the X that used to be branded on some slaves. Before long Malcolm X had become the leader of the Harlem temple. His eloquence brought him national attention as an advocate for Black Power, and he came to symbolize the black defiance of white racism in America.

Despite his success, however, Malcolm X became increasingly alienated from the movement. Finally in 1964 he broke away from the NOI and founded Muslim Mosque, Inc. Increasingly aware of the differences between NOI theology and that of traditional Islam, he converted to Sunni Islam and made the pilgrimage to Mecca, where he learned that Islam was not an exclusively black religion, as the NOI had taught. It was a life-changing experience. Changing his name to El Hajj Malik El-Shabazz, he began to teach Islam as a religion for all races. Less than a year later, in February 1965, he was assassinated while giving a speech in New York. Three members of the NOI were convicted of his murder, although some people suspected that the FBI's Counter Intelligence Program might have played a role in instigating the assassination (Lee 1996: 44).

Wallace Muhammad

The NOI itself showed a softening of its attitude towards whites in the early 1970s, along with an increasing willingness to work with other black organizations. When Elijah Muhammad, known as the Messenger, died in 1975, the leadership passed to his son Wallace, who took the NOI further towards the mainstream. He declared an end to the idea that all whites were devils; withdrew the demand for a separate black state; and helped put the NOI on a more solid financial basis. He also renamed the temples, adopting the Arabic word for mosque, 'masjid'. This, together with a new emphasis on studying the Qur'an, moved the NOI closer to Sunni Islam. In 1975 Wallace renamed the organization the World Community of al-Islam in the West, or WCIW.

Louis Farrakhan

Not all members of the former NOI agreed with these reforms, however. Among the dissenters was Minister Louis Farrakhan. In 1978 he broke with WCIW and formed a new organization modelled on the NOI. He restored the original name, reinstituted the Saviour's Day festival— which had been the group's most important holiday—and attracted a large number of members.

In 2001 a former member of the revived NOI published an account of his experience that was particularly critical of Farrakhan's financial dealings. According to Vibert L. White, Jr, members were pressured to donate large sums, and many struggling black-owned businesses were left with unpaid bills for their services to the organization, even as substantial amounts of money were finding their way to various members of the Farrakhan family (White 2001).

At the same time, Farrakhan appears to have courted African Muslim leaders, including Libya's Muammar Khadafi, for support. Perhaps this helps to explain why he has moved the NOI towards the Islamic mainstream by encouraging Islamic-style daily prayers and study of the Qur'an. The most difficult change he made was to drop the doctrine that identified Fard as Allah and Elijah Muhammad as his Messenger. In a 1997 conference, Farrakhan publicly affirmed that Muhammad was the last and greatest prophet of Allah (Walker 2005:495).

In 1995 Farrakhan organized a 'Million Man March' on Washington, DC, to draw attention to the role of the black male and to unite for social and economic improvement. The March was a joint effort sponsored by many black organizations, and most of the participants had a Christian background. As the main organizer, however, Farrakhan set the agenda. As Dennis Walker writes:

> The March was an Islamizing event. A range of Muslim sects were allowed to appear before the multitude and recite the Qur'an in Arabic on a basis of equality with the Christian and black Jewish clerics whom Farrakhan had inducted. It was a recognition in public space of Islam as part of the being of blacks that had had no precedent (Walker 2005: 508).

Although the March was criticized for excluding black women and promoting a Muslim agenda, as well as lacking transparency in accounting, it did bring several African-American organizations into fuller cooperation and helped draw public attention to the challenges faced by African Americans.

The Kabbalah Centre

The Kabbalah Centre in Los Angeles teaches a new form of spirituality based on traditional Jewish mysticism. As an organization, it traces its roots to a centre for Kabbalah studies founded in Jerusalem in 1922 by Rabbi (or Rav) Yehuda Ashlag. But the tradition stretches back through the sixteenth-century master Isaac Luria to the (probably) thirteenth-century text called the *Zohar* and beyond. The Centre itself claims that its teachings go back some four thousand years.

The National Institute for the Research of Kabbalah (later renamed the Kabbalah Centre) was founded in 1965 by Rabbi Philip S. Berg. Raised in New York City, he had trained as a rabbi but was not practising when, during a trip to Israel in 1962, he met Rabbi Yehuda Brandwein, the Kabbalist dean of a *yeshiva* in Jerusalem's Old City and a descendant of many famous Hasidic scholars. With Brandwein as his mentor, Berg became an active Kabbalist.

Berg's followers claim that he succeeded Rabbi Brandwein as leader of the entire Kabbalah movement, including leadership of the Jerusalem *yeshiva*. At the *yeshiva* itself, however, Brandwein's son Rabbi Avraham Brandwein is considered the leader, and the Kabbalah taught there is in no way new.

In itself, Berg's Kabbalah is not new either, but his approach to it is radically different. Traditionally, the study of Kabbalah was restricted to mature male Jews, aged 40 or older, who had already completed years of Talmudic studies. Yet Berg taught Kabbalah to his secretary, who would later become his wife and a leading figure in the movement herself. Within a few years, the Bergs set out to make Kabbalah available to the world at large: young and old, male and female, Jews and Goyim alike. This was the new dimension of Berg's Kabbalah, and it sparked a great deal of controversy in traditional Jewish circles.

On its website the Centre defines Kabbalah as 'ancient wisdom and practical tools for creating joy and lasting fulfillment now'. The emphasis on 'practical tools' is significant, for the purpose of Kabbalah study, as the Centre presents it, is to unlock the human potential for greatness. In fact, it is a fundamental tenet of Kabbalah (as it is of Eastern traditions such as Hinduism and Buddhism) that humans will be reincarnated over and over again, returning to this world as many times as necessary 'until the task of transformation is done' (Kabbalah Centre).

Another fundamental principle is that the reality perceived by our five senses is only a tiny portion of the totality, and that events occurring in the knowable 1 per cent of reality are the consequences of events in the unknown 99 per cent. Berg's followers maintain that their teachings enable people to perceive the 99 per cent of reality that normally remains unknown.

Practice

Kabbalists experience God in the world as the energy that underlies and imbues all things. As the sixteenth-century Kabbalist Moses Cordovero put it, even a stone is 'pervaded by divinity'. (A similar idea can be found in the non-canonical Christian Gospel of Thomas, which quotes Jesus as saying, 'Split a piece of wood, and I am there. Lift up the stone, and you will find me there.')

To illustrate the way God and the material world interrelate, Kabbalah uses a diagram usually referred to as the Tree of Life. The space above the tree represents the infinite nature of God. The tree itself pictures the ten **spherot**, shining circles of fire, representing the ten attributes of God in the world. The topmost circle represents the Crown (*Keter* or *Kether*). Below it the other nine circles are arranged in three sets, each with a circle in the left, centre, and right columns. Read from top down, these three sets represent the

---

Kabbalah: Thoughts on God

God's only desire is to reveal unity through diversity. That is, to reveal that all reality is unique in all its levels and all its details, and nevertheless united in a fundamental oneness (Kabbalist Aharon Ha-Levi Horowitz, 1766–1828; in Levi 2009: 929).

The essence of divinity is found in every single thing—nothing but It exists. Since It causes everything to be, no thing can live by anything else. It enlivens them. *Ein Sof* exists in each existent. Do not say, 'This is a stone and not God.' God forbid! Rather all existence is God, and the stone is a thing pervaded by divinity (Moses Cordovero, 1522–70; in Levi 2009: 937).

Shards of Light are drawn out of the destructive entities that reside within my being. Their life force is cut off and I am then replenished with Divine energy. Life grows brighter each and every day as billions of sacred sparks return to my soul! ('Focus in Front').

spiritual, intellectual, and material (earth-level) qualities of creation. The *spherot* in the right-hand column represent masculine attributes of God and those on the left feminine attributes. The *spherah* in the centre of the nine *spherot* is 'Glory', which brings harmony and interconnectedness among the lower nine *spherot*. Lines connecting the *spherot* illustrate the ways they interact.

The 10 *spherot* are numbered from top to bottom, and the 22 connecting lines are numbered 11 to 32, also from top to bottom. The total number of connecting lines corresponds to the number of letters in the Hebrew alphabet.

In an interesting twist on most theological systems, Kabbalah practitioners believe that their practices using the tree facilitate the flow of divine energy into the world. Whereas mainstream Judaism, Christianity, and Islam stress the absolute power of God, in Kabbalah God needs human effort to work in the world.

Kabbalists do not attempt to interpret the Bible literally; instead, they use a complex kind of numerology. The ancient Hebrews used regular letters as numbers, assigning their numerical value according to their position in the 22-letter Hebrew alphabet. Totalling the numbers in certain words could reveal hidden connections between them and lead to new interpretations. For example, it turns out that the numerical values of YHWH, the name for God revealed to Moses, and *aleph*, the first letter of the alphabet, are both 26. Kabbalists say this is significant because one of the words for Lord or Master in Hebrew, *aluph*, is based on the word *aleph*. Inspired by the numerological practices of ancient Kabbalah, modern Kabbalists maintain that determining the numerical value of one's name can lead to new insights.

One of those practices involves meditating on the 72 names for God, based on combinations of Hebrew letters that Kabbalah finds hidden in *Exodus* 14:19–21, the biblical account in which Moses calls to God for help before leading the people into the sea, as the Egyptian army pursues them. Kabbalists took these three verses, each having 72 letters in Hebrew, and developed 72 names of God by combining them into triads of three letters each. To get the first name, they took the first letter of verse 19, the last of verse 20, and the first of verse 21. The next name is composed of the second letter of verse 19, the second from last of verse 20, and the second of verse 21, and so on for a total of 72. These 72 names are then arranged in a grid with 8 columns and 9 rows. According to the Kabbalah Centre, the 72 Names of God 'work as tuning forks to repair you on the soul level'; each three-letter sequence 'act[s] like an index to specific, spiritual frequencies. By simply looking at the letters, as well as closing your eyes and visualizing them, you can connect with these frequencies' ('72 Names of God').

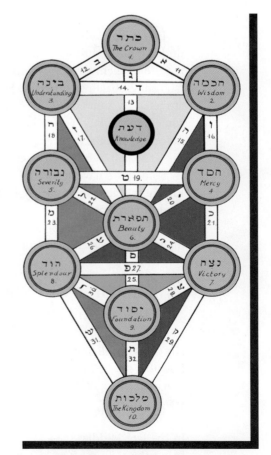

The Tree of Life (Mary Evans Picture Library/Alamy).

Many Kabbalists wear a bracelet of red wool string on the left wrist that is thought to provide protection against the 'evil eye' and other malevolent forces (David Silverman/Getty Images).

Traditional Kabbalah employs a dualistic symbolism of light and darkness, and many of the Centre's teachings focus on moving from darkness to light. For example, it stresses that instead of running away from adversaries, one should confront and learn from them, just as the biblical Jacob wrestled with the angel and gained the angel's blessing from the experience. Kabbalists see Jacob's angel as a personification of the personal darkness with which every individual must struggle in order to reach the light, and they understand the blessing as the divine light. The ego is seen as covered with a garment of darkness. Kabbalah practice helps to remove the darkness that covers the ego so as to reveal the light, the spark.

Like many other religious institutions, the Kabbalah Centre claims that its spiritual understanding fulfills other religions. In sharp contrast to most, however, it does not require its members to give up their former religious identities.

The Kabbalah Centre (like Scientology, below) has benefitted from the media attention attracted by some of its adherents. At the head of the celebrity list is Madonna, who has sometimes included references to Kabbalah in her lyrics (Huss 2005). However, with this notoriety, and the large sums of money donated by celebrities, have come questions about the Kabbalah Centre's finances and accounting.

Some Jews have accused the Centre of exploiting Kabbalah for worldly gain, which the Kabbalist tradition explicitly forbids. Others have charged that it goes too far in linking worldly happiness with Kabbalah practice. One leader of the Centre in London, England, was heavily criticized for seeming to suggest that the 6 million Jews killed in the Holocaust died because they did not follow Kabbalah practices to unblock the light.

RELIGIONS INSPIRED BY OTHER FORMS OF SPIRITUALITY

Not all new religions are offshoots of established mainstream religious traditions. We turn now to a selection of less conventional movements.

Wicca: The Witchcraft Revival

In the late Middle Ages, after centuries of condemning the remnants of 'pagan' tradition in northern Europe as 'witchcraft', the Roman Catholic Church mounted a systematic campaign to eradicate those remnants once and for all. Although accusations of witchcraft were frequent well into the 1700s, by the early twentieth century witchcraft was widely considered a thing of the past in industrialized societies: a matter of historical curiosity, but not in any way a living tradition.

Around the time of the Second World War, however, a movement emerged in England that claimed witchcraft to be the original religion of Britain and sought to revive the tradition. The leading figures in this movement were two men, Gerald B. Gardner and Aleister Crowley, but women's interest increased after 1948, when Robert Graves published *The White Goddess*, a work on myth that posited a mother goddess in European prehistory. Then Doreen Valiente, initiated into the movement in 1953, and produced a version of an existing text called *The Book of Shadows* that became a kind of a liturgical handbook for witchcraft.

The first modern use of the Old English word '**Wicca**' is attributed to Gardner in 1959. Within a few years, an Englishman named Alex Sanders, who claimed descent from witches in Wales, was attracting media attention to the movement; a 1969 film entitled *Legends of the Witches* was based on his writing. Sanders also initiated many witches who in turn founded covens (assemblies of witches) in Great Britain and continental Europe, but it is a Gardner initiate named Ray Buckland who is credited with introducing Wicca to the United States. Soon people with no connection to the Gardner lineage were establishing covens, and the name Wicca was becoming known outside the '**Craft**' itself.

It is difficult to estimate the current size of the Wicca movement, but sales of publications and reports of coven attendance suggest there are at least 85,000 adherents in North America, and perhaps four times as many around the world. The Covenant of the Goddess, established in California in 1975, is a kind of umbrella organization representing covens from a variety of traditions.

The feminist movement had a major impact on Wicca in North America. Zsuzsanna Budapest established a coven exclusively for women in 1971; her book *The Holy Book of Women's Mysteries* (1980) focuses on goddesses and rituals for women. Journalist Margot Adler became interested in the movement after listening to a tape produced by a witchcraft circle in Wales. Investigating other women's involvement in the Craft, she found that the visionary or aesthetic element played an important part, along with the mysteries of birth and growth, a concern for the natural environment, and particularly a sense of feminist empowerment. Feminism was also central to Starhawk (Miriam Simos), for whom the religion of the Goddess is the pulsating rhythm of life, and human sexuality is a reflection of the fundamentally sexual nature of the earth itself. At a lake high in the Sierra Nevada Mountains of California, she writes,

> it seems clear that earth is truly Her flesh and
> was formed by a sexual process: Her shakes
> and shudders and moans of pleasure, the orgasmic
> release of molten rock spewing forth
> in fiery eruptions, the slow caress of glaciers,
> like white hands gently smoothing all that
> has been left jagged (Starhawk 1982: 136).

In general, this kind of neopagan witchcraft seeks a return to primal nature and repudiates the classical Western religions that it holds responsible for repressing human sexuality. At the same time, its feminist emphasis challenges the patriarchal traditions of Judaism and Christianity. Although men can take an active part in it, Wicca is particularly empowering for women, and this has likely been part of its appeal.

Practice

Wiccans celebrate as many as eight *sabbats* (festivals) during the annual cycle or 'wheel of the year'. Four have fixed dates: Candlemas (1 February), May Day (1 May), Lammas (1 August), and Hallowe'en (31 October). The other four mark the important days of the solar cycle: the Spring and Autumn equinoxes and the Fall and Winter solstices.

Ideally, every Wiccan service would be held in the open air, but this is not always possible. Standard activities include healing rituals and celebrations of life-cycle events: birth, coming of age, marriage, death. Among the most important symbols are the circle, the four directions, and the four elements (earth, water, fire, air). Some of the rituals are symbolically sacrificial, paralleling (or parodying) the Christian Eucharist. Some covens announce upcoming services only by word of mouth and require that strangers be introduced by a trusted friend.

In 1993, members of the Covenant of the Goddess took part in the centennial World's Parliament of Religions in Chicago. In an age of interfaith acceptance, Wiccan priestesses and priests sought public and governmental recognition of their work as chaplains in hospitals, prisons, universities, and military units, but they could not provide any formal documentation of clerical training. To obtain the necessary credentials, some Wiccan leaders enrolled in Unitarian theological seminaries. Since then, the term 'witch' has begun to be used to distinguish credentialled clergy (group leaders) from lay adherents.

Scientology

The Church of Scientology was founded in 1954 by L. Ron Hubbard (1911–86). Official biographies emphasize the breadth of his experience and learning. As a boy in Montana, for instance, he was exposed to the traditional teachings of the Blackfoot nation. In his youth he was introduced to Freudian psychology by a mentor who had trained with Freud, and he learned about a variety of ancient spiritual traditions. As an adult he not only became a prolific author in various genres, including science fiction, but served as a naval officer in the Second World War and, severely wounded, assisted his return to health by discovering how to remove deep-seated blocks in his mind. Following his recovery he began to advocate a new theory of what the soul does to the body. He called this theory **dianetics**, from the Greek *dia* (through) and *nous* (mind or soul).

Hubbard's 1950 book *Dianetics: The Modern Science of Mental Health* sold millions of copies. Soon followers were forming groups across the US, and in 1954 they became the first members of the Church of Scientology. The Church's official website defines Scientology—a word derived from the Latin *scio* (knowing) and the Greek *logos* (study)—as 'knowing about knowing' and describes it as an 'applied religious philosophy'.

The Creed of Scientology begins with several generic statements about human rights, including freedom of expression, association, and religion. Reflecting Hubbard's belief that the underlying principle of all life forms is the drive to survive, it asserts that all humans have the right to defend themselves and the duty to protect others. At the same time it affirms that 'the laws of God forbid' humans to destroy or enslave the souls of others, that the spirit can be saved, and that the spirit alone can heal the body.

Scientologists understand the universe to consist of eight intersecting planes or 'dynamics', beginning with the self, the family, and so on at the bottom and moving up to the spiritual universe (the seventh dynamic) and the Supreme Being or Infinity (the eighth). The nature of the Infinity or God dynamic is not clearly defined. However, it seems to have less in common with the 'personal God' of Christianity, who knows, wills, and acts like a (super) human person, than with 'impersonal' principles or divinities such as the Dao of Daoism, the Brahman of the Hindu *Upanishads*, and the transcendent cosmic Buddha of some forms of Mahayana Buddhism.

Scientology uses the term '**thetan**' (pronounced 'thay-tan') for the soul. Each thetan is thought to be billions of years old. Like the atman of Hindu belief, the thetan is reincarnated, passing from one body to another at death.

Scientologists prefer to think of the movement as originating with its practitioners rather than with Hubbard himself. But he was its inspiration, he gave it direction from the first, and his writings and lectures constitute its religious literature. In a sense, the spread of Scientology began with the publication of *Dianetics* and its translation into numerous languages, even before the official founding of the Church in 1954. Various publications helped to spread Scientology to Britain and Europe. Today Scientologists have an organized presence in most countries.

As a strategy for spreading their influence Hubbard decided to focus on high-profile celebrities. 'Celebrity Centers' featuring posh facilities for practice and training, established in major cities of North America and Europe, succeeded in attracting several celebrities, whose names have added credibility to the organization.

Credibility was important because the movement was haunted by controversy. Several Scientologists, including Hubbard's wife, Mary Sue, were convicted of criminal activity involving the infiltration of various government agencies and theft in an effort (referred to by Scientology leaders as Operation Snow White) to remove documents thought to reflect badly on the operation. L. Ron Hubbard was named as an unindicted co-conspirator (United States vs Mary Sue Hubbard et al., 1979).

After Hubbard's death in 1986, the leadership passed to David Miscavige. As a boy growing up in Philadelphia, Miscavige had suffered from allergies and asthma, but was apparently cured following a dianetics training session. He joined Scientology in 1976, right at the time of Operation Snow White, and within three years rose from a cameraman filming Hubbard to an executive role, restructuring the various divisions so as to better conform to various laws and to protect Hubbard from personal liability. In the aftermath of the trial, Mary Sue Hubbard resigned from her leadership role and a new division was created under the leadership of Miscavige, who became chairman of the board of the Religious Technologies Center, charged with protecting the integrity of Hubbard's teachings. From this power base, he has served as the organization's paramount leader since 1986, although his role is that of an administrator rather than a spiritual leader.

As early as 1982, some dissenting followers of Hubbard were beginning to form alternative organizations outside the Church of Scientology, and this activity increased after

Hubbard's death. These organizations are known collectively as the 'Free Zone'. The name comes from Hubbard himself, who claimed that planet earth, under the galactic name Teegeeack, had been declared a 'free zone' millions of years ago. In that context, 'free' meant free of political or economic interference from other planets in the galaxy, but in the organizational context it meant free to follow Hubbard's teachings without payment to or interference from the Church of Scientology. One of the first Free Zone groups, Ron's Org, was founded in Germany in 1984 and now has members across Europe and the former Soviet Union. The Church of Scientology, which wants exclusive rights to Hubbard's practices, refers to **Free Zoners** as 'squirrels'—the equivalent of 'heretics'. Free Zoners themselves claim they are the ones who are faithful to the original teachings and practices of Hubbard.

Practice

In the 1960s Hubbard developed a step-by-step method for clearing the mind, or thetan, of mental blocks (called **engrams**) and restoring it to a state referred to as 'clear'. Engrams are the result of traumatic experiences, and they remain with the thetan until they are cleared, even carrying over from one life to the next. In some ways they are comparable to bad karma in the religions of India. Hubbard's process for clearing engrams, called '**auditing**', involves the use of a device called an '**E-meter**', which is supposed to indicate when an engram blockage has been discovered in the mind. The E-meter (electro-psychometer) was originally developed by a polygraph expert named Volney Mathison, who had noticed while doing lie detection sessions that subjects tended to give readable responses to words that triggered unconscious as well as conscious thoughts. Mathison and Hubbard knew each other because they both wrote science fiction, and Hubbard began to use the 'Mathison E-meter' in his dianetics practice. Although Mathison later distanced himself from Hubbard, the latter was able to get a patent on a modified version of the device. The Hubbard E-meter is manufactured at the movement's California headquarters and sold to members for use in auditing.

Another important practice—the equivalent of scriptural study—is the study of Hubbard's thought and writings (an area in which the movement works hard to preserve orthodoxy). This study is known as 'training' and students are encouraged to continue it, striving to reach ever-higher levels. Progress is called 'moving along the bridge' to total freedom, and it can take years of expensive auditing.

After students have made sufficient progress to be called Clear, 'advanced training' introduces some of Hubbard's imaginative science fiction concepts, among them the idea that an extraterrestrial named Xenu, the ruler of a galactic confederation, came to Teegeeack (earth) 75 million years ago, bringing with him thousands of aliens who had tried to revolt against his leadership. He put these political prisoners around volcanoes in which he detonated H-bombs. Then he captured the souls of the dead, now known as Thetans, and brainwashed them, implanting various ideas that we now associate with other religions. However, traces of their essences remain to this day, and some of their souls accumulated on the few bodies that were left. They are known as 'body thetans'. Those who complete all seven levels of this training are known as Operating Thetans (OTs).

Scientologists try to minimize the formation of new engrams in themselves or others. For example, Scientologist women are encouraged (though not required) to give birth in silence, in order to minimize the trauma of birth and therefore the creation of engrams in the infant thetan. Gestures are used for communication between the mother and attendants, and the mother is urged to minimize her cries of pain. Since Scientology prohibits drugs, the mother is also encouraged to give birth without the aid of painkillers.

Since Scientology does not anticipate any form of divine judgment after death, funeral services focus on celebrating the life of the deceased and wishing his or her thetan well in the next incarnation. After the funeral, friends and relatives of the deceased are encouraged to undergo auditing to rid themselves of the engrams resulting from grief. Scientologists may opt for cremation or burial. Hubbard was cremated, and before his death he discouraged the building of any elaborate memorials to him.

Scientology has come under intense public scrutiny and criticism for several reasons. Professional psychologists and other scientists are not sympathetic to the underlying claims of dianetics, and the fact that every step along the bridge costs more money has led some critics to charge that the entire program is designed to bilk money from the rich and gullible. Some critics have claimed that Hubbard once suggested to a meeting of science-fiction writers that, instead of writing for a penny a word, they could make millions by starting a new religion.

Marc Headley, a former Scientology believer and employee, broke with the movement after 15 years, escaping on a motorcycle with security personnel chasing him in a van until he crashed. Later he returned to rescue his Scientologist wife as well. In 2009 Headley published an autobiographical exposé of his years in Scientology. In *Blown for Good: Behind the Iron Curtain of Scientology* he describes his early years as a child of Scientologists who sent him to Scientology schools whenever they could afford it. Eventually he took a job with the organization. Promoted to the headquarters where the tapes, E-meters, and other equipment were manufactured, he happened to be chosen as the subject on whom Tom Cruise would practise auditing. In an interview with *The Village Voice*, Headley explained that, as Cruise's trainee, he was instructed to tell inanimate objects such as bottles or ashtrays to move in a certain way; when they did not move, Headley was instructed to move the objects himself and then thank them for moving. The purpose of this exercise, according to Headley, was to rehabilitate the mind's ability to control things and be controlled (Ortega 2009). He also claimed that employees lived and worked in sub-standard conditions for little or no pay, and were not allowed to leave the premises. In Scientology circles, critics such as Headley are known as Suppressive Persons, or SPs.

Despite the controversies that surround it, Scientology has been recognized as a valid new religion in several countries, including South Africa, Spain, Portugal, and Sweden. According to Headley, when the Internal Revenue Service of the United States granted Scientology tax-free status as a religious organization in 1993, Miscavige held a big meeting to announce that 'the war' was over.

The movement has had problems elsewhere, however, especially in France. In 1977 five Scientology leaders were found guilty of fraudulently coercing money from members; the next year Hubbard himself was found guilty of fraud; a well-known owner of a computer company lost a large order from the ministry of education after the French media ran a story about his Scientology affiliation in 1991; and in 2009 six leaders of the Scientology Celebrity Center of Paris were convicted of fraud and fined almost one million dollars (Erlanger 2009). In such cases, even the prosecution is careful to focus on Scientology's money-raising tactics rather than its spiritual beliefs.

Although it was founded only in the mid-twentieth century, Scientology now claims more than 12 million followers in over one hundred countries. Critics who believe that number to be grossly exaggerated suggest that it is based on the numbers of people who have ever bought a Scientology book or taken a Scientology course. Based on the quantities of E-meters and other supplies shipped during his time with the organization, Headley estimates that there were roughly 10,000 to 15,000 active Scientologists in the 1990s.

The Raëlian Movement

The Raëlian Movement traces its origins to a winter day in 1973 when a French journalist and racing enthusiast named Claude Vorilhon impulsively decided to drive to the site of an old volcano where he had enjoyed family picnics in the past. There he saw a small flying saucer hovering near the ground. An extraterrestrial creature—roughly 1.2 metres (4 feet) tall and resembling a bearded human with a greenish skin tone—then walked over and spoke to Vorilhon in French. In the course of this and subsequent encounters, the alien, Vorilhon came to know as Yahweh, recounted details of Vorilhon's own life and claimed that he had used telepathy to bring the Frenchman to this spot. Yahweh invited him inside the spaceship and told him that all life on earth was originally created in a laboratory by aliens called Elohim—the plural name sometimes used in the Torah to refer to the one God. The International Raëlian Movement translates 'Elohim' as 'those who came from the sky'.

Yahweh explained that a few weeks earlier he had used telepathy to urge Vorilhon to refresh his memory of the book of *Genesis* because he wanted to talk to him about it; now Vorilhon understood why, for no apparent reason, he had recently purchased a Bible and started to read it. The alien interpreted the *Genesis* story of God's creation of heaven and earth as a reference to the aliens 'from the sky', and the verse saying that the spirit of God moved over the face of the earth as a reference to the alien spacecraft. Continuing to instruct Vorilhon on the true meaning of *Genesis*, Yahweh said that a 'day' in the context of the six days of creation was equal to 2,000 earth years; that since the earth at that time was covered in water, the aliens had caused explosions in order to form the continents; and that they had used advanced scientific techniques to create the first plants and animals on earth in such a way that they would be able to reproduce themselves thereafter.

Despite minor differences in physical appearance (explained as the result of differences in the methods used by the various teams of Elohim scientists to create each group), the humans were formed 'in the image of' the Elohim themselves. This alarmed the Elohim back on the home planet, who feared that humans' intelligence might someday allow them to travel to the alien planet and cause trouble. Therefore it was decided that humans' scientific knowledge should be limited. The team working in what is now Israel, however, had created an unusually intelligent group of humans, and wanted to give them greater scientific knowledge. That team, Yahweh explained, was the 'serpent' that tempted Eve, while the 'Garden' from which Adam and Eve were expelled was in fact the laboratory of the Elohim. However, *Genesis* 6:4—in which 'the sons of Elohim' mate with the daughters of men—is interpreted literally.

The story of Noah and the flood in *Genesis* 7 is also given a novel twist. In the Raëlian interpretation, the flood is the result of nuclear explosions set off by the Elohim on the home planet who fear that humans have been given too much knowledge. Noah thwarts their plan by taking cells of each creature aboard an orbiting satellite; then, after the flood, he waits for the nuclear fallout to settle before returning to earth with a cargo that includes a pair of humans from each of the races created by the Elohim scientists.

Similarly, in the alien's account, the 'Tower of Babel' is not an actual tower but the name of a spaceship built by the Hebrews in partnership with the Elohim scientists who had been banished to earth for making humans too intelligent. This project so alarms the Elohim on the home planet that they thwart the progress of human science by scattering the Hebrews throughout the world. And God's order that Abraham sacrifice his son is translated into a test by the Elohim to see if the leader of the Hebrew scientists was still loyal to them. The New Testament gets some novel interpretations as well: for example, the resurrection of Jesus is attributed to cloning.

Yahweh told Vorilhon that he had been chosen to receive the truth because he had a Jewish father and a Catholic mother, and was a free-thinking opponent of traditional religion. He was told to change his name to Raël, 'messenger of the Elohim', to write down the message in book form, and to spread the word in anticipation of the Elohim's return.

Two years after his initial encounter, Raël reports, he was taken aboard a spaceship and transported to the planet of the Elohim, where he received further instruction and met with past religious leaders. He wrote an account of the visit in his book *The Message Given to Me by Extra-terrestrials*.

In 1974 Raël called a press conference in Paris to introduce his movement to the media. By 1980 the International Raëlian Movement had taken on most of the features of an organized religion: scripture, rituals, festival days, a communal building. It is organized hierarchically on the model of the Roman Catholic Church, with Raël himself at the pinnacle, like a pope, and various lesser officials with titles such as Bishop Guide and Priest Guide. Susan Jean Palmer (1995) notes that although the movement advocates gender equality and is libertarian about sexuality and gender roles, women are not well represented in the leadership hierarchy, especially at the upper levels.

The leadership hierarchy may reflect Roman Catholicism, but the Raëlian cosmology is nothing like that of traditional Christianity. Not only does it reject belief in gods of any kind, but it teaches that the whole of the observable universe is just a small atom of a larger structure, which is itself part of a larger one, and that every atom is a universe on the next smaller scale. Time and space are infinite in this cosmology, which runs on scientific principles without any need for divine command or intervention.

The Elohim are expected to return by 2035, but only on condition that humans are ready to welcome them, have tolerance for one another, and show respect for the environment. The Movement hopes one day to create an 'embassy' where the Elohim can interact with humans in a helpful way; ideally, this embassy would be located in Israel.

Raëlians reject the theory of evolution. Instead, they believe that life was brought to earth by the Elohim (who themselves were created by visitors from another planet), and that some day we earthlings in turn may take life to a different place. The term 'Intelligent Design', which some conservative Christians have promoted as an alternative to Darwinian evolution, has been adopted by Raëlians. But whereas for conservative Christians Intelligent Design is a way to get God and creationism back into the picture, for Raëlians it represents an alternative to both evolution and divine creation. The latest collection of Raël's writings about his UFO encounters has been published under the title *Intelligent Design: Message from the Designers*. In a postscript, Raël calls his approach a Third Way, between Darwin and *Genesis*. Since he holds that humans were created in a laboratory, he is confident this Third Way will one day be replicated in a laboratory by humans.

The Raëlian symbol is a swastika—best known today as the symbol of Nazism in Hitler's Germany—inside a six-pointed star that is said to be based on a design of interlocking triangles displayed on the spaceship during Raël's initial encounter with Yahweh. In fact, though, it seems identical to the Jewish Star of David. Raëlians claim that their swastika has nothing to do with Nazism, and point out that for thousands of years before its adoption by Hitler, it was a symbol of good luck and prosperity used in Buddhist, Jaina, and other religious traditions. They say that the symbol as a whole stands for the Elohim, while the swastika part represents infinite time and the hexagram infinite space. It reflects the Raëlian belief that the universe is cyclical, without beginning or end.

Practice

During Raël's second encounter with the Elohim he was taught a spiritual technique known as 'sensual meditation' or 'meditation of all senses', in which the meditator turns inward to experience the lesser universes within the atoms of his or her own body, and then turns outward to experience the greater universes beyond our own The goal is to awaken humans' highest spiritual potential by first awakening their physical sensibilities; eventually, the most adept will be able to visualize the planet of the Elohim.

There are four main Raëlian holidays: the first Sunday in April, celebrated as the day the Elohim created Adam and Eve; 6 August, the day of the Hiroshima bombing, which for Raëlians was the beginning of the Apocalypse; 7 October, the date that Raël met with Jesus, Buddha, and other past prophets aboard a spaceship during the second encounter; and 13 December, the day when Raël first encountered the Elohim.

Raëlians are expected to avoid mind-altering drugs, coffee, and tobacco, and to use alcohol either in moderation or not at all. They celebrate sensuality, advocate free love, and discourage traditional marriage contracts. The movement's liberal policy regarding marriage and sexual partners has made it an attractive religious home for gays and lesbians.

Becoming a Raëlian involves two ceremonies. First, initiates must renounce all ties to theistic religions.

Raël with a full-scale model of the spaceship he encountered in 1973 (Presselect / Alamy).

After this 'Act of Apostasy' comes a baptismal ceremony in which information about the initiate's DNA is supposedly transmitted to the Elohim.

As part of his effort to free humans from the constraints imposed by traditional religions, Raël has called for a massive 'de-baptism' campaign across Africa or (as he prefers to call it) the United Kingdom of Kama. He argues that 'spiritual decolonization' is a prerequisite for future development. The Movement has also been active in denouncing the practice of clitorectomy that is common in some parts of Africa, and has started a fundraising effort to pay for restorative surgery.

Perhaps because they reject the concept of the soul, Raëlians have taken a keen interest in the possibility of attaining a different kind of everlasting life through cloning. Clonaid, a Raëlian enterprise founded in France in 1997, has announced the births of several cloned babies, though none of these claims have been substantiated.

The movement does recognize religious figures such as Jesus and the Buddha as prophets, inspired by the Elohim to communicate as much of the truth as humans were able to absorb in their time. Raël identifies himself with Maitreya, the future Buddha who is expected to come when the world needs him, although Buddhists do not accept this identification. Just as Christianity sees itself as completing Judaism, and as Islam sees Muhammad as the 'seal of the prophets', Raëlians see their movement as the culmination of earlier religions, which incorrectly understood the role of the Elohim.

According to Raël, the Elohim told him that only 4 per cent of humans were advanced enough to understand the truth about them, so it is not surprising that the Raëlian mission has not made converts by the millions. Nevertheless, the International Raëlian Movement claims more than 65,000 members in 84 countries. Although it is not officially classified as a religion (because it rejects the idea of gods), some jurisdictions do recognize it as a non-profit organization; the first to do so was the province of Quebec, in 1977.

The New Age Movement

The expression 'New Age' has a wide range of connotations, including the biblical notion of an apocalypse in which God will intervene to restructure society, reward the righteous, and (in some scenarios) smite the wicked with long-overdue punishment. Among the millenarian Christian movements that have looked forward to the literal fulfillment of the prophecies in the biblical books of *Daniel* and *Revelation* are the Jehovah's Witnesses. For the Nation of Islam, however, the 'new age' would be one in which African Americans would emerge strong and triumphant. 'New Age' has also served as a generic term for a wide variety of loosely defined organizations. As we will see, New Age draws on both Eastern and Western traditions.

'New Age' was in use as early as 1907 as the title of a progressive British political and literary journal that introduced its readers to topics such as Freudian psychoanalysis. But with the 'consciousness revolution' of the 1960s came expectations of a different sort of 'new age'. The transpersonal psychology movement, for instance, emphasized spiritual insights and therapeutic techniques that were diametrically opposed to the mechanistic approach of orthodox Freudianism; the Esalen Institute in Big Sur, California, founded in 1962, became a centre of this movement, offering seminars, workshops, and encounter groups.

Not all New Age seekers were so disciplined. In 1967 the musical *Hair!* popularized the idea that the dawning of the Age of Aquarius would usher in a universal religion to replace the Christianity of the Piscean age. To some, the Aquarian age meant little more than freely available rock music or drugs. Those expectations came together in 1969, when as many as half a million young people congregated in a farmer's field near Woodstock, New York. By the late 1980s, 'New Age' had become a kind of shorthand term for a cluster of trends that included a quest for individual spiritual insight, expectations of both personal transformation and worldly success, the pursuit of physical healing and psychological peace through various self-help disciplines, and in some cases interest in astrology and psychic powers. Many New Age enthusiasts have published accounts of their personal transformation through some combination of New Age disciplines, diets, and cures.

Scholars looking for the historical roots of New Age spirituality often point to Emanuel Swedenborg, an eighteenth-century Swedish mystic who wrote about the evolution of the human soul; the nineteenth-century American Transcendentalist Ralph Waldo Emerson; or the Russian founder of the Theosophical movement, Helena P. Blavatsky, who claimed to have discovered the wisdom of the ages in Eastern traditions such as Hindu Vedanta. Those looking for antecedents of New Age therapeutic techniques often point to the sixteenth-century Swiss physician known as Paracelsus, who claimed that humans were subject to the magnetism of the universe. Two centuries later, the German physician Franz Anton Mesmer postulated that healing takes place through a kind of magnetism in bodily fluids (analogous to ocean tides), which he sought to manipulate. The effort to direct their flow, called mesmerism after him, was reflected in the development of hypnosis in the nineteenth century. As for what New Agers call 'channelling', the roots can be traced back at least as far as the nineteenth-century practice of the séance, in which the bereaved sought to make contact with their deceased loved ones through a 'spirit medium'. The use of gems and crystals was promoted in the first half of the twentieth century by the medium Edgar Cayce.

None of these earlier developments in itself constituted the New Age. But together they fertilized the spiritual soil of the English-speaking world, so that after the 1960s the New Age fascination with the exotic, the occult, the experiential, the curative, and the futuristic could take root and spread rapidly. Subjects that had been left on the sidelines of a scientific and technological age—astrology, hypnosis, alternative healing—were resurrected and, at a time of growing interest in subjects such as nutrition, ecology, and altruistic business ethics, entered the mainstream. All these could be seen as alternatives to orthodox religion, medicine, and society generally, and perhaps also to the exclusivist claims made by mainstream orthodoxies.

The metaphysical and therapeutic resources sketched so far came from outside or, at best, the margins of the major religious traditions discussed in this book. How did the New Age movement come to be so closely associated with religion? At least part of the answer can be found in its connections with Eastern religious traditions.

A prominent feature of the search for alternative modes of consciousness in the 1960s was a fascination with depths of awareness that traditions of Muslim Sufism, Hindu yoga, and Japanese Zen Buddhism in particular were believed to offer. The ancient Chinese divination manual known at the time as the *I Ching* (*Yijing* or *Classic of Changes*), became a bestseller, and many people were introduced to Asian religious symbolism through the writings of the Swiss psychologist Carl G. Jung and the Jungian comparative-religion scholar Joseph Campbell. 'Exotic' religions seemed to offer something that the familiar traditions of the West did not.

Across North America and Europe, young people in particular explored Chinese *qigong* and acupuncture, Indian yoga and ayurvedic medicine, and Buddhist meditation techniques. In India, Maharishi Mahesh Yogi's Transcendental Meditation movement attracted high-profile entertainers, including the Beatles, Mia Farrow, and Clint Eastwood, as devotees. Deepak Chopra, an endocrinologist practising in the West, returned to his native India to explore traditional ayurvedic medicine and proceeded to write and lecture about its compatibility with modern Western medicine. The Thailand-born and Western-educated Chinese master Mantak Chia, working in New York, has written extensively on the potential of Daoist techniques for healing and sexual energy. And the list goes on.

A recurring temptation, in the promotion of Asian disciplines and therapies, is to divorce the techniques from a comprehensive understanding of the cultural vocabularies in which they had developed. It is a temptation not only for consumers of these wares, but also for their providers. For example, **Eckankar**, a new religion introduced in the 1960s by the American Paul Twitchell, takes its name from 'Ik Onkar' ('the one om-expression'), a name for the transcendent God in the Sikh tradition. But though Twitchell claimed to have studied with a Sikh master in India, it was only one episode in a lifetime of 'soul travel' to supposed invisible worlds on levels above our earthly one. Eckankar holds that there has always been a living Eck master on earth, among whom have been ancient Greek and Iranian Muslim figures, and that Twitchell was the 971st in the series.

The New Age movement is thoroughly eclectic, and its diversity is part of its appeal. It is open to many possibilities, including female perspectives and leadership. As such, it stands in sharp contrast to the male-dominated structures of the established religions and professions. This may constitute one of its lasting contributions.

If there is a single word that sums up the spirit of the New Age, it might be 'holistic'. Implying a quest for wholeness, sometimes with an overtone of holiness, it was coined in the context of evolutionary biology to refer to the whole as something more than the sum of its parts. Holistic diets and therapies seek to treat the whole person, body and mind, and holistic principles are fundamental to the ecological movement; the Gaia hypothesis, for instance, sees the earth as a single organism whose survival depends on the interaction of all its components (a perspective central to James Cameron's film *Avatar*). New ages yet to come are bound to view ecological holism as an increasingly urgent goal.

New Thought

The term 'New Thought' encompasses a wide range of groups and individuals, from well-established organizations such as the Church of Divine Science, Unity Church, and Religious Science to bestselling contemporary authors such as Eckhardt Tolle and Rhonda Byrne. What all they have in common is their belief in positive thinking.

A formative influence on the New Thought movement was Phineas Quimby—the same mental healer who inspired Mary Baker Eddy to develop Christian Science. However, the New Thought churches have a broader conception of God and spirituality, and are not so exclusively Christian in their orientation. The Church of Divine Science, founded in the 1880s in San Francisco, teaches that God is present in all things, that evil is a fabrication of the human mind, and that humans can work healing miracles by drawing on the power of the divine. The Unity Church, or Unity School of Christianity, founded in 1889, sees itself as a form of Christianity, but holds that all religious traditions can be valid for their followers. It advocates 'affirmative prayer', in which practitioners focus not on the problems they wish to address (e.g., a particular illness) but on the results they hope to achieve (e.g., a particular state of health). Today Unity may be best known for the inspirational messages offered through its publication *Daily Word*. Finally, Religious Science was founded by Ernest Holmes in 1927 as a centre for mental healing along the lines advocated by Quimby. In his book *The Science of Mind* (1926) Holmes drew on Buddhist as well as Christian ideas. He stressed that his teachings were based not on fixed doctrines or revelations but on practical experience with what works to help people. He believed that humans, and his Religious Science, were 'open at the top', meaning that ideas and practices were still evolving.

Since the late 1990s, New Thought has enjoyed a surge of worldwide interest as a result of the media attention attracted by Eckhart Tolle and Rhonda Byrne. Ulrich Tolle, born in Germany in 1948, suffered severe depression for many years, but in 1977 a profound mystical experience transformed his life. Like many mystics before him, he experienced the dissolving away of the ego-centred, burden-laden self, leaving nothing but a deep sense of peacefulness. He took the name Eckhart in honour of the German Christian mystic Meister Eckhart (1260-1327?), moved to Vancouver, and published his first book, *The Power of Now*, in 1997. At first it sold only modestly, but after coming to the attention of Oprah Winfrey it became a blockbuster, as did his third book, *A New Earth* (2005). His writings draw on many sources, from Buddhism to the more mystical strains of Christianity. He maintains that most established religions have lost touch with the roots of true spirituality, that what prevents us from discovering our underlying spiritual nature is the ego, and that the key to transcending the ego is to be fully present in the here and now.

Rhonda Byrne, born in Australia in 1951, has become an influential New Thought spokesperson through her book *The Secret* (2006) and the film of the same title. Based on the prolific New Thought writings of William Walker Atkinson (1862–1932), Byrne's book is a kind of self-help manual that encourages readers to apply the power of positive thinking to all aspects of life, from weight control to personal success. Her more recent book, *The Power* (2010) has enhanced her status as the leading New Thought advocate.

Green Religion

A green movement is spreading across all religious traditions. In a global environment where so many moral or political issues pit different religious communities against one another, protection of the environment is a goal that all faiths can readily share. Religions that may not see eye to eye about god can work together to help an endangered species or lobby against the clear-cutting of a forest. The National Religious Partnership for the Environment is one example of the coalitions that have been formed to pursue this common cause.

Every religious tradition has some concern for nature, but Asian, African, and Native American religions appear to have a longer and stronger track record than their Abrahamic counterparts when it comes to incorporating that concern into their practice. More and more, people are searching their traditions for ecology-friendly principles and elements that lend themselves to the expression of ecological concern. A Buddhist group in Rochester, New York, for instance, has created an 'earth relief' ceremony that concludes with an interesting change in the wording of the 'merit transfer' prayer at the close. Traditionally, the participants in any such ritual would transfer the merit made by taking part in it to 'all living beings', but here the meaning of that phrase is made explicit:

> Tonight we have offered candles, incense, fruit, and tea,
> Chanted sutras [texts] and *dharani* [sacred words].
> Whatever merit comes to us from these offerings
> We now return to the earth, sea, and sky.
> May our air be left pure!
> May our waters be clean!
> May our earth be restored!
> May all beings attain Buddhahood!
>   (Rochester Zen Centre, 1992)

All the traditions arising in India share a worldview in which there is no radical distinction between humans and animals, rejecting the notion that only humans, and not animals, have souls. Hindus, Jains and Buddhists tell of a time where their gods or spiritual masters lived on earth as animals. Krishna five times took an animal form to save the earth from destruction. The Jain Tirthankaras and the Buddhas are said to have previously lived animal lives. The Hindu gods and goddesses have animal vehicles ('mounts') which are thought to represent them in animal form. Such stories, combined with the belief in rebirth over hundreds of lives in many kinds of bodies, promotes a spirituality that embraces all forms of life.

Some ecologically minded thinkers in the Abrahamic traditions have taken a fresh look at the passages in *Genesis* (1:26) and the Qur'an (2:30) in which God is said to have given humans dominion over all living things and made them his 'viceroys' on earth. They say that in the past these verses were interpreted as giving humans licence to do whatever they liked with the earth and its non-human inhabitants, but that this was not their intent: rather, they represent a divine dictate to care for the earth the way a responsible steward would. On this theological foundation, they say, it is possible to construct a comprehensive spiritual ecology.

But concern to protect the natural environment is not limited to the Abrahamic traditions. In rural Thailand, Buddhist 'ecology monks' have saved more than one forest from logging by conducting 'ordination' ceremonies in which a piece of saffron-coloured monk's cloth was tied around each tree. When the workers with chainsaws arrived, they refused to cut down the sacred trees despite orders from the multinational companies that had hired them to clear the land.

The International Islamic Green Movement, at its 2010 conference in Jakarta, called on Muslims to embrace ecological principles. Specific proposals included printing the Quran on paper from sustainable forests, using biodegradable replacements for plastic containers at mosques, and 'greening' the annual Hajj by, for example, banning plastic bottles and holding workshops on the concept of environmental stewardship in Islam (Green Prophet 2010).[1]

'Protecting Creation, generation to generation' is the motto of the Coalition on the Environment and Jewish Life, which focuses particular attention on climate change and energy policy and is working in partnership with a group called GreenFaith to make synagogues into models of environmental consciousness and education (COEJL).

The Forum on Religion and Ecology at Yale University seeks to promote interdisciplinary dialogue on environmental issues. Its directors, Mary Evelyn Tucker and John Grim (2001), have expressed confidence in the contributions that the world's religions can make to the development of 'a broader environmental ethics' based on a new awareness of the sacred dimensions of nature.

SCIENTIFIC AND SECULAR CHALLENGES TO RELIGIOUS AUTHORITY

Every religious tradition, in every age, has probably had its share of skeptics and critics, even if they have not able to make their views known. If the modern era seems to have produced more of them than any previous era, that's hardly surprising. Contemporary critics of religion do not constitute an organized movement, but some of them have attracted a significant following among people who might not otherwise have been motivated to examine the foundations of their own religious beliefs or to question whether religion is in fact a force for good in the world.

Among the best-known critics of religion today are the cultural critic and journalist Christopher Hitchens and the evolutionary biologist Richard Dawkins. Hitchens makes his position clear in the title of his 2007 book *God is Not Great: How Religion Poisons Everything*. Although he has been critical of Buddhism to the extent that it encourages people to set reason aside, his main targets are the monotheistic Abrahamic traditions. A brief summary of his argument has been widely quoted: 'Violent, irrational, intolerant, allied to racism, tribalism, and bigotry, invested in ignorance and hostile to free inquiry, contemptuous of women and coercive toward children: organized religion ought to have a great deal on its conscience' (p. 56). Dawkins, for his part, had written extensively on the mechanics of evolution through natural selection before taking direct aim at religion. For example, *The Blind Watchmaker* (1986) explained the natural processes through which all species of life on earth, including humans, evolved over millions of years—contrary both to the biblical narrative of creation and to the 'intelligent design' argument, according to which an organ as complex as a human eye could not have developed by chance. More recently, in *The God Delusion* (2006), Dawkins has laid out a detailed case against religious belief and for atheism.

Other scholars have examined religion itself from a scientific perspective. David Sloan Wilson, for instance, like Dawkins, is an evolutionary biologist. Instead of setting evolution and religion against one another, however, in *Darwin's Cathedral: Evolution, Religion, and the Nature of Society* (2002) he suggests that religion itself may represent a biological and cultural adaptation that gave certain human groups a survival advantage by creating social bonds that helped them to function as single units rather than collections of individuals. And the psychologist Justin L. Barrett, in *Why Would Anyone Believe in God?* (2004), suggests that belief in deities is a natural consequence of the human mind's disposition to look for the causal agents behind events. An observant Christian himself, Barrett sees no contradiction between belief and scientific understanding.

CONCLUSION

The new religious movements discussed in this chapter cover the spiritual landscape, from east to west to outer space. None of them represents a serious challenge to the influence of the established religions, and some may have already passed their peak in numbers, at least in North America. Since new religions typically need a strong, charismatic leader, most have trouble sustaining their unity and momentum after the founder's death. But others are still making significant gains in numbers, wealth, and influence.

The few that survive and prosper eventually become established as normal features in the religious landscape: 'religions' rather than 'new religions'. Judaism, Christianity, and Islam made this transition long ago. The Baha'i Faith and the Mormons have made it more recently. Which, if any, of the new religions that emerged in the twentieth century will survive into the twenty-second is impossible to tell from this vantage point, but is surely an interesting topic for debate.

Sacred Texts Table

Religion	Text	Composition/ Compilation	Compilation/ Revision	Use
Soka Gakkai	The *Lotus Sutra*	Probably composed in the early 1st century CE; considered the highest expression of Mahayana thought	Supplemented by writings of Nichiren and modern leaders	Read and chanted; the phrase 'Homage to the Lotus Sutra' is chanted as a mantra
Falun Dafa (Falun Gong)	*Falun Gong* by Li Hongzhi	First published in 1993. Li's works have been translated into most major languages	The English translation has been revised several times	Li's books and videos are used as guides to practice
ISKCON ('Hare Krishnas')	*Srimad Bhagavatam, Bhagavad Gita,* and other Krishna-centred devotional texts	Ancient Hindu texts of debatable date, now available in English and other major languages	Commentaries by Swami Prabhupada	Studied and chanted during puja

(continued)

Sacred Texts Table (continued)

Religion	Text	Composition/ Compilation	Compilation/ Revision	Use
LDS (Mormons)	The Bible, plus Smith's *The Book of Mormon*, *Doctrine and Covenants*, and *The Pearl of Great Price*	*The Book of Mormon* was published in 1830. *Doctrine and Covenants* (selected writings) in 1835; *The Pearl of Great Price* was compiled by F.D. Richards and published in England in 1851	All three texts have been revised at various times	Used in worship and for life guidance
Baha'i	The *Most Holy Book*, *The Book of Certitude*, *Hidden Words*, and *The Seven Valleys*	Written by Baha'u'llah between 1856 and 1873	Edited by 20th-century Baha'i leaders	The *Most Holy Book* is used as a source of legal guidance, The *Book of Certitude* for doctrine, *Hidden Words'* for ethical guidance, and *Seven Valleys* for mystical guidance
Nation of Islam	The Qur'an, plus Elijah Muhammad's *Fall of America* and *Message to the Blackman*	Elijah Muhammad's works date from the 1950s and '60s	Louis Farrakhan's *A Torchlight for America* (1993)	The Qur'an is studied, recited and used in Sunni services, along with *Muslim Daily Prayers*
Kabbalah Center	Hebrew Bible, The Zohar	The Kabbalah Center attributes the Zohar to Rav Shimon Bar Yochai rather than Moses de Léon	The Bible is interpreted through numerology and the 72 names of God	Spiritual practices of Zohar and related approaches are used to guide daily life
Wicca	Important early works include Graves' *The White Goddess* (1948) and *The Book of Shadows* (c. 1950)	Other publications added a feminist emphasis, such as *The Holy Book of Women's Mysteries*	Newer writers such as Starhawk have popularized the movement	Used in rituals and sabbats
Scientology	Hubbard's *Dianetics: The Modern Science of Mental Health* and *Scientology: The Fundamentals of Thought*	1950s		Used in 'auditing' process
Raëlian Movement	*Intelligent Design: Message from the Designers*	Published in 2005: a compilation of Raël's publications from the 1970s–80s	Other texts include *The Maitreyya* and *Sensual Meditation*	Teachings are studied and used as guidance for sensual meditation practice

Study Questions

1. What kinds of social and economic factors may contribute to the rise of new religious movements?
2. Why is the line between a 'cult' and a 'religion' so difficult to define?
3. Why do Eastern religions appeal so strongly to many people in the West?
4. Do all 'religions' have to involve belief in deities?
5. Can a set of beliefs and practices centred on extraterrestrial aliens be considered a 'religion'?
6. What are some of the factors that you think might attract some people to new religious movements?
7. How do new religious movements gain acceptance?
8. How do new religious movements tend to change over time?

Glossary

auditing The process used in Scientology to remove mental blockages.

Bab The individual expected to appear as the 'Gateway' to the new prophet in the Baha'i Faith.

bhakti Devotional faith, the favoured spiritual path in ISKCON.

cult Term for a new religion that typically demands unquestioning loyalty to a charismatic leader.

dianetics Hubbard's term for the system he developed to clear mental blocks.

Eckankar A new religion based on the teachings of Paul Twitchell.

E-meter A device used in Scientology to detect mental blocks.

engrams Scientology's term for mental blocks.

Falun The 'dharma or law wheel' said to be acquired through practice.

Free Zoners Individuals and groups teaching Hubbard's thought that are independent of Scientology International.

Hare Krishnas Informal name for the members of ISKCON, based on their chant.

ISKCON International Society for Krishna Consciousness.

Komeito A Japanese political party loosely associated with Soka Gakkai.

millenarian Term used to refer to the belief that the current social order will soon come to an end.

Mormons Another name for members of the Church of Jesus Christ of Latter-day Saints.

qi Spiritual energy (sometimes spelled *chi*).

qigong Exercises said to cultivate *qi*.

Scientology A new religion devoted to clearing mental blockages.

sect Sociological term for a group that breaks away from the mainstream of a given religion.

spherot The ten attributes of God in Kabbalah.

thetan Scientology's term for the soul or mind.

Vaishnava A Hindu who worships Vishnu and related deities.

Wicca A name for witchcraft.

Further Reading

Baha'u'llah. 1952. *Gleanings from the Writings of Baha'u'llah*, rev. ed. Wilmette, IL: Baha'i Publishing Trust. A good selection of Baha'i writings.

Barrett, David V. 2003. *The New Believers: A Survey of Sects, Cults and Alternative Religions*. London: Octopus Publishing Group. A good place to start on the topic of cults versus new religions.

Dan, Joseph. 2005. *Kabbalah: A Very Short Introduction*. Oxford: Oxford University Press. A useful introduction.

Dawkins, Richard. 2008. *The God Delusion*. New York: Mariner Books. A critique of religion from a scientific and atheistic point of view.

Drew, A. J. 2003. *The Wiccan Bible: Exploring the Mysteries of the Craft from Birth to Summerland*. Franklin, NJ: Career Press. An overview of Wicca.

Esslemont, John E. 1979. *Bahá'u'lláh and the New Era: An Introduction to the Bahá'í Faith*. 4th ed. Wilmette, IL: Baha'i Publishing Trust. The standard survey recommended by Baha'is.

Gallagher, Eugene V., William M. Ashcraft, and W. Michael Ashcraft, eds. 2006. *An Introduction to New and Alternative Religions in America*. 5 vols. Westport: Greenwood Press. Scholarly introductions to religious movements from colonial era to present.

Headley, Marc. 2009. *Blown for Good: Behind the Iron Curtain of Scientology*. Burbank: BFG Books. An autobiography of a former Scientologist turned critic.

Hitchens, Christopher. 2007. *God is Not Great: How Religion Poisons Everything*. New York: Twelve Books. An atheist's critique of religion's influence in social and political life.

Hubbard, L. Ron. 1956. *Scientology: The Fundamentals of Thought*. 2007. Los Angeles: Bridge Publications. The basics of Scientology as explained by its founder.

Lewis, James R., and J. Gordon Melton, eds. 1992. *Perspectives on the New Age*. Albany: State University of New York Press. One of the best assessments of the New Age phenomenon.

Li Hongzhi. 2000. *Falun Gong*. 3rd ed. New York: University Publishing Co. Master Li's introduction to Falun Dafa.

Miller, William McElwee. 1974. *The Baha'i Faith: Its History and Teachings*. Pasadena: William Carey Library. An outsider's perspective.

Muster, Nori J. 2001. *Betrayal of the Spirit: My Life behind the Headlines of the Hare Krishna Movement*. Champaign: University of Illinois Press. A critical view of ISKCON by a former adherent.

Ostling, Richard, and Joan K. Ostling. 2007. *Mormon America—Revised and Updated Edition: The Power and the Promise*. New York: HarperOne. An overview of the issues.

Porter, Noah. 2003. *Falun Gong in the United States: An Ethnographic Study*. N.p.: Dissertation.Com. Argues against the 'cult' label based on interviews and publications.

Seager, Richard H. 2006. *Encountering the Dharma. Daisaku Ikeda, Soka Gakkai, and the Globalization of Buddhist Humanism*. Berkeley: University of California Press. A scholarly overview.

Shinn, Larry D. 1987. *The Dark Lord: Cult Images and the Hare Krishnas in America*. Philadelphia: Westminster Press. An objective overview based on extensive interviews.

Starhawk. 1982. *Dreaming the Dark*. Boston: Beacon Press. One of many works by an important Wicca leader.

White, Vibert L., Jr. 2001. *Inside the Nation of Islam: A Historical and Personal Testimony by a Black Muslim*. Gainesville: University Press of Florida. An account made more interesting because it is written by someone involved in the movement and in organizing the 1995 March.

Recommended Websites

www.bahai.org   Site of the Baha'i religion.

www.falundafa.org   Site of the Falun Dafa organiztion.

www.finalcall.com   News site of the Nation of Islam.

www.internationfreezone.net   Portal for the Free Zoner alternative to Scientology.

www.iskcon.org   Site of the International Society for Krishna Consciousness.

www.kabbalah.com   Site of the Kabbalah Centre International.

www.lds.org   Site of the Church of Jesus Christ of Latter-day Saints, the Mormons.

www.komei.or.jp   Site of the New Komeito party, loosely affiliated with Soka Gakkai.

www.rael.org   Site of the International Raëlian Movement.

www.scientology.org   Site of the international Scientology organization.

www.sgi.org   Site of Soka Gakkai International.

www.wicca.org   Site of the Church and School of Wicca.

References

Amnesty International. 'Human Rights in China'. Accessed 10 March 2010 at http://www.amnesty.ca/blog2.php?blog=keep_the_promise_2&page=7.

Baha'i Prayers: A Selection of the Prayers Revealed by Bahá'u'llah, The Bab, and 'Abdu'l-Bahá. 1969. Wilmette: Bahá'í Publishing Trust.

Dawson, Lorne L. 2006. *Comprehending Cults: The Sociology of New Religious Movements*. Toronto: Oxford University Press.

Embry, Jessie L. 1994. *Black Saints in a White Church: Contemporary African American Mormons*. Salt Lake City: Signature Books.

Erlanger, Steven. 2009. 'French Branch of Scientology Convicted of Fraud'. *New York Times*. Accessed 10 March 2010 at http://www.nytimes.com/2009/10/28/world/europe/28france.html?_r=l.

'Focus in Front'. Accessed 10 March 2010 at http://www.kabbalah.com/newsletters/weekly-consciousness-tune-ups/focus-front.

Green Prophet. 2010. 'Saudis Listen to Call for Green Hajj". Accessed 13 April 2011 at www.greenprophet.com/2010/06/20/22890green-hajj-mecca/.

Huss, Boaz. 2005. 'All You Need is LAV: Madonna and Postmodern Kabbalah'. *Jewish Quarterly Review* 95, 4: 611–24.

Ikeda, Daisaku. 2008. 'Toward Humanitarian Competition: A New Current in History'. Accessed on 10 March 2010 at www.sgi.org/peace2009sum.html.

'Introduction: What Is Falun Dafa?'. Accessed 10 March 2010 at http://www.falundafa.org/eng/intro.html.

Kabbalah Centre. 'Reincarnation'. Accessed 10 March 2010 at http://www.kabbalah.com/node/434.

Lee, Martha F. 1996. *The Nation of Islam: An American Millenarian Movement*. Syracuse: Syracuse University Press.

Levi, Jerome M. 2009. 'Structuralism and Kabbalah: Sciences of Mysticism or Mystifications of Science?' *Anthropological Quarterly* 82, 4 (Fall).

Lewis, James R. 2003. *Legitimate New Religions*. Rutgers: Rutgers University Press.

Li Hongzhi. 2000. *Falun Gong*. 3rd ed. New York: University Publishing Co.

Ljungdahl, Alex. 1975. 'What Can We Learn from Non-Biblical Prophet Movements'. In *New Religions*, ed. Harlads Biezais. Stockholm: Almqvist & Wiksell International.

Olyan, Saul M., and Gary A. Anderson. 2009. *Priesthood and Cult in Ancient Israel*. Sheffield: Sheffield Academic Press.

Ortega, Tony. 2009. 'Tom Cruise Told Me to Talk to a Bottle: Life at Scientology's Secret Headquarters'. The Village Voice. Accessed 10 March 2010 at http://blogs.villagevoice.com/runninscared/2011/02/inside_scientol.php.

Prabhupada, A. C. Bhaktivedanta. 1968. *Teachings of Lord Chaitanya: The Golden Avatar*. New York: The Bhaktivedanta Book Trust.

———. 1972. *Bhagavad-gita As It Is*. New York: Collier.

Palmer, Susan Jean. 1995. 'Women in the Raelian Movement: New Religious Experiments in Gender and Authority'. In *The Gods Have Landed: New Religions from Other Worlds*, ed. James R. Lewis. Albany: State University of New York Press.

Rochester Zen Center, 'Earth Relief Ceremony' (unpublished manual, 1992), as cited by Kenneth Kraft, 'The Greening of Buddhist Practice'. www.crosscurrents.org/greening.htm#FN3.

Sahib, Hatim A. 1951. 'The Nation of Islam'. Master's thesis. University of Chicago. Cited in Lee 1996: 23.

'72 Names of God, The'. Accessed 15 March at http://www.kabbalah.com/node/432

Starhawk. 1982. *Dreaming the Dark*. Boston: Beacon Press.

Tucker, Mary Evelyn, and John Grim, 2001. 'Introduction: The Emerging Alliance of World Religions and Ecology'. *Daedalus: Journal of the American Academy of Arts and Sciences*. Fall.

Walker, Dennis. 2005. *Islam and the Search for African-American Nationhood: Elijah Muhammad, Louis Farrakhan and the Nation of Islam*. Atlanta: Clarity Press.

White, Vibert L., Jr. 2001. *Inside the Nation of Islam: A Historical and Personal Testimony by a Black Muslim*. Gainesville: University Press of Florida.

Note

Parts of this chapter, especially in the sections on the Mormons, Baha'i, Wicca, and New Age, incorporate material written by the late Will Oxtoby.

1. Trans. Thomas O. Lambdin; accessed 12 April 2011 at http://www.gnosis.org/naghamm/gthlamb.html.

Credits

Page 112, extract from *Zohar: The Book of Splendor*. New York: Schocken Books.

Page 113, extract from *Zohar: The Book of Splendor*. New York: Schocken Books.

Page 144, extract from *New English Bible*. 1970. New York: Oxford University Press; Cambridge: Cambridge University Press.

Page 195, From Martin Luther King, Jr, 'Letter from Birmingham Jail' Reprinted by arrangement with The Heirs to the Estate of Martin Luther King Jr., c/o Writers House as agent for the proprietor New York, NY. *Copyright 1963 Dr. Martin Luther King Jr.; copyright renewed 1991 Coretta Scott King.*

Page 230, extract from *Rabi'a the Mystic*. Copyright ©1928 Cambridge University Press. Reprinted with the permission of Cambridge University Press.

Page 230, extract from *Rabi'a the Mystic*. Copyright ©1928 Cambridge University Press. Reprinted with the permission of Cambridge University Press.

Page 231, extracts from *Legacy of Islam*, edited by Joseph Schacht, with C.E. Bosworth (1974). By permission of Oxford University Press.

Page 232, extract from *The Mystics of Islam*. Bloomington: World Wisdom.

Page 233, extract from *Rumi: Poet and Mystic*. Copyright © trans. 1950 G. Allen and Unwin.

Index